BUILDING A TREATY (
AND HUMAN R

GW01388362

The calls for an international treaty to elaborate the human rights obligations of transnational corporations and other business enterprises have been growing rapidly, due to the failures of existing regulatory initiatives in holding powerful business actors accountable for human rights abuses. In response, *Building a Treaty on Business and Human Rights* explores the context and content of such a treaty. Bringing together leading academics from around the world, this book engages with several key areas: the need for the treaty and its scope; the nature and extent of corporate obligations; the role of state obligations; and how to strengthen remedies for victims of human rights abuses by business. It also includes draft provisions for a proposed treaty to advance the debate in this contentious area and inform future treaty negotiations. This book will appeal to those interested in the fields of corporate social responsibility and business and human rights.

SURYA DEVA is an associate professor at the School of Law of City University of Hong Kong, and a member of the UN Working Group on Business and Human Rights. Deva's primary research interests lie in business and human rights, corporate social responsibility, India-China constitutional law and sustainable development. He has published extensively in these areas, and has advised UN/EU bodies, states, multinational corporations and civil society organizations on business and human rights matters. He is one of the founding editors-in-chief of the *Business and Human Rights Journal*.

DAVID BILCHITZ is Professor of Fundamental Rights and Constitutional Law at the University of Johannesburg and Director of the South African Institute for Advanced Constitutional, Public, Human Rights and International Law (SAIFAC). He is the Secretary-General of the International Association of Constitutional Law and was elected as a member of the South African Young Academy of Science. He has written extensively in the field of business and human rights and in 2013 he co-edited *Human Rights Obligations of Business* with Surya Deva.

BUILDING A TREATY ON BUSINESS AND HUMAN RIGHTS

Context and Contours

Edited by

SURYA DEVA
City University of Hong Kong

DAVID BILCHITZ
University of Johannesburg

CAMBRIDGE
UNIVERSITY PRESS

CAMBRIDGE
UNIVERSITY PRESS

University Printing House, Cambridge CB2 8BS, United Kingdom

One Liberty Plaza, 20th Floor, New York, NY 10006, USA

477 Williamstown Road, Port Melbourne, VIC 3207, Australia

314-321, 3rd Floor, Plot 3, Splendor Forum, Jasola District Centre, New Delhi - 110025, India

79 Anson Road, #06-04/06, Singapore 079906

Cambridge University Press is part of the University of Cambridge.

It furthers the University's mission by disseminating knowledge in the pursuit of education, learning and research at the highest international levels of excellence.

www.cambridge.org
Information on this title: www.cambridge.org/9781316648582
DOI: 10.1017/9781108183031

© Cambridge University Press 2017

First published 2017
First paperback edition 2018

A catalogue record for this publication is available from the British Library

ISBN 978-1-107-19911-8 Hardback
ISBN 978-1-316-64858-2 Paperback

CONTENTS

CONTRIBUTORS

DANIEL MAURÍCIO DE ARAGÃO is Associate Professor of Humanities and International Relations at the Federal University of Bahia (Brazil), where he coordinates the Academic Master on International Relations. He holds a PhD in International Relations from the Pontifical Catholic University of Rio de Janeiro. He is a lawyer with an LLM degree in Philosophy and Sociology of Law (Federal University of Santa Catarina). He has taken human rights courses at the International University of Andalusia (Spain), the Inter-American Institute of Human Rights (Costa Rica) and the University of Oxford (UK). In 2002–2005, he was the Executive Secretary of the Inter-American Platform of Human Rights, Democracy and Development. His current research and publications focus on critical globalization studies, business and human rights in the United Nations and international development cooperation. He is a member of the International Studies Association.

LARRY CATÁ BACKER is the W. Richard and Mary Eshelman Faculty Scholar and Professor of Law and International Affairs at the Pennsylvania State University. He served as Chair of the Faculty Senate of the Pennsylvania State University (2012–2013). He is the founder and director of the Coalition for Peace & Ethics, and has visited the University of California, Hastings College of the Law (1998) and Tulane Law School (2007–2008). His research focuses on governance-related issues of globalization and the constitutional theories of public and private governance, with a focus on institutional frameworks where public and private law systems converge. He is particularly interested in transnational problem-solving through law, broadly defined, including issues of corporate social responsibility, the relationship between state-based regulation and transnational systems of 'soft' regulation, state participation in private markets and the emerging problems of polycentricity where multiple systems might be simultaneously applied to a single issue or event, and problems of translation between Western and Marxist Leninist (especially Chinese) constitutional systems. He teaches courses in corporate law, transnational law and international organizations. His publications include *Lawyers Making Meaning: The Semiotics of Law in Legal Education* (2013) and *Signs in Law, A Source Book* (2014) (both with Jan Broekman), casebooks, *Elements of Law and the U.S. Legal System* (forthcoming 2017), *Law and Religion* (2015, with Frank Ravitch), *Comparative Corporate Law* (2002), an edited collection of essays, *Harmonizing Law in an Era of Globalization*, and a number of articles and contributions to published collections of essays. His work, especially on Chinese constitutional law and corporate social responsibility, has been translated into Chinese. Shorter essays on various aspects of globalization and governance appear on his essay site, 'Law at the End of the Day', http://lcbackerblog .blogspot.com.

DAVID BILCHITZ is Professor of Fundamental Rights and Constitutional Law in the Faculty of Law at the University of Johannesburg and Director of the South African Institute for Advanced Constitutional, Public, Human Rights and International Law (SAIFAC). He is also Secretary-General of the International Association of Constitutional Law (IACL). In 2012, he received a rating as an internationally acclaimed researcher by the National Research Foundation of South Africa and was appointed in 2015 to the South African Young Academy of Science for the most promising young researchers in South Africa. He has a BA (Hons) LLB cum laude from Wits University and an MPhil and PhD from the University of Cambridge. His monograph entitled *Poverty and Fundamental Rights* was published in 2007. He also has published two edited volumes, 14 book chapters and 37 journal articles, mostly related to fundamental rights. One of his specialities is in the field of business and human rights and he has related publications in the *South African Law Journal, SUR International Journal on Human Rights, Theoria*, the *Indiana Journal of Global Legal Studies*, the *Oxford Journal of Legal Studies* and the *Business and Human Rights Journal*. He has co-edited with Surya Deva a book entitled *Human Rights Obligations of Business: Beyond the Corporate Responsibility to Respect?* (published by Cambridge University Press in November 2013). He has also supervised reports in this field commissioned by the International Commission of Jurists and the SRSG's mandate. He has made submissions for reform in this area to the South African parliament, the King Commission on Corporate Governance and the Inter-Governmental Working Group on Business and Human Rights. He is on the editorial board of the *Business and Human Rights Journal* and on several other journals.

SHANE DARCY is a senior lecturer at the Irish Centre for Human Rights at the National University of Ireland Galway, where he teaches international criminal law and business and human rights. He is on the editorial board of the *Business and Human Rights Journal* and the Editorial Committee of *Criminal Law Forum*. He is the author of two monographs: *Judges, Law and War: The Judicial Development of International Humanitarian Law* (Cambridge University Press, 2014) and *Collective Responsibility and Accountability under International Law* (2007) and co-editor of two edited collections: *Judicial Creativity at the International Criminal Tribunals* (2010, w/Joseph Powderly) and *Truth Commissions and Courts* (2005, w/William A. Schabas). He has participated in human rights training, conferences and workshops in several countries including South Africa, China, Iran, Palestine, Iraq, Turkey, the United States and Russia. He is a member of the National Board of Amnesty International's Irish Section and runs the *Business and Human Rights in Ireland* blog.

SURYA DEVA is an associate professor at the School of Law of City University of Hong Kong, and a member of the UN Working Group on Business and Human Rights. Deva's primary research interests lie in business and human rights, corporate social responsibility, India-China constitutional law and sustainable development. He has published extensively in these areas, and has advised UN/EU bodies, states, multinational corporations and civil society organizations on matters related to 'business and human rights'. His books include *Socio-Economic Rights in Emerging Free Markets: Comparative Insights from India and China* (editor) (Routledge, 2015); *Human Rights Obligations of Business: Beyond the Corporate Responsibility to Respect?* (co-editor with David Bilchitz) (Cambridge University Press, 2013); *Confronting Capital Punishment in Asia: Human Rights, Politics, Public Opinion and Practices* (co-editor with Roger Hood) (Oxford University Press, 2013); and *Regulating Corporate Human Rights Violations: Humanizing Business* (Routledge, 2012). Deva is one of the founding editors-in-chief of the *Business and Human Rights Journal* (Cambridge University Press), and sits on the editorial board of the *Netherlands Quarterly of Human*

Rights and the *Vienna Journal on International Constitutional Law.* In 2014, he was elected a member of the Executive Committee of the International Association of Constitutional Law.

ERIKA GEORGE is the Samuel D. Thurman a professor of Law at University of Utah's S.J. Quinney College of Law. She teaches constitutional law, international human rights law, international environmental law and seminar courses on corporations and human rights. She earned her BA from the University of Chicago and her JD from Harvard Law School. She also holds an MA in International Relations from the University of Chicago. Prior to entering the legal academy, she was a corporate litigation associate with law firms in Chicago and New York City. The *BBC, The Economist, NBC News, CNN* and the *Christian Science Monitor* have reported human rights investigations she conducted as a research fellow for Human Rights Watch. Her current research explores the responsibilities of multinational corporations to respect international human rights and various efforts to hold corporations accountable for alleged rights violations. She is the author of *Incorporating Rights*, forthcoming.

KHALIL HAMDANI is a visiting professor at the Graduate Institute of Development Economics of the Lahore School of Economics, Pakistan. He holds a BA from The Johns Hopkins University and a PhD in Economics from Georgetown University. He served 29 years with the United Nations. He was a director in the United Nations Conference on Trade and Development (UNCTAD). He led UNCTAD's Division on Investment, Technology and Enterprise Development, which produces the annual *World Investment Report.* He created the United Nations programme on investment policy reviews, which was declared a 'valuable mechanism' by the G-8 Heads of State Summit in 2007. He has provided policy advice and training to investment officials in Africa, Asia, the Middle East and Latin America. He has published journal articles and co-edited with John Dunning a book on *The New Globalism and Developing Countries* (1997). His most recent publication is on the *United Nations Centre on Transnational Corporations* (2015).

LISA LAPLANTE is an associate professor at New England Law Boston, where she also directs the Center for International Law and Policy (CILP). Before entering academia, Professor Laplante earned her JD from New York University School of Law where she was a Root-Tilden-Kern Public Interest Scholar. Following graduation, she was a Furman Fellow with the Lawyers Committee for Human Rights (now Human Rights First) where she first began to work on the theme of business and human rights. She then spent half a decade in Latin America, beginning as a researcher with the Peruvian Truth and Reconciliation Commission as a grantee of the Notre Dame University Transitional Justice Program. She co-founded the Praxis Institute for Social Justice, where she served as deputy director. At Praxis, she oversaw multi-site research projects as well as directing trial monitoring projects. Her award-winning scholarship has been published by Cambridge University Press, other publishers and top law journals such as the *Yale Human Rights and Development Journal*, the *Virginia Journal of International Law* and the *Michigan Journal of International Law*, among others. Professor Laplante was invited to be a fellow at the Institute for Advanced Studies at Princeton in 2008 and then went on to become a visiting professor at Marquette Law School and then the University of Connecticut School of Law, where she was also visiting assistant professor and Richard D. Tulisano Human Rights Fellow. In 2012–2013 she served as the interim director of the University of Connecticut's Thomas J. Dodd Research Center, to help create programming on business and human rights.

SHELDON LEADER is founder and director of the Essex Business and Human Rights Project, and Professor of Law, University of Essex. His interest is in the relationship between economic non-state actors and human rights, drawing on political philosophy, labour law, company law and economic law. He negotiated, with the support of Amnesty International UK, the *Human Rights Undertaking* with British Petroleum: the first legally binding human rights instrument to accompany an international investment contract. Recent publications include 'Human Rights and the Constitutionalized Corporation' in *Multinationals and the Constitutionalization of the World Power System* edited by Stephane Vernac et al. (2017); 'Enterprise – network and enterprise – groups: the duty of care towards workers' in Adalberto Perulli and Tiziano Treu (eds.), *Enterprise and Social Rights* (2017); 'Statehood, Power, and the New Face of Consent.' *Indiana Journal of Global Legal Studies*, 23 (1), 127–142 (2016); 'Corporate Accountability', in M. Bovens, R. E. Goodin and T. Schillemans (eds.), *The Oxford Handbook on Public Accountability* (2014); 'Labor Rights in the World

Economy', in *Business and Human Rights*, L. Blecher et al. (eds.) (2014); 'Project Finance and Human Rights' in Bohoslavsky et al. (eds.), *Making Sovereign Financing and Human Rights Work* (2014). He received his PhD and BA from Oxford University, and his BA from Yale University.

CARLOS LOPEZ is the Senior Legal Advisor at the International Commission of Jurists (ICJ), and also a research associate to the Centre of International Studies, Barcelona. He joined the ICJ in January 2008 after six years of work in the United Nations in various posts, including work relating to the rule of law and democracy, economic and social rights and the right to development. He was lead legal advisor to the UN Commission of Inquiry into the Gaza Conflict (2009). Before that he worked for the ICJ (1998–1999), he worked for the Graduate Institute of International Studies in Geneva (2000) and for several international human rights organizations as well as national human rights NGOs in Peru. He holds a PhD and Masters in Public International Law (Graduate Institute of International Studies-Geneva University) and a Diploma in Sociology Studies and a law degree from the Catholic University of Peru.

RADU MARES is associate professor at the Raoul Wallenberg Institute of Human Rights and Humanitarian Law, and the Faculty of Law, Lund University, Sweden. With his background in international human rights law, he is specialized in the area of business and human rights, with a focus on multinational enterprises and global value chains. His work combines corporate social responsibility, corporate governance and transnational law perspectives. Mares has written about the relation between law and self-regulation, on corporate responsibilities in the mining industry and supply chain contexts, and more recently on the regulatory and governance implications of the UN Guiding Principles on Business and Human Rights. Mares has edited *The UN Guiding Principles on Business and Human Rights – Foundations and Implementation* (2012), and authored *The Dynamics of Corporate Social Responsibilities* (2008), 'De-centring human rights from the international order of states – The alignment and interaction of transnational policy channels' (*Indiana Journal of Global Legal Studies* 2016), and '"Respect" human rights: Concept and convergence' in Bird, Cahoy and Prenkert (eds.), *Law, Business and Human Rights – Bridging the Gap* (2014).

ROBERT MCCORQUODALE is the Director of the British Institute of International and Comparative Law in London. He is also a professor of

International Law and Human Rights, and former head of the School of Law, at the University of Nottingham, and a barrister at Brick Court Chambers in London. Previously, he was a Fellow and Lecturer in Law at St. John's College, University of Cambridge and at the Australian National University in Canberra. Before embarking on an academic career, he worked as a solicitor in commercial litigation with King & Wood Mallesons in Sydney and Herbert Smith Freehills in London.

Robert's research and teaching interests are in the areas of public international law and human rights law, including the role of non-state actors, and business and human rights issues. He has published widely in these areas. He has provided advice and training to governments, corporations, international organizations, non-governmental organizations and peoples concerning international law and human rights issues. Robert has published widely on business and human rights issues, including a large study on human rights due diligence in practice: http://human-rights-due-diligence.nortonrosefulbright.online/.

PETER MUCHLINSKI is Emeritus Professor of International Commercial Law at the School of Oriental and African Studies, University of London, and a door tenant at Brick Court Chambers in London. He is the author of *Multinational Enterprises and the Law* and has published extensively on transnational business regulation and, more recently, on business and human rights and comparative corporate law. He has acted as an adviser on international investment law issues for UNCTAD and has been a contributing author and member of the editorial team for the UNCTAD Papers on Issues in International Investment Agreements. He is currently a member of the editorial boards of the *Business Ethics Quarterly, The Yearbook of International Investment Law and Policy* and the *Business and Human Rights Journal*.

JUSTINE NOLAN is an associate professor in the Faculty of Law at UNSW Australia and Deputy Director of the Australian Human Rights Centre. She is a visiting scholar at the NYU Stern Centre for Business and Human Rights. She most recently published *Business and Human Rights: From Principles to Practice* (2016, co-edited with D. Baumann-Pauly). Prior to her appointment at UNSW in 2004, she was the director of the Business and Human Rights Program at the Lawyers Committee for Human Rights (now Human Rights First) in the United States. She is an editor of the *Australian Journal of Human Rights* and a member of the editorial board of the *Business and Human Rights Journal*.

MANOELA CARNEIRO ROLAND graduated with a Law degree from the Federal University of Viçosa, Minas Gerais, Brazil; she has a Master's degree in International Relations from the Catholic University of Rio de Janeiro (PUC-Rio) and PhD in International Law and Economic Integration at the State University of Rio de Janeiro (UERJ). She was Public International Law professor at PUC-Rio; course coordinator and professor of Constitutional Law at the Federal University of Viçosa, Minas Gerais, and is currently a professor at the Federal University of Juiz de Fora and Sub-Head of the Public Law Department. She teaches international public law and human rights at the MA in Law and Innovation. She also coordinates Homa – the Human Rights and Business Centre (www.projetodheufjf.com.br). Her research areas are human rights and business, public international law and international relations.

LORRAINE RUFFING is a development economist with extensive field experience in developing countries as well as with a wide range of development topics. She has worked for five different UN agencies. She earned an MA and PhD in Trade and Development from Columbia University, NY. She joined the UN Economic Commission for Europe in 1981 as an energy economist. Her next assignment was with UNCTC in New York where she led the work on transparency and disclosure in financial reporting entrusted to ISAR. She developed a demand-driven programme where ISAR pioneered disclosure in areas such as environmental accounting, corporate social responsibility, corporate governance as well as accounting by SMEs. She also undertook three seminal reports on the impact of TNC activities on the lands of indigenous peoples for the Sub-Commission on the Prevention of Discrimination and Protection of Minorities. This early work sparked off the Sub-Commission's further investigations into TNCs and human rights, which later resulted in the Human Rights Council's guidelines on business and human rights. When the UNCTC was abolished, she was selected to serve as the UNDP Deputy Representative in Uzbekistan. In 1995 she re-joined the remnant UNCTC staff in UNCTAD where she became a branch chief in charge of ISAR and enterprise development. Enterprise development included consolidating the EMPRETEC programme (for enterprise promotion) in Geneva as well as researching and initiating business linkages between TNCs and SMEs. Her recent book with Khalil Hamdani is on the *United Nations Centre on Transnational Corporations* (2015). Since retiring from UNCTAD, she has assisted the OECD to develop its annual publication on Financing SMEs and Entrepreneurs.

PENELOPE SIMONS is a professor at the Faculty of Common Law and a member of the Human Rights Research and Education Centre at the University of Ottawa. She has published widely in the area of business and human rights and is the co-author with Audrey Macklin of *The Governance Gap: Extractive Industries, Human Rights, and the Home State Advantage* (2014). She is also a co-author with J. Anthony VanDuzer and Graham Mayada of *Integrating Sustainable Development into International Investment Agreements: A Guide for Developing Country Negotiators* (2013). Her current research examines the human rights implications of domestic and extraterritorial corporate activity, international law and corporate impunity for violations of human rights, violence against women and resource extraction, as well as the intersections between transnational corporate activity, human rights and international economic law. She is a member of the editorial boards of the *Business and Human Rights Journal* and the Edward Elgar Series in Human Rights.

SIGRUN SKOGLY is Professor of Human Rights Law at Lancaster University (UK), where she also serves as Associate Dean for Postgraduate Studies in the Faculty of Arts and Social Sciences. She has written extensively on human rights obligations, and has several books and articles on extraterritorial human rights obligations, including *Beyond National Borders: Human Rights Obligations in International Cooperation* (2006) and *Universal Human Rights and Extraterritorial Obligations* (edited with Mark Gibney, 2010). She is a founding member of the Consortium on Extraterritorial Human Rights Obligations, and served as an expert in the group adopting the Maastricht Principles on States' Extraterritorial Human Rights Obligations in the area of Economic, Social and Cultural Rights in 2011.

LISE SMIT is research fellow in Business and Human Rights at the British Institute of International and Comparative Law. Previously, she was a practising advocate at the Cape Bar in South Africa. She has worked on business and human rights issues for the Business and Human Rights Resource Centre and the UN Global Compact Office. She was also law clerk to the Chief Justice of South Africa, Pius Langa, at the South African Constitutional Court. She has authored various publications in the area of business and human rights, including on human rights litigation against companies. Lise has an LLM in human rights law from the University of Stellenbosch, South Africa, and a Masters in International Law and Economics from the World Trade Institute in Berne, Switzerland.

BETH STEPHENS is a distinguished professor of Law at Rutgers Law School. She has written extensively on business and human rights, including 'Are Corporations People? Corporate Personhood under the Constitution and International Law', 44 *Rutgers Law Journal* 1 (2014) and 'The Amorality of Profit: Transnational Corporations and Human Rights', 20 *Berkeley Journal of International Law* 45 (2002). She has published a variety of articles on the relationship between international and domestic law, focusing on the enforcement of international human rights norms through domestic courts. Professor Stephens is currently an advisor to the American Law Institute's Restatement (Fourth) of the Foreign Relations Law of the United States. She has served as a legal consultant to a network of human rights groups formulating proposals for a new treaty on business and human rights. As a cooperating attorney with the Center for Constitutional Rights, Professor Stephens continues to litigate human rights cases, including *Mamani v. Berzain*, a lawsuit against the former president of Bolivia for the killing of civilians by troops under his command. Recent publications include 'The Alien Tort Statute, Kiobel, and the Struggle for Human Rights Accountability', in *For the Sake of Present and Future Generations* (William Schabas et al. (eds.), 2015), and 'The Curious History of the Alien Tort Statute', 89 *Notre Dame Law Review* 1467 (2014).

PREFACE

The power to impact upon human rights rests not only with states but also with powerful non-state actors such as businesses. This statement has always been true, but the power of non-state actors has become increasingly evident with the rise of globalization and interactions – commercial and otherwise – across borders. Business, for instance, has taken advantage of the new global order and brought with it both advantages and major challenges. The lack of adequate regulation of financial markets was a major contributing factor to the global financial crisis in 2008. Shocks such as these have highlighted the need for adopting global governance measures to address the new circumstances of increased and diffused private power.

Human rights are the central normative prong of the global world order since the Second World War and offer protection for the most fundamental interests of individuals. The rise of private power has also brought with it greater possibilities for the violation of human rights by businesses as well as opportunities for them to contribute towards the realization of such rights. Discussions around a possible treaty on business and human rights (BHR) are thus timely: one of the most important reasons for such a treaty is that it would expressly address some of the lacunas in international law that impact on the ability of victims of human rights violations by corporations to gain access to effective remedies.

The idea for this book germinated at an Asia-Pacific consultation about the proposed BHR treaty organized by the International Network for Economic, Social and Cultural Rights (ESCR-Net) and the International Federation for Human Rights (FIDH) in Chiang Mai in May 2015. The two editors participated in this consultation with civil society organizations (CSOs) and communities affected by corporate human rights violations as part of a Legal Group constituted by ESCR-Net and FIDH. The Chiang Mai consultation was part of a ground-breaking project, the Treaty Initiative, spearheaded by ESCR-Net and FIDH, in that it sought to provide CSOs working at the grassroots level and individuals affected by business-related human rights violations with an opportunity to inform the process of creating human rights norms at the international level. As part of this process, consultations were later held in Nairobi and Mexico City. The two editors are most grateful to ESCR-Net and FIDH for providing us with a unique opportunity of listening to the voices of victims of business-related human rights abuses and exploring with other experts legal solutions to the regulatory gaps that were exposed during these bottom-up consultations.

At the Asia-Pacific consultation and during subsequent exchanges, the two editors felt the need for concrete proposals concerning the proposed BHR treaty to be placed on the table as to how to address a number of regulatory problems raised at the international level, given that many states continue to show an unwillingness or incapacity to act against corporate violators of human rights at the domestic level. There has also been scepticism expressed by some states and other stakeholders about supporting a treaty process without seeing proposals concerning its content. Against this backdrop, the two editors, with the support of the International Commission of Jurists (ICJ), decided to organize a roundtable in Geneva in October 2015, where we invited selected leading BHR experts to address a number of core questions around the proposed treaty and to develop proposals concerning essential components thereof. With the exception of a few chapters, this book emerges from the excellent papers that were presented at that roundtable.

This book is a response to multiple legal and political challenges faced by the current process initiated by a June 2014 resolution of the Human Rights Council (HRC) to negotiate an international legally binding instrument to regulate the activities of transnational corporations (TNCs) and other business enterprises. In certain ways, the readers may also find this book to be a sequel to a 2013 book – *Human Rights Obligations of Business: Beyond the Corporate Responsibility to Respect?* – co-edited by the two editors, which offered a critical appraisal of the output emanating from the mandate of the UN Secretary General's Special Representative on business and human rights. The strong demands for a BHR treaty by civil society and many states just a few years after the unanimous endorsement of the Guiding Principles on Business and Human Rights by the HRC in June 2011 perhaps reflects the need to go beyond that framework, especially concerning the 'responsibility' of business to 'respect' human rights.

We thank the ICJ for the support they provided in hosting the round-table on which this book is based. The editors would also like to thank their respective institutions (the City University of Hong Kong and the University of Johannesburg) for their continued support of our academic work. We also make particular mention of the commitment of the governments of Ecuador and South Africa as well as of CSOs to ensure that the current treaty process achieves its goals. We do hope that the contributions in this volume will persuade at least some agnostic states to join the process in good faith and strengthen corporate accountability for human rights violations at the international level.

We are also very grateful to Kim Hughes, the Senior Commissioning Editor at Cambridge University Press, for her professionalism and support of this book project throughout the entire process. We express our gratitude to the entire Cambridge University Press team for the efficient production of this volume. We are also deeply grateful to the contributing authors to this volume: we were overwhelmed by the positive response of all the authors – many of whom are leaders in the BHR field – to our invitation to contribute to this project. Their hard work, co-operation, professionalism and patience enabled us to move from the roundtable to publication in a relatively short period. We also thank the anonymous reviewers of this book for their comments and suggestions which have helped to improve a number of features of the book.

Surya Deva would like to thank Swati, Vyom and Varun for standing with him in pursuit of all his academic endeavours and for being accom-modative of his long absences from home. He also expresses gratitude to his parents and other family members for offering unwavering support and encouragement over the years. Surya acknowledges invaluable insights about the proposed BHR treaty gained from interaction with diplomats, government officials, policy makers, scholars, students, law-yers, business representatives, trade union leaders, CSOs, social activists and affected communities.

David Bilchitz would like to thank the staff at the South African Institute for Advanced Constitutional, Public, Human Rights and International Law, a centre of the University of Johannesburg, which continues to provide a stimulating, intellectual family within which to conduct research and debate key questions around improving the human rights regime both domestically and internationally. He would also like to thanks his parents – Ruven and Cynthia – for their unconditional and unstinting love and support for all his endeavours. Last but not least,

David thanks his close family, friends and network of colleagues around the world for providing the social, emotional and intellectual support that enabled him to undertake and complete projects such as this.

We hope that this book will contribute towards the process of developing a BHR treaty, prove to be a catalyst for debating some of the concrete proposals contained therein and play an important role in informing the positions of states as well as CSOs in that regard. Even if international politics prevents the proposed treaty from coming to fruition soon, the contributions in this volume should offer enduring insights about the need for, and the content of, binding rules at both domestic and international levels in the BHR field. We hope, however, that history will bend towards the arc of justice and the international community will take another historic step in developing further the international human rights regime by adopting a BHR treaty.

Introduction: Putting Flesh on the Bone

What Should a Business and Human Rights Treaty Look Like?

DAVID BILCHITZ

I.1 The Tragic Story of Bougainville and Four Legal Problems

Bougainville is a small island to the east of Papua New Guinea.[1] It also happens to have one of the largest copper deposits in the world. In 1964, CRA Limited – a subsidiary of the large multinational corporation (MNC) Rio-Tinto – began mining exploration in the area. A local corporation – Bougainville Copper Limited (BCL) – was formed with a majority shareholding by CRA Limited and a minority by the Papua New Guinea government. BCL was granted rights over 12,500 hectares of land by the Australian colonial administration against the wishes of large segments of the indigenous communities who had inhabited the island for centuries. Compensation was to be paid to the existing landowners but was widely regarded as inadequate. Initially, royalties of just 1.25 per cent of mineral exports were to be paid to the Bougainville island administration itself with only 5 per cent (of that 1.25 percent) going to local landowners. BCL was also given a three-year tax holiday. The mining caused severe environmental pollution to the Jaba river system, with 150 million tonnes of mine tailing being released into the river. This affected the access of the population to much-needed food sources (such as fish from the river) and their very livelihoods were at stake given the importance of the river to their

---

[1] The paragraph below is a simplified account of a complex history drawn from the sources that follow. For a more detailed analysis of the events surrounding the mining and the civil war, see K. Laslett 'State Crime by Proxy: Australia and the Bougainville Conflict' (2012) 52 *British Journal of Criminology* 705–723; A. Regan 'Causes and Course of the Bougainville conflict' (1998) 33 *Journal of Pacific History* 269–285; H. Thompson 'The Economic Causes and Consequences of the Bougainville Crisis' (1991) 17 *Resources Policy* 69–85; and R.J. May 'Papua New Guinea's Bougainville Crisis' (1990) 3 *The Pacific Review* 174–177.

lives. In 1975, Australia granted Papua New Guinea independence and Bougainville was included as a part of this newly independent country. The unhappiness with the state of affairs surrounding the mine grew and, in the 1980s, this led to riots and the formation of a rebel group which armed itself. The Papua New Guinea administration sought forcibly to crush the rebellion that arose as the mine contributed a significant amount of revenue to its coffers. A bloody civil war ensued between 1989 and 1997 and between 15,000 and 20,000 people died. In 2001, a peace agreement was signed and there is currently an attempt to create reconciliation in a traumatized community. The mine remains closed.

I have begun this chapter with a concrete account of this tragic story as it raises a number of the key problems that provide the background against which the debate surrounding a treaty on business and human rights (BHR) is taking place. The demand made by a massive coalition of civil society organizations (CSOs) known as the Treaty Alliance as well as many academics for such a treaty arises against a backdrop of a number of core problems which have surfaced in recent years around the violation of human rights by businesses alone or in conjunction with states. Understanding these problems is key to addressing the main purpose of this book: to envisage what the content of a BHR treaty should include.

The first of these problems is what we might term the '*problem of corporate human rights obligations*'. The Bougainville case highlights the tremendous impact that businesses can have upon the human rights of individuals. For instance, the environmental devastation caused by the mining operations had an impact on the health of the people as well as their access to adequate food. The right to an adequate standard of living – which includes the right to food – and the right to highest attainable standard of physical and mental health are both protected in international human rights law.[2] Yet, when it comes to determining the obligations flowing from these rights, the focus has traditionally been on the role of the state in this regard. Although corporations can clearly have a severe effect on the enjoyment of these rights, there is no clarity in international law as to whether they have direct obligations flowing from these rights, and, if so, what the nature and extent of these obligations are. Moreover, international law often protects corporations and their commercial interests through international trade and investment regimes, without considering the impact of these activities upon human rights.

---

[2] See, for instance, articles 11 and 12 of the International Covenant on Economic, Social and Cultural Rights (entered into force 3 January 1976), 993 UNTS 3 (ICESCR).

The second problem is that many existing regulatory solutions focus on the recognized state obligation to protect individuals against harms caused by third parties such as corporations.[3] The Bougainville case, however, illustrates the fact that the state is often a co-perpetrator with corporations in violating human rights: in the worst cases seen internationally, the state perpetrates its own violations and so exacerbates corporate violations and, in other cases, it simply fails to act against the corporation where such violations take place. In the context of developing countries, states often desperately attempt to attract foreign investment and are reluctant to act against large MNCs. In some cases, institutional structures within the state are too weak and flawed to offer any hope of action to protect rights and provide remedies. States thus are often unable and/or unwilling to exercise their duty to protect. This is what we may refer to as the '*problem of weak state governance*'.

The third problem arises from the dominant form in which businesses are generally structured in the modern world. There are indeed many possible legal forms through which business can be conducted such as a partnership or sole proprietorship. Yet, the dominant business entity today is the corporation which offers its shareholders a number of benefits. The law confers on a corporation a separate legal personality, which in turn provides the basis for limiting generally the liability of shareholders to the capital they invest in the firm and for recognizing that the entity in question has the benefit of perpetual succession. Limited liability is designed to have a number of social and economic benefits through encouraging entrepreneurship, innovation and risk-taking. At the same time, it also has a number of risks, allowing individuals to limit their responsibility for social harms they cause through the pursuit of business through the corporate form, creating serious moral hazards.[4] The use of complex group structures of corporations with the creation of multiple subsidiaries is also a vehicle through which liability for social harms can be limited. Globalization has added to this complexity with group structures and shareholding taking place across international borders. In Bougainville, for instance, we see the creation of a new corporation on the island whilst the actual shareholding lies in other corporations in different parts of the world. The main corporation on the island is the focus of attention whereas the levers of power may actually lie elsewhere. Yet, it is

---

[3] The obligation to protect is widely recognized in international human rights law, for example, in the famous *Velasquez Rodriguez v. Honduras* Inter-American Court of Human Rights, (ser. C) no. 4 (July 29, 1988) paras. 172–174.

[4] See, for instance, Joel Bakan *The Corporation: the Pathological Pursuit of Profit and Power* (Penguin, 2004).

difficult to hold the actual decision-makers and those who benefit from human rights violations accountable. Similarly, complex supply chain structures in the global economy create a situation where multiple actors are involved across borders and it is difficult to pin-point responsibility or determine who holds actual control. Whilst the structures of doing business are interconnected, the law still often regards each corporation as a separate entity. We might call this the 'problem of corporate structure'.

Finally, many of these problems cumulatively lead to the difficulty for victims of human rights violations by corporations in gaining access to effective remedies.[5] The lack of a clear recognition of legal obligations upon corporations means that legal remedies are unavailable unless provided for within specific jurisdictions. Weak governance and complex corporate structures inhibit access to remedies too. There are several additional problems that arise here: where weak governance prevents an action in a particular jurisdiction, victims of human rights violations may seek a remedy in another country. Yet, jurisdictional doctrines such as *forum non conveniens* often pose serious difficulties in even commencing legal proceedings against a corporation across borders where courts need to be convinced as to why they should hear a case about a human rights violation taking place in another jurisdiction. There are also severe evidentiary obstacles to succeeding in a case in a different jurisdiction. These problems often make it difficult to gain a remedy in other countries. Currently, there are no legal fora at the international level which are set up to provide general relief to victims of human rights violations by corporations. The people of Bougainville are unlikely to succeed within the structures of Papua New Guinea, against BCL and there seem to be no alternative forum in which they can pursue their claims. This is what we might term the 'problem of access to remedies'.

I.1.1   A Treaty Process Commences and the Purpose of This Book

As we have seen, these four problems have a serious adverse impact on the realization of human rights for individuals. The question is whether it is possible to design legal solutions to these interconnected problems. The key purpose of doing so must remain squarely before us: that is, to prevent the violation of human rights and to advance the achievement thereof across the world. The growing recognition of the potential impact of corporations

---

[5] There is in fact a right to access a remedy under international law. See, for instance, Chapters 14 and 15 by Erika George/Lisa Laplante and Beth Stephens, respectively, in this volume. See also International Commission of Jurists, *Needs and Options for a New International Instrument in the Field of Business and Human Rights* (2014), 16.

upon human rights and the problems they create has stimulated a number of regulatory initiatives in the last 40 years. These have ranged from the attempt to draft a code of conduct for MNCs to encouraging a voluntary commitment on their part to respect human rights in terms of the United Nations Global Compact. A group of United Nations experts developed a document called the Draft Norms on the Responsibilities of Transnational Corporations and Other Business Enterprises which failed to gain widespread recognition at the international level. Thereafter, the United Nations appointed a Special Representative of the Secretary General on Business and Human Rights (SRSG), who developed the Guiding Principles on Business and Human Rights (GPs), which have achieved more widespread acceptance. I shall not engage in an analysis or detailed history of these initiatives on which there is much writing[6] other than to indicate that the state of affairs that exists in the world today is one where there is no adequate solution to the four problems identified above.

Against this backdrop, in June 2014, Ecuador and South Africa sponsored a resolution at the United Nations Human Rights Council 'to establish an open-ended intergovernmental working group on a legally binding instrument on transnational corporations and other business enterprises with respect to human rights'.[7] The mandate of this open-ended intergovernmental working group (OEIGWG) 'shall be to elaborate an international legally binding instrument to regulate, in international human rights law, the activities of transnational corporations and other business enterprises'.[8] Preliminary discussions about the nature, scope and content of the treaty took place during the first session of the OEIGWG, which was held in July 2015 and attended primarily by the states from the Global South as well as CSOs. These discussions continued during the second session held in October 2016, in which some developed countries as well as the European Union too engaged with the debate. The Chair-Rapporteur of the OEIGWG is expected to prepare elements of a draft text of the proposed treaty before the third session to be held in October 2017.

---

[6] See, the detailed analysis in S. Deva *Regulating Corporate Human Rights Violations: Humanizing Business* (Routledge, 2012) as well as the overview in D. Bilchitz and S. Deva 'The Human Rights Obligations of Business: a Critical Framework for the Future' in S. Deva and D. Bilchitz (eds.) *Human Rights Obligations of Business: Beyond the Corporate Responsibility to Respect?* (Cambridge University Press, 2013).

[7] Human Rights Council, 'Elaboration of an international legally binding instrument on transnational corporations and other business enterprises with respect to human rights,' A/HRC/RES/26/9 (14 July 2014).

[8] *Ibid.*

The current treaty process has triggered discussions around the world concerning both the desirability and possible content of the proposed BHR treaty. Whilst there remains uncertainty about whether a treaty will be adopted ultimately or not, the *process* of negotiating such a treaty in itself should prove to be valuable. It can, for example, help address the problems raised above through clarifying complex legal questions, concretizing human rights standards applicable to companies, bringing back the focus on removing obstacles to access to remedies in transnational litigation, and triggering a range of initiatives aimed at enhancing corporate accountability for human rights violations.

This book aims to play a role in this process through informing the ongoing debate about the value of a legally binding international instrument, debating complex and controversial issues concerning the treaty, and creating concrete proposals concerning the nature, scope and content of the proposed treaty. Indeed, some states and academics have held back from supporting this initiative as a result of doubts surrounding what such a treaty would look like. This book involves a number of leading scholars from all over the world attempting to rise to the challenge of defining the contours of the proposed BHR treaty and elaborating upon how it can solve a number of the pressing problems raised above.

The rest of this chapter will be structured as follows: the next part will present five arguments in support of such a treaty that respond directly to the four problems raised above. I will then consider some of the objections raised by treaty sceptics and provide responses. The last part of the introduction will outline our approach towards developing the content of the treaty and provide a thematic mapping of the contributions in this volume. It is important to emphasize that, whilst this introduction will engage with the debate around the 'why' question about the treaty, this book, in a sense, commences from the starting point that such a treaty would be desirable. The central purpose of the book is to develop an understanding of what such a treaty should contain and how the treaty might help in solving some of the existing regulatory challenges.

I.2   Can a Treaty Help Address the Four Problems?[9]

The four problems identified above cannot be solved without a change in the legal framework governing businesses and their operations across the

---

[9] This section and the next section dealing with objections to the treaty draw material from my recent article D. Bilchitz 'The Necessity for a Business and Human Rights Treaty' (2016) 1 (2) *Business and Human Rights Journal* 203.

world. Such a reform can take place in different ways: through domestic legal reforms, regional interventions, changes in international law or perhaps a combination of all of these. This section of the chapter considers five arguments as to the desirability of states creating binding international law on the subject through a new BHR treaty. These are not the only arguments that are possible and some other arguments have been canvassed in this very book. The arguments presented also provide some guidance on how the content of the treaty should be elaborated.

I.2.1   The Argument from Bindingness

The starting point for any discussion surrounding a treaty in this area must be a concern for the protection of human rights, which are articulated from the perspective of the beneficiaries of those rights.[10] Human rights are not specific about the agents that are required to realize them: what they entail are obligations on others both to desist from behaviour that would imperil these entitlements and to assist in the realization thereof.[11] The early historical contexts in which human rights claims arose – such as the French revolution where the oppressive exercise of state power needed to be addressed – meant that the focus was upon the obligations of the state in relation to the civil and political rights of citizens. However, those early origins do not mean that states are the only agents upon whom obligations fall to realize these entitlements. Indeed, the fact that rights are concerned with protecting the fundamental interests of individuals implies logically that they must have binding consequences for all agents who have the capacity to impact upon them.[12] The exact nature and distribution of these obligations amongst agents may of course vary: nevertheless, a necessary corollary of the institutionalization of human rights in international law

---

[10] See D. Bilchitz *Poverty and Fundamental Rights* (Oxford University Press, 2007), 74, in response to an objection by O. O'Neill, *Towards Justice and Virtue* (Cambridge University Press, 1996), 134.

[11] A. Kuper, 'Introduction: The Responsibilities Approach to Human Rights' in Andrew Kuper (ed.), *Global Responsibilities. Who Must Deliver on Human Rights?* (New York: Routledge, 2005), x.

[12] 'If human rights are aimed at the protection of human dignity, the law needs to respond to abuses that do not implicate the state directly.' Steven R Ratner, 'Corporations and Human Rights: A Theory of Legal Responsibility' (2001) 111 *Yale Law Journal* 443, 472. See also Florian Wettstein *Multi-National Corporations and Global Justice: Human Rights Obligations of a Quasi-Governmental Organisation* (Stanford University Press, 2009) 285; and David Bilchitz 'Corporations and the Limits of State-Based Models for Protecting Human Rights in International Law' (2016) *Indiana Journal of Global Studies* 143.

was that multiple agents – including businesses – would be bound by their requirements. The increased capacity of businesses in recent years to impact upon human rights provides added impetus for this development. The proposed BHR treaty will, therefore, provide a clear recognition and articulation of the important normative position that human rights under international law impose legally binding obligations upon businesses. In so doing, it would help address the problem of corporate human rights obligations identified above.

One of the main reasons why such a step is necessary is that the SRSG has created considerable uncertainty by asserting that international human rights law does not directly bind corporations legally (other than in relation to international crimes).[13] Corporations, the SRSG contended, should rather take account of human rights as they represent the social expectations of communities without which such bodies would lack a social license to operate.[14] The mandate thus took the retrogressive step of declaring the edifice of legally binding human rights in international law to be mere moral claims against corporations which could only entail social (rather than legal) censure. These circumstances demonstrate the need for an international treaty to recognize expressly that businesses have legal obligations under international human rights law. No vehicle other than an international treaty would establish this principle with the required clarity and authority.[15]

Recognizing the direct obligations of corporations under international law represents one potential route along which a treaty could be drafted in this area. There are also significant reasons why it is desirable for direct binding legal obligations to be recognized under international law.[16] Without doing so, it is only the state that can be held accountable for its own failure to protect individuals against harms by third parties. For

---

[13] Commission on Human Rights 'Interim Report of the Special Representative of the Secretary-General on the Issue of Human Rights and Transnational Corporations and Other Business Enterprises', E/CN.4/2006/97 (22 February 2006) (SRSG '2006 Interim Report') paras. 64–65. For a more detailed critique from which I draw some of the arguments in this section, see D. Bilchitz, 'A Chasm Between "Is" and "Ought"? A Critique of the Normative Foundations of the SRSG's Framework and the Guiding Principles' in Deva and Bilchitz, n. 6, 107–137.

[14] Human Rights Council, 'Protect, Respect and Remedy: A Framework for Business and Human Rights', A/HRC/8/5 (7 April 2008), para. 54 (2008 Framework).

[15] A. E. Boyle 'Some Reflections on the Relationship of Treaties and Soft Law' (1999) 48 *International and Comparative Law Quarterly* 901 at 903–904 recognizes that a treaty generally demonstrates a 'greater sense of commitment than a soft law instrument' and is particularly appropriate for the elaboration of human rights law.

[16] I also provide a theoretical reason in Bilchitz, n. 9. at 208.

example, in the Bougainville case, only Papua New Guinea could be held accountable and not the copper firm, BCL.[17] It seems fundamentally unfair, however, that the primary agent which is responsible for a harm is not capable of being held to account.

The recognition of binding obligations is particularly important when considering the connection between legal obligations and the right to have access to a remedy.[18] Without an understanding of the legal obligations corporations bear with respect to human rights, it will not be possible for victims of rights violations to claim access to a legal remedy against such a corporation. This is perhaps one of the strange features of the GPs: whilst recognizing in the third central pillar that victims of rights violations should have access to a *legal* remedy, they do not expressly recognize binding *legal* obligations of corporations for violations of human rights in the second pillar. Access to a remedy is itself a human right in international law[19] but how can a remedy be provided without recognition of a prior legal obligation? The role of a treaty in expressly recognizing that businesses have legally binding human rights obligations thus becomes the crucial precondition for providing legal remedies to individuals against such entities.

These arguments become particularly significant in contexts where the state cannot be held accountable. There are cases where the state cannot be shown to be culpable or complicit in the harm caused. Moreover, the state 'duty to protect' is not an absolute obligation; rather, it is formulated in such a way so as to require the state to exercise reasonable due diligence to ensure that it establishes the relevant legal frameworks and mechanisms to prevent third parties from harming human rights.[20] Without recognition of direct obligations upon corporations, there will be no possibility of corporate liability in scenarios where the state lacks legal culpability and no access to a remedy for the victims of those violations.

There are also circumstances where it is not possible to pursue remedies against a corporation within a particular state due to the problems of weak governance discussed above where states are unable or unwilling to

---

[17] A similar point can be made about the case of *Socio-Economic Rights Action Centre v. Nigeria* Communication 155/96, African Commission on Human and Peoples' Rights (2001) AHRLR 60 where the African Commission could not find any violations on the part of the corporation in question (Shell) but only the Nigerian government.

[18] I am indebted to Meghan Finn for highlighting this point to me.

[19] Article 2 of the International Covenant on Civil and Political Rights.

[20] *Velasquez Rodriguez v. Honduras*, n. 3, paras. 172 and 174.

comply with their 'duty to protect' obligations. There will be no possibility of holding corporations to account in another jurisdiction or before an international mechanism without recognition that there are legal obligations that they have violated. Only an international treaty has the authoritative nature to establish that corporations are bound by international human rights irrespective of whether states comply with their 'duty to protect' obligations.

I.2.2   The Argument from Mutual Assurance

It may be argued that there is no need for an international treaty to bind corporations directly as states currently are already under an obligation to enact a regulatory framework which establishes obligations of third parties – including businesses – in relation to human rights. Whilst we have seen that this duty to protect is often not sufficient to protect individuals' rights, a treaty will be desirable even on this reasoning.

As Sheldon Leader indicates in Chapter 3 in this book,[21] an international agreement such as a treaty can provide states with 'mutual assurance' that each will enact laws meeting certain minimum standards regulating corporate activity in relation to human rights. Without such an assurance, there will be little incentive for individual states acting on purely self-interested grounds to enact detailed regulation in this area which might have the effect of deterring investment. A treaty can help set minimum standards that domestic regulation for corporations must meet. Thus, even if states reject the possibility of recognizing direct human rights obligations for corporations under international law, there will still be merit in negotiating a BHR treaty. An indirect route could be followed whereby states accept the obligation to enact laws that place certain human rights obligations upon corporations and address problems in existing regulation. This approach is less desirable in solving the problems identified above and, in particular, might struggle to address the problem of weak governance. Nevertheless, there would still be some merit in pursuing such a treaty project. Indeed, this argument also demonstrates why corporations that seek to hold themselves to ethical standards and wish to avoid harming fundamental rights should welcome such a treaty. By having a global common standard set across the world for businesses, no longer will it be possible to compete on the

---

[21] Chapter 3.

basis of lowering human rights standards. Furthermore, the costs that ethical companies bear in upholding human rights will need to be borne by all other companies, thus levelling up the playing field rather than levelling down.

I.2.3   The Argument from Norm Development

Whether international law clearly recognizes that corporations have binding human rights obligations or places an obligation on the states to enact such obligations, many questions remain about the exact nature and extent of these obligations. In determining the exact obligations of business in relation to human rights, there is a need for much development both at the international and national levels.

The GPs do not adequately address this difficult issue. Corporations generally have a responsibility to respect human rights – '[t]his means that they should avoid infringing on the human rights of others and should address adverse human rights impacts with which they are involved'.[22] The position has an immediate intuitive appeal: corporations must avoid doing harm such as the environmental damage that occurred in Bougainville. However, as is recognized today in domestic, regional and international fora, the mere infringement of a human right is not sufficient to determine that an actionable wrong has been done.[23] A further step is necessary, namely, determining the justification for the infringement and whether the benefits achieved can be said to be proportional to the harms caused to the human right in question.[24] Moreover, in relation to corporations, there is also a prior question, namely, whether the infringement of rights flows from an obligation that falls upon or applies to a corporation.[25] Both questions are elided by a simple focus on a 'responsibility to respect human rights'.

There is also the important question as to whether corporations only have negative obligations not to harm human rights. The GPs focus on such negative obligations with a very limited role for positive

---

[22] Guiding Principles on Business and Human Rights: Implementing the United Nations 'Protect, Respect and Remedy' Framework (A/HRC/17/31), Principle 11.

[23] See K. Moller *The Global Model of Constitutional Rights* (Oxford University Press, 2012) 2–17.

[24] See, for example, the Canadian position in *R. v. Oakes* [1986] 1 S.C.R. 103 and, the South African position, *S v. Makwanyane and Another* [1995] ZACC 3; 1995 (3) SA 391, paras. 100 ff.

[25] See Ratner, n. 12, who provides a sophisticated approach to this question.

obligations.[26] Yet, that view has been strongly contested by several prominent scholars in the fields of philosophy, business ethics and law, who contend that there are good reasons why corporations should indeed be recognized as having at least some positive obligations in relation to human rights.[27] This issue of the contributions corporations can make positively to realizing rights is particularly important for developing countries and it is significant that the Human Rights Council resolution, regarding the proposed BHR treaty, specifically references the right to development.[28] If BCL had made a strong contribution to advancing the human rights of the people of Bougainville instead of violating them, perhaps it would still be able to mine.

The above discussion has underlined the need for greater clarity in relation to both the negative and positive obligations that corporations have in relation to human rights. The answer to this problem is to develop a mechanism that can elaborate upon international standards in relation to BHR. An international legally binding instrument would be the best vehicle through which to do so: it could set up a mechanism which would be able to provide guidance across the world as to the implications of human rights for corporations. This would be of importance for both a direct and indirect approach to corporate obligations. That mechanism would help determine a common, consistent and objective base standard that could be applied to business globally.

If we look to other international human rights treaties, we see that they establish committees which perform similar tasks. These various bodies have employed General Comments to provide clarification, development and persuasive interpretations of the obligations imposed in the covenants. There is thus a need for a similar mechanism for the release of authoritative guidance on the application of international human rights

---

[26] See, for example, instances in the 2008 Framework, n. 14 in relation to anti-discrimination, para. 55 and, in relation to due diligence, para. 56; and the 2009 Report of the SRSG A/HRC/11/13, at paras. 61–65.

[27] See, for instance, N. Hsieh, 'The Obligations of Transnational Corporations: Rawlsian Justice and the Duty of Assistance' (2004) *Business Ethics Quarterly* 14; F. Wettstein, n. 12, 311–333; S. Wood 'The Case for Leverage-Based Corporate Human Rights Responsibility' (2012) 22 *Business Ethics Quarterly* 63, 76–92; M. Santoro 'Post-Westphalia and its Discontents: Business, Globalisation and Human Rights in Political and Moral Perspective' (2010) 20 *Business Ethics Quarterly* 281, 291–292; I. M. Young 'Responsibility and Global Justice: a Social Connection Model' (2006) *Social Philosophy and Policy* 127–130; D. Bilchitz, 'Do Corporations Have Positive Fundamental Rights Obligations?' (2010) 125 *Theoria* 11–26; and Bilchitz, note 13, 126–136.

[28] Human Rights Council, n. 7.

to companies. The normative importance, universality and binding force of human rights (as explicated in the first argument above) renders it appropriate that their content be explicated by the most authoritative mechanism possible under international law which could only be established by a treaty.[29] Such a mechanism would help address the problem of specifying the implications of human rights for corporations and also address the problem of weak governance where states lack the capacity to develop their own authoritative standards.

I.2.4   The Argument from Competing Obligations

A BHR treaty is necessary because of the rapid pace at which international law has developed in the twentieth century in relation to commerce and trade across sovereign borders. International trade regimes – most notably the treaties relating to the World Trade Organization – have developed to govern free trade across the world. States have also entered into numerous bilateral and multilateral investment treaties ostensibly to promote economic development. These investment treaties, however, not only confer legal rights upon corporate investors but also create binding mechanisms to settle disputes. Importantly, all these changes in relation to international trade and commerce occur through binding legal frameworks.

The relationship between trade/investment regimes and human rights law is a large subject matter which cannot be addressed in detail here.[30] Nevertheless, it is necessary to address in international law the problem of conflicts that may arise between commercial legal regimes and the demands of human rights law. At present, with no clarity as to the legal obligations of corporations under international human rights law, and

---

[29] I recognize that the status of general comments is generally not taken to be as binding as the particular contents of a treaty. Nevertheless, they have a status and persuasiveness that flows from the fact that the committee which issues them derives its authority from a binding treaty. This is what I mean by 'strongly authoritative' (which is not equivalent to binding law). See, for example, International Law Association 'Final Report on the Impact of Findings of the United Nations Human Rights Treaty Bodies' (2004) at 5.

[30] See, for example, S. Joseph, *Blame It On the WTO?: A Human Rights Critique* (Oxford: Oxford University Press, 2013); J. Dine and A. Fagan (eds.), *Human Rights and Capitalism: A Multidisciplinary Perspective on Globalisation* (Edward Elgar, 2006); F. Abbott et al., *International Trade and Human Rights: Foundations and Conceptual Issues* (University of Michigan Press, 2006); and M. Jacob, 'International Investment Agreements and Human Rights' (2010) 3 *INEF Research Paper Series on Human Rights, Corporate Responsibility and Sustainable Development*.

with most statements of responsibility in existing instruments being at best soft law (such as the GPs),[31] international commercial obligations are likely to trump those flowing from human rights in most cases. The GPs by their very nature lack the capacity to address the fundamental imbalance between commercial and human rights obligations as they have a very weak normative force in international law. A key important role for a BHR treaty would be the express recognition by states that businesses have legal obligations in relation to human rights with a similar (or greater) level of bindingness to what commercial regimes have.[32] This would enable the recognition that the human rights obligations could well conflict with commercial treaty obligations in international law, but the latter would not automatically trump the former.

I.2.5   The Argument from Access to Remedies

A key concern in the field of BHR is the ability to gain access to remedies for victims of human rights violations by companies. As we saw, a range of legal issues come together to create a major problem of accountability for victims of corporate rights violations (which I term the accountability gap). To address this gap, several interventions are necessary which could best be accomplished by a treaty.[33] As we have seen in the first argument, the starting point is to recognize that corporations themselves have binding legal obligations in relation to human rights for which they can be held to account. Once this is established, it is necessary to put in place institutional fora where these obligations can be enforced by overcoming procedural and conceptual obstacles identified above. A treaty is essential in doing so and two primary options seem available in this regard.[34]

---

[31]   J. Nolan, 'The Corporate Responsibility to Respect Rights: Soft Law or Not Law?' in Deva and Bilchitz, note 6, 138.

[32]   There is an interesting and controversial question about the extent to which there is a hierarchy of norms in international law: see, for example, D. Shelton, 'Normative Hierarchy in International Law' (2006) 100 *The American Journal of International Law* 291; M. Koskenniemi, 'Hierarchy in International Law: A Sketch' (1997) 8 *European Journal of International Law* 566 and E. Wet and J. Vidmar, *Hierarchy in International Law: The Place of Human Rights* (Oxford: Oxford University Press, 2012). Human rights would be key candidates for norms that have a superior status given their rootedness in the dignity of individuals: as a matter of normative philosophy, they *should* have this status. Yet, as international law develops, there is no clarity as to whether human rights are recognized to have this prior status and how they intersect with other bodies of international law.

[33]   The reform of a number of doctrines of corporate law is amongst these, a matter I cannot consider here in any detail.

[34]   See also International Commission of Jurists, n. 5 at 9.

The first would be to allow the possibility of companies being held liable for the damage caused in a particular state (the 'host' state) in a forum that exists in a different jurisdiction where either the parent or contracting company is based (often referred to as the 'home state') and where there is a stronger institutional structure to enable access to a remedy, if access to an effective remedy cannot be attained in the host state.[35] One possibility would be for states across the world to agree in a treaty to provide that they would enact laws allowing for extraterritorial jurisdiction over corporations that violate human rights with some connection to them (together with relevant modifications to their corporate law).[36] Such a treaty provision could also help address technical difficulties that arise when extraterritorial jurisdiction is exercised: encourage cooperation surrounding such matters as gathering evidence, certifying statements, securing the attendance of witnesses in courts of a foreign jurisdiction and assisting victims with legal representation.[37] At the same time, such a binding international instrument could enunciate, for instance, legal principles that can aid accountability of a parent company for human rights abuses by its subsidiaries across territorial borders.

The alternative possibility to close the accountability gap would be to create an international mechanism or court which could adjudicate on civil and/or criminal claims against corporations where they have violated human rights.[38] Such a mechanism would hold jurisdiction over corporations that operate in multiple jurisdictions and/or where the judicial system is not operating effectively. Developing such a mechanism would be a less unwieldy solution to the accountability gap than the home-state liability solution, which would require laws to be passed in every country that would inevitably vary in their content and effect. Such a mechanism would not, however, need to be considered the exclusive

---

[35] S. Deva, 'Acting Extraterritorially to tame multinational corporations for human rights violations: Who should "Bell the Cat"?' (2004) 5 *Melbourne Journal of International Law* 37; and O. De Schutter 'Towards a New Treaty on Business and Human Rights' (2016) 1 (1) *Business and Human Rights Journal* 47, 55.

[36] Such an approach could be modelled on the provisions of the United Nations Convention against Corruption (UNCAC) (2003) A/58/422. See A. Ramasastry, 'Closing the Governance Gap in the Business and Human Rights Arena: Lessons from the Anti-Corruption Movement' in Deva and Bilchitz, note 6, 162.

[37] See De Schutter, note 35, at 65.

[38] D. Cassel and A. Ramasastry 'White Paper: Options for a Treaty on Business and Human Rights' (2015) 6 *Notre Dame Journal of International and Comparative Law* 1, 33--4 also canvass the possibility of an international arbitration tribunal that could be developed to perform this task.

forum in which such matters could be resolved and only come into play when domestic avenues are exhausted. Such a mechanism would be an ambitious international solution for an international problem: it would still, though, need state support to ensure judgements are enforced and would have to avoid many of the pitfalls faced by international adjudicatory fora in other spheres.

I.3   Are There Any Good Reasons Why a Treaty Should Not Be Pursued?

The five arguments outlined thus far provide an affirmative case for the BHR treaty: they represent particular strands of argumentation that, when added together, add weight to the case for such an instrument to address existing regulatory gaps, ambiguities and inflexible doctrines which impede the advancement of human rights where businesses are central actors. The problems identified are legal in nature and thus require a response that provides solutions that have a legal effect: a treaty would be the leading contender to fill these gaps. Yet, the voting pattern on the Human Rights Council resolution establishing the OEIGWG as well as the nature of states' participation in the first two sessions of the OEIGWG indicates that there is much disagreement on this topic, particularly between the Global North countries and the Global South countries.[39] It thus becomes important to consider and respond to some of the objections that have been raised against the proposed BHR treaty.[40] I consider three objections below that have been raised against the treaty: as will be seen, most of these objections to the treaty are rooted in practical or political concerns rather than in deep questions of law. Several other objections are dealt with in other parts of the book.[41]

I.3.1   The Scale of the Proposed Treaty: Too Ambitious?

Objections have been made that the proposed treaty could attempt to 'establish an overarching international legal framework – a global

---

[39]   20 countries voted in favour, 14 were against, and 13 abstained.

[40]   Whilst Ruggie has been the most prominent critic, I also consider other academic commentators.

[41]   See, for instance, the chapter by Surya Deva who discusses the objections surrounding the footnote limiting the scope of a potential treaty; and the attempt to confine such a treaty only to gross human rights violations. I have added my own views on these topics in Bilchitz, n. 9, 220–227.

constitution of sorts – governing transnational corporate conduct under international human rights law'.[42] The problem, as John Ruggie argues, is that there is a wide diversity of concerns that need to be addressed which cannot be captured by one comprehensive treaty. He writes that BHR 'encompasses too many complex areas of national and international law for a single treaty instrument to resolve across the full range of internationally recognised human rights'.[43] Moreover, '[a]ny attempt to do so would have to be pitched at such a high level of abstraction that it would be largely devoid of substance, of little practical use to real people in real places, and with high potential for generating serious backlash against any form of further international legalization in this domain'.[44]

It is no doubt true that the relationship between business 'and' human rights covers a wide range of issues. This is, however, precisely why a treaty is a good idea.[45] The proposed treaty will establish a legal framework and a number of general principles in terms of which some of these complex issues would be resolved. As pointed out in the arguments for a treaty, it would also need to establish a mechanism for norm development and, possibly, adjudication of particular disputes. The treaty would not be meant to address every single issue that arises in this complex arena but to create the legal 'basic structure'[46] in terms of which such legal matters would be resolved. In turn, this could have an impact on the domestic laws of states concerning the relationship between corporations and human rights. Indeed, this is precisely the structure through which international human rights treaties in general operate: they outline broad rights and principles which are then developed by the structures that the treaties create in various general comments and country reports. Such a process

---

[42] John Ruggie, 'Quo Vadis? Unsolicited Advice to Business and Human Rights Treaty Sponsors' (9 September 2014), www.ihrb.org/commentary/quo-vadis-unsolicitedadvice-business.html (last visited 20 January 2017).

[43] Ibid.   [44] Ibid.

[45] Indeed, it has been pointed out that the same objection could be lodged against the GPs, which attempt to cover the entire domain of BHR. S. Deva, 'Corporate Human Rights Abuses and International Law: Brief Comments' http://jamesgstewart.com/corporate-human-rights-abuses-and-international-law-brief-comments/ (last visited 20 January 2017) and J. Tasioulas, 'Human Rights, No Dogmas: The UN Guiding Principles on Business and Human Rights' http://jamesgstewart.com/human-rights-no-dogmas-the-un-guiding-principles-on-business-and-human-rights/ (last visited 20 January 2017). Ruggie's response – 'Life in the Global Public Domain: Response to Commentaries on the UN Guiding Principles and the Proposed Treaty on Business and Human Rights' http://jamesg stewart.com/lifein-the-global-public-domain-response-to-commentaries (last visited 20 January 2017) – is unconvincing, conflating principle with pragmatic considerations.

[46] See J. Rawls, The Law of Peoples (Harvard University Press, 2001), 3–10.

would indeed have important consequences for 'real people in real places'. There would also be no need to reinvent the wheel in particular areas: the treaty need not replace the excellent work done by a body such as the International Labour Organization; rather, it could simply incorporate many of the standards already developed by such bodies.

I.3.2   The Treaty Process: What Happens in the Short Term?

Concern has also been expressed about the fact that negotiating a treaty would be a long-term project. Ruggie, once again, contends that people whose rights are affected by businesses need some form of relief in the present and cannot wait for the vague hope that such a treaty will be adopted.[47] Moreover, such a treaty, he claims could distract from implementing the GPs which have already been accepted by consensus in the Human Rights Council.[48] Erika George also expresses concern about what will happen in the interim and that the advancements of human rights protections against business should not be conditional upon the negotiation of a successful treaty.[49]

It is indeed true that negotiating a BHR treaty will take time. However, this is not a reason to avoid such a process: indeed, the development of all international law norms takes time and this objection would counsel against embarking on any ambitious process to advance international law. Two significant legal developments in recent years – the Rome Statute establishing an International Criminal Court and the edifice of international environmental law – did not appear overnight and have taken years of negotiation and deliberation. It is also important to recognize that the very process of negotiating a treaty can be designed to embody a range of virtues which would apply irrespective of the nature of the final legal text: these could include increased discussion across the world of the issues around BHR; engaging with victims of corporate human rights abuses to understand the

---

[47] Ruggie, Quo Vadis, n. 42.
[48] *Ibid.* The United States government explained its vote against the establishment of the inter-governmental working group partially in this way. US Mission to the UN 'Proposed Working Group would undermine efforts to implement Guiding Principles' (June 26, 2014) https://geneva.usmission.gov/2014/06/26/proposed-working-group-would-undermine-efforts-to-implement-guiding-principles-on-business-and-human-rights/ (last visited 20 January 2017).
[49] See E. George, 'Incorporate Rights: Making the Most of the Meantime' http://jamesgstewart.com/incorporating-rights-making-the-most-of-the-meantime/ (last visited 20 January 2017). A similar worry is expressed by M. Taylor 'A Business and Human Rights Treaty: Why Activists Should Be Worried' www.ihrb.org/commentary/board/business-and-human-rights-treaty-why-activists-should-be-worried.html (last visited 20 January 2017).

problems they face in more detail; and the stimulation of focused and creative legal thinking by experts to solve the problems faced in this area, recognizing that a range of measures are necessary at the international, regional and domestic levels to address corporate obligations in relation to human rights.[50] Indeed, this very book is the result of the commencement of a concrete treaty process which has stimulated creative legal thought.

Having said that, clearly, for any human rights advocate, it is critical to have an eye not only on the long-term but the short-term too. One of the instruments which can assist in the shorter-term is the GPs. As a recent report produced by the International Commission of Jurists remarks, there is no need to consider the ongoing treaty process and the GPs as mutually exclusive: indeed, they can complement one another.[51] Organizations supportive of a treaty can make it clear that they expect states driving the treaty process to show their good faith in complying with the GPs and establish National Action Plans, for instance. The Human Rights Council has created a Working Group of experts to help advance the GPs and there is, consequently, an institutional mechanism in place to advance the BHR agenda in the interim period. In this way, the expansion of the GPs can themselves help to create the very environment in which a treaty becomes possible and be bolstered in turn by the development of hard law on this topic.[52]

I.3.3 International Politics: Is There Sufficient Consensus for a Treaty?

A major concern that has arisen relating to a treaty is its ability to command consensus amongst a wide variety of nations.[53] John Ruggie suggests two scenarios are likely: either negotiations will continue for a long period and eventually be abandoned, or an eventual treaty will only garner a few ratifications amongst small nations who lack the power adequately to address corporate abuses.[54]

---

[50] Ruggie's advocacy of polycentric governance (see 'Life in the Global Public Domain', n. 4) and Deva's integrated theory of regulation (developed in *Humanizing Business*, n. 6) need not be at odds with the formation of a treaty.

[51] International Commission of Jurists, n. 5, at 9. Ruggie too seems to accept this point: J. Ruggie, 'Closing Plenary Remarks, UN Forum Business and Human Rights' http://jamesgstewart.com/closing-plenary-remarks-un-forum-on-business-and-human-rights/ (last visited 20 January 2017).

[52] See Shelton, n. 32, at 320–321.   [53] Ruggie, 'Quo Vadis', n. 42.

[54] See J. Ruggie, 'Life in the Global Public Domain', n. 45, where he raises the spectre of the Migrant Workers Convention which came into force in 1990 but has not thus far been ratified by any migrant worker-receiving country.

This is a fundamentally conservative challenge: the fact that no consensus exists now is held out to be a reason to stop a process that addresses
significant problems in international law. The reality is that, if such an
approach were to have been followed, some of the most important developments in international law – which command large amounts of consensus today – would never have taken place. For instance, the Additional
Protocol II to the Geneva Conventions,[55] the birth of the World Trade
Organization and the Marrakesh Agreement,[56] and the development of the
International Criminal Court[57] were all rooted in significant disagreement
between countries which have, over time, garnered greater consensus.
Moreover, the fact that no consensus exists currently on a binding BHR
instrument is no reason to suggest it will never exist in future. Already,
there have been shifts in the approach of several countries and strong
campaigns by CSOs could also have an impact.

The world is changing with the economic power of non-Western states
and corporations growing.[58] It is highly significant that, apart from
Brazil, the rest of the BRICS countries (Brazil, Russia, India, China and
South Africa) supported the Human Rights Council resolution in favour
of the formation of the OEIGWG tasked with elaborating upon a treaty.
Should BRICS countries come out strongly in favour of such a treaty, and
eventually ratify it, it will at least be distinctly embarrassing for developed
countries in the Global North to oppose it. Moreover, if the Global South
countries actively embrace the proposed BHR treaty and require corporations with operations therein to adhere to its provisions, this will no
doubt become the de facto standard that companies utilize when evaluating their own conduct. Importantly, the nature of this treaty will mean
that corporations with strong links to states who refuse to ratify it can still
be held to account if they operate in states which ratify the treaty. That is a
good reason for developed states to change their attitude towards the
treaty and engage in the process. If they fail to do so, in time, their
opposition might become less relevant as the treaty's provisions will

---

[55] See S. Junod, 'Additional Protocol II: History and Scope' (1983) 33 *The American University Law Review* 29.
[56] S. Bhandari, 'Doha Round Negotiations: Problems, Potential Outcomes and Possible Implications' (2012) 4 *Trade, Law and Development* 356.
[57] F. Benedetti and J. Washburn, 'Drafting the International Criminal Court Treaty: Two Years to Rome and an Afterword on the Rome Diplomatic Conference' (1999) 5 (1) *Global Governance* 1.
[58] Ruggie, 'Closing Plenary Remarks', n. 51.

become the de facto international standard applicable to corporations (and thus potentially enter into customary international law).

I.4   Developing the Content of a Treaty

The discussion of arguments for the proposed BHR treaty provides some guidance as to what such a treaty should contain. However, it is also necessary to debate and consider concrete legal proposals to address at least the four legal problems identified above as well as others that may arise. That is the task of this book: to begin putting flesh on the bone of the proposed BHR treaty and, in so doing, respond to objections that this cannot be done. We have structured the book with chapters arranged around five thematic parts.

Part I of the book considers the case for an international treaty in its historical context. The first chapter, by Hamdani and Ruffing, considers a prior initiative to adopt a binding code of conduct for transnational corporations (TNCs) in the 1990s. It examines the past in order to high-light lessons the international community could and should learn from the failure to adopt this code. Simons, in Chapter 2, considers the value added by a BHR treaty to the existing regulatory landscape in that it will generate a sense of obligation to address corporate impunity for human rights violations. She argues that a framework treaty on BHR – which embodies an agreement on a thinner set of initial commitments but allows for the gradual evolution of other shared commitments in the long run – may be the best way forward at this stage. Leader (Chapter 3) continues in a similar vein to advance arguments in support of the treaty – namely, the development of coherence between legal regimes and mutual assurance between states – and the interactions between them. His argument supports a process whereby treaties are built up in this area initially through agreements between a narrow range of parties (such as developing countries in a particular region and sector). Once developed states realize that these treaties have implications for them, there will be greater impetus for a global treaty on business and human rights. Both Simons and Leader argue for a modesty of ambition if a treaty initiative is to be successful.

These insights – both historical and futuristic – provide the backdrop for Part II of the book, which grapples with the relationship between principles and politics in shaping the contours of the BHR treaty. Backer, in Chapter 4, considers the approach of 'principled pragmatism' adopted by Ruggie in his mandate. Backer suggests that an ideal treaty will not be achievable and seeks to develop a coherent set of principles to guide the manner in which pragmatic compromises are to be made. Aragão and Roland (Chapter 5), on the other hand, consider the role played by CSOs as a 'counter-hegemonic' force in the treaty process, especially to avert the dangers of corporate capture. They also highlight the relevance of social movements building international human rights norms 'from below'. The International Peoples Treaty on the Control of Transnational Corporations, they suggest, is a case in point. Deva's Chapter 6 also explores the interplay of competing principles as well as political considerations in relation to two concrete issues that will arise in treaty construction. First, he considers the regulatory targets of a treaty: this involves the questions whether the treaty should apply only to corporations that cross-borders (TNCs), entities which raise particular problems for international law. Second, he considers the subject matter of the treaty and whether it should only deal with situations where gross human rights violations are involved, or whether it should cover the full panoply of situations where international human rights are implicated.

Part III of the book examines the approach that any treaty should take in determining the nature and extent of corporate obligations. This is a complex question and is approached from several angles by the chapter authors. Bilchitz (Chapter 7) argues that the proposed treaty should outline an analytical framework for determining concrete obligations rather than outlining those obligations themselves. He suggests guidance can be gained from constitutional law in doing so, which allows for a balance to be achieved between considerations relating to those who are the beneficiaries of human rights and those arising from the nature of particular agents responsible for realizing those rights (agent-relative considerations). McCorquodale and Smit consider the celebrated concept of human rights due diligence introduced by the GPs in Chapter 8. They consider the approach to be adopted by any treaty towards the inclusion of this concept and address important theoretical and practical questions that arise in doing so. Nolan also engages the discussion of due diligence but in the context of considering the liability of corporations for the human rights violations that take place in their supply chains in Chapter 9. She considers both potential principles of liability as well as mechanisms for greater accountability across supply chains. Mares (Chapter 10), on the other hand, deals with the regulation of 'lead firms' – which are often TNCs – in global value chains, and especially the complex interplay between mandatory human rights due diligence processes and the separation of entities principle. He proposes a 'two-track legalization of human rights due diligence' to respond to two regimes of corporate responsibility that raise very different regulatory challenges: the 'cessation regime' of coercive solutions where the lead firm has direct involvement in the human rights violations, and the 'leverage regime' of softer legalization where the involvement is indirect. This part of the book thus seeks to address both the problem of corporate human rights obligations as well as the problem of corporate structures identified above.

Part IV of the book goes on to consider the role of the other main actors in this sphere (namely, states) in enforcing the human rights obligations of business. Lopez considers two main models for such a treaty in Chapter 11: one that imposes direct obligations on corporations and one that does so through the agency of the state. He argues that, even if a direct model is adopted, it will be effective only if it provides for clear obligations addressed to states regarding the implementation of the treaty at the national and international levels. Skogly in Chapter 12 turns her attention to the nature and extent of states' extraterritorial obligations under international human rights law to regulate the overseas conduct of companies incorporated therein. She responds to criticisms mounted against extraterritorial obligations and suggests that the proposed BHR treaty should build on the Maastricht Principles on States' Extraterritorial Obligations in the Area of Economic, Social and Cultural Rights. Clarifying and codifying states' extraterritorial obligations is necessary not only to uphold the universality of human rights but also to help in taming the 'race to the bottom'. Finally, Muchlinski in Chapter 13 examines the relevance of human rights to international investment law and arbitration, and then considers three alternative models – with varying degrees of impact – that the proposed BHR treaty may adopt to inject human rights into international investment agreements. He points out that if there is a political will, legal means are available to ensure that both investors and arbitrators do not ignore human rights. The treaty may, for example, draw inspiration from UNCTAD's Investment Policy Framework for Sustainable Development and require states to insert an express human rights clause in investment agreements that makes the observance of human rights by investors a precondition for the enjoyment of their rights.

Part V of the book considers specifically one of the key reasons behind demands for a legally binding international instrument, that is, improving access to remedies for the victims of human rights violations by business. George and Laplante (Chapter 14) discuss perspectives of diverse stakeholders on access to a remedy in relation to the current negotiations for a BHR treaty. To facilitate convergence on what such a remedy entails, they unpack both substantive and procedural aspects of the right to access a remedy under international human rights law. George and Laplante propose that the proposed BHR treaty should keep elements of restorative justice in mind, recognize the right to reparations, embrace pluralistic methods of dispute settlement and include an individual complaint mechanism. Stephens in Chapter 15 identifies obstacles in gaining access to effective remedies and highlights an important prerequisite for effective remedies, that is, the right to information. After sketching the substance of the right to an effective and adequate remedy, she outlines 'core require- . ments' for all remedial mechanisms and then proposes several specific mechanisms which the proposed BHR treaty may adopt to enhance access to justice for victims of corporate human rights abuses. In the final chapter in this segment of the book, Darcy considers the manner in which a BHR treaty can develop international criminal law to include remedies for victims of activities by corporations that constitute international crimes. The chapter also considers lessons for the treaty process that can be learnt from the development of international criminal law over the last two decades and the challenges faced in that regard.

Deva, in his concluding chapter, articulates the role of the proposed BHR treaty in the context of other regulatory initiatives (including the GPs) and highlights why the chances of a treaty coming into fruition are higher this time in comparison to two previous UN attempts to adopt a legally binding international instrument. He then outlines a number of principles that should guide negotiations about the content of the treaty and recommends some key elements of the treaty by building on proposals advanced in this volume. Deva's chapter also flags a few practical considerations that should be kept in mind to achieve the goal of accomplishing a treaty under the current process initiated at the Human Rights Council in June 2014.

As can be seen from the arguments in this chapter and throughout the book, a BHR treaty that tries to address the four problems identified above will perhaps be one of the most significant advances to take place in international human rights law. The development of such a treaty is not anti-business: it rather seeks to ensure that business operates within a framework that advances the most fundamental moral and legal aspects of the international order. Such a treaty would signal an end to impunity for business that still occurs in many contexts and correct an imbalance in the global governance system that tends to prioritize profits over people. It is hoped that this book will contribute to a wider recognition of the necessity of a BHR treaty for a fair and just international legal order as well as inform the debate about its exact contours.

PART I

Need for an International Treaty in a Historical Context

Lessons from the UN Centre on Transnational Corporations for the Current Treaty Initiative

KHALIL HAMDANI AND LORRAINE RUFFING

1.1 Introduction

The current treaty initiative on business and human rights within the Human Rights Council has precedents in the United Nations (UN). A first effort at addressing international business practice was in 1948 with the inclusion of investment and social responsibility provisions in the agreed Havana Charter for an International Trade Organization; but that charter was never ratified.[1] A second attempt was made in 1974 with the negotiation of a Code of Conduct on Transnational Corporations but that effort, which endured for twenty years, also did not succeed. Various subsequent, more focused efforts – as against illicit payments – have been adopted. However, an overarching legal framework covering the obligations and rights of transnational enterprises and their host and home countries has thus far proved elusive.

This paper draws lessons from the experience of the United Nations Centre on Transnational Corporations (UNCTC) for the current treaty initiative. The Centre was established in 1974 and abolished in 1992. In its lifetime, it did much research and advised governments but its inter-governmental Commission failed in its primary mission to conclude a code of conduct. This chapter recaps that experience.[2] In drawing lessons, we sidestep the intricate legal issues addressed by the other contributors to this book. Instead, our focus is on the broader institutional

---

[1] The Charter was adopted in the final act of the United Nations Conference on Trade and Employment held at Havana, Cuba, from 21 November 1947 to 24 March 1948.

[2] For a fuller account, see K. Hamdani and L. Ruffing, *United Nations Centre on Transnational Corporations: Corporate Conduct and the Public Interest* (Routledge, 2015). See also T. Sagafi-Nejad, in collaboration with J. Dunning, *The United Nations and Transnational Corporations: From Code of Conduct to Global Compact* (Indiana University Press, 2008) and S. Dell, *The United Nations and International Business* (Duke University Press, 1990).

context and political perspectives that underpin deliberations within the United Nations.

1.2   UN Successes and Failure (1974–1992)

The United Nations began serious efforts to establish a normative framework for the duties and rights of transnational corporations four decades ago, in the 1970s. It was a period of high anxiety. Scholars in France and Canada warned that TNCs were buying up their economies.[3] Trade unions in the United States lobbied against the export of jobs overseas. Governments in developing countries were nationalizing foreign affiliates incorporated in the colonial era. News of the involvement of foreign companies in the 1973 coup d'état in Chile unleashed a widespread public outcry, and the United States (US) Congress launched a series of hearings while the Government of Chile raised the matter in the UN. The basic concern was that TNCs operated beyond the reach of national sovereignty.[4] It was a universal concern, and the UNCTC was set up in 1974 to address it.

In response to the Chilean affair, the UN Economic and Social Council (ECOSOC) appointed by consensus a Group of Eminent Persons to study TNCs and their impact on society, and to recommend international action. Governments were concerned about the growing extraterritorial influence of TNCs, and wondered what their countries' position would be within this new and expanding world order. The term 'globalization' had not yet been coined. Raul Prebisch, the founding father of UNCTAD, voiced the hope of many in stating: 'It is indispensable to draw up new rules of the game'.[5]

The UN Group of Eminent Persons sought to be inclusive and embraced academics, politicians and businessmen. It also conducted public hearings. The report was unanimous in its recommendation that ECOSOC establish institutions for continuing to probe the issues raised by TNCs. The recommendation was endorsed unanimously by the General Assembly and, in November 1974, the UN Centre on Transnational Corporations

---

[3] See J. Servan-Schreiber, *Le Défi Américain* (Denoël, 1967) and K. Levitt, *Silent Surrender: The Multinational Corporation in Canada* (Macmillan, 1970).

[4] See R. Vernon, *Sovereignty at Bay: The Multinational Spread of U.S. Enterprises* (Basic Books, 1971) and R. Barnet and R Müller, *Global Reach: The Power of the Multinational Corporations* (Simon and Schuster, 1974).

[5] United Nations, *Proceedings of the United Nations Conference on Trade and Development*, 3rd session (1972), 365–369.

(UNCTC) was created. The Centre's work had three main foci: elaboration of a normative framework for TNCs, analytical research on TNCs and advisory services to developing countries to level the playing field with TNCs. These activities were all under the guidance of an intergovernmental Commission on Transnational Corporations of ECOSOC. Additionally, a body of 16 expert advisers from trade unions, business, civil society and universities was established to support the deliberations of the Commission. This mix of a secretariat, governments and independent experts continued the principle of 'inclusiveness' and gave the exercise legitimacy as well as generating a positive climate. At the same time, the Centre's tripartite mix of normative, analytical and advisory activities grounded its support to the Commission on facts and policy experience, gaining the respect of delegates, professionals and academics.

As to its normative work, the Group of Eminent Persons had advised an evolutionary approach: the long-term objective was an agreement on TNCs with the force of an international treaty along with machinery for its enforcement; the short-term objective was to begin with a code of conduct with the force of moral persuasion. The Eminent Persons had reasoned that it was premature to propose serious negotiations on a binding agreement and the machinery necessary for its enforcement. They thought that such a long-term objective required careful and extended preparations and discussion.[6] Accordingly, at its second meeting (March 1976), the Commission established an Intergovernmental Working Group on a Code of Conduct, chaired under the impartial leadership of Sweden.

The solid foundations of the endeavour deserve underlining. It responded to a universal need that was unanimously felt by all governments and it addressed that need in a consensual, rigorous and judicious manner that won legitimacy and authority. Those firm foundations sustained the endeavour through two decades of turbulence: the 1973 oil embargo and demands for a new international economic order, the ideological rhetoric of socialist countries, the debt crises of the 1980s and the market orthodoxy of the Washington Consensus.

The international community eventually failed to achieve the short-term goal of agreeing on a TNC code of conduct, despite its modesty, high priority and patient pursuit over 20 years. However, there were tangible and enduring contributions that redeemed the overall endeavour.

---

[6] United Nations, *The Impact of Multinational Corporations on Development and on International Relations* (1974), 54.

These included enhanced understanding generally, strengthened capabilities in developing countries and the emergence of a body of soft law on transnational corporations.

Research

UNCTC helped to better comprehend the transnational corporation. The Centre compiled statistics on foreign direct investment (FDI), and prepared studies on the industries and sectors in which TNCs operated, the nature of those operations and their impacts. Many of the findings challenged conventional wisdom. For example, while policymakers at the time were obsessed with the ownership of resources, the studies showed that control was more important than ownership. A contractual arrangement allowing a low equity share to be held by a TNC could be as or more disadvantageous to the host country than one permitting a high stake. A hotel management contract, for instance, could earn fees and royalties for a multinational hotel chain even if the state-owned facility were to operate at a loss, needed repair and accumulated unserviceable debt. The studies also showed that financial returns could have more tangible benefits than ownership *per se*. In mining agreements, a reduced equity stake could be negotiated by the state for increased investment in downstream activities and greater annual revenues to the country.[7] The Centre also showed that TNC activities involve a package of benefits and costs, and that capital investment is not necessarily the most important. Other potential benefits include technology transfer, managerial knowhow and entry into world markets. The Centre's investment reports and surveys showed that three-fourths of global technology rested within TNCs and two-thirds of world trade took place through TNCs or involved TNCs as either purchasers or sellers; in other words, countries that were closed to foreign direct investment and TNCs were not participating in complex production and in the more dynamic segments of global trade and technology transfer. As such benefits are not automatic, the Centre called for positive, not negative, engagement with TNCs, and for active, not passive, host country policies. The importance of active policies – once shunned by the so-called Washington consensus of the international financial institutions – was demonstrated by the successful

---

[7] For actual cases, see R. Allan 'Policy Advice', Reflection 6.1 in Hamdani and Ruffing, n. 2, 202.

development experience of the Southeast Asian economies and China. The Centre identified the shift from manufacturing to services and the potential developmental benefits of the services industries. The Centre highlighted the relationship between investment and trade, and also drew attention to TNC supply chains in 1990, years before the current fascination.

UNCTC was a small organization – some 50 professional staff – yet it issued a dozen or more reports and studies each year with the help of an interdisciplinary, international network of consultants and academics. The research topics included areas such as mining, transnational banking, pharmaceuticals, food and beverages, tourism, insurance, advertising, transfer of technology, creating business linkages between TNCs and local suppliers, and the environment. The studies revealed practices of TNCs and their impact on host countries. These constitute a vast library of knowledge on a subject poorly understood until recently.

The industry studies were balanced, and though corporate players vetted the drafts, the published reports were still criticized. The Centre was labelled anti-business; however, the truth is that UNCTC was neither against nor for TNCs. The aim was to demystify the TNC phenomenon, and to help governments understand it better at the intergovernmental and national level.

Advisory Services

The Centre advised developing countries in their dealings with TNCs. Although nationalization was a dominant practice in the 1960s and 1970s, a preferable option is renegotiation of contracts on more favourable terms to the host country. At the time, the major foreign investments were in the extractive industries, where the value of natural resources is additional to the costs of extraction and thereby confers a rent to either the producer (if the resources are undervalued) or the country (if overvalued). As there is no optimal pricing for natural resources, bargaining is an appropriate way to share the rent between the producer and country. Moreover, the bargaining power shifts in favour of the host country as the fixed investments already incurred by the TNC become obsolescent over time. Thus, the logic for renegotiation of investment contracts was evident. However, the host country officials typically lacked expertise, and renegotiations were often prolonged or derailed by unreasonable demands, or resulted in new deals that were no better than the original, or gave way to expropriation. UNCTC helped in several ways.

First, upon request, the Centre advised developing countries in contract negotiations. The outcomes were usually welcomed by both countries and companies. However, again, critics saw this as anti-business and interference with the market. Second, the Centre provided training for country officials through regional workshops on the complexities of contractual arrangements in such areas as mining and petroleum. Third, the Centre assisted countries in drafting laws, regulations and investment codes, which would lessen the need for arbitrary case-by-case handling of TNC deals. Fourth, the Centre helped countries establish institutions to interface with TNCs, not only with respect to approvals but also for benefiting from the best that TNCs can offer – capital, knowhow, access to world markets and stimulus to domestic enterprises.

The Centre's technical assistance was well received. China, Cuba, the Soviet Union and dozens of other developing countries and economies in transition sought the Centre's help when they opened up to foreign direct investment and TNCs in the 1980s. UNCTC implemented some 700 projects in its 18 years of technical assistance. The objective was never to attract investment at any cost, but to help countries attract the best package of benefits that TNCs can offer to meet their development needs.

Negotiating a Code of Conduct

The Intergovernmental Working Group on a Code of Conduct was an active body. All countries participated, including the United States and other developed countries. They met in 17 sessions over six years (1977–1982). They produced a text that was 90 per cent agreed; more than half of the 71 provisions were accepted, more than half of the rest could be settled without much effort and there were compromise formulations for the half-dozen difficult issues.

The working group reached early agreement on the standards for corporate conduct for TNCs. The draft code encompassed 20 standards relating to compliance with domestic laws and development policies, negotiation of contracts in good faith, respect for socio-cultural objectives, respect for human and labour rights, non-interference in political affairs, prohibition of bribery, transfer pricing, restrictive business practices, protection for the environment and consumers, transfer of

technology and disclosure of information. Regarding human rights standards, the focus of the working group was limited to non-discrimination.
TNCs were urged to conform to government policies on equality of
opportunity. TNCs were urged not to discriminate on the basis of race,
colour, sex, religion, language, social and national or ethnic origin, or
political or other opinion. This focus reflected the standards already
embodied in existing international instruments on human rights such
as the Universal Declaration of Human Rights, and the International
Covenant on Civil and Political Rights, which had become an integral
part of international law at the time. As such these recommendations
were not controversial and were easily accepted into the code.[8] All the
other standards were agreed thanks to common-sense wording (devoid
of narrow legal terminology); support of business (i.e., the Commission's
expert advisers); and conformity with parallel efforts, namely the *OECD
Guidelines on Multinational Enterprises* (1976) and the *ICC Guidelines
for International Investment* (1972). These latter guidelines were
prompted by the UN decision to embark on a code of conduct, and
could be seen as either a windfall for the code negotiations or as a pre-
emptive strike against the code that set the upper bar for what developed
countries would agree and made UN efforts seem redundant. In either
case, there was no quarrel in the working group on the need to codify
standards for corporate conduct.

Instead, the negotiations stalled on the need for norms on state
responsibility. Developed countries insisted on norms in four areas: the
applicability of international law, nationalization and compensation,
national treatment and settlement of disputes between host states and
TNCs. There was, however, a divergence of opinion between developed
and developing countries in these four areas. On the relevance of international law, OECD countries insisted that the code maintain its application regarding the treatment of foreign property and investments.
Socialist countries resisted the application of international law because
they held that the regulation of property relations fell outside its scope.
Some developing countries countered that international law norms were
not limited to the usual principles of state responsibility but were wider.
On nationalization and compensation, socialist and developing countries
joined ranks and objected to the compensation standards demanded by
OECD countries. On national treatment, developing countries argued

[8] UNCTC, *The United Nations Code of Conduct on Transnational Corporations* (United
Nations, 1986), 11.

that the principle of national treatment, if applied indiscriminately, could be detrimental to their development goals since their domestic enterprises were not as powerful as TNCs. While most delegations agreed that disputes should be submitted to the courts or other competent authorities of the host state, the OECD countries preferred a more vague formulation which merely encouraged the submission of such disputes to "competent national courts or authorities" *without* specifying the country concerned.[9] Overall, developing countries resisted the inclusion and wording of the norms on state responsibility, even though these are widely accepted today, and codified in their investment codes and bilateral and other agreements. The negotiations dragged on with little progress for another decade (1982–1992), and by then fatigue had set in on all sides.

The window of opportunity closed when the political atmosphere shifted radically and the pendulum swung from regulation to deregulation under the Reagan/Thatcher administrations. While Secretary of State Henry Kissinger, in a 1975 address to a special session of the UN General Assembly, pledged that the United States would support the work of the Commission on TNCs, Ambassadors Jeanne Kirkpatrick and Alan Keyes later warned in the early 1990s that the Centre was a major threat to the western civilization and way of life. In the view of the US State Department, the code was a relic of the past. The business lobby saw the Centre as anathema to the magic of the marketplace. A level playing field was not welcome in so far as it tried to counteract the tilt in favour of TNCs.

Additionally, developing countries became disenchanted. Those that wished a mandatory instrument were impatient with the evolutionary approach that had been suggested early on by the Group of Eminent Persons, and no longer believed that the short-term objective of a voluntary instrument, without an implementation mechanism, would lead to the desired long-term objective of a mandatory instrument. Other countries, mired in the debt crisis of the 1980s, were anxious to attract FDI, precipitating a race to the bottom. During one workshop, after a rousing lecture on how to fight against the abuses of TNCs, a participant asked, 'Now that you have told us how to fight multinationals, can you also tell us how to get them?'[10]

---

[9] S. Asante, 'Doctrinal differences on the code', Reflection 3.1 in Hamdani and Ruffing, n. 2, 91.

[10] K. Tapiola, 'The heritage of the code', Reflection 3.3 in Hamdani and Ruffing, n. 2, 110 at 115.

Overall, the focus of international investment agreements (IIAs) has shifted from investor responsibility to investor protection and establishing mandatory standards for the treatment of foreign investors by host governments. The surge in investor-friendly bilateral investment treaties in the early 1990s accelerated the demise of the code. However, the pendulum may have begun to swing back. There is, for instance, a growing awareness that the private dispute and arbitration mechanisms in IIAs are flawed in that they consider strictly the terms of the agreements and not the possible infringement of relevant national or international laws. Some governments are even revisiting past treaties.

1.3   Current Corporate Conduct and the Need for a Binding Treaty

The need for a normative international framework on corporate conduct across borders – balancing the rights with the duties of TNCs – is even more acute today given the exponential growth of FDI and the tremendous financial strength of transnationals compared to that of states. Global FDI flows have expanded from US$50 billion (1980–85) to over US$1.7 trillion in 2015.[11] The number of TNCs has expanded to some 100,000 and they have over one million affiliates.[12] Countries, both developed and developing, are now both home and host countries.[13] In some cases, their TNCs overshadow their governments in financial strength. For example, Apple's global cash position is more than three times that of the international reserves of the US government.[14]

A casual reading of the *Financial Times* gives evidence that good corporate governance and corporate social responsibility have yet to take hold among many TNCs. The following table lists various misdeeds and some of the offenders. Most of the misdeeds relate to economic misconduct but they also include human rights abuses. The root cause of most of these misdeeds is management's drive to maximize profits and share values, which imposes external costs on others. Thus, there is a link between economic misconduct and human rights abuses. Bilchitz points out that the financial misdeeds that caused the financial crisis in 2008

---

[11] UNCTAD, *World Investment Report 2016: Investor Nationality: Policy Challenges* (2016).

[12] Hamdani and Ruffing, n. 2, 246.

[13] The number of countries with outward FDI has more than doubled, rising from 68 in 1980 to 175 in 2013, see http://unctadstat.unctad.org.

[14] S. Ro, 'Apple Has More Cash on Hand than All These Different Countries' 7 April 2014 *Business Insider.*

imposed socio-economic costs on individuals, which limited their ability to meet their basic needs.[15]

Misdeeds	TNCs involved
Libor interest rate rigging	Barclays, Citigroup, Deutsche Bank, Goldman Sachs, HSBC, JP Morgan, Morgan Stanley, RBS, Standard Chartered, UBS, Rabobank, Societe Generale, Credit Agricole
Money laundering	HSBC (Mexico), JP Morgan (Madoff)
Mis-selling products such as mortgage-backed securities, insurance protection, tax shelters, credit card add-ons	J P Morgan, RBS, Credit Suisse, Bank of America, Deutsche Bank, Wells Fargo, Goldman Sachs, UBS
Manipulation of energy prices	Barclays
Foreign exchange manipulation	Deutsche Bank, Citigroup, Barclays, UBS
Bribery	Siemens, Alcoa, GSK, Eli Lilly, Sanofi, Pfizer, Danone, Caterpillar
Tax evasion	Apple, Google, Microsoft, HP
Tax avoidance advice or assistance	Big 4 audit firms, Credit Suisse, UBS
Abusive or illegal marketing practices	GSK, Eli Lilly, Sanofi, J&J
Concealing defective products	GM, Volkswagen, Ford
False info on product effectiveness/side effects	Novartis, Roche, Takeda, Eli Lilly
Child labour in supply chains	Samsung, British American Tobacco, Philip Morris International

There are at least four main reasons why there are so many transgressions against good corporate governance and corporate social responsibility. First, many TNCs are often too big and too complex to manage effectively. For example, General Motors (78th in US top 500 companies in 2015) with $155 billion in sales and over 200,000 employees failed to recall 2.6 million cars with faulty ignition switches because in the opinion

---

[15] D. Bilchitz, 'Socio-Economic Rights, Economic Crisis and Legal Doctrine' (2014) 12 (3) *International Journal of Constitutional Law*.

of some, 'General Motors was so dysfunctional that there was a failure to understand, quite simply, how the car was built.'[16]

Second, the view of many TNCs is short-term due to the pressure cooker of quarterly earnings reports. Senior executives are required to deliver progressive rises in short-term earnings. If they fail to meet their quarterly targets, the consequences can be quite negative in terms of share prices. Some TNCs, such as Coca Cola, McDonalds and ATT, have ended their practice of providing earnings guidance, stating they detract from creating a sustainable company in the long run.[17]

Third, given the frequency of economic transgressions TNC boardrooms seem to be ethics-free zones. Take the case of Deutsche Bank. How could the board miss such widespread operational practices as rigging the Libor rate, money laundering, mis-selling products, currency manipulation and false accounting for derivatives? This negligence results from the fact that corporations are punished for their misdeeds but their senior executives or their boards of directors are not. CEOs and board members, realizing they would probably not be prosecuted for risky actions, engage in 'moral hazards'. They know that it is the shareholders who end up paying the fines and penalties and the junior staff who go to jail.

Fourth, there is no effective compliance mechanism for company or industry codes through the use of verified and uniform corporate social responsibility (CSR) indicators. The CSR reports are seldom audited and companies can pick and choose among hundreds of CSR indicators, changing them each year so that comparisons over time or across companies are impossible.

The renewed drive for corporate governance and corporate social responsibility first came in the wake of corporate scandals at the beginning of this century in the United States and Europe (Enron, Ahold, Parmalat, Royal Dutch Shell). Enron catapulted corporate governance into the US public spotlight in 2001. It was then the largest bankruptcy in US history, causing a loss of 21,000 jobs, wiping out US$1.2 billion in employee savings and destroying the accounting firm Arthur Andersen. The response was a tremendous push to improve governance in the United States through the Sarbanes-Oxley Act 2002. The key provision required the CEO/CFO to certify that the financial statements contain no

---

[16] G. Tett, 'A Fragmented Corporate Structure is the Villain of the Piece' 13 July 2014 *Financial Times* 7.
[17] Knowledge@ Wharton, 'Shooting the Messenger: Quarterly Earnings and Short Term Pressure to Perform' 21 July 2010.

misrepresentations. Penalties for false certifications ranged from US$5 million to 20 years in prison.

There was a certain backlash against such regulation and TNCs began to subscribe to voluntary codes of corporate conduct at the company and the industry level. These have been criticized as being aspirational and vague but, most importantly, they lacked independent monitoring mechanisms. Of the 246 codes examined by the OECD, only 52 provided for external monitoring.[18] These codes were the business community's attempt at self-regulation in order to avoid more government regulations. Codes could deflect criticism and reduce the demand for external regulation.[19] Whatever their motivation, voluntary codes are a recognition of the need to integrate societal concerns into corporate policies and operations, but in the end it is not the code that is important but the conduct.[20]

The United Nations also championed corporate social responsibility in the form of the Global Compact to promote ethical business practices (2000). The Global Compact is a fairly non-committal initiative which asks that enterprises adhere to ten principles related to the environment, labour standards and human rights. There is no adequate verification mechanism. Currently, 8000 companies and 4000 non-businesses are members of the Compact.[21] While it has a growing following from many TNCs, the Global Compact has not been able to bridge the governance gap in the sphere of TNC behaviour and responsibility. In the eyes of critics it amounts to a whitewash – or in UN jargon a 'blue-wash' – as well as an effort to anaesthetize any future effort to establish an effective regulatory regime for TNCs.

The United Nations Human Rights Council has also undertaken initiatives in the realm of corporate social responsibility with its core framework of 'protect, respect, remedy' adopted in 2008. While it is the state's duty to 'protect' human rights, business has the lesser duty to 'respect' them. The framework to protect, respect and remedy was reinforced in 2011 by the UN Guiding Principles on Business and Human Rights, which guide states and business with the implementation thereof. However, as in the case of the global compact there is as yet no oversight mechanism to verify implementation.

---

[18] OECD, *Codes of Corporate Conduct: Expanded Review of their Contents* (OECD, 2001).
[19] R. Jenkins, *Corporate Codes of Conduct: Self-Regulation in a Global Economy* (UNRISD, 2001).
[20] H. Keller, 'Corporate Codes of Conduct and their Implementation: the Question of Legitimacy' (www.Yale.edu/Macmillan/HelenKeller, 2005).
[21] www.unglobalcompact.org.

Voluntary codes rely on reputational risk, which dissipates the further away an enterprise is from the ultimate consumer or if the enterprise is part of an oligopoly. For example, if the customers of Nike organize a boycott over child labour, it will likely be fairly effective. However, customers are not going to boycott Tiffany's over blood diamonds because of their uncertain origin. Likewise, they are unlikely to boycott their local gas station because of Exxon's or BP's environmental negligence. Furthermore, TNCs can ignore soft law such as codes or refuse to join compacts.

The growing dissatisfaction with 'voluntarism' led the Human Rights Council to vote upon and pass resolution 26/9 in 2014, which calls for the elaboration of a legally binding treaty to regulate the activities of TNCs and other business enterprises. Other business enterprises include those with a transnational character in their operational activities. The two initiatives – the Guiding Principles and the binding treaty – are being run in parallel. While some see the binding treaty as lessening the uptake of the Guiding Principles and its framework, the hope is that these initiatives will be complementary, whereby the Guiding Principles are seen as a necessary building block for the elaboration of a legally binding instrument; and the treaty is seen as a crucial complement to help bring the Guiding Principles into practice.[22]

The ineffectiveness of voluntary codes and compacts is evidenced by the growing laundry list of corporate scandals. Neither corporate codes nor moral censure nor national legal systems are entirely successful in curbing TNC misdeeds. If one examines the economic and environmental abuses in just four sectors – automotive, banking, energy and technology – public disapproval and national regulation have not had much impact on corporate conduct or culture (see earlier table). These abuses lead to violations of human rights as explained by Bilchitz. Indeed, during the first session of the open-ended intergovernmental working group established under Human Rights Council Res. 26/9, the working group's discussion enlarged the scope of the human rights that any potential treaty will cover. Delegates spoke of abuses in the areas of the environment, health, food, nutrition, workers' rights, women's rights, the right to development, rights in conflict zones and the right to free, prior and informed consent.[23]

---

[22] Human Rights Council, 'Report of the Open-ended Intergovernmental Working Group on Transnational Corporations and other Business Enterprises with Respect to Human Rights,' A/HRC/31/50 (10 July 2015).

[23] Ibid.

Volkswagen (VW) is the latest company to enter the hall of infamy. While its conduct is not as depraved as that of Ford, which used a cost/benefit analysis to keep its famous Pintos on the road even when they ignited upon rear-end impact, sending their passengers to a fiery death, Volkswagen is guilty of both environmental and economic misconduct. Since its diesel engines could not meet the stricter US air quality rules, it installed software to beat the tests in over 11 million diesel vehicles. It also understated carbon dioxide emission levels which enabled car owners to qualify for tax incentives to which they were not entitled – which is equivalent to tax evasion. The chairman of Volkswagen's supervisory board said that the cheating took place during a 'climate of lax ethical standards' where there was a tolerance for breaking the rules.[24] In an enterprise of this size (600,000 employees), when anything goes wrong, the management often professes ignorance, as in the case of Mr. Winterkorn, CEO of VW.[25] VW insists that it was the fault of 'rogue workers' yet to be identified.[26]

Barclays, as well as other big banks, has been in the dock and heavily fined for money laundering, manipulating Libor and Euribor, rigging foreign exchange rates as well as backing out of deals at the last second which were profitable to its clients but not to Barclays. It runs a 'dark pool' in which it engaged in a systematic pattern of fraud and deceit. It assigns safe ratings to toxic traders in the pool where the customer's stock order is 'fat and juicy prey'.[27]

After JPMorgan agreed to pay more than US$20 billion in fines and settlements for mis-selling mortgages, ignoring the Madoff Ponzi scheme and botching derivatives sales, its CEO was given a 75 per cent pay raise. This is another case of moral hazard where managers take excessive risks when they do not bear the consequences of failure. Despite all the attention paid to corporate governance and corporate social responsibility, many corporates, as we have seen, have not made them part of their business culture. Recent scandals 'violate the most basic ethical norms',

---

[24] J. Ewing, 'Volkswagen Cites 'Chain of Errors' in Emissions Cheating' 11 December 2015 *New York Times* B1.

[25] 'Martin Winterkorn Resigns as VW Boss over Emissions Scandal' 23 September 2015 and 'Prosecutors Open Preliminary Inquiry into VW's Martin Winterkorn' 28 September 2015 *Financial Times*.

[26] P. McGee and R. Wright, 'VW Management Back in Scandal Spotlight' 4 March 2015 *Financial Times* 15.

[27] J. Treanor and D. Rushe, 'Barclays Investigated in US over Dark Pool Activities' 26 June 2014 *Financial Times*.

said the IMF head, 'industry still prizes short-term profit over long-term prudence, today's bonus over tomorrow's relationship'.[28]

Trade associations for banking and energy have been trying to roll back or delay enactment of national reforms passed after the financial crisis. Goldman Sachs, Morgan Stanley and JPMorgan Chase routinely spend millions of dollars watering down the rules through their lobbying of both the EU Commission and the US Congress.[29] For example, the lobbyists for Wall Street have attempted to water down the rules established under the Dodd-Frank Wall Street Reform and Consumer Protection Act of 2010. These statutory interventions were adopted by the US Congress to end the abuses which caused the financial crisis. The aim of the legislation according to the White House is

> To prevent the excessive risk-taking that led to the financial crisis. The law also provides common-sense protections for American families, creating a new consumer watchdog to prevent mortgage companies and pay-day lenders from exploiting consumers. These rules will build a safer, more stable financial system-one that provides a robust foundation for lasting economic growth and job creation.[30]

The Dodd-Frank Act has 16 separate titles and required over 200 new rules to be enacted. The most controversial rule from the point of view of Wall Street is the Volker rule, which limits a bank's investment in speculative funds to 3 per cent of the bank's Tier 1 capital. Surprisingly, it also has rules covering other abuses stemming from conflict minerals and payments to foreign government officials.

Both the American Chamber of Commerce and the American Petroleum Institute have attacked the Dodd-Frank Act and have successfully blocked its full implementation through lawsuits. For example, Dodd- Frank requires the disclosure of oil and gas payments to foreign governments. However, the SEC disclosure rule was rendered vacuous by a US court, which said the SEC had miscalculated the scope of its discretion.

Exxon has deceived the public by its misinformation campaign about the impact of burning fossil fuels on climate change. While Exxon's own

---

[28] C. Lagarde, 'Economic Inclusion and Financial Integrity' – an Address to the Conference on Inclusive Capitalism, London, 27 May 2014 available at www.imf.org/external/np/speeches/2014/052714.htm.

[29] D. Robinson and T. Braithwaite, 'Goldman Forced to Reveal 14-fold Rise in Spending on EU Lobbying as Rules Bite' 29 April 2015 *Financial Times* 11.

[30] www.whitehouse.gov/economy/middle-class/dodd-frank-wall-street-reform, last accessed 01 September 2016.

scientists and research were 100 per cent aligned with expert consensus on human-caused global warming, Exxon funded 30 different organizations to undermine this scientific message and prevent policy action. After pledging to stop funding climate denial groups in 2007, it continued to fund the American Legislative Executive Council to indoctrinate US legislators with the idea that there is 'a great deal of scientific uncertainty' about climate change, thus inhibiting US negotiators from supporting a binding treaty on climate change.[31]

High-tech companies and pharmaceutical companies are among the leaders in tax evasion, using inversions to lower taxes and protect offshore cash. A tax inversion occurs when a domestic company becomes a subsidiary of a new parent company in another country for the purpose of falling under more beneficial tax laws. Typically, companies undertake inversions to lower tax domiciles. A popular tax inversion destination is Ireland, where the corporate tax rate is 12.5 per cent. Nine of the top ten pharmaceutical companies as well as leading tech companies including Apple, Google and Facebook now have operations in Ireland. Although inversions are not illegal, the companies have been branded as corporate deserters. By late 2014, such deals amounted to $186 billion.[32] The European Union has ordered Ireland to recover US$14 billion in back taxes from Apple. It appears that Apple didn't even pay the Irish tax rate of 12.5 per cent but less than 1 per cent between 2003 and 2014. Surprisingly, the US authorities were 'disappointed' with this ruling because according to some experts it might offer Apple a sweetheart deal to bring back its cash at an even lower tax rate than 12.5 per cent.[33]

1.4   Obstacles to a Binding Treaty and the Way Forward

If corporate conduct as described in Section 1.3 is so out of alignment with the public interest, then how can it be realigned? What are the chances for a normative framework in the form of a binding treaty on TNCs with respect to human rights (including economic, labour, social and environmental rights) being drafted, signed and implemented? Can the current treaty initiative evade the code's fate? Ninety per cent of the

---

[31] 'Two-faced Exxon: the Mis-information Campaign vs its Own Scientists' 25 November 2015, *The Guardian*.

[32] A. Ward and B. Jopson, 'US Casts a Pall over Planned Tax Inversions' 24 September 2014 *Financial Times* 5.

[33] S. Donnan, 'Political Leaders Voice Dismay at Verdict as Retaliatory Routes Explored' 31 August 2016 *Financial Times* 3.

content of the original code of conduct was not difficult to agree upon, just as the OECD guidelines were easily agreed. So too, the content of a binding treaty may not be the most difficult part of the exercise. The sticking points will be garnering universal acceptance by a large majority of states and its enforcement.

National Policy Spaces

The most important obstacle to the adoption of an international instrument and an enforcement mechanism is that states protect their national policy space. They prefer to curb TNC abuses through national regulation even though the diversity in national regulation leads to regulatory arbitrage. Take the case of the EU-US transatlantic trade pact. In 2014, it ran into trouble because the United States refused to include financial regulation in the pact as it preferred to rein in the excesses of its financial titans through national measures. According to the US trade negotiator, the United States was not 'open to creating any process designed to reopen, weaken or undermine implementation of Dodd-Frank'.[34] On the other hand, some EU politicians are unhappy with the proposed transatlantic trade pact because they feel it would lead to a dilution of environmental standards and workers' rights.[35] This impasse illustrates the difficulty of compelling domestic regulators to bring their standards into line with each other or, in other words, give up their national policy space.

Furthermore, to the chagrin of France, the United States applied its own rules to BNP, fining it US$8.7 billion for violating sanctions against Iran and Sudan. In the absence of a multilateral approach to TNC abuses, the strongest and longest national reach will dominate. It was best summed up by one of the chairs of the endless discussions on the code: 'If and when the United States comes to the realization that a code of conduct on transnational corporations is in its own national interest, then such a multilateral instrument will probably be concluded.'[36]

Besides States' protection of their national policy space and its extra-territorial reach beyond their national borders, there are also multiple national interests that will block a treaty at the global level. The

---

[34] S. Donnan, 'EU-US Trade Talks Hit Road Block over Banks' 17 June 2014 *Financial Times* 4.

[35] A. Chassany and S. Donnan, 'France Urges EU to Cease US Trade Talks' 31 August 2016 *Financial Times* 2.

[36] M. Marín-Bosch, 'An odorless code', Reflection 3.4 in Hamdani and Ruffing, n. 2, 118 at 121.

recalcitrance of the United States to engage in the treaty negotiations might be attributed, in part, to the fact that the US Congress is in the grips of partisan derangement in which the Tea Party conservatives neither compromise nor brook criticism of capitalism or the profit motive.

The context today for a binding treaty is very different from that of the last century. In the opinion of a former UNCTC executive director, 'we now face a much more complex and intricate matrix of home and host countries, TNCs and civil society with concurrent converging and conflicting interests between and within these four sets of diverse actors that cut across North-South lines'.[37] Perhaps the unique element of the present context is that civil society has grown in strength and cohesiveness and it is a major force behind the current initiative for a binding treaty. The Global Campaign to Dismantle Corporate Power and Stop Impunity has created a coalition of 190 social movements. It, along with the Treaty Alliance, has brought together over 600 social movements and states to press the Human Rights Council for a working group on TNCs and human rights. If civil society pushed successfully for the landmines treaty, then it might be able to put enough pressure on the states that are boycotting this initiative (the United States and EU) to ensure they come to the table.

Speed is important. The lengthy code negotiations created fatigue. Whilst the pendulum has once again swung in the direction of regulation and TNCs are being fined at the national level in record amounts, this trend might fade. As of late 2015, major banks in the United States and Europe have been fined upwards of US$260 billion for their misdeeds.[38] Yet they have paid these fines easily and have not suffered significant reputational damage nor have senior bank executives been charged with wrongdoing. The lack of such proceedings against top individuals has been called the 'immaculate corruption'.[39] Business practice and public sentiment may return to business as usual.

Fractured and Dissipated UN Efforts

The UN and its affiliated institutions and specialized agencies can provide normative leadership in drafting a binding treaty. The conduct of TNCs is being discussed in various forums such as the Global Compact,

---

[37] P. Hansen, 'The uniqueness of the Centre', Reflection 1.2 in Hamdani and Ruffing, n. 2, 32 at 37.

[38] L. Noonan, 'Banks Fine Tally since Crisis Hits $260bn' 28 August 2015 *Financial Times* 17.

[39] B. McLannahan, 'US Justice Department Urged to Act against Senior Bankers' 10 February 2016 *Financial Times* 4.

Human Rights Council and UNCTAD among others. These activities need alignment.

The *World Investment Report* has mapped the expanding number of BITs and IIAs. These instruments merit critical examination. The provisions of some investment agreements have allowed investors to challenge core domestic policies in the areas of environment, energy and health. In 2010, Philip Morris sued Uruguay and Australia over anti-smoking legislation. Lone Pine is challenging Canada over a moratorium against fracking in Quebec. Vattenfall is suing Germany for phasing out nuclear energy. Argentina has been sued 41 times by foreign investors for reforms implemented during its 2001 economic crisis and ordered to pay US$980 million in compensation.[40]

The rise in litigation – numbering 608 cases at the end of 2014 – has, according to UNCTAD, turned investor-state dispute settlement (ISDS) into the most controversial issue in international investment policy making. UNCTAD notes the systemic deficiencies in the ISDS regime such as the lack of transparency, the inability of the arbitrators to assess the validity of the states' acts, the lack of independence, inconsistency or mistakes in arbitral decisions, the high legal costs of arbitration, and the monopoly of certain legal firms over the conduct of arbitration.[41] The average award is over $500 million, and 60 per cent of the cases are decided in favour of the investor.[42] Civil society has been very vocal about the unfairness of arbitral tribunals, describing them as a privatization of justice.

UNCTAD has proposed a roadmap for the reform of the ISDS system, recommending a path of 'selective adjustments', which would, among other things, move towards rebalancing rights and duties through non-binding CSR provisions.[43] It sees systematic reform as daunting. However, this proposal is judged by civil society as 'totally insufficient'.[44] The proposal is also at variance with the dialogue in other UN circles

[40] C. Olivet and P. Eberhardt, *Profiting from Crisis: How Corporations and Lawyers are Scavenging Profits from Europe's Crisis Countries* (Transnational Institute and Corporate Europe Observatory, 2014).

[41] UNCTAD, *World Investment Report 2013: Global Value Chains: Investment and Trade for Development* (2013), 11–112.

[42] UNCTAD, *World Investment Report 2015: Reforming International Investment Governance* (2015), 116, 133 and 146.

[43] UNCTAD, *World Investment Report 2014: Investing in the SDGs: An Action Plan* (2014), 127.

[44] A. Villarreal, *Statement of Friends of the Earth Uruguay during a Side Event Global Campaign to Dismantle Corporate Power* (UNHRC Intergovernmental Working Group

where CSR is thought not to have legal weight and cannot protect human rights in a court of law. Some members of the Intergovernmental Working Group are advocating that any binding treaty must affirm the hierarchical superiority of human rights norms over trade and investment treaties. There is need for UNCTAD to elucidate the issues and mediate the differences, as UNCTC once did. Indeed, a report to the UN General Assembly (A/70/284 dated 5 August 2015) invites UNCTAD to convene a conference on IIAs.

Enforcement

If by some chance the obstacles to drafting and signing a binding treaty are overcome, how will it be enforced? The Global Campaign to Dismantle Corporate Power is calling for the creation of three new institutions to enforce the treaty and monitor its implementation. First, a treaty body (committee) could be established to monitor whether states and TNCs respect their obligations and implement the treaty. It could receive individual and collective complaints (like the OECD national contact points). Second, to complement this treaty body, a centre for monitoring TNCs could be created, and the former UNCTC provides a model for such a centre. It would have the mandate to analyse, investigate, document and inspect the practices of TNCs. It could also engage in capacity building with states that need assistance in dealing with TNCs to level the playing field.

Third, the treaty could establish a world court on TNCs and human rights that could impose appropriate sanctions and penalties when the normative framework is violated. The court could receive, investigate and judge complaints against TNCs. The court would consider the civil and criminal responsibility of TNCs and their executives, as well as the shared liability of TNCs for the activities of their subsidiaries, suppliers, licensees and subcontractors.[45] A standing international investment court could also replace existing mechanisms for investor-State arbitration. An investment court is being pursued in the Trans-Atlantic Trade and Investment Partnership – a recognition that a private model of adjudication is inappropriate for matters that deal with public law.[46] This lends some support to the necessity of creating a public body to deal with the abuses of TNCs.[47]

on Transnational Corporations and Other Business Enterprises with Respect to Human Rights, 6–10 July 2015).

[45] Global Campaign to Dismantle Corporate Power and Stop Impunity, *Eight Proposals for the New Legally Binding International Instrument on Transnational Corporations (TNCs) and Human Rights* (Transnational Institute, June 2015).

[46] (http://ec.europa.eu/trade/policy/in-focus/ttip). [47] See Human Rights Council, n.22.

1.5 Conclusion

An international regulatory framework for the activities of transnational corporations is a long-awaited objective of the United Nations. Although the negotiations on a code of conduct failed, the effort spawned international guidelines and declarations on transnational enterprises and foreign direct investment in the OECD (1977), the ILO (1977) and the World Bank (1992). In the UN, the General Assembly adopted a convention against corruption (2003), the Secretary-General launched a Global Compact to promote ethical business practice and the Human Rights Council endorsed Guiding Principles on business and human rights (2011). However, these initiatives have evolved in a piecemeal and unbalanced manner. The shortfalls include: a narrow focus on investor protection; a hortatory treatment of development provisions; the voluntary nature of guidelines on investor behaviour and conduct; neglect of sensitive issues such as fiscal and financial incentives (and the 'race to the bottom'); and the relative neglect of crucial issues such as human rights and sustainability.

The current treaty initiative within the Human Rights Council is timely but faces an uphill task. It is an important response to the resurfacing discontent with corporate behaviour. However, it has fragile foundations in contrast to the unanimity, legitimacy and authority that the code negotiations enjoyed. There may be benefit in presenting the demands more persuasively and in enlarging its constituency, enlisting broader segments of civil society, business and government without being subject to corporate capture. In addition, the UN should be more engaged in the initiative, and welcome the opportunity to bring coherence to its own disparate activities on investment and TNCs. Whatever the eventual outcome, it is sure to add to the global knowledge base, refine policy approaches and, hopefully, enlighten corporate practice. It is good to see the subject back on the UN agenda.

The Value-Added of a Treaty to Regulate Transnational Corporations and Other Business Enterprises

Moving Forward Strategically

PENELOPE SIMONS

2.1 Introduction

Three years after the Human Rights Council's (HRC) unanimous endorsement of the Guiding Principles on Business and Human Rights[1] (Guiding Principles), the HRC adopted a resolution to establish an open-ended intergovernmental working group (OEIGWG) with a mandate to 'elaborate an international legally binding instrument to regulate, in international human rights law, the activities of transnational corporations and other business enterprises'.[2] The resolution was contested, with 20 states voting in favour, 14 against and 13 abstaining.[3] Support for the development of the treaty is roughly divided along the lines of developing states and civil society organizations (CSOs) in favour and developed states and big businesses against.

The political resistance to developing an international instrument on this issue and the polarization between groups has been characteristic of attempts at the UN level to develop binding legal obligations for transnational corporations. The UN Draft Code of Conduct on Transnational Corporations,[4] which was negotiated over a period of about 20 years

---

[1] Human Rights Council (HRC), 'Guiding Principles on Business and Human Rights: Implementing the United Nations "Protect, Respect and Remedy" Framework', A/HRC/17/31 (21 March 2011).

[2] HRC, 'Elaboration of an International Legally Binding Instrument on Transnational Corporations and other Business Enterprises with respect to Human Rights', A/HRC/26/9 (14 July 2014).

[3] *Ibid.*

[4] Commission on Transnational Corporations, 'Proposed Text of the Draft Code of Conduct on Transnational Corporations' in United Nations Centre on Transnational Corporations, *Transnational Corporations, Services and the Uruguay Round Current Studies*, Annex IV, UN Doc ST/CTC/103 (1990).

within the UN Commission on Transnational Corporations, foundered over a number of issues including the disagreement between developing and developed states on whether the rules of conduct should be 'detailed and mandatory' or more general and voluntary.[5] More recently, the UN Draft Norms on the Responsibilities of Transnational Corporations and Other Business Enterprises with Regard to Human Rights[6] raised significant controversy and ultimately were aborted over their 'apparent attempt to impose [human rights] obligations directly on companies, in addition to parallel obligations on states'.[7]

There is a clear tide of support among developing states and CSOs for a treaty that will address the shortcomings of the Guiding Principles.[8] However, a number of developed states have refused to engage constructively with the process.[9] The first session of the OEIGWG that took place in early July 2015 was not well attended and delegates from the EU and

---

[5] S. D. Murphy, 'Taking Multinational Corporate Codes of Conduct to the Next Level' (2005) 43 (2) *Columbia Journal of Transnational Law* 389 at 404. See also Chapter 1 by Hamdani and Ruffing in this volume.

[6] Commission on Human Rights, 'Norms on the Responsibilities of Transnational Corporations and Other Business Enterprises with Regard to Human Rights', E/CN.4/Sub.2/2003/12/Rev.2 (26 August 2003).

[7] D. Kinley, J. Nolan and N. Zerial, 'The Politics of Corporate Social Responsibility: Reflections on the United Nations Human Rights Norms for Corporations' (2007) 25 *Companies and Securities Law Journal* 30 at 35.

[8] HRC, 'Report of the Human Rights Council on its 26th session', A/HRC/26/2 (27 June 2014); Republic of Ecuador, 'Statement on Behalf of a Group of Countries at the 24th Session of the Human Rights Council' (13 September 2013), http://business-humanrights.org/media/docu ments/statement-unhrc-legally-binding.pdf (last accessed 4 January 2017); Treaty Alliance Joint Statement, 'Enhance the International Legal Framework to Protect Human Rights from Corporate Abuse', www.treatymovement.com/statement (last accessed 4 January 2017); S. Deva, 'The Human Rights Obligations of Business: Reimagining the Treaty Business' (2014), http://business-humanrights.org/sites/default/files/media/documents/reimagine_int_law_ for_bhr.pdf (last accessed 4 January 2017); S. Shetty, 'Corporations Have Rights. Now We Need a Global Treaty on Their Responsibilities' (21 January 2015), www.theguardian.com/ global-development-professionals-network/2015/jan/21/corporations-abuse-rights-interna tional-law (last accessed 4 January 2017).

[9] Delegation of the United States of America, 'Proposed Working Group Would Undermine Efforts to Implement Guiding Principles on Business and Human Rights: Explanation of Vote: A/HRC/26/L.22/Rev.1 on BHR Legally-Binding Instrument, Delivered by Stephen Townley' (26 June 2014), https://geneva.usmission.gov/2014/06/26/proposed-working-group-would-undermine-efforts-to-implement-guiding-principles-on-business-and-human-rights/ (last accessed 4 January 2017); European Coalition for Corporate Justice (ECCJ), 'UN Treaty on Business and Human Rights Negotiation's ECCJ Daily Summary: Business & Human Rights Day 2: EU Disengagement & Lack of Consensus on Scope' (8 July 2015), www.corporatejustice.org/UN-Treaty-on-Business-Human-Rights-negotia tions-Day-2-EU-disengagement-Lack-of.html (last accessed 4 January 2017).

EU member states walked out of the meetings on the second day.[10] During the second session of the OEIGWG held in October 2016, the EU and certain EU member states participated in the meeting but maintained their reservations about the treaty process.[11] In addition, the International Chamber of Commerce has indicated that it was 'deeply disappointed' with the result of the vote and that a treaty would undermine the Guiding Principles and would 'risk shifting the responsibility to protect human rights from states to the private sector.'[12]

The lack of support for (and in some cases active resistance against) the proposed treaty project from developed states and business actors stands in stark contrast to the unanimous endorsement of the Guiding Principles by the HRC in 2011,[13] and significantly, to the HRC Resolution 26/22 adopted by consensus in support of the Guiding Principles the day after the adoption of the HRC resolution establishing the OEIGWG.[14] Among other things, Resolution 26/22 calls on states to develop national action plans (NAPs) to implement the Guiding Principles, and calls on businesses to respect human rights in their operations. The resolution extends the mandate of the Working Group on Business and Human Rights (WGBHR) for a further three years and calls on the UN High Commissioner for Human Rights in collaboration with the WGBHR 'to facilitate the sharing and exploration of the full range of legal options and practical measures to improve access to remedy for victims of business-related human rights abuses'.[15]

The former Special Representative of the United Nations Secretary-General on Business and Human Rights (SRSG), Professor John G.

---

[10] *Ibid.*, J. Ruggie, 'Get Real, or We'll Get Nothing: Reflections on the First Session of the Intergovernmental Working Group on a Business & Human Rights Treaty' (2015), www.hks.harvard.edu/index.php/content/download/77052/1729783/version/1/file/GET+REAL_Ruggie.pdf (last accessed 4 January 2017).

[11] ECCJ, 'UN Treaty Talks Day 1: The EU is in the Room, but is That Enough?', (25 October 2016), http://corporatejustice.org/news/321-un-treaty-talks-day-1-the-eu-is-in-the-room-but-is-that-enough (last accessed 14 June 2017).

[12] International Chamber of Commerce (ICC), 'ICC Disappointed by Ecuador Initiative Adoption' (30 June 2014), www.iccwbo.org/News/Articles/2014/ICC-disappointed-by-Ecuador-Initiative-adoption/ (last accessed 4 January 2017).

[13] HRC, 'Human Rights and Transnational Corporations and Other Business Enterprises', A/HRC/RES/17/4 (6 July 2011); S. Jerbi, 'UN Adopts Guiding Principles on Business and Human Rights – What Comes Next?' (17 June 2011), www.ihrb.org/commentary/un-adopts-guiding-principles-business-human-rights.html (last accessed 4 January 2017).

[14] HRC, 'Human Rights and Transnational Corporations and Other Business Enterprises', A/HRC/RES/26/22 (15 July 2014).

[15] *Ibid.*, paras. 2, 3, 7 and 10.

Ruggie, has weighed in forcefully in a variety of fora[16] against the treaty process, questioning the need for, and viability of, an overarching treaty on business and human rights. In January 2014, six months before the resolution was passed, Ruggie suggested that the HRC needed to keep its 'eye on the ball' in terms of implementing the Guiding Principles and that if it was going to consider 'further international legalization in this space, it should carefully weigh the extent to which different forms of legalization would be capable of yielding practical results where it matters most: in the daily lives of affected individuals and communities around the world'.[17]

Ruggie maintains that he is not against legalization *per se*, but that proponents need a more workable plan for moving forward:

> Further international legalization in business and human rights is inevitable as well as being desirable in order to close global governance gaps. About that there can be little doubt. The critical questions are how to get from here to there, and in what direction the 'there' should lie.[18]

For Ruggie, the Guiding Principles represent 'a new regulatory dynamic' which should be shored up by discrete treaties rather than superseded or complimented by a general treaty that develops substantive human rights obligations for business actors and requires home states to regulate the overseas activity of companies domiciled within their territory. Ruggie argues that this approach is neither necessary nor workable, and 'would likely end in largely symbolic gestures, of little practical use to real people in real places, and with high potential for generating serious backlash by undermining the credibility of

---

[16] J. Ruggie, 'A UN Business and Human Rights Treaty?' (28 January 2014), www.hks .harvard.edu/m-rcbg/CSRI/UNBusinessandHumanRightsTreaty.pdf (last accessed 4 January 2017); J. Ruggie, 'A UN Business and Human Rights Treaty Update' (1 May 2014), http://business-humanrights.org/sites/default/files/media/un_business_and_hu man_rights_treaty_update.pdf (last accessed 4 January 2017); J. Ruggie, 'Regulating Multinationals: The UN Guiding Principles, Civil Society, and International Legalization' in C. Rodriguez-Garavito (ed.), *Business and Human Rights: Beyond the End of the Beginning* (forthcoming), www.hks.harvard.edu/index.php/content/down load/74032/1678739/version/1/file/RPP_2015_04_Ruggie.pdf (last accessed 4 January 2017); J. Ruggie, 'Life in the Global Public Domain: Response to Commentaries on the UN Guiding Principles and the Proposed Treaty on Business and Human Rights' (2015), http://papers.ssrn.com/sol3/papers.cfm?abstract_id=2554726 (last accessed 4 January 2017); J. Ruggie, 'International Legalization in Business and Human Rights' (2015), www .hks.harvard.edu/m-rcbg/CSRI/research/WFLS.pdf (last accessed 4 January 2017); Ruggie, 'Get Real, or We'll Get Nothing', n. 10.

[17] Ruggie, 'A UN Business and Human Rights Treaty?' *ibid.*, 1–2.

[18] Ruggie, 'Get Real or We'll Get Nothing', n. 10, 1.

further international legalization in any form'.[19] He recommends the adoption of an approach of 'principled pragmatism' that would see the development of a few narrowly focused treaties (such as one that would clarify the applicability of international criminal law norms to business actors in relation to grave violations of human rights) to address the governance gaps 'that other means are not reaching'.[20]

Ruggie's comments on the treaty development process raise two distinct issues. First, what is the value-added of international law in the area of business and human rights and, in particular, an over-arching treaty? Second, if such a treaty can be justified, could it be achieved strategically without undermining the political support that exists for the Guiding Principles? Ruggie continues to be an influential voice in the area of business and human rights, and his opinion in this debate will weigh heavily with business actors and governments scep-tical about the push for a treaty, some of whom have articulated similar concerns. The next section of this chapter will therefore consider Ruggie's view of the role of international law in this area and his arguments for more targeted legalization, in light of a recent study that found that states are moving away from treaty development towards informal law making, and that, as a practical matter, in terms of legitimacy, compliance and enforceability, there appears to be little distinction between formal and informal law.[21] The subse-quent three sections will consider why a general treaty on business and human rights is a necessary addition to the global business and human rights regime. In particular, I will examine some of the key short-comings of the Guiding Principles and the extent to which such inadequacies limit their normative potential. This chapter will then explore the power dynamics behind the choice by states to address corporate impunity for transnational human rights violations through informal rather than formal international law and institutions in light of the bias of the international legal system in favour of business actors.

---

[19] Ruggie, 'International Legalization', n. 16, 4.
[20] *Ibid.*, 3. Bilchitz has been critical of the focus of the debate initiated by Ruggie, which he says 'commences from the wrong starting point'. In considering the proposal for a treaty, Bilchitz observes that one should first 'consider the reasons for a treaty on business and human rights, not the difficulties associated with achieving it'. D. Bilchitz, 'The Necessity for a Business and Human Rights Treaty' (2016) 1 (2) *Business and Human Rights Journal* 1 at 2.
[21] J. Pauwelyn, R., A. Wessel and J. Wouters, 'When Structures Become Shackles: Stagnation and Dynamics in International Lawmaking' (2014) 25 *European Journal of International Law* 733 at 762.

I will articulate the value-added of a treaty on business and human rights with reference to the theory of interactional international law advanced by Jutta Brunnée and Stephen Toope.[22] According to Brunnée and Toope, what distinguishes international law from other types of norms is the sense of obligation it generates. Such obligation is not established by meeting the formalities of international lawmaking, but rather through an interactional process of developing shared understandings around legitimate norms, and a practice of legality. Drawing on insights of Brunnée and Toope, I will consider the question of strategy and whether the push for an overarching treaty regime is feasible or, as Ruggie argues, a dangerous tactic that could ultimately undermine the consensus around the Guiding Principles. Finally, I will contemplate how the basis for a broad, robust and effective legal regime could be established through a framework treaty and address some of the concerns of critics, while at the same time entrenching in law a strategy for moving forward.

2.2 Informal versus Formal International Law: A Technical Distinction?

Ruggie's view on the utility of international law to address corporate impunity for human rights violations appears to have been consistent from the beginning of his tenure as SRSG until now. In his first report to the then Human Rights Commission in 2006, Ruggie stated that he had not ruled out a role for international law in the recommendations he would eventually make to it.[23] However, outside of his official reports, he pushed back against the notion of a broader treaty framework to address corporate impunity for transnational human rights violations.[24] He argued that international law could be most valuable in a supporting role to his policy recommendations 'as carefully crafted precision tools complementing and augmenting existing institutional capacities'.[25] The

---

[22] J. Brunnée and S. Toope, *Legitimacy and Legality in International Law: An Interactional Account* (Cambridge University Press, 2010).

[23] Commission on Human Rights, 'Interim Report of the Special Representative of the Secretary-General on the Issue of Human Rights and Transnational Corporations and Other Business Enterprises', E/CN.4/2006/97 (22 February 2006), para. 69 ('2006 Interim Report').

[24] J. Ruggie, 'Treaty Road Not Travelled' (May 2008), www.hks.harvard.edu/m-rcbg/news/ruggie/Pages%20from%20ECM%20May_FINAL_JohnRuggie_may%2010.pdf (last accessed 4 January 2017).

[25] J. Ruggie, 'Business and Human Rights: The Evolving International Agenda' (2007) 101 *The American Journal of International Law* 819 at 839.

Guiding Principles, he argues, have 'succeeded in generating the beginnings of a new global regulatory dynamic'.[26] Given this fact, he remarks
that it is ironic that 'human rights activists and some academic human
rights lawyers ... continually try to push the agenda back into the
conventional mould [of law]'.[27] He has referred to this behaviour as a
'"means-ends reversal", turning the quest for binding legal obligations
into an end in itself before sorting out what means – legal and non-legal,
different bodies of law or various areas of public and self-regulation – are
most promising for which contexts'.[28]

During his mandate as SRSG, Ruggie argued in response to critics of his
policy approach that the distinction between law and non-law was misleading. For example, he asserted that the stipulation, under the 'Respect,
Protect and Remedy' Framework and Guiding Principles, that business
actors engage in human rights due diligence is not voluntary (although
not enshrined in law) because 'there simply isn't any other way to demonstrate' respect for human rights.[29] In the context of the current debate,
Ruggie has continued to question the distinction between soft regulatory
initiatives and law. In defence of his position on the treaty project he has
said:

> Let there be no misunderstanding: this debate is not about legalization as
> such. Nor is it about the tired dichotomy between voluntary and manda-
> tory measures. Treaties, after all, are voluntary in that no state can be
> forced to adopt one, while the Guiding Principles, which are typically
> described as being voluntary, embody existing mandatory requirements
> and have given rise to new ones.[30]

The contention that there is no bright line between law and non-law finds
some support in a growing range of academic discourses, including the
literatures on corporate social responsibility, new governance, business
and human rights, transnational legal pluralism[31] and international law.
For example, a research project led by Joost Pauwelyn, Ramses Wessel

---

[26] Ruggie, 'Regulating Multinationals', n. 16, 14.   [27] *Ibid.*

[28] J. Ruggie, 'Remarks by SRSG John Ruggie for the Conference on "Business and Fundamental
Rights: The State Duty to Protect and Domestic Legal Reform"' (3 November 2008), p. 6,
https://business-humanrights.org/sites/default/files/reports-and-materials/Ruggie-remarks-
South-Africa-3-Nov-2008.pdf (last accessed 4 January 2017).

[29] J. Ruggie, 'Opening Statement to UK Parliament Joint Committee on Human Rights' (3 June
2009), www.business-humanrights.org/Documents/Ruggie-statement-UK-3-Jun-2009.pdf
(last accessed 4 January 2017).

[30] Ruggie, 'International Legalization', n. 16, 5–6.

[31] For a critical examination of these arguments and their applicability within the context
of the governance of transnational corporate behaviour that implicates human rights,

and Jan Wouters examined the recent turn away by states from treaty negotiation and towards informal international lawmaking. The authors define informal international lawmaking (IN-LAW) 'in contrast and opposition to formal *traditional* international lawmaking'.[32] IN-LAW goes beyond soft law[33] 'as it addresses not only informal output but also new and informal actors and processes'.[34] It 'is informal in the sense that it dispenses with certain formalities traditionally linked to international law' such as 'output, process, or the actors involved'.[35] However, it is '[l]imited to activities which involve public authorities (although private actors may also participate)'.[36] Assessing a range of informal international legal mechanisms, the authors found 'strong evidence that traditional international lawmaking is in a process of stagnation' and that '[n]ew, alternative forms of cross-border cooperation have emerged and gained prominence, especially since the 2000s'.[37]

According to Pauwelyn et al., their findings suggest, among other things, that one can no longer maintain the traditional view that international law is more effective and more legitimate than informal law.[38] Rather, these new forms of international governance can be legitimately developed, evoke behavioural change and can be as, or more, enforceable than treaty law. Although international law can be applied by international courts and tribunals as well as domestic courts, given the lack of a centralized system of sanctions, where there exists no specific

---

see P. Simons and A. Macklin, *The Governance Gap: Extractive Industries, Human Rights and the Home State Advantage* (Routledge, 2014), 81–93.

[32] J. Pauwelyn, 'Informal International Lawmaking: Framing the Concept and Research Questions' in J. Pauwelyn, R. Wessel and J. Wouters (eds.), *Informal International Law-Making* (Oxford University Press, 2012), 15.

[33] Boyle notes two distinct definitions of soft law. First of all, '[f]rom a law-making perspective the term "soft law" is simply a convenient description for a variety of non-legally binding instruments used in contemporary international relations by States and international organizations'. Second, the term can also refer to the distinction between rules that are clear and precise as opposed to more general norms or principles, whether or not the latter are found in legally binding instruments. See A. Boyle, 'Soft Law in International Law-Making' in S. Evans (ed.), *International Law*, 4th edn. (Oxford University Press, 2014), 119–120 and 126. It is the former definition that is applicable here.

[34] Pauwelyn et al., 'When Structures Become Shackles', n. 21, 743; J. Pauwelyn, R. A. Wessel and J. Wouters, 'Informal International Lawmaking: An Assessment and Template to Keep It Both Effective and Accountable' in J. Pauwelyn et al. (eds.), n. 32, 506.

[35] Pauwelyn, 'Informal International Lawmaking' n. 32, 13.

[36] J. Pauwelyn, 'Is It International Law or Not, Does It Even Matter?' in J. Pauwelyn et al. (eds.), n. 32, 141.

[37] Pauwelyn et al., 'When Structures Become Shackles', n. 21, 762.   [38] *Ibid.*

international judicial or arbitral mechanism, international law will not necessarily be enforceable. Additionally, international law only requires state consent. This 'thin' consent, which is often no more than a rubber stamp by a domestic legislature, does not necessarily add much legitimacy.[39] On the other hand, according to Pauwelyn, informal law seems to have equal and sometimes higher compliance rates than formal law, and courts 'tend to refer to non-binding instruments', despite the latter's informal legal status.[40] Moreover, in contrast to international law, the development of non-law instruments may include a diversity of actors in the process, including state agencies, business entities and CSOs, resulting in 'thicker' consent around the norms.[41]

These conclusions appear to support Ruggie's position on the distinction between the Guiding Principles and hard international law. They also raise the question: if there is no added benefit to having a general treaty on business and human rights – that is to say, the treaty would have no greater normative impact, nor generate better compliance rates nor be more enforceable than the Guiding Principles (and the consent for the Guiding Principles is 'thicker' than state consent for a treaty) – then why jeopardize the current support, and the nascent implementation, of this informal set of norms which fall within the realm of what Pauwelyn et al. describe as international law's 'dynamic face'?[42]

It is beyond the scope of this chapter to assess all of the case studies and other research from which Pauwelyn et al. draw their conclusions. Nonetheless, a number of observations can be made. First, the authors do not claim that informal law is always as, or more, legitimate, effective, enforceable than formal international law, or that the former should replace or displace formal international lawmaking. Indeed the study recognizes important accountability gaps in some informal law. Rather, these authors only specify that both informal and formal lawmaking 'can offer legitimate forms of cooperation'.[43] Second, it bears noting that the case studies upon which the findings are based include a wide range of diverse international policy initiatives from a variety of informal bodies

---

[39] Pauwelyn, 'Is It International Law or Not', n. 36, 148.
[40] *Ibid.*, 151. See, for example, *Choc v. Hudbay Minerals Inc et al.*, 2013 ONSC 998 (CanLII), where the Ontario Superior Court, dismissing the defendants' motion to strike, found that the plaintiffs had met the threshold of establishing a prima facie duty of care, based on, among other things, public statements the defendants had made about their adoption of the Voluntary Principles on Security and Human Rights.
[41] Pauwelyn, 'Is It International Law or Not', n. 36, 151.
[42] Pauwelyn et al., 'When Structures Become Shackles', n. 21, 763.   [43] *Ibid.*, 762.

or networks such as the G20 and Asia-Pacific Economic Cooperation, Financial Action Task Force, the Codex Alimentarius Commission, the Kimberly Process and the network that produced the United Nations Principles for Responsible Investment.[44] The 'Respect Protect and Remedy' Framework and the Guiding Principles, although mentioned as a form of informal lawmaking,[45] were not themselves studied. Third, while it may be possible to draw general conclusions about the effectiveness, enforceability and legitimacy of informal lawmaking as this study has done, it is important to remember that each informal law mechanism was developed in a particular political context, in relation to particular institutions and involving a different set of actors. Thus, while the choice by states of an informal law instrument to govern transnational business actors and their impact on human rights supports the finding of a trend towards informal lawmaking, one cannot simply conclude without further assessment that there is not much to distinguish the Guiding Principles from an international treaty addressing business and human rights.

The next three sections will critically assess the Guiding Principles and consider the value-added of a general treaty in the area of business and human rights. I will argue that while informal law like the Guiding Principles has an important role to play in addressing the governance gaps, Ruggie's claims about the Guiding Principles overstate their normative potential and misconstrue the need for, and value of, international law in this context.

2.3 The Normative Limits of the Guiding Principles on Business and Human Rights

Both informal law and treaties 'can be vehicles for focusing consensus on rules and principles, and for mobilizing a consistent, general response on the part of States'.[46] There are situations when informal law may be preferable for this purpose and may in the end be more authoritative than a treaty. For example, as Boyle notes, the 1992 Rio Declaration on Environment and Development (which both codified existing international law and elaborated new norms that, it was hoped, would develop into new rules of international law) 'secured immediate consensus support' at a time when it was not clear 'that a treaty with the same

---

[44] For the full list, see J. Pauwelyn, R. Wessel and J. Wouters, 'Introduction to Informal International Lawmaking' in J. Pauwelyn et al. (eds.), n. 32, 3–4.
[45] Pauwelyn et al., 'When Structures Become Shackles', n. 21, 738.   [46] Boyle, n. 33, 122.

provisions would carry greater weight or achieve its objectives any more successfully'.[47]

In the context of business and human rights, with the failure of the UN Draft Norms and the polarization that followed, it is not surprising that states (through the HRC and its predecessor) opted for a set of Guiding Principles and that this informal instrument was not negotiated between states, but rather developed by a UN human rights mandate holder. Unlike the Rio Declaration, however, the aim of the Guiding Principles was not to develop new norms of international human rights law. The goals and the outcome of this project were more limited. As Ruggie has pointed out, the normative contribution of the Guiding Principles 'lies not in the creation of new international law obligations but in elaborating the implications of existing standards and practices for States and businesses; integrating them within a single, logically coherent and comprehensive template'.[48] The choices that were made in terms of the content and language of the Guiding Principles have meant that they have not laid sufficient groundwork for the development of new norms of international law on home-state obligations to regulate transnational corporate conduct, human rights obligations for business actors and on access to effective remedies for victims of corporate-related human rights abuses.

This is not to say that the Guiding Principles have not played and will not continue to play an important role in shaping both the dialogue on business and human rights and developing important (albeit limited) expectations of state and business behaviour. They are the first set of universally accepted guidelines on business and human rights after decades of dissensus on this issue. They were developed with the benefit of broad consultation with stakeholders and, unlike the failed Draft UN Code of Conduct and the UN Draft Norms, the Guiding Principles have 'buy-in' from developed states and businesses. They have contributed to the clarification of the host state's obligation to *protect* human rights with respect to business activity, to the development of a distinct responsibility on the part of business to respect human rights (including the components of human rights due diligence), and to the understanding of the centrality of access to an effective remedy for victims of business-related human rights violations.

At the same time, the Guiding Principles have also been widely criticized for their failure to address adequately some of the most controversial issues regarding the governance of transnational business conduct, as well as for

---

[47] *Ibid.*   [48] Guiding Principles, n. 1, para. 14.

their misrepresentation of international human rights law. By soft-pedalling on these issues, the SRSG was able to garner the support of states, powerful business actors and international industry associations. This was a significant feat that may have been necessary following the polarization of parties around the UN Draft Norms.[49] But, it is these particular deficiencies that have arguably limited the normative potential of the Guiding Principles.

First, Pillar 1 of the Guiding Principles does not adequately address home-state regulation of transnational business activity and has arguably undermined current international human rights law on this point. Principle 2 merely encourages states to 'set out clearly the expectation that all business enterprises domiciled in their territory and/or jurisdiction respect human rights throughout their operations'.[50] The commentary on this principle very clearly asserts that states do not have an international human rights obligation to regulate the extraterritorial activities of businesses domiciled in their jurisdiction.[51] This was not only a retreat from the position Ruggie took in the 'Protect, Respect and Remedy' Framework,[52] but an inaccurate reflection of states' international human rights law obligations. As Olivier De Schutter points out, the Guiding Principles on this issue 'set the bar clearly below the current state of international human rights law [and]... in fact may have been encouraging states reluctant to accept such obligations to challenge the interpretation of human rights treaty bodies, despite the support the position of these bodies received both from legal doctrine and civil society, and from the International Court of Justice itself'.[53] Daniel Augustein and David Kinley argue that the way the Guiding Principles

---

[49] F. Wettstein, 'Normativity, Ethics, and the UN Guiding Principles on Business and Human Rights: A Critical Assessment' (2015) 14 *Journal of Human Rights* 162 at 178.

[50] Guiding Principles, n. 1, Principle 2.   [51] *Ibid.*, Principle 2 Commentary.

[52] See HRC, 'Protect, Respect and Remedy: A Framework for Business and Human Rights', A/HRC/8/5 (7 April 2008), para. 19 ('2008 Report'), which suggested that there was 'increasing encouragement' from international institutions, including UN treaty bodies, 'for home States to take regulatory action to prevent abuse by their companies overseas'.

[53] O. De Schutter, 'Towards a New Treaty on Business and Human Rights' (2015) 1 *Business & Human Rights Journal* 41 at 45–46. For a discussion about the extraterritorial obligations of states, see Skogly's chapter in this volume. With respect to the position of UN treaty bodies, see, for example, Committee on Economic, Social and Cultural Rights (CESCR), 'General Comment No. 14 (2000): The Right to the Highest Attainable Standard of Health (Art. 12 of the International Covenant on Economic, Social and Cultural Rights)', E/C.12/2000/4 (11 August 2000), para. 39; Convention on the Rights of the Child (CRC), 'General Comment No. 16 (2013) on State Obligations Regarding the Impact of the Business Sector on Children's Rights', CRC/C/GC/16 (17 April 2013), para. 43–45; Convention on the Elimination of All Forms of Discrimination against Women (CEDAW), 'Concluding Observations on the Combined Eighth and Ninth Periodic Reports of Sweden', CEDAW/

are drafted has actually diverted the focus of the debate away 'from states' extra-territorial obligations under human rights law to states' policy rationales to protect human rights in their international relations'.[54]

A second important defect of the Guiding Principles is their failure to articulate standards of corporate accountability linked to, or embedded within, international human rights law. As Justine Nolan writes, the fact that the SRSG chose to base the source of the corporate responsibility to respect human rights not in international human rights law 'but in a more inchoate and softer source' of 'societal-expectation'[55] may have increased the chance of acceptance of the Guiding Principles by states and business actors on a political level.[56] However, it has meant that the important second pillar of principles is 'non-authoritative' and is unlikely 'to induce strong normative change'.[57]

The Guiding Principles also divide, into two categories, the rights that businesses must consider as part of their responsibility to respect human rights. The first category includes those rights which are always applicable to business activity – namely the instruments included in the International Bill of Rights, and the principles drawn from the eight core ILO conventions as set out in the International Labour Organization's Declaration on Fundamental Principles and Rights at Work. The second category includes the rights of women, children, indigenous peoples, disabled peoples and the rights of other minority groups, relegating them to the status of 'additional standards' that business actors *may* need to consider in particular circumstances.[58] This classification of human rights is incompatible with, and undermines, the widely accepted doctrine of the indivisibility and interrelatedness of all human rights articulated in the Vienna Declaration and Programme of Action 1993.

Finally, in relation to the third pillar on access to remedy, Surya Deva has observed that the Guiding Principles fail to reflect adequately the internationally recognized human right to an effective remedy and the

---

C/SWE/CO/8–9 (7 March 2016), para. 35; HRC, 'Concluding Observations on the Sixth Periodic Report of Canada', CCPR/C/CAN/CO/6 (13 August 2015), para. 6.

[54] D. Augustein and D. Kinley, 'When Human Rights "Responsibilities" become "Duties": The Extra-Territorial Obligations of States that Bind Corporations' in S. Deva and D. Bilchitz (eds.), *The Human Rights Obligations of Business: Beyond the Corporate Responsibility to Respect?* (Cambridge University Press, 2013), 273.

[55] Social expectation is to be monitored and enforced in the 'courts of public opinion'. 2008 Report, n. 52, para. 54.

[56] J. Nolan, 'The Corporate Responsibility to Respect Human Rights: Soft Law or Not Law?' in Deva and Bilchitz (eds.), n. 54, 155.

[57] *Ibid.*, 160–161; Wettstein, n. 49, 167.

[58] Guiding Principles, n. 1, Commentary on Principle 12.

'rich' jurisprudence that has interpreted this right. He points out that 'access to remedy', rather than being anchored in the stand-alone right to an effective remedy, is treated as flowing from the state obligation to protect human rights.[59]

State uptake of the Guiding Principles has been far from spectacular. Some states have enacted reflexive legislation that encourages companies to undertake human rights due diligence. The French legislature has adopted a law that imposes obligations on large companies (5,000 or more employees domestically or 10,000 internationally) to develop and publish due diligence plans for avoiding adverse human rights, environmental or other social impacts.[60] The UK has enacted the Modern Slavery Act, which, among other things, requires commercial organizations either to report on the steps they are taking 'to ensure that slavery and human trafficking is not taking place' within their operations or their supply chains, or to report that they have 'taken no such steps'.[61] The 2015 regulations apply the Act to all companies supplying goods or services with an annual turnover of £36 million and which carry on business, or a part of their business, in the UK.[62] No state has yet enacted a more general law with incentive, facilitative and coercive compliance mechanisms and which directly requires companies to respect human rights in their overseas activities and to undertake preventative and ongoing action through human rights due diligence.

A small number of states have developed NAPs to implement the Guiding Principles and others have committed to do so.[63] However, a close reading of the existing NAPs suggests that there has been little movement by states in terms of legal and policy developments on key issues.[64] The International Corporate Accountability Roundtable (ICAR) and the European Coalition for Corporate Justice (ECCJ) assessed the

---

[59] S. Deva, 'Treating Human Rights Lightly: A Critique of the Consensus Rhetoric and the Language Employed by the Guiding Principles' in Deva and Bilchitz (eds.), n. 54, 102.

[60] Loi n° 924 du 21 février 2017 relative au devoir de vigilance des sociétés mères et des entreprises donneuses d'ordre.

[61] Modern Slavery Act 2015 (UK), sec. 54.

[62] *Ibid.*, s 54(2)(b) and (12) read with Regulations 2 and 3 of the Modern Slavery Act (Transparency in Supply Chains) Regulations 2015.

[63] Office of the United Nations High Commissioner for Human Rights (OHCHR), 'State National Action Plans', www.ohchr.org/EN/Issues/Business/Pages/NationalActionPlans .aspx (last accessed 4 January 2017).

[64] See, for example, UK Government, 'Good Business: Implementing the UN Guiding Principles on Business and Human Rights' (Cm 8695 September 2013), www.gov.uk/ government/uploads/system/uploads/attachment_data/file/236901/BHR_Action_Plan_- _final_online_version_1_.pdf (last accessed 4 January 2017). This was updated in May

development process and the substance of the NAPs launched by the UK, the Netherlands, Denmark and Finland[65] against 25 criteria developed by ICAR and the Danish Institute for Human Rights.[66] While ICAR and ECCJ noted some positive aspects in each of the NAPs,[67] they found that all four states failed 'to conduct national baseline assessments to inform the content of their NAPs'.[68] In terms of the substance, they found that all of the NAPs tended to focus on 'describing past actions' and did not adequately outline or commit to 'future action points'.[69] There was insufficient exploration of 'regulatory options', as opposed to 'awareness raising, training, research, and other voluntary measures'.[70] Each NAP also tended to 'focus on one or two of the Pillars of the UNGPs, leaving one or more of the Pillars inadequately addressed'. In particular, the NAPs gave little or no attention to Pillar 3 on access to remedy, despite the fact that they all acknowledged the latter's importance. Finally, the NAPs failed to address 'the circumstances of vulnerable groups, such as children or indigenous communities'.[71]

At the time of writing, only Denmark had indicated a willingness to move forward on the issue of extraterritoriality.[72] No states have committed to introducing sanctions and incentives to induce compliance with the corporate responsibility to respect human rights.[73] Additionally, as Ramasastry and Cassel point out, in the United States and the UK, access to judicial remedies for victims of corporate-related violations of human rights

2016, with almost no additional legal commitments: www.gov.uk/government/publica tions/bhr-action-plan (last accessed 4 January 2017).

[65] The International Corporate Accountability Roundtable (ICAR) and ECCJ, 'Assessments of Existing National Action Plans (NAPs) on Business and Human Rights' (November 2014), http://icar.ngo/analysis/napsassessments/ (last accessed 4 January 2017).

[66] ICAR and the Danish Institute for Human Rights (DIHR), 'National Action Plans on Business and Human Rights: A Toolkit for the Development, Implementation, and Review of State Commitments to Business and Human Rights Frameworks', http://icar.ngo/analysis/napsreport/ (last accessed 4 January 2017).

[67] ICAR and ECCJ, n. 65, 3–4.   [68] Ibid., 3.   [69] Ibid., 4.   [70] Ibid.   [71] Ibid.

[72] Danish Government, 'Danish National Action Plan – Implementation of the UN Guiding Principles on Business and Human Rights' (March 2014), 15, www.ohchr.org/Documents/Issues/Business/NationalPlans/Denmark_NationalPlanBHR.pdf (last accessed 4 January 2017).

[73] Canada's Enhanced CSR Strategy for the extractive sector does not require Canadian extractive companies to respect human rights in their overseas activities, although it does create incentives for corporations to engage in formal and informal mediation with the CSR Counsellor and the Canadian National Contact Point. See P. Simons, 'Canada's Enhanced CSR Strategy: Human Rights Due Diligence and Access to Justice for Victims of Extraterritorial Corporate Human Rights Abuses' (2015) 56 (2) Canadian Business Law Journal 167.

has actually been restricted since the Guiding Principles were adopted by the HRC in 2011.[74]

In terms of business uptake, the language of the business responsibility to respect human rights is becoming more widespread and this has helped to change the discourse and expectations on businesses. However, meaningful change in business practices has also been weak.[75] According to Nolan, '[w]hile the number of corporations prepared to adopt human rights policies may have risen, the few mechanisms for enforcing such policies remain largely embedded in soft law, that unless hardened, will have a very limited effect in preventing future violations of human rights by corporations'.[76]

The promise of the Guiding Principles has not so far been borne out *in practice* in the six years following their adoption by the HRC. The gaps in this informal instrument, along with the misrepresentation of international human rights law, have limited its potential to influence some of the most needed changes in state and business behaviour. Moreover, the misconstruction of core aspects of international human rights law might even, in the process, have undermined accepted understandings of states' international human rights obligations.

2.4 Informal Law, the Guiding Principles and Power

In contemplating whether there is a need for a general treaty on business and human rights, it is also important to consider the power dynamics that may be at play behind the choice to engage in informal rather than formal lawmaking in the area of business and human rights. Eyal Benvenisti has noted that 'governments, particularly those of relatively powerful States which set the rules, gain much from all types of [informal lawmaking]'.[77] In many instances, states will opt for soft law or informal law 'precisely and deliberately to avoid any obligation to comply'.[78] This may allow them to

---

[74] D. Cassel and A. Ramasastry, 'White Paper: Options for a Treaty on Business and Human Rights' (May 2015), 7, http://business-humanrights.org/sites/default/files/documents/whitepaperfinal%20ABA%20LS%206%2022%2015.pdf (last accessed 4 January 2017).

[75] See, for example, Worldwide Movement for Human Rights (FIDH), 'Briefing Paper: Business and Human Rights: Enhancing Standards and Ensuring Redress' (March 2014), www.fidh.org/IMG/pdf/201403_briefing_paper_enhance_standards_ensure_re dress_web_version.pdf (last accessed 4 January 2017).

[76] Nolan, n. 56, 161.

[77] E. Benvenisti, 'Towards a Typology of Informal International Lawmaking Mechanisms and their Distinct Accountability Gaps' in J. Pauwelyn et al. (eds.), n. 32, 306.

[78] C. Chinkin, 'Normative Development in the International Legal System' in D. Shelton (ed.), *Commitment and Compliance: The Role of Non-Binding Norms in the International*

agree on 'more detailed and precise provisions' or to 'avoid the domestic treaty ratification process, and perhaps escape democratic accountability for the policy to which they have agreed',[79] or even to give them more control over the outcome. To date, most powerful states (supported and prodded by influential business actors) have insisted that informal self-regulatory rules and mechanisms are sufficient to govern effectively the behaviour of transnational corporations and, as noted above, they have successfully resisted the development of formal international law on this issue.[80] At the same time, such states have used formal international law and institutions over time to protect and facilitate transnational corporate activity through international trade and investment law while undermining the ability of many developing states to control and regulate transnational corporate actors.[81]

For example, Ruggie himself has recognized the regulatory constraints that international investment agreements can impose on host states. He has noted that, through arbitration or the threat of arbitration, 'a foreign investor may be able to insulate its business venture from new laws and regulations, or seek compensation from the Government for the cost of compliance'.[82] As a result, states may find it difficult to fulfil their obligations under international human rights law to exercise due diligence to protect individuals and communities from corporate-related human rights abuses. Impecunious developing state governments may be faced with a choice between a potential international arbitral suit by a foreign investor that could cost approximately $8 million to defend[83] and result in an award of millions or even billions of dollars,[84]

Legal System (Oxford University Press, 2000), 25; See also M. A. Pollack and G. C. Shaffer, 'The Interaction of Formal and Informal International Lawmaking' in J. Pauwelyn et al. (eds.), n. 32, 269, who argue that states choose to engage in informal lawmaking not only because it may be more flexible and efficient, but because 'they seek to promote their preferred interpretation of law in the most propitious forums available'.

[79] Boyle, n. 33, 121.   [80] Murphy, n. 5; UN Draft Norms, n. 6; Kinley et al., n. 7.

[81] P. Simons, 'International Law's Invisible Hand and the Future of Corporate Accountability for Violations of Human Rights' (2012) 3 (1) Journal of Human Rights and the Environment 5 at 19–29.

[82] HRC, 'Towards Operationalizing the "Protect, Respect and Remedy" Framework', A/HRC/11/13 (22 April 2009), para. 30 ('2009 Report').

[83] United Nations Conference on Trade and Development (UNCTAD), World Investment Report 2013: Global Value Chains: Investment and Trade for Development (United Nations Publication, 2013), 112.

[84] J.E. Viñuales, 'The Environmental Regulation of Foreign Investment Schemes under International Law' in P. Dupuy and J. E. Viñuales (eds.), Harnessing Foreign Investment to Promote Environmental Protection Incentives and Safeguards (Cambridge University Press, 2011), 274.

or complying with their international human rights obligations. Such a state may thus be forced to refrain from taking the regulatory or policy action necessary to protect the rights of individuals from corporate abuses where to do so might contravene their obligations under international investment law. Additionally, the economic and social interventions of the World Bank and International Monetary Fund, including through the imposition of conditionalities for loans, have often favoured foreign investors while undercutting the capacity of such states to undertake the social reform necessary to, among other things, respect, protect and fulfil human rights.[85] Business actors therefore benefit from the weakened regulatory capacity of developing host states and robust international laws and enforcement mechanisms that facilitate and support their activities.[86]

It is no surprise that the call for a general treaty on business and human rights has been led by developing states. According to Benvenisti, the choice by states to use informal law and institutions can be for the purpose of constraining 'the behaviour of third, usually weaker, States' by limiting their opportunities 'to resist new norms or even to participate in their shaping'.[87] It is arguable that the failure of the Guiding Principles to include a clear obligation on home states to regulate transnational behaviour of corporate nationals or binding international human rights obligations for transnational business actors, coupled with the insistence that a treaty is unnecessary, maintains in place the international legal structures that limit the governance capacity of weaker states. The Guiding Principles do little to address the bias of international law that favours business activity above human rights or to enhance the capacity of developing countries to govern foreign investors in a manner consistent with their international human rights obligations.

Formal law and institutions, on the other hand, can empower weaker states by reducing 'the political gap along the North-South axis'.[88] The fact that weaker states have used international courts and tribunals to challenge the actions of more powerful states suggests that they perceive these formal institutions as an effective means for constraining their more powerful counterparts.[89] The 85 developing states that tabled the treaty resolution before the HRC view the Guiding Principles as an important, but insufficient, step to addressing corporate impunity for transnational violations of human rights. They argue that the development of an international treaty is

---

[85] M. Salomon, 'International Economic Governance and Human Rights Accountability', *LSE Law, Society and Economy Working Papers* (September 2007), 9–10, http://eprints.lse.ac.uk/24622/1/WPS09-2007Salomon.pdf (last accessed 4 January 2017).

[86] Simons, n. 81, 85.   [87] Benvenisti, n. 77, 299.   [88] *Ibid.*, 307.   [89] *Ibid.*

necessary in order to provide 'for enhanced State action to protect rights and prevent the occurrence of violations'.[90]

The Guiding Principles also do little to address the *structural* bias of the international legal system, including international law's relationship with domestic law, which contribute to the preferential treatment of business activity.[91] In addition to the international economic laws and institutions, public international law turns a blind eye to transnational corporate groups, treating them as disaggregated entities and leaving their conduct to be regulated by domestic law in the jurisdictions in which they operate or are incorporated.[92] These laws and practices, coupled with domestic corporate laws that protect the integrity of the doctrines of separate legal personality and limited liability, and impose fiduciary duties on directors and managers to operate in the best interests of the corporation (which is often seen as the maximization of profit) were developed 'through careful and deliberate design' and are 'part of a dysfunctional global legal architecture'[93] which helps to perpetuate corporate human rights impunity. Despite the revisions some states have made to corporate law to integrate certain corporate social responsibility obligations,[94] neither the soft 'responsibility to respect human rights' nor the exhortations of other intergovernmental and multi-stakeholder initiatives[95] will be sufficient to counter the legal obligation on directors and officers to maximize profit for the shareholders,[96] or the other imbalances embedded in the international legal system.[97]

Benvenisti notes that informal lawmaking can also 'mask governmental concessions to powerful private actors'.[98] The power dynamics

---

[90] 'Statement on Behalf of the Group of Countries at the 24th Session of the Human Rights Council', n. 8.

[91] Simons, n. 81, 29–34.

[92] J. Crawford and S. Olleson, 'The Character and Forms of International Responsibility' in M. Evans (ed.), *International Law*, 4th edn. (Oxford University Press, 2014), 446.

[93] S. Turner, *A Global Environmental Right* (Routledge, 2013), 32 and 116–17. Turner here is referring to the impact of the ensemble of these laws on the environment and notes that they are the 'root-causes' or 'drivers' of environmental degradation. But an analogy can be drawn with respect to their impact on human rights.

[94] See, for example, S. Deva, 'Socially Responsible Business in India: Has the Elephant Finally Woken Up to the Tunes of International Trends?' (2012) 41 *Common Law World Review* 299.

[95] Such as, for example, the OECD Guidelines for Multinational Enterprises, the Global Compact, the Voluntary Principles on Security and Human Rights, the IFC Performance Standards, the Equator Principles, the Extractive Industries Transparency Initiative or the Global Reporting Initiative.

[96] Simons and Macklin, n. 31, 87–88.   [97] Simons, n. 81, 39–40.

[98] Benvenisti, n. 77, 306–307.

at play behind the development and refinement of the Guiding Principles were evident in the final version of the Principles presented to the HRC. Many large businesses and influential industry groups engaged in the mandate of the SRSG, and provided comments on his drafts reports, advocating against laws and legal mechanisms.[99] Deva demonstrates that despite the broad consultation undertaken by the SRSG,[100] in the end, the voices and critiques of the less powerful actors (mainly CSOs and some developing states) were taken less seriously and generally not accommodated compared to the concerns and critiques of business actors. Deva points to the draft and final versions of the Guiding Principles and the fact that the latter did not reflect the recommended changes of a wide range and number of CSOs 'in terms of broadening the scope of corporate human rights responsibilities, enforcement mechanisms, or the removal of barriers experienced by victims in seeking judicial remedies'.[101]

In short, Ruggie's assertion that the role of international law in addressing corporate impunity for human rights violations should be limited to discrete '"precision tools" . . . focused on specific governance gaps that other means are not reaching'[102] is misconceived and short-sighted. The Guiding Principles, with their significant shortcomings, will not ensure sufficient behaviour change by states or businesses. Nor can they begin to redress the power imbalances of an international legal system that favours business activity over the protection of human rights. While formal international law in the form of a general treaty on business and human rights is not a silver bullet, it has the potential to address the gaps left by the Guiding Principles and to contribute towards countering the bias of international law in this context.

---

[99] See, for example, International Organization of Employers (IOE), International Chamber of Commerce (ICC), and Business and Industry Advisory Committee to the OECD (BIAC), 'Joint initial views of the IOE, the ICC and the BIAC to the Eighth Session of the Human Rights Council on the Third report of the Special Representative of the UN Secretary-General on Business and Human Rights' (May 2008), http://business-humanrights.org/sites/default/files/reports-and-materials/Letter-IOE-ICC-BIAC-re-Ruggie-report-May-2008.pdf (last accessed 4 January 2017) (arguing against a global ombudsman on business and human rights); IOE, ICC and BIAC, 'Joint Statement on Business & Human Rights to the United Nations Human Rights Council' (30 May 2011), http://business-humanrights.org/sites/default/files/media/documents/ioe-icc-biac-submission-to_the-un-hrc-may-2011.pdf (last accessed 4 January 2017) (advising against creating a follow-up mechanism to the Guiding Principles with the capacity receive complaints).

[100] Importantly, victims of corporate-related human rights abuses were not central to these consultations. See Deva, 'Treating Human Rights Lightly', n. 59, 83–84.

[101] *Ibid.*, 85–86.   [102] Ruggie, 'International Legalization', n. 16, 3.

2.5   The Value-Added of a Treaty Regime on Business
and Human Rights

One could argue that there are two core characteristics that distinguish law from other norms: obligation and the potential for establishing formal compliance mechanisms. In their book, *Legitimacy and Legality in International Law: An Interactional Account*, Jutta Brunnée and Stephen Toope put forward a theory to explain why a horizontal system of law, like international law, is able to generate an internal sense of bindingness for states. For Brunnée and Toope, 'obligation is the "value-added" of law, distinguishing it from social desiderata, airport signs, or the rationalist proposition that "obligation" is a mode of action chosen by actors to signal credible commitment'.[103] However, they caution that formal lawmaking itself (e.g., by complying with the requirements of the Vienna Convention on the Law of Treaties) is not what differentiates law from social norms. 'Although formal indicators provide useful indicia of the existence of binding rules and, of course, "validity" on the terms of the system, they are not enough to identify "law" because formality alone is not strong enough to generate fidelity.'[104] Rather, it is the combination of shared understandings, acceptance of the legitimacy of the norms in question and a practice of legality that generates the obligatory force of law.[105] International actors must work to build shared understandings around both 'the role of law' and 'candidate norms'.[106] According to Brunnée and Toope, such norms must meet Lon Fuller's eight criteria of legality: they must be 'general, prohibiting, requiring, or permitting certain conduct', made public, prospective, clear, non-contradictory, realistic, constant and there must be 'congruence between legal norms and the actions of officials operating under the law'.[107] Adhering to these criteria will enhance the legitimacy of the norms for the actors to whom they are addressed.[108] Law that meets these criteria, Brunnée and Toope argue, 'facilitates interaction on the basis of mutual respect and reciprocity and, therefore, fosters the commitment of states and other actors to their joint enterprise'.[109] Finally, while formal law can develop from informal instruments, actors must engage in a practice of

---

[103] Brunnée and Toope, *Legitimacy and Legality in International Law*, n. 22, 41–42.
[104] *Ibid.*, 46–47.   [105] *Ibid.*, 217.
[106] J. Brunnée and S. Toope, 'Interactional, International Law: An Introduction' (2011) 3 (2) *International Theory* 308.
[107] *Ibid.*, 310.
[108] Brunnée and Toope, *Legitimacy and Legality in International Law*, n. 22, 27.
[109] *Ibid.*, 76.

legality to transform the shared understandings into shared legal understandings. They must create 'spaces and opportunities for ongoing [legal] interaction'.[110] According to Boyle, treaties may be more effective in developing consensus around norms than informal law 'because they indicate a stronger commitment to the principles in question and to that extent they may carry greater weight than a soft law instrument'.[111] Moreover, he notes that the 'argument for using a treaty rather than a soft law instrument is stronger in the case of new law-making or the revision of existing law, such as the renegotiation of the law of the sea or the elaboration of human rights law'.[112]

Furthermore, like domestic law, through which one can harness a range of incentive, facilitative and coercive mechanisms to induce compliance,[113] a treaty can establish a range of hard and soft formal international compliance mechanisms and mandate the creation of other compliance mechanisms at the domestic level, including private remedies in domestic courts. Informal law and informal mechanisms, on the other hand, that are not embedded or linked to a legal framework, are less likely to be effective.[114] Börzel and Risse demonstrate that transnational governance initiatives are unlikely to be effective where the state plays no role in coercion or providing a 'shadow of hierarchy'.[115] Compliance mechanisms, however, cannot simply be tacked on to a treaty. Rather, to be effective 'enforcement measures . . . compliance mechanisms or dispute settlement, must be embedded in the shared understandings and the practice of legality that generate interactional law and, through it, obligation'.[116]

The general approach of powerful business actors to international law is Janus-faced and speaks to the recognition of these special characteristics of law. On the one hand, these actors pursue and/or support the development of formal law with hard compliance mechanisms both domestically and internationally in order to protect and support their activities. At the international level, the proliferation of international trade and investment agreements, both bilateral and

---

[110] *Ibid.*, 124. [111] Boyle, n. 33, 122. [112] *Ibid.*

[113] Simons and Macklin, n. 31, 20–21.

[114] Nolan argues that soft law is most effective when it is positioned to be 'precursor to hard law' or when it operates within a framework of hard law or supplements the latter. Nolan, n. 56, 157.

[115] T.A. Börtzel and T. Risse, 'Governance without a State: Can it Work?' (2010) 4 *Regulation & Governance* 113.

[116] Brunnée and Toope, *Legitimacy and Legality in International Law*, n. 22, 111.

multilateral, is a classic example. On the other hand, they actively oppose the development of unilateral home-state regulation[117] or an international treaty on business and human rights that might undercut profits and they insist that their activities should be 'regulated' by informal forms of normativity.

2.6　Interactional International Law and Moving beyond the *Status Quo*

A treaty is of course not a panacea. Treaties have well-known inherent weaknesses that Ruggie and others have pointed out, for example: their creation is a long-term process; once a treaty is adopted, states may decide not to ratify it; states that have ratified may not implement their obligations; treaties may be difficult to enforce at the international level; options for enforcement may rely heavily on domestic law and hence require state implementation and cooperation. Yet some of the same allegations can be made about informal law standards, and, as noted above, are indeed some of the central problems with the Guiding Principles. As Florian Wettstein remarks, '[t]he GPs effectively hand the regulatory authority for any binding, enforced or even merely monitored measures back to the governments, which have proven in the past that they are hardly willing to go it alone'.[118]

Nevertheless, the limitations of treaties and the process of their development do not undermine their value nor justify their exclusion 'from the array of regulatory tools that could be employed to target transnational corporate behaviour'.[119] I have argued elsewhere that a treaty on this subject need not replace current informal forms of regulation but rather should operate alongside them.[120]

Throughout his mandate as the SRSG, Ruggie claimed that international law had a role to play in his overall strategy to address the governance gaps

---

[117] For example, a major lobbying effort was launched by the Canadian mining industry that eventually defeated Bill C-300 (An Act Respecting Corporate Accountability for the Activities of Mining, Oil or Gas in Developing Countries, 3rd Sess, 40th Parl, 2010–2011), which would have imposed obligations on extractive companies to comply with certain human rights and environmental standards when operating in developing states. See B. Curry, 'Lobbying Blitz Helps Kill Mining Ethics Bill' Globe and Mail (27 October 2010), www.theglobeandmail.com/news/politics/lobbying-blitz-helps-kill-mining-ethics-bill/article1215704/ (last accessed 4 January 2017).

[118] Wettstein, n. 49, 166.

[119] Simons and Macklin, n. 31, 20. We make this claim with respect to unilateral home-state regulation, but it applies equally to international law.

[120] Simons, n. 81, 39.

with respect to business conduct that violates human rights.[121] Yet, he has never laid out a plan for what that role might be, apart from cautioning against a general treaty (both then and now) and recommending (among other options) the development of a discrete treaty to clarify the legal norms applicable to business where they engage in behaviour that violates international criminal law standards. For Ruggie, this latter option is the only politically viable one. He has argued that '[i]f present dynamics continue, the process is likely to yield one of two outcomes: no treaty at all, or one that squeaks through to adoption but is ratified by few if any major home countries and thus would be of no help to the victims in whose name the negotiations were launched'.[122] He points out that there is no broad consensus on 'meaningful legal liability standards for corporate abuse' of the full range of human rights. Moreover, any treaty would need to address extraterritorial regulation of transnational corporations, and state practice on this issue does not support this.[123]

Ruggie is correct that the treaty project needs to be approached strategically. However, this does not necessarily mean settling for what is immediately possible based on the current position of states or that the push for a broader treaty will necessarily undermine the Guiding Principles. His call for a targeted treaty, around which state consensus may already exist, is not sufficiently forward-looking. According to Brunnée and Toope, actors involved in lawmaking are not bound to 'defer to existing practice'.[124] The development of law should be seen as a process, which is often long and sometimes hard fought. Political consensus to develop law does not simply appear; it needs to be built and nurtured. The establishment of the International Criminal Court, the negotiation and adoption of the Convention on the Prohibition of the Use, Stockpiling, Production and Transfer of Anti-Personnel Mines and on their Destruction,[125] the Convention on the Elimination of All Forms of Discrimination Against Women[126] and the principle of non-discrimination all required the

---

[121] See, for example, '2006 Interim Report', n. 23, para. 65; Ruggie, 'Business and Human Rights', n. 25, 839; Ruggie, 'Treaty Road Not Travelled', n. 24, 43.

[122] Ruggie, 'Get Real, or We'll Get Nothing', n. 10, 1.

[123] Ruggie, 'International Legalization', n. 16, 4–5. On the extraterritorial dimension of the duty to protect, the UK has consistently stated that such duty is limited to a state's territory and jurisdiction and that there is no obligation to regulate the transnational activities of UK corporations. This position is reiterated in the UK NAP for implementing the Guiding Principles. See 'Good Business', n. 64, 8.

[124] Brunnée and Toope, *Legitimacy and Legality in International Law*, n. 22, 33.

[125] Adopted 18 September 1997, entered into force 1 March 1999.

[126] Adopted 18 December 1979, entered into force 3 September 1981.

building and maintenance of consensus or shared understandings. If promoters of the climate change regime did not attempt to move forward at
various stages because the United States or China were unsupportive of the
process, international lawmaking would have never gone forward in this
area.[127]

There is a strong basis of support for the Guiding Principles, and the
shared understandings that they reflect can be used as a springboard for
moving forward.[128] There is currently a groundswell of political support
for a treaty on business and human rights with over 85 states and 600
CSOs supporting the call for a treaty.[129] The EU did participate in the
second session of the OEIGWG. The new Canadian government, which
took office on 4 November 2015, has pledged to re-engage with the UN[130]
and may at the very least participate in the OEIGWG process in future.

According to De Schutter, the political dissensus between proponents
and opponents of the treaty development process is not as wide as 'the
voting patterns seem to suggest. The suspicion towards the Ecuador-
South Africa proposal is in fact largely a matter of perception' that this is
an attempt to refight old battles over the New International Economic
Order or the UN Draft Norms.[131]

Even if a more modest approach to lawmaking is initially necessary,
any such plans need to be embedded in a larger long-term strategy to
ensure that the eventual treaty regime covers the breadth and complexity
of issues and problems. The development of a treaty is an ongoing
process and, while some shared understandings are necessary to make
lawmaking possible, according to Brunnée and Toope, 'a morally cohe-
sive "community"' is not.[132] Even where there is dissensus, 'thin initial
commitments to legality are possible and shared legal understandings

---

[127] Brunnée and Toope, *Legitimacy and Legality in International Law*, n. 22, 129, 136
and 141.

[128] S. Deva, 'Moving Forward in the Implementation of the UN Guiding Principles on
Business and Human Rights' (27 October 2016), www.ohchr.org/Documents/
HRBodies/HRCouncil/WGTransCorp/Session2/PanelVSubtheme1/SuryDeva.pdf (last
accessed 4 January 2017).

[129] S. Deva, 'The Human Rights Obligations of Business', n. 8, 1.

[130] See, for example, Liberal Party of Canada, 'Statement by Prime Minister-designate Justin
Trudeau on United Nations Day' (October 24 2015), www.liberal.ca/statement-by-prime-
minister-designate-justin-trudeau-on-united-nations-day/ (last accessed 4 January
2017); J. Trudeau, 'Minister of Foreign Affairs Mandate Letter' (Prime Minister
of Canada Justin Trudeau), http://pm.gc.ca/eng/minister-foreign-affairs-mandate-
letter#sthash.mxTrplLG.dpuf (last accessed 4 January 2017).

[131] De Schutter, 'Towards a New Treaty', n. 53, 43.

[132] Brunnée and Toope, *Legitimacy and Legality in International Law*, n. 22, 44.

may deepen through communities of practice. That is the hard work of international law.'[133]

The next section will consider some of the merits of, and obstacles to, the OEIGWG negotiating a framework treaty that would allow an incremental approach to law making and give time for CSOs, states, business actors and other stakeholders to develop deeper and broader shared understandings, but without compromising the future coverage of the legal regime.

2.7 A Framework Treaty on Business and Human Rights

Several scholars have assessed the strengths and weaknesses of a range of options for a treaty on business and human rights, including the idea of a framework treaty.[134] According to Douglass Cassel and Anita Ramasastry:

> The main advantage of initially adopting a 'framework' treaty like the Vienna Convention [for the Protection of the Ozone Layer 1985] ... is that it might swiftly secure broad agreement by States. Its general principles could be taken from the already widely supported UN Guiding Principles. More difficult or specific issues could then be deferred to future protocols, without holding up the entire negotiating process (possibly for years), or limiting the number of Parties to an eventual treaty to only the most supportive States.[135]

They also note that early consensus on an agreement of this sort might help to 'ease the way for further negotiations on more challenging issues'.[136]

In light of the current resistance from most of the developed states to the mandate of the OEIGWG, developing a framework treaty could be the most promising way forward. It may be able to accommodate many of the desires of the treaty proponents by facilitating agreement on some baseline issues and establishing a strategic plan for moving forward embedded in international law. At the same time, it could address some of the main concerns of opponents to the treaty process.

Given its slow development and the fact that the global climate regime has not yet produced an 'emissions regime capable of averting dangerous climate change',[137] the UN Framework Convention on Climate Change

---

[133] *Ibid.*, 82.
[134] See, for example, Cassel and Ramasastry, n. 74; De Schutter, 'Towards a New Treaty', n. 53.
[135] Cassel and Ramasastry, n. 74, 22.   [136] *Ibid.*
[137] Brunnée and Toope, *Legitimacy and Legality in International Law*, n. 22, 219.

1992[138] (UNFCCC) may not appear to be a model that proponents of the business and human rights treaty would want to emulate. However, the UNFCCC may offer some useful guidance in terms of its structure and the 'institutions and opportunities for repeated, long-term engagement between states parties and other actors, and between these actors and the norms of the regime' that it established in relation to an extraordinarily complex regulatory problem.[139] The UNFCCC sets out the overall objective of the treaty and seeks to apply this to any related legal instruments that are adopted, and establishes a set of principles and commitments of the parties.[140] It also creates, among other things, institutions such as a Conference of the Parties (CoP) with the power to adopt proposed amendments to the Convention and its Annexes and the power to adopt protocols to the Convention.[141]

Brunnée and Toope point out that the UNFCCC was adopted based on a thin set of shared procedural understandings that spawned procedural legality. This demonstrates 'that interactional law can emerge without strong substantive agreement among parties'.[142] As compared with the situation that existed at the time the UNFCCC was negotiated, the advantage in the area of business and human rights is that there exists a relatively broad consensus around some substantive norms. Thus, a framework treaty on business and human rights could potentially include more substantive commitments up front than the UNFCCC.

The Guiding Principles have been widely endorsed by states and business actors and represent the emerging global standard for the conduct of these actors. Provisions setting out the principles of the regime could recognize the Guiding Principles as an important step forward in addressing the governance gaps related to business conduct. A provision on state commitments could include, among other things, an obligation on parties to implement in domestic law the key aspects of the Guiding Principles within a specified timeframe. This would help to address the concern raised by critics, including the United States, that there has been insufficient time to implement the Guiding Principles and that the treaty regime will undermine them.[143] It would also put

---

[138] United Nations Framework Convention on Climate Change (adopted 9 May 1992, entered into force 21 March 1994) (UNFCCC).
[139] Brunnée and Toope, *Legitimacy and Legality in International Law*, n. 22, 219.
[140] UNFCCC, n. 138, arts. 2–4.   [141] *Ibid.*, arts. 7 and 15–17.
[142] Brunnée and Toope, *Legitimacy and Legality in International Law*, n. 22, 217.
[143] Delegation of the United States of America, 'Proposed Working Group', n. 9.

developed states in a position to demonstrate their professed commitment to implementing the Guiding Principles.

A framework approach to the business and human rights treaty project would also address the charge that the problems of business and human rights are too complex to be dealt with in a single treaty. As Cassel and Ramasastry observe, this format would allow for incremental development of a business and human rights regime through a range of protocols that could deal with some of the more controversial issues,[144] as well as addressing specific business sectors that may each pose distinct problems for the protection of human rights.

Additionally, negotiating a framework treaty could also address the concern raised by Ireland that the OEIGWG was 'not equipped to deal effectively with this hugely complex task of considering the gaps and challenges currently faced by victims of human rights violations by business' compared with bodies with technical expertise like the International Law Commission.[145] Once in force, a framework treaty would shift the next stage of lawmaking to the Conference of the Parties. The UNFCCC establishes two subsidiary bodies to support the lawmaking role of the CoP for the climate change regime: one to provide the CoP with 'information and advice on scientific and technological matters relating to the Convention', and the other to support the CoP in assessing and reviewing implementation of the Convention by states parties.[146] Analogous bodies could be established in a business and human rights framework treaty to provide technical advice on complex legal and technological issues that may arise in the development of protocols and to oversee state implementation of their obligations.

Another core concern put forward by Ruggie and others is that powerful states like the United States, who oppose the treaty negotiation process, will not ratify any treaty that is eventually adopted by the negotiating states.[147] The advantage of the framework approach is that it would allow time for international and domestic actors to engage with these states to attempt to develop shared understandings. As Brunnée and Toope note, '... shared understandings are collectively held background knowledge, norms or

---

[144] Cassel and Ramasastry, n. 74, 22.
[145] Ireland to the HRC, 'Explanation of Vote, Elaboration of international legally binding instrument on TNC's and Other Business Enterprises with respect to human rights', www.dfa.ie/media/dfa/alldfawebsitemedia/ourrolesandpolicies/int-priorities/human rights/Explanation-of-vote-transnational-corporations-human-rights.pdf (last accessed 4 January 2017).
[146] UNFCCC, n. 138, arts. 9 and 10.   [147] Ruggie, 'International Legalization', n. 16, 5.

practices; but these understandings do not simply exist, or miraculously emerge as agreed among actors. They are *shared* understandings precisely because they are generated and maintained through social interaction.'[148] To ensure the development of a robust ambitious legal regime, stakeholders must 'work to construct shared understandings ... through more and more interaction'.[149] The OEIGWG already provides one such forum for developing shared understandings at the international level, and any framework treaty could establish institutions, such as those discussed above, for creating additional sites for legal interactions between stakeholders. According to Brunnée and Toope, intergovernmental organisations and treaty institutions are 'especially well placed' to nurture repeated legal engagement between actors.[150]

Treaty proponents will also have to work at the state level to generate shared understandings domestically, not only in support of an international regime but in order to develop domestic law. Domestic law can 'act as a catalyst for other states to develop similar regulatory frameworks' and can also foster the development of shared understandings at the global level.[151] As Ramasastry points out, it was the US Foreign Corrupt Practices Act that spurred the development of a range of binding international treaties on bribery and corruption.[152] Stakeholders can use the process of developing NAPs as a platform for developing domestic shared understandings for a broader response by states than that currently demanded by the Guiding Principles.

The framework approach, however, may not satisfy treaty proponents who would like to see the early development of binding rules on corporate legal liability, home-state regulation and access to effective remedies for victims of corporate-related human rights violations.[153] Additionally, De Schutter points out that the burden of reporting requirements under a framework convention, along with the financial costs associated with establishing and operating the treaty bodies may make the framework approach less appealing to states. The latter is a particular concern given the growing reluctance of states to establish international monitoring bodies.[154] This reluctance may be reflected in the turn by states towards informal international lawmaking to address global governance problems.

---

[148] Brunnée and Toope, *Legitimacy and Legality in International Law*, n. 22, 64.
[149] *Ibid.*, 33.   [150] *Ibid.*, 103.   [151] Simons and Macklin, n. 31, 271.
[152] R. Ramasastry, 'Closing the Governance Gap in the Business and Human Rights Arena: Lessons from the Anti-Corruption Movement' in Deva and Bilchitz (eds.), n. 54, 163.
[153] Cassel and Ramasastry, n. 74, 22.   [154] De Shutter, 'Towards a New Treaty', n. 53, 57.

2.8 Conclusion

The problem of corporate impunity for human rights violations is exceedingly complex and will need to be tackled from all normative angles both at the international and domestic level.[155] The Guiding Principles represent a vital and necessary step towards this goal. Nonetheless, Ruggie's view of the respective roles for the Guiding Principles and treaty law reflects a misunderstanding of the value-added of law in the business and human rights context. The gaps in the Guiding Principles and their misconstruction of international human rights law undermine their potential to effect, on their own, necessary change in the behaviour of states and businesses. Additionally, the bias of the international legal system which favours and supports business activity over the protection of human rights cannot be counterbalanced solely by informal law: rather, it requires formal international law and institutions to address state and business conduct. Finally, a treaty on business and human rights developed through an interactional process (where shared understandings are transformed into shared legal understandings through a practice of legality) will develop an internal sense of obligation that the Guiding Principles, in their current form as informal law, do not have.

This critical treaty project needs to be developed in a careful and strategic manner. However, Ruggie's strategy for moving forward is too unambitious. As discussed above, there is no need to settle for what can be agreed upon immediately.[156] The widespread support for the Guiding Principles and the presence of a large number of developing states and CSOs that support the development of a general treaty is a good basis from which to foster more extensive consensus around a thicker set of shared understandings that go beyond the Guiding Principles. However, treaty proponents will have to work hard both domestically and internationally to ensure that, at the very least, the EU continues to engage constructively with treaty negotiations. The importance of having the support of the EU cannot be underestimated. As Pollack and Shaffer note, 'the EU has increasingly played an important entrepreneurial role in global governance, from standard-setting to financial regulation, with informal norms once again leading the way and gradually giving way to more formal agreements' and it was a core supporter of a legal approach to addressing climate change.[157]

---

[155] Simons, n. 81, 43.
[156] Brunnée and Toope, *Legitimacy and Legality in International Law*, n. 22, 33.
[157] Pollack and Shaffer, n. 78, 255 and 260.

The negotiation of a framework treaty on business and human rights might be the best way forward at this stage. This would allow for lawmaking based on a thinner set of initial commitments, while at the same time embedding a long-term strategic plan in a formal legal framework that will 'accelerate collective learning, and the gradual convergence on certain practices'.[158] Treaty promoters, impatient to see a comprehensive treaty in place, will need to accept that such developments cannot be accomplished overnight. As Brunnée and Toope note, '[t]here is no possibility of simply imposing significant social change by fiat in the absence of some degree of social consensus, expressed in practice'.[159] A treaty regime on business and human rights that addresses the full complexity of the problem and tackles controversial issues like extraterritorial regulation by home states and human rights obligations for business actors will require time for the development of deeper and broader shared legal understandings around these crucial issues.

[158] De Shutter, 'Towards a New Treaty', n. 53, 57.
[159] Brunnée and Toope, *Legitimacy and Legality in International Law*, n. 22, 32.

3

Coherence, Mutual Assurance and the Rationale for a Treaty

SHELDON LEADER[*]

My aim here is to explore the links between two leading reasons for having a binding treaty on business and human rights: the goal of achieving policy coherence and the goal of achieving mutual assurance between states. These two objectives can interact with one another, and their interaction is not usually investigated. Doing so can help shape the design of a treaty in a more promising direction than it might otherwise take. It will also reveal how a treaty is a more urgent need than is often acknowledged. The text is followed by proposed sections in a treaty that reflect the argument.

3.1 Policy Coherence as a Goal

As the UN Secretary-General urged in his Report on the post-2015 sustainable development agenda, there is a need to remedy the '. . . policy incoherence between current modes of international governance in matters of trade, finance and investment on the one hand, and our norms and standards for labour, the environment, human rights, equality and sustainability on the other and to ensure investment policies that are in line with the Guiding Principles.'[1] Doug Cassel and Anita Ramasastry, in their recent excellent portrayal of the potential elements in a treaty, point to two levels at which this need for policy coherence is felt: national and international. At the level of national law they remind us that the UN Guiding Principles '. . . call on States to ensure that their laws and institutions affecting business are coherent with their duty to protect

---

[*] I would like to thank the two editors for their project leadership and contributors to this volume for their insightful comments which have made a substantial difference to the arguments presented in this chapter.

[1] UN Secretary General, 'The Road to Dignity by 2030 – Synthesis Report by the UN Secretary General on the post 2015 Agenda' (A/69/700, paras. 95 and 105). http://docu ments.tips/documents/sg-synthesis-report-road-to-dignity-by-2030.html.

human rights,' and this points to the need for coherence between human rights norms and '... corporate law and securities regulation, investment, export credit and insurance, trade and labour as well as professional codes regulating the legal profession.'[2] At the level of international agreements, Cassel and Ramasastry point to the need that '... States ... maintain adequate domestic policy space to meet their human rights obligations when pursuing business-related policy objectives with other States or business enterprises. In this spirit, states might agree to include human rights protections in future investment and trade treaties. They could also agree to add human rights standards to the terms of existing treaties.'[3]

3.1.1   Two Types of Coherence

All this is well and good, but what are we actually looking for in this call for more policy coherence? It is a need that carries different degrees of normative force. At a minimum, the call for coherence among different branches of the law focuses on the fact that the demand to respect human rights might be present in some sets of norms and missing in others, all within the same legal system. There can be, as in some of the examples to follow, an obligation on a state to respect human rights in one instrument, such as a human rights treaty, and an obligation on the state in another instrument, such as an investment treaty, to do things that the human rights treaty forbids. Those interpreting the investment treaty might be able to avoid formal contradiction between legal obligations here by declaring that the human rights treaty has no relevance to its construction. A treaty linking business and human rights would take aim at this exclusion, stipulating that human rights requirements must explicitly or implicitly form part of the corpus of all legal disciplines regulating business.

Notice, however, that there are two ways of filling out this demand. One approach can aim to secure the presence of the rights in all the right places, but pragmatically leave the interpretation of any given right open to vary with context. States parties to the treaty will have come to their

---

[2] D. Cassel and A. Ramasastry *White Paper: Options for a Treaty on Business and Human Rights*, Prepared for the American Bar Association, Center for Human Rights and The Law Society of England and Wales (May 2015) p. 35. https://business-humanrights.org/sites/default/files/documents/whitepaperfinal%20ABA%20LS%206%2022%2015.pdf.

[3] *Ibid.*

support for the instrument with very different convictions about the ground and extent to which economic actors should be held accountable to society for their activities. Wherever possible, on this approach, solutions to particular cases and problems should be sought by drawing on the least controversial aspects of the fundamental principles linking business and human rights.[4] It follows that those drafting a future treaty should be content to leave a great deal unsaid: aiming to provide a broad framework of principles that generate the least controversy and within which particular solutions will hopefully emerge in the future. Where there is a clash between the cost of observing human rights norms and attending to business gains, on this pragmatic approach, resolution of the conflict might, depending on where the balance of forces lies, see human rights take second place over operative business interests where the two compete.[5]

A stronger conception of coherence is different. It aims not only to place the term 'human rights' in all relevant parts of the law, but to generate a unified coverage and set of priorities for human rights as they compete with other principles and interests across the norms shaping business activity. These features will be explored below, but at this point it is important to notice a concern that these two approaches to coherence share: a worry about the fragility of consensus around the treaty project. Whereas the first approach, pursuing a milder form of coherence, does so out of a concern to preserve support for the treaty via doing the least to perturb the other legal principles and convictions framing business activity – be they in corporate, investment or trade law – the second approach fears that it is precisely this approach that is a recipe for long-term decline in the support for, and creative shaping of, a place for human rights in economic activity. It favours pressing for principles that may be initially unattractive to one or another party in ongoing dialogues, but which they can be brought to see are credibly anchored in human rights principles that apply in areas other than business activity, and which could be plausibly built upon.

Before looking further at the more ambitious species of coherence, it is important to back up and set it off against the milder form.

---

[4] C. Sunstein, 'Incompletely Theorized Agreements in Constitutional Law' 2007 Public Law and Legal Theory Working Paper No 147, Law School, University of Chicago passim http://ssrn.com/abstract_id=957369.
[5] S. Deva, 'Treating Human Rights Lightly?' in *Human Rights Obligations of Business* S. Deva and D. Bilchitz eds. (Cambridge University Press, 2013), 78 at 100.

3.1.2   Looking Further Into the Milder Form of Coherence

At its most basic, as already said, the call for coherence takes aim at the fact that human rights requirements might be present in some areas of law regulating business activity but absent in others. For example, a state might find itself bound to refrain from applying its changed domestic law to an infrastructure project, where the change is aimed at improving labour conditions, because it had previously signed a stabilization clause in an investment contract by which it promised not to alter applicable law for the lifetime of the project. At the same time, under the terms of a human rights treaty the state may be obligated to make and to apply precisely those legislative changes.[6] Those adjudicators interpreting the stabilization requirement within the four corners of investment law often ignore these human rights obligations of the state, obliging the latter to pay possibly large amounts of compensation for changing domestic law as its human rights obligations require, but which the investment agreement prohibits. As has been often pointed out, the result can be a harsh burden on poorer states. If a treaty on business and human rights insisted that interpretations of investment agreements had to 'take account' of the potential impact of those agreements on human rights norms binding on a state party, this requirement, even in such a weakly formulated form, could widen the scope of attention of those interpreting investment instruments. It would be an example of mild coherence. The Canada/Senegal Investment Agreement provides an example. It states that:

> Each Party should encourage enterprises operating within its territory or subject to its jurisdiction to voluntarily incorporate internationally recognized standards of corporate social responsibility in their practices and internal policies such as statements of principle that have been endorsed or are supported by the Parties. These principles address issues such as labour, the environment, human rights, community relations and anti-corruption. Such enterprises are encouraged to make investments whose impacts contribute to the resolution of social problems and preserve the environment.[7]

In this way, human rights can make their appearance in another domain of law. The appearance in this instrument is indeed modest, being simply

---

[6] On this clash see S. Leader, 'Human Rights, Risks, and New Strategies for Global Investment' (2006) 9 *Journal of International Economic Law* 657–705.

[7] Agreement Between Canada and the Federal Republic of Senegal for the Promotion and Protection of Investments, Article 3 www.international.gc.ca/trade-agreements-accords-commerciaux/agr-acc/fipa-apie/senegal-agreement.aspx?lang=eng.

an encouragement to business to voluntarily adopt a human rights standard. Nevertheless, it would no longer be possible for someone interpreting and applying the terms of investment law in this treaty to say that a concern for human rights is totally irrelevant to their doing their job. It then becomes legitimate for a tribunal to invoke this part of the Senegal/Canada investment agreement in order to deal with a borderline question of interpretation of the investment contract when, say, the scope of a stabilization clause is unclear. Human rights are brought in from the cold and made potentially relevant to an answer: it is a step towards mild coherence.[8]

With due adjustments, this requirement could migrate from its location in a bilateral investment treaty to a global one – to a treaty on business and human rights – and it could be a provision spread to other fields of law governing relevant commercial activity. Indeed, the prospect of movement towards this minimal level of coherence might be opened by the Transatlantic Trade and Investment Partnership (TTIP). A draft of the investment chapter in the agreement submitted by the EU contains an article stating that:

> The provisions of this section shall not affect the right of the Parties to regulate within their territories through measures necessary to achieve legitimate policy objectives, such as the protection of public health, safety, environment or public morals, social or consumer protection or promotion and protection of cultural diversity.[9]

'Human rights' are not explicitly referred to in this draft, unlike the Senegal/Canada investment agreement, but neither are they clearly excluded. If a state defends a departure from the relevant terms of the TTIP Agreement treaty as being justified for the sake of the 'social protection' it allows the state to favour one of the benchmarks for such

[8] Via a clear statement in the objects clause of an investment agreement, human rights can move from being simply relevant to investment promotion through to having a stronger position. This could, if suitably framed and coordinated with the preamble, give the obligation to respect such rights priority over other goals of the treaty when and if there is a conflict. This would be a step towards what is here termed strong coherence, to be elaborated on below. See the important discussion of this point in J. Anthony VanDuzer, P. Simons and G. Mayeda (2012) 'Integrating Sustainable Development into International Investment Agreements: A Guide for Developing Countries' pages 92–94. www.iisd.org/pdf/2012/6th_annual_forum_commonwealth_guide.pdf (last accessed January 6, 2017).

[9] European Commission: Draft Transatlantic Trade and Investment Partnership, Article 2 *"Investment and regulatory measures/objectives"* Tabled and made public on12 November 2015. http://trade.ec.europa.eu/doclib/docs/2015/november/tradoc_153955.pdf.

protection could be the criteria provided by the human rights norms binding on that state. On the other hand, if human rights are not imported by those charged to interpret the TTIP agreement, such that they understand a state party not to be entitled to deploy human rights as part of their social policy objectives, we have a potential failure of minimal coherence: a gap appears between the presence of human rights requirements binding on a state from one source, such as a human rights treaty, and the state's inability to rely on such rights coming from another source in a trade and investment agreement.

Even if this egregious gap were closed via interpretation, mild coherence still permits an interpretation of 'necessity' in the TTIP formulation above in a way that allows a state to pursue its policy of social protection in a way that, from among alternative policy choices reasonably available, does least to hamper the commercial objectives of the treaty: a priority which may conform with orthodox interpretations of trade and investment treaties but, as discussed below, is the opposite of that pursued by principles in human rights instruments.[10]

A final example of a potential role for mild coherence with human rights norms takes us from the state to decision-making by the private commercial company. Here, there can be a clash between a company's 'external' obligation – as an entity – to a local population, and the company directors' 'internal' obligation – owed to the enterprise to work for its best interests as a matter of company law. A recent instance has arisen around the controversial Phulbari open-pit coalmine project in Bangladesh.[11] At least 40,000 people are predicted to be displaced if the project goes ahead in its present form, with 10,000 due to receive alternative land. The rest of that population is directed towards what the company itself admits is a precarious future in unfamiliar urban environments with a cash sum that studies have shown is likely to dissipate quickly.[12]

---

[10] See on this point S. Leader 'Human Rights and International Trade' in P. Macrory et al. (eds.) *Understanding the World Trade Organization: Perspectives from Law, Economics and Politics* (Springer, 2005) Section 5 (D).

[11] International Accountability Project / World Development Movement, *Complaint to the UK National Contact Point under the Specific Instance Procedure of the OECD Guidelines for Multinational Enterprises concerning GCM Resources (UK)*Initial assessment of complaint (2013); Final statement (2013) (www.gov.uk); see also Brief by the Essex Business and Human Rights Project (On file with the author).

[12] Summary of the Report of the Expert Committee to Evaluate Feasibility Study Report and Scheme of Development of the Phulbari Coal Project, (2007) p. 7. (On file with the author.)

GCM Resources, a UK company developing the project via a subsidiary, was challenged before the OECD's UK National Contact Point to withdraw from or reduce the scale of the mine because of its likely damage to food security, health, shelter and other core rights arising from the Project.[13] GCM replied that to do so would lead its directors to fail to fulfil their fiduciary obligation under the UK's Companies Act, 2006 to 'promote the success of the company for the benefit of its members [i.e. shareholders – SL] as a whole'.[14] While the statute adds the requirement that in carrying out this duty to shareholders the directors are to 'have regard to the impact of the company's operations on the community',[15] there is no mention in the text of human rights violations as guidelines in assessing those impacts. While the company did not ignore the human rights objections lodged by the complainants, its directors felt able to read their obligations under the UK legislation in a way that did not give them significant weight.

> The Directors may not have the capacity to surrender the contract. GCM is a UK Company and consequently its Directors are obliged to comply with UK law. The UK Companies Act requires that a director of a company must act in the way that he considers, in good faith, would be most likely to promote the success of the company for the benefit of its members as a whole, albeit taking into account a number of factors.[16]

The UK National Contact Point did not comment on this argument. The issue remains open for it. Once again, human rights are not mentioned in the text of the Companies Act. If they are not imported by interpretation, in the name of coherence, then a gap opens: it is possible that human rights law would condemn Bangladesh for allowing this damaging and poorly compensated displacement of such massive numbers of people. However, on their reading of the relevant UK company law, which the UK National Contact did not explicitly reject, the directors considered that they were obligated to the company to accept that damaging displacement as the price to pay for assigning ultimate priority to shareholder interests.

The arguments advanced in the Phulbari case take us a step further. Notice that the company was willing to admit the potential relevance of

---

[13] Supra n 12 paras. 52–70, at pp. 13–16.
[14] The applicable law for the purpose of an OECD National Contact Point hearing was the Companies Act, 2006 s. 172.
[15] *Ibid.*, s. 172 (d).
[16] GCM Resources plc, Point by Point Response to Complaint under the OECD Guidelines for Multinational Enterprises Appendix II, paras. 9–10, at p. 35.

human rights to the issues, but once these were taken into account it was argued that the rights still did not have enough strength to displace the fundamental conviction that when a clash emerges between those human requirements and the primacy of shareholder interests, the latter must prevail. In other words, the weight assigned to the rights placed them in a secondary position as compared with shareholder rights, which continued to have primacy.[17] On the strategy behind the search for mild coherence, this relegation can make sense. Human rights make an entrance into business decision-making, but they do so in a way that does least to upset the core priorities assigned to shareholder interests in corporate law. This could appeal to a strategy of preserving consensus among those with very different conceptions of the legitimacy of corporate power: human rights are admitted as relevant, but a version of the weight of those rights is delivered that is designed to work as smoothly as possible with the pre-existing priorities found in the UK's corporate practice. Over time, this is not likely to be enough for a durable consensus around a treaty, and the reason for this inadequacy merits a closer look.

3.1.3   Levels of Precision vs Levels of Consensus

In a recent comment on the role of business in meeting the UN's Sustainable Development Goals, the Institute for Business and Human Rights said that:

> The Sustainable Development Goals are based largely on the hope that business really has hitched its wagon to the sustainability locomotive, and fear that a closer look might reveal that it has not. The resulting consensus – don't ask, don't tell – signals a temporary alliance of business enthusiasts and sceptics.[18]

This diagnosis signals a wider problem that is fundamental for agendas linking business and human rights. It can be called the paradox of precision. On the one hand, we need to be more precise about the features of human rights that can guide business behaviour in difficult cases. On the other hand, there is an attraction in keeping things agreeably general:

---

[17] On the distinction between a primary and collateral role for human rights in economic regulation, see S. Leader: 'Collateralism' in R. Brownsword (ed.) *Global Governance and the Search for Justice* (Hart Publishing: 2005), 53–67.

[18] Institute for Human Rights and Business, *State of Play: Business and the Sustainable Development Goals* (2015), 16.

the more these features are spelled out in detail, the greater the risk that this will generate fundamental disagreement among the parties concerned. A provisional consensus risks coming apart as an uneasy business community on one side faces a restive civil society on the other. Yet, at the same time, we need to know enough details of the content and weight of human rights if they are to be effective guides in orienting business activity as framed in such norms as corporate or investment law. Both sides want relative precision and both sides also fear it, since they know that they might disagree over the crucial details precision delivers.

If, in this context, these standards are to be taken seriously the parties confronting one another need to be able to operate by tracing a line between a legitimate, if regrettable, *impact* on a human right and a *violation* of that right. Those who want to undertake projects that will disrupt lives, and those who wish to protect populations from such disruption, both want to be able to trace such a line. This demands continually greater precision if human rights are to generate precise interventions able to complement the law that carries on without such norms. At the moment, to warn businesses that human rights are at stake in their operations often opens a door to victims, but does not help them to go through that door. That is, they are not helped towards achieving a just legal outcome any more than they would have been were human rights not to have been mentioned at all. Instead, victims' advocates frequently fall back on the classical law of tort, contract, company law, etc. To invoke human rights in such situations is often, once the excitement dies down, to invoke a technically redundant element. A treaty linking business and human rights can help change this state of affairs. It can move the parties along from asking whether a human right is at stake per se in business activity towards asking at what level of strength and detail the right is to operate.

There is no option to stand still here. All sides need a degree of precision necessary to decide convincingly on a concrete case in the light of human rights requirements, and all sides face the prospect of a destructive impasse as time goes on if they push hard for their own version of those requirements. There are then two ways to proceed: one is to hold on to the strategy behind mild coherence and hope that it delivers the concrete results in particular disputes that all sides in those disputes will ultimately endorse as legitimate. Another is to opt for strong coherence. As indicated earlier, the former approach is inclined to aim at the least displacement of the objectives traditionally underpinning corporate and investment law, while bringing human rights into account. In doing this, however, there is, despite appearances, a fundamental shift of priorities – and a price to be paid for the shift. Whereas human rights instruments typically allow their guarantees to be overridden by the need to pursue other competing objectives, including commercial ones, they do so by adjusting the pursuit of those objectives in a way that does least damage to the underlying human rights at stake.[19] The cases and principles examined above do the opposite: the version of human rights protection that is admitted is the one that does the least damage to commercial objectives. Over time, victims confronting this result will see that human rights receive less weight than they do in other domains where they are a central, rather than collateral, part of the agenda. A two-speed result threatens: one giving a stronger role to human rights concerns outside of the regulation of business activity, and the other inside it.

It should be possible to avoid this result by assigning the same weight to a human right across all domains framing business activity: to pursue, that is, strong coherence.

3.1.4   Towards Strong Coherence

As indicated earlier, this form of coherence looks to fashion a consistent series of principles capable of reshaping crucial parts of the body of norms, and not just adding another rule to those already present in the corpus.[20] For this to happen, it is not enough to make sure that the expression 'respect human rights' appears in all the relevant sets of laws governing business activity. The basic principles informing those norms must be ranked and given effect in a consistent way in the light of human rights requirements. This can require re-working certain priorities at the heart of commercial practice. In turn, this shift in priorities can call for reshaping some of the basic elements in corporate, investment and related areas of the law. This can affect rules such as those defining the company director's fiduciary duty to the company, or the separation of parent and subsidiary corporate liability.

---

[19] S. Leader, 'Collateralism' supra n. 19 at 55 and S. Leader, 'Two Ways of Linking Economic Activity to Human Rights' (2005) 185 *International Social Science Journal* 541 ff.

[20] It is a form of consistency central to the work of Ronald Dworkin. See, for example, his notion of law's integrity in *Law's Empire* (Fontana, 1986) chs 6 and 7.

3.1.4.1   Strong Coherence and the Fiduciary Obligations of Company Directors

What is at stake can be seen in two examples. The first takes us back to the Phulbari coal mine in Bangladesh. Here, to recall, the directors of the mining company GCM were seeing their obligations to the population around the mine through the prism of an overall fiduciary obligation to maximize shareholder value. Even when acknowledging the Companies Act's requirement that they 'have regard' for the impact of the mine on local communities, they shaped the scope of that duty through what they took to be the requirement in the Act that any such attention to social impacts must be given in a way that does least damage, from among reasonably available alternatives, to corporate revenue. For this reason, they dismissed the call for a reduced initial size of the mine, which would have required it to be developed in phases: a measure that would have given local populations more of an opportunity to adjust. That option, the company argued, would go against investor interests, as it would reduce annual revenue even though it would still leave the project profitable.[21] Even if human rights were admitted in this reasoning, such that they form part of the fiduciary concerns for the well-being of the company as required by UK legislation, that insertion would still allocate those rights to a collateral role. That is, the company could have acknowledged that it has to attend to the rights of the affected population, but it could still insist that a way of respecting those rights had to be found that did least damage to investor returns. The basic priorities in the objectives of corporate law remain intact, with a secondary position assigned to human rights.[22]

A strategy of strong coherence, using as a benchmark the principles underpinning human rights instruments, inverts this order of priorities. While acknowledging that such rights may have to be compromised in order to meet competing commercial demands, it insists that a way has to be found of meeting those demands, among reasonably available alternatives, that does least damage to the rights, not the other way around.[23] For instance, staying with the example of internal displacement balanced against the economic gains produced by projects such as the Phulbari coal mine, the Office of the United Nations High Commissioner for Human Rights has said that

---

[21] Supra n.16.

[22] See elaborations of this point under 'directions of adjustment' between rights in S. Leader, 'Three Faces of Justice and the Management of Change' January 2000 63 *Modern Law Review* 55–83 S. Leader, 'The Place of Labour Rights in Foreign Direct Investment' in *Global Labor and Employment Law* A. Morris and S. Estreicher (eds.) (Kluwer, 2010), 579–596.

[23] *ibid.*, passim.

States must give priority to exploring strategies that minimize displacement. Comprehensive and holistic impact assessments should be carried
out prior to the initiation of any project that could result in development-
based eviction and displacement, with a view to securing fully the human
rights of all potentially affected persons, groups and communities, including their protection against forced evictions.[24]

The World Commission on Dams looks more closely at the balance
between human rights and commercial return. It has formulated guiding
principles that can be applied to displacements from land arising from a
wide range of activity. It demands that reasons be given explaining '. . . why
the quantity of land proposed to be acquired is necessary and justified in
relation to the purpose of the project.'[25] The 'necessity' of a given use of
land must, in the view of the Commission, be set against the requirement
that it pursues the least displacing of the alternative project strategies
available. This can call for compromise, since the Commission presses
for accepting a smaller scale for some projects in return for significant
gains to those affected in the local population: which is precisely the
approach that the mining company rejected in Phulbari. In relation to
dams, for example, the Commission argues that '. . . small reductions in
height of a large dam may dramatically reduce displacement, with a
proportionately much smaller fall in benefits.'[26]

> The UN Global Compact draws such a line. In its advice about operatio-
> nalising higher human rights standards, it anticipates that meeting greater
> demands of this sort can result in significant extra costs to business. It then
> recommends fixing '. . . a threshold of losses incurred by an investor, above
> which the host state will share the economic burden of compliance', while
> below that threshold the extra costs would be for the investor to bear.[27]

---

[24] UN OHCHR, 'Basic Principles and Guidelines on Development Based Evictions and
Displacement' *Annex 1 of the report of the Special Rapporteur on adequate housing* A/HRC/
4/18, para. 3, www.ohchr.org/Documents/Issues/Housing/Guidelines_en.pdf (last accessed 7
January 2017).

[25] World Commission on Dams, 'Dams, Displacement, Policy and Law in India' http://
siteresources.worldbank.org/INTINVRES/214578-1112885441548/20480074/
DamsDisplacementPolicyandLawinIndiasoc213.pdf (last accessed 7 January 2017).

[26] *Ibid.*

[27] This is in the analogous context of higher costs resulting from limiting the effect of stabilization clauses in order to allow host states to respect ongoing human rights standards. UN
Global Compact, 'Human Rights and Business Dilemmas Forum, "Stabilisation Clauses",
Suggestions for Responsible Business,' para. 27, available at http://human-rights.unglobal
compact.org/dilemmas/stabilisation-clauses/#.Umf6e5ReuXR (last accessed on 7 January
2017).

Via this path, human rights standards can penetrate quite far into a company's calculation of costs and benefits. In these statements, special weight is assigned to human rights considerations leading to a call for compromise on the company's search for optimal returns. This could in turn have a strong impact on orthodox understandings in corporate law of directors' fiduciary duty to their company, mentioned earlier.[28] It is an impact that goes further than the strategy of mild coherence is likely to find comfortable.

At the moment, the positions advanced by the company in the Phulbari case, including those it takes which are open to human rights concerns, express what can be called a two-world view: one set of internal standards links the director and the company, and another quite different set of external standards links the company, as an entity, and the state. Internally, the directors are – they argue – bound as fiduciaries to treat human rights concerns as exceptional and secondary factors: taking them away from their core obligations towards investors. Their allegiance to the short and long-term interests of shareholders leads them to reject the call for scaling down the initial size of the mine, followed by a later phase when the first is completed. Whatever concessions are made by the company to the need to take other measures to respect the human rights of those affected, such as prior consultation with those affected, this measure of size reduction could considerably alleviate the inroad on their basic rights. It is rejected by the company even though no evidence was submitted that it would significantly damage overall profit. Externally, the picture is quite different. The human rights obligations of Bangladesh point in the opposite direction. Its primary duty is to protect its population by requiring the company to look for alternative measures that would have a less damaging impact on human rights. Profitability would have to be adjusted so as to make this possible. The state would then require the company, as an entity, to do what the directors do not consider themselves internally entitled to do under corporate law principles. If the orthodox conception of the director's duty to the company remains in place, while

---

[28] See the analysis of the director's fiduciary duty in this context in D. Bilchitz and L. Ausserladscheider Jonas, 'Proportionality, Fundamental Rights and the Duties of Directors' 2016 *Oxford Journal of Legal Studies* 1–27; for a differently framed argument see S. Leader, 'Participation and Property Rights' (1999) 21 *Journal of Business Ethics* 97–109; 'Gouvernement d'entreprise et droits des salariés' in S. Leader and P. Lokiec, Pascal, *Revue de droit du travail*, (Paris: Dalloz, 2008), 3, 201–203 ; S. Leader 'Labour Rights in the World Economy' In L. Blecher et al. (eds.), *Corporate Responsibility for Human Rights Impacts* (Washington DC: American Bar Association, 2013).

the company as an entity is also called on to respect human rights, a clash of obligations emerges. Company directors can claim that their fiduciary obligations to shareholders dominate, with the risk – as in Phulbari – that this is thought to prevent their steering the company towards the same degree of respect for human rights that the state must display.

A treaty linking business and human rights can close this gap, as will be argued in Part II. It can provide that the same standards govern the state's duty to protect its population's rights from damage by private actors, the company's duty as an entity, and the directors' own duty to act in the best interest of that company. The benchmark provided by the state's obligation would be carried through into the directors' fiduciary duty to promote the success of their company. All sets of norms would be integrated, with the priority assigned to human rights when balanced against other competing interests. It would be a step towards strong coherence across the collection of norms regulating business activity.

3.1.4.2   Strong Coherence and Corporate Structure: The Example of the Corporate Veil

A second example of the potential in strong coherence moves from deliberations in the boardroom to the place of that boardroom and the company itself within a wider corporate structure. Here, there is another potential threat to human rights that a treaty could address. It emerges in the ever-present problem of the 'corporate veil'. This element of corporate law continues to bedevil the search for a way of making responsibility follow the locus of corporate power. Parent companies are, barring exceptional circumstances and jurisdictions, often treated as legally separate entities from their subsidiaries. Liabilities are usually confined to the subsidiary that caused an accident or signed a commercial contract, while the parent has no more obligation arising from what its subsidiary has done than does any other shareholder in a limited liability company.

At the same time, de facto control over key policies and practices of the subsidiary is usually in the hands of the parent, sometimes accompanied by regular transfers of assets from the subsidiary to head office. If, in this situation, we simply declare that corporations are to 'respect human rights', we don't have enough in hand to know when this classic separation between the liability of parent and subsidiary does and does not contribute to violations of those rights. Invoking human rights concerns takes us no closer to seeing when it is appropriate to pierce the corporate veil, or indeed when it is appropriate to sidestep the veil without piercing it by increasing the range of a parent company's responsibility for its subsidiary's behaviour via an extension of the parent's duty of care.[29] Matters are not greatly improved if we add provisions which mention human rights like those in the Canada/Senegal Investment Agreement, seen above. This tells us that enterprises are encouraged in the name, inter alia, of human rights to '... make investments whose impacts contribute to the resolution of social problems and preserve the environment.'[30] A good deal more precision is needed if this element of the treaty can be turned to helping answer hard questions about what is and is not to be tolerated in the preservation of parent companies from liability.[31]

It is possible for a treaty linking business and human rights to say more, and with a level of detail that gives human rights real purchase in dealing with potential abuses of the 'corporate veil'. Consider the agreement among member states of the Economic Community of West African States (ECOWAS). The Community has produced a measure that can be seen as a regional and sectorial species of treaty on business and human rights.[32] The measure, in the form of a directive, provides as part of its formal commitment to human rights that member states are to require of mining companies that they obtain free, prior and informed consent of local communities before exploration begins and prior to each subsequent phase of mining and post-mining operations. Companies are to maintain consultations and negotiations on important decisions affecting local communities throughout the mining cycle. The companies must also set up socio-economic development funds to which mining rights-holders shall contribute by law for the development of new capacity in the affected local communities.[33]

This is a step towards giving priority to human rights concerns that strong coherence demands. As the ECOWAS Directive puts the requirement, '... Member States, holders of mining rights and other mining related business entities have a *primary*[34] obligation ·to respect

[29] Cf. *Chandler v Cape Industries* EWCA Civ 525 (25 April 2012).

[30] *Agreement Between Canada and the Federal Republic of Senegal for the Promotion and Protection of Investments*, Article 3 www.international.gc.ca/trade-agreements-accords-commerciaux/agr-acc/fipa-apie/senegal-agreement.aspx?lang=eng.

[31] For a strong example of a human rights requirement of greater scope and depth, see VanDuser, Simons and Meyeda, supra n. 8 pp. 309–316.

[32] ECOWAS Directive C/DIR.3/05/09 on the Harmonization of Guiding Principles and Policies in the Mining Sector, Article 16. See also discussion of the ECOWAS Directive in *Mining and Human Rights in Senegal*, Amnesty International 2014 www.amnesty.nl/sites/default/files/public/p4350_senegal_mining_report_-_web_en.pdf.

[33] *Ibid.*, Article 16 para. 7.   [34] Emphasis mine, SL.

and promote recognized human rights including the rights of women, children and workers arising from mining activities.'[35] Without wanting to read too much into a single word, this claim of primacy for human rights does give a central rather than a collateral place to human rights on the business agenda.

It is also precise and concrete enough in its requirements that member states are given the guidance about elements of corporate behaviour that must be targeted. The states can in turn reshape – if necessary by further agreement among themselves – rules in their corporate law necessary to give effect to this primacy of human rights-driven requirements about appropriate levels of consultation and about the establishment of capacity-development funds for the locals affected. In particular, the member states have a basis for turning back to their own corporate laws and amending them so as to hold parent companies liable for claims by victims against subsidiaries arising from violation of these consultation and development fund requirements. In these and allied areas picked out by human rights instruments and principles, the liability could be extended to those companies within the corporate group which have the resources and/or the relevant control to compensate adequately or to prevent damage.[36] This would not be a total collapse of the separation between parent and subsidiary liability but would instead be an intervention that was precisely targeted, integrating human rights requirements into a principle at the heart of corporate law. It would pursue a strong form of coherence.

If the strong version of coherence sought in these examples is a desirable objective what role might a treaty play in achieving it? This is the next question to consider.

3.2   Strong Coherence via a Treaty on Business and Human Rights

The prospects for a treaty depend on who is sitting around the table and on what it is that motivates them to negotiate a treaty in the first place. Consider a classic and important reason for entering into a treaty: the creation of mutual assurance among the parties to the agreement. If states agree on a common set of human rights standards guiding business, such

---

[35] *Ibid.*, Article 15 para. 1.

[36] For an application of this approach to the liability of the Royal Dutch Shell group, see *Corporate Liability In a New Setting: Shell and the Changing Legal Landscape for the Multinational Oil Industry in the Niger Delta*, by the Essex Business and Human Rights Project (2012), pp. 5155. http://www.essex.ac.uk/ebhr/activities/default.aspx.

as those in the UN Guiding Principles, then it makes sense that, once agreed, these standards cease being sites of competition among those states – even as they carry on competing in other ways – on pain of triggering a well-known problem known as the 'race to the bottom'. For, what starts as being a shared view about the desirability of a certain level of human rights protection afforded by business can end up being undermined – not because each state has changed its basic priorities and come to think it fundamentally right to lower that protection, but because without agreed sanctions to enforce the shared view, it is frightened that a competitor will draw inward investment away from it if it does not weaken that commitment. All the concerned states end up worse off – as measured by their own standards – because they cannot trust one another to hold to the standard that they each initially subscribed to: the race to the bottom is on.[37]

3.2.1   Host State and Home State Concerns

While this is a well-known problem, it actually comes in several varieties: each with different potential impacts on the design of a treaty and each having a particular impact on the goal of strong policy coherence. The difference is located in the concerns of states that are primarily hosts to inward investment on the one hand and, on the other, those that are primarily home to the companies making such investment. While each might seek competitive assurance against a race to the bottom, they are looking at different threats and at different parties doing the threatening. For example, the states in ECOWAS have been concerned that international mining companies might play one member state off another in choosing the regulatory environment in which the companies find it easiest to work. Having made their initial commitment to protecting human rights at a level of significant detail in the mining industry, the member states are, via this directive, coordinating their efforts via a regional and sector-focused version of a treaty on business and human rights. As one analyst puts it, a key objective of this Directive is 'lessening competition ... between the member states'.[38] In other words, it aims to remove mutually undermining competition among ECOWAS members over requirements

---

[37] For an exploration of this phenomenon see Mancur Olson, *The Logic of Collective Action: Pubic Goods and the Theory of Groups* (Revised edn. Harvard University Press, 1971); S. Leader, *Freedom of Association* (Yale University Press, 1992), ch. 7.

[38] Mayer Brown *Recent Legal Developments in the Mining Sector of West African States* page 2 www.mayerbrown.com/files/Publication/.

they impose on business: all the ECOWAS member states wish to impose these requirements, but each member might be tempted to weaken its commitment to doing so out of fear of what its neighbour might do.

While states that are *hosts* to international mining activity, often in the developing world, share this interest, other states – no less involved in international mining, but as *home* states in the developed world – share a different interest. Canada and Senegal, for example, do not risk compet-ing with one another for inward investment – not, that is, in the same way that Senegal and Mali might compete. Canada may indeed welcome a measure of regulatory competition between the latter two states as good for Canadian mining interests in the region. On the other hand, Canada does share with, for example, the United States or certain states in the EU an interest in setting similar controls on the responsibilities of the parent companies for their MNCs operating abroad. If one home-state jurisdic-tion is stricter than is the other then they might find that corporate head-quarters migrate to the less stringent – with the attendant loss of corporate tax revenue and jobs.[39]

Of course, the differences among home and host states are not quite this stark. Countries normally labelled hosts to the activities of transnational companies may also be homes to large transnational parent companies, such as India and Brazil, and many that are homes to outward investment are also hosts to certain inward investment activities of transnationals. Thus, Senegal might worry about its domiciled parent companies migrat-ing to less regulated environments in the same way that Canada does. Yet, this is unlikely to include the fear that the Senegalese parent will move to Canada, whatever the formalities of a bilateral investment agreement allowing for two-way corporate investment might provide.[40] Equally, Canada might fear that Senegal can provide a comparatively low level of labour rights protection and so draw employment away from Canada's shores via the latter's businesses transferring some of their operations to the cheaper operating environment. This worry can and does provoke strong reactions from civil society in developed countries, acting to protect

---

[39] There are factors in any given sector that may well deter capital flight from home countries, such as favourable insurance services, tax laws and investment services avail-able to nationals. These would weigh against but do not always eliminate the capital flight concern. I am grateful to Penelope Simons for this point.

[40] Agreement between Canada and the Federal Republic of Senegal for the Promotion and Protection of Investments, Article3 www.international.gc.ca/trade-agreements-accords-commerciaux/agr-acc/fipa-apie/senegal-agreement.aspx?lang=eng (last accessed 7 January 2017).

labour, health and environmental standards. These issues prompt a search for a floor of mutual guarantees, as seen in the section of the investment agreement between Canada and Senegal mentioned above.[41] However, a home country in the developed world will nevertheless be concerned that over the wide range of other potential human rights concerns that apply to business, the hands of its companies should not be tied unduly when operating in host countries. Canada might therefore be willing to see a regulatory race to the bottom between host countries in West Africa, for example, anxious to attract inward investment while wanting to avoid such a race between itself and other similarly placed home countries wanting to encourage outward investment for their companies.

Therefore, there are at least two distinct races to the bottom that threaten: one manifested in worries shared among home countries about being undercut as they vie for favourable conditions for their capital-exporting businesses and the second, in distinct worries, shared among host countries about being undercut as they vie for the best terms for their capital-importing activities. It is tempting to deny this by pointing to the fact that both sets of countries largely accept the human rights standards applying to business as set out in the UNGPs. Support by states is overwhelmingly in favour of the Guiding Principles, and this can seem like an inducement to take human rights off the table as items of competition between all states, without dividing them between home and host states. However, this accord on the Principles may deliver less than it appears to: within that envelope of agreement there is room for strong divergence about the scope and weight of a relevant human right when deployed to deal with a particular type of situation. When countries' interests are as strongly differing as are those in our examples, consensus among them risks unravelling if pushed too hard to solve particular problems. There arises the paradox of precision referred to earlier. Precision is simultaneously necessary and is an obstacle: it is necessary if the promise of mutual assurance against being undercut is to have any efficacy in stopping a race to the bottom, and it is an obstacle since the level of consensus among states needed to make progress is difficult to obtain. How, if at all, can a treaty help here?

Both home and host countries might reach agreement on what was identified earlier as a mild level of coherence. They might eventually agree, to go back to an earlier example, that human rights obligations should be included in the fiduciary obligations that directors owe to their

---

[41] Canada – Senegal Investment Agreement, Article 16 supra n. 9.

companies. However, these countries are likely to disagree strongly over
what the concrete impact of human rights standards should be on the
content of that fiduciary obligation. Imagine that ECOWAS members
were to propose, as a provision of a global treaty to which Canada was
asked to agree, that states parties to the treaty impose on companies
within their jurisdiction an obligation corresponding to the detailed
requirements that ECOWAS has enacted for mining companies. This
would include the duty to maintain consultations and negotiations on all
important decisions affecting local communities throughout the mining
cycle.[42] Canada may well resist, preferring to fall back on the precedent of
the more general, voluntary provisions of its Investment Agreement with
Senegal stating, as we have seen it do, that '... Each Party should
encourage enterprises operating within its territory or subject to its
jurisdiction to voluntarily incorporate internationally recognized standards of corporate social responsibility in their practices and internal
policies ...'[43]

This has the ingredients of an impasse between host and home states:
an impasse which leads many to predict an interminable wait before the
key terms of a treaty can be agreed by all concerned. However, the parties
and the issues they face are not standing still. While debates about a
global treaty go on, Senegal, other member states in ECOWAS and many
others in mineral-rich areas face pressures – at times amounting to
violent protests – from local populations evicted by mining activity
from their homes, suffering damage to their health and family disintegration. Domestic social and political pressures could lead these states to
insist, in the name of human rights, on detailed matters of consultation
and protection for local populations – equivalent to those that the
agreement to produce the Mining Directive contains. If there were no
such mutual undertaking, these states would have less confidence in
pressing companies investing in their economies to take the more costly
route of spending on measures that can avoid social damage in advance,
as the Directive does. Without the mutual assurance that the Directive is
designed to help deliver, the state is thrown back onto the blunt instrument of suppressing protest as it emerges. That can be all that remains in
its reserve of measures. These states face urgent needs in their local
populations that other states that are home to the major enterprises do

---

[42] They could back up their argument by pointing to the resemblance between their
consultation requirements and those of the IFC in its performance standards. See IFC
Performance Standard 1.
[43] Supra n. 7.

not face. The latter are therefore likely to be more cautious about entering into a tight, enforceable human rights requirement. They are thus likely to resist strong coherence.

In short, the members of ECOWAS, and other host states similarly situated, have good reason to opt *among themselves* for strong rather than weak coherence on human rights standards. They have particular reason to try to close the gap between broad human rights provisions and their concrete implications in the realm of business activity. The prospect for strong coherence is greater if the range covered by a treaty is regional and/or sectorial rather than if it is global. On the other hand, the pursuit of a global treaty will correspondingly weaken the attractions of a policy of strong coherence, forcing us to be content to achieve the milder version.

Much turns on the choices to be made between these two strategies. We can either aim at strong coherence or, going in the opposite direction, human rights will move into a 'two-speed' regime mentioned earlier: having greater strength outside of the world of business than they do within that world. If we go down the latter path we fuel disillusionment, together with the slow atrophy of support by some and the increasingly cynical deployment of the label 'human rights' by others.

3.3   Conclusion

This argument supports the construction of a treaty on business and human rights built on consensus among an initially narrow scope of parties within a given region and/or sector. It is a consensus that can gradually spread beyond those borders – particularly once home countries realize that host countries are making robust treaties among themselves that carry consequences for the former. The initial benefits of this strategy should show themselves quickly. The mutual assurance such a treaty can provide could give those hosts facing similar international commercial pressures to lower social standards a basis for resisting doing so – as a group with its members able to count on one another. At the same time, it is such smaller scale treaties that should be able to encourage host governments to give the human rights they guarantee their proper content and weight in the name of coherence with human rights standards developed in other areas of law and policy – a coherence that is not shrunken due to these rights being introduced into the unfamiliar terrain of business activity. Without support from such an instrument, national efforts to give effect to the UN Guiding Principles are likely to be weakened by the persistent fear that one's competitors are not going to live up to the standards they profess to embrace. If we are to make further progress nationally, we need mutual assurance internationally – but on a scale that allows nations similarly placed in the world economy to move ahead with greater confidence. Such a treaty fills an urgent need.

3.4   Draft Treaty Clauses Relating to Elements in the Chapter

The following draft provisions are directed at the goals of strong coherence and mutual assurance that have been discussed.

3.4.1   Preamble (Elements)

Whereas it is essential that a Treaty be able to provide assurance that each state party undertakes to the others that it will observe the Treaty's requirements,

Whereas it is recognized that appropriate sanctions be designed and deployed for failure to respect the said undertaking,

Whereas it is the object and purpose of this Treaty to govern the relationship between states, non-state actors in the economy, and natural persons by applying national and international human rights law, and

Whereas human rights law is to be given priority wherever it is in conflict with other bodies of law governing business activity . . .

3.4.2   General Interpretive Protocol (Elements)

The parties agree that the body of law included in Annex I shall be interpreted in accordance with the requirements of instruments included in Annex II together with relevant provisions of customary international law. [Note: Annex I includes relevant provisions of regulating business activity, including but not limited to corporate, labour, competition, intellectual property, data management and investment law. Annex II includes all elements of national and international human rights law applicable to the parties].

The object and purpose of the provisions in Annex 1 shall have added to them the object and purpose of giving effect to the rules and principles of the provisions in Annex 2. Where the provisions in Annex 1 are in conflict with those of Annex 2, priority is to be given to Annex 2. For the avoidance of doubt, the parties must find a method of implementing the provisions of Annex 1 that, from among reasonably available alternatives, imposes the least burden on and/or provides the greatest opportunity to further the rights provided in Annex 2.

Any party to this Treaty can bring a complaint to [an Authority] alleging failure by another party to respect the requirements of the foregoing paragraphs.

3.4.3   Application to Corporate Laws in Annex 1(Elements)

The Parties agree to incorporate into their laws relating to companies the following provisions:

Directors must execute their duties in a manner that implements their company's obligation to respect and adequately remedy the rights guaranteed by the provisions in Annex 2 and in compliance with the priority for human rights as provided for the General Interpretive Protocol.

The individual's fiduciary duty to the company of which he or she is director shall include respect for the relevant human rights of all stakeholders.

For associated companies [Note: a term to be defined so as to capture the features of a corporate group], liability for damage to the rights indicated in Annex 2 is to be shared among all associates which are or have been in a position to contribute significantly to compensating and/or preventing that damage. For the avoidance of doubt, where such damage to human rights has happened, no associated company will benefit from limitations on liability for the acts of another associated company which would otherwise apply.

PART II

Principles and Politics Shaping the Treaty's
Contours

4

Principled Pragmatism in the Elaboration of a Comprehensive Treaty on Business and Human Rights

LARRY CATÁ BACKER

'It was on a dreary night of November that I beheld the accomplishment of my toils. With an anxiety that almost amounted to agony, I collected the instruments of life around me, that I might infuse a spark of being into the lifeless thing that lay at my feet. It was already one in the morning; the rain pattered dismally against the panes, and my candle was nearly burnt out, when, by the glimmer of the half-extinguished light, I saw the dull yellow eye of the creature open; it breathed hard, and a convulsive motion agitated its limbs.'[1]

4.1 Context

In June 2011, the UN Human Rights Council unanimously endorsed the UN Guiding Principles on Business and Human Rights (UNGP).[2] This act represented the culmination of a contentious and often failed process that had started in the 1970s as international organizations sought to figure out a way of creating a set of quasi-public 'social' responsibilities of corporations engaged in economic activity across borders.[3] Yet the

---

[1] M. Shelley, *Frankenstein or the Modern Prometheus* (Lackington Hugh Harding Mavor & Jones, 1818), ch. 5.

[2] United Nations Office of the High Comm'r for Human Rights, *Guiding Principles On Business And Human Rights: Implementing The United Nations 'Protect, Respect And Remedy Framework*, (Geneva and New York. 2011) www.ohchr.org/Documents/Publications/GuidingPrinciplesBusinessHR_EN.pdf (30 August 2016).

[3] Generally, see L. C. Backer, 'Multinational Corporations, Transnational Law: The United Nation's Norms on the Responsibilities of Transnational Corporations as a Harbinger of Corporate Social Responsibility as International Law,' (2006) 37 *Columbia Human Rights Law Review* 287; K. P. Sauvant, *Looking Back, Looking Ahead: What Lessons Should we Learn from Past UN Efforts to Adopt a Code of Conduct for Business?* Institute for Human Rights and

endorsement did not silence criticism[4] – it merely sharpened it.[5] Amnesty International set the tone for the post-endorsement critique, which stressed that the 'guiding principles enjoy broad support from business, precisely because they require little meaningful action by business', that 'governments fail to regulate companies effectively, . . . that companies working in many countries evade accountability and proper sanctions', and as a consequence what became the UNGPs 'fail to meet this challenge. Amnesty International believes they must be strengthened. We have offered constructive advice, based on years of investigative experience, to help the process. We will continue to do so.'[6]

Indeed, this constructive advice from Amnesty International, along with the views of a growing number of civil society organizations, together with developing states led by the UN delegation for Ecuador and South Africa, became a call for a comprehensive treaty on business and human rights shortly after the UNGP endorsement.[7] The civil society elements framed their efforts around a 'Global Movement for a Binding Treaty' whose purpose was to enhance the international legal framework

Technology (16 April 2015), www.ihrb.org/commentary/looking-back-looking-ahead.html (last accessed 3 September 2016). The reference to quasi-public social responsibility harks back to the foundational debate from which the UNGP emerges – the debate within corporate law, of the extent of the duty of an enterprise to society, namely, its public role. That debate touched on the nature of the corporation (as a state construct or as the state recognition of an organic construct) from out of which a host of obligations to shareholders, local communities, the 'nation' or society might be extracted – and exploited in societal norms and law. The internationalization of this debate occurred from the 1970s in the context of reactions to a complex set of factors including the beginnings of the emergence of globalization and its governance gaps, and the rise of the power of integrated supply chains overseen by apex corporations that appeared increasingly autonomous of states. That project of internationalization and legalization was then appropriated to the emerging discourses of human rights so that by the beginning of the twenty-first century, it became common place to think about corporate social responsibility as a legal, international and human rights issue.

[4] See, e.g., H. Williamson, 'Rights Groups Slam UN Plan for Multinationals' *Financial Times*, 17 Jan 2011.

[5] See, e.g., Amnesty International, CIDSE, ESCR-Net, Human Rights Watch, International Commission of Jurists, International Federation for Human Rights (FIDH) and Rights and Accountability in Development (RAID), 'Joint Civil Society Statement on the draft Guiding Principles on Business and Human Rights' 14 Jan 2011, www.fidh.org/IMG/pdf/Joint_CSO_Statement_on_GPs.pdf (last accessed 3 September 2016).

[6] W. Brown, Sr. Director for International Law and Policy, Amnesty International, Letter: Stronger UN Draft On Human Rights Abuses Needed, *Financial Times*, 20 January 2011.

[7] See, D. Cassel, Remarks: 'Does the World Need a Treaty On Business and Human Rights? Weighing the Pros and Cons, Introduction of Topic' Notre Dame London Centre 14 May 2014, http://international.nd.edu/assets/133113/may_14_cassel_remarks.pdf. (last accessed 4 September 2016).

to protect human rights from corporate abuse.[8] Leading voices in the business community, on the other hand, reaffirmed their commitment to a governance framework for business and human rights without a treaty.[9]

All this activity bore fruit in 2014, when the UN Human Rights Council established an Open-Ended Intergovernmental Working Group on Transnational Corporations and Other Business Enterprises (IGWG) with respect to human rights, and mandated the working group to 'elaborate an international legally binding instrument to regulate, in international human rights law, the activities of transnational corporations and other business enterprises'.[10] At the same time, the Human Rights Council affirmed adherence to the principles of the UNGP, adopting by consensus a resolution put forward by Norway and supported by 44 co-sponsors supporting further operationalization of the UNGP.[11] The latter resolution included a request that the UN Working Group on Business and Human Rights prepare a report considering, among other things, 'including the benefits and limitations of a legally binding instrument'.[12] Many of the states that supported the Norway resolution remain hostile to the treaty project.[13]

The UN Human Rights Council directed the newly created IGWG to devote its first two sessions to 'conducting constructive deliberations on the content, scope, nature and form of the future international instrument'.[14] At its first session, civil society refined its expectations for the scope and coverage of a treaty instrument under the mandate.[15] The

[8] See, e.g., Treaty Alliance, Statement, www.treatymovement.com/statement/ (last accessed 30 August 2016).

[9] See, United States Council for International Business, Statement: 'Employers Reaffirm Commitment to UN Principles on Business and Human Rights' 30 June 2014, www.uscib.org/employers-reaffirm-commitment-to-un-principles-on-business-and-human-rights-ud-4771/ (last accessed 3 September 2016).

[10] Human Rights Council, 'Elaboration of an international legally binding instrument on transnational corporations and other business enterprises with respect to human rights' A/HRC/RES/26/9 (14 July 2014).

[11] Human Rights Council, Resolution: 'Human Rights and Transnational Corporations and other Business Enterprises' 26th Sess. Agenda item 3, A/HRC/26/L.1 (23 June 2014).

[12] Ibid., at para. 8.

[13] See, J. Ruggie, Remarks: 'The Past as Prologue?: A Moment of Truth for UN Business and Human Rights Treaty, Institute for Human Rights and Business' (8 July 2014), www.hks.harvard.edu/m-rcbg/CSRI/Treaty_Final.pdf (last accessed 15 August 2016).

[14] M. Espinosa, 'Report on the first session of the open-ended intergovernmental working group on transnational corporations and other business enterprises with respect to human rights, with the mandate of elaborating an international legally binding instrument' HRC 31st Sess, Agenda Item 3, A/HRC/31/50 (5 February 2016).

[15] See, ibid., supra, at paras. 21–105.

IGWG organized the sessions around a number of broad concepts framing structuring principles.[16] As might be expected at this early stage,
there was little consensus on these questions except at a very high level of
generality.[17] There may also be some fundamental disagreement between
the position of the states supporting the treaty project and their civil
society allies.[18]

Such initial stage setting is usually of little interest except for what it
might suggest of the underlying tensions that will be built into both the
process and product of the treaty elaboration enterprise. And thus, the
work to date suggests two principal challenges for the treaty-making
project – the first looks to consensus on the underlying principles and
objectives; the second is the extent to which the provisions of a treaty
must conform strictly to principle. Both touch on issues of coherence and
vision. And both suggest the need for a set of principles to be developed
for pragmatic choices to be made that move from conceptualization to a
draft treaty.[19] The first focuses on the political and the ordinary politics of
consensus building. The second focuses on framework and method, that
is, on the methods that guide consensus and the ultimate expression of
that consensus in the presentation of an elaboration that represents the
agreement of at least the advocates of the treaty process. With respect to
the first point, it might be argued that consensus building is ultimately

---

[16] The resulting report summarized the discussion by stakeholders and other invited
persons on their sense of the commitment by states (*Ibid.*, paras. 37–39; paras. 67–77),
principles (paras. 40–54), the 'legal nature' of the corporation (paras. 55–61) and their
legal liability (paras. 88–97), scope of human rules (paras. 62–66), enhancing enterprise
responsibilities (paras. 78–87) and remediation mechanism (paras. 98–105).

[17] Consider the various statements proffered to the working group by civil society organization
around its first session. Statement may be accessed at http://business-humanrights.org/en/
binding-treaty/intergovernmental-working-group-sessions (last accessed 3 August 2016).

[18] See, ESCR-Net Corporate Accountability Working Group, 'Statement,' http://business-
humanrights.org/sites/default/files/media/documents/cawg_statement_re_un_hrc_reso
lution_text.pdf (last accessed 3 September 2016) They noted: '[S]ome States involved in
the negotiation are attempting to qualify this text with the following definition: "Other
business enterprises" denotes all business enterprises that have a transnational character
in their operational activities, and does not apply to local businesses registered in terms of
relevant domestic law. The inclusion of this restrictive definition in the resolution text is a
damaging development, which would result in a missed opportunity to ensure a level
playing field for all corporations worldwide, while also ensuring that all corporate human
rights violations are addressed by future international normative developments.' *Ibid.*).

[19] Discussed in L. Backer, 'Ruminations 64: Can Pragmatism Be Principled? A View From
the Efforts to Elaborate to Comprehensive Treaty for Business and Human Rights' Law at
the End of the Day, 3 September 2016, http://lcbackerblog.blogspot.com/2016/09/rumina
tions-64-can-pragmatism-be.html (last accessed Sept. 4, 2016).

uninteresting as law, though it might be valuable as sociology or politics, or helpful with interpretation issues. With respect to the second point, some might suggest both contradiction and irrelevance. There is contradiction because of a false presumption of the opposition of pragmatism and principle – that indeed, the essence of the pragmatic is unprincipled. There follows irrelevance, because there is a desire to approach treaty-making in the grand nineteenth-century style misattributed to the Second Reich's Bismarck: 'Gesetze sind wie Würste, man sollte besser nicht dabei sein, wenn sie gemacht warden.'[20]

This chapter proposes to peek inside the sausage of treaty elaboration, and examine the premises usually left to the historian, the sociologist and the theorist. Those charged with the elaboration of a treaty – as well as the stakeholders (states and civil society actors) working in the shadows to ensure that it takes a specific shape – are motivated by a grand principle, the necessity of public international law to manage the multinational enterprise in its operations. However, that grand principle neither describes the character nor quality of the object or the specific language of the treaty that might incorporate it. The realization of grand principle could take a variety of forms, with substantially distinct effects, and remain true to the simple ideal of a treaty. Like Dr Frankenstein, treaty framers will patch together a creature of international law in their own image. They will gather parts from the charnel houses of several generations' worth of ideas and cobble them together to produce a creature whose animation will fulfil the underlying ambition of the IGWG mandate.[21] To build this creature is to build a body of whose character is the operational sum of a host of choices. But the process of choice – the pragmatic turn – is itself bounded by principle. Not just the grand principle, but those that shape the 'character' of the project and thus helps guide the development of provisions that give principle effect. The failure of principle in choice will leave the creature stillborn. Its

---

[20] F. Shapiro, 'Quote. . . Misquote' *The New York Times Magazine* (July 21 2008) ('Laws, like sausages, cease to inspire respect in proportion as we know how they are made.' John Godfrey Saxe, 1869).

[21] Cf. Shelley, *Frankenstein*, n. 1. ('The materials at present within my command hardly appeared adequate to so arduous an undertaking, but I doubted not that I should ultimately succeed. I prepared myself for a multitude of reverses; my operations might be incessantly baffled, and at last my work be imperfect, yet when I considered the improvement which every day takes place in science and mechanics, I was encouraged to hope my present attempts would at least lay the foundations of future success. Nor could I consider the magnitude and complexity of my plan as any argument of its impracticability.' *Ibid.*, ch. 4).

application, however, may also produce a monster that consumes its creator. Principled pragmatism is unlikely to win much sympathy among many of those bent to the task of assembling a bricolage of parts for the animation of the creature that is the comprehensive treaty. The invocation of the term by John Ruggie as the core of his approach to the development of the Protect-Respect-Remedy framework that became the UNGP[22] has been a source of great criticism.[23] And yet, treaty elaboration will require the same sort of judgements under similar constraints to embed, unobscured, those principles that produce a relational system that provides a material basis for the socio-legal processes[24] involved in the management of business behaviours with human rights consequences.[25]

The chapter first considers the great key framework principles that might be extracted from the mandate for treaty elaboration of the IGWG. Those principles provide the objectives and substantive principles around which a comprehensive treaty will be elaborated. The chapter then turns to the consideration of two levels of principles that may be used to guide pragmatic choices in treaty elaboration. The first touches on the great framework principles that give the treaty its structure and coherence within the objectives of the mandate. These suggest the range of ideological choices that must serve as a starting point for *treaty drafting that is principled.* Pragmatism follows from the need to choose

---

[22] J. Ruggie, 'Interim Report of the Special Representative of the Secretary-General on the Issue of Human Rights and Transnational Corporations and Other Business Enterprises,' E/CN.4/2006/97, 2006, ¶ 81 ('As indicated at the outset, the SRSG takes his mandate to be primarily evidence based. But insofar as it involves assessing difficult situations that are themselves in flux, it inevitably will also entail making normative judgments. In the SRSG's case, the basis for those judgments might best be described as a principled form of pragmatism: an unflinching commitment to the principle of strengthening the promotion and protection of human rights as it relates to business, coupled with a pragmatic attachment to what works best in creating change where it matters most – in the daily lives of people.'). See also R. Mares, 'Business and Human Rights After Ruggie: Foundations, the Art of Simplification and the Imperative of Cumulative Progress' in R. Mares (ed.), *The UN Guiding Principles on Business and Human Rights –Foundations and Implementation* (Martinus Nijhoff Publishers, 2012), 1.

[23] Cf. W. van Genugten and N. Jägers, Editorial: 'Corporations and human rights: moving beyond "Principled Pragmatism" to "Ruggie-Plus,"' (March 1 2011).

[24] Cf. N. Luhmann, *Social System* (Stanford University Press, 1995).

[25] Cf. E. Cardoso and I. Miola, 'The Treaty on Transnational Corporations and Human Rights: Mapping Positions, Stakes and Strategies in the Global South (Brazil, India, Indonesia, and South Africa)' (Sao Paulo, February 2016), http://csnbricsam.org/wp-content/uploads/2013/08/The-Treaty-on-Transnational-Corporations-and-Human-Rights.pdf (last accessed 4 September 2016).

among these framing principles or work through ways of blending them that avoid incoherence of the treaty as a whole. The second touches on issues of the application of framing principles in the actual drafting of treaty provisions. Distinct framing principles privilege or emphasize distinct sets of provisions. Coordinating principle and actual provisions – or moderating that connection – suggests the scope of pragmatism that most take for granted (as the routine 'wheeling and dealing. of negotiation). The pragmatic bridges the provisions of a treaty instrument and their usually unstated normative frameworks, the purpose of which is to ensure coherence and fidelity to the basic ideological foundation of the draft.

4.2   The Assumptions Underlying the Intergovernmental Working Group Mandate

In order to make sense of the treaty project itself, it might be useful to seek to extract a set of coherent and organizing principles that are meant to be manifested and advanced through the provisions of a treaty as envisioned by the Human Rights Council. What precisely is the objective of the IGWG and of the treaty it is to elaborate? A good starting point is the mandate of the IGWG itself. At its narrowest, the mandate is quite specific and divided into three parts. First, the mandate establishes 'open-ended intergovernmental working group on transnational corporations and other business enterprises with respect to human right'.[26] Second, it charges that the IGWG 'elaborate an international legally binding instrument to regulate, in international human rights law, the activities of transnational corporations and other business enterprises'.[27] Third, the mandate directs the focus of the work of the IGWG during its first two sessions: it must engage in 'constructive deliberations on the content, scope, nature and form of the future international instrument, in this regard'.[28] The mandate sets a deadline and specifies the product of its charge – the preparation of 'elements for the draft legally binding instrument for substantive negotiations at the commencement of the third session of the working group on the subject, taking into consideration the

---

[26] Human Rights Council, 'Elaboration,' supra n. 10 'Elaboration of an international legally binding instrument on transnational corporations and other business enterprises with respect to human rights' U.N. Human Rights Council, A/HRC/RES/26/9, supra, para. 1.
[27] *Ibid.*   [28] *Ibid.*, para. 2.

discussions held at its first two sessions'.[29] Those objectives suggest not merely an objective but an ideology too around which structural principles for treaty elaboration may be framed.

First, states are privileged in this enterprise of treaty elaboration. There will be no repeat of the tripartite formula that marked the tempestuous but more contemporary process producing the UNGP. Instead, power is vested in an intergovernmental working group representing states. Others may be consulted, as is now the habit of the UN agencies.[30] Civil society groups, including business, no longer have even the appearance of privileged participation in this process that is meant to be, formally at least, state driven.[31] This is no secret. The Resolution stresses 'that the obligations and primary responsibility to promote and protect human rights and fundamental freedoms lie with the State, and that States must protect against human rights abuse within their territory and/or jurisdiction by third parties, including transnational corporations'.[32]

Second, the mandate stays close to traditional approaches to international law making. There does not appear to be a charge for the transformation of legal or economic orders. Nor does it imply a transformed role for international law above or within states. The object is an international legally binding instrument. That might reference a traditional treaty which, unless it assumes a role of *jus cogens*, may be adopted or rejected by states as they see fit, and may be adopted with such reservations as suits the adopting states. Nor does it imply an obligation to transpose the instrument, *binding in international law against states*, into the domestic legal orders of any state, though the treaty may itself provide a substantially unenforceable obligation to give effect domestically to its provisions. The conventional ideology, then, appears to assume the possibility that a single comprehensive treaty will produce a potentially large number of legally effective variants.

Third, the object of this internationally binding instrument is the regulation, in international law, of the activities of a subset of economic enterprises. The meaning of 'in international law' is quite flexible. For conservatives, it means no more than describing the obvious constraints on the applicability of international law – in other words, the treaty

---

[29] *Ibid.*, para. 3. The mandate also sets a time for the first session of the IGWG (para. 4) and reserves to itself an oversight role (para. 9).
[30] Discussed in P. Willets, 'The Cardoso Report on the UN and Civil Society: Functionalism, Global Corporatism or Global Democracy?'(2006) 12 (3) *Global Governance* 305.
[31] Human Rights Council, 'Elaboration,' supra n. 10, para. 5.
[32] *Ibid.*, supra n. 10, para. 1.

would impose obligations on states under international law, but with no direct effects on enterprises or individuals, except to the extent they transpose obligations upon corporations into their domestic legal orders. For others, it could mean substantially broader obligations flowing from the treaty itself, though these remain undefined. Beyond the domestic legal order, international law also constrains the legitimate projection of the domestic legal order of one state into the territory or jurisdictional space of another. There is room for such projection, to be sure, and powerful states tend to project to the extent they can or desire, but the embrace of a principle of extraterritoriality would appear to stretch the mandate, or at least to interpret it broadly.

Fourth, the scope of coverage is limited to 'international human rights law'. That appears, on the one hand, to be broad: there is a lot of international human rights law, and some international tribunals have sought to treat human rights instruments as fundamentally different in character from the other international law treaties.[33] However, it is also narrow – it does not include international human rights norms or other writings that do not have the effect of international law. It appears, though, that the mandate builds ambiguity into this portion thereof, 'recalling' the Universal Declaration of Human Rights and the 1986 UN General Assembly Declaration on the Right to Development.[34] Nevertheless, the recalling of various non-binding norms and declarations in addition to some of the more fundamental instruments of international human rights law does not have the effect of transforming non-binding declarations into binding law, even international law. To achieve that result, any comprehensive treaty on business and human rights elaborated would have to create international law expressly. Such a back-door method of legalizing and extending the effect of these instruments would be clever, indeed, but would depend on the agreement of states that would bind themselves to them – and only to the extent of their willingness to be bound. It does suggest, however, the *ideology* that these non-binding instruments advance – an ideology the foundation of which

---

[33] Inter-American Court, *The Effect of Reservations on the Entry Into Force of the American Convention on Human Rights (Arts. 74 and 75), IACHR*, Series A, No. 1, ¶ 29 (Advisory Opinion OC-2/82 (sept. 24, 1982): 'In concluding these human rights treaties, the States can be deemed to submit themselves to a legal order within which they, for the common good, assume various obligations, not in relation to other states, but towards all individuals within their jurisdiction'). But see, A. Orakhelashvili, 'Restrictive Interpretation of Human Rights Treaties in the Recent Jurisprudence of the European Court of Human Rights' (2002) 14 (3) *European Journal of International Law* 529.

[34] Human Rights Council, 'Elaboration,' supra n. 10, Preamble.

conflates norm and law at the international level and assumes the legal effect of instruments that are recognized as socially compelling.

Fifth, though the state is the driver of human rights legalization, international organizations play a leadership role as the source of that legalization. The interplay between international legalization, national context, democratic principles and global harmonization remains unresolved. The tension between states as the operative engine of human rights implementation and international organizations as the source of law continues an old conversation about the nature and role of international law and its relation to the constitutional orders of states.[35] On the one hand, it suggests the sort of easy extraterritorialization that civil society embraced in the form of pre-Kiobel[36] US juridical jurisdictional conceits. On the other, it suggests the paramount role of international organizations as the source of superior law binding on states and administered through their courts.[37]

Sixth, the potentially transformative potential of the comprehensive treaty project is itself intimated but not declared through the traditional method of 'recalling', 'bearing in mind' and 'taking into account' in the Mandate's preamble. These bring within the framework of elaboration not just the UNGP, and their ideology of fidelity to the limitations of international law and the state system on which it is built, but also the rich history of efforts, especially by developing states, to transform the character of economic globalization and to impose substantial restrictions on transnational enterprises, especially those with apex entities in developed states. To that end, the production of an international legally binding instrument may be interpreted as being substantially broader than a treaty: it might suggest the broadness of the UN Norms[38] to bind

---

[35] Generally L. Henkin, *International Law: Politics and Values* (Springer, 1995) (origins of present state system and its consequences for shaping the form and constraints of international law with an emphasis on sovereign and equal nation-states).

[36] *Esther Kiobel v. Royal Dutch Petroleum* 133 S Ct 1659 (2013).

[37] See, UNGP, supra n. 2 S. Skogly, 'Regulatory Obligations in a Complex World: States' Extraterritorial Obligations Related to Business and Human Rights' in Surya Deva and David Bilchitz (eds.), *Business and Human Rights: Exploring the Contours of a Treaty* (Cambridge, forthcoming 2016). Cf., 'Maastricht Principles on Extraterritorial Obligations of States in the Area of Economic, Social and Cultural Rights' (23 January 2013), www.etoconsortium.org/nc/en/library/maastricht-principles/?tx_drblob_pil%5BdownloadUid%5D=23 (last accessed 3 August 2016).

[38] Norms on the Responsibilities of Transnational Corporations and Other Business Enterprises with Regard to Human Rights, ECOSOC, 55th Sess., U.N. Doc. E/CN.4/Sub.2/2003/12/Rev.2 (26 August 2003) (the UN Norms). The effective mandatory character of the Norms and relationship to domestic law is discussed in Backer, supra n. 3.

enterprises and individuals, as well as states, and to embed itself within domestic legal orders despite constitutional barriers to such an action in national law. Indeed, the Mandate was careful to take into account 'all the work undertaken by the Commission on Human Rights and the Human Rights Council on the question of the responsibilities of transnational corporations and other business enterprises', the body of which includes the Norms themselves, and the ideologies that supported the Norms.

Seventh, the other constraint on treaty elaboration is the object of regulation – the activities of transnational corporations and other business enterprises. A broad reading would suggest this includes all enterprises in global production chains. A narrow reading would suggest that this includes only enterprises, whether organized as corporations or in other forms, which are transnational in character. And indeed, the drafters of the resolution, in a footnote made clear their intent in this regard that the instrument was to apply only to transnational entities.[39] But even at this early stage that aspect of the mandate has met resistance. A recent analysis suggests the extent of the rupture.[40]

The IGWG mandate, then, provides the borders within which a discussion of framing principles may be attempted, and then used to further the project of treaty elaboration. It is, in effect, an invitation to make choices about the principles that will be used to guide choices that will produce provisions the aggregated effects of which will further the structuring principles from which they were framed. The importance of the IGWG's first session objective, which was 'to collect inputs, including written inputs, from States and relevant stakeholders on possible principles, scope and elements of such an international legally binding instrument'[41], becomes clearer in this context. The only objective for which there is agreement – and it is an important one – is that states are directed to elaborate a draft of an international legally binding document through the IGWG. Further, this document is to be constrained by existing international human

---

[39] Human Rights Council, 'Elaboration' supra n. 10, at n. 1. That footnote 1 provides '"Other business enterprises" denotes all business enterprises that have a transnational character in their operational activities, and does not apply to local businesses registered in terms of relevant domestic law.'

[40] See, Cardoso and Miola, The Treaty on Transnational Corporations and Human Rights, supra n. 25 ('focusing on TNCs – is more often advanced by CSOs and social movements from the global South. The second view, in turn, can be identified in the contributions of proponents from varied origins, but mostly from CSOs from the global North, as well as from representatives of the corporate sector and the European Union.' p. 18).

[41] Human Rights Council, 'Elaboration' supra n. 10.

rights *law*, and must apply only to *transnational* corporations and other business enterprises. These terms are subject to substantial interrogation in the course of a three-year progression from *intention* to *realization* of treaty elaboration with respect to which a range of framing principles is suggested. It is those principled frameworks that the chapter considers next.

4.3   The Principles Underlying the Elaboration of a Coherent Treaty

The consideration of the great framework principles that might be extracted from the mandate for treaty elaboration of the IGWG suggested the broad objectives and substantive principles around which a comprehensive treaty will be elaborated. Yet, the Mandate neither suggests the choice nor the principles for making that decision. This raises the first of the great issues that must be confronted and resolved in the movement towards a treaty: a choice among competing framing principles, which may not be entirely complementary, and indeed in most respects are incompatible in the effects that flow from their implementation. These can be divided into three broad categories: *status quo, evolutionary or re-characterization* and *transformative* objectives. These are further refined by secondary framework objectives that are structural and methodological but also ideologically driven. These include framework treaty objectives, institutional objectives and systemic objectives. Each is briefly discussed in turn and from that the contours of principled pragmatism are sketched.

Status Quo objectives are the most conservative. A very narrow reading of the ideological implications of the mandate might suggest that it requires nothing more of the state than the conversion of the UNGP themselves into an instrument of international law, yet retaining its non-binding character. This might take the form of a Treaty that would embrace the UNGP as recommendations addressed by governments to enterprises, that is, as a code of responsible conduct that governments have committed to promoting. That upsets no traditional law or principle. It does not confront the great principles of corporate autonomy, of the limits of national jurisdiction, or of the substantial legal limitations to the determination of liability among groups of enterprises engaged in production chain relations. This is an approach that preserves the appearance of having created 'law' without affecting the legal relationships of the parties under 'law'.

Evolutionary or re-characterization objectives might be understood as an incrementalist approach. The incrementalism inherent in this approach embodies both a principle (move the business and human rights project 'forward') and a pragmatic choice (constraining treaty provisions so that they modify but do not substantially change the status quo). This approach is grounded in embracing the 'stage-setting' elements of the mandate; that is, to frame a treaty that can provide a basis for movement towards a more transformative goal but to do it in a way that opens possibilities while not coercing them. At bottom, this seeks to embrace the UNGP but also to improve them[42] by using a treaty instrument to transform the UNGP second Pillar responsibilities to respect into domestic law. This moves the 'status quo' objectives substantially forward by embedding the second pillar into law. As such, this approach avoids the difficulties of forcing states to change their relationship to international law, while adding the legal dimension to corporate societal obligations that had been among the biggest criticism of the UNGP's polycentric approach. Evolutive and re-characterization objectives suggest a fidelity both to the project of internationalization and of legalization of the substantive norms around which a law of business and human rights may be constructed. However, it also relies on national judiciaries to enforce this new international law within their domestic orders. Additionally, it remains silent on the scope of a state's duty to protect human rights, leaving that entirely to the willingness of states, under international law, to adopt such duties in the first instance. States like the United States are making it clear that they intend to draw away from rather than embrace multilateralism in ordering their domestic legal systems.[43] Moreover, this approach might sacrifice uniformity and interpretive coherence across states, encouraging both forum and rule shopping. It might also produce a willingness to accept *incrementalism*.[44]

---

[42] See, e.g., 'Joint Civil Society Statement' supra, n. 5.

[43] See Draft Executive Order, 'Moratorium on New Multilateral Treaties' (25 January 2017, available http://apps.washingtonpost.com/g/documents/world/read-the-trump-administra tions-draft-of-the-executive-order-on-treaties/2307/ and discussed in Larry Catá Backer, 'The 45th Presidency and Multilateral Treaties–Fear, Loathing and a Repudiation of 20th Century Americanism' Law at the End of the Day 2 February 2017, available http://lcback erblog.blogspot.com/2017/02/the-45th-presidency-and-multilateral.html#more.

[44] Cf., S. Block-Lieb and T. Halliday, 'Incrementalisms in Global Law making' (2007) 32 *Brooklyn Journal of International Law* 851 ('Consensus building – for that is what produces global law – takes time and political skill. Once we conceptualize incrementalism in these terms, a theoretical and empirical agenda opens up that includes but far exceeds insolvency lawmaking.' *Ibid.*, 902).

Incrementalism may produce a tolerance of fracture – the piecemeal negotiation of provisions of a treaty that does not produce coherence or the elaboration of a singular vision, but instead produces a framework that permits further negotiation and refinement as a work in progress and through application.[45]

Transformative objectives represent the broadest reading of the ideological principles embedded in the mandate. They involve furthering the project of internationalization through law beyond the state but imposed through the state.[46] Transformative objectives offer a number of variations – the choice among which may reflect pragmatic considerations (reflecting the views of critical stakeholders, furthering privileged agendas and ensuring the completion of the elaboration project). These variations speak to four distinct approaches to the construction of an internationalized legal order: (1) an ideology-objective of constructing a stronger unified system of global law administered through states; (2) the construction of a global law administered through a global governmental apparatus; (3) the creation of a centralized prosecutorial and remedial mechanism; and (4) a transformation of the ground rules of globalization itself. It might also veer toward *utopianism* – the objective being to frame a distinct vision of the world that will serve as a touchstone for the future (like the Universal Declaration of Human Rights) without any expectation that a treaty looking anything like the vision will come into force – at least in the short run.

The choice of any of these framing principles is plausible under the mandate. The way in which the IGWG is to choose among them is impliedly pragmatic: it is grounded in the obligation to collect inputs at the first IGWG meeting from states and relevant stakeholders. Those inputs would provide a principled way of making a choice 'on possible principles, scope and elements', one based on the strength of collective sentiment among those involved in the treaty elaboration process. That choice is not mandatory: it is possible to avoid any systematic and coherent approach and to disaggregate the process and seek input solely with respect to the cluster of provisions powerful groups might like to see

---

[45] But consider S. Deva, 'Treating Human Rights Lightly: A Critique of the Consensus Rhetoric and the Language Employed by the Guiding Principles' in S. Deva and D. Bilchitz (eds.), *Human Rights Obligations of Business: Beyond the Corporate Responsibility to Respect?* (Cambridge, 2013), 78.

[46] Cf. N. Krisch, *Beyond Constitutionalism: The Pluralist Structure of Postnational Law* (Oxford, 2010) (international orders as the new constitutional centre beyond the nation-state).

in a treaty. That certainly would amount to an embrace of a status quo or evolutionary approach at its base, but one in which coherence would be lost. In its place would be a collection of provisions that could be strategically connected only by their location within a single document denominated 'treaty' and given the effect of 'law'.

However, plausibility leaves unanswered the question of choice. Ironically, that choice may well depend on the international climate in the coming years. Between 2011 and 2014, with the success of multilateralism evidenced by the UNGP themselves, evolutionary and even well-directed status quo framing principles might have been the optimal strategy for a treaty effort designed to further the project of human rights legalization. But from 2016, the changed climate for multilateralism among key state actors – including principally the United States, which moved from being suspicious to openly hostile to multilateralism that does not touch on issues of extradition, national security or trade[47] – might change the calculus. Indeed, the more likely that powerful states will seek to ensure any treaty effort is unsuccessful, the more valuable will be an aggressive embrace of transformative objectives in treaty writing. The object would shift from signing and ratification to setting out a clear vision for the future. On the other hand, the withdrawal of the United States from engagement with multilateral efforts like a comprehensive business and human rights treaty might provide other states with the opportunity to group together to produce a workable evolutionary treaty objectives framework, with the understanding that the United States would not participate. But that lack of participation would serve as a trap for the United States – its companies would have to adhere to any treaty in those places where the treaty would be effective (i.e., ratified and transposed into a domestic legal order without reservations). The transformative model would be most effective where US withdrawal becomes an aggressive effort to coerce other states to treat such treaties as fundamentally illegitimate.[48]

These emerging realities affecting choices among these framing objectives then require a greater focus on the set of secondary principles. The

---

[47] See Donald J. Trump, Inaugural Address, Washington, DC, 20 January 2017 available www.whitehouse.gov/inaugural-address, Larry Catá Backer, Ruminations 69/Democracy Part 38: 'Behold, how good and how pleasant it is for brethren to dwell together in unity!': On President Trump's Inaugural Speech, Law at the End of the Day, 21 January 2017 available http://lcbackerblog.blogspot.com/2017/01/ruminations-69democracy-part-38-behold.html.

[48] See, Backer, 'The 45th Presidency and Multilateral Treaties' supra, n. 43.

employment of these secondary principles, focused on institutional and methodological issues, might well help guide the specific provisions that could be drafted to enhance the likelihood that any of these framing objectives could achieve the overall goal of producing a treaty that will be signed and ratified. These principles, touching on framework, institutional and systemic considerations, are each briefly considered in turn.

Framework or treaty format objectives touch on those matters relating to the process of treaty elaboration. They move the discourse from principle in the elaboration of a treaty to the principled pragmatics of the treaty's construction. There are several issues of importance to consider in this context. The first touches on principles of transparency. The more transparent the treaty elaboration, the more likely there will be broader and deeper participation. The less transparent and more controlled the process the more limited the participation. Transparency touches on the fidelity to democratic or mass principles in international norm-making, something that neither the great states nor the great civil society organs have a history of fostering. The second issue touches on principles of participation. If transparency makes it possible to access the process, participation goes to the opening of a place at the negotiating table. For the most part, it is unlikely that broad participation will be facilitated – the transaction, expertise and capital costs of participation tend to be high. And the inability to break into established networks of influence and communication might make it impossible to participate effectively. The third issue focuses on principles of implementation, focused on the operationalization through states or international organizations. Here one confronts the unresolved tensions about the internationalization of law and the autonomy of states. Structurally, centring internationalization of law might be best served through legal unification and by the delegation of administration to a centralized international body. However, centring national autonomy would favour state-based and contextually sensitive administration, with a weaker central authority and limited supportive roles for the international sphere.

Institutional objectives touch on a parallel set of principles that affect those concerning the operational elaboration of the treaty discussed above. What makes these objectives different is that they touch on principles of institutional organization and relational order, rather than on normative principles in the first instance.[49] These require a sense of the placement of the administrative centre of the treaty norms. An

---

[49] Cf. J. Alvarez, *International Organizations as Lawmakers* (Oxford, 2006).

internationalizing focus would result in a move towards establishment of a centralized administration in an international organization. A more state-centred approach would devolve operations to the states with a much less elaborate system for inter-state communication. The former enhances coherence and harmonization but reduces state autonomy. The later enhances state autonomy but reduces the coherence of the norms. A treaty of the sort contemplated by the mandate will likely require an international apparatus of some sort. Yet, the character and scope of such an apparatus is not apparent on the face of the Mandate.

Systemic objectives, last, bring the focus back to core principles. The treaty represents, at its foundation, an operationalization and elaboration of the principle of law over governance, of the state over the enterprise and of public rather than private governance structures. The treaty can be understood as an exercise in preserving the privilege of law as the form of legitimate regulatory governance. The treaty, in its entirety, represents the articulation of an emerging system one sees clearly for the first time here: one in which states retain the only legitimate authority to create law binding on individuals, but that states cede to international organizations the authority to create the rules that states are required to transpose into their domestic law and administer in accordance with international standards. More specifically, one comes face to face with the tension between the *legal obligations of states under international law* – that is to other states – and the *constitutional obligations of states* under national constitutional traditions to their own polities. Within these international organizations that appropriate legislative authority, issues of democratic deficits,[50] already troublesome where powerful states and multilateral actors impose their sense of internationalized norms on developing states, will only be exacerbated through the process of elaboration of a treaty in which influence, privilege and power predominate in its construction.

The framework choices now become clear – as do the consequences of choice for shaping the basic approach to treaty elaboration. Yet, they are also complex. The Mandate permits, and indeed sketches, a broad matrix of possible aggregations of ordering and structural principles that can frame coherent approaches to treaty drafting. Each combination pro-duces a coherent approach to valuing the utility of the potentially large

---

[50] On democratic deficits, see generally, A. Aman, Jr., *The Democracy Deficit: Taming Globalization Through Law Reform* (NYU Press, 2004) (democratic values furthered through administrative engagement on global level in lieu of markets-driven harmonization).

set of possible specific treaty provisions that can be combined to maximize its effectiveness in implementing the ordering principles. And
conversely, each provides a method for evaluating the negative effects
of particular provisions to the integrity of the ordering vision that gives
the treaty its coherence. That ability to assess coherence to principle and
objectives provides the essential element to the task of pragmatic decision-making in treaty construction out of principle.

The assessment of the effects of provisions suggests the character of the
treaty – its aggregate object. And the measure of the value of those
aggregated effects may only be made by reference to the principles that
the effects producing provisions are meant to enhance. *'The means
employed for the exercise of choice is the foundation of the pragmatic
challenge in treaty elaboration.* The principles that serve as the standards
against which the value of effects producing factors are measured serve as
the principles that guide pragmatism – that is that guide choice among
plausible alternative constructions of a treaty. *It is in this sense that one can
speak about principled pragmatism* – that is the application of standards of
value to the choices that must be made among competing choices whose
aggregations produce effects that change dramatically the conception of
the object that they affect.'[51] I have suggested the complexity of the interplay.[52] These provide a crude map of the possible framing principles that
can serve as the objectives of the treaty and the standards against which
proposed provisions might be assessed (the principle and the pragmatism).
One can better understand how the conflict of principles hidden by a set of
common objectives themselves reflect the necessity of normative choices.
And conversely, how the normative choices mask conflicts of objectives
and principles. Those choices are usually framed, not in the more abstract
discussion of principle and fidelity to bigger picture ideals, framed in a
coherent structure, but in the give and take of the negotiation of specific

---

[51] See L. Backer, Ruminations 64: Can Pragmatism Be Principled? With Application to the
Elaboration to Comprehensive Treaty for Business and Human Rights" Law at the End of
the Day (3 September 2016), http://lcbackerblog.blogspot.com/2016/09/ruminations-64-
can-pragmatism-be.html (last accessed 4 September 2016) ('*The means employed for the
exercise of choice is the foundation of the pragmatic challenge in treaty elaboration.* The
principles that serve as the standards against which the value of effects producing factors
are measured serve as the principles that guide pragmatism – that is that guide choice
among plausible alternatives constructions of a treaty. *It is in this sense that one can speak
about principled pragmatism* – that is the application of standards of value to the choices
that must be made among competing choices whose aggregations produce effects that
change dramatically the conception of the object that they affect.')

[52] Table from Backer, Ruminations 64, supra, n. 19 (reproduced with permission).

provisions. It is to the relationship of those choices to the matrix of principle that the chapter next turns.

4.4 The Manifestation of Principles in Treaty Provision Drafting

It is here, at this stage of the consideration of the framing principles for the elaboration of a treaty, that most discussion is centred.[53] These suggest an objectives-based pragmatism.[54] It is unlikely, then, that the elaboration of the treaty will be preceded by an agreement on principle. Instead, those involved in the treaty process will likely use the drafting process itself – the elaboration of the implementation provisions of the treaty – to embed their principles and ideology. This approach prevents deadlock but also avoids accountability. This chapter has posited that such objectives-implementation-based approaches might benefit from a principles-based and systemic approach to the elaboration of a more or less complete system for the regulation of the human rights impacts of economic activity. Indeed, the danger of an approach that is grounded in the aggregation of perfectly plausible single suggestions for parts of a treaty would create precisely the sort of creature that either cannot be animated – or worse, a creation that might be turned on its creators.[55] Having suggested the aggregation of principle and objective that form the foundation of the treaty elaboration project, it becomes necessary to develop principles for the exercise of choices among them.

Negotiation will tend to focus on three classes of technical provisions, all of which look ideologically adrift, but each of which is embedded with principle and the choices of ideology moving the elaboration project forward. These classes of provisions include structural provisions,

---

[53] For an excellent analysis see D. Cassel and A. Ramasastry, White Paper: Options for a Treaty on Business and Human Rights, Prepared for American Bar Association, Center for Human Rights and The Law Society of England and Wales, (American Bar Association, May 2015), https://business-humanrights.org/sites/default/files/documents/whitepaperfinal%20ABA%20LS%206%2022%2015.pdf (last accessed 4 September 2016).

[54] See, e.g., A. Gutman and D. Thompson, 'The Mindsets of Political Compromise' (2010) 8 (4) *Reflections* 1125, www.upenn.edu/president/images/president/pdfs/Mindsets-Political-Compromise-Amy-Gutmann-2010.pdf (last accessed 2 September 2016).

[55] One can ascertain a sense of this challenge and the means by which other international bodies have sought to deal with it in the context of the Climate Treaty Draft. See, e.g., John H. Cushman, Jr., 'New Climate Treaty Draft Still a Tangled Mess, but Growing Clearer' *Inside Climate News* (27 July 2015) https://insideclimatenews.org/carbon-copy/27072015/new-climate-treaty-draft-tangled-clearer-paris-talks-UN (last accessed 7 December 2016). Cf. A. Margalit, *On Compromise: And Rotten Compromises* (Princeton University Press, 2010).

substantive provisions and process provisions. These inter-connections are discussed in turn.

Substantive provisions touch on the normative heart of the treaty. The provisions go to the issue of the human rights that are to be legalized and enforced against enterprises (and others). The plausible variations on possible provisions and approaches follow from the embrace of any variation of the framing principles. A transformationalist perspective, for example, might approach the issue of rights coverage by using treaty elaboration to produce a *catalogue of legally cognizable rights under international law* and eventually under the domestic legal orders of states. The difficulty for transformationalists would consist in the contents of that catalogue. A number of alternative approaches are possible. The Treaty could elaborate this catalogue of rights – and even frame new ones as it likes. Alternatively, the Treaty might itself create a secretariat or other body with the authority to elaborate those catalogues of rights. A third alternative would follow the form of the Rome Statute[56] and vest an intergovernmental organization with the authority to further elaborate human rights from one or several sources.[57] However, an adherent of status quo framing principles would reject this approach, and those provisions. They might be inclined to approach the issue as collateral to the treaty objective and choose provisions that merely reference the conventional obligations of states within current international law, now directed as well to transnational enterprises. Evolutionary principles would reject both approaches in favour of a more limited approach, one that might merely legalize the UNGP 2nd Pillar and create an international obligation for states to embed this in their domestic orders. Plausible under this approach would be additional provisions to establish a centralized administration to promote coherence or to permit states to develop their own contextually based implementation regimes.

---

[56] Rome Statute of the International Criminal Court, art. 25, July 17, 1998, 2187 U.N.T.S. 90 (entered into force 1 July 2002).

[57] On the governance or regulatory authority within the Rome Statute framework, see, e.g., Elements of Crimes ICC-ASP/1/3(part II-B) (2011) www.icc-cpi.int/NR/rdonlyres/ 336923D8-A6AD-40EC-AD7B-45BF9DE73D56/0/ElementsOfCrimesEng.pdf (last accessed 20 July 2016); see also, A. Kuenyehia, 'The International Criminal Court: Challenges and Prospects, Annual Lecture on Human Rights and Global Justice, Center for International Law and Justice (CILJ)' (2010) 6 *Florida A&M University Law Review* 89.

The same classification of plausible alternatives, and their assessment, focuses on the issue of the objects of regulation as well as rights-holders.[58] Beyond individuals, others might also hold rights. In many constitutional traditions, juridical persons are also entitled to the protections of fundamental rights, including corporations.[59] More interestingly, there is no logical reason why the constraints of human rights in institutional activities ought not to extend to civil society actors, religious institutions and to international organizations themselves. The assessment of inclusion will thus be tested against framing principles and its expression tested against second order structure and methodological principles.

Substantive provisions will also have to confront a number of important technical issues with important substantive consequences, such as treaty triggers, sovereign immunity, complicity and the scope of the liability. There are two principle ways of triggering rights protection, status (only identified enterprises bear the burdens of the treaty) or transactions (only specified transactions will trigger liability).[60] Sovereign immunity touches on issues of protection against state liability or amenability to litigation, with respect to its obligations under the treaty.[61] In the human rights context, transformationalists might argue that states ought to be stripped entirely of their sovereign immunity. Yet less developed states might find this works to the advantage of developed states that can afford to bear the risk and which have governmental structures in place better able to mitigate risks.[62] Complicity touches on the legal effects of involvement in or facilitating the acts of states.[63] Evolutionary principles might incline towards provisions that impose

---

[58] Cf., M. Fox, Comment: 'What's So Special About Multinational Enterprises?: A Comment on Avi-Yonah' (2004) 42 *Columbia Journal of Transnational Law* 551; and generally W. Baxter, 'Choice of Law and the Federal System' (1963) 16 *Stanford Law Review* 1; L. Kramer, 'Rethinking Choice of Law' (1990) 90 *Columbia Law Review* 277.

[59] See, e.g., *Citizens United v. Federal Election Commission*, 558 U.S. 310 (2010).

[60] There are exceptions. The German Enterprise law might provide a framework that could be internationalized. See, e.g., T. Raiser, 'The Theory of Enterprise Law in the Federal Republic of Germany' (1988) 36 (1) *The American Journal of Comparative Law* 111. Yet any attempt to create a new juridical person out of the parts of a multi-entity system, of which the autonomy of the individual parts is a central concept in the enterprise law of virtually every state, may prove to be a difficult problem indeed.

[61] Cf., I. Diaz, 'A Critique of Proposals to Amend the Foreign Sovereign Immunities Act to Allow Suits Against Foreign Sovereigns for Human Rights Violations' (2002) 32 *University of Miami Inter-American Law Review* 137.

[62] Discussed in L. Backer, 'Ideologies of Globalization and Sovereign Debt: Cuba and the IMF' (2006) 24 *Penn State International Law Review* 497.

[63] Discussed in the UNGP, supra, n. 2, ¶ 17 Commentary.

liability on companies that are involved in the wrongful acts of states; transformationalists might also include liability, for states involved in the wrongful acts of companies should be equally liable along with the principal actor.[64]

Structural Provisions touch on issues of the operation of the substantive provisions of the treaty itself. A fundamental issue touches on the character of the treaty – whether it is self-executing,[65] whether it ought to have direct effect[66] and, in the most transformative aspect, whether the Treaty or some of its substantive elements ought to be recognized as *jus cogens*.[67] Under status quo principles, most of these alternatives embedded in treaty provisions would be unacceptable;[68] although, a modification of legal hierarchies within states might not.[69] Even here, however, a structural principle of state authority would incline towards a permissive rather than mandatory approach since some states assert full authority to interpret international law in their domestic legal order.[70]

Another set of structural issues goes to the institutional structures that may be built around the treaty.[71] Alternatives focus on the construction of an international institutional architecture which, in some cases, is seen

---

[64] See, e.g., R. Thompson, A. Ramasastry and M. Taylor, 'Translating Unocal: The Expanding Web of Liability for Business Entities Implicated in International Crimes' (2009) 40 *George Washington University International Law Review* 841; A. Mamolea, 'The Future of Corporate Aiding and Abetting Liability Under the Alien Tort Statute: A Roadmap' (1998) 51 *Santa Clara Law Review* 79; A. Ramasastry, 'Secrets and Lies? Swiss Banks and International Human Rights' (1998) 31 *Vanderbilt Journal of Transnational Law* 325.

[65] See, e.g., *Medellín v. Texas*, 552 U.S. 491 (2008).

[66] Direct effect has been well refined within the law of the European Union. See, e.g., S. Robin-Olivier, 'The Evolution of Direct Effect. Stocktaking, Problems, Projections' (2014) 12 (1) *International Journal of Constitutional Law* 165.

[67] Vienna Convention on the Law of Treaties (1969), U.N. Doc. A/CONF.39/27.

[68] T. Meron, 'On a Hierarchy of International Human Rights' (1986) 80 *American Journal of International Law* 1.

[69] Consider, e.g., German Basic Law art. 25 ('The general rules of international law shall be an integral part of federal law. They shall take precedence over the laws and directly create rights and duties for the inhabitants of the federal territory') www.btg-bestellservice.de/pdf/80201000.pdf (last accessed 20 June 2016).

[70] See, e.g., L. De Jesus, 'The Inter-American Court on Human Rights' Judgement in *Artavia Murillo v. Costa Rica* and Its Implications for the Creation of Abortion Rights in the Inter-American System of Human Rights' (2014) 16 *Oregon Review of International Law* 225, 243 (referencing Juzgado Federal de Salta No. 1 [Juzg. Fed.] [Federal Court of Salta No. 1], 8/7/2013, 'Lodi Ortiz Andrea Melisa-Larran Cristian c. Swiss Medical s/ amparo,' Expte. No. 61000007/13, (Arg.).)

[71] Cf. L. Helfer, 'Understanding Change in International Organizations: Globalization and Innovation in the ILO' (2006) 59 *Vanderbilt Law Review* 649, 657–670.

to be essential. These can take a variety of forms – from a secretariat with a small staff that provides some centralized support and monitoring capacities, to a full-blown quasi-governmental apparatus with the authority to develop interpretations and elaborations of basic treaty provisions. A third set of structural issues goes to the problem of states in weak governance and conflict zones.[72] There are a number of models developed by international actors in recent years to engage this question.[73] The UNGP address the issue in part, focusing on the problems for enterprises in conflict zones.[74]

Process provisions revolve around the scope and nature of judicial remedies. These are more complex than merely the choice of remedial mechanism: they touch on issues of the judicialization of social relations, of the distribution of power among political actors and the judiciary, and on accountability for a remedial mechanism that at once must be responsive to law as a political instrument and protected from political influence in specific instances.[75] One set of issues touches on *judicial interpretation*,[76] with alternatives ranging from national control to international control through a centralized judicial body akin to a regional human rights court.

Another set of issues is tied more directly to *access to remedies*. The nature of those provisions will be heavily dependent on the principles to be advanced by the treaty, whether they be evolutionary or transformational, and whether they are intended to respect national customs and traditions or burst through them. Among these are issues of access to courts,[77] universal jurisdiction[78] and

---

[72] Discussed in L. Backer, 'Corporate Social Responsibility in Weak Governance Zones' (2016) 13 *Santa Clara Journal of International Law* 297.

[73] Chief among them the *Organization for Economic Cooperation and Development, OECD Risk Awareness Tool For Multinational Enterprises in Weak Governance Zones (2006)* www.oecd.org/daf/inv/corporateresponsibility/36885821.pdf (last accessed 10 June 2016).

[74] UNGP, supra, n. 2 Principles ¶¶ 7, 17 and 23.

[75] R. Hirschl, *Towards Juristocracy: The Origins and Consequences of the New Constitutionalism* (Harvard University Press, 2004); C. Harlow, 'Global Administrative Law: The Quest for Principles and Values' (2006) 17 *European Journal of International Law* 187; generally, J. Waldron, *Law and Disagreement* (Oxford, 1999).

[76] Cf., M. Van Alstine, 'Dynamic Treaty Interpretation' (1998) 146 *University of Pennsylvania Law Review* 687; S. Seck, 'Transnational Business and Environmental Harm: A TWAIL Analysis of Home State Obligations' (2011) 3 *Trade, Law & Development* 164 (in the context of reconsidering the character of extraterritoriality).

[77] See, e.g., R. Sandefur, 'The Fulcrum Point of Equal Access to Justice: Legal and Nonlegal Institutions of Remedy' (2008) 42 *Loyola L.A. Law Review* 949.

[78] There are those among treaty proponents who might embrace the idea of the universal jurisdiction of all states over all objects of international law with respect to violations of international *law*. For the argument that universal jurisdiction over violations of

non- judicial remedial mechanisms.[79] For example, those under the OECD Guidelines for Multinational Enterprises have at times substantially broadened standing and even venue rules.[80] Similar issues arise as well with respect to rules of joint and several liability. These provide a back-door to the transformation of modern corporate law and corporate governance principles by permitting liability across autonomous juridical personalities without the need to change the form or national principles through which they are created and regulated.

One can now suggest the connection between the substantive provisions and the structuring principles. Consider the issue of a simple provision that might read something like this: 'The International Bill of Human Rights constitutes the fundamental law of every State adhering to this Treaty, is explicitly self-executing, and its provisions will be given direct effect by individuals in the courts of every adhering State.' The provision consists of three integrated effects. The first is substantive – the provision would require all states to transpose a quite specific set of international law and norms into its domestic legal order. The second is structural – the provision would provide for direct effect of its obligations, producing legal rights for individuals at the time the treaty is effective. And the third is procedural – the provision would open the courts of all adhering states to claims of individuals based on the substantive rights provided. However, the application of framework principles would yield substantially different approaches to the drafting of this provision, with substantially different results. Status quo principles may yield a provision in which adhering States may opt into such a provision, but which would otherwise be aspirational and discretionary in all respects. On the other hand, evolutionary approaches might yield a provision that seeks to make some or all of the provision mandatory, depending on the interpretation of the mandate. It might make all of its components mandatory but provide an opt-out for States. Or it might make the substantive provision mandatory but refrain from either direct

---

international law already exists within the jurisprudence of the United States, see, J. Paust, 'Kiobel, Corporate Liability, and the Extraterritorial Reach of the ATS' (2012) 53 *Virginia Journal of International Law Digest* 18, 18–35, 20–29. See generally M. Cherif Bassiouni, 'Universal Jurisdiction for International Crimes: Historical Perspectives and Contemporary Practice' (2001) 42 *Virginia Journal of International Law* 81.

[79] See, e.g., G. de Beco, *Non-Judicial Mechanisms for the Implementation of Human Rights in European States* (Bruylant, 2009).

[80] See, e.g., *Initial Assessment by the UK National Contact Point for the OECD Guidelines for Multinational Enterprises: Survival International and Vedanta Resources plc*, 27 March 2009, available www.business-humanrights.org/Links/Repository/969215/jump.

effect or self-execution. The transformative approach might make the entire provision mandatory and enforceable against any state and any enterprise in the courts of any other state. Institutional and systemic considerations would then shape the centring of the provision and its institutional structures, depending on whether the principle of strong international or strong national focus is adopted. With the former, one might expect additional treaty provisions creating a centralized international interpretation mechanism, an international secretariat for technical assistance and accountability, and perhaps even an interpretive court. With the latter, one would expect a greater tolerance for national approaches and more significant protections for national resolution. Structuring flexibility among these alternatives is given coherence by the cross-cutting framework and methodology principles. They provide clarity both for drafting and negotiating of a treaty where the object is coherence rather than a symbolic gesture constructed out of what one can achieve. They provide the principles on the basis of which the treaty can be given concrete form and coherence by providing a framework that can be used to assess provisions in light of the principles adopted for the elaboration of the treaty, that is, to make principled pragmatic choices.

The circle is now complete. Choices among treaty provisions must be assessed against standards, which are themselves derived from coherent framing principles. Those principles themselves are understood only in the context of the effects they produce through the provisions adopted. 'Principles speaks to normative choice; pragmatism speaks to its embedding in context, to an assessment of the truth or value of principle or beliefs in terms of the success of their practical application.'[81] These considerations bring one back to the larger point of pragmatics, especially as practised within these technical but highly significant rules.

The elaboration of the treaty will not be an elaboration of principle but give expression to structures of rights and the remedial mechanisms to vindicate them. It will not serve as a manifesto of ideological purity, or of the consensus ideology of human rights in the international sphere, but be a roadmap for the legalization of obligation in states and enterprises. That roadmap, those structures and that framework, will be built through the construction of a coherent, deep and complex system of obligation, rights and remedies – of directions to states, to the international community, to enterprises and individuals. It is code-building at its most complex and the extension of judicial authority beyond its current limits.

[81] *Ibid.*

The elaboration of the treaty is, at bottom, an exercise in pragmatism in the service of a specific set of objectives.

4.5   Conclusion

Where does this discussion leave the treaty movement? In a sense, it suggests the fundamental difficulties of coherence in the project of human rights legalization at the international level.[82] It also suggests, again, the difficulties of legalization as a basis for the regulatory governance of societal behaviours in the economic sphere. That difficulty is augmented precisely because all stakeholders have been united in the objective of achieving a treaty, but not on the principles that must be given effect by its provisions (and against which the choice among provision ought to be made). 'What is clear for the moment is that the politics of the drive toward a treaty, and the defense of the UNGP, has produced a mountain of sloppy thinking. Or better, perhaps, a landscape littered with rhetorical tropes (in the form of academic and policy arguments) that veil both framing principle, the character of choice and its effects, and the principles that may be necessary to assess and choose among alternatives.'[83]

The influential and powerful stakeholders in the international community driving the treaty elaboration process will have their creature. They will assemble from the charnel houses of international law and policy the bits and pieces of a creature that is made in their image. However, that bricolage of legalization will require more than the act of aggregation to animate it – to produce from this assemblage a self-referencing[84] system that furthers the objectives for which it was created. The chapter has suggested a way to think through these structuring issues, and a means for practising principled pragmatism in the assessment and choice among the large number of variants that together will serve as the provisions that will give the treaty its form and effects, out of which its framework principles may be advanced.

---

[82] See also Chapter 3 by Sheldon Leader in this book.   [83] *Ibid.*
[84] The self-referencing nature of a coherent system refers to its relational self-production that governs its capacity to have contacts with its environment. It touches on the framing of a system that can operate autonomously by itself, producing all necessary rules from the application of the principles that set it apart from other systems of rules or operation. See, R. Poli, 'The Complexity of Self-Reference: A Critical Evaluation of Luhmann's Theory of Social Systems' (April 2010) 50 Università degli Studi di Trento Dipartimento di Sociologia e Ricerca Sociale, Quaderno, http://web.unitn.it/files/quad50.pdf (last accessed 3 September 2016).

The Need for a Treaty

Expectations on Counter-Hegemony and the Role of Civil Society

DANIEL M ARAGÃO AND MANOELA C ROLAND

5.1 Introduction

Over the last three decades, a growing number of studies have shown how legal privileges bestowed on transnational corporations (TNCs) have increased their economic and political power.[1] When perusing research on neoliberal hegemony, corporate power and the absence of effective global governance mechanisms for addressing current world challenges, it becomes more evident that there is a gap between the rights and the responsibilities of corporations. This gap puts the call for peoples' control over corporations at the centre of demands on governance.

This chapter aims to reflect on opportunities generated by the current negotiations of a treaty within an Open-ended Intergovernmental Working Group (OEIGWG), namely, for building counter-hegemony and the role of civil society in this process. First, it presents an analysis on 'hegemony' as an essential concept for understanding world order and the role that international organizations play in the legitimatization of the system. While there are divergent opinions as to whether it is possible to build counter-hegemony by engaging with international organizations, most civil society organizations (CSOs) share the view that the current governance space within international organizations – and at the United Nations (UN) in particular – should not be entirely abandoned and could be used to strengthen social demands.

Section 5.3 of the chapter then presents the trajectory of the debate on 'human rights and business'[2] (HRB) at the UN in the lead up to the

---

[1] See S. Gill and A. C. Cutler (eds.), *New Constitutionalism and World Order* (Cambridge University Press, 2014); S. Soederberg, *Corporate Power and Ownership in Contemporary Capitalism* (Routledge, 2010); J. H. Zubizarreta and P. Ramiro, *Contra la Lex Mercatoria* (Icaria, 2015); P. Muchlinski, *Multinational Enterprises and the Law*, 2nd edn. (Oxford University Press, 2007)

[2] We prefer to call it HRB rather than 'business and human rights' (BHR) to stress the normative hierarchy of human rights over business interests.

current negotiations on a binding instrument for TNCs. This debate has the potential to challenge two decades of a neoliberal approach to this issue at the UN. Finally, the chapter points to the role of global civil society in this debate. Here, the analysis will highlight the role of global civil society in getting the binding instrument Resolution 26/9 passed in the Human Rights Council (HRC) in June 2014, and during the OEIGWG's First Session on the treaty which took place in Geneva in July 2015. It will also identify strategic next steps that could be taken in order to guarantee effective participation of CSOs and to ensure that the voices of the victims are heard by all stakeholders.

This chapter presents a critical analysis of the ways in which the UN adopted a neoliberal approach to human rights and development, and observes how the current treaty process represents an opportunity for the UN to put back on track a people-centred approach to human rights. This perspective shines light on civil society participation in the process based on the experience of the First Session (public speeches and the UN live webcast) of the OEIGWG. We draw attention to the obligation of states to protect the treaty negotiations from corporate capture and the need to learn from social initiatives on how to build human rights norms 'from the below'. From this perspective, it is suggested that mechanisms to prevent corporate capture of the process be put in place. It is also indicated how the UN treaty process could learn from the normative dimension of the International Peoples Treaty on the Control of Transnational Corporations (Peoples Treaty),[3] a document produced by a large number of CSOs and social movements around a global campaign to confront corporate abuses of human rights.

5.2   Building Hegemony and Counter-Hegemony through International Organizations

What is the purpose of an international treaty on HRB? To understand what is at stake in this debate, one must first discuss the role of inter-governmental organizations and their norms in the current world order. There are several ways of looking at these international organizations. Theoretical approaches to international relations diverge on the political significance, the functionalities and potentialities of international

---

[3] 'International Peoples Treaty on the Control of Transnational Corporations' (December 2014), www.stopcorporateimpunity.org/wp-content/uploads/2016/11/PeoplesTreaty-EN-mar2015-1.pdf (last accessed 30 December 2016).

organizations.[4] Institutions such as international organizations, human rights and global civil society are intrinsic to the liberal theoretical tradition of international relations. As a result, they have been historically associated to the process of capitalist expansionism worldwide. However, they have also represented the ways in which social struggles gained space and visibility in the international sphere.

This chapter uses Robert Cox's Neo-Gramscian approach to international relations, particularly his approach to hegemony in the world order and the role played by international organizations in that context.[5] Based on Gramsci's studies at the national level, Cox applies Gramsci's concept of hegemony and other related concepts such as historic bloc, passive revolution and *transformismo* to the international political arena. He differentiates hegemony from dominance: 'A period in which a world hegemony has been established can be called hegemonic and one in which dominance of a hegemonic kind prevails, nonhegemonic'.[6] The idea of hegemony has to do with convergence or consensus on a kind of world order 'expressed in universal norms, institutions and mechanisms which lay down general rules of behavior ... rules which support the dominant model of production'.[7] While the creation of international organizations or, more generally, their institutionalization is connected to hegemonic strategies, this process is not limited to the quest for hegemony: 'Institutions may become the anchor for such a hegemonic strategy since they lend themselves both to the representation of diverse interests and to the universalisation of policy'.[8]

Gramsci's approach on hegemony and Cox's adaptation of it for his analysis of the world order is of particular relevance to the discussion of the current hegemonic project centred on corporate power and its globalizing neoliberal ideology. It is also central to understanding the role of international organizations (such as the UN) in the dissemination

---

[4] See, for instance, the debates brought by M. Barnett and M. Finnemore, *Rules for the World: International Organizations in Global Politics* (Cornell University Press, 2004); C. Murphy, *International Organization and Industrial Change: Global Governance since 1850* (Oxford University Press, 1994); L. L. Martin and B. Simmons, 'Theories and Empirical Studies of International Institutions' (1998) 4 *International Organization* 52; J. Mearsheimer, 'The False Promise of International Institutions' (1994/95) 3 *International Security* 19.

[5] R. Cox, 'Gramsci, Hegemony and International Relations: An Essay in Method' (1983) 12 *Millennium Journal of International Studies* 162.

[6] *Ibid.*, 170.   [7] *Ibid.*, 172.

[8] R. Cox, 'Social Forces, States and World Orders: Beyond International Relations Theory' in R. O. Keohane (ed.), *Neorealism and its Critics* (Columbia University Press, 1986), 204 at 219.

of ideas and consensus building. Institutional changes reflect changes occurring in the hegemonic project. This chapter discusses the challenges stemming from the context in which a binding instrument for TNCs on human rights is being negotiated. Special attention should be given to the specific ways international organizations can promote and help perpetuate a hegemonic project. Cox notes:

> Indeed, international organization functions as the process through which the institutions of hegemony and its ideology are developed. Among the features of international organization which express its hegemonic role are the following: (1) they embody the rules which facilitate the expansion of hegemonic world orders; (2) they are themselves the product of the hegemonic world order; (3) they ideologically legitimate the norms of the world order; (4) they co-opt the elites from peripheral countries; and (5) they absorb counterhegemonic ideas.[9]

When Cox first wrote on the issue of hegemony in international relations in the early 1980s, he described the process of the internationalization of the world economy, which he and other scholars such as Stephen Gill and William Robinson later referred to as 'capitalist neoliberal globalization'. In this context, they make reference to the emergence of a 'transnational capitalist class'[10] or 'globalizing elites'[11] as part of changes to state structures and the global structure of production. This means that even the states which have developed citizen rights and democratic institutions tend to adapt to the rules of a 'market civilization'.[12] Gill describes 'market civilization' as a world order that 'involves a more "liberalized" and commodified set of historical structures, driven by the restructuring of capital and a shift politically, to the right ... This process involves the spatial expansion and social deepening of economic liberal definitions of social purpose and possessively individualist patterns of action and politics.'[13] Gill identifies this process as part of the dialectic of integration and disintegration. For example, the integration of markets leads to social disintegration due to setbacks in historical achievements in the area of human rights and democracy.

In the past few decades, TNCs have gained more power than ever, which has been guaranteed, among others, by international/regional/bilateral free trade and investment agreements. These agreements give

---

[9] Cox, 'Gramsci, Hegemony and International Relations', n. 5, 172.
[10] Cox, 'Social Forces, States and World Forces', n. 8, 234; W. I. Robinson, *A Theory of Global Capitalism* (Johns Hopkins University Press, 2004).
[11] S. Gill, *Power and Resistance in the New World Order* (Palgrave Macmillan, 2003).
[12] *Ibid.*   [13] *Ibid.*, 117.

prerogatives to corporations, thus treating them as special subjects in the international system. However, no responsibilities and effective constraints can be imposed on their worldwide expansion. The adaptation of national, regional and international law to satisfy market interests or to harmonize them with *lex mercatoria* is what Gill calls 'new constitutionalism'.[14]

Corporations continue to gain more economic, political and juridical power at the global level, which is not counterbalanced by the establishment of effective rules to hold them responsible for their direct and indirect participation in human rights violations. As special subjects with an unusual amount of power in the global arena, they take part in central governance spaces and decisions that force constraints upon states and international organizations. The opposite is not true: other actors such as CSOs do not seem to have the strength needed to impose regulations on corporations. Ensuring compliance with human rights obligations is constantly left to a set of flexible, voluntary and self-regulated norms that these unusually fortunate subjects define for themselves: 'the importance of corporations in the global political economy may lie precisely in their disintegration, in their ability to continually define and redefine the limits of their risks and responsibilities'.[15]

However, resistance to corporate power has increased since the 1990s, with mass protests being held in parallel to the meetings of international economic organizations. A few notable examples include the 'Battle in Seattle' during the World Trade Organization Ministerial Meeting in 1998 and the convergence of social movements and CSOs at the World Social Forum, whose first edition was held in 2001. These new forms of transnational resistance 'pointed to the inability of ruling groups to sustain hegemony in *civil society*'.[16] Although it is not clear what direction a counter-hegemonic project will take in the years to come, grassroots and global justice movements continue to fight to contest or define the agendas of international organizations. Their goal is often to stop global policies – mainly those proposed by public-private partnerships and that promote a private corporate approach to governance – from advancing.

---

[14] 'In effect, new constitutionalism confers privileged rights of citizenship and representation to corporate capital, whilst constraining the democratization process that has involved struggles for representation for hundreds of years.' *Ibid.*, 132.

[15] L. Amoore, 'Making the Modern Multinational' in C. May (ed.), *Global Corporate Power* (Lynne Rienner Publisher, 2006), 47 at 62.

[16] Robinson, n. 10, 175.

In the 1990s, while neoliberal policies were being implemented by state policymakers, major human rights conferences were taking place at the international level, spreading the promises of liberal internationalism. By the end of the decade, it became clear that these promises would not be consolidated under the same culture of rights that was promoted before. The Global Compact and the Millennium Development Goals (MDGs) became the symbols of the new flexible and pragmatic approaches to which the UN would give priority. At the same time, however, UN mandate holders such as the special rapporteurs used to participate regularly in counter-hegemonic spaces such as the World Social Forum. This fuelled expectations that the UN would continue to play its historical role in liberal (and not neoliberal) terms. The next section analyses the challenges presented by the UN initiatives, or what may be called their deviation.

5.3   Human Rights and Business: The Role of the United Nations

Due to the state-centric logic of the international order, states are recognized as the main subjects of international law: they must comply with human rights standards and have the responsibility of remedying violations. This logic is also justified by the fact that states have always been the main potential human rights violators. However, as the globalization of business activity has been intensifying since the 1970s, there are growing demands in both national and international spheres for more effective mechanisms to protect human rights violations by corporations. This is because the strengthening of corporate power has not been accompanied by the improvement of instruments to regulate business activity, especially in relation to human rights violations.

International economic organizations such as the World Bank and the International Monetary Fund have played an essential role in promoting free trade agreements and capitalist globalization. In the 1990s and 2000s, the UN also converted to neoliberal globalization by associating itself with TNCs through initiatives such as the Global Compact and several public-private partnerships set up to perform the roles of the UN, its agencies and funds. One of the architects behind this political shift was John Ruggie, an intellectual who argues for a social constructivist view of international relations. This is particularly evident in his earlier approach to multi-lateralism and his current defence of globally embedded liberalism.[17]

---

[17]   See J. Ruggie, 'International Regimes, Transactions, and Change: Embedded Liberalism in the Postwar Economic Order' (1982) 2 *International Organization* 36; J. Ruggie,

During his position as the UN Assistant Secretary-General for Strategic Planning (1997–2001), Ruggie developed the Global Compact. Later, he worked as the Secretary-General's Special Representative for Business and Human Rights (SRSG) during 2005–2011 and drafted the Guiding Principles on Business and Human Rights (GPs). His view on multilateralism is clearly opposed to that of Robert Cox:

> Cox clearly distinguishes between multilateralism, which he sees as a potential transformative force, and the existing multilateral organizations, which in his view generally serve to extend the historic bloc of production forces and their authority. As regards the question of political purpose, we may conclude that Ruggie can be seen as a defender of domestic social intervention as an appropriate and potentially effective complement to an organized liberal economic order. Cox, by contrast, can be read as more skeptical, seeing international social interventionism as a necessary response to the limitations of the multilateral system.[18]

Developing countries organized around the so-called New International Economic Order had some level of influence in the UN during the 1960s and 1970s, particularly through the creation of two organizations with a mandate specifically on development: the United Nations Conference on Trade and Development Agreements (UNCTAD) and the United Nations Development Programme (UNDP). There were also attempts to create structures to investigate the activities of TNCs and to draft a code of conduct for their operations.[19] In comparison to that period, the UN during the period between the 1990s and the 2000s seemingly adopted an approach that was more favourable towards the networks that articulate and promote transnational capitalism (the International Chamber of Commerce, the World Economic Forum and the World Council for Sustainable Development, among others). Initiatives such as the Global Compact and the MDGs are the products of this new UN approach to HRB, whose logic has been incorporated into the mainstream through the use of terms such as 'corporate social responsibility' (CSR), 'voluntary', 'guidelines', 'programmatic goals' and 'social minimum'. Hence, the pragmatic depoliticization of the UN development

---

'Multilateralism: The Anatomy of an Institution' (1992) 3 *International Organization* 46; J. Ruggie, 'Reconstituting the Global Public Domain: Issues, Actors, and Practices' (2004) 4 *European Journal of International Relations* 10.

[18] B. Bull and D. McNeill, *Development Issues in Global Governance: Public-Private Partnerships and Market Multilateralism* (Routledge, 2007), 28.

[19] See Chapter 1 by Hamdani and Ruffing in this volume.

agenda is a reflection of the gradual adaptation of the organization to the emerging neoliberal concept of governance.[20]

To explain the evolution of the business and human rights agenda at the UN, Surya Deva and David Bilchitz divide the process into three phases.[21] The first phase was from 1972 to 1990 and involved the creation of the Commission on Transnational Corporations by the UN Economic and Social Council and the presentation of the Draft Code of Conduct for Transnational Corporations. The second phase lasted from 1997 to 2005. During this phase, the Sub-Commission on the Promotion and Protection of Human Rights, which was a subordinate body of the then Human Rights Commission, established a working group with a mandate to present an overview of the working methods and activities of TNCs.

An important moment during this second phase was the launch of the Global Compact under the leadership of the then UN Secretary General Kofi Annan in 2000. The approach of the Global Compact was the opposite to that of the Draft Norms on the Responsibility of Transnational Corporations and Other Business Enterprises with regard to Human Rights[22] presented to the Human Rights Commission in 2003 by the Sub-Commission's working group. The proposed Draft Norms were rejected by the Human Rights Commission. This decision brought to light the dispute between two factions/approaches: one that seeks to avoid confronting corporate power and thus proposes more lenient rules in an unbinding voluntary framework, and another composed of civil society activists who pursue a counter-hegemonic strategy that defends the adoption of effective and enforceable mechanisms to hold corporations responsible for human rights violations. The second group was more closely identified with the Draft Norms at the time.[23]

The third phase, from 2005 to 2011, corresponded to the appointment of Ruggie as the SRSG. In 2008, Ruggie presented his 'Protect, Respect and Remedy' Framework to the HRC. Based on this Framework, Ruggie

---

[20] D. M. Aragão, *Responsabilidade como Legitimação: Capital Transnacional e Governança Global na Organização das Nações Unidas*, PhD Dissertation (Pontifícia Universidade Católica do Rio de Janeiro, Instituto de Relações Internacionais, 2010).

[21] D. Bilchitz and S. Deva, 'The Human Rights Obligations of Business: Acritical Framework for the Future' in S. Deva and D. Bilchitz (eds.), *Human Rights Obligations of Business: Beyond the Corporate Responsibility to Respect?* (Cambridge University Press, 2013), 1 at 4–10.

[22] Sub-Commission on the Promotion and Protection of Human Rights, 'Norms on the Responsibilities of Transnational Corporations and Other Business Enterprises with Regard to Human Rights', UN Doc. E/CN.4/Sub.2/2003/12/Rev. 2 (2003).

[23] Deva and Bilchitz, n. 21; Aragão, n. 20.

in 2011 presented the GPs[24] to the HRC, which unanimously endorsed them. The GPs postulate that corporations merely have a 'responsibility' – as opposed to a legal 'duty' – to respect human rights.

It is important to note that Kofi Annan intended to adapt the UN to the structural challenges created by the acceleration of the globalization process in the 1990s. Consequently, the discourse behind initiatives such as the Global Compact focused on the need to globalize international organizations by transcending the limits of a state-centred or intergovernmental framework, as corporations and social organizations were already globally based.[25] One problem with the UN strategy is that it naturalizes the status of corporations – and not states – as key actors in the global political economy. In such a perspective, change is only possible within the rules of the game imposed by these agents and therefore, 'there is a danger that seeking to account for or explain global transformation in terms of corporate power takes business knowledge as a given and further normalizes the framing of social change in managerial terms'.[26]

The current treaty process is one where, after four decades, forces opposed to the voluntary regimes finally succeeded in the HRC adopting a resolution for a mandatory instrument to force corporations to assume their responsibilities in the area of human rights. Their goal is to challenge measures that end up reinforcing global business activities. The origins of this initiative can be traced back to the creation of the UNCTAD in the mid-1960s and the third world movement for what was called a New International Economic Order in the 1970s. The history of the demand for corporate regulation at the UN reflects the resistance of peoples, communities, CSOs and governments from the 'Global South' to the arbitrary and predatory actions of increasingly powerful companies, notably transnational ones.

In a broader context, the neoliberal logic permeating the current UN approach to development takes a pragmatic approach to partnerships with the private sector, which is believed to share UN goals on global development.[27] This perspective is evident in the recently adopted

---

[24] Human Rights Council, 'Guiding Principles on Business and Human Rights: Implementing the United Nations "Protect, Respect and Remedy" Framework', A/HRC/17/31 (21 March 2011).

[25] Aragão, n. 20.   [26] Amoore, n. 15, 63.

[27] J. P. Thérien and V. Pouliot, 'The Global Compact: Shifting the Politics of International Development?' (2006) 1 *Global Governance: A Review of Multilateralism and International Organizations* 12.

Sustainable Development Goals and their reinforcement of public-private partnerships as an innovative and efficient model for managing social policies. These partnerships work both ways: they lend legitimacy (1) to transnational capitalism, as corporations appear to be engaged in global issues promoted by the UN (what has been labelled by social activists as 'bluewashing'), and (2) to the UN which, by showing its adaptability to a neoliberal global order, is able to guarantee its funding, even if it means reinforcing the present hegemonic project. As Gill explains, a 'perspective becomes hegemonic when the theories and arguments it entails, and the social forces it embodies come to prevail in setting the agenda for debate and policy in a given historical situation'.[28]

Both the Global Compact and the GPs focus on a flexible approach to obtaining the commitment of the business community to human rights obligations. Referring to the Global Compact, David Held notes that it is possible that a first move was made to 'engag[e] companies in the promotion of core UN universal principles' since if 'this [leads] to the entrenchment of human rights and environmental standards in corporate practices, that would be a significant step forward'.[29] As time has shown and several academic and activist articles have highlighted, the Global Compact has not accomplished those expectations.[30] Held, for example, noted that 'if this is to be something other than a voluntary initiative, vulnerable to being sidestepped or ignored, then it needs to be elaborated in due course into a set of codified and mandatory rules … This would require a new international treaty, laying down elements of universal jurisdiction and clear avenues of enforcement.'[31]

In summary, mere voluntarism is not enough to respond to the historical demands for the protection of human rights against corporate activities. The international human rights system was built to give priority to binding mechanisms. In the past, the UN played an essential role in advancing national legal frameworks that are often grounded in UN human rights norms. Therefore, both states and the UN have a duty to

---

[28] Gill, n. 11, 168–169.
[29] D. Held, 'Reframing Global Governance: Apocalypse Soon or Reform' in D. Held and A. McGrew (eds.), *Globalization Theory: Approaches and Controversies* (Polity Press, 2007), 250.
[30] See S. Deva, 'Global Compact: A Critique of UN's "Public-Private" Partnership for Promoting Corporate Citizenship' (2006) 34 *Syracuse Journal of International Law & Commerce* 107; J. Nolan, 'The United Nations' Compact with Business: Hindering or Helping the Protection of Human rights?' (2005) 24 *University of Queensland Law Journal* 445.
[31] Held, n. 29, 250.

reconcile themselves with the history of human rights and work towards a binding instrument that best meets the aspirations of the peoples affected by recurring and severe human rights violations perpetrated not only by states but also by companies. The fragility of remedies at the national level requires efforts to strengthen the international human rights system by adopting mandatory norms to effectively force corporations to assume their responsibility and guarantee remedy to the victims.

5.4 Global Civil Society: Expectations on and Strategies for the Treaty

The idea of global civil society is interrelated with the history of international organizations. In the last few decades, international organizations themselves have become more inclusive and several non-state actors have intensified their collaboration (demands, financing, dialogue) with these organizations. On the one hand, one finds transnational capitalism seeking legitimacy and thus building hegemony by using all means to exert influence on global governance processes. On the other, there are CSOs, advocacy networks and social movements that have been investing some of their efforts to target agendas, campaigns, conferences and norms of international organizations (e.g., those related to the UN and its agencies and funds).

Some academics have denounced the idea of global civil society being part of a (neo)liberal approach to politics, while others see a promising role for civil society at the global level.[32] Although it is true that the work of several organizations ends up strengthening global capitalist power, there is also a long history that connects civil society struggles to resistance to national and transnational human rights violations. From the time of the activist mobilizations against human rights violations committed by specific states from the 1950s to the 1980s to the current initiatives of the World Social Forum and the global justice movement to oppose new kinds of global authority, there has been a strategic shift in their approach.[33] Collaboration with the UN has been an essential part of this struggle. Falk refers to this shift as 'new globalism':

---

[32] For a profound analysis on this subject, see M. Kenny and R. Germain, 'The Idea(l) of Global Civil Society' in R. Germain and M. Kenny (eds.), *The Idea of Global Civil Society: Politics and Ethics in a Globalizing Era* (Routledge, 2005), 1–15.

[33] R. Falk, 'Human Rights and Global Civil Society: On the Law of Unintended Effects' in P. Gready (ed.), *Fighting for Human Rights* (Routledge, 2004), 33 at 40.

Global civil society self-constructed as a political reality arose out of an oppositional mentality. Such attitudes were shaped in the crucible of activism associated with human rights during the Cold War, and in relation to the anti-colonial and anti-apartheid movements ... Given the expanded agenda of human rights, as including the framework of global authority structures, this effort to promote global democracy and global justice by transnational social activism could be understood as a new direction of the world human rights movement.[34]

With the advent of accelerated globalization and the multiplication of human rights violations linked to businesses, many CSOs have opted for globalizing resistance since the early 1990s. However, the UN responses so far (Global Compact and the GPs) fall far short of global civil society expectations. Even when some CSOs are engaging with these soft and voluntary initiatives, it is clear for most organizations that a stronger response is still needed. That is why the legitimacy of the UN is currently being tested by the negotiations for a treaty. Are the states and the system of states so intertwined with TNCs that their only option is to attempt to prevent such a treaty from being passed? Is it only the states from the Global North that fear the treaty due to the interests of their TNCs in exploiting people in the Global South? In which ways can the negotiations and the treaty itself help the victims?

This section aims to analyse the role of global civil society in the official and informal negotiating spaces for the treaty, while focusing on its capacity to mobilize and influence. The goal is not to come to a diagnosis on how determinant civil society advocacy was for the approval of Resolution 26/9 or to assess its current capacity to influence treaty negotiations in order to obtain more ambitious human rights protections. Rather, the purpose here is to develop an understanding of the nature of global civil society's contribution to this process and its transnational strategy of networking on the subject of HRB.

During the negotiating process, global civil society brought fundamental debates on the mechanisms and premises needed to hold business enterprises responsible for their human rights violations. They did so by using a progressive and innovative approach to the potential of directly applying international human rights norms to business, based on a logic that seeks to break with pro-business parameters of CSR. At the same time, there is lack of consensus among organized civil society entities and movements on issues such as expectations about the treaty's content, the

---

[34] *Ibid.*, 40 and 45.

way to negotiate it and even its necessity in light of the GPs. Differences on these issues prevented CSOs from adopting a unanimous position on the proposed treaty, or even the GPs for that matter.

The differences amongst CSOs on the treaty issue can be better understood when analysed according to Robert Cox's definition of civil society in his Neo-Gramscian theoretical framework. Cox notes that social movements and other groups that are part of organized civil society do not constitute a monolithic organism, since they tend to dispute space within what is categorized as global civil society.[35] Thus, there are groups that defend hegemonic premises and thereby contribute to the reproduction of transnational capitalism, while others engage in initiatives to confront the system or build counter-hegemony. It should be highlighted that in each of these two approaches there are multiple views and positions on which could be the best strategy to undermine or preserve the dominant logic.

When arguing in favour of the adoption of a binding international instrument on HRB, one common point shared among CSOs identified with a counter-hegemonic dimension of global civil society was their dissatisfaction with the existing regulatory frameworks on the human rights responsibilities of business actors, including the GPs. Therefore, one essential input from social organizations was to identify deficiencies or gaps in existing regulatory initiatives and propose changes that could be made to end the impunity that is part of the universe of business responsibility. Some of those proposals are related to elements that may positively influence a binding instrument on HRB.

As discussed in more details in section 5.5 of this chapter, among the strategies developed by civil society, special attention should be paid to the process of elaborating the Peoples Treaty. The process was officially launched in 2012 by the Global Campaign to Dismantle Corporate Power and Stop Impunity at the Peoples' Summit held in parallel to the Rio+20 Conference.[36] The importance of this process is that it created an interface for bringing hundreds of national, regional and international CSOs and social movements that take part in transnational networks together to elaborate the Peoples Treaty and the value given to producing the document 'from the below'. In this approach, the content and the means to protect the victims of corporate human rights abuses are to be

---

[35] R. Cox, 'Civil Society at the Turn of the Millennium: Prospects for an Alternative World Order' (1999) 25 (1) *Review of International Studies* 3.

[36] 'Campaign Materials', www.stopcorporateimpunity.org/?page_id=2059 (last accessed 30 December 2016).

identified through direct dialogue with affected communities and groups of victims, so as to come closer to what affected peoples understand as a more adequate way to guarantee the protection of their dignity from violations resulting from business activities.

Strategic concepts such as 'globalization from below' or 'bottom-up globalization' inform the possibilities for a counter-hegemonic agenda to confront corporate power in the current stage of global capitalism. What is at stake is the extent to which international human rights law is capable of absorbing social demands that oppose neoliberal globalization. As Santos notes: 'At stake is, first of all, the inquiry into the possibility of the counter-hegemonic use of a hegemonic tool such as law. Secondly, the inquiry is into non-hegemonic traditions of law and legality and the possibility of its mobilization in counter-hegemonic struggles.'[37]

Global civil society has always played an important role in advancing HRB regulations at the UN level by both pressing for more rigorous protections and questioning the effective commitment of companies towards UN human rights norms. The push for voluntary CSR norms is perceived as the result of the co-optation of formal regulatory spaces at the UN by business interests. One of the aspects that illustrate the importance of this contribution is precisely global civil society pressure exerted to contest the generic nature of the Global Compact, the dissolution of the working group which drafted the UN Norms and the refusal to adopt the 2003 Draft Norms. This pressure forced the then UN Secretary-General Kofi Annan to respond to the demands, but the response he gave was not the one the CSOs expected. Kofi Annan named Ruggie, the mentor of the Global Compact, as the SRSG, thereby putting the chances of building mandatory norms on hold for several years.

The double standards at the UN in relation to capitalist globalization – or, in other words, the UN support for business interests, which is contrary to its primary purpose of responding to the concerns of those affected by human rights violations – has also marked the path taken by the business and human rights agenda at the UN until now. In this scenario, CSOs that were more closely connected to the victims of violations played a historical role in delegitimizing some initiatives and presenting counter-hegemonic proposals at the same time. For example, after the unanimous approval of the GPs by the HRC, while some CSOs

---

[37] B. S. Santos, 'Beyond Neoliberal Governance: The World Social Forum' in B. S. Santos and C. A. Rodríguez-Garavito (eds.), *Law and Globalization from Below: Towards a Cosmopolitan Legality* (Cambridge University Press, 2005), 29 at 60.

are willing to build on the GPs, others see convergence around the GPs as a way to depoliticize the debate. These groups defend a counter-hegemonic agenda on HRB with a view to get a UN treaty passed and a tribunal with the power to try denunciations against corporations set up.

As stated by Gonzalo Berrón, former coordinator of the Hemispheric Social Alliance and member of the Global Campaign to Dismantle Corporate Power and Stop Impunity, the international situation for the fight for binding responsibilities for corporations in relation to human rights violations improved after the global economic crisis 'in which financial corporations were exposed for their involvement in the types of crime and irresponsible actions that led to a breakdown in the United States and later in Europe. This gave more visibility to the problem.'[38] The adoption of Resolution 26/9 in June 2014 was considered a surprising victory for global civil society. It was obtained against a backdrop of a growing number of reports of human rights violations by companies and an alarming diagnosis regarding the 'architecture of impunity'[39] that supports these economic actors and against which the GPs do not produce any significant results.

However, there is considerable disbelief in the ability of the UN to host a process of dialogue and mediation between victims of human rights violations, companies and states. The corporate capture of the UN, particularly in the 'business and human rights' agenda, was the central issue of a document entitled *Corporate Influence on the Business and Human Rights Agenda of the United Nations* published in June 2014 by MISEREOR, Brot für die Welt and Global Policy Forum.[40] Among several strategies presented in the document to counter the business

---

[38] L. C. Faria Jr., *A Batalha de Davi Contra Golias: Uma Análise Neogramsciana da Agenda das Nações Unidas em Direitos Humanos e Empresas*, Dissertação de Mestrado (Universidade Federal de Juiz de Fora, 2015), 141.

[39] On the 'architecture of impunity', Diana Aguiar and Raphaela Lopes observe: 'while the human rights norms to protect the peoples and common goods are not regulated by a system that force actors to comply with them, the norms that protect the rights of investors – especially large transnational corporations – are mandatory and binding in character. This difference generates an imbalance, which is the result of the so-called architecture of impunity in which transnational corporations are the main beneficiaries of the complicity of states and international organizations.' D. Aguiar and R. Lopes, 'Campanha Global: Desmantelemos o Poder Corporativo e Coloquemos Fim à Impunidade!' (25 June 2012) www.rebrip.org.br/noticias/campanha-global-desmantelemos-o-poder-corporativo-e-coloquemos-fim-a-impunidade-9076/ (last accessed 30 December 2016).

[40] J. Martens, *Corporate Influence on the Business and Human Rights Agenda of the United Nations, Working Paper* (MISEREOR, Brot für die Welt and Global Policy Forum, 2014).

strategy of co-optation and capture, there is the demand for 'the UN, its specialized agencies and its member states [to] adopt clear mandatory guidelines and policies for their relationship with corporations and establish comprehensive and enforceable individual and institutional conflict of interest policies, including mechanisms to allow for public scrutiny'.[41]

The report released by the International Commission of Jurists (ICJ) in June 2014, *Needs and Options for a New International Instrument in the Field of Business and Human Rights*,[42] systematizes the concerns raised by civil society that are often presented as challenges to be tackled through the treaty process. This document is the result of a consultation ICJ carried out with three main objectives: identify the existence of gaps in human rights protections in relation to corporate activity; determine if there is the need for a new international instrument to fill these gaps; and finally, identify the options on the nature, scope and elements of the instrument, if necessary, as well as the appropriate institutional forum for its elaboration and adoption. One key importance of this report lies in its methodology, which included interviews with experts, debates and extensive public consultation.[43]

The ICJ and hundreds of other CSOs have manifested their support for the treaty. Based on the documents referred to above and the Peoples Treaty, some specific recommendations – which aim to truly change the current state of affairs in relation to the corporate responsibility on human rights at the international level – are listed below:

1. It is important to adopt a binding instrument. The GPs were approved only after the regulatory content that could make corporate human rights responsibilities binding had been removed. This confirms the existence of an 'architecture of impunity'.
2. There is a need to abandon the logic of multi-stakeholderism in several UN initiatives, particularly in the negotiations on the treaty. Priority should be given to the identification of the victims' standpoint and prevention of the corporate capture of the treaty process. The problems inherent in the multi-stakeholder approach are aptly summed up as follows:

> The key question remains whether the current mainstream approach based on voluntarism and a broad consensus of all 'stakeholders' – a term which includes victims as well as offenders of human rights

---

[41] *Ibid.*, 28.
[42] International Commission of Jurists, *Needs and Options for a New International Instrument in the Field of Business and Human Rights* (ICJ, 2014).
[43] *Ibid.*, 5.

violations – is the right way to go. The evidence of ongoing human rights violations and aggressive lobbying strategies by transnational corporations suggests that it is not. It is important to re-establish a clear distinction between those who should regulate and the party to be regulated and to reject any discourse that obfuscates the fact that corporations have a fundamentally different 'primary interest' from that of government, UN agencies, CSOs and social movements: their prime interest – enshrined in their fiduciary duty – is to satisfy the interests of their owners and shareholders. The stakeholder discourse blurs this important distinction between the different actors.[44]

3. The scope of the treaty should not be restricted to the concept of serious or gross violations, as there is a risk that economic, social and cultural rights might be left out of that category. All kinds of violations perpetrated by companies must be covered and victims must be ensured maximum reparation, while the mechanisms are adjusted to the reality of each group. It is believed that the adoption of a methodology that ensures greater participation of the victims in cases would foster a creative dynamic capable of allowing for the recognition of all categories of rights, violations and reparations. This would strengthen the legal demands of those affected by business human rights violations.

4. Access to justice must be guaranteed. The urgent need to improve mechanisms to hold TNCs accountable for extraterritorial violations, together with the procedural imbalance between the victims of violations and corporations appear recurrently in the debate. Arguments in favour of establishing the criminal responsibility of corporations at the international level and the creation of an international court to impose sanctions on these companies for human rights violations should be considered.

5. The joint efforts of UN agencies to promote the creation of devices that integrate a system for monitoring and exchanging information on human rights violations committed by TNCs and to improve the transparency of national and transnational cases' situation should be reinforced. The goal should be to establish a plan based on a preventive approach in relation to business compliance with human rights norms, and guarantee an effective remedy framework to ensure that sanctions are effectively imposed on corporations and victims receive adequate reparation.

---

[44] Martens, n. 40, 28–29.

5.5   The Peoples Treaty and the Global Campaign as a Strategic Reference Point for the Proposed Treaty

The launch of the Global Campaign to Dismantle Corporate Power and Stop Impunity in 2012 united several voices that were already contesting the fundamentals of capitalist hegemony. There were various counter-hegemonic initiatives under way at that time, including a demand for a treaty on business and human rights. Advanced debates at the Third World Conference on Human Rights (Vienna+20) in June 2013, and in the first UN Regional Forum on Human Rights and Business in August 2013 in the city of Medellín, Colombia, were followed by an Ecuador-led statement released during the 24th session of the HRC.[45] Ecuador's statement highlighted the urgent need to move beyond the provisions of soft law, despite the historical efforts that the GPs represent.

The Global Campaign builds on a 'bottom-up' movement which was already under way in other related areas. For example, a network of CSOs and social movements from Europe and Latin America joined forces in the form of the Enlazando Alternativas initiative to strengthen resistance to free trade agreements. Free trade agreements weaken human rights guarantees, as well as existing mechanisms that can impose some limits on the concentration of power of transnational capital and its influence in the territories. During the 2000s, Enlazando Alternativas held three hearings of the Permanent Peoples' Tribunal (PPT), which gave greater visibility to more than 40 cases of human rights violations caused by European companies in Latin America.[46] The evidence presented by the affected communities during the PPT sessions brought to light the systematic behaviour of TNCs.

When the Global Campaign to Dismantle Corporate Power was launched, it started with a long series of consultations on how to build and adopt rules to hold TNCs responsible for what was already understood as 'crimes' at the global level. The Campaign also decided to prepare a Peoples Treaty as a document that would reflect the outcome of the struggles of CSOs and social movements against human rights violations perpetrated by corporations. The focus, therefore, was more comprehensive, as Campaign members sought to further their understanding of the forms of organization

---

[45]   Human Rights Council, 'Statement on behalf of a Group of Countries at the 24th Session of the Human Rights Council: Transnational Corporations and Human Rights' (September 2013), http://business-humanrights.org/sites/default/files/media/docu ments/statement-unhrc-legally-binding.pdf (last accessed 30 December 2016).

[46]   Enlazando Alternativas, 'The European Union and Transnational Corporations in Latin America: Policies, Instruments and Actors Complicit in Violations of the Peoples Rights', www.enlazandoalternativas.org/IMG/pdf/TPP-verdict.pdf (last accessed 30 December 2016).

of corporate power and the need to dismantle it and put an end to their impunity.

Initially, a working group was set up to initiate the process. In February 2013, the first draft of the preamble and the legal dimension was presented. The methodology included a consultation with 20 activist-experts in order to come up with a draft Treaty that would then be submitted for discussion to all organizations and movements linked to the Global Campaign. The Campaign members were also asked to submit the proposals emerging from their struggles to compose the 'Alternative Dimension' of the treaty. Two months later, a second and more elaborate version of the Peoples Treaty was completed.

Finally, in June 2014, after a period of consultation with Campaign members, the draft text was approved and presented during the 'stop corporate crime and impunity' week of mobilization held in Geneva. Between July and November 2014, new texts were added to the Alternative Dimension, and at a Global Campaign meeting in Geneva on 28 November 2014, the document was finally approved for broader global consultations.

Since then, various consultations have been held around the text of the Peoples Treaty. The importance of this document lies in its ability to bring organizations and social movements together on the issue of HRB, encourage a systematic and technical convergence of agendas and lend political legitimacy to the treaty. Another aspect is also the use of this text as a tool to support critical positions within civil society and for engaging in dialogue with states or corporations. Ultimately, this document helps CSOs to be more prepared to deal with issues that arise during the negotiating process. This, in turn, will strengthen their ability to push negotiations towards a treaty on the human rights obligations of business.

The current counter-hegemonic demand to re-politicize and reregulate may find opportunities in the UN negotiations for a binding instrument. Global civil society strategies such as the Global Campaign and the development of creative initiatives such as the Peoples Treaty have the potential to add to these efforts. In discussing alternatives to the crisis in the world order brought on by the emergence of neoliberal hegemony, Cox argues that:

> the cure can only come, perhaps as a first stage, through world regions, and ultimately at the global level; and it can only come there if it is firmly based in global society. A dual approach is involved: the building of

sufficient foundation in social organization at the base; and a creative response and initiative through multilateralism.[47]

Section D of the Peoples Treaty[48] entitled 'Legal Dimension' contains several provisions that should be part of a peoples-centred approach to HRB in the proposed binding international instrument. Although we recommend an attentive reading of all the provisions of the Peoples Treaty, we highlight below some of these provisions to reveal the creative and counter-hegemonic potential that the Peoples Treaty has as a reference to the provisions of the proposed UN treaty.

The Peoples Treaty seeks to impose obligations on three sets of actors: TNCs, international economic-financial institutions and states. Like other legal persons, TNCs 'have the obligation to respect the rule of law and must face sanctions if they do not' comply with rules under international human rights instruments.[49] The Peoples Treaty bases this obligation of private individuals (including legal person) on Article 29 of the Universal Declaration of Human Rights and other international conventions.[50] The Peoples Treaty further stipulates that as international legal entities, international economic-financial institutions '– and the members of their decision-making bodies (single-person or collegiate) – are legally liable for the violations of civil, political, social, economic, cultural and environment rights that they commit, or help to commit, either through their actions or by omission.'[51] The Peoples Treaty does not, however, absolve states from their human rights obligations. It provides: 'The fact that a human rights violation is committed by private actors does not exempt the State from its obligation to guarantee, protect and promote these rights, and to provide affected communities with access to compensation through adequate judicial means.'[52]

One key issue for the proposed UN instrument will be about the definition of a 'TNC'. The Peoples Treaty provides the following definition:

> Transnational corporations are individual entities, or groups of economic entities, that conduct activities in more than one country, regardless of the legal framework they adopt in the country of origin and the country where they carry out their activity, and that are considered both as an individual

---

[47] R. Cox, 'Globalization, Multilateralism and Democracy' (1992), 9, http://acuns.org/wp-content/uploads/2009/04/Robert-Cox.pdf (last accessed 30 December 2016).

[48] The Treaty is divided into an Introduction and five sections: Section A: Context and Background; Section B: Justification; Section C: Preamble; Section D: Legal Dimension; and Section E: Alternatives Dimension. Peoples Treaty, n. 3.

[49] *Ibid.*, para. 1.1.   [50] *Ibid.*   [51] *Ibid.*, para. 1.2.   [52] *Ibid.*, para. 1.3

and a group. A transnational corporation is any company that is made up of a parent company established according to the laws of the country in which it was created, which sets up operations in other countries through foreign direct investment or other economic-financial practices, without creating a local company, or through subsidiaries registered as local companies in accordance with the host country's legislation.[53]

One key general principle laid down by the Peoples Treaty is the hier-archical supremacy of human rights law over trade and investment laws. It declares that 'international human rights law – including international labour law and international environmental law – is hierarchically super-ior to national and international trade and investment norms, due to its binding nature and as *erga omnes* obligations'.[54] The Peoples Treaty acknowledges that the existing 'social, labour and environmental clauses incorporated into trade and investment treaties and agreements are more declarative provisions than mandatory ones' and therefore recommends that 'their regulatory weight must be changed to make them hierarchi-cally superior to the principles related to trade and investment norms.'[55]

The need for stronger and clearer extraterritorial state obligations is another issue that the proposed UN treaty would have to grapple with. On this issue, the Peoples Treaty builds on the Maastricht Principles on the Extraterritorial Obligation of States in the area of Economic, Social and Cultural Rights and lays down several provisions stressing the states' extraterritorial human rights obligations.[56] It, for example, provides:

> States where transnational corporations' headquarters are based may be charged for criminal involvement and liability in human rights violations when they pressure or try to force countries to sign trade and investment agreements that do not protect the rights of citizens and peoples, or if they do not incorporate complaint mechanisms when the implementation of the treaties generate such violations.[57]

Furthermore, the Peoples Treaty tries to articulate the notion of 'shared liability' in the context of allocation of liability within corporate groups. It provides that there 'is a shared liability between transnational corpora-tions and their subsidiaries (de jure or de facto) and their chain of suppliers, licensees and subcontractors. As they are connected to the TNC through their economic practices, they share liability for violations of civil, political, social, economic, cultural and environmental rights.'[58]

---

[53] *Ibid.*, para. 1.1.   [54] *Ibid.*, para. 2.9.   [55] *Ibid.*, para. 2.13.   [56] *Ibid.*, paras. 2.18–2.21.
[57] *Ibid.*, para. 2.18.   [58] *Ibid.*, para. 3.4.

Last but not least, the Peoples Treaty enumerates international crimes,[59] and proposes the establishment of a World Court on Transnational Corporations and Human Rights to adjudicate such crimes. The proposed World Court 'must be complementary to universal, regional and national mechanisms . . . that affected individuals and communities have access to . . . in order to obtain justice for violations of civil, political, social, economic, cultural and environmental rights.'[60] Such a 'Court would be responsible for receiving, investigating and judging complaints against transnational corporations, States and international economic-financial institutions for human rights violations and for civil and criminal liability in international economic, corporate and ecological crimes.'[61]

5.6   Conclusion

This chapter sought to respond to one central question: what are the expectations for building counter-hegemony in the negotiations on the treaty and how does global civil society contribute to this process? Over the past two decades, the UN has mostly adhered to the neoliberal and global capitalist hegemonic project. Its recent initiatives on HRB served to legitimize TNCs' globalizing goals, instead of holding them accountable for human rights violations. The neoliberal shift at the UN betrays the liberal promises in the UN Charter and the history of its human rights norms and instruments. Current negotiations on a treaty for TNCs regarding human rights could represent an opportunity for the UN to effectively engage with and commit to counter-hegemonic demands grounded in the primacy of human rights. What is at stake is whether the UN and the member states' commitments made to corporations via several public-private partnerships still allows them to develop regulations and mechanisms that could constrain business's privileged status of rule and authority in contemporary global politics. Active participation of global civil society in the treaty negotiation may, to some extent, contribute to overcoming corporate capture on the process.

   The engagement of global civil society in the treaty negotiations is part of a bigger struggle against corporate power and impunity. The Global Campaign and other related initiatives have both a normative and a strategic role that is essential to advancing the negotiations for the treaty. As a counter-hegemonic project, the Peoples Treaty also serves as a reference point that should inform the negotiations of the proposed

---

[59] *Ibid.*, paras. 5.1–5.3.   [60] *Ibid.*, para. 6.5.   [61] *Ibid.*

treaty within the UN fold. Alternatives framed as 'globalization from below' are being put forward and the UN has an opportunity to advance in the direction of a greater commitment to peoples' struggles. Both the content of the Peoples Treaty and the strategies developed by the Global Campaign offer the ground for advancing beyond the current bases of global governance, while calling for reregulation and repolicitization. This is the path to building counter-hegemony in the current state of world order.

6

Scope of the Proposed Business and Human Rights Treaty

Navigating through Normativity, Law and Politics

SURYA DEVA

6.1 Introduction

One of the most contentious issues so far in the current treaty process has been the 'scope' of the proposed instrument:[1] should the proposed treaty follow the model adopted by the Guiding Principles on Business and Human Rights (GPs)[2] and apply to all types of business enterprises, or should its applicability be limited to TNCs and other business enterprises with a transnational character in their operational activities? This discussion in my view is about the *regulatory targets* of the treaty. Although so far the frictions have mostly related only to the regulatory targets of the treaty, the scope question has another prong: the *subject matter* of the instrument. Should the proposed treaty cover all international human rights, or only selected gross or serious violations of human rights? These two prongs are interlinked in that the ambit of one will have an impact on the other and in

---

[1] The European Union (EU) and many other states from the Global North did not participate in the first session of the OEIGWG due to the proposed treaty targeting only TNCs. See C. Lopez and B. Shea, 'Negotiating a Treaty on Business and Human Rights: A Review of the First Intergovernmental Session' (2015) 1 *Business and Human Rights Journal* 111. The EU and some other states participated in the second session held in October 2016 only after a 'footnote' in the programme of work provided that the discussions in the session 'can include TNCs as well as all other business enterprises'. Human Rights Council, 'Second session of the open-ended intergovernmental working group on transnational corporations and other business enterprises with respect to human rights' www.ohchr.org/EN/HRBodies/HRC/WGTransCorp/Session2/Pages/Session2.aspx (last accessed 20 January 2017).

[2] Human Rights Council, 'Guiding Principles on Business and Human Rights: Implementing the United Nations "Protect, Respect and Remedy" Framework', A/HRC/17/31 (21 March 2011) (GPs).

154

turn influence the scope of the treaty in addressing business-related human rights abuses. For instance, if the treaty applied only to a particular type of corporations but covered all human rights or alternatively applied to all business enterprises but focused only on gross human rights violations, it will in the end have a narrow scope.

This chapter analyses the legal as well as political feasibility of various options related to the twin scope-related aspects of the proposed treaty. In terms of regulatory targets, the chapter will examine three potential options – from the treaty covering all types of business enterprises to being limited to TNCs. Due to a number of normative, legal and political reasons elaborated below, I will argue that the treaty should *ideally* apply to all business enterprises. However, if a consensus cannot be built amongst states to apply the treaty to all types of businesses, then a 'hybrid option' should be used to break the deadlock. This hybrid option could be operationalized in a number of ways. For example, while the main treaty could apply only to TNCs and other business enterprises with a transnational character, an Optional Protocol could extend its relevant provisions to all other types of business enterprises.

Regarding the subject matter of the treaty, this chapter explores three options. I will contend that the proposed treaty should not be limited to 'gross' human rights violations, because such a narrow focus might not be able to capture how people are suffering in diverse ways, especially in the Global South, from human rights abuses linked to corporate activities aimed at profit-maximization. I argue that the treaty should, therefore, cover all internationally recognized human rights, though a differentiation could be made in terms of available remedies for violations, e.g., criminal prosecution could follow only for 'gross' human rights abuses. To operationalize this idea, I propose that the treaty should include an annexure listing nine core human rights conventions adopted by the UN, eight fundamental ILO conventions, 'plus' the Universal Declaration of Human Rights (UDHR), the Rio Declaration on Environment and Development 1992 (Rio Declaration) and the UN Declaration on the Rights of Indigenous Peoples (UNDRIP). This is labelled as the 'core+' option.

However, before dealing with these two specific questions, section 6.2 of this chapter will describe the interplay between 'normative objectives' and 'political considerations' in relation to the current treaty process. A legally binding international instrument is needed not for the sake of it, but to fill certain governance gaps left by existing regulatory initiatives, including the GPs.[3] While a treaty may not be able to fill all the existing regulatory gaps, it should assist in overcoming at least some of the obstacles in holding corporations accountable for human rights violations. These normative objectives, which should have a bearing on the scope of the treaty, are, however, at odds with competing political considerations guiding the position of various states vis-à-vis the treaty. The idea of a legally binding international instrument is not new.[4] Nor is the strong opposition of many states – mostly developed states from the Global North – and business enterprises to the necessity or feasibility of such a treaty.

If we were to have a treaty on business and human rights (BHR), resolving this clash between normative objectives and political considerations will be critical to come up with a draft text which has a reasonable level of acceptance amongst states. Taking the scope of the proposed treaty as a concrete example, this chapter will show how it is possible to navigate through this clash by using creative legal solutions.

6.2   The Treaty Road: Clash between Normativity and Politics

What should guide the discussion about the proposed BHR treaty? At least two sets of variables are crucial. The first are normative objectives – linked to the high normative value enjoyed generally by the currency of human rights at the international level – behind the push for a legally binding international instrument to tame corporate power. It is trite that the current state of regulatory affairs makes it extremely difficult for the victims of corporate human rights abuses to seek justice against both states or corporations[5] and a treaty could help in redressing this situation,

---

[3] For limitations of the GPs, see Surya Deva and David Bilchitz (eds.), *Human Rights Obligations of Business: Beyond the Corporate Responsibility to Respect?* (Cambridge: Cambridge University Press, 2013); FIDH, 'Briefing Paper on Business and Human Rights: Enhancing Standards and Ensuring Redress' (March 2014).

[4] See S. Deva, 'The Human Rights Obligations of Business: Reimagining the Treaty Business', http://business-humanrights.org/sites/default/files/media/documents/reimagine_int_law_for_bhr.pdf (last accessed 10 October 2016).

[5] See G. Skinner, R. McCorquodale and O. De Schutter, *The Third Pillar: Access to Judicial Remedies for Human Rights Violations by Transnational Business* (ICAR, CORE and ECCJ, 2013); Amnesty International, *Injustice Incorporated: Corporate Abuses and the Human Rights to Remedy* (London: Amnesty International, 2014); J. Jerk, 'Corporate Liability for Gross Human Rights Abuses: Towards a Fairer and More Effective System of Domestic Law Remedies', a report prepared for the Office of the UN High Commissioner for Human Rights (2014), www.ohchr.org/Documents/Issues/Business/DomesticLawRemedies/StudyDomesticLawRemedies.pdf (last accessed 20 January 2017).

at least partially.[6] Political considerations – which will include economic, foreign policy and other interests that guide the political stand taken by states at the international level – are the second set of variables having a bearing on the fate of the proposed treaty.

Logically thinking, there should be a correlation between these two sets of variables. If human rights are important global values accepted by states and there are well-documented barriers in gaining access to an effective remedy, then the negotiation position of states should be informed, at least to some extent, by the desire to put in place a binding international framework of corporate accountability for human rights abuses. In practice, however, this correlation seems to be missing, as many states continue to employ human rights selectively to serve their political or economic goals. The challenge, therefore, is to strike a balance: the key will be to infuse as much normativity as possible in moulding the position taken by states, rather than merely sacrificing normative objectives at the altar of political considerations.

6.2.1 Normative Objectives

If the proposed BHR treaty is going to add any value to the existing regulatory landscape, it should try to accomplish some of the key normative objectives elaborated below.

6.2.1.1 Redress Multiple Asymmetries

The intersection of (transnational) business with human rights has brought to the surface several asymmetries in the current human rights framework, which the proposed treaty should try to address. The first asymmetry arises from the predominantly state-centric human rights discourse and (inter)national human rights instruments, which discourage the imposition of direct human rights obligations on non-state actors such as corporations.[7] For historic reasons, duties in relation to

---

[6] See D. Bilchitz, 'The Necessity for a Business and Human Rights Treaty' (2016) 1 *Business and Human Rights Journal* 203; ICJ, 'Needs and Options for a New International Instrument in the Field of Business and Human Rights' (June 2014), http://icj.wpengine.netdna-cdn.com/wp-content/uploads/2014/06/NeedsandOptionsinternationalinst_ICJReportFinalelecvers.com pressed.pdf (last accessed 10 October 2016); Deva, 'Reimagining the Treaty Business', n. 4.

[7] The traditional distinction between 'subjects' and 'objects' of international law is, however, becoming increasingly problematic. R. Higgins, *Problems and Process: International Law and How We Use It* (Oxford University Press, 1994), 49–55; S. Deva, 'Human Rights Violations by Multinational Corporations and International Law: Where from Here?' (2003) 19 *Connecticut Journal of International Law* 1, 50–54; R. McCorquodale, 'The

such rights developed – subject to certain exceptions[8] – with reference to states. However, it does not mean that other non-state entities are (or should be) free from such duties.[9] As Joseph Raz rightly points out, 'there is no closed list of duties which correspond to the right ... *A change of circumstances may lead to the creation of new duties based on the old right* ... This dynamic aspect of rights, *their ability to create new duties*, is fundamental to any understanding of their nature and function in practical thought.'[10]

Human rights are not uni-relational: if the objective is to protect human dignity, then duties need not be confined to the state-individual matrix.[11] In fact, the nature of violators – public agencies or private actors, national or transnational, big or small – matters little for the victims. Therefore, the proposed treaty should acknowledge that companies have human rights obligations independent of states, something what the GPs already do albeit in a non-obligatory manner. Raz's 'change of circumstances' threshold could be easily satisfied at this point of time. The illustrative examples of such a change can include some of the following:

- the outsourcing of essential public services such as education, health, water, sanitation, telecommunication and electricity by the state to private corporate actors creates a situation where profit considerations dictate the availability of, and access to, basic human needs;[12]
- the privatization of war and security enabling private military and security companies (PMSCs) to violate human rights at will, thus breaking the hitherto monopoly of states in this sphere;[13]

Individual and the International Legal System' in M. D. Evans (ed.), *International Law*, 4th edn. (Oxford University Press, 2014), 280 at 281–284.

[8] See, for example, duties imposed by international humanitarian law. Moreover, the Indian Constitution of 1950 did conceive – much before the evolution of the horizontal effect human rights – certain fundamental rights to be binding even on private actors. Granville Austin, *The Indian Constitution: Cornerstone of a Nation* (Clarendon Press, 1966), 51, and generally M. Singh, 'Fundamental Rights, State Action and Cricket in India' (2006) 13 *Asia Pacific Law Review* 203.

[9] For instance, Section 8(2) of the Constitution of South Africa 1996 provides: 'A provision of the Bill of Rights binds a natural or a juristic person if, and to the extent that, it is applicable, taking into account the nature of the right and the nature of any duty imposed by the right.' See generally D. Oliver and J. Fedtke (eds.), *Human Rights and the Private Sphere: A Comparative Study* (Routledge-Cavendish, 2007).

[10] J. Raz, *The Morality of Freedom* (Clarendon Press, 1986), 171 (emphasis added).

[11] On this point, see also Bilchitz's chapter 7 in this volume.

[12] See S. Narula, 'The Right to Food: Holding Global Actors Accountable under International Law' (2005) 44 *Columbia Journal of Transnational Law* 691.

[13] See, for example, Human Rights Council, 'Report of the Working Group on the use of mercenaries as a means of violating human rights and impeding the exercise of the right

- the emergence of public-private partnerships for big infrastructure projects with direct impact on the lives as well as human rights of people affected by such projects;[14] and
- the expectation from business to contribute to achieving the Sustainable Development Goals (SDGs).[15]

Second, the proposed treaty should redress the asymmetry between the increasingly *transnational* operations of companies and the predominantly *territorial* nature of human rights law as well as constitutional law. The rise of transnational governance in many areas such as climate change, terrorism, child-trafficking, corruption, money laundering and tax evasion is a direct response to address a disjunction between the physical territory of states and the virtual operations or effects of corporate activities at the transnational level.[16] The treaty may respond to this asymmetry by either imposing explicit extraterritorial obligations on states or creating a supra-state regulatory framework at the regional or international level.

Third, the treaty should also try to create a 'level playing field'[17] for both states and victims of business-related human rights violations vis-à-vis TNCs by addressing the current power imbalance between the two sides. While (developing) states experience such a power imbalance in negotiating investment or trade agreements[18] and attracting foreign

---

of peoples to self-determination', A/HRC/15/25 (2 July 2010); F. Francioni and N. Ronzitti (eds.), *War by Contract: Human Rights, Humanitarian Law and Private Contractors* (Oxford University Press, 2011); E. Moyakine, *The Privatized Art of War: Private Military and Security Companies and State Responsibility for their Unlawful Conduct in Conflict Areas* (Intersentia, 2014).

[14] S. Deva 'Public-Private Partnerships: Keeping Human Rights on the Radar' in Pradeep Mehta (ed.), *Mainstreaming Public Private Partnership in India* (New Delhi: CUTS Institute for Regulation & Competition, 2012), 85; M.B. Likosky, *Law, Infrastructure and Human Rights* (Cambridge University Press, 2006).

[15] UN General Assembly, 'Transforming our World: the 2030 Agenda for Sustainable Development', A/Res/70/1 (21 October 2015), paras. 28 and 67. See also Business & Sustainable Development Commission, *Better Business Better World* (2017).

[16] The SRSG rightly identified 'governance gaps' created by transitional and outsourcing-based operations of MNCs being the key problem. Human Rights Council, 'Protect, Respect and Remedy: A Framework for Business and Human Rights', A/HRC/8/5 (7 April 2008), para. 3 ('2008 Report').

[17] FIDH, 'Comments in relation to the Workshop on Human Rights and Business organized by the Permanent Mission of Ecuador and the South Center', http://business-human rights.org/sites/default/files/media/documents/fidh_written_comments_workshop_ecua dor.pdf (last accessed 20 January 2017).

[18] See Columbia Centre on Sustainable Investment, *International Investment and the Rights of Indigenous Peoples* (16 November 2016), http://ccsi.columbia.edu/files/2016/11/

direct investment (FDI),[19] victims often face such an imbalance in litigating against companies. Case studies – from the Bhopal gas disaster[20] to the more recent Shell settlement for Nigerian oil spills[21] – show that TNCs generally tend to deny any responsibility for human rights abuses linked to their actions unless they are subjected to significant pressure, whether inside the court through litigation or outside the court through civil society campaigns.

6.2.1.2   Respond to 'Hard Cases'

The proposed treaty should be able to deal with governance gaps visible in certain 'hard cases' of corporate human rights violations.[22] The idea of 'hard cases' refers to a cocktail of two broad types of situations. The first situation concerns instances in which a company sees no clear business case for complying with its human rights responsibilities (e.g., the company in question has no public goodwill to protect, or the company is engaged in a business activity like tobacco which is socially reprehensible). The second type of situation relates to circumstances in which states are unable or unwilling to regulate effectively the activities of private actors.

The response of the GPs, for example, to the hard cases has been overly optimistic, to put it mildly. The former SRSG found that most serious human rights violations were taking place in 'weak governance zones' or

---

Workshop-on-International-Investment-and-the-Rights-of-Indigenous-Peoples-Outcome-Document-November-2016.pdf (last accessed 20 January 2017).

[19] Creating an environment conducive to investment and business by TNCs could trigger a 'race to the bottom' or deregulation of norms related to labour laws, safety of workers or the environment. A concrete example is provided by lax (or no) safety standards adopted by a Kentex manufacturing factory in the Philippines, which resulted in the death of 72 workers in a fire, because the government was eager to improve its ranking in World Bank's 'ease of doing business' index. I. Pietropaoli, 'Philippines Factory Fire: 72 Workers Need not have Died', *The Guardian*, 8 June 2015, www.theguardian.com/global-development-professionals-network/2015/jun/08/philippines-factory-fire-72-workers-unions-human-rights (last accessed 20 January 2017).

[20] Amnesty International, *Clouds of Injustice: Bhopal Disaster 20 Years On* (Amnesty International, 2004); S. Shetty, 'Thirty Year On from Bhopal Disaster: Still Fighting for Justice' (2 December 2014), www.amnesty.org/en/articles/news/2014/12/thirty-years-bhopal-disaster-still-fighting-justice/ (last accessed 20 January 2017).

[21] 'Shell announces £55m payout for Nigeria oil spills', *The Guardian* (7 January 2015), www.theguardian.com/environment/2015/jan/07/shell-announces-55m-payout-for-nigeria-oil-spills (last accessed 20 January 2017).

[22] See S. Deva, 'Multinationals, Human Rights and International Law: Time to Move beyond the 'State-Centric' Conception?' J. Letnar Černič and T. Van Ho (eds.), *Human Rights and Business: Direct Corporate Accountability for Human Rights* (Wolf Legal Publishers, 2015) 27.

'conflict zones'.[23] Nevertheless, the GPs expect those very states at the centre of conflict or weak governance to exercise effectively their duty to protect people against human rights violations perpetuated by companies.[24] This expectation is very unrealistic, considering that even in normal circumstances states are generally unreliable in protecting human rights against corporate behaviour. For example, in the Philippines it is the government which is using a special paramilitary unit – the Investment Defence Force – to secure large-scale development projects against resistance by displaced indigenous people.[25] Similarly, in cases where there is no clear 'business case' for human rights, there may not be enough incentives for companies to carry out their 'responsibility to respect' diligently in the absence of any legal bite flowing from the GPs[26] or without CSOs having an institutionalized role as informal watchdogs.

The treaty should, therefore, find a way to respond to governance gaps in 'hard cases'.[27] It may, for instance, harness the potential of CSOs in enforcing international human rights norms, especially in those cases where states fail to act against powerful companies. Recognizing the key accountability role that CSOs can play, Melish and Meidinger, for example, make a case for the GPs to have a fourth 'participate' pillar.[28] Alternatively, accountability mechanisms could be created at the regional and international level, or triggers for extraterritorial obligations of states could be elaborated by building on the Maastricht Principles on Extraterritorial Obligations of States in the area of Economic, Social and Cultural Rights.[29]

---

[23] HRC, '2008 Report', n. 16, paras. 47–49.

[24] GPs, n. 2, Principle 7. Commentary on Principle 7 though rightly conceives a role for the 'home' states of TNCs operates in conflict zones.

[25] ESCR-Net and FIDH, 'Shaping the treaty on business and human rights: views from Asia and the Pacific', 11 May 2015, www.escr-net.org/node/365922 (last accessed 20 January 2017). See also Human Rights without Frontiers et al., *Police in the Pay of Mining Companies: The Responsibility of Switzerland and Peru for Human Rights Violations in Mining Disputes* (December 2013).

[26] Ruggie though thinks that there are 'several bites'. J. Ruggie, *Just Business* (Norton, 2013), 101–102.

[27] For some regulatory options in the context of home states, see P. Simons and A. Macklin, *The Governance Gap: Extractive Industries, Human Rights, and the Home State Advantage* (Routledge, 2014).

[28] T. M. Melish and E. Meidinger, 'Protect, Respect, Remedy *and Participate*: "New Governance" Lessons for the Ruggie Framework' in R. Mares (ed.), *The UN Guiding Principles on Business and Human Rights: Foundations and Implementation* (Leiden: Martinus Nijhoff Publishers, 2012), 303.

[29] Regarding states' extraterritorial obligations, see Chapter 12 by Skogly in this volume.

6.2.1.3   Improve Victims' Access to Remedies

The proposed treaty must improve access to effective remedies for victims of human rights violations by corporations. It can do so, among other measures, by removing well-documented conceptual, substantive or procedural obstacles that victims face in holding companies accountable: these barrier include corporate law principles of separate legal personality and limited liability, the doctrine of *forum non conveniens*, the difficulty of attributing criminal liability to corporations, the lack of legal aid and the high cost of litigation, and the difficulties involved in enforcing judgements in overseas jurisdictions.[30]

The GPs acknowledge these obstacles for victims in gaining access to remedies, but hardly suggest any concrete measures that states should take to improve access to justice.[31] The treaty could adopt several measures to address barriers faced by affected communities in accessing effective remedies. First of all, the proposed treaty can outline legal reform options for states to reduce, if not totally eliminate, obstacles in access to remedies for the victims of corporate human rights abuses. Considering that states have diverse legal systems and traditions, it might be desirable to propose to states a few options to strengthen access to remedies. It may, for instance, be worthwhile to draft Model Laws to provide states with *concrete* guidance as to what legislative and policy adjustments they should make to embed the human rights obligations of business in domestic, bilateral, regional and international governance regimes.

Second, the treaty should create regional and/or international remedial mechanisms to complement mechanisms (whether judicial or non-judicial) at the national level. At the international level, the treaty should, at the minimum, create a body of experts with the power to issue authoritative interpretations, develop standards and accept individual complaints from

---

[30] Amnesty International, *Injustice Incorporated*, n. 5; R. Meeran, 'Tort Litigation against Multinational Corporations for Violations of Human Rights: An Overview of the Position Outside the United States' (2011) 3 *City University of Hong Kong Law Review* 1; P. Blumberg, 'Asserting Human Rights against Multinational Corporations under United States Law: Conceptual and Procedural Problems' (2002) 50 *American Journal of Comparative Law* 493; S. Deva, 'Corporate Code of Conduct Bill 2000: Overcoming Hurdles in Enforcing Human Rights Obligations against Overseas Corporate Hands of Local Corporations' (2004) 8 *Newcastle Law Review* 87.

[31] This gap is somewhat filled by OHCHR's Accountability and Remedy Project. See Human Rights Council, 'Improving accountability and access to remedy for victims of business-related human rights abuse, Report of the United Nations High Commissioner for Human Rights', A/HRC/32/19 (10 May 2016).

victims of corporate human rights abuses. Establishing an international court to adjudicate complaints against TNCs appears ambitious at this stage. Nevertheless, the treaty may require states to explore, in good faith, the possibility of establishing a new international forum (or extending the jurisdiction of an existing forum like the International Criminal Court) to deal with gross human rights abuses committed by corporations.

Third, considering the transnational character of human rights violations by business, the treaty should establish a system of mutual assistance and cooperation amongst states.[32] Such cooperation should ideally extend to all relevant stages of judicial proceedings – from collection of evidence to enforcement of judgements.

Fourth, as companies can and do violate all types of human rights,[33] it will be vital that the proposed treaty offers remedial responses for all human rights violations, though the exact nature of these responses may vary. For example, whereas civil remedies (e.g., compensation, injunction and public apology) should be available for all types of human rights violations, criminal prosecution may be appropriate only for certain more serious human rights abuses.

6.2.1.4   Trigger Creation and Compliance of Norms

Last but not least, the proposed international treaty, as part of a 'continuous upward-downward cycle' of norm creation,[34] should facilitate the creation as well as compliance of human rights norms at various levels and by various types of actors. Treaties tend to trigger reform of domestic legal frameworks in states which ratify them. However, the BHR treaty may be useful even in states not ratifying it. To illustrate, courts may use an international treaty – even in the absence of a domestic legislation implementing it – as a reference point to develop principles suitable to respond to corporate violations of human rights.

---

[32] See O. De Schutter, 'Towards a New Treaty on Business and Human Rights' (2016) 1 *Business and Human Rights Journal* 41, at 61–66. See also A. Ramasastry and D. Cassel, 'White Paper: Options for a Treaty on Business and Human Rights' (2015) 6 *Notre Dame Journal of International and Comparative Law* 1.

[33] HRC, '2008 Report', n. 16, paras. 51-52; FoEI, 'Oral Statement by Friends of the Earth International (FoEI) at the side event organized by the missions of Ecuador and South Africa at the UNHRC session in Geneva, March 12-13 on human rights and the operations of transnational corporations and other business entities', http://business-human rights.org/sites/default/files/media/oral_statement_foei_at_unhrc_side_event_in_gen eva_on_binding_rules_for_corporations.pdf (last accessed 20 January 2017).

[34] See S. Deva, *Regulating Corporate Human Rights Violations: Humanizing Business* (Routledge, 2012), 202–203.

For example, if the treaty has a provision about mandatory human rights due diligence on the part of corporations, this requirement could be used to define the contours of the duty of care in a given situation.[35] Similarly, national human rights institutions could employ the human rights due diligence requirement stipulated in the treaty to develop guidelines for business as long as doing so is not inconsistent with the domestic legal framework.

A BHR treaty should also mount pressure on corporations to comply with human rights norms. A company incorporated in a non-ratifying state may be required to comply with the treaty provisions while doing business in a state which has ratified the treaty. Moreover, the proposed treaty should result in the empowerment of CSOs and law firms working in the BHR area: it will enhance their leverage to negotiate directly with companies and secure beneficial human rights terms for affected communities in private settlements.

6.2.2   Political Considerations

If we analyse the voting pattern of states regarding the HRC resolution adopted in June 2014 as well as the stand taken by states during the first two sessions of the open-ended intergovernmental working group (OEIGWG) held in July 2015 and October 2016, it becomes clear that the position of many states was not informed by the normative objectives outlined above. Rather, political considerations must have dictated their decision to oppose the proposed BHR treaty, because these very states otherwise champion human rights in the international arena and support the evolution of binding regional or international instruments in the field of trade and investment.

In terms of political considerations related to the current treaty process, states can be divided into four broad camps.[36] In the first camp are states – mostly developed countries from the Global North – which are supportive of the GPs but are against the treaty project. Their opposition to the treaty process embodies several stands: that the 'footnote' of Resolution 26/9 arbitrarily excludes local or domestic companies from purview of the

---

[35] See D. Cassel, 'Outlining the Case for a Common Law Duty of Care of Business to Exercise Human Rights Due Diligence' (2016) 1 (2) *Business and Human Rights Journal* 179.

[36] I develop this typology based on my participation in the first two sessions of the OEIGWG as well my interaction with a range of stakeholders over the last few years.

treaty, that a discussion about treaty will break the consensus built around the adoption of the GPs, that the treaty discussion will divert the attention from implementing the GPs through national action plans or otherwise, and that it will take many years before a treaty could be negotiated. In terms of the scope of the treaty specifically, some states in this camp may tolerate a BHR treaty which is narrow in terms of its subject matter but applies to all business enterprises.

The second camp belongs to developing states from the Global South which are supportive of the current treaty process, but they do not see much value in implementing soft international norms like the GPs. Their scepticism about soft human rights norms stems from the failure of such past initiatives in holding TNCs accountable. They also feel that a legally binding international instrument is needed to deal with companies which operate at a transnational level and that equity demands 'hard' trade/investment law be matched by 'hard' international human rights law. In terms of the scope of the treaty specifically, the states in this camp aspire to have a treaty which covers all human rights but applies only to TNCs.

In the third camp are those states which have no deep engagement with either of the two processes (the GPs as well as the treaty). Over a period of time, the number of disengaged states in this camp is coming down and it is inevitable that such states will either join one of the first two camps or migrate to the fourth camp described below. This may, therefore, be regarded as a transitory camp.

The fourth camp comprises states which are supportive of both regulatory initiatives. Rather than finding any conflict between the GPs and the proposed treaty, they see them as complementary to each other. In terms of the scope of the treaty specifically, states in this camp tend to adopt a flexible approach: while all corporations can violate all human rights, certain types of corporations (e.g., TNCs) may be treated differently for the purpose of regulation.

The chances of negotiating a treaty would increase if more and more states occupy the fourth complementary camp. That could only happen if states from the first two camps (especially from the first camp) cross over to the fourth camp. Despite political considerations at play and pressure from business on states in the first camp, such a movement may still take place in future. After all, the divide between the first two camps is artificial and misinformed. If one supports the GPs and the ideas underpinning them (i.e., corporations have human rights responsibilities independent of states and victims should have access to effective remedies), then one can hardly oppose binding regulations at the domestic or international level.

Conversely, it would be almost indefensible for a treaty-supporting state to reject the GPs altogether. The advocacy on the part of CSOs might expose states in the first two camps to abandon a false dichotomy between the GPs and the proposed treaty.

Moreover, once the treaty-sceptic states in the first camp realize that their political positions in the twenty-first century are still being informed by the economic conditions that prevailed in the second half of the twentieth century, some of them might have to abandon their blind opposition to the treaty. Developed countries did not favour a binding international instrument at a time when the flow of FDI was almost uni-directional (from developed to developing countries) because of a per-ception that such a regulatory tool would harm their economic interests or the business interests of TNCs incorporated therein. However, this landscape has undergone significant changes in recent years, as TNCs from developing countries are emerging on the global stage. For example, in the 2016 Fortune Global 500 list, there are 134 companies from the United States and 52 from Japan, as compared to 103 from China and 7 each from India and Brazil.[37] This scenario is very different from what the world had experienced during most of the twentieth century when almost 90 per cent of the TNCs were based in the United States, Europe and Japan. Moreover, the outflow of FDI from developed economies has been generally declining from a 'one-way' position of dominance, while the outflow from developing and transition economies is on the rise. The World Investment Report 2013 indicated that the FDI outflow from developed countries fell from 88 per cent in 2000 to 65 per cent in 2012 – during the same period, there has been an almost three-fold increase in the FDI outflow from developing and transition economies.[38]

Having laid out normative objectives and political considerations vis-à-vis the treaty generally, the next two sections of this chapter will examine the interplay between these two sets of variable in relation to the scope of the proposed BHR treaty.

---

[37] 'Fortune Global 500', http://beta.fortune.com/global500/list/ (last accessed 16 August 2016).

[38] UNCTAD, *World Investment Report 2013: Global Value Chains: Investment and Trade for Development*, 4. The FDI outflow from developed countries was 61 per cent in 2014, which increased to 72 per cent in 2015. Nevertheless, it is clear that FDI is no longer one-directional. UNCTAD, *World Investment Report 2016 – Investor Nationality: Policy Challenges*, 5–7.

6.3   Regulatory Targets of the Treaty

The issue of regulatory targets revolves around the controversial 'footnote' in the HRC Resolution 26/9, which establishes the OEIGWG 'to elaborate an international legally binding instrument to regulate, in international human rights law, the activities of transnational corporations and other business enterprises'.[39] This footnote in the Preamble reads: '"Other business enterprises" denotes all business enterprises that have a transnational character in their operational activities, and does not apply to local businesses registered in terms of relevant domestic law.'[40] However, the main text of Resolution 26/9 provides that the first two sessions of the OEIGWG 'shall be dedicated to conducting constructive deliberations on the content, scope, nature and form of the future international instrument'.[41] This may suggest that the scope of the proposed treaty remains an open question. In fact, the programme of work for the second session held in October 2016 had expressly provided – in order to secure the EU's participation – that discussions in the session 'can include TNCs as well as all other business enterprises'.[42]

It should be noted at the outset that the footnote language is conceptually ambiguous and perhaps contradictory. Logically speaking, the term 'other business enterprises' should mean something other than TNCs. The footnote defines 'other business enterprises' to denote all business enterprises that have a 'transnational character'. But if so, should they not be already be covered within the definition of 'TNCs'? Moreover, the second limb of the footnote – that the definition of other business enterprises 'does not apply to local businesses registered in terms of relevant domestic law' – is somewhat meaningless, because all companies (including TNCs) are registered under domestic law of some country. In order to make sense of this footnote, it is arguable that the intent is to apply the treaty to TNCs and such other companies which have a transnational character, but exclude domestic companies whose operations are completely confined to the territory of any one state.

The proposal for the treaty not to apply to domestic businesses is rooted in the belief – held by many states in the Global South as well as by several states supporting the resolution – that a treaty is required only

---

[39] Human Rights Council, 'Elaboration of an international legally binding instrument on transnational corporations and other business enterprises with respect to human rights', A/HRC/RES/26/9 (26 June 2014), para. 1, http://daccess-dds-ny.un.org/doc/UNDOC/GEN/G14/082/52/PDF/G1408252.pdf?OpenElement (last accessed 20 January 2017).

[40] *Ibid.*, footnote 1.   [41] *Ibid.*, para. 2.   [42] See n. 1.

to deal with TNCs and business enterprises which operate at a transnational level. This belief is consistent with one of the normative objectives
highlighted above, i.e., addressing the asymmetry between transnational
operations of companies and the predominantly territorial nature of
human rights law. Furthermore, developing countries are apprehensive
that if the treaty applied to all types of business enterprises, their local and
small-scale companies might be subjected to heavy burdens flowing from
international human rights norms.

Many other developed states from the Global North, on the other
hand, oppose the idea of any future treaty being limited to TNCs: they
think that doing so will put their TNCs at an economic disadvantage. Such
states also point out that applying the treaty to a narrow set of companies
will also be impractical from the perspective of implementation.

There are three broad options on how the treaty may deal with the
regulatory targets issue. Normative objectives and political consideration
alluded to earlier in the chapter play out differently in each of these
options.

6.3.1   Focusing on More Difficult Regulatory Targets

One obvious option for the OEIGWG will be to follow strictly the
footnote text of Resolution 26/9,[43] so as to exclude domestic business
enterprises from the purview of the treaty and focus merely on the
activities of TNCs and other business enterprises with operations of a
transnational character.

It is not very clear whether the footnote in the resolution will capture
the supply chain partners of TNCs or not. Ideally, the treaty should reach
TNCs' entire supply chain because that is where most violations occur for
most TNCs' operations, particularly in labour-intensive industries.[44] The
ambiguity in the phrase 'business enterprises with a transnational character' may offer the treaty drafters some leeway to include suppliers of
TNCs. The term 'transnational character' could, for instance, be defined
more broadly to capture those local business enterprises which have
some transnational element, e.g., offering products or services outside

---

[43] The interventions made by several states (such as South Africa, Pakistan, India, China,
Russia, Egypt, El Salvador and Indonesia) during the First Session of the OEIGWG
stressed that the intent behind the footnote should be respected.

[44] EIRIS, 'A Risky Business? Managing core labour standards in company supply chains'
December 2009, p. 11, www.eiris.org/files/research%20publications/CoreLabourStandards
ReportDec09.pdf (last accessed 20 January 2017).

the country of incorporation; direct sourcing of materials from overseas suppliers; or having overseas investors and/or directors. Alternatively, this result could be achieved by the treaty mandating parent companies to conduct human rights due diligence processes within their supply chains,[45] or by developing the idea of complicity in the context of a lead company and its suppliers.[46]

An obvious advantage of this option will be to keep the treaty manageable – this consideration will be especially relevant at the enforcement stage because any remedial mechanism cannot possibly deal with an unlimited number of complaints or cases against a vast number of companies. One could also justify this option on the grounds that as TNCs are undoubtedly more difficult regulatory targets,[47] regulating their behaviour should be taken up as a matter of priority. Moreover, this option may solidify the coalition amongst pro-treaty states: not only the states which voted for Resolution 26/9 but also other developing countries may prefer this option for two interconnected reasons. First, a treaty is likely to enhance the leverage of developing countries against powerful TNCs in multiple ways, e.g., providing an explicit basis to take regulatory measures (including extraterritorially) against companies; and operating as a bargaining tool when negotiating trade and investment agreements. Second, a narrow focus of the treaty may give developing states some comfort that their small-scale local companies will not be burdened to comply with onerous global human rights standards.

In terms of disadvantages, this option would prove to be highly divisive: it is very unlikely that the developed countries will ever agree to an international instrument which applies only to TNCs. From the perspective of victims of human rights violations by corporations, limiting the treaty to TNCs – which by definition exclude many companies only with domestic operations, but which have an equally adverse effect on the enjoyment of human rights – will be problematic. It is also arguable that making a distinction between TNCs and other business enterprises with domestic operations will offend the principle of non-discrimination. If it is

---

[45] See, for example, California Transparency in Supply Chains Act of 2010; Modern Slavery Act 2015 (UK).

[46] Jungk, for example, examines four principles (enabling, causality, severity and power) as a potential basis to identify the responsibility of a company for the conduct of its suppliers. M. Jungk, *Complicity in Human Rights Violations: A Responsible Business Approach to Suppliers* (Danish Institute for Human Rights, 2006).

[47] B. Stephens, 'Corporate Liability: Enforcing Human Rights Through Domestic Litigation' (2001) 24 *Hastings International & Comparative Law Review* 401.

irrelevant whether the violator of a human right is a state agency or a non-state actor, why should a distinction based on where a company operates matter?

6.3.2   Reaching All Business Enterprises

The second option in terms of regulatory targets will be to negotiate a treaty which applies to all types of businesses. This option could be achieved, as pointed out earlier, by contending that the 'scope' of the treaty under the HRC resolution remains an open question.

The most significant advantage of adopting this option will be to bring developed countries to the negotiation table and in turn help in achieving the OEIGWG mandate of crafting a treaty. Undoubtedly, this option will also be sounder normatively, as it will not differentiate between companies based on the reach or nature of their operations and in turn afford protection to potential victims against all types of corporate behaviour. Another practical advantage of this option will be to avoid the need for constructing an agreeable definition of 'TNC', a task which is likely to prove very difficult because an entity could be considered 'transnational' in view of multiple alternative variables (e.g., shareholding, operations, business relations, location of offices, nationality of shareholders and directors). One should also not forget that 'TNC' is hardly a legal term: neither municipal corporate laws nor international law generally recognize incorporation of a company as a TNC.[48]

Adopting this option, on the other hand, may result in some pro-treaty states withdrawing from the treaty negotiations. Also, negotiating 'limiting principles' of the treaty – principles that will help each company to identify their exact human rights responsibilities and differentiate corporate responsibilities from state responsibilities – would be much more difficult if the treaty were to apply to all types of business enterprises irrespective of their size, sector, location, ownership and structure.[49]

Under international law, both the above options are feasible. It appears, however, that the increasing trend in the twenty-first century is more towards adopting instruments which apply to all types of enterprises, rather than merely TNCs. For example, the 1976 OECD Guidelines for Multinational Enterprises applied to 'multinational enterprises' operating

---

[48]   There may be certain exceptions like the EU law allows the incorporation of a European Company to operate throughout the EU countries.

[49]   Unless the treaty adopts a 'process-' – as opposed to 'outcome-' – oriented approach, as done by the GPs.

in the territories of OECD countries.[50] The 1977 ILO Tripartite Declaration of Principles Concerning Multinational Enterprises was similarly limited to 'multinational enterprises' *operating in* the territories of the ILO member states.[51] However, after the revision of both these instruments in 2000, their scope was extended to other enterprises too.[52] For instance, the 2000 version of the OECD Guidelines applied to multinational enterprises '*operating* in or *from*' the territories of OECD countries.[53] The revised Guidelines not only asked MNCs to observe the provisions 'wherever they operate',[54] but also expected them to encourage their 'business partners, including suppliers and sub-contractors, to apply principles of corporate conduct compatible with the Guidelines'.[55] In the same vein, the 2000 version of the ILO Declaration provided that the 'principles laid down in the Declaration do not aim at introducing or maintaining inequalities of treatment between multinational and national enterprises. They reflect good practice for all.'[56]

Building on these developments, the 2003 UN Draft Norms on the Responsibilities of Transnational Corporations and Other Business Enterprises not only applied to TNCs, but also 'other business enterprises' – such as contractors, suppliers, licensees or distributors – if (1) they had any relation with a TNC, (2) the impact of its activities was not entirely local, or (3) the activities involved violations of the right to security.[57] It is worth noting that while the Draft Norms' application was not limited to TNCs, it did not extend either to all types of businesses operating in all situations.

The GPs in 2011 took the final step forward by abolishing the distinction between TNCs and other business enterprises and posited that all

---

[50] OECD Declaration on International Investment and Multinational Enterprises, 21 June 1976, reprinted in 1976, *ILM*, vol. 15, 967 at 968. Para. 8 of the Guidelines provided a definition of 'multinational enterprises'. *Ibid.*, at 971.

[51] ILO Tripartite Declaration of Principles Concerning Multinational Enterprises and Social Policy, 16 November 1977, reprinted in 1978, *ILM*, vol. 17, 422 at 423.

[52] Deva, *Humanizing Business*, n. 34, 80, 90.

[53] OECD Declaration and Decisions on International Investment and Multinational Enterprises: Basic Texts, DAFE/IME(2000)20, 8 November 2000, p. 5.

[54] *Ibid.*, p. 9 (para. I.2).   [55] *Ibid.*, p. 11 (para. II.10).

[56] ILO Tripartite Declaration of Principles Concerning Multinational Enterprises and Social Policy, November 2000, para. 11. See also ILO Tripartite Declaration of Principles Concerning Multinational Enterprises and Social Policy, March 2017, para. 5.

[57] Norms on the Responsibilities of Transnational Corporations and Other Business Enterprises with Regard to Human Rights, U.N. Doc. E/CN.4/Sub.2/2003/12/Rev.2 (2003), paras. 20–21.

business enterprises have a responsibility to respect human rights.[58] Considering the incremental extension of the scope of initiatives regulating corporate behaviour over the last four decades and the unanimous endorsement of the GPs by the HRC, it will be quite difficult politically to take a step back and limit the scope of the proposed treaty only to TNCs and other business enterprises with transnational operations, unless this treaty is seen as the first of many subsequent treaties in the BHR field.

6.3.3   Taking a Hybrid Route

The above two options represent two extreme positions taken by two camps of states described earlier in the chapter: one camp supporting the treaty process, while the other opposing it. Considering that the success of drafting a treaty as well as its implementation would require a broad consensus amongst states from both these groups, I will explore a middle path to bridge the divide between the two camps.

The 'hybrid option' may be to draft a treaty that applies to all business enterprises, but to have certain special provisions to deal with TNCs as the more difficult regulatory targets. Special provisions for TNCs in the proposed treaty may relate to mutual assistance and cooperation amongst states in investigating violations and in enforcing judgements; explicitly obligating states to regulate the conduct of TNCs extraterritorially; providing rules to govern the liability of parent companies for human rights abuses committed by their subsidiaries; and providing for rules to limit the corporate misuse of the doctrine of *forum non conveniens*.

This option could be operationalized in a number of ways. A *soft hybrid* would be where most of the treaty provisions focus on TNCs' operations, but the Preamble and/or General Principles acknowledge that all business enterprises have an obligation to comply with human rights norms. The *strong hybrid* would entail the treaty containing some general parts applicable to all types of business enterprises and a few parts applicable only to TNCs and other companies with a transnational character. The strong hybrid option could also be achieved by adopting an optional protocol model: the main treaty only applies to TNCs, whereas an optional protocol extends the application of the treaty provisions, as far as they are relevant, to all local business enterprises with no

---

[58] 'These Guiding Principles apply to all … business enterprises, both transnational and others, regardless of their size, sector, location, ownership and structure.' GPs, n. 2, General Principles. See also Principle 11 and the Commentary.

'transnational character'. Such an Optional Protocol should also stipulate principles with reference to which the extent of human rights obligations of small- and medium-size enterprises could be differentiated from those of TNCs and other business enterprises with a 'transnational character' (e.g., the reasonable level of due diligence measures will vary, among others, as per the size of an enterprise).

The hybrid option canvassed here will have several advantages. Apart from being a potential 'ice breaker' between the two camps of states, this option will not result in sending any inadvertent signal that international law or the global community is only concerned about human rights violations by TNCs. At the same time, this option will be a legitimate response to the problems created by the disjunction between (inter) national human rights law and the transnational operations of some business enterprises.

6.4   Subject Matter of the Treaty

The subject matter issue is reflective of the debate about whether the proposed treaty should be limited to 'gross' human rights violations by business or not. The debate here is underpinned by a normative aspiration to put in place a treaty which covers all civil, political, social, economic and cultural human rights and the political feasibility of negotiating a narrower treaty around which it might be easier to build consensus. This debate is also somewhat reflective of the historical divide between civil and political rights on the one hand and the economic, social and cultural rights on the other. Closely connected with this divide is the manner in which different sets of human rights were given priority traditionally by the Global North and the Global South, respectively.

In relation to the subject matter, there are at least three broad options for the proposed BHR treaty, which I will now elaborate upon. Irrespective of which option is chosen, the OEIGWG would have to make another drafting choice: the treaty may either prescribe the human rights obligations of companies with reference to existing international human rights treaties or enumerate them precisely after suitable modifications if any.[59] While the first approach will be definitely easier, it might not provide companies with enough guidance, as it is difficult to transplant the state-centric text of certain human rights treaty provisions directly onto

---

[59] A combination of these models may also be adopted, e.g., the 2003 UN Norms.

the private actors. However, the second approach of negotiating the exact obligations of companies is likely to prove very contentious in practice. The solution here may lie in the proposed BHR treaty enumerating a list of international human rights instruments applicable to business and stipulating some general principles with reference to which the obligations of corporations could be ascertained in a specific context.

6.4.1   Gross Human Rights

Some states and scholars suggest that the scope of the proposed treaty, at least to begin with, should be limited to gross human rights abuses. Ruggie, for instance, is in favour of binding regulation only to target 'gross violations'.[60]

As there is no definite certainty or consensus yet on what the term 'gross' means under international human rights law,[61] there is some leeway to interpret the term in a manner which is broader than,[62] say, the four crimes covered by the ICC Rome Statute[63] or even broader than the territory occupied by international corporate crimes.[64] It is arguable that a number of factors – such as the character of the right, the magnitude of the violation, the vulnerability of victim and the impact of the violation – may determine which violations are regarded as 'serious'

---

[60] J. Ruggie, 'Life in the Global Public Domain: Response to Commentaries on the UN Guiding Principles and the Proposed Treaty on Business and Human Rights' (23 January 2015), p. 5, http://ssrn.com/abstract=2554726 (last accessed 20 January 2017).

[61] See Zerk, 'Corporate Liability for Gross Human Rights Abuses', n. 5, 25–28. Although Ruggie moots the idea of a carefully crafted legal instrument that deals with 'worst' human rights abuses, he does not elaborate clearly what these rights are. Ruggie, *Just Business*, n. 26, 200. On another occasion, he mentioned that international crimes such as 'genocide, extrajudicial killings, and slavery or slavery-like practices' are obvious candidates for such a category. J. Ruggie, 'A UN Business and Human Rights Treaty? An Issue Brief' (28 January 2014), pp. 5, http://business-humanrights.org/media/documents/ruggie-on-un-business-human-rights-treaty-jan-2014.pdf (last accessed 20 January 2017).

[62] See the online symposiums on corporate accountability: http://jamesgstewart.com/list-of-previous-symposia/ (last accessed 20 January 2017).

[63] The ICC Rome Statute covers four international crimes: genocide, crimes against humanity, war crimes and the crime of aggression.

[64] See A. Ramasastry and R. C. Thompson, *Commerce, Crime, and Conflict: Legal Remedies for Private Sector Liability for Grave Breaches of International Law – A Survey of Sixteen Countries* (FAFO, 2006); J. Stewart, 'The Turn to Corporate Criminal Liability for International Crimes: Transcending the Alien Tort Statue' (2014) 47 *New York University Journal of International Law and Politics* 1.

under international human rights law.[65] Bassiouni noted that 'the term "gross violations of human rights" has been employed in the United Nations context not to denote a particular category of human rights violations per se, but rather to describe situations involving human rights violations by referring to the manner in which the violations may have been committed or to their severity'.[66] It is also worth noting that the 1993 Vienna World Conference on Human Rights Declaration extends the notion of gross and systematic violations to include 'torture and cruel, inhuman and degrading treatment or punishment, summary and arbitrary executions, disappearances, arbitrary detentions, all forms of racism, racial discrimination and apartheid, foreign occupation and alien domination, xenophobia, poverty, hunger and other denials of economic, social and cultural rights, religious intolerance, terrorism, discrimination against women and lack of the rule of law.'[67]

Although the term 'gross' is susceptible to a broad interpretation, it is really doubtful whether proponents of this option have such an interpretation in mind, because it would be easier to build international consensus only if gross human rights violations are defined narrowly. More importantly, from the perspective of victims of corporate human rights violations, the option of such a narrow treaty will not be very helpful (unless states agree to negotiate additional instruments in specific areas on a continuous basis),[68] because such a treaty might not cover a great majority of human rights abuses committed by companies all over the world. Calls for negotiating a narrow treaty that deals only with egregious abuses is also reflective of the Global

---

[65] Geneva Academy, 'What amounts to "a serious violation of international human rights law"?' (September 2014), p. 5, www.geneva-academy.ch/docs/publications/Briefings%20and%20In%20breifs/Briefing%206%20What%20is%20a%20serious%20violation%20of%20human%20rights%20law_Academy%20Briefing%20No%206.pdf (last accessed 20 January 2017).

[66] 'Report of the Independent Expert on the Right to Restitution, Compensation and Rehabilitation for Victims of Grave Violations of Human Rights and Fundamental Freedoms, Mr M. Cherif Bassiouni, submitted pursuant to Commission on Human Rights Resolution 1998/43', para. 85.

[67] Vienna Declaration and Programme of Action, World Conference on Human Rights, 1993, para. 30.

[68] For example, a multiplicity of treaties could be adopted to 'troubleshoot particular kinds of corporate human rights violations, e.g., a treaty to combat the targeting of children by the tobacco industry.' J. Tasioulas, 'Human Rights, No Dogmas: The UN Guiding Principles on Business and Human Rights' (30 January 2015), p. 4, http://ssrn.com/abstract=2561420 (last accessed 20 January 2017).

North's prioritization of civil and political rights over economic, social and cultural rights.[69] For people living in the Global South – who suffer disproportionately due to business-related human rights abuses – the latter set of rights are equally, if not more, important. There are no sound reasons why the displacement of indigenous peoples for mining, emission of (and/or exposure to) hazardous chemicals, compulsory pre-employment pregnancy testing of women and illegal land-grabs by companies should be taken less seriously than slavery or genocide.

6.4.2   Core Human Rights

This option would involve extending the scope of the proposed treaty to the 'core' list of internationally recognized human rights that the GPs recommend companies to follow 'at a minimum': that would include 'the International Bill of Human Rights (consisting of the Universal Declaration of Human Rights and the main instruments through which it has been codified: the International Covenant on Civil and Political Rights and the International Covenant on Economic, Social and Cultural Rights), coupled with the principles concerning fundamental rights in the eight ILO core conventions as set out in the Declaration on Fundamental Principles and Rights at Work.'[70]

Alternatively, the BHR treaty could go beyond the International Bill of Rights and refer to all nine core international human rights treaties: the International Convention on the Elimination of All Forms of Racial Discrimination (ICERD); the International Covenant on Civil and Political Rights (ICCPR); the International Covenant on Economic, Social and Cultural Rights (ICESCR); the Convention on the Elimination of All Forms of Discrimination against Women (CEDAW); the Convention against Torture and Other Cruel, Inhuman or Degrading Treatment or Punishment (CAT); the Convention on the Rights of the Child (CRC); the International Convention on the Protection of the Rights of All Migrant Workers and Members of Their Families (ICMW); the International Convention for the Protection of All Persons from Enforced Disappearance

---

[69] S. Deva, 'Corporate Human Rights Abuses and International Law: Brief Comments', (28 January 2015), http://jamesgstewart.com/corporate-human-rights-abuses-and-international-law-brief-comments/ (last accessed 20 January 2017).
[70] GPs, n. 2, Principle 12 with Commentary.

(CPED); and the Convention on the Rights of Persons with Disabilities (CPRD).[71]

In terms of filling in governance gaps and from the perspective of potential victims of corporate human rights abuses, this option – especially if it included all nine core human rights conventions – will have a significant advantage over the first option limited to gross human rights violations. Although all human rights instruments could be traced to the UDHR or the ICCPR and the ICESCR, human rights require a particular 'lens' and 'specification' when dealing with specific groups of people like children, women, migrants workers and persons with disabilities. The language of the International Bill of Rights does not unfortunately offer such a sensitive treatment of human rights. In this way, this option would also be beneficial for corporations by providing them with much more clarity and specific guidance about the contours of specific human rights.

At the same time, as compared with codifying a narrow list of gross human rights violations, this option would be much more difficult to accomplish given the divisions and differences of opinion amongst states and considering that not all states have ratified some of these core treaties. Moreover, even the extended 'core' list of human rights under this option will not include many important instruments relating to labour rights, environmental rights and the rights of indigenous peoples. Consequently, the proposed treaty will not directly capture many business-related human rights abuses experienced by individuals and communities all over the world. This leads me to consider another option below.

6.4.3   Core+ Human Rights

The third option for the proposed BHR treaty may be to go beyond 'hard' international human rights law instruments, as human rights in certain areas have not yet been codified in treaties. The rights of indigenous peoples, who are being violated routinely by business, are a case in point:[72] unless the UNDRIP is referenced in the BHR treaty, the right

---

[71] OHCHR, 'The Core International Human Rights Instruments and their Monitoring Bodies' www.ohchr.org/EN/ProfessionalInterest/Pages/CoreInstruments.aspx (last accessed 20 January 2017).

[72] The ILO's Indigenous and Tribal Peoples Convention of 1989 is an exception to this situation.

of indigenous peoples to provide (or withhold as the case may be) 'free, prior and informed consent' may not get adequate recognition.

To operationalize this option, the treaty should include all human rights contained in the following international instruments: nine core international human rights conventions enumerate above; the UDHR; the UNDRIP; the Rio Declaration; and eight fundamental ILO conventions (i.e., the Freedom of Association and Protection of the Right to Organise Convention 1948, the Right to Organise and Collective Bargaining Convention 1949, the Forced Labour Convention 1930, the Abolition of Forced Labour Convention 1957, the Minimum Age Convention 1973, the Worst Forms of Child Labour Convention 1999, the Equal Remuneration Convention 1951, and the Discrimination (Employment and Occupation) Convention 1958).

CSOs may find this comprehensive option attractive because it will capture not only all civil, political, economic and cultural rights, but also labour rights and environmental rights. Another key advantage of this option will be an implicit acknowledgement of the principle of non-derogation of international human rights norms: the proposed BHR treaty should not be taken as making soft international law norms irrelevant for corporate operations. On the other hand, this option will perhaps be the most difficult in terms of getting political traction within the HRC. It would also raise questions as to how states can apply certain human rights treaties to business without subjecting their own conduct to such treaties by ratification.

6.5   Conclusion

This chapter has highlighted the clash between 'normative objectives' and 'political considerations' regarding the proposed BHR treaty. This clash is visible both in relation to the desirability-cum-feasibility of the treaty generally as well as with reference to the scope of the treaty specifically. This clash has the potential to derail – for the third time – the process at the UN level to negotiate a legally binding international instrument on the human rights obligations of business. It is not, however, impossible to navigate through this clash by employing creative legal solutions. Taking the 'scope' of the treaty, which relates to the footnote of the HRC resolution 26/9, as a concrete example, this chapter outlined how this could be done in relation to both the *regulatory targets* and the *subject-matter* of the proposed BHR treaty.

Since 'the corporate form of the abuser is irrelevant' for the victims of corporate human rights abuses[73] and any attempt to limit the treaty's scope only to TNCs would inevitably result in lawyers advising enterprises how to bypass the given definitional contours,[74] the proposed BHR treaty should ideally apply to all types of business enterprises.[75] At the same time, it cannot be denied that TNCs are more difficult regulatory targets and that regulatory measures – both at national and international levels – often decide to target certain types of actors as a matter of regulatory priority. In order to bridge the divide between the two extreme options outlined in this chapter (only TNCs versus all business enterprises), I have proposed that a *hybrid option* should be considered. The hybrid option should also be able to resolve, at least partially, the clash between normative objectives and political considerations.

As far as the subject matter of the proposed treaty is concerned, it may be easier to build a political consensus for a treaty which focuses only on 'gross' human rights violations. However, I have argued in this chapter that such a narrow treaty – even if the term 'gross' is defined somewhat broadly – might not cover a great majority of human rights abuses committed by businesses all over the world. It would thus mostly serve a symbolic purpose for the victims of business-related human rights abuses. Therefore, I have proposed a 'core+ option' under which core international conventions related to human rights and labour rights as well as three declarations (UDHR, UNDRIP and Rio Declaration) will be referenced in the Annexure to the proposed BHR treaty.

Both the options recommended here – the 'hybrid option' and the 'core+ option' – regarding the scope of the proposed treaty could be operationalized by incorporating the elements of these proposals in the Preamble as well as other relevant provisions of the treaty. An initial attempt is made below as to how this could be done. In short, if states show a political will to protect human rights from violation by private actors and if businesses 'walk the talk' regarding their responsibility to respect human rights under the GPs, legal solutions that strike a balance

---

[73] J. Ruggie, 'Quo Vadis? Unsolicited Advice to Business and Human Rights Treaty Sponsors', www.ihrb.org/commentary/quo-vadis-unsolicited-advice-business.html (last accessed 20 January 2017).

[74] Deva, 'Brief Comments', n. 69.

[75] Darcy argues that a focus on TNCs might be too narrow. Shane Darcy, 'A new business and human rights instrument?' p. 6, https://businesshumanrightsireland.wordpress.com/2015/04/13/key-issues-in-the-debate-on-a-binding-business-and-human-rights-instrument/ (last accessed 20 January 2017).

between competing normative objectives and political considerations surrounding the current treaty process can be found. This chapter has tried to demonstrate this with reference to the scope of the proposed BHR treaty.

Preamble (paragraphs limited only to the 'scope' question)

'*Acknowledging* that all types of business enterprises can violate all universal, inalienable, interrelated, interdependent and indivisible human rights,

Considering that transnational corporations and other business enterprises with a "transnational character" pose special regulatory challenges, this Convention focuses only on such business enterprises as a matter of regulatory priority,

Affirming that the human rights norms laid down in this Convention should be treated as good practices for all types of business enterprises,

Encouraging states to ratify the Optional Protocol to this Convention to extend the provisions of this Convention, as far as relevant, to all other business enterprises with no transnational character.'

Applicability of the Convention

'(1) This Convention shall apply to:
   (a) states and intergovernmental organizations; and
   (b) transnational corporations and other business enterprises with a transnational character, unless a state party ratifies the Optional Protocol to this Convention to extend its provisions to all types of business enterprises.

 (2) For the purpose of clause (1)(b), a 'transnational corporation' is a corporation which operates in more than one country or jurisdiction through its subsidiaries or affiliates (howsoever structured or defined) and exercises some level of control over such subsidiaries or affiliates.

 (3) For the purpose of clause (1)(b), a 'business enterprise with a transnational character' will include a business enterprise which has some transnational element in its business operations, such as that it directly offers products or services outside the country of incorporation, or it directly sources materials from overseas suppliers.

(4) States and all other actors mentioned in clause (1) shall comply with all instruments mentioned in Annexure A to this Convention to deal with business-related human rights abuses.

(5) The human rights obligations of actors mentioned in clause 1(b) shall be ascertained, on a case by case basis, with reference to the human rights instruments directed at states, but with due regard to their identity distinct from that of the state and in accordance with the general principles laid down in this Convention.'

Optional Protocol

'(1) State parties to this Convention shall consider ratifying the Optional Protocol to this Convention.

(2) On ratification of the Optional Protocol, the provisions of this Convention, except Chapters [related to provisions specific to TNCs such as states' extraterritorial obligations, applicable law and forum in trans-border cases, and states' obligation to provide mutual assistance and co-operation] shall extend to all other business enterprises with no transnational character.

(3) The Optional Protocol shall specify, among others, the principles with reference to which the extent of human rights obligations of small- and medium-size business enterprises could be differentiated from those of transnational corporations and other business enterprises with a transnational character.'

Annexure A

'Universal Declaration of Human Rights 1948

International Covenant on Civil and Political Rights 1966

International Covenant on Economic, Social and Cultural Rights 1966

International Convention on the Elimination of All Forms of Racial Discrimination 1965

Convention on the Elimination of All Forms of Discrimination against Women 1979

Convention against Torture and Other Cruel, Inhuman or Degrading Treatment or Punishment 1984

Convention on the Rights of the Child 1989

International Convention on the Protection of the Rights of All Migrant Workers and Members of Their Families 1990

International Convention for the Protection of All Persons from Enforced
   Disappearance 2006
Convention on the Rights of Persons with Disabilities 2006
Freedom of Association and Protection of the Right to Organise
   Convention 1948
Right to Organise and Collective Bargaining Convention 1949
Forced Labour Convention 1930
Abolition of Forced Labour Convention 1957
Minimum Age Convention 1973
Worst Forms of Child Labour Convention 1999
Equal Remuneration Convention 1951
Discrimination (Employment and Occupation) Convention 1958
Declaration on the Rights of Indigenous Peoples 2007
Rio Declaration on Environment and Development 1992'

PART III

Nature and Extent of Corporate Human Rights
Obligations

Corporate Obligations and a Treaty on Business and Human Rights

A Constitutional Law Model?

DAVID BILCHITZ

7.1 Introduction: Developing an Analytical Framework for Determining Corporate Obligations

The proposed business and human rights (BHR) treaty will be unique amongst human rights treaties. Whereas most general treaties outline the human rights all individuals may claim,[1] other treaties enumerate the rights that particularly vulnerable groups such as women or children may claim.[2] Where these treaties lay out obligations, it is generally the state that is expressly identified as being responsible for protecting and realizing these rights. A BHR treaty, in contrast, will, in all likelihood, need to be different in order to fulfil its objectives: instead of outlining the entitlements that individuals have, it will need to focus on the regulation of a particular class of non-state actors – businesses or corporations[3] – to ensure that they do not harm the human rights of individuals[4] and that they play their part in contributing towards their realization.

---

[1] The two most general treaties outlining the universal fundamental rights of all individuals are the International Covenant on Civil and Political Rights (entered into force 23 March 1976), 999 UNTS 171 (ICCPR) and the International Covenant on Economic, Social and Cultural Rights (entered into force 3 January 1976), 993 UNTS 3 (ICESCR).

[2] See, for example, the Convention on the Elimination of Discrimination against Women (entered into force 3 September 1981) 1249 UNTS 13 (CEDAW) and the Convention on the Rights of the Child (entered into force 2 September 1990) 1577 UNTS 3 (CRC).

[3] These terms are not identical: businesses can refer to a variety of legal forms such as a sole proprietor, partnership or corporations. Corporations are just one form of business entity but the most popular given the benefits the structure offers such as limited liability and perpetual succession. In this paper, I will focus on the obligations of corporations.

[4] I prefer the term fundamental rights, which places an emphasis on the importance of these rights and also recognizes that they are not limited to only members of the human species

There are two main models for a treaty to regulate corporations in this regard: the first retains a focus on the obligations of the state to protect individuals against the violation of their rights by third parties such as corporations (or to require certain actions of corporations to facilitate the realization of rights).[5] This 'indirect' model would basically place an international legal obligation on the state to ensure that corporations do not violate the human rights of individuals;[6] however, corporations would lack any obligations flowing directly from international human rights law.[7]

The 'direct' model, on the other hand, would involve recognizing that there are in fact direct obligations imposed upon corporations by international human rights law or that such obligations should be created by states. I have argued elsewhere that this idea is already contained in international human rights law and should not be regarded as a radical departure.[8] Irrespective of whether that position is accepted or not, the direct model would require both recognition that corporations are bound by human rights provisions and some guidance or mechanism to determine the nature and extent of these obligations.

Even if the proposed treaty adopts an indirect model, it will be critical to specify some guidelines as to the human rights obligations each particular state must impose on corporations within its jurisdiction. Otherwise individual states would essentially be given free rein to regulate as they see fit, which, in many instances, would lead to inadequate protections and in turn, reduce the effectiveness of such an instrument in realizing the goal of advancing the protection of human rights globally.

(which appears arbitrary and unjustifiable). For the sake of consistency with the practice of other authors in the rest of this book, I will use the term 'human' rights in this chapter.

[5] Such an obligation is well accepted in international human rights law and was first persuasively articulated in the case *Velasquez Rodriguez v. Honduras* (1989) 23 I.L.M. 291; (1988) Inter-A.C.H.R. (Ser. C) No.4, paras. 166–177.

[6] As will be seen in the argument below, I argue that corporations should have both 'negative' and 'positive' obligations and thus the state may also, on this model, be responsible for ensuring that corporations realize their positive obligations too.

[7] I have explored the indirect model for recognizing corporate obligations and its shortcomings in D. Bilchitz, 'Corporations and the Limits of State-Based Models for Protecting Fundamental Rights in International Law' (2016) 23 *Indiana Journal of Global Legal Studies* 143, at 149–157.

[8] See D. Bilchitz, 'A chasm between "is" and "ought"? A critique of the normative foundations of the SRSG's Framework and the Guiding Principles' in S. Deva and D. Bilchitz (eds.), *Human Rights Obligations of Business: Beyond the Corporate Responsibility to Respect?* (Cambridge: Cambridge University Press, 2013) 111–114. See also A. Clapham, *Human Rights Obligations of Non-State Actors* (Oxford University Press, 2006).

Furthermore, such an approach would lead to a wide-ranging assortment of regulatory regimes which would fail to offer a degree of uniform protection for individuals across the world. Such a situation could undermine a key rationale for the treaty: to avoid competition between jurisdictions regarding their regulatory regimes governing the BHR landscape which, in the worst case scenario, could lead to a 'race to the bottom'.[9] Thus, even on the indirect model, it would be highly desirable for an international treaty to outline a minimum set of specific human rights obligations that each state must impose on the corporations within its jurisdiction.

Consequently, both the direct and indirect models of regulating corporations are likely to require some approach to be adopted in the text of a treaty towards determining the obligations of corporations in relation to human rights (whether flowing from international law or domestic legislation). Although both approaches will need some guidance on how to approach corporate obligations, in this chapter, I will focus on the direct model and explore how a treaty should approach determining the obligations of corporations.

In addressing this question, it is important to recognize that what is being sought is not a full specification in the treaty of the obligations of corporations in relation to every specific human right.[10] Such a goal would be impossible to achieve within a treaty. Instead, the goal for the relevant treaty provision should be to provide an analytical framework that provides some guidance as to how these obligations can be determined in a particular context. Concrete obligations can later be specified in more detail by treaty bodies or domestic courts on a case by case basis. Within domestic constitutional contexts too, a similar problem arises in constitutional design as to how to create an analytical framework for determining corporate (and, indeed, state) obligations which can later be utilized by courts (and other actors) rather than providing a full specification of concrete obligations. The South African constitution, in particular, has included in its bill of rights a provision directly recognizing that juristic persons have obligations in this regard.

In this chapter, I consider four different approaches to formulating an analytical framework that addresses the obligations of corporations at a level of abstraction necessary for a treaty provision. The first approach utilizes the

---

[9] For an elaboration of this argument, see Chapter 3 by Leader in this volume.

[10] There is also an important question that arises as to which rights are the subject of obligations for corporations: this matter is dealt with in Chapter 6 by Deva in this volume.

notion of a 'sphere of influence' to determine corporate obligations. This approach was adopted by the Draft Norms on the Responsibilities of Transnational Corporations and other Business Enterprises (Draft Norms).[11] After providing the historical context that led to this approach, I engage with some of the key critical elements of the concept of 'sphere of influence' in order to understand its strengths and inadequacies. The discussion highlights that this approach alone cannot provide the desired framework. Nevertheless, it does highlight a number of normative factors that must be taken into account in any adequate treaty provision.

In the second part of the chapter, I consider the 'negative obligation' approach, which focuses on restricting corporate obligations only to a particular type of duty, namely negative obligations. This criterion has been utilized by the former Special Representative of the Secretary General on Business and Human Rights (SRSG) – Professor John Ruggie – at the international level in the form of the Guiding Principles on Business and Human Rights (GPs).[12] This approach has also been suggested by a provision of the South African Constitution. Whilst I provide several reasons why this approach is neither fully adequate nor desirable, an investigation of the normative impetus behind it also suggests which aspects thereof need to be addressed in any acceptable framework provision.

The next part of the chapter considers the 'nature of the rights' approach, which is drawn from the provision in the Constitution of South Africa. This criterion focuses on the nature of the rights in question to help determine the obligations of corporations. The manner in which this criterion has been developed by the South African Constitutional Court is promising in that it includes both considerations relating to the impact of corporate conduct on the rights of beneficiaries (or victims) as well as considerations that take into account the particularities of certain agents (agent-relativity). Unfortunately, this approach has factors pulling in different directions and there is no overarching framework identified thus far in South African case law to resolve these tensions in determining corporate obligations.

---

[11] Commission on Human Rights, Sub-Commission on the Promotion and Protection of Human Rights, 'Norms on the Responsibilities of Transnational Corporations and Other Business Enterprises with Regard to Human Rights', E/CN.4/Sub.2/2003/12/Rev.2 (26 August 2003) (Draft Norms).
[12] Human Rights Council, 'Guiding Principles on Business and Human Rights: Implementing the United Nations' "Protect, Respect and Remedy" Framework', A/HRC/17/31 (21 March 2011) (Guiding Principles).

The final part of this chapter outlines a 'two-stage approach' to determining corporate obligations in relation to human rights which can capture some of the strengths of the other approaches. This approach flows from recent thinking in drafting constitutional provisions around determining general human rights obligations in a range of jurisdictions around the world and draws on the widespread notion of proportionality. The first stage of this approach attempts to capture the interests of individuals that are at stake and the potential infringement that corporations can have upon those interests: it is thus beneficiary-orientated. The second stage involves considering the justifiability of any infringement upon those interests. It does so by considering the purpose of the infringement and involves a general use of the proportionality enquiry to determine whether the benefits of the infringement can justify the harms to the right. That enquiry, I shall contend, allows agent-relative considerations to be taken into account and can capture the key normative issues that are necessary in determining corporate obligations. It can also provide a structured enquiry that will allow the nature and scope of corporate obligations to be developed incrementally by dedicated mechanisms that should be created for this purpose.

All of these approaches are considered given that each of them highlights normative factors that are of importance in the construction of an analytical framework for corporate obligations in a treaty. Appreciating even the deficiencies of these approaches is helpful in understanding what needs to be done to correct these weaknesses. I will end this chapter by proposing a draft provision for the treaty that draws on the insights gained from the critical analysis of these four approaches conducted in this chapter.

7.2 The Development of a 'Sphere of Influence' Approach

Since the 1970s, there has been discussion of developing an international law framework in relation to corporations. In this part of the chapter, I consider the first attempt to outline corporate obligations, which was rather minimalist in character, and then turn to the distinct approach to this question that emerged in a subsequent document focused on the notion of a 'sphere of influence'.

7.2.1   The Draft Code

The first attempt to create a binding code of conduct for transnational corporations (TNCs) culminated in the 1990s with a proposed text being published in the form of the Draft Code of Conduct on Transnational

Corporations.[13] The document was very much entwined with the politics of its time and, particularly, the conflict between developed and developing countries.

The Draft Code clearly wished to strengthen the role of the state and was concerned that state sovereignty may be undermined by TNCs. In relation to human rights, it has a rather brief provision which required that:

> Transnational corporations shall respect human rights and fundamental freedoms in the countries in which they operate. In their social and industrial relations, transnational corporations shall not discriminate on the basis of race, colour, sex, religion, language, social and national origin, or political or other opinion. Transnational corporations shall conform to government policies designed to extend equality of opportunity or treatment.[14]

This provision is noteworthy as it does recognize a general direct obligation upon TNCs to 'respect' human rights and fundamental freedoms. The conservative legal thinking of the time would have been opposed to the recognition of any direct obligations upon non-state actors. It is not entirely clear whether the language used was meant, at the time, to limit the direct obligations of corporations simply to the obligation to 'respect' as it has been understood in human rights law. That understanding would involve only imposing a largely negative obligation upon corporations to avoid harming rights.[15] Such a narrow approach would, in a sense, be at odds with other aspects of the Draft Code which envisaged a larger role for TNCs in the development of societies. Having laid out that general obligation upon corporations, the Draft Code articulated a specific obligation to avoid discrimination on various grounds as well as an obligation to implement positive discrimination measures that were developed by governments. There is no clear justification offered as to why the focus in this key human rights section lies on only one particular right amongst the full panoply of the rights in the international bill of rights:[16] such an approach does not appear desirable as it is likely to create a hierarchy amongst human rights.

---

[13] 23 ILM 626 (1984) (Draft Code). For the history of this document and background to it see the chapter in this volume by Hamdani and Ruffing.

[14] *Ibid.*, art. 14.   [15] Such an approach will be evaluated in the next part of this chapter.

[16] One major question for any treaty will be the list of applicable rights which can range from a minimal approach (including only the international bill of rights) to a more maximal approach (including the full range of international human rights treaties and even possibly non-binding declarations). I am in favour of the more minimal approach which will be capable of capturing most of the violations caused by corporations.

7.2.2 Draft Norms

The next attempt to codify and to develop progressively the international law relating to corporate obligations took place with the release of the Draft Norms in 2003. This document emerged from an expert working group appointed by the Sub-Commission on the Promotion and Protection of Human Rights. The Sub-commission approved the Norms but, unfortunately, they attracted much criticism and eventually were declared by the Commission on Human Rights to have 'no legal standing'.[17] Whilst they were never formally adopted by the Commission, the approach adopted by the group of experts to the obligations of business and the criticism thereof merits more detailed attention.

The Draft Norms begin in their preamble to recognize that 'transnational corporations and other business enterprises, their officers, and their workers have, inter alia, human rights obligations and responsibilities'.[18] Having recognized that business enterprises have direct obligations, the Draft Norms go on to elaborate the approach towards such obligations as follows:

> States have the primary responsibility to promote, secure the fulfilment of, respect, ensure respect of, and protect human rights recognised in international as well as national law, including assuring that transnational corporations and other business enterprises respect human rights. Within their respective spheres of activity and influence, transnational corporations and other business enterprises have the obligation to promote, secure the fulfilment of, respect, ensure respect of, and protect human rights recognized in international as well as national law.[19]

This key provision does a number of things. First, it recognizes that states have the primary obligations to ensure human rights are realized which include a duty to protect individuals against violations by corporations. We can call this 'the primacy principle'. Second, it recognizes that TNCs and other business enterprises have the obligations – subject to the limitations discussed below – to 'promote, secure fulfilment of, respect, ensure respect of, and protect' human rights. These words include both negative and positive obligations under international human rights law. These obligations can be further specified as duties to avoid depriving individuals of rights (to respect); duties to protect from deprivation by third parties (to protect) and duties to aid the

---

[17] Commission on Human Rights, Agenda Item 16, E/CN.4/2004/L.73/Rev.1 (16 April 2004), para. (c).
[18] Draft Norms, n. 11, Preamble. [19] *Ibid.*, para. 1.

deprived (to fulfil).[20] Third, the above provision, when read with the definitions section, adopts an expansive view of the human rights in relation to which these obligations apply. Article 23 of the Draft Norms states that human rights include 'civil, cultural, economic, political, and social rights, as set forth in the International Bill of Human Rights and other human rights treaties, as well as the right to development and rights recognized by international humanitarian law, international refugee law, international labour law, and other relevant instruments adopted within the United Nations system'.[21] Finally, the provision contains two limiting principles in relation to the obligations of corporations: that corporations are not understood to have the primary responsibility for the realization of these rights; and that their obligations apply only within their respective 'spheres of activity and influence'.

The Draft Norms then include specific provisions which specify the obligations of corporations in relation to a few particular rights, which were perhaps regarded as being particularly important in the context of corporate activity: the rights to equality, to security of the person, worker's rights, consumer protection, environmental protection and non-corruption. There is then a further general provision:

> Transnational corporations and other business enterprises shall respect civil, cultural, economic, political, and social rights, and contribute to their realization, in particular the rights to development; adequate food and drinking water; the highest attainable standard of physical and mental health; adequate housing; privacy; education; freedom of thought, conscience, and religion; and freedom of opinion and expression; and refrain from actions which obstruct or impede the realization of those rights.[22]

I shall now engage critically with some of the elements of this approach.

7.2.3   The Primacy Principle

The primacy principle articulated in the Draft Norms accords priority to state obligations in relation to human rights. One of the motivations for this may well have been to dispel the fear often expressed that states may seek to avoid their own duties by hiding behind and/or transferring their

---

[20] I take this language from the work of Henry Shue, *Basic Rights* (Princeton University Press, 1980), which inspired the development of the framework of duties to respect, protect and fulfil.

[21] Draft Norms, n. 11, para. 23.   [22] *Ibid.*, art. 12.

responsibilities in this area to corporations.[23] Placing priority on state obligations, however, is problematic as it fails to capture adequately the equal normative status of the human rights obligations in relation to varied agents as well as the empirical realities of their power today. From a normative point of view, human rights are ultimately focused on protecting the worth or dignity of individuals. That dignity requires that their most foundational interests in freedom and well-being are guaranteed. The focus of human rights is on ensuring that rights-bearers have their interests realized: it does not specify any agent that has primary responsibility in this regard. Given the initial focus of human rights discourse on limiting the power of oppressive states, it is understandable why there was an early emphasis placed on the responsibility of the state. Yet, in our current world, it is quite clear that non-state actors may themselves have a similar level of power over individuals. Consider, for example, guerrilla groups who control an area where they are fighting a civil war. Similarly, a corporation which is the sole source of employment and economic development in a state with weak governance has enormous power. Normatively, there is no reason why the obligations of the non-state actors in these settings should not be of an equal strength to those of the state. To assert the primary responsibility of the state in this regard sets up a hierarchy of obligation which may not reflect at all the reality of the agents who have the most power to impact upon human rights in a particular situation.

Such an approach also, misleadingly, suggests that the obligations of corporations are of a 'lesser import', which will often not be true due to the foundational manner in which they can impact on the rights of individuals. The distinction between primary and secondary responsibility is also not helpful in any manner as a principle for determining what the exact obligations of a corporation are.

The primacy principle places the focus on the obligations of the state and corporations vis-à-vis one another. Whilst I argue against the language of primacy for the state, I do believe that there is an underlying normative concern that merits attention: the need to consider the nature and particularities of different agents when determining their obligations. If this is so, it is likely that the obligations of the state and the

---

[23] The SRSG expressed this worry on several occasions in his reports. See, for instance, Commission on Human Rights, 'Interim Report of the Special Representative of the Secretary-General on the Issue of Human Rights and Transnational Corporations and Other Business Enterprises', E/CN.4/2006/97 (22 February 2006), para. 68 ('Interim Report').

corporation will differ, given the fact that they have different institutional natures and functions. It will thus be important to develop an approach that can capture the particular nature of the corporation in defining their obligations without resorting to an understanding that their obligations are in some sense secondary. This leads us into a consideration of methods for distinguishing obligations of states and corporations: I will now turn to the 'sphere of influence' approach adopted in the Draft Norms.

7.2.4   The Sphere of Influence

The notion of 'sphere of influence' had already become influential within the domain of corporate social responsibility when it was included in the Draft Norms. The idea involves a spatial metaphor which conditions corporate responsibility on the extent of its influence. It is perhaps an analogue of an attempt to define the 'jurisdiction' of a corporation: the state's jurisdiction lies, mostly, within its territorial borders; the jurisdiction of a corporation lies within its 'sphere of influence'. The problem is that the notion of 'sphere of influence' has a much greater vagueness than the territorial boundaries of the state and the question is whether that can be remedied.[24]

The 'influence' of a corporation has been recognized to occur within certain domains and to be more intensive in some domains as opposed to others. The core idea behind this approach is that the greater the influence, the more responsibility a corporation has. The idea links up with developments in the realm of stakeholder theory, which recognizes that a corporation should be understood not merely in relation to the shareholders who invest in it, but in relation to all stakeholders upon whom it has an impact.[25] Stakeholder theory holds that there are a number of stakeholders which are affected by company activities: these include employees, customers, shareholders, contractors, investors and members of local communities. The obligations of a corporation will vary in relation to the relationship a company has with a particular group.

---

[24] Though the territory of the state is pretty clear and defined, its influence beyond its borders and the extent of its consequent extraterritorial obligations perhaps also raise similar difficulties.

[25] R. E. Freeman, *Strategic Management: a Stakeholder Approach* (Cambridge University Press, 2010) 46. See also R. E. Freeman et al., *Stakeholder Theory: the State of the Art* (Cambridge University Press, 2010).

The 'sphere of influence' notion does seem to include a number of features which are normatively significant. The first is that the impact or potential impact of the corporation on human rights needs to be considered when determining their obligations. The second feature is that there may be a continuum of obligations which range from the more extensive to the less extensive. In a sense, we see an analogue here to principles that exist in relation to the state as well: the more intrusive the impact upon fundamental interests, the more extensive the obligations of agents may be.[26] Finally, the notion of 'sphere of influence' seems to embody that there must be a limit to corporate obligations and that there is a point at which it is not fair to hold them accountable for wrongs that occur.

These attractive features are no doubt some of the reasons why the idea was included in the Draft Norms. Yet, at the same time, the concept has come in for detailed criticism which has highlighted several of its shortcomings.[27] The first critique concerns what is meant by 'influence'. Lehr and Jenkins, for instance, have critiqued the notion, claiming that the idea lumps together ideas of 'proximity, impact, control, benefit and political influence'.[28] The notion is thus dependent, they claimed, upon a range of underlying normative ideas and in itself, it is irredeemably vague. They claim that it is necessary to disentangle these various aspects to arrive at a notion that is useful in determining corporate obligations. Some of the underlying ideas, too, are not adequate to address the range of corporate obligations and are either too wide or too narrow. The idea of 'benefit', for instance, may seem too wide a notion to couch a definitive obligation upon: corporations may well benefit from certain unjust social structures or laws though it is not clear how this conditions their obligations. On the other hand, the idea of 'proximity' may be too narrow: if

---

[26] Such a principle has, for instance, been articulated by the South African Constitutional Court in relation to the right to privacy where the intrusion into the domain of the home – where an individual can expect the greatest privacy – will require a greater level of justification than intrusions into privacy at the workplace. See, for instance, *Bernstein v. Bester* 1996 (2) SA 751 (CC) para. 67.

[27] See, for instance, Human Rights Council 'Clarifying the Concepts of "Sphere of Influence" and "Complicity"', A/HRC/8/16 (15 May 2008) ('Companion Report'); K. Macdonald, 'Rethinking "Spheres of Responsibility": Business Responsibility for Indirect Harm' (2011) 99 *Journal of Business Ethics* 549.

[28] A. Lehr and B. Jenkins, 'Business and Human Rights – Beyond corporate spheres of influence' (12 November 2007) available at https://business-humanrights.org/en/business-and-human-rights-%E2%80%93-beyond-corporate-spheres-of-influence (last accessed 18 July 2016).

understood in the sense of geographical proximity, it fails to account for the ability of corporations today to damage the environment far away from the location of a factory or the power of an internet-service provider to cause harm to the privacy of individuals literally on the other side of the world.[29] The ideas of 'causation' and 'control' also require further unpacking, as too restrictive an understanding may well not be able to take account of the complex responsibilities of corporations, for instance, for their subsidiaries or businesses in supply chains which they do not directly control. In view of such criticisms the SRSG reached the conclusion that what matters in determining corporate obligations is the 'company's web of relationships and activities'.[30]

I would like to add a further critique which is important in this context. The 'sphere of influence' idea connects the range of influence and the consequent obligations of corporations vis-à-vis particular stakeholders. Thus, in general, a corporation is understood to have a greater influence and therefore more extensive obligations in relation to employees. However, this may not always be the case: for instance, the impact of a corporation's operations may be extensive on a local community living near a mine and, at least, equal in its effects to those of the corporation on the rights of employees.[31] It does not therefore make sense to determine the obligations of a corporation in relation to particular stakeholders such as employees: in this sense the idea is too rigid by identifying in advance the particular stakeholders upon which there is more or less impact. It would be better to focus upon the impact of particular activities on the interests of individuals and thus determine obligations in relation to avoiding potential violations.

This analysis of the 'sphere of influence' approach has identified a number of important issues that will need to be considered in determining corporate obligations. At the same time, it is not itself an adequate basis for determining corporate obligations. I now turn to consider an

---

[29] HRC, 'Companion Report', n. 27, para. 15.   [30] *Ibid.*

[31] For instance, consider an example as to whether a corporation may view the personal communications of employees on office computers provided to employees for performing their work. On the one hand, the 'sphere of influence' idea may require a high level of protection for the right to privacy of employees given the strong impact the corporation can have on their lives in this area. On the other hand, given the very close nature of its relationship with employees, the company may also have the greatest justifiable claim in these circumstances to monitor their communications (something a person, for instance, with a more distant relationship would lack). How does the sphere of influence idea help determine the specific obligations of corporations in this case? In a sense, the notion simply amplifies the normative conflict involved without providing any means to resolve it.

approach that has been suggested both in the constitutional law context as well as within the international sphere in the GPs.

7.3 An Approach Focused on the Nature of Corporate Obligations: Do Corporations Only Have Negative Obligations?

An analogue of the current debate at the international level has occurred in the realm of domestic constitutional law where, in the drafting of recent constitutions, the question has arisen as to whether to impose obligations upon non-state actors.[32] South Africa's Constitution is one of the most advanced in the world in this regard and includes a provision which envisages the direct application of constitutional rights to private bodies. Section 8(2) of the Constitution reads as follows: 'A provision of the Bill of Rights binds a natural or a juristic person if, and to the extent that, it is applicable, taking into account the nature of the right and the nature of any duty imposed by the right.'[33]

A similar provision is included within the recent Kenyan Constitution of 2010, which provides in section 20(1) that the 'Bill of Rights applies to all and binds all state organs and all persons'. The Kenyan constitution, however, contains no further provisos or guidance as to how it will apply to persons other than the state.

The South African Constitution, however, attempts to provide some basis for determining the extent to which the bill of rights places obligations on private actors. It recognizes that there are three possibilities:[34] a right may not have any implications for a private party; a right may apply

---

[32] The issue has been the subject of discussion and development in many jurisdictions prior to this. See, for instance, in India, M. Singh, 'Fundamental Rights, State Action and Cricket in India' (2006) 13 *Asia Pacific Law Review* 203; in Germany, the concept of Drittwirkung, developed in the *Lüth case* BVerfGE 7, 198 (1958) and A. Sajo and R. Uitz, *The Constitution in Private Relations: Expanding Constitutionalism*. (Eleven International Publications 2005); and in the United States, E. Chemerinsky, 'Rethinking State Action' (1985) 80 *Northwestern University Law Review* 503.

[33] There is some complexity as to the effect of this provision and whether it operates any differently to the indirect horizontal doctrine. The reason for this is that section 8(3) appears to envisage that the manner in which section 8(2) will apply lies in developing doctrines of the common law. Nevertheless, the provision, on its face, recognizes that private actors are directly bound by the bill of rights and provides some criteria to determine that. See, for instance, N. Friedman 'The South African Common Law and the Constitution: Revisiting Horizontality' (2014) 30 *South African Journal on Human Rights* 63–88.

[34] The analysis here is drawn from D. Bilchitz 'Corporate Law and the Constitution: Towards Binding Human Rights Responsibilities for Corporations' (2008) 125 *South African Law Journal* 754–789.

fully to a private party; and a right may apply partially to a private party. Clearly, it will be necessary to determine the circumstances under which the right applies and the manner in which it does: the notion of applicability is circular without more. Two criteria are identified in that regard: the nature of the right must be taken into account, and second, the nature of any duty imposed by the right must be taken into account. This South African Constitutional provision requires further interpretation as it is not entirely clear what is meant by each variable and how these variables determine the resultant obligations. In any international instrument, it would be desirable to provide additional guidance. In doing so, though, it is instructive to consider the manner in which the South African Constitutional Court has interpreted these provisions and whether that can provide any guidance in determining a suitable approach at the international level. I will in this part of the chapter consider an approach based on the nature of the duty criterion and, in the next part, consider the nature of the right criterion.

7.3.1   The Nature of the Duty Imposed by the Right: Only Negative Obligations?

Section 8(2) seems to indicate that the nature of duty imposed by the right may affect its applicability, or the extent of its applicability, to private parties. The manner in which this criterion applies is quite unclear on its face: the nature of the duty might, in terms of this provision, render it inapplicable to both natural and juristic persons; on the other hand, it is possible that the applicability of obligations may vary with the kind of private entity that is under consideration. The importance of the provision is that it indicates that considerations relative to particular agents ('agent-relative considerations') may help determine the extent of obligations held by private entities.

The Constitutional Court has had very few opportunities to engage with the implications of this criterion. In the case of *Governing Body of Juma-Masjid Primary School v. Essay N.O.*,[35] the Court was faced with a complex matter where the government had established a school on the property of a private trust. The government failed to pay the rentals and additional expenditure that it owed the trust and the trust decided to evict the school from its premises. The Court had to determine both the obligations of the state and that of the private trust in these circumstances

---

[35] [2011] ZACC 13.

in relation to the right to education of learners attending the school. Importantly, the Court overturned a finding by the High Court that the trust lacked any direct obligations in relation to the right to education. Nevertheless, it reasoned that the ambit of these obligations had to be restricted: the trust did not have an obligation to provide basic education nor to lease its property to the government. The trust's obligations were largely negative, and were framed by the Court as being 'not to impair the learners' right to a basic education'.[36] In a crucial paragraph, the Court reasoned as follows:

> This Court, in *Ex Parte Chairperson of the Constitutional Assembly: In re Certification of the Constitution of the Republic of South Africa*, made it clear that socio-economic rights (like the right to a basic education) may be negatively protected from improper invasion. Breach of this obligation occurs directly when there is a failure to respect the right, or indirectly, when there is a failure to prevent the direct infringement of the right by another or a failure to respect the existing protection of the right by taking measures that diminish that protection. It needs to be stressed however that the purpose of section 8(2) of the Constitution is not to obstruct private autonomy or to impose on a private party the duties of the state in protecting the Bill of Rights. It is rather to require private parties not to interfere with or diminish the enjoyment of a right.[37]

The Court, in this case, appears to affirm the principle that, in general, the duties of private parties will be conceived of in a negative manner: these involve, at least the duty to avoid harming individuals through their own actions (the 'duty to respect' in the context of international human rights law). The reference to indirect breaches of this obligation may well also include obligations upon private parties to avoid harm to individuals through the actions of others closely connected to them (the 'duty to protect' in the context of international human rights law). The justification for this conception lies in an attempt to recognize the impact private parties can have on human rights but also to avoid too much interference with private autonomy and saddling private parties with the duties of the state.

This conception of the obligations of private actors is similar to that adopted by the SRSG in his 2008 Framework and later in the GPs. Whilst in these documents the SRSG did not, in general, recognize that there are direct legal obligations upon corporations under international law (in contrast to the binding obligations recognized by the Constitutional

---

[36] *Ibid.*, para. 60. [37] *Ibid.*, para. 58.

Court under the South African Constitution), he articulated that corporations have a responsibility to respect human rights rooted in societal expectations. The responsibility to respect essentially involves a negative obligation to 'avoid causing or contributing to adverse human rights impacts through its own activities' and to 'seek to prevent or mitigate adverse human rights impacts that are directly linked to their operations, products or services, by their business relationships even if they have not contributed to those impacts'.[38] It does also include a requirement that there be positive steps taken where this is necessary to avoid such harm. The positive steps include businesses putting in place relevant policies to avoid harm and engaging in a human rights due diligence process to identify, prevent, mitigate and account for how they address their impacts on human rights.[39] However, all these positive duties flow from a conception of corporate obligations that is essentially 'negative' in character, namely, being focused on avoiding harm to rights whether through their own actions or those of other third parties.[40]

The SRSG explains the reasons underlying the approach adopted by his mandate in a similar manner to the reasons provided by the Constitutional Court of South Africa. He contends that corporations must be understood to have a limited role in relation to human rights given their specialized nature. He writes:

> While it may be useful to think of corporations as "organs of society" as in the preambular language of the Universal Declaration, they are specialized organs that perform specialized functions. They are not a microcosm of the entire social body. By their very nature, therefore, corporations do not have a general role in relation to human rights as do States; they have a specialized one.[41]

Wider social obligations upon corporations, he contends, may undermine 'the company's own economic role and possibly its commercial viability'.[42] The SRSG also raises questions about the legitimacy of corporations performing a wide range of social functions and, in some cases,

---

[38] Guiding Principles, n. 12, Principle 13.   [39] Ibid., Principle 15(b).

[40] I have previously demonstrated the primacy of negative obligations in the SRSG's work in D. Bilchitz 'The Ruggie Framework: An Adequate Rubric for Corporate Human Rights Obligations?' (2010) 12 Sur International Journal on Human Rights 199, 206.

[41] Commission on Human Rights, 'Interim Report', n. 23, para. 66.

[42] Human Rights Council, 'Business and Human Rights: Further Steps Towards the Operationalization of the "Protect, Respect and Remedy" Framework', A/HRC/14/27 (9 April 2010), para. 64.

taking over responsibilities that are the domain of governments.[43] Steven Ratner, in a seminal journal article on determining corporate obligations, contends too (with very limited discussion) that corporations should not in general have positive obligations actively to be involved in realizing rights. He notes that doing so would be to 'ask too much of the corporation, especially at this stage of the international legal process, when the broad notion of business duties in the human rights area is just emerging'.[44]

7.3.2 Why the Negative-Positive Distinction Should Not Be Used as a Framework to Delineate Corporate Obligations

This approach raises the question as to whether it is justifiable as an analytical framework to distinguish corporate obligations on the basis that they have only a 'negative' character, including at most the duties to respect and protect as understood in international human rights law.[45] Such a conception would mean that corporations have no obligations positively to assist in the realization of rights where no harmful activities of their own (or those they are connected to) are involved. This approach raises several complex considerations which a number of authors (including myself) have engaged elsewhere.[46] In this chapter, I shall not be able to deal with this question in detail, but will present four central arguments against a conception of corporate obligations that simply limits them to negative obligations.

First, the 'negative-positive' distinction is not sufficient as an analytical framework for determining the extent of corporate obligations. It excludes

---

[43] *Ibid.*, para. 64. In this regard, he also mentions the fact that corporations could undermine government capacity and engage in strategic gaming with the government in relation to the provision of goods.

[44] S. Ratner, 'Corporations and Human Rights: a Theory of Legal Responsibility' (2001) 111 *Yale Law Journal* 443, at 517. Ratner goes on to say that to require proactive steps to promote human rights 'seems inconsistent with the reality of the corporate enterprise'. *Ibid.* at 518.

[45] Whilst the duty to protect requires positive actions, it is also largely focused on the avoidance of harm by third parties (at least in the SRSG's articulation and thus is properly considered as part of the 'negative' conception of corporate obligations).

[46] See, for instance, N. Hsieh, 'The Obligations of Transnational Corporations: Rawlsian Justice and the Duty of Assistance' (2004) *Business Ethics Quarterly* 14; F. Wettstein, *Multi-National Corporations and Global Justice: Human Rights Obligations of a Quasi-Governmental Institution* (Stanford: Stanford University Press, 2009); D. Bilchitz, 'Do Corporations Have Positive Fundamental Rights Obligations?' (2010) 125 *Theoria* 11–26; and Bilchitz, 'A Chasm', n. 8, 107.

corporations from having positive obligations but it fails to provide any guidance on how to capture the nature and range of the negative obligations of corporations.[47] Determining what falls within the ambit of such obligations is not trivial: do corporations harm privacy rights by monitoring emails of employees? Do they harm freedom of expression rights by forbidding senior executives from commenting on political events on their personal Twitter accounts? These illustrative questions cannot be answered simply by saying corporations have 'negative' but not 'positive' obligations: there is a need for more guidance in any analytical framework on how to determine the more specific obligations of corporations.

Second, excluding corporations from the ambit of positive obligations would render them highly exceptional entities. Both Kantian and utilitarian ethical theories recognize that individuals have, at least, some positive moral obligations on fundamental ethical concerns: if this is so for individuals, it is hard to see why corporations – structures behind which often lie conglomerations of individuals – should be exempted. In order to claim an exemption from positive obligations, it would be necessary to provide reasons why the particularities of a corporation as an agent should allow it to be so exempted. Considering that the structure usually involves multiple individuals who own and control the corporation and that the corporate form enables corporations to wield significant economic power, corporations should have stronger not weaker positive obligations than individuals.[48] Those considerations would also support rendering these moral obligations legal.

The third argument is consequentialist in nature. If we want to improve the well-being of individuals across the world, it is necessary to recognize that corporations have certain positive obligations.[49] In the modern world, corporations are one of the central prongs of the economy. They are present in countries around the world and create as well as accumulate large amounts of social wealth. They play a key role in the well-being of many individuals who are reliant on them for employment. In short, corporations have the potential as well as the power to make a major impact on human rights and, in some cases, their operations affect the capacity of the state to realize such rights. To obviate the need to

---

[47] I have elaborated upon this argument in D. Bilchitz, 'The Necessity for a Business and Human Rights Treaty' (2016) 1:2 *Business and Human Rights Journal* 203, 210–211.

[48] I have developed this argument in more detail in Bilchitz, 'A Chasm', n. 8, 128–132.

[49] I have considered this argument and the potential of corporations to assist in the fight against global poverty in Bilchitz, 'The Ruggie Framework', n. 40, 124–125.

consider the positive role such major actors can play in the realization of human rights would hamper seriously the realization of these rights.

The final argument is rooted in a consideration of the nature of corporations as agents.[50] Corporations are themselves creatures of statute: they cannot exist without a law enabling their creation. In creating laws, legislatures cannot themselves be motivated simply to enrich private individual interests; that would be an illegitimate exercise of their power. The normative basis for the exercise of legitimate legislative power must be founded in a commitment to advance the interests of all members of society and, to do so, in a manner that demonstrates the equal importance of every individual in the society.[51] The protection of human rights is a core purpose that flows from this principle of equal importance: in performing their tasks, legislators must thus have the realization of such rights as one of their core goals.

This purpose must, consequently, be considered when evaluating the reasons behind the creation of the corporate form. The corporate entity, which provides a number of important social benefits, limits the liability of those who invest in it. As such, individuals are willing to take more risks, which in turn enhances innovation and, indeed, economic growth. All these activities can increase the ability of individuals to gain access to various human rights through increased employment, improved technology and much else. Thus, the very underlying reasons for the creation of corporations involve a consideration of its social purpose and its relation to the realization of human rights.

At the same time, the corporate form is a medium through which individuals are able to advance their own personal interests. An understanding of the nature of corporate actors thus involves recognizing that they have a dual aspect: they are meant to operate both in the self-interest of their shareholders and also advance a range of social benefits including advancing human rights. That dual aspect means that private autonomy and profit is not the only interest to be considered in developing an understanding of corporate obligations; it is also necessary to consider whether the underlying social purposes behind the creation of the form are being realized.

However, any conception of positive corporate human rights obligations has to recognize the need for a clear difference between corporations

---

[50] See also Bilchitz, 'Positive Obligations', n. 46, 19–23 for an extended version of this argument.

[51] See R. Dworkin, *Sovereign Virtue* (Harvard University Press, 2000) 1.

and governments in relation to positive obligations. Corporations are generally designed to achieve social benefits indirectly through their ordinary operations, whereas all activities of governments must be designed expressly to achieve these goods. The indirect manner in which corporations are meant to advance human rights is key to understanding the extent of their positive obligations. In determining these obligations, it is suggested that any future BHR treaty should include a number of normative factors that can guide decision-making bodies in determining the nature and extent of corporate positive obligations. These factors should include, at least, the following:

- Given the reasoning above, it is clear, as a starting point, that corporations cannot exclusively focus on achieving business goals such as maximizing profits in a manner that inhibits the advancement of human rights. As such, they have a positive duty actively to consider fundamental rights and to align their business interests with them. That understanding may in fact require taking decisions that are not optimal from a point of view focused purely on the achievement of profits. Thus, for instance, trying to increase already substantial profits may lead corporations to retrench employees who are not absolutely essential in a context with poor employment prospects. Technological advances in petrol pumps could, for instance, allow South African gas station owners to retrench the large number of petrol attendants in the country. Yet, to do so would lead to large numbers of additional people being unemployed with the consequent impact on their families' access to social and economic rights. Gas station owners could still make a profit in this scenario even though the business model of employing attendants may be less efficient than not doing so. The social benefits and effect on the human rights of employees outweighs this cost in efficiency. This example demonstrates the need for positive obligations upon corporations actively to align their advancement of business goals with fundamental rights concerns in decision-making. At the same time, as a corporation is not equivalent to the state, such an alignment must still ensure that some autonomous space remains for the corporation to achieve its economic goals.[52] Whilst no corporation can ignore its impact upon fundamental rights, these two dimensions will affect the extent of corporate obligations in particular situations.

---

[52] An attempt to address a methodology that can be required of directors of companies in balancing these competing factors is considered in D. Bilchitz and L. Ausserladscheider Jonas 'Proportionality, Fundamental Rights and The Duties of Directors' (2016) 36 *Oxford Journal of Legal Studies* 828–854.

- Another key factor relates to the extent to which the sphere of activity of a corporation is closely connected to the realization of human rights (such as the rights to health and education). For example, pharmaceutical companies, which are involved in the development and production of critical medicines, seek to make profits from the fact that what they produce connects to very basic needs of individuals. As such, in such contexts, it would be particularly justifiable to place on them a duty to ensure the affordability of any critical medicines they develop and the extent of their obligations may be greater.
- The structure of the market and dominance of a corporation therein may also affect the extent of its positive duties. If certain corporations have a monopoly over the production of an essential good – such as bread – that seriously affects human rights, it would seem justifiable to place stronger positive obligations upon them to ensure accessibility and affordability of bread to individuals.
- Another connected factor relates to the dependency or vulnerability of individuals to particular corporate actors. This factor would justify placing greater positive obligations on an entity in proportion to the increased vulnerability of individuals to it.
- The final suggested factor would be the extent to which corporate activity affects the ability of government organs to realize the state's positive obligations. This factor recognizes that there is a connection between corporate behaviour in a market and the government's own ability to realize human rights. Corporations, for instance, affect the labour market and are often able to attract the most talented employees away from the public sector, which in turn has an adverse effect on the government's capacity to fulfil its obligation to realize rights. This is a complex issue to solve, but it points to the need to recognize an obligation upon corporations not to undermine the government's ability to achieve its goals and to modify its behaviour accordingly.

The upshot of this section has been to argue that the negative-positive obligations distinction is neither adequate nor desirable as a basis for the formation of an analytical framework to help determine corporate obligations in a future treaty on business and human rights. The proposed treaty should not in any way deny that corporations have a role to play in advancing such rights in a positive manner. At the same time, it should be emphasized that none of the arguments outlined above suggest that the positive obligations of corporations should be articulated in a manner that is identical to those of the state. The particular nature of corporations may limit the extent of their positive obligations; it does not, however, exempt them from performing some such obligations.

7.4   An Approach Focused on the 'Nature of the Rights'

As mentioned above, the South African Constitution identifies the 'nature of the right' as an important component in determining the obligations of non-state actors. However, without any further clarity, these words are rather vague. The Constitutional Court first considered the interpretation thereof in the case of *Khumalo v. Holomisa*.[53] In that case, the Constitutional Court was faced with a defamation claim between two sets of private parties (one of which was a major media publishing house): it was thus required to consider whether the right to freedom of expression could be applied directly between two private parties. In addressing this question, the judgement can be understood to refer to three factors which were of importance in deciding whether a right should be held to be 'applicable' to private parties. First, it mentioned that a court needs to consider 'the intensity of the right'.[54] Whilst this factor is not entirely clear, it would seem to require an understanding of the right's importance within the wider constitutional order as well as the reasons lying behind its protection. This is a crucial starting point in determining corporate obligations as it helps understand whether there is any individual interest in a particular context that requires protection against corporate invasion. We might call this the 'justification component'.

Second, the court needs to consider the potential invasion of the right by persons other than the state. This seems to place the impact of a corporation on a human right squarely in focus. The difficulty here is that it is not clear how far the notion of 'potential' extends: clearly, actual impact will need to be considered but it might be unfair to hold corporations to account for impacts which are very unlikely or remote. The focus of this criterion is on the potential impact upon beneficiaries of a right. We might call this, therefore, the 'impact component'.

Third, the court should consider the nature of the parties before it and whether the right has a particular significance in relation to their role within the broader society. Since the case itself concerned the media, and freedom of expression is central to its operation, the right was held to be

---

[53] 2002 (5) SA 401 (CC).
[54] *Ibid.*, para. 33. See also I. Currie and J. De Waal, *The Bill of Rights Handbook* (Juta, 2013) 48 who suggest that this phrase is opaque but probably relates to the 'scope of the right'.

directly applicable to the private parties in that case. This factor thus involves what may be termed 'agent-relative' considerations and the effect they have on the obligations of particular agents.[55] There might be particular factors which provide grounds for certain agents to have obligations which others do not. We might call this 'the agent-relative component'.

All these elements seem to be normatively relevant and provide an attractive rubric for determining corporate obligations under international human rights law. At the same time, there are some difficulties. This approach first suggests that certain human rights may not be 'applicable' to a private actor such as a corporation. This appears to contradict recent developments in the BHR field with the GPs stating the following:

> Because business enterprises can have an impact on virtually the entire spectrum of internationally recognized human rights, their responsibility to respect applies to all such rights. In practice, some human rights may be at greater risk than others in particular industries or contexts, and therefore will be the focus of heightened attention. However, situations may change, so all human rights should be the subject of periodic review.[56]

This statement, however, need not be understood as at odds with the South African constitutional law approach: whilst potentially all rights can be impacted upon by private actors, in reality, it is necessary to determine degrees of impact on rights. The approach adopted by the Constitutional Court of South Africa does not immediately state that any right is 'inapplicable' to private bodies: rather it develops the tests of justification, impact and agent-relativity to determine whether such rights are applicable and, if so, the extent to which they should be regarded as such. Given that there is a large degree of similarity between internationally recognized human rights and those in domestic bills of rights, it is unlikely that the conclusions regarding the applicability of a right or the extent thereof will be different in these two spheres. At the same time, the possibility of reduced applicability should be admitted even at the international level with, for instance, the right to a fair trial in Article 14 of the International Covenant on Civil and Political Rights largely having application to the state (though private actors would have a duty not to interfere with these rights).

---

[55] Macdonald explains that agent-relative accounts of responsibility concur on the central proposition that 'attributions of responsibility rest solely or at least primarily on facts about agents and their relations to certain harmful or favourable events or states'. Macdonald, n. 27, 550.

[56] Guiding Principles, n. 12, Commentary on Principle 12.

The second set of problems, which are more difficult to answer, relate to the way in which these factors are specified and the relation between them. There is some under-specification in each factor which leads to a lack of clarity as to when obligations should be imposed or not: what kind of impact is sufficient to impose an obligation? What are the relevant factors relating to the agents themselves that play a role in determining the obligations that may be imposed? Do the latter factors relate to the role of corporations in society as a whole or in specific sectors?[57]

Moreover, these factors may pull in differing directions. The potential impact upon the beneficiary of a right may support the imposition of a strong obligation; on the other hand, the particular nature of an entity, may push towards no obligation being recognized or the attenuation thereof. For instance, in relation to whether a corporation may monitor content on the computers it gives to its employees, the potential of a corporation to violate the privacy of employees may well push towards recognizing widespread and strong obligations to avoid such monitoring and interferences with their privacy. At the same time, the fact that the corporation is an employer and has an interest in its reputation and productivity may well also provide a justification for limiting the privacy of its employees, restricting their legitimate expectations of privacy and thus reducing the scope of its obligations in that regard.[58]

The identification of these factors is important analytically: yet, we still need some kind of rubric within which to determine how to resolve the normative conflicts identified. We saw a similar problem arise in relation to the sphere of influence approach discussed earlier. In the next part of this chapter, I propose an analytical framework drawn from constitutional law that can assist with such a balancing enquiry and can be included in the proposed BHR treaty to assist in determining corporate obligations.

7.5   Moving towards a Two-Stage Enquiry into Corporate Obligations

One approach to determining corporate obligations is to address the enquiry as a species of a larger question concerning how to determine the

---

[57] These are questions which I cannot address in detail in this chapter but are important for further consideration.

[58] I have sought to consider the specific obligations of corporations in relation to the right to privacy in D. Bilchitz 'Privacy, Surveillance and the Duties of Corporations' (2016) *Journal of South African Law* 45.

scope of obligations of any agent in relation to human rights. Constitutional documents have generally addressed this broader question in the context of providing a method for specifying state obligations. Increasingly, in more modern constitutions, there is some convergence on the approach to be adopted in this regard to the extent that some authors have referred to this as a 'global model of constitutional rights'.[59] Constitutions in Canada, South Africa and Kenya, for instance, outline what may be termed a two-stage enquiry.[60] The first stage involves interpreting the rights, which requires understanding their underlying justification and the interests they protect. A determination is then made as to whether certain conduct (or an omission) is a prima facie infringement of that right.

The second stage then involves considering whether that infringement is justifiable or not. Usually, this involves what may be termed a proportionality enquiry, which includes the following steps:[61]

- The first step is to determine the purpose of any infringement and whether it is legitimate within the constitutional scheme. This step is vital as it signifies that there needs to be a very good reason for any right to be infringed.
- The second step concerns a determination of whether there is a rational connection between the means adopted to limit the right and the purpose of the limitation (this may be termed the 'suitability' enquiry). If the means are not designed to achieve the purpose, then there is no good reason to limit the right in this way.
- The third step involves understanding whether or not the means adopted to limit the right are necessary to achieve the purpose. This step itself can be broken down further and involves considering whether there is an alternative that sufficiently realizes the purpose but has a lesser impact on the right (this may be termed the 'necessity' enquiry).[62] This part of the enquiry highlights the fact that it will be

---

[59] K. Moller, *The Global Model of Constitutional Rights* (Oxford University Press, 2012).

[60] Even though their texts differ from these aforementioned constitutions, the German Constitutional Court essentially follows such an approach, as does the European Court on Human Rights in interpreting the European Convention on Human Rights.

[61] The proportionality enquiry has been subject to much analysis. One of the seminal works in this regard is that of R. Alexy, *A Theory of Constitutional Rights* trans. J. Rivers (Oxford University Press 2002), whose analysis I draw upon.

[62] I have attempted to examine in more detail the necessity enquiry and its components in D. Bilchitz, 'Necessity and Proportionality: Towards a Balanced Approach?' in L. Lazarus, C. McCrudden and N. Bowles, *Reasoning Rights* (Hart, 2014).

unjustifiable to violate a right more than is necessary to achieve the purpose.

- The final step of the proportionality enquiry involves considering whether or not the benefits of the limitation are proportional to the harms caused to the right (often termed the 'proportionality in the narrow sense' enquiry).[63] This step involves a more holistic balancing enquiry after considering the other steps as to whether the importance of the purpose (and the means adopted towards its realization) can ultimately justify the infringement of the right in the particular circumstances.

The proportionality test essentially provides a structured analytical framework for determining when the limitation of a right is justifiable or not and for addressing the normative conflicts that arise in this regard. It does not generate automatic results and is dependent upon a number of sub-enquiries. It is critical to determine the weight to be accorded to the right vis-à-vis the purpose of the limitation in any such evaluation.

The usefulness of this model is borne out by its adoption in many fora which have to adjudicate upon human rights. The question is whether it could be adapted to assist in determining the obligations of corporations in relation to human rights. I shall argue that it can be and that it in fact provides a promising analytical framework for inclusion within a future BHR treaty.

7.5.1 Corporations and the Two-Stage Enquiry

As has been outlined above, the first stage of the enquiry requires an understanding of the right and whether conduct (or an omission) provides a prima facie infringement of the right in question. In the corporate context, this stage of the enquiry involves the first two elements of the South African Constitutional Court's test outlined above (under the 'nature of the rights' approach), namely, considering the justification/ nature of the right as well as the potential impact of a corporation upon such a right. In constitutional approaches to human rights that involve two-stages, the first stage often allows for a wider construction of a right so as to capture the range of impacts upon the underlying interests it

---

[63] These components of the test have been developed in seminal cases such as, in Canada, in *R v. Oakes* [1986] 1 SCR 103; and, in South Africa, in *S v. Manamela* (2000) 3 SA 1 (CC). For a more detailed analysis of these components, see A. Barak *Proportionality: Constitutional Rights and their Limitations* (Cambridge University Press, 2012).

protects. There is always the second stage in terms of which the obligations flowing from these interests can be narrowed. This is conducive to more analytical clarity than one-stage approaches which immediately conflate questions surrounding the interests protected by a right with the reasons for limiting it. This first stage of the enquiry is also beneficiary-focused: it seeks to determine which fundamental interests of a beneficiary are implicated in particular circumstances and the impact upon them. Placing this focus at the first stage of the enquiry is very important as it situates the interests and concerns of potential victims of human rights violations by corporations as being primary.

However, the fact that there may be a prima facie infringement of an interest of a beneficiary is not determinative. There may be good reasons why that interest cannot be realized, or there may be reasons why a particular agent may lack the obligation to protect that interest in question. I contend that the second stage of the enquiry may be helpful, particularly, in determining when a particular agent such as a corporation has an obligation or not. The first step in this regard would be to determine whether or not there is a legitimate purpose for any infringement. The legitimacy of any purpose should, of course, be linked to the nature of the particular agent. The state may, for instance, justify some surveillance of citizens' emails on the grounds of national security. On the other hand, a corporation could not generally use such a justification – rather, it would need to relate any surveillance to the objectives of the company such as regulatory compliance or ensuring no harm is done to its brand. There is some complexity here given the understanding discussed above that corporations are formed to achieve social objectives, though generally achieved indirectly through the pursuit of their business interests. This understanding of the particularities of the agent in question would inform whether a purpose is legitimate or not. A corporation could not, however, claim anti-social purposes – such as destroying the environment or undermining a democratically elected government – as legitimate given that part of its reasons for incorporation relate to achieving social goods. Since the question of purpose requires an understanding of the nature of the corporations and their role within a particular society, it would take account of the South African court's third agent-relative criterion.

The matter would not, however, end here. A measure may not be designed well to realize a purpose and be overly intrusive in relation to rights. This is where the suitability and necessity enquiries would be of importance in deciding whether a measure rationally relates to the identified purpose and whether there are alternatives that could do so with a lesser impact on rights. Here again, the purpose would be important but not determinative: corporations would have obligations to adopt measures that do not too severely impact upon rights. In the email example provided above, it would have to be determined whether monitoring email in fact aids the purposes of the firm. Moreover, it would also need to be considered whether the infringement of privacy could be lessened, for instance, by filters that only monitor particular sets of work-related mails and/or communicating the policy of monitoring to employees.

Finally, an overarching assessment of proportionality between the benefits of achieving the purpose and the harm to the human rights in question would be necessary. Even if the other tests were passed, a major violation of a right could never be sanctioned for a flimsy purpose. On the other hand, a very important purpose could justify a minor violation of a right. Some infringement of privacy rights might, for instance, be justifiable in the work place in order to protect the business so long as it does not too severely intrude upon that right. Once again, at this stage, the dual aspect of a corporation would become important in deciding on the weight to be attached to the purpose it claims. If it meets the rather minimal legitimacy test when determining the purpose, a question would still arise as to the relationship between the business-related goals of the corporation and fundamental social purposes, such as the impact on human rights. The overarching proportionality assessment conducted at this stage would also allow for wider considerations of fairness to enter into the picture in terms of determining corporate obligations.

The approach adopted here would thus commence with an evaluation of rights, their implications and whether particular conduct or omissions give rise to any obligations. It is likely at the first stage that the net of corporate obligations will be cast widely. The starting point is thus beneficiary or victim-orientated. The second stage would involve considering reasons to limit the obligations of corporations in these circumstances either for reasons relating to their nature or for reasons relating to the normative considerations underlying any potential limitation. The two-stage enquiry thus helps to ensure normative clarity about both beneficiary-orientated and agent-relative considerations without mixing the two sets of distinct consideration: yet, it offers an overarching framework within which to evaluate them in relation to one another. It also allows for the determination of these obligations incrementally: it is not necessary to achieve a once-and-for-all specification of these obligations but they can be determined in relation to particular circumstances.

7.6 Conclusion and Draft Provisions

In this chapter, I have sought to consider what would be an appropriate analytical framework that should be included in any BHR treaty to determine the nature and extent of corporate human rights obligations. This question is distinct from determining the exact obligations but rather requires a consideration of the relevant normative factors that could provide guidance in any framework instrument. In doing so, I have considered attempts to capture the ambit of these obligations in both international law and constitutional law. First, I considered an approach that was focused on the notion of the 'sphere of influence' of a corporation: it highlighted the importance of considering the impact of a corporation on different stakeholders; the possibility that its obligations must be conceived of as lying on a continuum and the key idea that there are limits to these obligations. It, however, conflated too many normative considerations and was misleading in several respects, for instance, in connecting the nature of an obligation with a particular stakeholder.

The second approach, popular both in international and constitutional law, has been to confine the ambit of corporate obligations to negative obligations. Yet, we saw why such an approach failed on its own terms to provide adequate guidance in relation to negative obligations, as well as why it does not capture the dual aspect of corporations, renders them exceptional entities without good reason and would fail to harness the potential of a powerful actor to address major challenges such as global poverty. In engaging with this approach, I suggested some general principles that will be of importance when outlining a framework for determining the positive obligations of corporations.

The third 'nature of the rights' approach was drawn from South African constitutional law. It considered the applicability of three factors in determining corporate obligations: the underlying justification and importance of a right, the impact (or potential impact) of a corporation on the right, and the nature and role of corporations in society. Whilst these factors are all relevant to a determination of corporate obligations, unfortunately, the Constitutional Court of South Africa has merely outlined the factors without explaining how they interact and what an overarching framework could be for determining corporate obligations.

Finally, I considered the applicability of a 'two-stage' approach to corporations that is dominant in constitutional law worldwide in determining the human rights obligations of the state. The two-stage enquiry involves both a focus on beneficiary-orientated considerations (relating to the impact on the rights of victims) as well as agent-relative reasons (providing grounds to justify infringements or omissions in certain cases). I argued that, with suitable modifications, this approach can usefully help provide a broad analytical framework for determining corporate obligations in relation to human rights.

I have sought to engage with each of these approaches as they all highlight aspects that are of importance in providing an analytical framework within which to determine corporate obligations. Although drafting a provision that can capture the key insights of the different approaches canvassed in this chapter is not easy, an attempt is made below.

7.6.1   Obligations of Corporations under International Human Rights Law

(1) State parties to the present covenant recognize that corporations have legal obligations flowing from the human rights enumerated in the international bill of rights, which includes the International Covenant on Civil and Political Rights and the International Covenant on Economic, Social and Cultural Rights.

(2) The specific nature and extent of the legal obligations of a corporation corresponding to each human right should be determined on the basis of the following two-stage enquiry applicable to both actions and omissions of a corporation:

(a) whether the right is prima facie infringed by the corporate behaviour that is impugned in the particular circumstances; and

(b) whether the prima facie corporate infringement of the right mentioned in clause (a) is justifiable taking into account the following factors:

   i. the purpose of any infringement;

   ii. whether there is a rational relationship between the infringement and the purpose identified in sub-clause (i);

   iii. whether there is an alternative that sufficiently realizes the purpose identified in sub-clause (i) and has a less restrictive impact on the right; and

iv. whether there is a proportionality between the benefits to be achieved by a corporation by the infringement and the harms caused to the right.

(3) In applying the proportionality principle under clause (2)(b)(iv) and in determining the weight of any purpose justifying an infringement, the following factors should be considered:

(a) the recognition that corporations have an underlying social purpose which affects how they pursue their business interests;

(b) the responsibility assumed by corporations in relation to particular holders of human rights;

(c) the proximity (which need not be physical proximity) of any infringement of the rights of individuals from the operations of a corporation or its business partners;

(d) the extent to which a corporation has any control or leverage over its subsidiaries or other third party (such as contractors) that perpetrated the infringement; and

(e) the capacity of a corporation to affect the rights in question.

(4) In determining the obligations of corporations to take positive measures to assist in the realization of human rights and the extent of those obligations, the following factors should be considered:

(a) the duty upon a corporation to aligns its business interests with the realization of human rights and the extent to which it has done so;

(b) the extent to which the sphere of activity of a corporation is closely connected to the realization of human rights;

(c) the structure of the market in relation to particular goods or services;

(d) the dependency or vulnerability of individuals to particular corporate actors;

(e) the extent to which corporate activity affects the ability of government organs to realize the state's positive obligations; and

(f) the extent to which the recognition of positive obligations would affect the ability of a corporation to achieve its economic goals.

Human Rights, Responsibilities and Due Diligence

Key Issues for a Treaty

ROBERT MCCORQUODALE AND LISE SMIT

8.1 Introduction

Human rights due diligence is a key concept of the Guiding Principles on Business and Human Rights (Guiding Principles).[1] Linking the three pillars, human rights due diligence is a means by which business enterprises can identify, prevent, mitigate and account for the harms they cause, contribute to, or to which they are directly linked.[2] Human rights due diligence is thus at the core of the responsibility of all business enterprises to respect human rights, and this needs to be acknowledged within any treaty in the area of business and human rights.

In order for a treaty to include human rights due diligence, it is necessary both to clarify the concept and to understand its practical implications. This is made more difficult as the Guiding Principles seem to use the term 'human rights due diligence' in a variety of ways.[3] These diverse usages, in turn, cause confusion about the extent of the business enterprise's responsibility to respect human rights and about the situations in which adverse human rights impacts give rise to responsibilities to provide a remedy.

This chapter will set out the possible different meanings of 'human rights due diligence' and how they could apply to business enterprises. It

[1] Human Rights Council, 'Guiding Principles on Business and Human Rights: Implementing the United Nations "Protect, Respect and Remedy" Framework', A/HRC/17/31 (21 March 2011).
[2] Five of the 31 Guiding Principles (17–21) appear under the heading 'Human Rights Due Diligence', and it is also referred to in GP15, as well as in relation to the State's duty to protect human rights (GP 4), and in the Commentary to other GPs.
[3] The term 'human rights due diligence' is primarily used as a noun in the Guiding Principles, with the word 'process' added to the term to describe the action of conducting human rights due diligence – see below.

will examine the scope of the meanings in order to determine which legal standard (if any) would need to be applied if there is to be a treaty obligation. It will also consider the implications of the application of a standard of human rights due diligence to matters such as state regulation of business enterprises and parent company liability for the actions of subsidiaries. Finally, it will set out some possible treaty provisions.

8.2   Meanings of Human Rights Due Diligence

The term 'due diligence' has been used in relation to obligations on states and in relation to business management, which might be why it was chosen by the Special Representative of the Secretary General on the issue of Human Rights and Transnational Corporations (SRSG).[4] Each of these uses will be explored here both in terms of their meanings and in relation to the legal consequences, if any, that attach to different meanings. After this, there is analysis of the term 'human rights due diligence' under the Guiding Principles.[5]

8.2.1   States and Due Diligence

'Due diligence' has been a term used for many decades in relation to the state's legal obligations under human rights treaties.[6] International courts and supervisory bodies have made clear that states have human rights obligations in relation to all violations of human rights, even when those violations are caused by non-state actors:

> An illegal act which violates human rights and which is initially not directly imputable to a State (for example, because it is the act of a private person or because the person responsible has not been identified) can lead to international responsibility of the State, not because of the act itself, but because of *the lack of due diligence* to prevent the violation or to respond to it as required by the [American] Convention [on Human Rights].[7]

---

[4] J. Ruggie, *Just Business: Multinational Corporations and Human Rights* (Norton, 2013).

[5] For a more detailed exploration of the meanings of human rights due diligence, see J. Bonnitcha and R. McCorquodale, 'The Concept of "Due Diligence" in the UN Guiding Principles on Business and Human Rights' (2017) *European Journal of International Law*. Our thanks to Jonathan Bonnitcha for all his work in this area.

[6] See R. Pisillo-Mazzeschi, *Responsabilité de d'état pour violations des obligations positives relatives aux droits de l'homme*, (2009) 333 *Collected Courses of the Hague Academy of International Law*, Chapter III.

[7] *Velasquez Rodriguez Case*, Judgement of July 29, 1988, Inter-ACtHR (Ser. C) No. 4 (1988) at para. 172 (emphasis added). See also, e.g. *Rubio v. Colombia* (161/1983), (1988)

As the UN Human Rights Committee explained in its General Comment
31 on the International Covenant on Civil and Political Rights, due
diligence defines the standard of conduct expected of a state in preventing, investigating and remedying infringements of human rights by
private parties:

> The positive obligation on States Parties to ensure Covenant rights will
> only be fully discharged if individuals are protected ... against acts
> committed by private persons or entities that would impair the enjoyment
> of Covenant rights ... There may be ... violations by States Parties of
> those rights, as a result of States Parties' permitting or failing ... to *exercise
> due diligence* to prevent, punish, investigate or redress the harm caused by
> such acts by private persons or entities.[8]

An illustrative example is the case of *Social and Economic Rights Action
Centre v. Nigeria,*[9] where the African Commission on Human and
People's Rights held that the State of Nigeria breached its human rights
obligations both through its own actions and in respect of the actions of
the relevant oil company. These findings were based on the State's failure
to require basic health and environmental impact studies, the failure to
require oil companies to consult affected communities, and the failure to
investigate attacks on communities and campaigners, or to punish the
perpetrators of these attacks.[10] The Commission referred to the standard
of care in its finding: 'the care that should have been taken... [was that]
which would have protected the rights of the victims of the violations
complained of'.[11]

Hence the state is under an obligation to satisfy a certain standard of
conduct[12] – that of due diligence – in preventing and responding to the
conduct of third parties, as part of their ongoing legal obligations. This is
a standard of conduct that requires the state to conduct, for example,

HRC Report, G.A.O.R., 43rd Sess., Supp. 40, 190 [11], *Ergi v. Turkey* (App. 23818/94)
(1998) 32 EHRR 388; *Timurtas v. Turkey* (App no 23531/94) (2000) ECHR 13 June
2000; and *A v. UK* (App no 25599/94) (1999) 27 EHRR 611.

[8] Human Rights Committee, General Comment 31, Nature of the General Legal Obligation
on States Parties to the Covenant, U.N. Doc. CCPR/C/21/Rev.1/Add.13 (2004) at para. 8
(emphasis added).

[9] *Social and Economic Rights Action Centre (SERAC) v. Nigeria* (2001) AHRLR 60 (ACHPR
2001). See also *Tatar v. Roumanie* (App no 67021/01), ECtHR 27 January 2009) at para. 88.

[10] *Ibid.*, paras. 5–7, 41, 53 and 61.   [11] *Ibid.*, para. 54.

[12] The International Law Association has considered that 'due diligence is concerned with
supplying a standard of care against which fault can be assessed': International Law
Association (ILA), Study Group on Due Diligence in International Law, Second Report,
July 2016, www.ila-hq.org/en/study-groups/index.cfm/cid/1045 (last accessed 7
September 2016).

investigations about human rights violations, even if they were perpetrated by a non-state actor such as a business enterprise.[13] Indeed, such a standard of conduct is even higher than the 'reasonable person' test in the common law of negligence and the equivalent in civil law legal systems,[14] though it comes from a similar foundation.[15] For example, due diligence as a standard of conduct has been considered in national law as being 'to exercise due diligence to prevent something being done is to take all reasonable steps to prevent it'.[16]

This legal obligation on a state is confirmed by the first Guiding Principle:

> States must protect against human rights abuse within their territory and/
> or jurisdiction by third parties, including business enterprises. This
> requires taking appropriate steps to prevent, investigate, punish and
> redress such abuse through effective policies, legislation, regulations and
> adjudication.[17]

The importance of this obligation on a state is made clear by it being one of just two of the Guiding Principles that uses the word 'must', showing that the obligation is of a mandatory nature.[18]

---

[13] See, for example, *Commission Nationale des Droits de l'Homme et des Libertes v. Chad*, African Commission on Human and Peoples' Rights, (1995) Communication No. 74/92, and *Jordan v. UK*, Application No 24746/94 (Unreported European Court of Human Rights, Trial Chamber, 4 May 2001), para. 143, where the European Court of Human Rights considered that the conduct of the investigation, the coroner's inquest, delay, the lack of both legal aid for the victim's family and the lack of public scrutiny of the reasons of the Director of Public Prosecutions not to prosecute, was a violation of Article 2 ECHR.

[14] See C. Van Dam, 'Tort Law and Human Rights: Brothers in Arms – On the Role of Tort Law in the Area of Business and Human Rights' (2011) *JETL* 221 at 237: 'It is well-known that the standard of care is differently framed in the various jurisdictions. In common law, the test consists of two elements (duty of care and breach of duty), in German law, three (*Tatbestand, Rechtswidrigkeit, Verschulden*), and, in French law, one (*faute*). The common feature is whether the defendant has acted like a "reasonable man" (addressed under *faute, Verschulden* or breach of duty). The other elements (duty of care, *Tatbestand*) serve as control mechanisms, particularly in areas like governmental liability, mental harm, and omissions.'

[15] R. Zimmerman, *The Law of Obligations: Roman Foundations of the Civilian Tradition* (Oxford University Press, 1996), 1009.

[16] *Tesco Supermarkets Ltd v. Nattrass* [1972] AC 153 (UK House of Lords) at p. 23.

[17] GP 1.

[18] The other mandatory obligation is in GP 25: 'As part of their duty to protect against business-related human rights abuse, States must take appropriate steps to ensure, through judicial, administrative, legislative or other appropriate means, that when such abuses occur within their territory and/or jurisdiction those affected have access to effective remedy.'

8.2.2   Business and Due Diligence

In business management practice, 'due diligence' is normally understood to refer to a process of investigation conducted by a business to identify and manage commercial risks:

> [Due diligence is] . . . [t]he process by which a buyer of or an investor in a company, asset or business investigates the records of the target to support its value and find out whether there are matters on which it requires further information or which it should use as a platform to renegotiate the price.[19]

Therefore, due diligence is a risk management process whereby a business enterprise can satisfy itself – if it so chooses – that it – or a business with which it wishes to be connected – is meeting certain governance standards or preventing future risk to its business.[20] While the scope and extent of a due diligence process will vary according to the nature and context of the transaction,[21] such a business management due diligence is frequently understood to be 'voluntary' in contexts where there is no legal enforcement process in relation to considering business risks.[22]

However, sometimes there are legal requirements of due diligence placed by a state on a business enterprise in specific circumstances. For example, national environmental legislation often requires environmental impact assessments to be done before a mining exploration license may be granted.[23] Similarly, health and safety regulation may require certain steps to be taken by an employer.[24] Some legislation relies on the concept of due

---

[19] Thomson Reuters, Practical Law Company Due Diligence, http://uk.practicallaw.com/5-107-6162 (last accessed 13 September 2016).

[20] See O. Martin-Ortega, 'Human Rights Due Diligence for Corporations: From Voluntary Standards to Hard Law at Last?' (2013) 31 *Netherlands Quarterly of Human Rights* 44, 51, who notes that, essentially, 'due diligence is a procedural practice to assess risk in a company's own interest'.

[21] See D. Godfrey, 'Transactional Skills Training: All About Due Diligence' (2009) *Transactions Tenn. J. Bus. L.* 357 at 358.

[22] There may be other pressure for business enterprises to conduct due diligence, such as industry standards: see D. McBarnett, 'Corporate Social Responsibility beyond the Law, through the Law, for Law: The New Corporate Accountability' in D. McBarnett, A. Voiculescu and T. Campbell (eds.), *The New Corporate Accountability* (Cambridge University Press, 2007). Though business management due diligence processes often include legal risks within their scope, this concerns commercial judgement about these potential liabilities.

[23] For example, see section 79 of the South African Mineral and Petroleum Resources Development Act 2002 read with Chapter 5 of the National Environmental Management Act 107 of 1998.

[24] For example, section 27 of the Australian Work Health and Safety Act (2011) (NSW).

diligence in defining disclosure and reporting requirements. For example, the US Dodd-Frank Wall Street Reform and Consumer Protection Act 2010[25] requires that publicly traded companies report to the US Securities and Exchange Commission if their products contain minerals obtained from the conflict in the Democratic Republic of Congo. In order to undertake this disclosure, the business must 'exercise due diligence on the source and chain of custody of such minerals'.[26] Other legislation can allow a business to use due diligence as a defence, such as the UK Bribery Act 2010, which creates an offence where a company fails to prevent bribery committed by a person associated with the company,[27] but provides for a defence where the company can prove that it had 'adequate procedures' (such as due diligence) in place to prevent such bribery.[28]

This type of legislation informs and regulates the business management due diligence process. It even reasserts it as a 'process' and not a legal standard of conduct, as reporting of the process is the main method of compliance. Even the UK Modern Slavery Act 2015, which deals with a human rights issue directly, only requires business enterprises to report on the steps they are taking to eradicate slavery and human trafficking in their own operations and in their supply chains.[29] There is no requirement in this, or most other national legislation, for business enterprises to address and remediate their human rights impacts. Thus business management due diligence remains a process, and is not a standard of conduct with legal consequences for lack of compliance.

8.2.3   Guiding Principles and Due Diligence

The concept of 'human rights due diligence' was introduced by the Guiding Principles on the basis that:

---

[25] Dodd-Frank Wall Street Reform and Consumer Protection Act 2010, Pub.L. 111–203, H. R. 4173.

[26] *Ibid.*, Section 1502 (p), I.A (i).   [27] UK Bribery Act 2010, Section 7(1).

[28] *Ibid.*, Section 7(2). 'Due diligence' is such an 'adequate procedure': UK Ministry of Justice, *Guidance on the Bribery Act 2010*, www.gov.uk/government/uploads/system/uploads/ attachment_data/file/181762/bribery-act-2010-guidance.pdf at 20–31 (last accessed 13 September 2016). See also the European Union (EU) Transparency Directive, which applies to large extractive and logging companies, and requires country by country reporting on material payments made to governments: EU Directive 2013/50/EU.

[29] Section 54 UK Modern Slavery Act 2015. It applies to all companies supplying goods or services with an annual turnover of £36 million and which carry on business, or a part of their business, in the UK: Section 54(2)(b) read with Regulation 2 of the Modern Slavery Act (Transparency in Supply Chains) Regulations 2015. Similarly, see California Supply Chain Transparency Act 2010, Senate Bill No. 657, Chapter 556, 30 September 2010.

> To discharge the [corporate] responsibility to respect [human rights]
> requires due diligence. This concept describes the steps a company must
> take to become aware of, prevent and address adverse human rights
> impacts.[30]

However, there is no definition of 'human rights due diligence' given in
the Guiding Principles. Later, the UN Office of the High Commissioner
for Human Rights in their Interpretive Guide to the Guiding Principles
defined 'human rights due diligence' as follows:

> [Due diligence is] a measure of prudence, activity, or assiduity, as is
> properly to be expected from, and ordinarily exercised by, a *reasonable
> and prudent [person or enterprise]* under the particular circumstances; not
> measured by any absolute standard, but depending on the relative facts of
> the special case. In the context of the Guiding Principles, human rights
> due diligence comprises an ongoing *management process* that a reasonable
> and prudent enterprise needs to undertake, in light of its circumstances
> (including sector, operating context, size and similar factors) to meet its
> *responsibility to respect human rights.*[31]

This interpretation suggests human rights due diligence is about a combination of the legal standard of conduct (of reasonableness) and a
business management process, in relation to human rights impacts.
This disparity of elements has the potential to create confusion as to
the legal consequences, if any, of the failure to conduct human rights due
diligence. It is the issue of legal consequences/liability that may be crucial
in dealing with human rights due diligence in a treaty.

The Guiding Principles do state that '[t]he responsibility of business
enterprises to respect human rights is distinct from issues of legal liability
and enforcement, which remain defined largely by national law provisions
in relevant jurisdictions'.[32] Nevertheless, in relation specifically to human
rights due diligence its Commentary offers a different perspective:

> Conducting appropriate human rights due diligence should help business
> enterprises address the risk of legal claims against them by showing that
> they took every reasonable step to avoid involvement with an alleged

---

[30] Human Rights Council, 'Protect, Respect and Remedy: A Framework for Business and
Human Rights: Report of the Special Representative of the Secretary General on the Issue
of Human Rights and Transnational Corporations and Other Business Enterprises', A/
HRC/8/5 (7 April 2008) (SRSG, '2008 Report'), at para. 56.
[31] UN Human Rights Office of the High Commissioner for Human Rights, 'The Corporate
Responsibility to Respect Human Rights: An Interpretive Guide' (OHCHR, 2012) at 4
(emphasis added).
[32] Commentary to GP 12.

human rights abuse. However, *business enterprises conducting such due diligence should not assume that, by itself, this will automatically and fully absolve them from liability for causing or contributing to human rights abuses.*[33]

This indicates a link between the conducting of human rights due diligence and legal liability, which is relevant for a treaty.

The Guiding Principles do give some guidance on the scope of the *process* of human rights due diligence. In GP 17, there are four components of a human rights due diligence process listed, being that a business enterprise should take steps to: identify; prevent; mitigate; and account for any actual or potential adverse human rights impacts.[34] The Guiding Principles also list relevant factors which may determine the scope of the human rights due diligence process required in each individual context, such as the size of the business enterprise, the nature and country of its operations, and the extent of leverage over third parties.[35] They also indicate that human rights due diligence should take into account all human rights,[36] though they allow for prioritization, provided that priority is given to those risks that are most severe or irremediable.[37] This does not mean that there is appropriate human rights due diligence by focussing solely on what the business enterprise itself pre-determines are the 'salient' human rights (being those human rights most at risk from the business enterprise's activities).[38] Instead, a business enterprise should first determine its human rights impacts before it prioritizes its human rights due diligence actions. This was confirmed by the Norwegian National Contact Point for the OECD Guidelines on Multinational Enterprises when it

---

[33] Commentary to GP 17 (emphasis added). The Commentary to GP 23 gives an example of legal compliance issues that business must face in dealing with gross human rights abuses.

[34] GP 17 (as linked to GP 15).   [35] GP 17(b) and its Commentary.

[36] Commentary to GP 18 states that human rights impact assessments may be integrated into other processes, but 'should include all internationally recognized human rights as a reference point, since enterprises may potentially impact any of these rights'.

[37] GP 24. The Commentary to GP 24 notes that severity is not an absolute concept in this context, but is relative to the other human rights impacts that the business enterprise has identified.

[38] OHCHR, *Interpretive Guide*, 9: 'The most salient human rights for a business enterprise are those that stand out as being most at risk. This will typically vary according to its sector and operating context. The Guiding Principles make clear that an enterprise should not focus exclusively on the most salient human rights issues and ignore others that might arise. But the most salient rights will logically be the ones on which it concentrates its primary efforts.' Cf. C. Rees and R. Davis, 'Salient Human Rights Issues: When Severe Risks to People Intersect with Risks to Business' in D. Baumann-Pauly and J. Nolan (eds.) *Business and Human Rights: From Principles to Practice* (Routledge, 2016), 103.

found that a major pension fund investor breached its human rights due diligence obligations by failing to have any strategy 'on how to react if it becomes aware of human rights risks related to companies in which [it] invested, apart from child labour violations'.[39]

One other important aspect of the human rights due diligence process under the Guiding Principles is that it is an ongoing process. The Guiding Principles provide that human rights due diligence 'should be ongoing, recognizing that the human rights risks may change over time as the business enterprise's operations and operating context evolve'.[40] Most forms of business management due diligence consist of a once-off process which takes place before a specific transaction and is completed once the transaction takes place. By asserting that it is an ongoing process, the Guiding Principles set out a process that is closer to the human rights obligations on states.

The other way in which the meaning of human rights due diligence under the Guiding Principles is closer to the standard of conduct under the state's human rights obligations is that the focus is on human rights *impacts*. Human rights due diligence is concerned with the risks to rights-holders – in terms of the impacts on them, and not on the risks to the business enterprise. While business management due diligence is about the commercial risks to the business (even including a risk of liability for human rights impacts) or, sometimes, to other stakeholders (such as consumers, employees and shareholders under legislation), its focus is not on the prevention of the risks to the rights-holder. In addition, human rights due diligence expects every business enterprise to consider the human rights impacts of its own operations as well as those of third parties with which it has business relationships, such as those in its value chain. Further, while 'human rights impacts' is not defined in the Guiding Principles, it does seem to be equated there with human rights violations under international law. This is seen by the Commentary to GP 12, which makes clear that '[b]ecause business enterprises can have an impact on virtually the entire spectrum of internationally recognized human rights, their responsibility to respect applies to all such rights',

---

[39] The Norwegian National Contact Point for the OECD Guidelines for Multinational Enterprises, *Complaint from Lok Shakti Abhiyan, Korean Transnational Corporations Watch, Fair Green and Global Alliance and Forum for Environment and Development v. Posco (South Korea), Abp/Apg (Netherlands) And Nbim (Norway)*, Final Statement, 27 May 2013 at 6.

[40] GP 17(c). The Commentary to GP 12 notes that 'situations may change, so all human rights should be the subject of periodic review'.

with the examples given of these rights being the major global human rights treaties and instruments,[41] including the rights of particularly vulnerable groups.[42] Thus the Guiding Principles do seem to establish that 'human rights impacts' of companies should be interpreted in the same way as 'human rights violations' by states. This further equates human rights due diligence with human rights obligations of states.

Therefore, the meaning and scope of human rights due diligence under the Guiding Principles uses the business management due diligence idea of a 'process', as well as the standard of conduct of states required under international human rights law. This approach indicates that it cannot be a tick-box procedure, as simply having conducted a business management due diligence process will not be sufficient because the standard of conduct must also be met.[43] There are sufficient indications in Guiding Principles, as shown above, that there are standards of conduct by which a business enterprise might be measured. This enables some connection with the creation of legal obligations under a treaty.

As is clear from the above, states already have a legal obligation to provide for appropriate legislation and effective enforcement of human rights adherence by business enterprises. They also have legal obligations

[41] The Commentary to Principle 12 states: 'An authoritative list of the core internationally recognized human rights is contained in the International Bill of Human Rights (consisting of the Universal Declaration of Human Rights and the main instruments through which it has been codified: the International Covenant on Civil and Political Rights and the International Covenant on Economic, Social and Cultural Rights), coupled with the principles concerning fundamental rights in the eight ILO core conventions as set out in the Declaration on Fundamental Principles and Rights at Work. These are the benchmarks against which other social actors assess the human rights impacts of business enterprises.'

[42] The Commentary to Principle 12 also states: 'Depending on circumstances, business enterprises may need to consider additional standards. For instance, enterprises should respect the human rights of individuals belonging to specific groups or populations that require particular attention, where they may have adverse human rights impacts on them. In this connection, United Nations instruments have elaborated further on the rights of indigenous peoples; women; national or ethnic, religious and linguistic minorities; children; persons with disabilities; and migrant workers and their families. Moreover, in situations of armed conflict enterprises should respect the standards of international humanitarian law.'

[43] On related issues see B. Fasterling and G. Demuijnck, 'Human Rights in the Void? Due Diligence in the UN Guiding Principles on Business and Human Rights' (2013) 116 *Journal for Business Ethics* 799; A. Nacvalovaite, A. Zapesochny and M. Jones, 'Integrating Concern for Human Rights into the Mergers & Acquisitions Due Diligence Process' (2013) *Good Practice Note to the UN Global Compact Human Rights Working Group* (26 July 2013), www.unglobalcompact.org/docs/issues_doc/human_rights/ Human_Rights_Working_Group/MandA_GPN.pdf (last accessed 13 September 2016).

to provide an effective remedy for human rights violations, because '[f]or rights to have meaning, effective remedies must first be available to redress violations. This requirement is implicit in the Convention [on the Rights of the Child] and consistently referred to in the other six major international human rights treaties.'[44] As there is a link between human rights due diligence and remediation, it is evident that there are legal consequences in this area.

Accordingly, the language of human rights due diligence, as introduced by the Guiding Principles, provides a combination of meanings in order to craft a novel notion of a 'human rights due diligence'. This shows that a human rights due diligence process is necessary in order to identify, prevent, mitigate and account for how business enterprises address their impacts on human rights, both directly and through their business relationships. It also shows that there is a standard of conduct developed that is designed to be similar to that of states' obligations under international human rights law.

In order to ensure compliance with human rights due diligence as a legal requirement or legal standard, business management due diligence processes would need to become more widespread, integrated and systematic, with a focus on human rights impacts and not just commercial business risks. The focus on identification and prevention would need to be extended to provide for ongoing monitoring and tracking processes. Thus, human rights due diligence under the Guiding Principles is unique in nature: it will thus be necessary that the treaty should assert the meaning of 'human rights due diligence' in the Guiding Principles and not stray from it.

8.3   Implications of Human Rights Due Diligence

In setting out the human rights due diligence approach in the Guiding Principles, there are both process elements and standard of conduct elements, as was shown. When examining the consequences of this understanding in a binding treaty, matters of legal obligation are raised. In order to explore this further, three consequences will be considered: state obligations; parent company liability; and human rights due diligence as a defence.

---

[44] The UN Committee on the Rights of the Child, *Effective Remedy and Corporate Violations of Children's Rights* (UN, 2011), para. 1.2. See also Amnesty International, *Injustice Incorporated: Corporate Abuses and the Human Rights to a Remedy* (AI, 2014) pp. 16–20.

8.3.1   Obligations on States

Due diligence under human rights law places a legal obligation on states to act to prevent, investigate and remediate violations of human rights by business enterprises. This is reaffirmed by the Guiding Principles. In order to link this with the corporate responsibility to respect human rights and to conduct human rights due diligence, a treaty could require states to ensure business enterprises conduct human rights due diligence in national legislation.

As was shown, national legislation in relation to business management due diligence in areas connected to human rights impacts, such as the US Dodd-Frank Act and the UK Modern Slavery Act, as well as the EU non-financial reporting directive,[45] generally require reporting by business enterprises. Reporting is an important step, and can lead to codes of conduct and good business practices, and shape corporate behaviour as business enterprises can be incentivized by these regulations.[46] However, the current legislation is limited in its impact without effective compliance mechanisms.

Introducing mandatory human rights due diligence as a legally binding process on all business enterprises in a state would be consistent with both the state's human rights treaty obligations and the Guiding Principles. The method of doing this could vary from state to state. It could be included in core corporate legislation, such as being part of directors' duties. For example, directors could be held accountable for a failure to act with due diligence concerning the company's human rights impacts.[47] This would be stronger than some current legislation, which requires directors to take into account social or environmental considerations as part of their fiduciary duties.[48] In the absence of clear legal

---

[45]   The EU Directive on non-financial reporting (Directive 2014/95/EU).

[46]   See A. Ewing, 'Mandatory Human Rights Reporting' in D. Baumann-Pauly and J. Nolan (eds.) *Business and Human Rights: From Principles to Practice* (Routledge, 2016), 284; see also R. McCorquodale, L. Smit and, S. Neely and R. Brooks, 'Human Rights Due Diligence in Law and Practice: Good Practices and Challenges for Business Enterprises' (2017) 2 *Business and Human Rights Journal* 195–224.

[47]   For example, in the South African case of *Minister of Water Affairs and Forestry v. Stilfontein Gold Mining Co Ltd* 2006 (5) SA 333 (W), the directors of a company were held liable for all resigning simultaneously instead of complying with a water directive order.

[48]   For example, the UK Companies Act 2006 requires directors to 'have regard' to such matters as 'the impact of the company's operations on the community and the environment' as part of their duties (Section 172 (1) (d)), and the South African Companies Act 2008 allows the Government to prescribe social and ethics commitments for companies (Section 72 (4)).

accountability, corporate and directors' duties may be interpreted narrowly.[49] However, it has been persuasively shown that using the public law concept of proportionality in the legislation or by courts would enable an appropriate balancing of human rights and commercial interests in this area.[50]

Whichever approach is adopted by states, it is essential that appropriate monitoring is included, with an effective compliance/enforcement mechanism. This could be through fines, deregistration or criminal sanctions. However, as the SRSG noted:

> State regulation proscribing certain corporate conduct will have little impact without accompanying mechanisms to investigate, punish, and redress abuses. Victims face particular challenges when seeking personal compensation or reparation as opposed to more general sanction of the corporation through a fine or administrative remedies.[51]

Thus, it is essential that remedies to victims of the human rights impacts of business enterprises be included in corporate regulation in this area.

Some recent legislative proposals indicate a movement by some states to make human rights due diligence a more direct obligation on business enterprises. For example, legislation which has been passed in France and proposed by Switzerland,[52] and by the Council of Europe's Recommendations on Human Rights and Business,[53] have all considered this. It is not yet clear how compliance with these provisions would be enforced, though they are certain to be tested in courts, with the test presumably to be that of a legal standard of conduct. In other instances, the human rights due diligence process itself is not

---

[49] See, for example, *Parke v. Daily News* [1962] Ch 927, where the Court held that directors' duties are typically not interpreted to factor in matters other than profit-making. While the Australian Stock Exchange Corporate Governance Principles and Recommendations of 2014 contradict this position, the case has not been overruled.

[50] D. Bilchitz and L. Ausserladscheider Jonas, 'Proportionality, Fundamental Rights and the Duties of Directors' (2016) *Oxford Journal of Legal Studies* 1.

[51] SRSG 2008 Report, paras. 82 and 88.

[52] Swiss Coalition for Corporate Justice (SCCJ), 'The initiative text with explanations', Factsheet V, available at http://business-humanrights.org/sites/default/files/documents/150421_sccj_factsheet_5_-_responsible_business_initiative.pdf (last accessed 13 September 2016). The French law is considered in the next section.

[53] Council of Europe, Recommendation CM/Rec(2016)3 of the Committee of Ministers to Member States on human rights and business, adopted on 2 March 2016. See also the UK Parliament's Joint Committee on Human Rights Inquiry in Business and Human Rights Report in 2017: (https://www.publications.parliament.uk/pa/jt201617/jtselect/jtrights/443/443.pdf, where they recommend a mandatory duty to prevent human rights impacts.

strictly required by law, but the conduct which it seeks to prevent or identify is prohibited by law. Examples include anti-bribery and money-laundering legislation, which is not always specific about the required steps, but imposes significant penalties where a failure to conduct due diligence results in a breach.[54]

A human rights due diligence provision in a treaty on business and human rights needs to reassert the state's obligations under international human rights law as expanded in the Guiding Principles. It could require states to compel business enterprises to carry out human rights due diligence processes, through corporate law or other legislation. It could place a mandatory duty on business enterprises to exercise due diligence with respect to human rights in all its operations. This would need to be supported by strong compliance and enforcement mechanisms. Thus the treaty could include a requirement on states to introduce legislation (or other forms of regulation) for the enforcement of human rights due diligence. This would also be consistent with the human rights due diligence obligations on states themselves.

8.3.2   Parent Company Liability

One particular challenge which arises in the application of human rights due diligence as a legal obligation is the issue of parent company liability for the conduct of its subsidiaries.[55] While the Guiding Principles deliberately refer to 'business enterprises' in order to include all forms of business enterprise, a key part of many transnational companies is a relationship of parent and subsidiary.[56] The general international legal principle is that a corporate entity has separate legal personality from its shareholders.[57] Courts are traditionally reluctant to 'pierce the corporate veil'.[58] However, there are exceptions, with an example of piercing of the

---

[54] For example, the UK Bribery Act 2010.

[55] See G. Skinner, R. McCorquodale and O. de Schutter, 'The Third Pillar: Access to Judicial Remedies for Human Rights Violations by Transnational Business' (ICAR, CORE, ECCJ, 2013) at 59–61.

[56] A survey of the world's largest 500 companies shows that they employ 67 million people worldwide and are represented by 33 countries: http://beta.fortune.com/global500 (accessed 13 September 2016). Joint ventures are another common method of business relationship.

[57] See *Solomon v. Solomon* [1897] AC 22.

[58] See, for example, *Faiza Ben Hashem v. Shayif* [2008] EWHC 2380 (Fam), where the English High Court found that a court cannot pierce the corporate veil merely because it would be 'in the interest of justice' to do so; rather, there must be some impropriety 'in the

corporate veil being the South African case of *Ex Parte Gore NO.*[59] This case considered section 20(9) of the South African Companies Act 2008, which provides a statutory basis for piercing the corporate veil in cases of an 'unconscionable abuse of the juristic personality of the company as a separate entity'.[60] The Court found that this statutory provision will 'inevitably operate ... to erode the foundation of the philosophy that piercing the corporate veil should be approached with an à priori diffidence ... [and that its] unqualified availability ... militates against an approach that it should be granted only in the absence of any alternative remedy.'[61] This remedy can be invoked by any 'interested person' or by a court of its own motion, and, the Court found that an 'interested person' includes someone whose human rights (as set out in the South African Bill of Rights) have been affected.[62]

Further, a few recent and ongoing cases demonstrate that the scope of a parent company's duty of care for the actions of its subsidiaries will depend on the factual circumstances and legal factors such as effective control and foreseeability.[63] Relevant issues may include the extent to which the parent has a direct relationship with the affected rights-holders or control over the subsidiary's on-the-ground operations,[64] and whether the parent has issued public statements as to its transnational standards of conduct.[65] Moreover, the test to meet the due diligence standard is not only what the business enterprise knew, but what it ought to have known.[66] As such, a parent company with subsidiaries in a state with

---

sense of misuse of the company structure to avoid or conceal liability' at paras. 159--64. See also *VTB Capital PLC v. Nutritek International* [2012] EWCA Civ 808.

[59] *Ex Parte Gore NO and 37 Others NNO (in their capacities as the liquidators of 41 companies comprising King Financial Holdings Ltd (in liq) and its subsidiaries* 2013 (3) SA 382 (WCC).

[60] R. Cassim 'Hiding Behind the Veil' (2013) 34 *De Rebus* October 2013 35.

[61] *Ex Parte Gore NO* note 59, at para. 34.

[62] *Ibid.*, para. 35. See L. Smit 'Binding corporate human rights obligations: A few Observations from the South African Legal Framework' (2016) 1 *Business and Human Rights Journal* 349.

[63] *Choc v. Hudbay Minerals Inc* 2013 ONSC 1414 (Canada). See also Y. Aftab 'The Intersection of Law and Corporate Social Responsibility: Human Rights Strategy and Litigation Readiness for Extractive-Sector Companies' (2014) 60 *Rocky Mt. Min. L. Inst.* 19–1.

[64] *Chandler v. Cape PLC* [2012] EWCA Civ 525; See, more generally, G. Skinner, *Parent Company Liability: Ensuring Justice for Human Rights Violations* (ICAR, 2015), 20.

[65] *Choc v. Hudbay Inc*, note 63, at para. 26.

[66] See C. Van Dam 'Tort Law and Human Rights: Brothers in Arms – On the Role of Tort Law in the Area of Business and Human Rights' (2011) *Journal of European Tort Law* 221.

well-documented human rights risks will not be able to escape liability based on a lack of knowledge about the local practices.[67]

In addition, there has been legislation passed in 2017 in France that imposes a duty of care (*'devoir de vigilance'*) on certain parent companies in relation to subsidiaries over which they hold 'exclusive control', as well as in relation to its subcontractors and suppliers.[68] This applies human rights due diligence as a legal standard, and courts would use a contextual interpretation to determine whether the parent company has complied with the appropriate standard rather than simply undertaking a 'process'.[69]

Therefore, in light of all these developments, there are now sufficient national legal examples to support a treaty provision to require parent companies to conduct human rights due diligence with respect to their subsidiaries. This would expand considerably the effects of undertaking a human rights due diligence process and the number of potential human rights impacts it would cover.[70]

8.3.3   Due Diligence as a Defence

In some cases, proving that due diligence has been undertaken can afford a defence against liability[71] or provide for a reduction in sentence.[72] For example, the UK Food Safety Act creates a due diligence defence to a range of offences relating to the preparation and supply of food that is 'injurious to health'.[73] The defendant needs to 'prove that he took all

---

[67] For example, see *Guerrero and others v. Monterrico Metals PLC.* [2009] EWHC 2475 (Q. B.) and Amnesty International Canada's arguments in *Choc v. Hudbay Minerals Inc* 2013 ONSC 1414 (Canada) at para. 37.

[68] Art. L. 225-102-4 and L.225-102-5 of the French Commercial Code.

[69] G. Skinner, *Parent Company Liability: Ensuring Justice for Human Rights Obligations* (ICAR, 2015) at 18.

[70] See further in the chapter by Justine Nolan in this book.

[71] See, for example, section 90 (1) of the UK Financial Services and Markets Act 2000, section 11(b)(3)(A) of the US Securities Act 1933, and section 7(2) of the UK Bribery Act 2010 read with UK Ministry of Justice, Guidance on the Bribery Act 2010, 20–31.

[72] See, for example, §8B2.1. of the United States Sentencing Commission '2011 Federal Sentencing Guidelines Manual', available at www.ussc.gov/guidelines-manual/2011/ 2011-8b21 (accessed 26 February 2015), where it is stated: 'The prior diligence of an organization in seeking to prevent and detect criminal conduct has a direct bearing on the appropriate penalties and probation terms for the organization if it is convicted and sentenced for a criminal offense.'

[73] The General Food Regulations 2004 S.I. 3279 made under the UK Food Safety Act 1990 and the Food Hygiene (England) Regulations 2006 S.I. 14 under Article 9 of Regulation (EC) No. 178/2002; Regulation (EC) No. 1642/2003.

reasonable precautions and exercised all due diligence to avoid the commission of the offence by himself or by a person under his control.'[74] In *Tesco v. London*[75] the UK High Court explained this provision as follows:

> There are two elements which have to be established for this defence [of due diligence] to succeed ... [first, the] defendant has to show the establishment of an effective system to avoid the commission of an offence, that is the precautions have to be established, and secondly it has to ensure that the system it had established is observed and followed.[76]

This interpretation confirms that due diligence is not simply a process in terms of which companies can simply tick certain boxes. Instead, as discussed above, courts look at the adequacy and effectiveness of the process and whether the process was implemented in practice.

Similarly, the US Federal Securities Act of 1933 creates a defence if the defendant director can establish that she or he 'had, after reasonable investigation, reasonable ground to believe and did believe ... that the statements therein were true and that there was no omission to state a material fact'.[77] The test is a two-fold one: there must be a process of 'reasonable investigation'; and the defendant must have reasonably believed that the statements were true and complete.[78] This test, where both procedure and substance is required, can be found in other due diligence defences, such as section 731 of the Australian Corporations Act[79] and section 72 of the Canadian Forest and Range Practices Act 2014. For example, the latter provides:

---

[74] UK Food Safety Act 1990, Section 21, and Regulation of the Food Hygiene (England) Regulations 2006.

[75] *R. (on the application of Tesco Stores Ltd) v. City of London Corp* [2010] EWHC 2920 (Admin).

[76] *Ibid.* at para. 4.

[77] US Securities Act 1933, Section 11(b)(3)(A). The courts and jurists describe this provision as a 'due diligence' defence: *Herman & MacLean v. Huddleston*, 459 U.S. 375, 382 (1983); and W. Sjostrom 'The Due Diligence Defense under Section 11 of the Securities Act of 1933' (2005) 44 *Brandeis Law Journal* 549.

[78] Sjostrom, *ibid.*, 574.

[79] Section 731(1) of the Australian Corporations Act 2001 provides:
  (1) A person does not commit an offence against subsection 728(3), and is not liable under section 729 for a contravention of subsection 728(1), because of a misleading or deceptive statement in a prospectus if the person proves that they:
    (a) *made all inquiries (if any) that were reasonable* in the circumstances; and
    (b) after doing so, *believed on reasonable grounds* that the statement was not misleading or deceptive.

> For the purposes of a determination of the minister under section 71 or 74, no person may be found to have contravened a provision of the Acts if the person establishes that the
>
> (a) *person exercised due diligence* to prevent the contravention,
> (b) person reasonably believed in the existence of facts that if true would establish that the person did not contravene the provision, or
> (c) person's actions relevant to the provision were the result of an officially induced error.

As in the *Tesco* case above, the court, in deciding whether the defendant has complied with its human rights due diligence obligations, would both enquire as to the existence of a process and the adequacy of this process. This is information more readily available to the business enterprise than to the claimants. Indeed, if the business enterprise had conducted human rights due diligence processes in order to prevent human rights abuses, it would have this information in its possession regardless of whether a claim is brought.

Therefore, due diligence when used as a defence places the onus on the corporate defendant. The business enterprise would then need to show that it has done all that could be required of it in the relevant context. This is a significant step, as otherwise human rights claimants would need to demonstrate all elements of the alleged violation, including that the business enterprise failed to have adequate procedures in place. If human rights due diligence were to be enacted as a defence in the treaty, victim claimants would only need to establish the existence of an adverse human rights impact. In this way, the shifting of the onus through due diligence as a defence in the treaty would significantly facilitate access to remedies for corporate human rights victims.

8.4   Conclusion

Human rights due diligence is a key aspect of the Guiding Principles. It needs to be present in any treaty as it provides a standard that is both objective and context-specific. What a prudent or reasonable business enterprise does in relation to the human rights impacts its activities cause, contribute to or are linked with can be judged through legal means, while taking into account the particular circumstances of the business enterprise's own operations or that of a third party. As such, it is not the exact equivalent of a state's human rights legal obligations, though it has similarities, and can be used for all business enterprises regardless of sector, size and structure. It sets out a clear and concise responsibility that companies should adhere to and states can regulate.

It is evident that the meaning of 'human rights due diligence' in the Guiding Principles is a new term and includes a combination of a business management due diligence process, the state's legal obligation of due diligence under international human rights law and a legal standard of conduct. It application is still developing and will be influenced by state and international law and other regulation, as well as judicial determinations. Accordingly, we consider that the treaty should not aim to prescribe the exact content of due diligence but should restate the terminology and scope of human rights due diligence as set out in the Guiding Principles. The meaning of 'human rights due diligence' can then be developed through treaty interpretation at national and international levels.

We recommend that having a human rights due diligence process should be a mandatory legislative requirement. This would require every business enterprise to carry out human rights due diligence for its own human rights impacts as well as for those within its value chain, including subsidiaries, suppliers and other third parties. This sets out a legal standard and the treaty provision would allow states to do this whichever way they choose to in their domestic legal framework. This approach not only allows more states to ratify the treaty, it also corresponds with the Guiding Principles in that the scope of adequate human rights due diligence should be context-specific, and it is also consistent with the principles of international law in terms of which detailed regulation primarily takes place at the domestic level.

There needs to be strong compliance mechanisms in place for human rights due diligence. While reporting is important for transparency, for remedies and for incentivizing the best practice of business enterprises, enforcement is also necessary, as self-regulation is problematic. A compliance mechanism will afford stakeholders and regulators the ability to monitor and enforce the implementation of the duty to undertake human rights due diligence. In this way, the treaty provisions will also contribute to states' compliance with the third pillar of the Guiding Principles by allowing for access to a remedy for corporate human rights impacts.

The treaty requirements should make clear that human rights due diligence must apply to the impacts of business enterprises themselves, as well as to the impacts of those third parties with which they are linked, in accordance with the Guiding Principles. It must also be expressly stipulated that the state duty to regulate these impacts applies regardless of whether these impacts took place within the jurisdiction of the relevant state. In this way, the treaty will overcome the current gap in accountability caused by questions around transnational (or extraterritorial) impacts, as well as the barriers imposed on victims by the concepts of the separate corporate identity of parent companies and subsidiaries.

Similarly, human rights due diligence lends itself towards a defence, not least as the Guiding Principles note that 'conducting appropriate human rights due diligence should help business enterprises address the risk of legal claims against them by showing that they took every reasonable step to avoid involvement with an alleged human rights abuse'.[80] However, with such a defence, the onus is placed on the business enterprise once a claimant has shown an adverse human rights impact.

Further, we recommend that the treaty places legal obligations on business enterprises. This is consistent with the view of the Guiding Principles that '[b]usiness enterprises need to know and show that they respect human rights. They cannot do so unless they have certain policies and processes in place'.[81] These provisions would replicate the processes and scope set out in the Guiding Principles, being to identify, prevent, mitigate and account for how business enterprises address their impacts on human rights, both directly and through their business relationships. It also would reinforce the position in the Guiding Principles that 'business enterprises conducting such due diligence should not assume that, by itself, this will automatically and fully absolve them from liability for causing or contributing to human rights abuses'.[82] Hence, if states and business enterprises comply with the treaty provisions concerning human rights due diligence, they will be both implementing the Guiding Principles and clarifying that these are legal obligations.

APPENDIX

Possible Human Rights Due Diligence Treaty Provisions

State Obligations

1. Each State Party to the treaty undertakes to ensure that all business enterprises domiciled within its territory and/or subject to its jurisdiction, including state-owned enterprises, carry out mandatory human rights due diligence processes and provide periodic reports on them in order to meet their responsibility to respect

---

[80] Commentary to GP 17.   [81] Commentary to GP 15.   [82] Commentary to GP 17.

human rights, notwithstanding that the actual or potential human rights impacts have or may occur outside the relevant State Party's territory or jurisdiction.

2. Each State Party shall take the necessary steps, in accordance with its constitutional processes, to adopt such laws or other measures to establish a standard of conduct for business enterprises undertaking human rights due diligence processes, including a responsibility to identify, prevent, mitigate and account for how they address their impacts on human rights both of their own activities and of those with whom they have business relationships.

3. Each State Party undertakes to monitor and enforce the implementation of any laws or other measures adopted in accordance with this article, preferably through judicial mechanisms.

4. Where a State chooses to allow a defence of human rights due diligence where a business enterprise has caused, contributed to or is directly linked through a business relationship to an adverse human rights impact, then it shall create a defence if the business enterprise can prove that it took all reasonable precautions, had an effective policy and procedure in place, and exercised human rights due diligence to prevent the adverse impact.

Business Enterprises

1. All business enterprises must carry out human rights due diligence processes to identify, prevent, mitigate and account for how they address their impacts on human rights.

2. Human rights due diligence processes must include identification, prevention, mitigation and remediation of all adverse human rights impacts that the business enterprise may cause or contribute to through its own activities, or which may be directly linked to its operations, products or services by its business relationships with other state or business parties in any territory or jurisdiction.

3. Human rights due diligence processes must be ongoing and include assessing actual and potential human rights impacts, integrating and acting upon the findings, tracking responses and communicating how impacts are addressed.

4. The scope of the human rights due diligence a business enterprise is required to carry out in the circumstances will depend on factors such as, but not limited to:
   a. The size of the business enterprise;
   b. The risk of severe human rights impacts;
   c. The nature of the business enterprise's operations;
   d. The context of its operations;
   e. The state of its relevant operations;
   f. Whether the impact is caused or contributed to by the business enterprise itself or by a third-party entity in its value chain;

g. If caused or contributed to by a third party in the business enterprise's value chain, the extent to which the business enterprise has leverage over the relevant third party's conduct, the manner in which the business enterprise exercises its leverage and the extent to which it seeks to increase its leverage;

h. Any other circumstances which may be relevant.

5. Where a business enterprise has caused, contributed to or is directly linked through a business relationship to an adverse human rights impact, it shall be a defence for the business enterprise to prove that it took all reasonable precautions, had an effective policy and procedure in place, and exercised all due diligence to prevent the adverse impact.

9

Human Rights and Global Corporate Supply Chains

Is Effective Supply Chain Accountability Possible?

JUSTINE NOLAN

Corporate accountability for human rights currently rests upon an incomplete patchwork of legal and non-legal frameworks that vary from country to country and industry to industry. Increasing demands for corporate human rights accountability are now enveloping the myriad corporate actors and activities within a company's supply chain.[1] The supply chain[2] is an area of potential commercial (including reputational) risk for companies. Evolving acceptance of a company's responsibility to respect all human rights[3] is making it more difficult for businesses to disassociate themselves from human rights violations that inevitably arise in many global supply chains. This developing and expansive concept of corporate responsibility for human rights is influencing the way states are framing legislative responses, as well as how some companies

---

[1] I. Mamic, 'Managing Global Supply Chains: The Sports Footwear, Apparel and Retail Sectors' (2005) 59 *Journal of Business Ethics* 81–100; R. M. Locke, *The Promise and Limits of Private Power* (New York: Cambridge, 2013); S. Wheeler, 'Global Production, CSR and Human Rights: The Courts of Public Opinion and The Social Licence To Operate' (2015) 19(6) *The International Journal of Human Rights* 757–778.

[2] Supply chains may be variously labelled value chains or production chains sometimes with distinction, see G. Gereffi and K. Fernandez-Stark 'Global Value Chain Analysis: A Primer', Center on Globalization, Governance & Competitiveness, Duke University (May 31 2011), www.cggc.duke.edu/pdfs/2011-05-31_GVC_analysis_a_primer.pdf (last accessed *date*).

[3] Human Rights Council, 'Guiding Principles on Business and Human Rights: Implementing the United Nations "Protect, Respect and Remedy" Framework: Report of the Special Representative of the Secretary-General on the issue of Human Rights and Transnational Corporations and Other Business Enterprises', A/HRC/17/31 (21 March 2011).

are responding to the exposure of human rights violations in their supply chains.[4]

However, the rhetoric around the broad acceptance of a company's responsibility to respect human rights has not assuaged the ambiguity that surrounds human rights supply chain responsibilities. In most industries, large companies now rely on a series of contractors and suppliers in a range of countries to produce and transport their products. Today's global supply chains link individual workers with large and small companies across national, political and cultural boundaries. Broad and sometimes amorphous supply chains begin with the process of sourcing raw materials, and then involve a multiplicity of actors who are involved in developing and distributing the product in order to bring it finally to the consumer market. Any desire to compartmentalize human rights responsibilities to a particular company or within particular geographical boundaries is exacerbated by direct and indirect corporate linkages in global supply chains. Each company along that supply chain has a responsibility to respect human rights – but where does that responsibility begin and end? Is the supply chain inherently integrated into the operations of the lead company at the top end of the chain? When is it reasonable to hold a company accountable for actions that may have occurred because of the actions of other (legally separate) firms? What legal mechanisms (such as due diligence or reporting) might be used to regulate human rights responsibilities within a supply chain?

This chapter begins (Section 9.1) by discussing the increasing centrality of supply chains in global production and argues that global supply chains are now an intrinsic part of the operations of many global companies. Section 9.2 highlights the use of transparency and reporting legislation to regulate human rights behaviour in supply chains. In some cases, this is done by mandating human rights due diligence reporting requirements and in others by attaching legal liability to companies for failing to comply both with the due diligence expectations and the reporting requirements. In this respect, this chapter contributes to the scholarship on the intersectionality of corporate law and human rights responsibilities[5] by focusing in

---

[4] See the discussion in this report on the role of authorized and unauthorized subcontractors in supply chains as a way some companies delimit their responsibility for the Rana Plaza disaster in 2013; S. Labowitz and D. Baumann-Pauly, 'Business As Usual Is *Not* An Option: Supply Chains and Sourcing After Rana Plaza' (2014) 14, www.stern.nyu.edu/cons/groups/content/documents/webasset/con_047408.pdf.

[5] P. Redmond, 'The Thrall of Shareholder Value: Implications For Corporate Social Responsibility and Directors' Duties' (2006) 58(2) *Keeping Good Companies* 79–83; P. Muchlinski, 'Implementing the New UN Corporate Human Rights Framework: Implications for Corporate Law, Governance and Regulation' (2012) 22 *Business Ethics*

particular on the value of mandating human rights due diligence and reporting by corporations and attaching penalties for non-compliance. Finally, Section 9.3 considers the factors to take into account in drafting a general provision in a future business and human rights treaty that attempts to regulate corporate human rights responsibilities in global supply chains.

9.1   The Increasing Centrality of Supply Chains in Global Production

The industries and activities encompassed in supply chains have increased since the 1990s and 'cover not only finished goods but also components and subassemblies... affecting not just manufacturing industries, but also energy, food production and all kinds of services'.[6] The multi-layered nature of a supply chain means that suppliers may be difficult to trace and therefore regulate. Supply chains can be fluid and while the first tier of suppliers may be easily identified, those suppliers in lower tiers are not so visible and may enter and exit supply chains at various points.[7] The OECD illustrates the complexity and multi-layered nature of a supply chain when defining a mineral supply chain:

> The process of bringing a raw mineral to the consumer market involves multiple actors and generally includes the extraction, transport, handling, trading, processing, smelting, refining and alloying, manufacturing and sale of end product. The term supply chain refers to the system of all the activities, organisations, actors, technology, information, resources and services involved in moving the mineral from the extraction site downstream to its incorporation in the final product for end consumers.[8]

Increasingly, companies do not generally own or operate the end factories in which their goods are produced and they may contract with hundreds, sometimes thousands, of different suppliers annually.[9] Nike, for example, sources its products from over 655 factories, engaging more

---

Quarterly 145; V. Harper Ho, 'Of Enterprise Principles and Corporate Groups: Does Corporate Law Reach Human Rights?' 52 Columbia Journal of Transnational Law 113–172.

[6] G. Gereffi, 'Global Value Chains in a post-Washington Consensus World' (2014) 21(1) Review of International Political Economy 9, 10.

[7] Labowitz and Baumann-Pauly, 'Business As Usual', n. 4, 14.

[8] OECD (2013) OECD Due Diligence Guidance for Responsible Supply Chains of Minerals from Conflict-Affected and High-Risk Areas: Second Edition, OECD Publishing, 14 http://www.oecd.org/daf/inv/mne/GuidanceEdition2.pdf.

[9] Locke, The Promise, n. 1.

than one million workers across more than 42 countries.[10] Walmart, one of the world's largest and most powerful retailers, sells its goods in '11,500 stores under 72 banners in 28 countries and e-commerce sites in 11 countries each week. With fiscal year 2016 revenue of $482.1 billion, Walmart employs 2.2 million associates worldwide.'[11] Walmart acknowledges that it has 'thousands of businesses around the world that proudly call themselves Walmart suppliers'.[12] Apple publicly acknowledges its top 200 suppliers but does not state how many more lie beneath them.

The challenges associated with regulating human rights issues arising in multi-jurisdictional supply chains, along with civil society pressure to improve working conditions, has led (some) companies to take a more proactive role in internalizing responsibility for regulating the workplaces producing their goods. Self-regulation is a familiar theme in discussions on business and human rights, and many global brands and transnational companies operating complex supply chains that span multiple jurisdictions have increasingly adopted codes of conduct to address human rights issues in their supply chain operations. Some have also joined forces in multi-stakeholder organizations to streamline their approach to regulating human rights issues.[13] Following the public criticism that Nike faced in the mid-1990s, the company established a specific department tasked with working to improve factory conditions. In 1998, the then-CEO of Nike, Phillip Knight, acknowledged that '[t]he Nike product has become synonymous with slave wages, forced overtime, and arbitrary abuse' and stated, 'I truly believe the American consumer doesn't want to buy products made under abusive conditions.'[14] Today Nike declares that one of its:

---

[10] Current as at December 2016: Nike, 'Frequently Asked Questions', http://nikeinc.com/pages/frequently-asked-questions. Nike is one of the world's largest suppliers of athletic shoes and apparel and a major manufacturer of sports equipment, with revenue in excess of US$32 billion in 2016: Nike, 'Nike, Inc. Reports Fiscal 2016 Fourth Quarter and Full Year Results' http://s1.q4cdn.com/806093406/files/doc_financials/2016/Q4/FY'16-Q4-NIKEINC-Press-Release-FINAL.pdf (last accessed 6 December 2016).

[11] Walmart, 'Our Story', http://corporate.walmart.com/our-story (last accessed 6 December 2016).

[12] Walmart, 'Suppliers', http://corporate.walmart.com/suppliers (last accessed 6 December 2016).

[13] D. Baumann-Pauly, J. Nolan, S. Labowitz and A. van Heerden, 'Setting and Enforcing Industry-Specific Standards for Human Rights: The Role of Multi-Stakeholder Initiatives in Regulating Corporate Conduct' in D. Baumann-Pauly and J. Nolan (eds.), *Business and Human Rights: From Principles to Practice* (Routledge, April 2016), 107--27.

[14] M. Nisen, 'Why the Bangladesh Factory Collapse Would Never Have Happened To Nike' *Business Insider Australia* (9 May 2013) www.businessinsider.com/how-nike-solved-its-sweatshop-problem-2013-5.

responsibilities as a global company is to play a role in bringing about positive, systemic change for workers within our supply chain and in the industry. We've run the course – from establishing a Code of Conduct . . . to pulling together an internal team to enforce it . . . and working with external bodies to monitor factories and work with stakeholders.[15]

Walmart's 2014 Sustainability Report acknowledges the multi-layered and deep nature of its supply chain and states that it is 'committed to supporting the informal supply chain, which ranges from the small supplier to artisan home workers'.[16] Apple's 2009 Supplier Responsibility Progress Report highlighted a specific problem in its supply chain – namely, the recruitment of migrant workers by its suppliers. The report noted that Apple's suppliers used multiple third-party labour agencies to source workers from other countries and it was common practice to charge workers a recruitment fee. In response, Apple updated its Supplier Code of Conduct and issued a standard for the Prevention of Involuntary Labor.[17] In 2014 Apple announced that, starting in 2015, no worker employed on an Apple line could be charged any recruitment fees.[18] Since 2008 Apple has required its suppliers to reimburse what it regards as excessive recruitment fees.[19]

Each of these examples evidences the willingness of (some) global companies to acknowledge the vital nexus that exists between the operations of their contractors and subcontractors and the company's ultimate goods and services. The supply chain has become an intrinsic part of the lead firm's operations but is generally composed of separate legal entities. Acknowledging the relevance of a firm's suppliers, however, is not the same as accepting that lead companies could or should assume legal liability for wrongdoing by suppliers in their production chains. Requiring or 'requesting' suppliers to fund the reimbursement of recruitment fees or to pay increased wages in their factories is an acknowledgement of the

---

[15] Nike, 'Sustainability', http://about.nike.com/pages/sustainability.

[16] Walmart, 'Walmart 2014 Global Responsibility Report', 61, https://cdn.corporate.wal mart.com/db/e1/b551a9db42fd99ea24141f76065f/2014-global-responsibility-report.pdf.

[17] Apple Inc., 'Apple Supplier Responsibility Standards', www.apple.com/supplier-responsi bility/pdf/Apple_Supplier_Responsibility_Standards.pdf.

[18] Apple Inc., 'Apple Supplier Responsibility 2014 Progress Report', 10, www.apple.com/ supplier-responsibility/pdf/Apple_SR_2014_Progress_Report.pdf.

[19] In 2014, Apple required its suppliers to reimburse US$3.96 million in excess fees to over 4500 foreign contractors, bringing the total reimbursements to US$20.96 million to over 30,000 foreign contract workers since it began addressing this issue in 2008, Apple Inc., 'Apple Supplier Responsibility 2014 Progress Report', 10 www.apple.com/supplier-responsibility/pdf/Apple_SR_2014_Progress_Report.pdf.

universalization of global responsibility for supply chain operations, and suggests a degree of leverage on the part of the lead firm to influence the conduct of the supplier. It does not, however, necessarily transform that responsibility into legal liability for lead firms.[20] Nevertheless, public statements about the breadth, depth and interdependent nature of supply chains are a welcome step and a far cry from the narrower perspective and 'denial of responsibility' approach of companies involved in the Bhopal disaster just a few decades earlier.

Beyond a company's self-identification of the relevance of its supply chain, various soft law initiatives that have emerged since the late 1990s have also recognized the importance of the link between a company and its suppliers from a human rights regulatory perspective. In 2000, the United Nations (UN) launched the Global Compact, an initiative that asked business leaders to 'embrace, support and enact, within their sphere of influence',[21] a set of ten principles in the areas of human rights, labour, the environment and anti-corruption. In a subsequent and quite different UN initiative a few years later, the draft UN Norms on the Responsibilities of Transnational Corporations and Other Business Enterprises referred to a company's 'sphere of activity and influence' as a means of delineating corporate responsibility for human rights.[22] Neither initiative defined 'sphere of influence', although in a later briefing paper the UN Office of the High Commissioner for Human Rights noted

---

[20] However, legal developments in a very select few cases in Canada seem to signal an increased willingness by an Ontario court to impute the wrongs of a subsidiary operating in a foreign country to the parent corporation. See, for example, *Choc v. Hudbay Minerals Inc*, 2013 ONSC 1414. In *Hudbay*, a group of indigenous peoples from Guatemala sued Hudbay Minerals Inc., a Canadian corporation, and its Guatemalan subsidiary, Compañia Guatemalteca De Niquel (CGN), for alleged human rights abuses at a Guatemalan mining project owned through CGN. The Plaintiffs brought their claims in Ontario, not Guatemala. Hudbay applied to strike the claims on the basis that the claims improperly relied on 'piercing the corporate veil' or ignoring the separate corporate personalities of Hudbay, a Canadian corporation, and CGN, its Guatemalan subsidiary. Hudbay further argued that the Plaintiffs were seeking to impose a supervisory liability on parent corporations over their foreign subsidiaries. Hudbay's applications were dismissed, and the action allowed to proceed against it and its Guatemalan subsidiary in an Ontario Court. Also see: *Chevron Corp v. Yaiguaje*, 2015 SCC 42.

[21] The concept of sphere of influence was used in the first iteration of the Global Compact but was revised in 2011 and the language of the Global Compact now mirrors the terms and concepts set out in the Guiding Principles and references to 'sphere of influence' have been removed.

[22] United Nations' Norms on the Responsibilities of Transnational Corporations and Other Business Enterprises with Regard to Human Rights, U.N. Doc E/CN.4/Sub.2/2003/12/ Rev.2 (2003), para. A.1.

that the concept encompasses a company's internal and external business networks, including its relationships with joint venture partners and government authorities.[23] This concept of a corporate 'sphere of influence' began to be widely used in corporate social responsibility discourse[24] and implied the need for companies to use their influence to respect human rights beyond the ambit of their immediate operations. However, as noted in 2008 by the UN Special Representative for Business and Human Rights, Professor Ruggie, the concept was arguably too broad and ambitious to apply with any degree of rigour and he abandoned the terminology in the subsequent UN Guiding Principles on Business and Human Rights (Guiding Principles).[25]

The most recent business and human rights initiative emanating from the UN, the 2011 Guiding Principles,[26] notes that a company's responsibility to respect human rights applies not only to the company's 'own activities' but also to those impacts that are 'directly linked to their operations, products or services by their business relationships, even if they have not contributed to those impacts'.[27] The Commentary accompanying the Guiding Principles clarifies that business relationships include 'business partners, entities in its value chain, and any other non-state or state entity directly linked to its businesses operations, products or services'.[28] The Guiding Principles thus clearly anticipate the need for companies to accept that their responsibility to respect human rights goes beyond the bounds of the enterprise (i.e., formally affiliated entities) to reach extended networks of third parties. As the OECD has observed, '[m]ultinational enterprises, like their domestic counterparts, have evolved to encompass a broader range of business arrangements and organizational forms. Strategic alliances and closer relations with suppliers and contractors tend to blur the boundaries of the enterprise.'[29]

The question of what suffices as a 'direct link' in the Guiding Principles is left open and potentially narrows corporate exposure. However,

---

[23] OHCHR Briefing Paper, 'The Global Compact and Human Rights: Understanding Sphere of Influence and Complicity' (OHCHR, Geneva, 2004), 18–19.

[24] J. Ruggie, 'Report of the Special Representative of the Secretary-General on the Issue of Human Rights and Transnational Corporations and other Business Enterprises; Clarifying the Concepts of "Sphere of influence" and "Complicity"', A/HRC/8/16 (15 May 2008), http://198.170.85.29/Ruggie-companion-report-15-May-2008.pdf. See also the critique of the concept in Chapter 7 by Bilchitz in this collection.

[25] Ibid., para. 4.   [26] Human Rights Council, 'Guiding Principles', n. 3.

[27] Ibid., Principle 13.   [28] Ibid.

[29] OECD (2011), OECD Guidelines For Multinational Enterprises, www.oecd.org/daf/inv/mne/48004323.pdf.

further guidance provided by the Office of the High Commissioner for Human Rights (OHCHR) indicates that the 'direct link' concept should be interpreted broadly. One example provided by the OHCHR notes that a 'company's operations, products or services may be directly linked to an adverse impact through a business relationship if one of its suppliers subcontracts work, without its prior knowledge, to contractors.'[30] Many of these business relationships will lie beyond the formal legal bounds of the corporate enterprise and this example advocates for the inclusion of authorized and unauthorized subcontractors as being directly linked to lead firms. Despite the willingness of the Guiding Principles to acknowledge the breadth and depth of a supply chain, the terminology does not directly attribute legal liability to the lead firm for the activities of its suppliers. Indeed, the Guiding Principles introduce an element of caution into the attribution of responsibility by acknowledging that the extent to which a company might need to take 'appropriate action' in order to prevent or mitigate adverse human rights impacts will depend first on whether the company itself caused or contributed to the impact or whether it was involved because of its business relationships, and second the extent of its leverage in addressing the adverse impact.[31] Thus, while the corporate responsibility to respect human rights applies to each and every company along the supply chain, the extent of action that the Guiding Principles envisage for particular companies in that chain may vary and is left open to interpretation.

9.2   Mandating Due Diligence and transparency as a Mechanism to Regulate Global Supply Chains

Various legal attempts to regulate supply chains in order to address negative impacts on human rights have begun to emerge in recent years. Legislation imposing due diligence requirements on lead firms is contributing to an evolving understanding of what actions might be

---

[30] OHCHR, 'Frequently Asked Questions About The Guiding Principles On Business And Human Rights' (2014), 32 www.ohchr.org/Documents/Publications/FAQ_PrinciplesBuss inessHR.pdf. Further, Ruggie notes that '[t]he Framework documents make clear that due diligence necessitates enterprise-wide monitoring across all jurisdictions in which an MNE does business and includes not only an assessment of the companies' actual and potential human rights impacts, but also analysis of the local business context and its relationships with business partners.' Ruggie, n. 24, 19–22.

[31] Guiding Principle 19 defines leverage as the 'ability to effect change in the wrongful practices of an entity that causes harm', Human Rights Council, 'Guiding Principles', n. 3. See discussion at n. 54.

required from a company with respect to the prevention and/or mitiga-tion of human rights violations in its supply chain. This section will discuss legislative attempts to increase the transparency of supply chains by imposing due diligence and reporting requirements on both the separate corporate entities within that chain and overarching obligations placed on the lead firm. The requirement for companies to conduct human rights supply chain due diligence imposes some level of account-ability on the lead firm for, at a minimum, reporting and disclosing the actions of its suppliers downstream. Whether such accountability might then lead to legal liability being attached to a company for a supplier's wrongdoings is a further question.

The corporate responsibility to respect human rights as set out in the Guiding Principles is not framed in legal terms but this does not necessarily prevent binding legal duties emerging from this concept, most obviously as flowing from the concept of due diligence. The Guiding Principles encourage companies to conduct due diligence as a means by which the company discharges its responsibility to respect human rights.[32] The Guiding Principles' focus on due diligence bor-rows heavily from corporate law principles which embed due diligence within corporate governance processes. While the focus of corporate due diligence processes is on identifying material risks (i.e., financial, legal, reputational etc.) to the company, human rights due diligence is aimed at ascertaining risks to a broader set of stakeholders, including rights-holders, individuals and communities that may be negatively impacted upon by the company's operations.[33] Human rights due diligence is expected to cover not only the company's own activities, but also those to which it might be directly linked via its business relationships. However, while there is no legal obligation in the Guiding Principles either to conduct such an assessment or to publish the results, some states have recently adopted legislation that takes the discretionary element out of human rights due diligence and requires lead firms to report on certain activities of other companies within their supply chain.

---

[32] Human Rights Council, 'Guiding Principles', n. 3, Principles17 [II.A.17] and 18 [II.A.18].
[33] For a discussion on the difference between the use of the notion of due diligence in the corporate sphere and in the human rights sphere in relation to corporations, see Chapter 8 by McCorquodale and Smit in this collection. See also on the materiality of human rights risks more generally C. Williams, '" Knowing and Showing" Using U.S. Securities Law to Compel Human Rights Disclosure' (2013), http://icar.ngo/wp-content/uploads/2013/10/ICAR-Knowing-and-Showing-Report5.pdf.

Mandatory supply chain due diligence highlights the intersectionality between international human rights law and domestic corporate governance frameworks. The 'conventional wisdom ... [which] maintains that corporate law is largely irrelevant to questions of human rights'[34] is changing, but there are still a number of theoretical challenges to overcome in clarifying the human rights responsibilities of each company in a supply chain and to what extent they might be connected. Foremost among these issues are the dual principles of separate legal personality and limited liability, which are barriers to attributing legal liability to a company for the practices of its suppliers. These general corporate principles assume a model 'under which the liability of the shareholders or members of a corporate is limited only to the value of their shareholding'.[35] 'Piercing the corporate veil' to make shareholders liable for the debts of the company is contentious, even where the shareholder is another company.[36] Transparency legislation that mandates reporting from a lead firm about the activities of its suppliers and in some cases (discussed below) attaching liability to the lead firm for the actions of its suppliers begins to, at least partially, blur traditional distinctions around corporate separate legal personality. Global corporate accountability for human rights that would permit (or require) one company to assume some level of responsibility (ranging from reporting to legal liability) for human rights impacts arising from the actions of another company challenges these dual principles of corporate law.[37] In a world of global supply chains, where a global company might have business relationships with tens or hundreds of suppliers which are intrinsic to the company's operations, it is arguable that the circumstances in which a separate legal identity can be used as a shield to *avoid* liability for the human rights

---

[34] Harper Ho, n. 5, 113.

[35] K. Amaeshi, K. Osji and P. Nnodim, 'Corporate Social Responsibility in Supply Chain of Global Brand: A Boundaryless Responsibility?' (2008) 81(1) *Journal of Business Ethics* 223–234 at [*] citing the case of *Salomon v. Salomon & Co.* 1897.

[36] H. Anderson, 'Piercing the Veil on Corporate Groups in Australia: The Case for Reform' (2009) 33 *Melbourne University Law Review* 333––67, 334.

[37] While corporate law itself allows for limited exceptions to these dual principles, the circumstances in which courts have been willing to 'pierce the corporate veil' are the exception rather than the rule. For a survey of veil-piercing doctrine and practice, see, e.g., K. Strasser, 'Piercing the Veil in Corporate Groups' (2005) 37 *Connecticut Law Review* 637; R. Thompson, 'Piercing the Corporate Veil: An Empirical Study' (1991) 76 *Cornell Law Review* 1036;. H. Easterbrook and D. R. Fischel, 'Limited Liability and the Corporation' (1985) 52 *University of Chicago Law Review* 89, 89 as cited by Anderson, 'Piercing the Veil', n. 36, 341. Also see discussion of *Choc v. Hudbay Minerals Inc* at n. 20.

wrongdoings of another entity with which it is directly linked should be exceptional rather than the norm.[38]

There is a latent potential for corporate governance frameworks to incorporate legal liability for human rights violations in supply chains, and recent legislative developments are indicative of an emerging trend to broaden the scope of what lead firms should at least be aware of, if not accountable for, in their supply chains. Reporting by itself does not guarantee accountability. Rather, reporting is a tool that has the power to advance accountability by increasing transparency around corporate operations which may then trigger pressure to improve corporate human rights performance not only of the lead firm but also of those companies with which it is linked. The discussion below highlights various models which have emerged relatively recently to encourage greater transparency in supply chains. Some of these models have inbuilt legal liability that can be attached to firms along the supply chain. Other models focus more purely on reporting but they too can have legal consequences.

9.2.1   Transparency Legislation: Imposing legal Obligations on Firms in a Supply Chain to Report

In 2015, the United Kingdom passed the Modern Slavery Act, which mandates transparency in supply chains.[39] The Act requires companies[40] to prepare an annual statement describing steps that they have taken to ensure that slavery and human trafficking is not present in their operations or in any of their supply chains, and to publish information on the company's web site.[41] The statement may include information about the organization's structure, company's policies, due diligence processes, risks, performance indicators and training relating to slavery and human trafficking.[42] If the company has not taken any such steps, it

---

[38] See generally, Anderson, 'Piercing the Veil', n. 36. See further discussion in Section 9.5.
[39] *Modern Slavery Act* 2015 (c.30) (UK), s.54.
[40] The disclosure obligation in s.54 applies to 'commercial organizations' which are defined as bodies corporate (wherever incorporated) or partnerships (wherever formed) and which 'carry on business, or part of a business' in the UK. The entity must supply goods or services (although there is no requirement that they be supplied in the UK) and it must have a total turnover or group turnover – that is, the total turnover of a company and its subsidiaries – of £36 million or more.
[41] *Modern Slavery Act* 2015 (c.30) (UK), s.54(4), s.54(7). The Act applies to companies with total turnover above £36 million. *Ibid.*, s.54(2)(b).
[42] *Modern Slavery Act* 2015 (c.30) (UK), s.54(5).

must issue a statement to that effect.[43] The scope of the disclosure obligation is opaque because the Act does not define 'supply chain'. There are no financial or other penalties attached to non-compliance with the disclosure obligation; instead, the Act aims to harness the power of the consumer to demand and use information to help prevent slavery and exploitation.[44] Early analysis[45] of the first 75 statements published shows that only 29 per cent of them complied with the Act's basic procedural requirements, namely, that the statement is approved by the Board and signed by a company director (or equivalent) and available on the homepage of the company's website. Further, the analysis also disclosed that of the six content areas on which information may be included, such as organizational structure, company policies and due diligence, only nine statements covered the six suggested areas. Although it is only early in the life of the Modern Slavery Act, such analysis suggests that reporting requirements that are broadly framed and do not couple transparency with any penalty for non-compliance may not be the most effective mechanism for achieving the type of transparency which may be converted into accountability.

The UK legislation was modelled on, but is potentially broader than, the California Transparency in Supply Chains Act passed a few years earlier.[46] Since 2012, large retailers and manufacturers doing business in California have been required to disclose on their websites the extent to which the company engages in verification of product supply chains to address risks of slavery, forced labour and human trafficking. Specifically, the company must state whether it (1) engages in verification of product supply chains to evaluate and address risks of human trafficking and

---

[43] *Modern Slavery Act* 2015 (c.30) (UK), s.54(4)(b). The Act provides for enforcement through injunction or specific performance. *Ibid.*, s.54(11).

[44] United Kingdom, *Parliamentary Debates*, House of Commons, 28 February 2012, 174 (Fiona McTaggert MP).

[45] The analysis was conducted by civil society organizations, the CORE Coalition and the Business and Human Rights Resource Centre, 'Register of Slavery & Human Trafficking Corporate Statements Released To Date To Comply With UK Modern Slavery Act' (2016), http://business-humanrights.org/sites/default/files/documents/CORE%20BHRRC% 20Analysis%20of%20Modern%20Slavery%20Statements%20FINAL_March2016.pdf. For a registry of statements made under the *Modern Slavery Act*, see Business and Human Rights Resources Centre, http://business-humanrights.org/en/registry-of-slavery-human-trafficking-statements-under-uk-modern-slavery-act.

[46] *California Transparency in Supply Chains Act*, Ca. Civ. Code § 1714.43. The Californian Act potentially limits the scope of the legislation as it refers to the 'direct supply chain for tangible goods offered for sale' s.1714.43(a)(1). Also the Act only applies to retail sellers or manufacturers *operating in California* with more than US$100 million in gross receipts.

slavery; (2) conducts audits of suppliers to evaluate supplier compliance with company standards for trafficking and slavery in supply chains; (3) requires direct suppliers to certify that materials incorporated into its products comply with laws regarding slavery and human trafficking; (4) maintains internal accountability standards and procedures for employees or contractors who fail to meet company standards regarding slavery and trafficking; and (5) provides company employees and management with training on human trafficking and slavery. Importantly, the Act does not actually require covered retailers to do any of the five things listed above: they must simply say on their websites whether or not they do them. These mechanisms do not set mandatory standards for what due diligence must look like, nor do they hold companies directly legally accountable for actual adverse human rights impacts connected to their operations. There is no penalty for failing to take steps, only for failing to disclose whether or not a company engages in supply chain due diligence. The Act does not address what constitutes appropriate due diligence. The sanction for non-compliance is potential injunctive relief by the California State Attorney General, meaning that companies will not face a monetary penalty for failure to disclose, but that they will receive an order from the Attorney General to take specific action.

Another example of transparency legislation that is narrowly tailored to focus on a particular issue is s.1502 of the US Dodd-Frank Act, which requires all listed companies to report on the sources of minerals used in their products that originate from the Democratic Republic of Congo (DRC) or adjoining countries.[47] The purpose of this provision is to provide greater transparency about how the trade in minerals is potentially fuelling and funding the armed struggle in the DRC; functionally, it relies on the adverse reputational impact of such a disclosure rather than mandating penalties for actually sourcing minerals from conflict-afflicted regions.[48]

---

[47] *Dodd-Frank Wall Street Reform and Consumer Protection Act*, Pub. L. No. 111-203, 124 Stat. 1376 (2010). In addition, s. 1504 of the Act addresses financial transparency by requiring all listed oil and mining companies to disclose the revenues they pay to governments worldwide.

[48] G. A. Sarfaty, 'Shining Light on Global Supply Chains' (2015) 56(2) *Harvard International Law Journal*, 419–463. Section 1502 does impose penalties for not reporting or complying in good faith (see Conflict Mineral, 77 Fed. Reg. at 56,280. Also the information filed by companies is subject to s.18 of the *Securities Exchange Act* 1934 which attaches liability for any false or misleading statements. Sarfaty's study of the first set of Conflict Minerals Reports submitted to the Securities Exchange Commission up to June 2014 argues that these reports exhibited a low level of compliance with due diligence requirements and

Due diligence and reporting requirements are a first step in linking transparency with accountability. Each of these three pieces of legislation is designed principally to produce information about steps taken by companies to conduct supply chain due diligence on specific human rights issues, and to force companies that have not engaged in due diligence to say so publicly.[49] For example, the Californian Act presents a disclosure requirement, as opposed to presenting required measures to be undertaken by a retailer, manufacturer or similar business to prevent the utilization of slave labour or implement operational changes. However, the lack of mandatory measures to be implemented throughout the Act, as well as its limitation on the ability to pursue private claims, might lull companies into a false sense of security concerning the possibility of litigation, as even transparency legislation 'without teeth' can lead to negative repercussions for business. One of the laws' purposes here is to provide consumers with critical information that may allow them to distinguish companies based on the merits of their efforts taken to tackle this issue. The disclosure obligations establish social and legal expectations of what is expected of companies and provide consumers with crucial information with which they could pursue other legal options to hold the companies accountable.

In August 2015, two separate lawsuits, one filed against Costco[50] and the other against Nestlé,[51] alleging the use of slave labour in each company's supply chain demonstrate the potential link between transparency and accountability. Both lawsuits were filed in California and separately

identified several obstacles to achieving broader compliance, including that: '(i) international norms on supply chain due diligence are in their infancy; (ii) the proliferation of certification standards and in-region sourcing initiatives are still evolving and often competing; and (iii) inadequate local security and weak governance inhibit the mapping of mineral trade and the tracing of minerals in the region' at 4.

[49] O. De Schutter, A. Ramasastry, M. Taylor and Robert C. Thompson, 'Human Rights Due Diligence: Role of the State' (December 2012), 46, http://humanrightsinbusiness.eu/wp-content/uploads/2015/05/De-Schutter-et-al.-Human-Rights-Due-Diligence-The-Role-of-States.pdf: '[I]t is a disclosure statute that simply asks companies to tell the public what they do, and to publish this on their website with a conspicuous link to the pertinent information.'

[50] *Sud v. Costco Wholesale Corp.*, 15-cv-03783, U.S. District Court, Northern District of California (San Francisco).

[51] *Barber v. Nestlé USA Inc.*, 15-cv-01364, U.S. District Court, Central District of California (Los Angeles). In November 2015 Nestle disclosed that it had found forced labour in it supply chain and published a report by civil society organization Verite disclosing this: Verite, 'Recruitment Practices and Migrant Labor Conditions in Nestlé's Thai Shrimp Supply Chain' (2015), www.verite.org/sites/default/files/images/NestleReport-ThaiShrimp_prepared-by-Verite.pdf.

accused the companies of knowingly supporting a system of slave labour in their supply chain to import seafood products into the United States. As of late 2016, both cases have been dismissed.[52] The lawsuits stemmed in part from the disclosure expectations set by the California Transparency in Supply Chains Act and argue that the alleged use of forced labour in the corporate supply chain is inconsistent with the company's mandated disclosures. For example, the Costco lawsuit alleged that various public disclosures by Costco were fraudulent and misleading because, despite public statements by the company that it does not tolerate human trafficking and slavery in its supply chain, it continued to sell seafood products to consumers that are allegedly the result of slave labour. In its 2015 Trafficking in Persons report[53] examining human trafficking in 188 countries, the US State Department cited concerns about slave labour in Thailand's fishing industry and found fault in the Thai government's record in fighting exploitation. Some of the practices alleged to be occurring in the Thai fishing industry include torture, chaining of workers and the killing of those who seek to escape illegal fishing vessels. Neither Costco nor Nestlé were accused of expressly engaging in such practices; rather, the accusations concerned supplier relationships with companies that are sourcing seafood from suppliers that do engage in such practices. Both of these lawsuits utilized consumer law as the tool to attempt to attach supply chain legal liability

---

[52] *Barber v. Nestlé USA Inc.*, Order Granting Defendant's Motion to Dismiss, December 9, 2015: www.csrandthelaw.com/wp-content/uploads/sites/2/2016/01/Nestle-dismissal.pdf. The plaintiffs did not allege that Nestlé did not comply with the Supply Chains Act, rather that Nestlé was obligated to make additional disclosures at the point of sale regarding the likelihood that a given can of its Fancy Feast product contains seafood sourced by forced labor. Nestlé's argument that this claim is barred by the safe harbour doctrine because the California Legislature already considered the disclosures that large companies with potential forced labour in their supply chains need to make to consumers, and elected not to require the disclosures was successful. In *Sud v. Costco Wholesale Corp* the plaintiff alleged that Costco knew, but did not disclose to consumers, that feed for prawns sold at Costco was sourced from slave labour, human trafficking and other illegal labour abuses. The plaintiff also alleged that statements on Costco's website required by the *California Supply Chain Transparency Act* were misleading. The case was dismissed for lack of standing as the plaintiff was unable to provide proof that she had purchased the affected prawns from Costco. Specifically, the plaintiff had stated in her complaint that she had purchased prawns that came from two suppliers in Thailand and Costco provided evidence that the prawns she purchased came from Vietnam and Indonesia. The Court granted the plaintiff leave to amend her complaint. See Order on Motions to Dismiss, *Sud v. Costco Wholesale Corp.*, No. 15-cv-03783-JSW (N.D. Cal. Jan. 15, 2016), ECF No. 76.
[53] United States Department of State, 'Trafficking in Persons Report' (July 2015), p[*], www.state.gov/documents/organization/245365.pdf.

to the lead firm by alleging that the companies are fraudulently misre-presenting how their supply chain operates.[54] Flowing from the disclosure obligations set out in the Californian legislation, the lawsuits treat the practices of Costco's and Nestlé's suppliers as intrinsic to the lead firm's operations and argue that lead firms have a responsibility to be fully cognizant of the practices of their tiered suppliers so that any statements made by the lead firm are consistent with corporate practices that flow throughout the supply chain.

9.2.2   Transparency Legislation: Attaching Direct Legal Liability to Firms in Supply Chains

While the American and British legislative developments discussed above mandate disclosure, they do not directly impose civil or criminal liability on lead firms for the downstream acts of other companies in their supply chain. However, transparency legislation can also be crafted to expressly attach legal liability up and down a supply chain for particular wrongdoings occurring anywhere in that chain. This type of legislation emphasizes the link between control and/or leverage and responsibility. If a lead firm at the top end of the supply chain can control the size, design, quantity and quality of a product, and possesses potential leverage to influence the working conditions of those producing the goods, it is then both fair and effective to align that power with legal responsibility.

Attaching specific obligations to lead firms in a supply chain to con-duct due diligence downstream is a potentially effective mechanism in regulating supply chains. However, the power relationship between lead firms and subsequent tiers of suppliers is a 'complicating factor in the implementation of supply chain regulation'.[55] Often, 'it is the firm at the top of the chain that makes the decision to structure its enterprise through subcontracting relationships, presumably because such a struc-ture allows the firm to increase profits by lowering the costs and risk of liability that come with being a direct employer'[56]; and thus that firm may

---

[54] *Nike, Inc. v. Kasky*, 123 S.Ct. 2554 (2003) was somewhat of a precursor to these human rights/consumer-oriented actions in which Mr. Kasky contended that Nike's commu-nication (regarding its labour practices) contained significant misstatements of fact and thus was actionable under California's unfair competition and false advertising laws. The parties settled out of court before any finding on the accuracy of Nike's statements was made.

[55] Sarfaty, 'Shining Light', n. 48, 13.

[56] J. Gordon, 'Joint Liability Approaches to Regulating Recruitment' (2014) Fordham Law Legal Studies Research Paper No. 2518519, 2.

be able to monitor and influence suppliers down the chain to act in a responsible manner. Accordingly, companies in such a position of power may have the capacity to exercise leverage over actors in the supply chain via their strategic position at the apex of the chain. However, this may not be true for all entities. If a lead firm lacks 'the purchasing power to hold suppliers captive'[57] they will have a lower capacity to influence the suppliers' practices. 'Leverage' (defined as the 'ability to effect change in the wrongful practices of an entity that causes harm'[58]) is relevant here in terms of the applicability of attaching legal liability to the lead firm for a supplier's practices downstream.[59] The application of such leverage is not restricted to influencing behaviour that is dependent on the existence of a legal relationship with other supply chain actors. Leverage refers more broadly to the company's ability to affect another company's practices via their strategic position in the chain. Gereffi argues that there has been a fundamental shift in the last few decades 'from what had been "producer-driven" commodity chains to "buyer-driven" commodity chains' culminating in a power shift whereby buyers, particularly large transnational retailers and brand-name companies, have increased leverage over other firms in the supply chain.[60] The legislative examples below illustrate a

---

[57] Sarfaty, 'Shining Light', n. 48, 14.

[58] Human Rights Council, 'Guiding Principles', n. 3, Principle 19.

[59] The concepts of leverage and control have some overlap here depending on how they are defined. Control can be used in a strict legal sense to connote control via ownership. For example, in the context of commodities trading, control of a company means 'the power to exercise a controlling influence over the management or policies of a company whether through ownership of securities, by contract, or otherwise'. 17 CFR 160.3 [Title 17 – Commodity and Securities Exchanges; Chapter I – Commodity Futures Trading Commission; Part 160 – Privacy of Consumer Financial Information]. However, control may also be defined as the ability of a company to exert practical influence over another entity to influence change. For example, the Australian *Corporations Act* 2001 – SECT 50AA defines control more in the context in which leverage is used in this chapter.

'(1) For the purposes of this Act, an entity controls a second entity if the first entity has the capacity to determine the outcome of decisions about the second entity's financial and operating policies.

(2) In determining whether the first entity has this capacity:
   (a) the practical influence the first entity can exert (rather than the rights it can enforce) is the issue to be considered; and
   (b) any practice or pattern of behaviour affecting the second entity's financial or operating policies is to be taken into account (even if it involves a breach of an agreement or a breach of trust).'

[60] G. Gereffi, 'Global Value Chains in a post-Washington Consensus World' (2014) 21(1) *Review of International Political Economy* 9–37, 10. Also, G. Gereffi, J. Humphrey and T. Sturgeon, 'The Governance of Global Value Chains' (2005) 12(1) *Review of International Political Economy* 78–104.

variety of mechanisms used to attach legal liability to such entities (generally the lead firm or the company at the top of the chain) for the activities of other (non-related) firms in that supply chain.

In the early 2000s, a number of State governments in Australia introduced supply chain regulation in response to a strong and sustained civil society campaign focused on safeguarding the rights of home-based workers in the clothing industry.[61] The Australian legislation sets up a regulatory framework that requires the insertion of contractual tracking mechanisms in supplier contracts to follow production and mandate disclosure up and down the supply chain. Liability for contraventions of the laws is imposed on lead companies in order to shift the overarching legal responsibility to the top of the supply chain. This legislation has a number of distinctive features.

First, the legislation broadens the traditional approach to defining employment by deeming home-based workers or outworkers to be employees in order to defeat commercial arrangements that might otherwise undermine the employee status, for instance, by classifying workers as 'independent contractors'. In many cases, the immediate 'employer' may not be the controlling entity. Control may be shared by a number of key players in the supply chain or be wielded by a firm that sits outside the traditional employment relationship. The Australian laws effectively extend the scope of industrial relations law to deal with work arrangements and contracts that are common in supply chains, and which are often beyond the reach and definitions of traditional employment relationships. This deeming mechanism also then provides a clear legal basis upon which workers can recover unpaid entitlements from lead companies further up a particular supply chain.

Second, the provisions impose obligations on successive parties (other than the retail sector) in the contracting chain to ensure that outworkers receive their lawful entitlements (rights of recovery). The legislation provides for a recovery mechanism whereby the outworkers are entitled

---

[61] The FairWear campaign (http://fairwear.org.au/) was a significant force that led to the introduction of successive legislative amendments including: *Industrial Relations (Ethical Clothing Trade) Act 2001* (NSW) and s 175B *Workers Compensation Act 1987* (NSW): *Industrial Relations (Fair Work) Act 2005* (SA); *Outworkers (Improved Protection) Act 2003* (Vic); and *Industrial Relations and Other Acts Amendment Act 2005* (Qld). Also see generally, I. Nossar, R. Johnstone and M. Quinlan, 'Regulating Supply Chains to Address the Occupational Health and Safety Problems Associated with Precarious Employment: The Case of Home-Based Clothing Workers in Australia' (2004) 17 *Australian Journal of Labour Law* 137.

to claim unpaid entitlements throughout the supply chain up to and including the principal manufacturer. The recovery mechanism is also innovative in that it reverses the traditional onus of proof, so that unless the relevant firm can prove that a claimant worker has not done the work or that the claim calculation is erroneous, the company will be obliged to pay the claimed wages within a specified time.

Third, the mandated disclosure requirements operate up and down the supply chain, in that retailers are obligated to establish whether outworkers are being used in the production of their goods, and suppliers at all levels are obligated to provide that information to parties further up the chain. The information is then provided by the retailer to a designated trade union so that the supply chain is transparent and able to be monitored.

Finally, the legislation is supplemented by a voluntary mechanism administered by a multi-stakeholder initiative – Ethical Clothing Australia[62] – that accredits businesses operating in this specific sector and assists companies with the process of mapping their supply chain and verifying that all workers within it are receiving their legal entitlements. This legislation, like the other examples below is focused on a narrow issue – here, the treatment and entitlements due to homeworkers – and a specific sector – namely, apparel. This means that the legislation can be specific and targeted in attaching liability for wrongdoing to disparate actors in the supply chain.

Another regulatory technique that might be applied to supply chains is a specific mechanism utilized in the construction sector in the European Union. 'Chain liability regimes' potentially allow any firm in a supply chain to be held accountable for the debts of suppliers, including sub-contractors, in that chain.[63] One study notes the limited and selective use of such regimes but discusses the different variations of chain liability arrangements (all focused in the construction sector) that can be found in certain countries of the European Union.[64] The legislative mechanisms as exemplified in this study highlight two different techniques used to link firms legally in the EU construction industry:

---

[62] www.ethicalclothingaustralia.org.au/

[63] K. Lukas, 'Human Rights in the Supply Chain: Influence and Accountability' in R. Mares (ed.), *The UN Guiding Principles on Business and Human Rights: Foundations and Implementation* (The Hague: Brill, 2012), 163.

[64] M. Houwerzijl and S. Peters, 'Liability in Subcontracting Processes in the European Construction Sector' European Foundation for the Improvement of Living and Working Conditions (2008), www.ft.dk/samling/20121/almdel/beu/spm/69/svar/931966/1199657.pdf.

joint and several liability – this only applies at one level of the employment relationship, that is, when a subcontractor does not fulfil its obligations regarding payments, for example, to the Inland Revenue; in such instances, the contractor, together with the subcontractor, can be held liable by the Inland Revenue for the entire debt of the subcontractor; chain liability – this applies not only in relation to the contracting party, but also to the whole chain. In this case, the Inland Revenue may address all parties in the chain for the entire debt of a subcontractor.[65]

This type of legislation appears to have been only selectively developed to date and is narrowly targeted.[66] For example, the three main categories of obligations covered by the chain liability arrangements are minimum wages, social security contributions and taxes on wages. The purpose of this type of legislation is to hold the company with the most extensive financial resources ultimately accountable for certain debts in the supply chain. What both the EU construction and Australian home-based workers legislation do is re-characterize a series of discrete contracts (that are technically separate and confined to distinct corporate entities) into a broader and contiguous contractual arrangement spread throughout the supply chain that ultimately reveals 'features of an organizational hierarchy similar to those found within an integrated firm'.[67] The purpose of such 're-engineering' of relationships within the supply chain is to ensure that liability for wrongdoings, for example, non-payment of wages, is actionable against one or other company in that chain. This legislative technique acknowledges the inherent interconnectedness of firms within those supply chains and reflects the modern sensibility that what purports to be separate is not in fact so.

A third model of transnational supply chain regulation which combines due diligence requirements with civil and criminal liability is exemplified by the Illegal Logging Prohibition Act recently established in Australia.[68] This Act incorporates due diligence requirements which obligate the importers and processors of timber to initiate verification and certification processes in order to ensure the imported timber was not illegally logged.[69]

---

[65]   Houwerzijl and Peters, *ibid.*, 2.

[66]   Houwerzijl and Peters, *ibid.* This study notes that national liability regimes for the construction sector have been developed in Austria, Belgium, Finland, France, Germany, Italy, the Netherlands and Spain.

[67]   H. Collins, *Regulating Contracts* (Oxford University Press, 1999), 250–251. [NB to author: also check *Michael Rawling – A Generic Model of Regulating Supply Chain Outsourcing* www.rsrt.gov.au/default/assets/File/exhibits_draftRSRO/TWU38.pdf]

[68]   *Illegal Logging Prohibition Act 2012* (Cth).

[69]   The *Illegal Logging Prohibition Amendment Regulation* 2013 requires that importers and processors undertake due diligence processes from 30 November 2014. There is an 18-month transition period during which the Australian government will seek to assist and

If an importer or processor intentionally, knowingly or recklessly imports or processes illegally logged timber they could face significant penalties, including up to five years imprisonment and/or heavy fines. This hybrid legislation deliberately targets the firm at the top end of the supply chain (and utilizes civil and criminal liability) as a means of deterring illegal activities downstream. It is a potentially useful model for overcoming regulatory challenges that may arise in host states including an unwillingness or inability to enforce their own labour, human rights and environmental laws.[70]

Ultimately, however, laws – whether national or international – are only as strong as their enforcement capacity. The laws discussed above are relatively nascent in terms of their implementation and their potential effectiveness in regulating transnational supply chains remains to be tested. The scope of these laws challenges the traditional corporate law framework, which supports limited liability and the separate entity doctrine. In essence, what these laws are attempting to do is bring a broader and arguably more modern sensibility to determining which entities might be traditionally understood as falling within a corporate group. The use of the term 'business enterprise' throughout the Guiding Principles arguably reflects this broader interpretation. Transnational supply chains are an intrinsic part of most modern corporate operations. This is reflected not only by the approach of global brands and large

---

educate companies about the due diligence requirements. Section 7 sets out the four step due diligence process. Step 1 is information gathering (the importer must obtain as much of the prescribed information as is reasonably practicable); Step 2 is an option process that involves assessing and identifying risk against a prescribed timber legality framework (section 11) or a country-specific guideline (once they are prescribed); Step 3 is risk assessment (section 13); and Step 4 is risk mitigation (section 14) which should be adequate and proportionate to the identified risk. Illegally logged timber is defined broadly in the *Illegal Logging Prohibition Act* 2012 (Cth) as timber 'harvested in contravention of laws in force in the place (whether or not in Australia) where the timber was harvested' (Section 7).

[70] Another potential model is US procurement regulations which require federal contractors who supply products on a list published by the Department of Labor to certify that they have made a good-faith effort to determine whether forced or indentured child labour was used to produce the items listed (US Department of State, Bureau of Democracy, Human Rights and Labor, *US Government Approach on Business and Human Rights* (2013)). Federal contractors providing supplies acquired or services to be performed outside of the United States, with a value greater than US$500,000, must provide a compliance plan and certification after completing due diligence, that no contractor or subcontractor is engaged in human trafficking. Violations can result in termination of a federal contract. (United States Federal Register, 'Federal Acquisition Regulation; Ending Trafficking in Persons; Final Rule', 80 Fed. Reg. 4967 (2 March 2015)).

retailers as to how they structure their operations, but also emerging soft and hard laws which aim to guide businesses as to how they can better respect human rights while operating within a complex corporate web of supply lines.

Legislation that purports to regulate transnational corporate activities will encounter potential enforcement obstacles including language barriers, non-transparent or inaccessible legislative information, difficulties in proving violations in cross-border judicial proceedings and, of particular importance, vagueness in legislative definitions and mandated due diligence requirements. However, some of the models discussed above include innovative techniques (such as the reversal of the onus of proof[71] or carefully prescribed duties of investigation[72]) that could be useful when considering the application of mandatory human rights due diligence requirements and legal liability at a global level. What these examples demonstrate is how due diligence can be hardened and used as a basis for attaching legal liability to firms throughout a supply chain rather than simply as a non-binding risk assessment process. Due diligence can be a process designed to ensure that companies meet certain legal standards: in order to comply and avoid penalty, the companies must discharge their duty to investigate and assess certain risks.[73]

---

[71] *Industrial Relations (Ethical Clothing Trade) Act 2001* (NSW).

[72] *Illegal Logging Prohibition Act 2012* (Cth).

[73] Some recent (if limited) case law on human rights liability suggests certain courts might be willing to examine the reality of corporate group operations to determine where responsibility should lie for human rights infringements in the context of tort or contract liability. See earlier discussion of *Choc v. Hudbay Minerals Inc* at n. 20. Also, in *Chandler v. Cape plc* [2012] EWCA Civ 525 the UK Court of Appeal, for the first time, imposed liability on a company for a breach of its duty of care to an employee of its subsidiary. A decision of the US National Labor Relations Board in *Browning-Ferris Industries of California, Inc. d/b/a BFI Newby Island Recyclery, and FPR-II, LLC d/b/a Leadpoint Business Services, and Sanitary Truck Drivers and Helpers Local 350, International Brotherhood of Teamsters* (Case 32-RC0109682, 2 August 2015 National Labor Relations Board (362 NLRB No. 186)) also highlights the potential to look behind contractual arrangements to assess which business should be held to account for human and labour rights obligations. The challenge is to determine who the 'employer' is and thus who might be liable for redress if problems occur. In *BFI*, the Board held that two or more entities are joint employers if they share and codetermine matters governing essential terms and conditions of employment. The Board explained that the initial inquiry is whether a common law employment relationship exists, meaning whether the alleged joint employer has the right to control the employees' work, and, if so, whether the assumed joint employer possesses sufficient control over employees' essential terms and conditions of employment to permit meaningful collective bargaining. The impact and scope of these isolated decisions is not clear and while both may be confined to their very particular facts, it is also arguable that business entities, depending on the extent of control (or leverage) they have over their franchisees or subcontractors, may be considered to be joint

9.3   Inclusion of Supply Chain Regulatory Provisions in a Business and Human Rights Treaty

In considering the development of a business and human rights treaty, the inclusion of provisions aimed at regulating corporate human rights responsibilities in supply chains seems essential given not only the preponderance and reliance on supply chains in bringing goods to market but also because of their potential as a repository of corporate human rights violations. At the annual conference of the International Labour Organization (ILO) in June 2016, the question of whether global supply chains need new rules and regulations figured prominently on the agenda. The final ILO conference conclusions highlight the need for a more formal examination of governance gaps within global supply chain and consideration of whether new international standards are required to protect workers in supply chains. Specifically, the ILO conference noted that governments have a responsibility to:

> [c]reate an enabling environment to help enterprises strengthen their contribution to sustainability and decent work throughout their business operations, help them to identify sector-specific risks and implement due diligence procedures in their management systems. Governments should also clearly communicate on what they expect from enterprises with respect to responsible business conduct and could consider whether further measures, including regulation, are needed if these expectations are not met.[74]

In light of the ILO's 2016 discussions and the relatively recent development of the legislative initiatives discussed above, arguing for the inclusion in a future business and human rights treaty of regulatory provisions aimed at protecting the rights of workers in supply chains is both necessary and urgent. However, the form of such a provision is likely to be controversial. Reliance on the regulatory techniques of due diligence and reporting seems a logical starting point in drafting such a provision. However, a number of

---

employers of workers whose contract is with another corporate entity, and thus legally liable for their working conditions. In this case, it was argued that BFI was a joint employer because of BFI's involvement in hiring and firing decisions, wage limitations, hours of work, training and safety requirements and the supervisory systems imposed on workers. This notion of substantive control or leverage may potentially be a useful mechanism for legislatures seeking to allocate liability on the basis of mandated due diligence requirements.

[74] International Labour Conference, Provisional Record, 105th Session, Geneva, 'Fourth Item on the Agenda: Decent work in Global Supply Chains Reports of the Committee on Decent Work in Global Supply Chains: Resolution and conclusions submitted for adoption by the Conference' (May–June 2016) para. 16(e) www.ilo.org/wcmsp5/groups/public/–ed_norm/–relconf/documents/meetingdocument/wcms_489115.pdf.

questions that were highlighted in the introductory section of this chapter remain relevant: How broadly should a supply chain be described? How prescriptively should due diligence be defined? Should due diligence processes vary from sector to sector or be narrowly focused on specific issues such as forced labour? If due diligence applies separately to all entities within a supply chain, should lead firms in the chain be subject to specific requirements holding them accountable for both reporting on downstream activities and potentially liable for wrongdoings in that chain?

9.3.1 Defining a Supply Chain

In defining a supply chain, treaty drafters should look to soft and hard law guidelines that are already in place and include a comprehensive definition of a supply chain, not limited to the first-tier suppliers. For example, the OECD Due Diligence Guidance[75] adopts a deep approach and includes all suppliers from the sourcing of raw material to the final product in its supply chain definition; the US Foreign Corrupt Practices Act[76] attaches liability to a company through its supply chain vendors.[77] The broad and inclusive approach of defining a supply chain as set out in the OECD Due Diligence Guidance is an approach to be recommended.

9.3.2 Defining Due Diligence

The Guiding Principles provide a broad framework that sets out the general parameters of what companies should take into account in conducting human rights due diligence assessments.[78] They state that the 'process should include assessing actual and potential human rights impacts, integrating and acting upon the findings, tracking responses, and communicating how impacts are addressed'.[79] However, the term 'impacts' – the crucial

---

[75] OECD (2013), *Due Diligence Guidance*, n. 8. Also see, OECD (2015), *Due Diligence Guidance for the Responsible Supply Chains in the Garment and Footwear Sector, Draft for Consultation* www.oecd.org/daf/inv/mne/Due-Diligence-Guidance-Responsible-Supply-Chains-Textiles-Footwear.pdf.

[76] *Foreign Corrupt Practices Act 1977*, as amended, 15 U.S.C. §§ 78dd-1.

[77] The US Department of Justice has stated that one of the best practices of a FCPA compliance program includes the right to conduct audits of the books and records of the agents, business partners and suppliers or contractors to ensure compliance. See: *USA v. Panalpina World Transport (Holdings)* Docket Number 10-CR-769, a Deferred Prosecution Agreement.

[78] Specifically Human Rights Council, 'Guiding Principles', n. 3, Principles 17–-0.

[79] Human Rights Council, 'Guiding Principles', n. 3, Principle 17.

element to which due diligence is addressed – is not defined and it may be clearer to refer to violations of international human rights in future legislation.[80] The Guiding Principles also note that human rights due diligence may 'vary in complexity with the size of the business enterprise, the risk of severe human rights impacts, and the nature and context of its operations.'[81] Some of the legislative approaches to mandating due diligence are narrowly targeted towards a particular issue. For example, the Dodd-Frank Act requires companies to conduct due diligence on the source and chain of custody of conflict minerals emanating from the DRC. The Illegal Logging Prohibition Act is prescriptive in its approach to mandating due diligence as related specifically to the source of certain imported timber into Australia. Supply chain arrangements are not static[82] and will vary from sector to sector and amongst firms. Treaties by their nature tend to be broad and somewhat abstract and the supply chain provisions would necessarily reflect this broadness but will differ in one clear respect from the Guiding Principles because such treaty provisions would not be optional but rather be cast as legal obligations. In order to capture sector specificities, one option may be to attach sector-specific guidelines or 'regulations' to a treaty (to be drafted at a later date), setting out a narrower set of investigative issues to consider when conducting due diligence in that sector.

To date, only France has introduced a comprehensive and mandatory human rights due diligence law. The Corporate Duty of Vigilance Law 2017 requires large French companies[83] to identify and prevent adverse human rights (and environmental) impacts, including those resulting

---

[80] S. Deva, 'Treating Human Rights Lightly: A Critique of the Consensus Rhetoric and the Language Employed by the Guiding Principles' in S. Deva and D. Bilchitz, *Human Rights Obligations of Business: Beyond the Corporate Responsibility to Respect?* (Cambridge University Press, 2013), 78–104.

[81] Human Rights Council, 'Guiding Principles', n. 3, Principle 17.

[82] G. Gereffi, J. Humphrey and T. Sturgeon, 'The Governance of Global Value Chains' (2005) 12(1) *Review of International Political Economy* 78–104, 96.

[83] The law applies to any company established in France with at least 5,000 employees within the company head office and its direct and indirect subsidiaries, whose head office is located on French territory, or that employs at least 10,000 employees within the company and its direct and indirect subsidiaries, whose head office is located on French territory or abroad. It has been estimated that about 100-150 companies currently meet this definition. Judges were initially granted the power to impose fines for failure to implement a plan, ranging from 10 to 30 million euros, however this was struck down by the French Constitutional Court: European Coalition for Corporate Justice, 'Last hurdle overcome for landmark legislation: French Corporate duty of vigilance law gets green light from Constitutional Council' (24 March 2017) <http://corporatejustice.org/news/435-last-hurdle-overcome-for-landmark-legislation-french-corporate-duty-of-vigilance-law-gets-green-light-from-constitutional-council>

from their supply chains. Specifically, companies must implement, and report annually on, a 'vigilance plan' in line with the Guiding Principles' concept of due diligence. The plan must assess the company's human rights risks, as well as risks associated with its subsidiaries, subcontractors or suppliers with whom the company maintains an established business relationship. Once identified, companies are required to take appropriate action to mitigate risks or prevent serious violations, to create risk alert mechanisms in conjunction with trade unions, and monitor and assess the efficiency of its measures. Interested parties may enforce non-compliance with the law through the courts. This law represents the most promising advance to date in mandating human rights due diligence, although its enforceability and impact on practice remains to be seen.

The proposed bill was weakened during the parliamentary process following opposition from business. A provision to reverse the burden of proof in international corporate accountability cases, requiring the company concerned to prove that it was not in control of the activities of its subsidiaries and subcontractors (akin to the Australian homeworkers legislation) was removed from the final text. It is suggested here that a provision that connects due diligence and reporting with legal liability as discussed below is more likely to be effective and diligently implemented by companies than a provision that does not.

9.3.3   Accountability for Human Rights Violations in a Supply Chain

The various legislative models discussed above use different techniques to connect due diligence requirements with legal liability. Some aim to make corporate practices transparent and allow legal sanctions to be attributed indirectly via other legal principles, such as consumer law. Others directly incorporate civil or criminal penalties in the legislation. Due diligence provisions that directly incorporate penalties are more likely to be an effective deterrent against corporations operating in a manner that violates international human rights. Contractual risk allocation may be effective in certain circumstances in shielding or indemnifying a firm for the wrong-doings of its suppliers, but such risk allocation would not protect the company or its officers from criminal liability via domestic laws. Moreover, contractual indemnification does not remove responsibility in the terms set out in the Guiding Principles where a firm has the leverage to effect change. It also does not prevent reputational risk. In the face of a human rights scandal, investors and consumers are unlikely to be appeased by corporate recourse to a legal indemnification clause. A treaty might also provide that demonstrated good faith due diligence could be raised as a defence to, or at least a proportional mitigation of, criminal or civil liability.[84] Guidance in this respect could be obtained from various anti-bribery and corruption laws that have been implemented both nationally and internationally. The UK Bribery Act 2010, for example, takes into account the fact that companies implemented 'adequate proce-dures' to prevent bribery in their operations as a defence to a charge of a company's failure to prevent bribery.[85] Provisions incorporating both penalties for, and defences to, alleged misconduct could give business a strong incentive to exercise due diligence, without depriving them of the ability to defend themselves or depriving victims of a remedy for serious violations of human rights.[86]

In summary, inclusion of supply chain accountability provisions in a future business and human rights treaty should take account of the following factors:

(1) the definition of a supply chain should extend beyond the first tier of suppliers;
(2) the requirements of due diligence could borrow from the framework set out in the Guiding Principles but the provision should also encourage the development of sector specific-guidelines which can provide more specificity around due diligence requirements (see the Illegal Logging Prohibition Act);
(3) the provision should include penalties for non-compliance – options may include civil penalties (fines) for non-compliant reporting or inadequate due diligence and civil and criminal liability for viola-tions such as non-payment of wages, trafficking and slavery (along the lines of the legislative models set out in the European chain liability regimes or the Illegal Logging Prohibition Act);

[84] S. Michalowski, 'Due Diligence and Complicity: A Relationship in Need of Clarification' in S. Deva and D. Bilchitz, *Human Rights Obligations of Business: Beyond the Corporate Responsibility to Respect?* (Cambridge University Press, 2013), 218–242. See also Chapter 8 by McCorquodale and Smit in this collection which addresses this issue as well.
[85] D. Cassel and A. Ramasastry, 'White Paper: Options For A Treaty On Business And Human Rights' March 2015, 99. Also, courts and the US Department of Justice take certain factors into consideration when assessing criminal fines for companies prosecuted under the U.S. Foreign Corrupt Practices Act including: whether high-level personnel were involved in or condoned the conduct, whether the organization had a pre-existing compliance and ethics program, voluntary disclosure, cooperation and acceptance of responsibility.
[86] *Ibid.*

(4) the provision could provide a defence for companies that could demonstrate they had robust due diligence programs in place; and

(5) innovative provisions that mandate disclosure requirements that operate up and down the supply chain; reversal of the onus of proof and deeming all workers to be 'employed' in the supply chain and a mix of public and private monitoring schemes (as per the Australian homeworkers legislation) should be considered.

In terms of drafting a provision for a business and human rights treaty regarding supply chain regulation, this chapter supports the draft provisions set out in Chapter 8 and would also add the following article:

(1) A business enterprise shall commit an offence if it fails to conduct reasonable due diligence as set out in the State Parties regulations. The penalty for failing to conduct reasonable due diligence shall be established by the State Party.

9.4   Conclusion

The regulation of global supply chains creates opportunities and challenges in improving the practices of corporate entities with respect to human rights. Any future treaty that mandates due diligence will provide an opening for states and international human rights bodies to adopt a stronger stance in guiding the activities of firms typically operating beyond the jurisdictional reach of individual states. Supply chain regulation which requires lead firms to take a principal role in monitoring and reporting on their supply chains, and which may also transfer some level of legal accountability to that firm for the downstream activities of its suppliers, necessarily incorporates a mix of public and private actors in the regulatory framework. The legislative frameworks discussed in this paper have been driven in part by campaigns involving unions, non-governmental organizations, consumers, investors and workers. This push from the 'ground-up' has caught the attention of legislators, who are beginning to develop legal frameworks that challenge the traditional separate legal personality and limited liability concepts that govern corporate law, so as to universalize the implementation of corporate human rights duties. An international treaty that mandates due diligence assessments and recommends penalties for non-compliance will further spur national laws that reiterate such standards – a crucial step towards developing an environment and business culture that values human rights.

10

Legalizing Human Rights Due Diligence and the Separation of Entities Principle

RADU MARES

10.1 Introduction

The United Nations Conference on Trade and Development (UNCTAD) in its 2013 *World Investment Report* wrote that 'Today's global economy is characterized by global value chains (GVCs), in which intermediate goods and services are traded in fragmented and internationally dispersed production processes. GVCs are typically coordinated by TNCs, with cross-border trade of inputs and outputs taking place within their networks of affiliates, contractual partners and arm's-length suppliers. TNC-coordinated GVCs account for some 80 per cent of global trade.'[1] In such GVCs, 'lead firms', or TNCs, use a variety of devices to operate internationally through their 'suppliers': subsidiaries/affiliates (foreign direct investment), contractual partner firms (non-equity modes of collaboration) and arm's-length transactions.[2] Lead firms affect how a developing countries enter the GVCs: 'Countries' participation and role in GVCs and their value-added trade patterns are often shaped by TNCs' decisions on where to invest and with whom to partner.'[3] In the last twenty years most countries increased participation in GVC and the UNCTAD indicates that 'for the majority of smaller developing economies with limited resource endowments there is often little alternative to development strategies that incorporate a degree of participation in GVCs. The question for those countries is not whether to participate in GVCs, but how.'[4]

Against this backdrop, the chapter deals with the regulation of lead firms to prevent and address human rights abuses occurring in supplier operations. The encompassing notion of GVCs covers equity-

---

[1] UNCTAD, *World Investment Report 2013, Global Value Chains: Investment and Trade for Development* (2013), 10.
[2] *Ibid.*, 141–144.   [3] *Ibid.*, 176.   [4] *Ibid.*, xxiv and 175.

based and contract-based multinational enterprises (MNEs),[5] whether vertically integrated or operating with various degrees of autonomy.[6] What these multinational groups and networks have in common is that they are economically coordinated, but remain composed of legally separated entities incorporated in several jurisdictions. Parent companies are not liable for their subsidiaries due to the separate corporate personality and limited liability bedrock principles of company law; companies are not liable for third parties such as contractors and subcontractors. This is the principle of legal separation of entities. To discuss the regulation of human rights responsibilities of MNE, the following research questions are raised: how is the principle of legal separation of entities reflected in current legal discussions on business and human rights (BHR), why are current treatments problematic and what alternative way forward could be adopted for lawmakers and the UN treaty process?[7]

To answer these questions, the chapter revisits and emphasizes the principle of legal separation of entities. A core proposition here is that ongoing proposals to pass new human rights due diligence (HRDD) regulations and hold lead firms accountable should not override too quickly this principle and the policy considerations it embodies. This principle's staying power cannot be discounted. More attention needs to be given to the ramifications of this principle in the transnational (cross-border) BHR context. With this cautionary analysis, rather than foreclosing the legalization of lead firms responsibility under current and potentially forthcoming laws, this chapter sets the analytical stage for a fresh look at transnational regulation of GVCs and seeks to explain the specificity, difficulties and openings arising in regulating lead firms (from the top of the GVC).

The analysis holds that the transnational BHR setting evolves under the spectre of redirection of GVCs: legal pressure on the lead firm creates liability risks and compliance burdens that may result in a compliance

---

[5] T. Muchlinski, *Multinational Enterprises and the Law* (Blackwell, 1995), 62–73.

[6] For a definition of MNEs, see Organisation for Economic Co-Operation and Development, *OECD Guidelines for Multinational Enterprises* (2011) para. I.4.

[7] In June 2014, the Human Rights Council set up an open-ended intergovernmental working group with the mandate 'to elaborate an international legally binding instrument to regulate, in international human rights law, the activities of Transnational Corporations and Other Business Enterprises'. Human Rights Council, 'Elaboration of an international legally binding instrument on transnational corporations and other business enterprises with respect to human rights', A/HRC/26/L.22/Rev.1 (24 June 2014), para. 1.

strategy to redirect the value chain away from high-risk zones. Therefore, regulating lead firms should be mindful of three 'first-order' principles in the transnational BHR context, that is, fundamental considerations of corporate law (legal separation of entities), international law (national sovereignty) and human rights law (leverage for rights-holders). In this way, the main thesis is that the legalization task is not a straightforward one of just moving beyond soft law (e.g., Guiding Principles on Business and Human Rights (GPs)) and corporate voluntarism towards hard law (treaty), and is not merely about striving to make HRDD mandatory for lead firms in as coercive way as possible, and thus ultimately hold MNEs and GVCs accountable and offer rights-holders remedies against lead firms. Once these principles and difficulties are recognized, the chapter proposes as a way forward a regulatory perspective that on the one hand valorises the entire spectrum of legalization options from the less coercive end (e.g., transparency regulations) to the more coercive end (e.g., liability for damage and fines),[8] and on the other hand accounts for a multitude of transnational policy channels impacting GVCs.

Section 10.2 of the chapter introduces the legal separation of entities principle and reviews how several regulatory proposals deal with it. Section 10.3 pinpoints the specificities of the transnational BHR area and examines precedents of legally mandating HRDD as a way to overcome legal separation hurdles. Section 10.4 then sets the analytical stage for a comprehensive legalization perspective that is able to account for recent developments in multiple policy areas. The last section contains recommendations for the UN treaty process as it highlights choices and pitfalls waiting for legalization proponents.

10.2   The Legal Separation of Entities Principle – Staying Power and Challenges

The principle of legal separation of entities and the policy considerations it embodies are a cross-cutting issue – cutting across all human rights, industries and types of business enterprises – at the core of current legalization discussions in the BHR field. The principle is meant to facilitate expansion of economic activity and efficiency by localizing liability with the direct wrongdoer, the subsidiary, supplier or other

---

[8]   A. Ramasastry and D. Cassel, 'White Paper: Options for a Treaty on Business and Human Rights' (2015) 6 *Notre Dame Journal of International & Comparative Law* 1 (documenting the wide spectrum of instruments from the comparatively weak end simply mandating public reporting to the strong end with civil and criminal remedies.)

business partner.[9] The principle thus prevents the moving upwards of liability for harm to the lead firm, the moving of liability up the value chain of MNEs, unless the lead firm's own contribution to harm can be established (the separation principle is irrelevant) or the law imposed on the lead firm an obligation to act regarding suppliers (exception from the separation principle). The downside of localization is that the victims of harm are bound to the local judicial and regulatory regime with all its dysfunctionalities specific to less developed countries, face various hurdles in pursuing the lead firm even when its wrongful conduct seems to exist, and thus run the real risk of corporate impunity prevailing. This raises lasting questions about who bears the risks and harvests the opportunities of accelerated economic exchanges: about the fairness of economic globalization.

10.2.1 Justification and Controversy

The principle of legal separation of entities is well recognized in most jurisdictions.[10] As a general rule, one is not liable for the harms created by third parties.[11] Originally meant to limit the exposure of individuals from bearing the liabilities of the company they invested in, the principle now offers protection also to companies that operate through subsidiaries and contractors. Although such business enterprises are economically coordinated, the multitude of entities involved in the enterprise remain legally separated with their own assets and liabilities. The public policy explanations of the counterintuitive privilege of limited liability and the separate personality principle more broadly have to do with efficiency considerations and stimulation of large-scale economic activity.[12]

---

[9] A. P. Solé et al, *Human Rights in European Business: A Practical Handbook for Civil Society Organisations and Human Rights Defenders* (Tarragona Centre for Environmental Law Studies, 2016), 45–50.

[10] Human Rights Council, 'Human rights and Corporate Law: Trends and Observations from a Crossnational Study Conducted by the Special Representative, Addendum 2 to the Report', A/HRC/17/31/Add.2 (23 May 2011), paras. 31 and 49; *Barcelona Traction, Light and Power Company, Limited*, I.C.J. Reports 1970, 35.

[11] US tort law, for example, lays down principles such as 'there is no duty so to control the conduct of a third person so as to prevent him from causing physical harm to another' and 'the employer of an independent contractor is not liable for physical harm caused to another by an act or omission of the contractor'. American Law Institute, *Restatement (Second) of Torts* (1977) § 315 and § 409.

[12] P. Blumberg, 'Limited Liability and Corporate Groups' (1985–1986) 11 *Journal of Corporation Law* 611–616 (noting, and criticizing, common arguments that the limited

MNEs employ a wide variety of structures to expand operations globally but are commonly split into equity-based and contract-based. For MNEs that are equity-based, the limited liability privilege applies: this legal innovation introduced in the nineteenth century makes a shareholder – whether an individual or a parent company – not liable for a subsidiary's deeds even though it 'owns' it, that is, it owns shares and could thus influence the subsidiary's activities.[13] The separation of entities here is not genuine, but the result of a legal fiction. However as the UK Supreme Court observed, 'the separate personality and property of a company is sometimes described as a fiction, and in a sense it is. But the fiction is the whole foundation of English company and insolvency law.'[14] For MNEs that are contract-based, following contracting out production or distribution tasks to layers of suppliers and distributors, the separation of entities is genuine, not a fiction, as such suppliers have not been created and are not 'owned' by the lead firms. There is no privilege of limited liability involved as there is no ownership relationship, so the liability for the third party misconduct does not exist.[15] However, the ability to significantly influence the contractor or a supplier further down the value chain may exist.[16]

This legal separation of entities principle creates opportunities to increase efficiency in legitimate ways but also to accidentally or even deliberately externalize costs on society. This dark side of the principle is revealed when the subsidiary cannot be compelled by the domestic legal regime to bear the full costs for the risks and harms its operations create. The subsidiary might have insufficient assets to compensate the damage, become bankrupt and cease to exist. Alternatively, the subsidiary might have plenty of assets but the legal regime of the host state, due to weaknesses of all kinds, fails to detect or punish adequately the company's

---

liability principle facilitates diversification of portfolios, encourages risk taking and reduces monitoring costs).

[13] UNCTAD, *World Investment Report 2016, Investor Nationality: Policy Challenges* (2016), 129.

[14] *Prest v. Petrodel Resources Ltd & Ors* [2013] UKSC 34 (12 June 2013), para. 8. See also P. Ireland, 'Limited Liability, Shareholder Rights and the Problem of Corporate Irresponsibility' (2010) 34 *Cambridge Journal of Economics* 837.

[15] '[S]ince the employer has no power of control over the manner in which the work is to be done by the contractor, it is to be regarded as the contractor's own enterprise, and he, rather than the employer, is the *proper party to be charged with the responsibility of preventing the risk, and bearing and distributing it . . .*' (emphasis added). American Law Institute, *Restatement (Second) of Torts*, n. 11, Section 409, Comment b.

[16] UNCTAD, *World Investment Report 2013*, n. 1.

misconduct, which is often the case in developing countries. In both situations, the rights-holders are inclined to direct their case against the lead firm and its assets, and seek justice in the home country's courts. At this juncture, the principle of legal separation of entities is universally seen as a significant barrier to access to remedies.[17] Legal systems have developed doctrines to counter formalistic and automatic defences based on legal separation.[18] However, lifting of the corporate veil remains confined in applicability and firmly within the realm of exception to the rule, which inherently warns against liberal interpretation and extensions.

Far from a developing country problem only, the limited liability privilege has come under sustained 'attack' in highly developed countries with advanced rule of law and judicial systems. The protection offered to parent companies places tort victims (non-consensual creditors) at a severe disadvantage by denying them reparations for damage suffered if the subsidiary cannot compensate them. These extremely sophisticated challenges[19] to the limited liability privilege in tort law have proved unsuccessful in reshaping the law. As Muchlinski noted, the 'enterprise liability' doctrine is exceptionally employed in some areas of law – tax, environmental, disclosure laws – but 'in relation to tort liability enterprise analysis has made virtually no impact'.[20] Still proposals advancing 'enterprise liability', which disregards legal separation of entities and holds the entire group of entities liable for damages, continue to be put forward.[21] A hard look at history serves as a reminder about the staying

---

[17] Human Rights Council, 'Guiding Principles on Business and Human Rights: Implementing the United Nations "Protect, Respect and Remedy" Framework', A/HRC/17/31 (21 March 2011), Principle 26.

[18] For instance, in *Choc v. Hudbay Minerals Inc.*, 2013 ONSC 1414, the Ontario Superior Court laid down the three situations where a court can disregard legal separation (para. 45): the parent company makes use of the subsidiary for fraudulent purposes (fraud), the subsidiary is an agent of the parent company (complete control) and the lawmakers created a duty on the parent company (statutory liability). If that the parent company's own conduct is negligent (direct negligence) can be proven, the legal separation becomes irrelevant.

[19] H. Hansmann and R. Kraakman, 'Toward Unlimited Shareholder Liability for Corporate Torts' (1991) 100 *Yale Law Journal* 1897; N. A. Mendelson, 'A Controller-Based Approach to Shareholder Liability for Corporate Torts' (2002) 102 *Columbia Law Review* 1203.

[20] P. Muchlinski, 'Limited Liability and Multinational Enterprises: A Case for Reform?' (2010) 34 *Cambridge Journal of Economics* 920. See also V. H. Ho, 'Theories of Corporate Groups: Corporate Identity Reconceived' (2012) 42 (3) *Seton Hall Law Review* 879.

[21] A. A. Berle, Jr., 'The Theory of Enterprise Entity' (1947) 47 *Columbia Law Review* 343; M. Dearborn, 'Enterprise Liability: Reviewing and Revitalizing Liability for Corporate Groups' (2009) 97 *California Law Review* 195.

power of the legal separation principle and for sizing up this key obstacle for current legalization discussions in BHR.

The message that the corporate accountability movement sends out is compelling: outsourcing business does not mean outsourcing responsibility.[22] Outsourcing production, distribution or other business functions in settings where human rights are at high risk of infringement and non-remediation does not mean the company became insulated from abuses 'tainting' its goods and services. The thrust of the argumentation is to make MNEs responsible for their culpable actions and omissions, that is, to hold lead firms accountable for their harmful decisions with rippling effects in suppliers' operations and/or to condemn lead firms when they passively stand by as their business partners infringe the rights of workers, consumers or local communities. And still, in dealing with the specific issue of legal separation of entities, will proponents of legalization of MNE responsibilities note the staying power of the separation principle, as limited liability survived sustained attacks that hardly made a dent in law? Or will they point to exceptions and see them as symptoms of a nascent and fundamental trend away from legal separation? The proposals can then harbour varying levels of ambition for reform. Will proponents suggest an overhaul of the principle and be content to rehearse the same arguments scholars promoting 'enterprise liability' put forward decades ago? Or will proponents settle for carving exceptions from the principle with narrow legalization proposals in recognition that the principle (and the policy considerations behind it) has to be taken seriously?

The principle of legal separation of entities cannot be merely regarded as a legal technicality or a lasting pro-business bias that new regulations could simply reverse under sustained advocacy and moral weight of human rights imperatives. The quest for legalizing a lead firm's responsibilities is bound to confront the principle (and the policy considerations lying behind it) and should not lose sight of the ramifications behind this principle in the transnational BHR context. Unless a more analytical way is found to set the stage for legalization in the BHR context in relation to the separation principle, the variety of proposals will oscillate between unfeasibility and narrowness with significant blind spots regarding the operation of law in the transnational BHR area. The next section analyses

---

[22] Institute for Human Rights and Business, *State of Play – The Corporate Responsibility to Respect Human Rights in Business Relationships* (IHRB, 2012), 3 (examining six types of business relationships).

proposals for legalization of corporate human rights responsibilities that range on a continuum from a principled and complete rejection to varying accommodations of the separation principle.

10.2.2 Dealing with the Separation of Entities Principle – A Brief Review of Legalization Proposals

10.2.2.1 Limited Approaches

Limited approaches to BHR legalization make different inroads in the territory occupied by legal separation principle. They reveal multiple ways in which the lead firm's responsibility can be defined in order to reduce frictions with the principle. The result, however, is a legalization of a corporate responsibility to respect human rights that is narrower than the broad scope it received in the GPs. The price to pay for holding lead firms liable is, in other words, a limited coverage of such liability regimes.

Skinner advances a carefully delineated approach and proposes to 'enact legislation to disregard limited liability of parent corporations for claims of customary international human rights violations and serious environmental torts' subject to a number of conditions such as operations in a high-risk host country and victims being unable to obtain remediation in the host country.[23] The proposal is addressed to US lawmakers and has a narrow coverage of rights and situations, but is coupled with strong remediation through a strict liability standard[24] favourable to plaintiffs.[25] This prioritization of severe abuses[26] for a legalization effort is consistent with Ruggie's end of mandate suggestion on international legalization.[27] In this way, Skinner's proposal carves an exception from the limited liability principle rather than downplaying its importance or proposing a wholesale rejection. Skinner considered that

---

[23] G. Skinner, *Parent Company Accountability – Ensuring Justice for Human Rights Violations* (International Corporate Accountability Roundtable, 2015), 3.

[24] See Human Rights Council, 'Improving accountability and access to remedy for victims of business-related human rights abuse, Report of the United Nations High Commissioner for Human Rights', A/HRC/32/19 (10 May 2016), paras. 11, 16 and 20.

[25] *Ibid.*, 27.

[26] CorA Network for Corporate Accountability and German Human Rights Forum, *Position Paper on Business and Human Rights – Expectations of a German Action Plan* (2013), 14–15.

[27] *Recommendations on Follow-Up to the Mandate*, Mandate of the Special Representative of the Secretary-General on the Issue of Human Rights and Transnational Corporations and other Business Enterprises, 2011.

the 'enterprise liability' doctrine of holding MNEs liable without careful limitations is 'not feasible. . . is simply too broad, and as such, would not likely gain any traction with legislators.'[28]

De Schutter deems as most promising two approaches, to be pursued separately or in tandem.[29] One is concentrating on the home state's duty to protect human rights by regulating lead firms,[30] while the other option refers to enhancing legal mutual assistance between host and home states. The latter approach does not challenge legal separation of entities, but holds that even the current limited space of holding MNEs accountable is not valorized fully due to evidentiary and procedural impediments that make it impossibly hard for plaintiffs to make a case against the parent company, as seen in the Bhopal and Chevron cases.[31] A like-minded twin approach informs the recent debates in the French parliament around the 'duty of vigilance': the legislative initiative, discussed below, initially proposed a statutory HRDD obligation on lead firms coupled with a reversed burden of proof to facilitate the foreign plaintiff's access to remedies in French courts.

The draft Statute of a World Court of Human Rights[32] also promotes a limited approach to corporate accountability as it indicates that attribution of responsibility among corporations would draw on state responsibility principles.[33] The upside of such allocation of responsibility would be a unitary international law approach to corporate and state responsibility.[34] However, due to the high thresholds for control and assistance that entail state responsibility,[35] the corporate responsibility for third party conduct would in effect be significantly narrower than what the GPs propose and the corporate social responsibility (CSR) movement has advocated for the last 20 years. Responsibility would be confined to a minority of BHR cases where the lead firm is directly involved in its

---

[28] Skinner, n. 23, 17. See also Dearborn, *Enterprise Liability*, n. 21.
[29] O. De Schutter, *Towards a Legally Binding Instrument on Business and Human Rights*, CRIDHO Working Paper 2015/2 (2015).
[30] See also O. De Schutter et al., *Human Rights Due Diligence: The Role of States* (International Corporate Accountability Roundtable, 2012), 53.
[31] De Schutter, *Towards a Legally Binding*, n. 29, 41–42.
[32] J. Kozma, M. Nowak and M. Scheinin, *A World Court of Human Rights – Consolidated Statute and Commentary* (European University Institute, 2010).
[33] *Ibid.*, art. 6.1.
[34] A. Clapham, *Human Rights Obligations of Non-State Actors* (Oxford University Press, 2006), 268 (endorsing this unitary treatment to inform the scope of corporate responsibilities under international law).
[35] International Law Commission, *Draft Articles on Responsibility of States for Internationally Wrongful Acts*, U.N. Doc. A/56/10 (2001), arts. 4-11 and 16-18.

supplier's harmful conduct by controlling or assisting it. As such, the Statute's approach generates virtually no friction with the legal separation of entities principle. This emphasis on direct involvement of parent companies transpires also from recent English and Canadian judgements in negligence law, discussed below. In those cases, a parent company's direct involvement allows a court to establish a duty of care resulting in the parent company's liability for its own wrongful conduct.

In short, such limited legalization approaches seek to enact new statutory law or test the boundaries of current case law (usually the law of negligence) in order to hold the lead firm accountable. Such proposals manage much better the tension with legal separation: they carefully carve exceptions to the principle or leave it untouched altogether to concentrate on other obstacles to remedies that plaintiffs face when seeking redress in home-state courts. However, all these proposals fall short of the stated ambition of the treaty movement to deliver a comprehensive hard law instrument covering all human rights impacts and all types of involvement of lead firms.

10.2.2.2   Extensive Approaches

Expansive approaches to legalization display increased frictions with the legal separation of entities principle. They employ various argumentation strategies.

The first strategy emphasizes the normative force of human rights that should take precedence over other considerations. This 'trumping normativity' argument is to a large extent self-explanatory in its choice to not stumble into legal separation or entertain lengthy discussions about balancing competing policy considerations.[36] Such approaches explicitly acknowledge the foundational character of principle for business operations, reject it openly in the quest to expand the responsibilities of lead firms and at times explicitly advocate systemic change and transition to other economic systems.[37]

The second strategy embraces established concepts of responsibility in international human rights law ('respect, protect, fulfil') and international

---

[36] D. Bilchitz, 'A Chasm Between "Is" and "Ought"? A Critique of the Normative Foundations of the SRSG's Framework and the Guiding Principles' in S. Deva and D. Bilchitz (eds.), *Human Rights Obligations of Business, Beyond the Corporate Responsibility to Respect?* (Cambridge University Press, 2013) 137.

[37] The 'Global Campaign to Dismantle Corporate Power and End Impunity' seeks 'the extension of a parent company's responsibility with affiliates, suppliers and subcontractors'. www.stopcorporateimpunity.org/?page_id=5530 (last visited 20 January 2017).

law ('legal personality') to cover corporate responsibilities and economic globalization. This 'reapplication of international law' argument can be discerned in the works of Clapham[38] and De Schutter[39] inspired by the 2003 UN Draft Norms.[40] With the arrival of the SRSG mandate, this conceptualization of corporate responsibilities has been reversed and restricted to 'respect' human rights only.

The third strategy invokes legalization precedents wherein lead firms are held accountable in spite of the legal separation of entities principle. Such approaches deliberately downplay the fundamental character of legal separation. The tensions with the principle are initially acknowledged[41] but quickly forgotten. The principle might be recognized as a legal reality and of obvious importance to business activity, but these approaches see no reason why exceptions – small or large indeed – could not be carved in the future,[42] especially in an area like human rights. The search for precedents in other legal areas employs reasoning by analogy and engages in 'slippery slopes' from direct to indirect involvement in suppliers' abuses. For example, the International Corporate Accountability Roundtable[43] acknowledges the wide recognition of the principle in legal systems, peruses case law and regulations in detail, only to put forward a sweeping hard legalization of HRDD. Thus, the report covers the less direct involvement of the lead firm (it 'either controls or should have controlled' subsidiaries and suppliers) and couples it with a strong sanction (lead firm be 'civilly liable for human rights violations').[44] This effectively delocalizes liability of the supplier and moves it wholesale up the value chain to the lead firm.

---

[38] Clapham, n. 34, 230–232.
[39] O. De Schutter, 'Transnational Corporations as Instruments of Human Development' in P. Alston and M. Robinson (eds.), *Human Rights and Development: Towards Mutual Reinforcement* (Oxford University Press, 2005).
[40] Sub-Commission on the Promotion and Protection of Human Rights, *Commentary on the Norms on the Responsibilities of Transnational Corporations and Other Business Enterprises with Regard to Human Rights*, E/CN.4/Sub.2/2003/38/Rev.2 (2003), art. 1 (the definition of state and corporate responsibilities has a deliberately symmetric formulation using identical terms.)
[41] International Commission of Jurists, *Needs and Options for a New International Instrument in the Field of Business and Human Rights* (ICJ, 2014), 13.
[42] Y. Queinnec and W. Bourdon, *Regulating Transnational Companies – 46 Proposals* (Forum for a New World Governance, 2010).
[43] G. Skinner, R. McCorquodale and O. De Schutter, *The Third Pillar: Access to Judicial Remedies for Human Rights Violations by Transnational Business* (International Corporate Accountability Roundtable, 2013).
[44] *Ibid.*, 69.

Such delocalization of liability often resulting from these expansive approaches is addressed in some soft law instruments. The annex to the 2000 version of the OECD Guidelines contained: 'The question whether parent companies should assume responsibility for certain financial obligations of subsidiaries as part of good management practice raises complex problems in view of the limited liability principle embodied in adhering countries' national laws. The Guidelines cannot supersede or substitute for national laws governing corporate liability. They do not therefore imply an unqualified principle of parent company responsibility.'[45] Furthermore, in 2011 the OECD Guidelines were updated and brought in line with the GPs. The Guidelines now reflect verbatim the cause/contribute/linkages typology of involvement introduced by the GPs (Principle 13), but with a meaningful addition: 'This is not intended to shift responsibility from the entity causing an adverse impact to the enterprise with which it has a business relationship.'[46]

Without further disaggregation and careful reflection on first-order principles at play in the transnational BHR context, such laborious legal analysis encourages the reader to pursue a simplistic and incoherent understanding of the legalization paths ahead. This 'legalization precedents' argument seeks to impress that the legal separation of entities principle is far from sacrosanct and it might actually be crumbling under a growing number of exceptions in a multitude of legal fields.[47] Used alone or in conjunction with the other argumentative tools, the 'legalization precedents' approach requires a closer look at those precedents and what they really say about the policy considerations behind the legal separation principle.

10.3   Precedents of Due Diligence Legalization

With an eye to recent regulatory and judicial developments, one might legitimately wonder why the caution, if not an altogether misplaced deference to the legal separation of entities principle, a business law principle that is coming under attack from so many directions and seemingly losing ground on so many fronts? Transparency laws and HRDD regulations have emerged to address human rights abuses in MNE operations. Some cover supply chains where not even an

---

[45] OECD, 'OECD Guidelines for Multinational Enterprises: Text, Commentary and Clarifications' (Report No DAFFE/IME/WPG(2000)15/FINAL) (2001), 10.
[46] OECD Guidelines, n. 6, Section II.A.12.   [47] De Schutter et al., n. 30; Dearborn, n. 21.

investment link is required for the lead firm to be held accountable. Courts have held that lead firms might owe a duty of care to rights-holders under established negligence law principles. Precedents of imposing due diligence obligations in other policy areas are also readily identifiable. Not only are legislation and case law in flux but they are also fully aligned with the idea of HRDD enshrined in the widely endorsed GPs. At the end of the day, would all these developments not offer irrefutable evidence that strong legalization of due diligence is possible in more and more situations and the legal separation of entities principle is in retreat?

Therefore, why not seek to comprehensively legalize HRDD in the BHR field so that all MNEs acquire obligations to ensure that their subsidiaries and suppliers comply with all human rights? Why not just legalize HRDD, turn soft law into hard law? Such precedents in case law and statutory law are noteworthy indeed, but they should be carefully read for how they refer to the separation principle. A closer look at these judicial and legislative precedents will soon temper such argumentation and optimism and reveal the continued relevance of the separation principle. In addition, the specificities of the transnational BHR context are worth reflecting on before drawing easy analogies with precedents from other policy areas featuring DD obligations. The ramifications of legal separation in the transnational BHR setting are worth reflecting on.

10.3.1   Judicial and Legislative Precedents regarding a Human Rights Due Diligence Obligation

Judicial precedents supporting a HRDD obligation come from two recent notable English and Canadian cases in tort law. These cases contemplate a parent company's duty of care leading to liability for its subsidiary's harmful operations. However, in both cases the courts write explicitly and at length that this is not a challenge to the legal separation principle. They should not be construed as a vindication of enterprise liability reasoning but as instances of liability derived from the parent's own faulty conduct, from its own involvement in harmful activities of sub-sidiaries. Instead of being downplayed, the legal separation of entities principle is reaffirmed in the strongest terms. In *Chandler v. Cape*, the judge wrote: 'I would emphatically reject any suggestion that this court is in any way concerned with what is usually referred to as piercing the corporate veil. A subsidiary and its company are separate entities. There is no imposition or assumption of responsibility by reason only that a company is the parent company of another company.'[48] Furthermore, the judgement draws on precedent to affirm that 'there is in general no duty to prevent third parties causing damage to another'.[49] In *Choc v. Hudbay Minerals*, the plaintiffs rely not on piercing the corporate veil, but primarily on the 'direct negligence as against Hudbay [parent company], separate and distinct from claims framed in vicarious liability'.[50] Indicating that the limited liability principle is not being overlooked, the court noted that 'there were competing policy reasons concerning the recognition of a duty of care between a Canadian mining company and individuals harmed by security personnel at its foreign operations'.[51]

A legislative precedent is offered by France, as the French Parliament in February 2017 adopted a law which obliges large companies to exercise vigilance in relation to its subsidiaries and suppliers.[52] The process began in 2013, drawing on the momentum created by the GPs and the shocking factory collapse at Rana Plaza, Bangladesh. The original proposal envisaged a HRDD legal regime characterized by a new legal duty of care (a 'duty of vigilance' to prepare, publish and implement a vigilance plan) falling on the lead firm, a liability standard that allows companies a DD defence, a reversed burden of proof in favour of the plaintiffs through a rebuttable presumption of lead firm responsibility and sanctions in the form of civil damages and fines.[53] Both the 2013 and 2015 parliamentary reports dedicated ample space to the legal separation of entities principle and also noted regulatory developments in several fields of law that render this main obstacle increasingly 'friable'.[54] Notably though, the proposal explicitly steered clear from strong features such as strict or vicarious liability. Actually, the draft law drew multiple limitations: the law applied only to serious risks and damages, and liability was based on fault. As the proposal progressed in the French Parliament, the HRDD

---

[48] *Chandler v. Cape* [2012] EWCA (Civ) 525, para. 69. [49] *Ibid.*, para. 63.

[50] *Choc v. Hudbay Minerals Inc.*, 2013 ONSC 1414 (Ontario Superior Court), 3. See also paras. 24–25.

[51] *Ibid.*, 3.

[52] ECCJ, 'Corporate duty of vigilance: Another step forward towards the French law's adoption' (30 November 2016), http://corporatejustice.org/news/353-corporate-duty-of-vigilance-another-step-forward-towards-the-french-law-s-adoption (last visited 20 January 2017).

[53] Proposition de loi relative au devoir de vigilance des sociétés mères et des entreprises donneuses d'ordre (6 November 2013) www.assemblee-nationale.fr/14/propositions/pion1519.asp (last visited 20 January 2016).

[54] D. Auroi et al., 'Rapport relative au devoir de vigilance des sociétés mères et des entreprises donneuses d'ordre', (21 January 2015), sec. I.B.2, www.assemblee-nationale.fr/14/rapports/r2504.asp (last visited 20 January 2016).

regime was weakened to the detriment of plaintiffs; for example, the initially planned reversal of the burden of proof has been abandoned in order to exclude the possibility that the law in practice would result in vicarious liability.[55] The gradual tightening of the legislative proposal demonstrates lawmakers' preoccupation to proceed carefully in moving liability upwards to the lead firm for subsidiary's harmful operations as the law will carve an exception from the legal separation principle. In addition, frictions with host state sovereignty are revealed by the National Front's enthusiasm for this 'protectionist' law.[56]

This analysis of legalization precedents is a cautionary one. The policy considerations surrounding the legal separation of entities principle reasserted themselves vigorously in recent legislative and judicial processes establishing duties of care and obligations to exercise due diligence. Court judgements entertain only cases of demonstrable involvement of parent companies; they applied well-established principles of negligence law and in the process reaffirmed strongly the continued relevance and fundamental importance of the legal separation principle. The French legislature, far from becoming oblivious to the policy considerations behind legal separation, is engaged in crafting a HRDD legal regime that is more limited and softer than some would deem appropriate to coerce MNEs into compliance. The result is a limited legalization of HRDD to keep frictions with the legal separation of entities principle at manageable levels.

10.3.2   First-Order Principles: The Specificity of the Transnational Business and Human Rights Context

It might be appealing to think of imposing a HRDD obligation on lead firms as merely pushing back against a business-friendly principle, of ranking fundamental human rights imperatives over profitability of large companies. The fact remains that lead firms subjected to such potential HRDD obligations can comply by strengthening their human rights efforts or by redirecting their global value chains. The latter compliance

---

[55] The French Duty of Vigilance Law (translated into English by ECCJ), https://business-humanrights.org/sites/default/files/documents/Texte%20PPL_EN-US.docx (last visited 20 June 2017). For a commentary, see ECCJ, 'French Corporate Duty Of Vigilance Law: Frequently Asked Questions' (23 February 2017), https://business-humanrights.org/sites/default/files/documents/French%20Corporate%20Duty%20of%20Vigilance%20Law%20FAQ.pdf (last visited 20 June 2017).

[56] Auroi et al., n. 54, sec. II.

strategy has significant ramifications. Therefore, legalization proposals should account for the specificity of the transnational BHR context through three first-order principles in business law, international law and human rights law. This chapter argues that legalization of HRDD creates frictions with the legal separation of entities principle, which in turn can generate frictions with the sovereignty of host states and with the very imperative of realizing human rights in an economically integrating world. Such frictions should be acknowledged and legalization proposals should be designed to keep such frictions at manageable levels.

(1) The legal separation of entities principle is widely seen as the bedrock of company law. It is not an outright, formal obstacle for lawmakers contemplating a statutory HRDD. While courts are bound to observe the separation principle, lawmakers can carve out exceptions to the principle. However, the risk-management and public policy considerations behind the principle do not become irrelevant when legalizing HRDD through statutory action. In deciding how to comply with the new regulations, companies remain free to sell a subsidiary, divest from joint ventures or redirect supply chain away from high-risk zones. If they are deprived of the protection offered by legal separation, companies contemplating international trade or investment decisions will ponder whether the risks and costs of compliance are worth taking.[57] Simply disengaging from suppliers in high-risk zones remains a legitimate compliance strategy for lead firms. This is a real possibility that requires analysis of the specific supply chains, including discerning the position of host states in those specific value chains.[58]

A widely ratified treaty would solve the collective action problem of states and would make it much harder for lead firms to relocate operations as states agree to hold them to the same standards of corporate responsibility instead of engaging in a 'race to the bottom'. Furthermore, a strong legal obligation of HRDD would make companies take human rights seriously instead of sheltering under the legal separation shield. Until such widely ratified treaty exists, the spectre of relocation value chains has to be confronted as it affects the very process of forging, or not, a treaty. The understating of international legalization cannot foreclose

---

[57] An illustration comes from the EU as it contemplated legalizing lead firms' responsibilities regarding conflict minerals in conflict-torn DRC: 'we want to avoid companies disengaging from such regions as an easy way to comply with the Regulation' European Commission, *Frequently asked questions – Responsible sourcing of minerals originating conflict-affected and high-risk areas: towards an integrated EU approach* (5 March 2014).

[58] UNCTAD, *World Investment Report 2013*, n. 1, 144–147.

the discussion precisely where it has to begin: what are the implications of accepting that companies might redirect their value chains away from high-risk zones as a compliance response to legalizing lead firms' HRDD in home states? Thus, increasing frictions with the legal separation of entities principle – through the redirection of value chain spectre – brings into play the other two first-order principles.

(2) The second principle at play concerns state sovereignty under international law. A legalization of lead firms' responsibilities that in effect diverts global value chains away from the host state denies it the opportunities from participating in the global economy according to its own sovereign developmental path. Although some might argue that sovereignty is a myth, concerns of national sovereignty are not misplaced, particularly now as developing countries show an ever-growing desire for increased international trade and investment as witnessed by the multitude of free trade agreements being negotiated in recent years.[59] Hard legalization strategies targeting lead firms can be seen in host states as protectionist moves,[60] as illegitimately linking trade and human/labour rights in spite of developing countries' explicit resistance to the idea when the WTO was set up.[61]

Therefore, legalizing the lead firm's HRDD responsibilities cannot overlook a global development, trade, investment context where sovereign states highly prize their integration in global value chains.[62] For sure, this is not an argument against legalization, but an explanation that legalization of HRDD targeting lead firms increases friction with host state sovereignty. To reduce such frictions with international law's fundamental principle, the legalization of HRDD could be narrowed to limited settings, or softened into weaker legalization forms, or maintained as planned (hard legalization and broad coverage of human rights)

---

[59] World Trade Organization, *Regional Trade Agreements*, www.wto.org/english/tratop_e/region_e/region_e.htm (last visited 20 January 2016). UNCTAD, *International Investment Agreements*, http://investmentpolicyhub.unctad.org/IIA (last visited 20 January 2016).

[60] The ILO Declaration on Fundamental Principles and Rights at Work 1998 stresses that 'labour standards should not be used for protectionist trade purposes ... and the comparative advantage of any country should in no way be called into question'.

[61] D. Kinley, *Civilising Globalisation: Human Rights and the Global Economy* (Cambridge University Press, 2009), 47. See also Clapham, n. 34.

[62] On the importance of 'global value chains' in shaping trade law, see European Commission, *Trade for All: Towards a More Responsible Trade and Investment Policy* (2015) 10, 20 and 22.

if the host state agrees to take the risk of redirection of value chains (through a treaty).

(3) The third principle concerns international human rights law. The necessity of taking a wide variety of legislative and other measures to protect the rights-holders is well established in this body of law.[63] In the transnational BHR context scarred by deep governance gaps, this variety of measures translates into the overriding aim to mobilize all forms of private and public leverage to systematically increase the protection of the rights-holder harmed by business operations. This principle can be discerned clearly in the GPs, which clarify that the responsible course of action for a company that does not cause or contribute to infringements is first to exercise leverage, and second to disengage from its abusive suppliers.[64] This sequencing reflects a priority that rights-holders should be supported through all sources of leverage possible. The GPs draw on 'principled pragmatism' and the polycentric governance model[65] of driving change through public, corporate and civil governance (variety of measures). The possibility of value chains redirecting as a response of legalizing lead firms' HRDD is immediately problematic for the GPs as it severs transnational channels of exercising leverage and of international human rights law as it tries to reinvent itself in a globalized economy. Furthermore, rights-holders and those acting in their support tend to see redirecting value chains away from high-risk zones as unproductive and desirable only as a last resort and in rather extreme circumstances. This is also clearly reflected in the UN Norms,[66] and in NGO advocacy.

While harvesting leverage is desirable, legalizing such leverage is not a straightforward task. Legalizing leverage in a too coercive way may result in destroying the leverage altogether, as companies will consider reorienting their value chains to escape the compliance burden and liability risks. The legislatures seeking lead firms' accountability have a delicate

---

[63] Human rights treaties urge states to take 'the necessary steps . . . laws or other measures as may be necessary to give effect to the rights' (art. 2.2 of the International Covenant on Civil and Political Rights) and secure rights 'by all appropriate means' (art. 2.1 of the International Covenant on Economic, Social and Cultural Rights).

[64] Guiding Principles, n. 17, Principle 19, Commentary.

[65] J. Ruggie, 'Life in the Global Public Domain: Response to Commentaries' (5 February 2015) http://jamesgstewart.com/author/john-g-ruggie (last visited 20 January 2017). For a critique, see T. J. Melish, 'Putting "Human Rights" Back Into the UN Guiding Principles on Business and Human Rights: Shifting Frames and Embedding Participation Rights' in Cesar Rodriguez-Garavito (ed.), *Business and Human Rights: Beyond the End of the Beginning* (Cambridge University Press, 2017) 76.

[66] UN Norms, n. 40, para. 15.c.

balancing task in not setting the bar too low (making the legalization effort less significant in the BHR field) or too high (risking redirecting the value chains away from high-risk zones). As detailed below, to reduce frictions with this leverage principle under international human rights law, the legalization of HRDD should, on the one hand, distinguish between two settings of BHR based on the direct or indirect involvement of the lead firm in its suppliers' abusive operations, and on the other hand reassess the continuum of harder to softer legalization options.

This legalization perspective posits that three first-order principles are at play and interacting in the transnational BHR context, and that the difficulty for legalization comes from the possibility that lead firms subjected to strong legalization in their home states could comply by redirecting global supply chains away from high-risk zones. Some objections could be raised. First, MNEs will not necessarily redirect their value chains: MNEs might have no feasible alternative but stay and comply, or they might chose to stay and bear or pass to consumers the costs of compliance. If value chains do not get redirected, then the interrelations of the first-order principles will not really unfold, there will be no sovereignty objections and the rights-holders will only benefit from the added safeguards. This objection requires a case by case analysis of supply chains to identify where the risk of redirecting is significant and where it is not, given the specificities of each supply chain. But one would be hard pressed by reality to deny the operation of the three first-order principles once the possibility of redirection arises. For the time being, the majority of BHR treatments of legal separation and legalization of MNE responsibilities seem less concerned about such dynamics and principled difficulties brought by the redirection spectre.

The second objection would be that host states would not object to legalizing lead firms' responsibility but instead support a treaty that would solve their collective action problem. Through a treaty, states would address the 'race to the bottom' pitting developing countries against each other as they compete to attract international investment and trade. With no objections from host states and no place for MNEs to relocate, a broadly ratified treaty would see the interaction of the three first-order principles not unfold. That would allow a strong legalization of MNEs responsibilities in their home countries; the choice would solely be between human rights normativity and the legal separation of entities principle. The reality is that developing countries continue to compete fiercely in the global market place and have varying commitments to human rights. There seem to be divergent developmental models that currently appeal to host states seeking integration in the global economy.[67] Some states pursue a path to development and integration in the global economy that builds on social and environmental safeguards (the 'development with human rights' path). Signals for this model are sent by those developing states that have agreed at bilateral and regional levels that trade treaties should incorporate some labour and human rights protections. However, some states signal their attraction to the 'prosperity through trade' model which promises accelerated economic growth and development uncluttered by human rights sensitivities. A recently documented restriction of space for civil society activism[68] indicates the willingness of these governments to pursue rapid economic development and grasp the opportunities economic globalization and liberalized global markets offer without getting bogged down in protracted debates, dissent and individual complaints that respect for human rights enables. The UN treaty process sits squarely in the midst of this clash of development models.

Access of rights-holders to remedies in home-state courts is an area lagging behind, and made observers refer to Pillar three in the GPs as the 'forgotten pillar'. Clearly, home states are not eager to delocalize liability and move it upwards to lead firms in value chains, and seem to shy away from discussing judicial remedies in the few National Action Plans on BHR adopted so far. As shown before, it was well-established principles of negligence law, rather than new legislative action, that in a few jurisdictions have offered justice to foreign plaintiffs and this holds only for straightforward involvement of lead firms in supplier misconduct. In a more promising legal development, there are new regulations in home states requiring action from lead firms, such as reporting regulations.[69] These laws neither offer remedies to victims nor are particularly prescriptive regarding expected action. Also, as the French example demonstrates, strong legal regimes that were proposed initially get weakened later in the political process. Such 'softer legalization' as well as the reluctance to provide judicial remedies against lead firms surely can be explained through the home state's lack of political will to saddle own MNEs with burdensome obligations and liability risks.

---

[67] F. Fukuyama, 'Exporting the Chinese Model', *Project Syndicate* (12 January 2016).

[68] Special Rapporteur on the Situation of Human Rights Defenders, 'Global Trends in Risks and Threats Facing Human Rights Defenders', A/70/217 (2015), para. 35.

[69] Directive 2014/95/EU of the European Parliament and of the Council on Disclosure of Non-Financial and Diversity Information by Certain Large Undertakings and Groups (2014).

Be this as it may, more fundamentally this analysis suggests that softer legalization of lead firms' responsibilities can also be explained as a necessary way to minimize frictions with the host state's sovereignty, the need to maintain rather than sever the leverage for promoting human rights through value chains, and to not displace wholesale the legal separation of entities principle on which business risk management relies. These are the three first-order principles in business law (legal separation), international law (sovereignty) and human rights (leverage) that proposals for legalizing MNE responsibilities should not lose sight of, particularly as these three principles are tightly interrelated due to the presence of global value chains. This, however, is not an argument for legal stalemate. Lead firms do not have a carte blanche to continue business as usual in the global economic landscape explained herein by the three first-order principles.

The legalization discussion should not be reduced to one about overcoming the legal separation principle and about a simple choice between human rights normativity and pro-business privileges. Instead, the analytical stage for legalizing HRDD should be staged carefully (1) by separating the two contexts of lead firms' involvement and (2) by explaining when harder (more coercive) and softer (less coercive) legalization options are feasible tools to manage frictions with first-order principles. Once the appropriate space for coercive, hard legalization strategies directed at lead firms is clarified, the question will be how to reason constructively about softer legalization strategies, as well as non-legalistic strategies of change, rather than dismissing them as inherently insufficient in face of fierce completion and the profit motive? This analysis holds that *limited* harder legalization and *softer* legalization regimes can both reduce frictions with the three first-order principles. Furthermore, recent and multiple openings in the global economic landscape can render softer legalization more effective when these developments are analysed together than in isolation.

10.4   Setting the Analytical Stage for a Comprehensive Legalization Perspective

The above discussion of HRDD legalization precedents and the specificities of the transnational BHR context impressed that the legal separation of entities has to be taken seriously given its ramifications. Less coercive, softer legalizations of lead firms' responsibilities should not be seen as mere reflections of insufficient political will and/or mere stepping stones on a longer road to overcome the separation principle. The analysis herein suggests that these less coercive legalizations represent the end of the line due to unmanageable frictions with first-order principles in transnational BHR setting. Where does that leave the legalization analysis and agenda? This section differentiates situations where coercive instead of softer measures against lead firms are warranted, and proposes a way to valorize softer legalization in the human rights regime.

10.4.1 Unpacking the Legalization of Human Rights Due Diligence: Two Regimes and Two Objectives

The GPs put forward a responsibility of lead firms that stretches deep into value chains. The responsibility to respect covers direct and indirect forms of involvement in human rights abuses. In other words, the lead firm should address adverse impacts that it causes, contributes to or is merely directly linked to through its goods, services and operations, wherever they might be in the value chain. The HRDD notion outlines the key management steps expected from businesses, while the 'corrective action' element clarifies that a responsibility to act requires *ceasing* the causation or contribution and, in the linkages scenario, it entails *exercising leverage* over the suppliers, and if that is unsuccessful, *disengaging* from them.[70]

From a root cause perspective,[71] the GPs put the spotlight on two clearly separable root causes of value chain abuses: on the one hand, a lead firm's own decisions that lead directly or more remotely to adverse impacts throughout the value chain, and, on the other hand, the failures in the host state's regulatory regime that allow the supplier to infringe rights with impunity. The two root causes carry fundamental implications for legalizing the responsibility to respect. Thus, depending on the root cause, the lead firms' responsibility to respect becomes a *responsibility to cease harmful conduct* (when the lead firm's decisions 'caused' the impacts) and, respectively, a *responsibility to exercise leverage* over the third party (when the lead firm is merely 'linked' to impacts) before termination of the relationship should be contemplated. Therefore, one must differentiate between the 'cessation' regime and the 'leverage'

---

[70] Guiding Principles, n. 17, Principles 13, 17 and 19.
[71] R. Mares, 'De-centring Human Rights from the International Order of States: The Alignment and Interaction of Transnational Policy Channels' (2016) 23 *Indiana Journal of Global Legal Studies* 171, 177–179.

regime as the two regimes raise different challenges for the legalization of HRDD.

In the 'cessation regime', harder legalization in the form of *coercion* and instituting a *prohibition* for harmful conduct should not be objectionable even in a value chain context. There are two scenarios that can be identified. The first is that of *direct involvement* of the lead firm contributing to harm either as one of the multiple causes at play or as an accomplice that aids or abets the perpetrator.[72] Such contributions to a supplier's harmful operations can be approached through classical civil and criminal liability lenses; there are both precedents and legal principles to rely upon to cover such torts and crimes even though they are, as here, transnational.[73] The second scenario refers to the *prohibitions to trade* for specific goods such as gems (conflict diamonds) and illegally harvested good. These are exceptional cases where lawmakers decided it is preferable to block trade, to exclude some 'tainted' goods and services from global supply chains. Rather than being based on established principles of civil or criminal liability, these regulations are driven by public policy to create special liability regimes. For both these scenarios, an important question arises: what place would softer legalization occupy in the 'cessation regime'? 'Softer' legalization appears inherently not up to the task of ensuring the company is ceasing its harmful conduct and stops importing tainted goods. A core company's direct involvement or pull force (market demand as a buyer of tainted goods) appears as a root cause that has to be eliminated and dealt with vigorously. None of the three first-order principles creates major difficulties in this 'cessation' regime if home states decided to apply coercion on the lead firms for not ending their involvement.

The 'leverage regime' is different. Here the task of legalization is not one of prohibition, but of *mobilizing* and *guiding leverage*. The GPs reflect this concern by sequencing the appropriate action expected under the 'linkages' scenario as leverage first, terminate relationship second (Principle 19). The regulatory aim is to legalize the exercise of leverage, rather than to legalize a separation from harmful operations of suppliers as in the 'cessation regime'. Any harder legalization targeting the lead firms has to be assessed against the real danger of destroying the leverage added by the value chain rather than securing that leverage. Again, the

---

[72] OHCHR, *The Corporate Responsibility to Respect Human Rights: An Interpretive Guide* (2012), 16–17 (offering a diagram explaining 'contribution').

[73] See the transnational litigation pursued by the British law firm Leigh Day, www.leigh day.co.uk/International-and-group-claims (last visited 20 January 2017).

question is what place would softer legalization occupy here? When coercive strategies appear inappropriate due to frictions with the three first-order principles, softer legalization strategies suddenly become more meaningful. However, the next question is how to still ensure that softer strategies are actually making a difference?

10.4.2 The Two-Track, Multi-Channel Perspective on the Legalization of Due Diligence: Harder and Softer Legalization

To answer the key question of how less coercive, softer strategies can make a difference in the BHR field, this chapter suggests a *multi-channel perspective*. To valorize softer legalization of lead firms' responsibilities it is necessary to refocus the regulatory lenses and expand the field of view to see clearly the entire value chain. As detailed elsewhere,[74] there are promising developments in five transnational policy streams: international trade law, international human rights law, development aid, home-state laws with extraterritorial effects and 'corporate social responsibility' (CSR). This multi-channel perspective accounts for several transnational policy channels that are impacting the global value chains, particularly the two root causes mentioned above. The softer legalization of lead firms' responsibilities is then to be analysed not in isolation, but in conjunction with other transnational policy tools. Despite controversies, the most surprising opening in the BHR landscape is the channel of trade law where a growing number of free trade agreements now contain social clauses[75] and the 2015 EU trade strategy paper refers to 'human rights' 25 times.[76]

There are a few aspects about the multi-channel perspective worth emphasizing. First, such policy channels should be *accounted* for instead of quickly being dismissed as weak, pro-business, non-legal or of limited applicability. They carry precious leverage that the struggle for human rights cannot afford to waste. Second, a closer look at these channels reveals increasing *alignment* towards internationally recognized human rights standards and *interaction* among channels as witnessed by myriads of cross references and joint programs. This creates opportunities to harvest and deliver more effectively their combined leverage to protect

---

[74] Mares, n. 71.
[75] International Institute for Labour Studies, *Social Dimensions of Free Trade Agreements* (ILO, 2013), 19 (finding that the number of trade agreements with labour provisions has increased from four in 1995 to fifty-eight in 2013).
[76] European Commission, n. 62.

human rights. Third, there is an increased *root cause orientation* in recent BHR thinking.[77] On the one hand, MNEs began to expressly acknowledge their own harmful decisions rippling through their value chains.[78] So, also, do home states requiring more transparency and contemplating the use of public procurement to drive change through value chains. On the other hand, the root cause orientation extends to host state weaknesses as well. The trade channel where free trade agreements now incorporate labour clauses displays a root cause orientation by insisting on strengthened host state regulations to monitor and enforce rights in supplier operations. Furthermore, international human rights law mechanisms in the UN make copious use of the GPs to extract information and sensitize both host and home states to hold companies in value chains accountable. Also, developments in investment law emphasize regulatory space so that host states maintain ability to regulate for the public good and fight back against overreaching international investors.

Encouraging as these openings are, they still amount to no more than softer legalization as they fall short of coercing companies and states. It is necessary therefore to explain how it could ever matter where the competitive market pressures and profit motive are so strong and where the stakes (human rights) are so high. How will softer legalization make a difference? The above multi-channel perspective on BHR is a view on legalization which seeks to gather strength by bundling together weak strands (softer legalization and non-legal options in various transnational channels) into a 'rope' that targets root causes of tainted value chains rather than symptoms. This is a picture of a transnational regulatory regime that comes to terms with the multiple though limited tools in its arsenal, and the 'rope from weak threads' is the answer to frictions with the first-order principles in the transnational BHR context. It is not simply about insufficient political will to 'hold MNEs accountable' but about designing carefully calibrated policy mixes. The mix valorizes softer legalization strategies and non-legal incentives created by states, markets and civil society activism.

This analysis highlights recent openings in the global economic landscape and emphasizes the importance of softer legalization and non-legal

---

[77] See, for example, Global Agenda Council on Human Rights, *Shared Responsibility: A New Paradigm for Supply Chains* (World Economic Forum, 2014).

[78] Nike reported that it 'continued to assess root causes of excessive overtime . . . [It was able to establish that 68 per cent of incidents analyzed] were attributable to factors within Nike's control, primarily forecasting or capacity planning issues, shortened production timelines and seasonal spikes.' Nike, Inc. *FY10/11 Sustainable Business Performance Summary*, 20, 53 (2012).

incentives in their own right and is necessary to navigate around the three first-order principles specific to the transnational BHR context. A comprehensive legalization perspective on BHR should account for and explain how these policy channels together 'work' the transnational supply chains from both ends. In short, the treaty process pondering on legalizing the lead firm's HRDD should 'see' the channels, and see them not in isolation[79] and only for their weakness (softer legalization), but in ensemble to detect how they begin to interact[80] and target root causes of abuse in value chains.[81]

The principle of legal separation of entities is an essential filter through which to detect and explain tensions in the transnational BHR field as the human rights movement is finding its voice(s) on legalizing HRDD. The legalization perspective herein is a two-track strategy that confronts with harder legalization the excesses of legal separation in the 'cessation regime' and that largely bypasses with softer legalization the principle in the 'leverage regime' by using multiple policy channels. Through this 'chipping and bypassing' strategy, a global BHR regime can be built to encompass the two regimes: harder, coercive law solutions for the cessation regime and a less legally coercive, 'rope' solution for the leverage regime.

Forging a 'rope out of weak threads' raises typical difficulties of having an arrangement with so many moving parts and constantly negotiating the tensions between economic, political and human rights imperatives. But a comprehensive and feasible legalization alternative is difficult to identify. Indeed, a frontal attack on the separation principle leads the legalization discourse either directly in the 'expansive approach', which would seek to dismantle the separation principle with predictable outcomes, or towards some 'limited approach', which would cover a narrow territory in BHR and leave the rest of the territory under a large blind spot. Reducing the legalization agenda to hard, most coercive legal solutions and to lead firms cannot eliminate human rights abuses from value chains, and furthermore obscures first-order principles and critical regulatory dynamics surrounding global value chains.

---

[79] UNCTAD, *World Investment Report 2013*, n. 1, 144–47 (noting that 'TNC efforts beyond the first-tier level of suppliers are especially fraught with challenges and require public policy assistance and collective action within multi-stakeholder initiatives.')

[80] O. Dilling, 'From Compliance to Rulemaking: How Global Corporate Norms Emerge from Interplay with States and Stakeholders' (2012) 13 *German Law Journal*.

[81] European Parliament, 'Joint Motion for a Resolution on the Second Anniversary of the Rana Plaza Building Collapse and Progress of the Bangladesh Sustainability Compact' (28 April 2015).

10.5   Implications and Recommendations for the Treaty Process

The UN treaty process should pursue a broad legalization agenda. It could cover both direct and indirect types of involvement by lead firms and employ different forms of legalization (harder and softer forms) and non-legal incentives. Strategically, it should seek to capture all sources of leverage available and combine them in order to address root causes of infringements in the value chain and maximize transnational leverage for human rights. Another advantage of a comprehensive legalization perspective resides in highlighting rather than obscuring the multitude of legalization streams on the table. Instead of facile analogies among very different BHR settings and among different legal areas where DD obligations are present, there would be no contamination among such specific contexts. Keeping settings separate in a comprehensive framework would clarify where harder legalization options are imperative and where the 'strong rope from weak threads' approach is required, and also explain why.

The UN instrument should pursue a comprehensive, but two-track, legalization strategy which recognizes that two regimes (cessation and leverage regimes) raise different legalization challenges. The importance and appropriateness of harder, coercive measures in the 'cessation regime' is indisputable. Different streams of harder legalization could be pursued and their relationship to the legal separation of entities principle explained: first, severe abuses might require exceptional responses like bans on trade or strict, vicarious liability of lead firms (both represent a narrow *exception* to legal separation on public policy grounds); second, direct involvement of lead firms causing or significantly contributing to harm (such involvement raises *no frictions* with legal separation); and third, mutual legal assistance among home and host states (such assistance works *within the confines* of legal separation and tackles other obstacles to judicial remedies).

Softer legalization and non-legal incentives should not be quickly discarded as falling short of a hard law ideal of legalization in the BHR field. Instead, their crucial role in the 'leverage regime' should be recognized, their necessity and significance explained. That requires a view of legalization in the 'leverage regime' that, on the one hand, does not lose sight of first-order principles specific to the transnational BHR context, and on the other hand, focuses on the mobilization, alignment, complementarity and interaction of policy channels to maximize and direct leverage towards root causes. A multi-channel perspective on legalization as proposed herein could account for public and private leverage, delivered through human rights and economic channels,[82] using softer and harder forms of legalization. The fundamental aim of a carefully calibrated policy mix is to deliver cleaner global value chains while not diverting value chains away from host states that committed to a 'development through human rights' path in a highly competitive global market place.

10.6   Proposed Text of Treaty Provisions

The proposed BHR treaty should incorporate the following elements rooted in the analysis undertaken in this chapter.

The business responsibility to respect human rights applies to own operations and to those outsourced to value chains irrespective of ownership or contractual forms of coordination within business enterprises.

The business responsibility for value chains applies where there is causation, contribution or direct linkages to human rights impacts irrespective of the tier of the value chain where the impact occurs.

The content of the business responsibility is informed (i) by the principles of human rights due diligence as elaborated in the Guiding Principles, and (ii) by demonstrating "reasonable care" as informed by regulatory obligations and authoritative standards specific to the industry or the human rights issue and with due regard to factual circumstances.

Legalization of business responsibility for value chains does not assume an unqualified principle of lead firms' responsibility for supplier operations, but reflects the degree of culpability of the relevant company, unless strict or absolute liability is deemed appropriate to address particularly high risks of severe human rights impacts.

Culpable business conduct in the form of causation and contribution requires legislature to compel, under legal sanction, business to cease harmful conduct and take corrective actions to prevent reoccurrence and remediate the adverse impacts.

Culpable business conduct in the form of direct linkages to adverse impacts requires a mix of legislative and other measures to maximize leverage and, if not feasible, terminate relationships with non-compliant business partners. This policy mix includes more

---

[82] L. Backer, 'Sovereign Investing and Markets-Based Transnational Rule of Law Building: The Norwegian Sovereign Wealth Fund in Global Markets' (2013) 29 *American University International Law Review* 1.

coercive or less coercive measures imposed on lead firms to be chosen in light of the possible redirection of value chains as a compliance strategy.

Regulatory measures applied to lead firms have to be assessed against and reconciled as far as possible with basic principles applicable in the cross-border context of global value chains: national sovereignty (international law), maximum leverage for rights-holders (human rights law) and legal separation of entities in value chains (business law). To safeguard against undesirable or premature redirection of value chains and ensure the goal of harvesting maximum leverage for the benefit of rights-holders, policy mixes have to be informed by ex-ante and ex-post regulatory impact assessments in the specific value chain context of the industry.

Regulatory measures to ensure responsible business conduct and remedies in value chains shall be taken in a number of transnational policy channels:

- *International human rights mechanisms* should fulfil their mandates to monitor and engage in constructive dialogue with host and home states around business-related human rights impacts by making regular use of the Guiding Principles and specific standards of responsible business conduct.
- *International trade agreements* should include human rights and labour standards clauses that create cooperation, monitoring and remedial mechanisms. International investment agreements should also safeguard the regulatory space of host states and reflect a joint commitment of host and home states to responsible value chains.
- *International development cooperation* should facilitate multi-stakeholder initiatives, support the capacity of various private and public actors to fulfil their role in complex regulatory regimes, and overall facilitate policy coherence through targeted interventions.
- *The corporate social responsibility practices of businesses* should be recognized and disseminated for their ability to detect and innovatively address root causes of value chain problems, whether in their own decision-making process or in institutional frameworks of host and home states.
- *Home states of lead firms* should take legislative and other measures regarding lead firms and in this way apply indispensable leverage at their end of value chains, in a way mindful of the spectre of redirection of value chains and designed to seek reinforcement of actions occurring at other stages of the value chain.

The primary obligation of host states under international law to secure human rights in their jurisdiction is reaffirmed and shall be reinforced by the aforementioned transnational policy channels bracketing global value chains. Strengthening the regulatory framework for global value chains requires increased policy coherence so that transnational channels align and reinforce each other to maximize leverage and direct it to root causes of human rights infringements throughout the global value chain.

10.7   Conclusion

The task of regulating lead firms cannot escape the spectre of value chains being redirected away from high-risk zones, which triggers profound national interests of states not willing to forfeit their integration in the global economy and raises unintended effects for the protection of rights-holders. Three first-order principles are defining for the transnational BHR context and shape legalization options: the legal separation of entities (business law), national sovereignty (international law) and rights-holders' interest in maximum leverage being mobilized by the BHR regime (human rights). The specificity of the transnational BHR context requires therefore setting the analytical stage differently from a broad rhetoric to 'hold MNEs accountable', to mandate stringent HRDD obligations for lead firms and provide remedies to victims against lead firms.

Three implications were drawn to deliver a comprehensive BHR legalization perspective. First, a *two-track legalization of HRDD* should be pursued given that there are two regimes of corporate responsibility that raise very different regulatory challenges. Coercive solutions would be appropriate for direct involvement of the lead firm (the 'cessation regime') and softer legalization solutions are warranted where involvement is indirect (the 'leverage regime'). That explains why and where softer legalization is necessary in the BHR field.

Second, to clarify how softer legalization could matter in driving real change, the chapter puts forward a *multi-channel perspective* on BHR. Five channels can be identified where recent favourable developments can be detected: international trade law, international human rights law, development aid, home-state laws with extraterritorial effects and CSR. Although most of these developments amount to softer legalization only, the emerging BHR regime cannot afford to discard any sources of leverage. The way to make softer legalization count is for the legalization project to aim to deliver a 'strong rope from weak strands' (softer legalization and non-legal options) to overcome the weaknesses of these channels assessed in isolation.

Third, this perspective could inform a *comprehensive BHR instrument that could complement and reinforce the GPs*. Through the lenses offered by the legal separation of entities principle, this chapter shows the trappings of current conceptualizations of legalizing the BHR field and explains why reverting to the pre-GPs way of reasoning about regulating MNEs is not advisable. This analysis puts forward the imperative of grasping the place of more coercive, harder legalization in policy mixes, and the complexities that follow, if a comprehensive instrument is envisaged. This analysis adds a legalization layer on the polycentric governance outlook embodied in the GPs. The result would be a genuine complementarity between the UN treaty process and the GPs, rather than an appealing but superficial soft law-hard law complementarity.

This two-track, multi-channel regulatory perspective affirms that legalization in BHR is necessary and begins to answer the question of how softer legalization and non-legal incentives could drive change in the face of strong competitive pressures and profit motive. The legalization of HRDD is not about moving liability upwards towards the lead firm through coercive means but is a project of mobilizing leverage from multiple sources to rid value chains of human rights abuses through carefully designed policy mixes. The legalization of HRDD is not simply about moving beyond soft law and corporate voluntarism through coercive means targeted primarily at lead firms but about conceiving policy mixes adapted to the mobility of global value chains and thus deliver a regulatory regime able to navigate a course around first-order principles specific to the transnational BHR area. This is an outlook that combines private and public governance as it pursues the lead firm's responsibility in tight coordination with other transnational policy channels, not in isolation from them.

PART IV

Role of States in Enforcing Human Rights
Obligations

11

Human Rights Legal Liability for Business Enterprises

The Role of an International Treaty

CARLOS LOPEZ

The creation by the United Nations Human Rights Council in June 2014 of an Intergovernmental Working Group to elaborate a legally binding instrument to regulate Transnational Corporations (TNCs) and other business enterprises in the field of human rights[1] has reignited a series of theoretical controversies that were put – temporarily and partially – to rest during the process of elaboration of the UN Guiding Principles on Business and Human Rights (Guiding Principles). Some of those issues have a long history in the business and human rights debates, but others are new emerging issues relating to the form and content of the new legally binding instrument. One key issue is whether an international agreement, such as the one to be discussed in an intergovernmental setting, will be capable of creating international human rights obligations (or responsibilities) for business corporations (whether national or transnational). And, if so, what would be the nature and form that those obligations will take in the proposed agreement? The answer to this question may not be as simple as it appears at first sight since it is tied to a number of other questions such as the way those obligations would be implemented and enforced within domestic jurisdictions and abroad, and the creation, or not, of the necessary national or international mechanisms for that purpose. The issue also has ramifications for the debates about corporations as – possible – subjects of international law, and the kind of international law norms that should be addressed to those corporations. More generally, it has to do with the character and effectiveness of the proposed international

---

[1] Human Rights Council, 'Resolution 29/9 Elaboration of an International Legally Binding Instrument on Transnational Corporations and other Business Enterprises with Respect to Human Rights' A/HRC/29/RES/9, (26 June 2014).

agreement, which is expected to go beyond a simple restatement of obligations or responsibilities to provide States and other actors with the means effectively to apply them in practice.

Some of these questions were partially set-aside at the start of the term of the UN Special Representative of the Secretary General (SRSG) on the issue of business and human rights (for a total of six years between 2005 and 2011). The UN Norms on the Responsibilities of Transnational Corporations and Other Business Enterprises with Regard to Human Rights drafted by the UN Sub-Commission on the Protection and Promotion of Human Rights[2] (UN Sub-Commission) made legal obligations for corporations its central theme. In his first interim report (2006), the SRSG concluded that the Norms prepared by the UN Sub-commission could not be a restatement of the current international human rights law because, with a few possible exceptions, this law did not bind corporations.[3] The SRSG 2007 report conducted a mapping of international law arriving at the same conclusion, but again left the possibility open that international criminal law actually applies to corporations.[4] The Framework and ensuing Guiding Principles prepared by the SRSG were based on the assumption that business corporations' human rights responsibilities are not based on any international legal obligation but on social expectations. In fairness, the SRSG's reports never rejected the possibility that international agreements may create direct obligations for business corporations, although he refused to follow the treaty path during his mandate.[5]

---

[2] Sub-Commission on the Protection and Promotion of Human Rights 'UN Norms on the Responsibilities of Transnational Corporations and Other Business Enterprises with Regard to Human Rights', E/CN.4/Sub.2/2003/12/Rev.2 (26 August 2003).

[3] Commission on Human Rights, 'Interim Report of the Special Representative of the Secretary-General on the Issue of Human Rights and Transnational Corporations and other Business Enterprises', E/CN.4/2006/97, (22 February 2006), paras. 60–61.

[4] Commission on Human Rights, 'Business and Human Rights: Mapping International Standards of Responsibility and Accountability for Corporate Acts, Report of the Special Representative of the Secretary-General on the Issue of Human Rights and Transnational Corporations and other Business Enterprises', A/HRC/4/35 (19 February 2007), at para. 8. For a critique to the SRSG stance making no link between international crimes and human rights violations, see S. Deva, 'Multinationals, Human Rights and International Law: Time to Move beyond the "State-Centric" Conception' in J. Letnar Cernic and T. Van Ho (eds.) *Human Rights and Business: Direct Corporate Accountability for Human Rights* (The Netherlands: Wolf Legal Publishers, 2015), 27 35–36.

[5] In a 2008 publication explaining its position, the SRSG stated: 'negotiations on an overarching treaty now would be unlikely to get off the ground, and even if they did the outcome could well leave us worse off than we are today.' See, J. Ruggie, 'Business and Human Rights: Treaty Road Not Travelled' *Ethical Corporation*, (May 2008), 42–43.

However, while the path set by the SRSG on business and human rights within the United Nations adopted a non-legal approach to corporate human rights responsibility, the issue of legal responsibilities under international law came to the surface several times in other contexts. This was notably the case in the context of litigation in the United States under the Alien Tort Statute.[6] The discussion in that context largely focusses on whether there exists customary international criminal law binding on corporations in the absence of international treaties that do so. The terms of the debate today are more focused on what kinds of legal obligations and/or liability for business corporations an international agreement (a treaty) can create and how to do that.

Rather than a full revision of the somewhat old general debate between direct or indirect obligations for non-state actors such as corporations, the present chapter explores what an international treaty can reasonably achieve in relation to the human rights obligations or responsibilities of corporations. It suggests that whatever the option that is finally developed in relation to models of direct or indirect obligations (or a combination of the two) for corporations under international law, the character of a treaty as an international agreement concluded between states, plus the need to ensure the effectiveness and enforceability of the treaty provisions naturally and logically reserves a key role for state-based institutions and machinery. With this in mind, the first part of the chapter will recall some of the main concepts and principles of international law that are relevant in this context and clarify the ways international treaty law has in practice dealt with the issue of obligations for business corporations. The second part will provide an outline of how a new international treaty on business and human rights may deal with the issue.

11.1   International Law and Human Rights Obligations for Business Corporations

Today it is indisputable that States as the main – perhaps not the sole – subjects and makers of international law have the capacity to bestow rights and obligations on third parties, including intergovernmental

---

[6]   See generally, L. F. H. Enneking, *Foreign Direct Liability and Beyond* (The Hague: Eleven International Publishing), 77 and ff.; B. Stephens, 'Translating Filartiga: A Comparative and International Law Analysis of Domestic Remedies for International Human Rights Violations' (2002) 27 *Yale Journal of International Law* 1.

organizations and private economic entities such as business corpora-tions.[7] The International Court of Justice's (ICJ) opinion in the *Reparations case*[8] is usually seen as laying a foundational doctrine whereby non-state actors may have such rights and obligations as States their creators, decide to bestow on them. But, in fact, that doctrine finds its foundations in the jurisprudence of the Permanent Court of International Justice, at the beginning of the twentieth century.[9]

This doctrine also fuels the debate on whether corporations have or can possibly have some form of international legal personality. International personality is seen by many, in somewhat circular reason-ing, as a necessary prerequisite for a subject to enjoy international rights and obligations. At the same time, international personality seems to be acquired only by those subjects that enjoy rights and/or obligations. In a well-known paragraph, the ICJ held:

> The subjects of law in any legal system are not necessarily identical in their nature or in the extent of their rights, and their nature depends upon the needs of the community. Throughout its history, the development of international law has been influenced by the requirements of international life, and the progressive increase in the collective activities of States has already given rise to instances of action upon the international plane by certain entities which are not States.[10]

This paragraph has led some authors to discern a derived and limited personality for non-State entities, as opposed to original and plenary personality that belongs only to States.[11] There is also a representative

---

[7] N. Rodley, 'Non-State Actors and Human Rights' in S. Sheeran and N. Rodley (eds.) *Routledge Handbook of International Human Rights Law*, (Routledge, 2013), 525; C M. Vazquez, 'Direct vs. Indirect Obligations of Corporations under International Law' (2004) 43 *Columbia Journal of Transnational Law* 930; S. Deva, 'Multinationals, Beyond the "State-Centric" Conception'. n. 4, 38.

[8] *Reparations for Injuries Suffered in the Service of the United Nations*, ICJ Advisory Opinion, ICJ Reports 1949, 174.

[9] *Jurisdiction of the Courts of Danzig*, Advisory Opinion, 1928 P.C.I.J. (ser. B) No. 15 (Mar. 3) 17–8.

[10] *Reparations case*, n. 8, 178.

[11] V. Chetail, 'The Legal Personality of Multinational Corporations, State Responsibility and Due Diligence: The Way Forward' in D. Alland, V. Chetail, O. de Frouville and J. E. Viñuales (eds.), *Unity and Diversity of International Law. Essays in Honour of Prof. Pierre-Marie Dupuy* (Boston/Leiden: Martinus Nijhoff Publishers, 2014), 105, 110 and ff; In support, *Legality of the Use by a State of Nuclear Weapons in Armed conflict*, ICJ Advisory Opinion, ICJ Reports 1996 at 66 is also cited: 'International organizations. . . are invested by the States which create them with powers, the limits of which are a function of the common interests whose promotion those States entrust to them.'

current in international law that would prefer to underplay the concept of 'international subjects' or 'international personality' and instead talk about the relevant non-State actors as 'participants' in the international legal system. This approach would avoid the inconveniences posed by the classical concepts of international legal personality as a prerequisite to enjoy rights and obligations under international law.[12]

That States have the power to endow other private entities with rights and obligations through the conclusion of international agreements does not automatically lead to the conclusion that they have already done so in the area of human rights, or that they must do so in the near future. States usually create rights and obligations for other entities when there is sufficient understanding and consensus about the necessity and usefulness of those entities having rights and/or obligations to perform functions deemed relevant for the international community.

Several authors argue that international law already recognizes rights and obligations for business corporations in the field of human rights.[13] International law seems to offer a few instances in which rights and obligations have been directly addressed to corporations (or even individual businesspersons or investors). The majority of international conventions establish indirect obligations for private actors, including corporations, by creating State duties to enact legal obligations for corporations or enterprises as a matter of domestic law.[14] Many cases presented as instances of 'direct' obligations are in fact examples of specific standards (on labour and other areas) addressed directly to non-State actors and defined in international agreements but the implementation of which is always left to the states concluding and ratifying the agreement. In these cases, the States are the only actors who bear international responsibility for breach of those obligations and the only ones ultimately held accountable at the international level.

---

[12] R. Higgins, *Problems and processes: International Law and How we use it* (Clarendon Press, 1995), 274.

[13] See generally N. Jägers, *Corporate Human Rights Obligations: in Search of Accountability*, Intersentia; S. Deva, 'Multinationals, Beyond the State-Centric Conception' n. 4, 38–39; J. Letnar Cernic, 'An Elephant in the Room of Porcelain: Establishing Corporate Responsibility for Human Rights' in J. Letnar Cernic and T. Van Ho (eds.), *Human Rights and Business: Direct Corporate Accountability for Human Rights*, (Oisterwijk: Wolf Legal Publishers, 2015), 131, 146; D. Bilchitz, 'Corporations and the Limits of State-Based Models for Protecting Fundamental Rights in International Law' (2016) 23 *Indiana Journal of Global Legal Studies*, 143.

[14] V. Chetail, 'The Legal personality?' n, 11, 115; Vazquez, 'Direct vs Indirect Obligations' n. 7, 948; J. H. Knox, 'Horizontal Human Rights Law' (2008) 102 *American Journal of International Law* 18–27.

Indeed, several conventions on labour rights and standards concluded within the International Labour Organization address directly 'employers' (which could be a natural person or a corporation) in a peremptory way, using the word 'shall'. Among many others, the ILO Convention 170, Article 13 provides in part:

> Employers shall make an assessment of the risks arising from the use of chemicals at work, and shall protect workers against such risks by appropriate means, [. . .][15]

The United Nations Convention on the Law of the Sea (UNCLOS) Article 137(1) and (3) provides that no juridical person shall appropriate any part of the ocean floor beyond the limits of national jurisdiction nor claim or exercise any rights on its resources. The Warsaw Convention on Air Transportation also directly addresses obligations to air carriers: 'a carrier shall be liable for damage' sustained by a passenger under certain circumstances.[16] It has also been claimed[17] that Article III(1) of the International Convention on Civil Liability for Oil Pollution Damage provides for direct obligations for corporations:

> the owner [a natural person or a corporation] of a ship at the time of an incident, or, where the incident consists of a series of occurrences, at the time of the first such occurrence, shall be liable for any pollution damage caused by the ship as a result of the incident.

Although not directly focussing on corporations, international criminal law can also be seen to provide instances of international agreements imposing direct obligations on non-state actors such as individuals. For instance, the Convention against Genocide prohibits the commission of genocide by both states and individuals. The Rome Statute for the International Criminal Court defines a series of crimes that individuals can commit and establishes the possibility of a direct jurisdiction of the International Criminal Court being exercised over individuals accused of committing any of those crimes.

---

[15] C170 – Chemicals Convention, 1990 (No. 170). See also, among many others, C174 – Prevention of Major Industrial Accidents Convention, 1993 (No. 174), C176 – Safety and Health in Mines Convention, 1995 (No. 176), C119 – Guarding of Machinery Convention, 1963 (No. 119).

[16] Convention for the Unification of Certain Rules Relating to International Transportation by Air, 12 October 1929, L.N.T.S. 11.

[17] Deva, n. 4, 42. This and other conventions are listed in the introduction to the Sub-Commission Norms indicating that they provide for direct duties for corporations.

An argument frequently used to justify the need for an international agreement that provides directly binding obligations on business corporations is to highlight that international law already recognizes that business corporations have a wide range of rights or standards of protection. International obligations directly binding on corporations would serve as a counterbalance to the rights they have already acquired. For instance, corporations have substantive rights under the European Convention on Human Rights: to freedom of expression under Article 10,[18] and the right to property under the Protocol 1 to the Convention, amongst others.

In fields other than human rights, companies are also said to be accorded rights under foreign investment international law in relation to expropriation, compensation and national treatment of their investments in contracting countries. In addition to customary international law, myriad bilateral investment treaties (BIT) and free trade agreements (FTA) contain standards that are generally seen as providing rights for investors.[19]

---

[18] European Convention for the Protection of Human Rights and Fundamental Freedoms ETS 005 (entered into force 3 September 1953); *Autronic AG v. Switzerland*, European Court of Human Rights, A. 178, 22 May 1990, para. 47; Protocol 1 to the European Convention for the Protection of Human Rights and Fundamental Freedoms, Article 1 Right to Property. See also M. Addo, 'The corporation as a victim of human rights violations' in M. Addo (ed.) *Human Rights Standards and the Responsibility of Transnational Corporations* (The Hague: Kluwer Law International, 1999), 187–196.

[19] The nature of rights and protections under investment protection agreements is far from uncontroversial. While a majority trend seems to see them as rights directly benefiting investors, others still believe that they are not more than 'derivative' rights flowing from the reciprocal rights and obligations established between the States that concluded the agreements. See, Z. Douglas, 'The Hybrid Foundation of Investment Treaty Arbitration' (2003) 74 *British Yearbook of International Law*, 163–164; C. Foster, 'A New Stratosphere? Investment Treaty Arbitration as 'Internationalized Public Law' (2015) 64 *International Law Quarterly*, 476. The standards on 'expropriation' or 'nationalization', 'compensation' and 'national treatment', among others, are frequently the matter of controversy in ongoing disputes before arbitral tribunals. Appleton provides one often cited definition: 'The term "expropriation" carries with it the connotation of a "taking" by a governmental-type authority of a person's "property" with a view to transferring ownership of that property to another person, usually the authority that exercised its de jure or de facto power to do the "taking"'. Barry Appleton, 'Regulatory Takings: The International Law Perspective' (2002) *NYU Environmental Law Journal* 46. When an expropriation is deemed illegal, the victim of it is entitled to receive compensation, which is one form of reparation to injuries caused by an internationally wrongful act. It is commonly due when the property cannot be subject of restitution to the legitimate owner, and covers any 'financially assessable damage including loss of profits insofar as it is established.' 'Draft articles on responsibility of States for internationally wrongful acts', *Yearbook of the International Law Commission* 2001. National treatment can be defined as a principle whereby a host country extends to foreign investors treatment that is at least as favourable as the treatment that it

In terms of procedural rights, corporations and individual business-persons have rights to file complaints before the European Court of Human Rights under the European Convention and its First Optional Protocol. Similar procedural rights of action exist in relation to international arbitral tribunals or panels under a growing number of investment and trade agreements alleging the violation of the protections granted in these treaties.[20]

The instances of obligations 'directly' binding on business corporations discussed above are, upon closer analysis, part of a more complex international law system. Rather than creating 'direct' duties under international law for private third parties it is more accurate to see these conventions as part of a multi-layered system where substantive norms or standards aimed also at private actors are defined in the international agreement but the signatory States assume the international obligations to apply them domestically by concluding and ratifying the agreements.[21] This is so in all cases where there is not an international jurisdictional body such as a tribunal where the private actor can obtain direct enforcement of its rights or the obligations can be directly enforced. The latter option currently exists only in the International Criminal Court that has jurisdiction over individuals and the international tribunals to which investors can have recourse to protect their rights under investment and trade agreements.

John Knox has proposed a horizontal human rights regime in the image of a 'pyramid' of correlative obligations addressing private duties in four ways that can be particularly useful here.[22] At the lowest and broadest level of the 'pyramid', human rights law 'contemplates' the general duties of states to regulate and prevent abuses by private parties, leaving to them the flexibility to decide on the specific measures to be adopted. At this level are located most of the current international human rights treaties, which broadly rest on the general state's 'duty to protect' and 'due diligence' obligations. In the next level, human rights law 'specifies' the content of the private duties or responsibilities that governments have the obligation to impose under domestic law. In this level

accords to national investors in like circumstances. In this way, the national treatment standard seeks to ensure a degree of competitive equality between national and foreign investors. See UNCTAD, *National Treatment* (Geneva, 1999).

20 See, for instance, the 1965 Convention on the Settlement of Investment Disputes between States and Nationals of other States, *ILM* 4, 1965 at 532, article 25.

21 Vazquez, 'Direct vs. Indirect Obligations' n. 7, 935.

22 Knox, 'Horizontal Human Rights Law' n. 14, 18.

could be located some recent conventions that contain specific provisions on corporate legal liability, such as the UN Optional Protocol on the Sale of Children and Child Pornography, or the Convention against Transnational Organised Crime, but also the series of corporate-related standards developed by some UN monitoring bodies in relation to human rights treaties. The third level entails human rights law 'directly' placing obligations on private corporations but leaving their enforcement with governments and domestic law, and the fourth and highest level of involvement of human rights law means the creation of an international machinery such as the International Criminal Court to directly enforce obligations imposed on private actors. However, as noted by Knox, in this fourth level, the 'direct' character of the obligation for the private actor does not depend on the existence of an international body to enforce it,[23] but on the language used in the formulation of the obligation and the intention of the parties to the agreement.[24]

This framework assists in better understanding the existing and possible future international obligations for business corporations. While many ILO Conventions provisions define and address substantive standards to be respected by employers, each Convention clearly States that it 'shall be binding only on those Members of the ILO whose ratifications have been registered with the Director-General', placing these conventions in the third level of Knox's pyramid. In the current state of international law, only States can ratify these conventions. The tripartite structure of the ILO adds an element of employers' consent to the substance of the conventions by means of their participation in the negotiations and adoption thereof, but that participation cannot be equated to an act of ratification. The 1992 Convention on civil liability for oil pollution damage sets out the grounds of civil liability of 'ship owners' as defined in the Convention, but it then falls in line with conventional treaty law when it comes to the concrete application of those standards and liabilities. Its Article IX provides for the obligation of each Contracting Party to 'ensure that its Courts possess the necessary jurisdiction to entertain such actions for compensation'. These and other

---

[23] Some authors seem to suggest the opposite: Vazquez, 'Direct vs. Indirect Obligations', n. 7, 940--41; Olivier De Schutter, 'Towards a New Treaty on Business and Human Rights' (2016) 1 *Business and Human Rights Journal* 58–59. Jernej agrees with Clapham that the 'direct' character of the obligations does not depend on the existence of an international machinery. See Letnar Cernic, 'An Elephant in the Room of Porcelain', n. 13.

[24] Knox, 'Horizontal Human Rights Law', n. 14, 30–31.

similar conventions can hardly be seen as establishing 'direct' obligations for private parties, nor as a radical departure from the existent paradigms of international law.

An additional pair of concepts may be useful also for understanding how legal rules operate and what can be expected from an international agreement such as the one in prospect: the concepts of primary and secondary rules in domestic or international legal orders. The former are rules that define rights and obligations while the latter are rules that define how rules of the first type are recognized as part of the system, how they are created and modified, and how they are subject to adjudication and enforcement.[25] While the first type of rules defines rights and obligations, the second type defines how they are made and rendered operative. This distinction between primary and secondary norms is not a simple difference between substantive and procedural rules but a distinction between the substance of the rights and obligations and all that is necessary for them to be operative and effective.

Perhaps the best-known practical application of this conceptual pair is its incorporation in the International Law Commission's Articles on the 'Responsibility of the State for Internationally Wrongful Acts'. The introduction to the commentaries to these Articles highlights that they are concerned with secondary rules rather than with primary rules that define the substance of rights and obligations under international law. Those rules are the ones that come into operation when a breach of an international obligation occurs and, therefore, do not define the content of the rules that have been breached but the consequences of the breach.[26]

---

[25] H. L. A. Hart, *The Concept of Law* (Oxford: Clarendon Press, 1993), 78–79. Hart described the distinction between primary and secondary rules as follows:

> 'Under rules of the one, which may well be considered the basic or primary type, human beings are required to do or abstain from certain actions, whether they wish to or not. Rules of the other type are in a sense parasitic upon or secondary to the first; for they provide that human beings may by doing or saying certain things introduce new rules of the primary type, extinguish or modify old ones, or in various ways determine their incidence or control their operations.'

[26] General Assembly, 'Report of the International Law Commission', Fifty-third session, 2001 *General Assembly Official Records* Fifty-sixth session, Supp. No. 10 (A/56/10), pp. 59–61. See also J. Crawford, 'The ILC Articles on Responsibility of States for Internationally Wrongful Acts: A Retrospective' (2002) 96 *American Journal of International Law* 876; G. Abi-Saab, 'Cours Général de Droit International Public' *RCADI*, 1987-VII, (The Hague/Boston/London: Martinus Nijhoff Publishers, vol. 207, 1996) 125.

In the field of corporations and human rights, Nicola Jägers used a framework with slightly different terminology, material rights/duties versus proceedings/responsibility/examinations, to explain how corporations may be the subjects of international law because they have material rights and duties even if enforcement mechanisms or procedures for those duties do not exist or are weak (at the international level).[27] Within this framework, for instance, customary international criminal law can be said currently to apply to business corporations: while the substance of the rule defining the crimes attributable to a company may already exist under international customary law, there is not yet a court or mechanism with the jurisdiction to apply or enforce it. Indeed, it has been strongly argued elsewhere that the US Military Tribunal in Nuremberg found corporations to have committed crimes under international law such as deportation, slave labour, killings and pillage, but they were not actually tried nor sentenced because the US Military Tribunal just like the International Military Tribunal operating in the same setting had no jurisdiction to try and convict corporations, but only natural persons.[28] While the tribunal seems to have found grounds to find corporations criminally responsible, it could not exercise jurisdiction over them.

However, the distinction between primary and secondary rules in international law does not necessarily correspond to the dichotomy of substantive/enforcement mechanisms. In fact, primary and secondary rules of international law refer, on one side, to the content of the international obligation and, on the other side, to the consequences of its violation (i.e., the obligations of reparation, the rights of the injured party, circumstances precluding the wrongfulness of the act, etc.). Secondary rules are not immediately related to institutions or mechanisms of enforcement of rules (i.e., courts or administrative organs). If the existence of a set of secondary rules defining the content and consequences of a breach by a business corporation of its substantive international obligations is considered essential to confirm the existence of those very obligations, then the current absence of that set of secondary norms poses a serious challenge to the theory that corporations already have obligations under international law.

---

[27] Jägers, 'Corporate accountability', n. 13, 26–27.

[28] A. Clapham, 'The Question of Jurisdiction under International Criminal Law over Legal Persons: Lessons from the Rome Conference on an International Criminal Court' in M. Kamminga and S. Zia-Zarifi (eds.), *Liability of Multinational Corporations under International Law* (Kluwer Law International), 170–171.

As seen above, in most treaties that are seen as containing some sort of 'direct' duties addressed to corporations, there is no definition of the consequences of the corporations' breach of their obligations, nor have such consequences developed in customary law, at least not in a codified manner. Treaties among States generally leave their implementation to governments and domestic law, and sometimes an international body such as a tribunal serves as a complementary mechanism. This last option has so far been exceptional, and only used in relation to individuals and for a limited number of the most serious crimes. Generally, treaty-based international obligations remain with the ratifying States which are required to adopt measures, legal or otherwise, to place rights and duties on corporations at the domestic level under pain of incurring international responsibility if they breach their obligations.

Traditionally, there have been strong objections to the notion of direct human rights obligations for private actors (including corporations), and to the idea that human rights treaties would apply horizontally. These objections are generally grounded in the belief that applying rights and obligations under international law will likely impact upon the power of nation States and their authorities exclusively to regulate and control a creature born under their own national law. International obligations directly binding on business corporations would be autonomous and independent from obligations arising from national legislation, which may give rise to situations of potential conflict. This 'natural' resistance from (some) States[29] – as the opposition by most States to the Sub-Commission project of Norms in 2003–2004 shows – could be a defining element in the debates.

On the other hand, recognizing 'direct' duties of corporations without at the same time setting an effective system of remedies for the victims of rights violations, enforcement of those duties and guaranteeing due process may only serve at the end to undermine the protection of human rights and favour authoritarian states' rule.[30] Too many States are willing to relinquish their human rights obligations by transferring them to private corporations or other entities. The adoption at the international level of a catalogue of duties for corporations without correlative States' obligations may encourage governments who argue that human rights obligations, until then only binding upon them, are now also shared with (or are transferred altogether to) private (not

---

[29] Vazquez, 'Direct vs. Indirect Obligations', n. 7, 950.
[30] See generally Knox, 'Horizontal Human Rights Law', n. 14, 1–47.

democratically elected) corporations. At the same time, international human rights obligations for corporations may embolden governments that are ready to 'condition' the respect of corporate economic rights to their delivering (or good behaviour) in relation to their own human rights obligations. Finally, while the notion of 'direct' obligations for corporations under international law without an international enforcement machinery may be an appealing concept for many, it is not yet clear why they are necessary and how they will strengthen in practice the protection of individuals' and communities' rights without a robust functioning State-based system for their enforcement.

11.2 Implementation and Enforcement of Corporate Human Rights Responsibilities: What an International Treaty Can Achieve

International treaties are instruments used by States to create obligations binding upon them on issues of common concern. Under international law, treaties are agreements between two or more parties that produce legal effects for those parties and are governed by international law.[31] A central principle for the existence and operation of treaties is the rule that treaties are based on the consent of the parties and are binding only upon the parties to them and must be performed in good faith (*pacta sunt servanda*). So fundamental is this principle in the law of treaties that rights and obligations established under a given treaty do not bind third parties unless they explicitly accept them (Article 34 and 35 of the VCLT, with the exception of the relevant provisions in the UN Charter). Rights created by treaty for the benefit of third parties are treated somewhat differently. International law accepts that the consent of the third party can be presumed 'so long as the contrary is not indicated, unless the treaty otherwise provides' (Article 36 VCLT).[32]

Individuals and corporations are nationals of States and subject to the domestic laws of that state. Business corporations are clearly creatures of domestic law and up until now are not formally parties to international agreements governed by international law. But business corporations

---

[31] M. Shaw, *International Law*, Third Edition, 560–561; A. Pellet and P. Daillier,. *Droit international public*, 5th Edition, 117. The Vienna Convention on the Law of Treaties (VCLT), article 2, defines a treaty as: 'an international agreement concluded between states in written form and governed by international law, whether embodied in a single instrument or in two or more related instruments and whatever its particular designation'.

[32] Shaw, *ibid*, pp. 580–581 ; Pellet et al., *ibid.*, pp. 243–244.

have been given rights under certain treaties that have also created procedural rights to file claims before international tribunals. Already in 1928, the Permanent Court of International Justice recognized it as perfectly possible under international law.

> ...[A]ccording to a well-established principle of international law, [...] an international agreement, cannot, as such, create direct rights and obligations for private individuals. But it cannot be disputed that the very object of an international agreement, according to the intention of the contracting Parties, may be the adoption by the Parties of some definite rules creating individual rights and obligations and enforceable by the national courts. [...] The intention of the Parties, which is to be ascertained from the contents of the Agreement, taking into consideration the manner in which the Agreement has been applied, is decisive.[33]

Only in a few cases have international conventions 'directly' addressed obligations to corporations in the strict sense of the term under international law without the intermediation of the State. Most of those cases occur in the field of labour standards where many conventions directly set standards of conduct for employers, and also in the field of international criminal law with the Rome Statute on an International Criminal Court and the most recent Amending Protocol to the African Court of Justice. It may be more exact to regard those treaties as lawmaking or norm-making, setting standards of conduct applicable to all, including business corporations. But even in those cases only States that have ratified the relevant conventions can violate them and be responsible under the law of state responsibility for international wrongful acts. There may be thus a need to develop an international regime of corporate responsibility equivalent to the system of international law of responsibility of States for wrongful acts.

In any case, it is clear that an international treaty can potentially create 'direct' obligations for corporations if such is the intention of the parties to the treaty, but it may assign the task of enforcement to other actors such as States or international tribunals. For the 'direct' obligation to exist, the intention of the parties to the treaty should be transparent from the text of the treaty. In the current debate about a treaty to regulate transnational corporations there is not yet clarity about that intention. What kind of obligations or responsibilities may be created and for what purpose? What kind of enforcement mechanisms will be adopted? These

---

[33] *Jurisdiction of the Courts of Danzig*, Advisory Opinion, 1928 P.C.I.J. (ser. B) No. 15 (Mar. 3) 17–18.

are issues among several others that are still open to debate. The answers to these questions are likely to be guided by the assessment of the necessity of creating 'direct' obligations. In this context, advocacy on the need to create an international regime of accountability for corporations and of access to an effective remedy for affected individuals and communities may be crucial.

Calls for 'direct' obligations for companies under international law aim to overcome the many perceived obstacles in the existing 'state-centred' system: weakness, unwillingness or corruption of national state bodies and authorities to adopt and enforce national legislation, monitor it and hold corporations to account. Obligations 'directly binding' on corporations and, hopefully, enforced by international mechanisms would sideline the need for state action. The proponents of 'direct' obligations for companies still have to propose, however, in more specific terms what 'direct' obligations have to be imposed on corporations[34] and what kind of institutions and mechanisms will have the task of implementing and enforcing those obligations.

One option is to leave implementation to corporations themselves and to the so-called civil society with the help of the 'court of public opinion'. This option is not far from the model followed in the UN Guiding Principles which, although not binding, clearly sets a global standard of conduct for business enterprises: the responsibility to respect all human rights and to carry out human rights diligence processes. The Guiding Principles do not, however, explicitly assign States or other actors the task of implementing or enforcing those standards. A treaty creating 'direct' obligations for corporations, even if legally binding, without an external (national or international) mechanism of monitoring and accountability will not go much further than the Guiding Principles. Another option, or perhaps a variation of the first one, is to leave the task of implementation and enforcement implicitly to national courts through the 'direct' application of international treaties that are said to be self-executing. The specific requirements and hazards in the practical application of that doctrine show its potential and limitations in practice. Those who embrace this option would have to carry a survey of state practice in relation to self-executing treaties to ascertain the feasibility of this option.

A third option is the creation of an international court (or the expansion of the ICC jurisdiction). However, apart from the obvious hurdles

---

[34] See Chapter 7 by Bilchitz, who attempts to provide an analytical framework for determining corporate obligations in a future treaty.

relating to costs and political support for this alternative, international tribunals' efficacy rests largely on the commitment, cooperation and efficiency of national mechanisms. Even the International Criminal Court takes over a case only when the national state is unwilling or unable to act. Furthermore, the operation and effectiveness of a tribunal such as the ICC relies heavily on the cooperation of States party to the tribunal's statute, from the investigation and arrest of suspects or indicted persons to the execution of tribunal orders and decisions.

Another option is the one that has been followed in most cases, including in international treaties relating to human rights. In this model, States are required to enact legal liability for business corporations following specific standards or definitions provided in the treaty itself, and to provide access to remedies and other enforcement through domestic law. This is the model followed by the Optional Protocol to the Convention on the Rights of the Child on the Sale of Children and Child Pornography – OPSC – which so far is the only example of a human rights convention (excluding those within the Council of Europe and the ILO) that does so. Article 3(4) of this protocol[35] provides as follows:

> Subject to the provisions of its national law, each State Party shall take measures, where appropriate, to establish the liability of legal persons for offences established in paragraph 1 of the present article.
>
> [sexual exploitation]
> [transfer of organs],
> [forced labour],
> [illegal adoption of a child],
> [child prostitution].
>
> Subject to the legal principles of the State Party, such liability of legal persons may be criminal, civil or administrative.

---

[35] See Optional Protocol to the Convention on the Rights of the Child on the sale of children, child prostitution and child pornography, adopted under General Assembly resolution A/RES/54/263 of 25 May 2000 (entered into force on 18 January 2002). Article 3(4) of the Optional Protocol builds on the model previously adopted in the UN Convention on organized crime and the Convention against corruption, among others. See also Council of Europe, Convention on the protection of the environment through criminal law, adopted on 4 November 1998, Strasburg http://conventions.coe.int/Treaty/EN/Treaties/Html/172.htm (Accessed 28 March 2014). See also Convention on the Protection of Children against Sexual Exploitation and Sexual Abuse (article 26 and 27); The Convention on Action Against Trafficking in Human Beings (articles 22 and 23); The Convention on Cybercrime (articles 12 and 13); the Criminal Law Convention on Corruption (articles 18 and 19); Convention on preventing and combating violence against women and domestic violence (article 12.2).

There is also provision for legal liability for company directors, managers and other employees. The Optional Protocol states that the provisions on legal liability of corporations are without prejudice to the corresponding responsibility of individuals.[36]

This model was influenced by the UN Convention on Transnational Organized Crime and the OECD anti-bribery convention, among others. For many people, this could be a suitable model: the standards of liability are defined in international law, but it remains the task of the national State to implement them within their jurisdiction. An international tribunal may be a useful complement to be established in a separate associated protocol at a later stage.

One of the hurdles in this and other similar models is the need to achieve a consensus on the content of the standards or grounds of liability (i.e., a definition of the offences or violations that will give rise to legal responsibility), and also on the kind of corporate legal liability (civil, criminal or administrative) that the treaty will include. On this latter issue, the Optional Protocol on the sale of children as well as most other conventions accepting legal liability for corporations do so in an eclectic way: contemplating the various ways in which legal liability for corporations can be practised at the domestic level. Those ways are civil (giving rise to compensation for material and moral damages), criminal (aimed at the prosecution of criminal offences in defence of societal values and interest) or administrative (giving rise to fines and other penalties imposed by administrative authorities for lack of respect for administrative regulations) liability.

11.3   Concluding Remarks

International treaties can establish norms and standards of conduct applicable to business corporations as long as the intention of the parties to the treaty to do so is clear and becomes explicit in the text of the treaty. By doing so, the prospective treaty on transnational corporations and other business enterprises would not be moving away from the current paradigm of international law (sometimes described as 'state-centred') which, some may argue, already presents some instances of 'direct' obligations for private actors. However, a mere set of definitions of corporate obligations without at the same time setting out a system for their implementation and/or enforcement will be no more effective than

---

[36] See Chapter 16 by Darcy in this volume.

a declaratory statement and will not overcome some of the shortcomings that the UN Guiding Principles are said to present. If a declaratory statement is intended, the most appropriate instrument for that purpose is not a legally binding instrument but a declaratory one. Yet, if what is pursued is to create a system of legal accountability of corporations and better access to remedies for the victims of corporate abuse, then much more attention needs to be paid to the state-based bodies and mechanisms that will be the enforcement mechanisms.

Creating rights and obligations by treaty can only be possible if it is seen as responding to the needs of the international community. The need for States to create 'direct' international obligations for corporations in any of its forms and combinations still must be demonstrated. One of the arguments in favour of 'direct' obligations for corporations is the perception that very often States fail or are unable duly to discharge their duty to protect human rights under international law, leaving corporations that violate human rights immune from sanction. This is especially so in situations of conflict or weak governance, but even developed economies with powerful functioning state institutions are perceived as 'captured' by business interests. Existing instruments such as the Guiding Principles on business and human rights, relying on the foundational principle that the State has a duty to protect, are said to have failed in hard cases where business has no interest in respecting rights.[37] According to this argument, imposing obligations directly onto corporations without the intermediation of the national State would solve the problem. However, the proponents of this argument also fail to offer an option that will go beyond a mere 'declaratory' instrument without effective implementation. It is also argued that the enormous economic and political power of business corporations[38] and the effects of globalization make state structures that are expected to regulate and monitor business conduct – ensuring their respect for human rights – ineffective in practice. Governments and even international organizations are 'captured' by corporate interests. In this context, doing away with the 'corrupt' and 'inefficient' State by imposing direct obligations on corporations seems to be the solution. However, it is hardly an argument in favour of human rights to weaken or do away with the need for a key instrument for their

---

[37] Deva, 'Multinationals, Move beyond the "State-Centric" Conception', n. 4.
[38] See written submissions by several NGOs to the first session of the Open-Ended Intergovernmental Working Group at: www.ohchr.org/EN/HRBodies/HRC/WGTransCorp/Session1/Pages/WrittenContributions.aspx.

protection, which is the democratic State based on rule of law principles and representing and working for the public good.

New international mechanisms such as an international criminal, civil or human rights tribunal for corporations – although in itself not a bad idea – are difficult to create, at least in the short term, and are potentially very costly and slow. It would also be erroneous to believe that the solution to all problems of domestic protection of human rights against corporate abuse lies with an international body. It seems difficult to escape from the conclusion that state-based mechanisms will have to be given a prominent role in the implementation and enforcement of those internationally defined 'direct' obligations for corporations, if such is the choice finally made, and therefore the State as such will continue to play its intermediary role. This is so even in the case where an international court or tribunal with jurisdiction over corporations is put in place. The vast majority of existing international courts operate under principles that grant national law and States the primary role. Even the International Criminal Court operates under the principle of complementarity (article 17 of the Rome Statute), whereby the Court will assume jurisdiction only when the State is unable or unwilling to do so, or under the other cases foreseen in the Rome Statute. To dispense with the State as the primary bearer of human rights obligations seems not only unrealistic but may also be counterproductive to the very final end of the treaty process: to enhance the protection of human rights against corporate abuses. Rather than outright dismissal, the State needs to be reinforced with additional tools to perform its protective functions, including expanded jurisdiction and international legal cooperation. At the same time, safeguards need to be put in place within the State that counteract corruption and undue influence from corporate interests, and which strengthen its democratic and rule of law roots.

Regulatory Obligations in a Complex World

States' Extraterritorial Obligations Related to Business and Human Rights

SIGRUN SKOGLY

12.1 Introduction

The discourse on business and human rights (BHR) has developed over the past two to three decades with changing emphases: from no link between the two at all, through the concepts of corporate social responsibility with voluntary standards and processes, to calls for direct responsibility for human rights violations by businesses themselves, and states' obligations to protect individuals from infringement by private entities such as corporations. Throughout these debates, there are a number of recurring themes in terms of the role of the state and their obligations. The traditional human rights approaches negate a direct role of business in human rights violations, as per definition, only states are obligation holders. Furthermore, this tradition also focuses on a one-dimensional approach to human rights obligations where the *domestic* state is the only possible human rights obligations holder within its territory. Consequently, this tradition has hampered a more nuanced approach to obligations in a complex, globalized world.

In recent years, there has been increased debate about the limitations of this one-dimensional approach to human rights obligations, and it should be emphasized that this debate has not come about because of the 2014 UN Human Rights Council's resolution to start the drafting process of a legally binding international instrument on BHR.[1] Over the past few decades, human rights lawyers, practitioners, international institutions

---

[1] Human Rights Council, 'Elaboration of an International Legally Binding Instrument on Transnational Corporations and Other Business Enterprises with respect to Human Rights', A/HRC/Res/26/9 (25 June 2014).

and non-governmental organizations (NGOs) have repeatedly argued for more diverse approaches to human rights obligations, and the time may now have come to find ways to address this through binding international law provisions.

This diverse attention to the content of human rights obligations has addressed several different aspects, such as whether non-state actors may have human rights obligations, and how this relates to state obligations; whether human rights obligations are exclusive to one state at the time, or whether they can be combined in some concept of shared or joint obligations with other actors (including other states); whether state obligations are restricted to its domestic territory or they go beyond this geographical sphere; and finally whether states can be complicit in human rights violations committed by other states or other non-state actors.

Amongst these varied approaches to the subjects and the content of obligations, a strong and growing recognition that human rights obligations are not necessarily confined to a state's territory has emerged.[2] This work has challenged the notion of territorial confinement of obligations, and is commonly labelled as extraterritorial human rights obligations.[3] A major milestone in this work was the adoption of the Maastricht Principles on States' Extraterritorial Obligations in the Area of Economic, Social and Cultural Rights (Maastricht Principles) in September 2011.[4] However,

---

[2] There is a rapidly growing literature in this field, but some of the central contributions can be mentioned: M. Gibney, K. Tomasevski and J. Vedsted-Hansen, 'Transnational State Responsibility for Violations of Human Rights' (1999) 12 *Harvard Human Rights Journal* 267; F. Coomans and M. T. Kamminga, *Extraterritorial Application of Human Rights Treaties* (Intersentia, 2004); S. Skogly, *Beyond National Borders: States' Human Rights Obligations in International Cooperation* (Intersentia, 2006); R. Wilde, 'Legal "Black Hole"? Extraterritorial State Action and International Treaty Law on Civil and Political Rights' (2005) 26 *Michigan Journal of International Law* 739; M. Salomon, *Global Responsibility for Human Rights: World Poverty and the Development of International Law* (Oxford University Press, 2007); R. McCorquodale and P. Simons, 'Responsibility Beyond Borders: State Responsibility for Extraterritorial Violations by Corporations of International Human Rights Law' (2007) 40 *Modern Law Review* 598; M. Gondek, *The Reach of Human Rights in a Globalizing World: Extraterritorial Application of Human Rights Treaties* (Intersentia, 2009); M. Gibney and S. Skogly (eds.), *Universal Human Rights and Extraterritorial Obligations* (University of Pennsylvania Press, 2010); M. Langford et al., *Global Justice, State Duties: The Extra-Territorial Scope of Economic, Social and Cultural Rights in International Law* (Cambridge University Press, 2013).

[3] For a critical analysis of the terminology used in debates regarding extraterritorial human rights obligations, see M. Gibney, 'On Terminology: Extraterritorial Obligations' in Langford et al., n. 2.

[4] Maastricht Principles on Extraterritorial Obligations of States in the Area of Economic, Social and Cultural Rights (September 2011), www.etoconsortium.org/

while the concept of extraterritorial obligations (ETOs) is gaining increasing interest and acceptance in regional human rights courts[5] and the UN human rights mechanisms,[6] the general recognition of such human rights obligations among states is still missing.

In other areas of international law, the right and obligation to regulate the conduct of agents of the state (and also private actors) when they act extraterritorially is often recognized. For example, Section 72 of the United Kingdom's Sexual Offences Act (2003) makes it a criminal offence to engage in sexual activity with a person under the age of 16 within and outside the borders of England, Wales and Northern Ireland.[7] Furthermore, in compliance with the United Nations Convention for the Suppression of Financing of Terrorism 1999, many countries have passed legislation to enable a pursuit of individuals and institutions that fund terrorism. For instance, the United States has,

> in conjunction with other initiatives, enacted a substantial body of post 9/11 laws and regulations that define new crimes, create new civil causes of action, expand the jurisdictional reach of U.S. laws, and enhance the authority of U.S. prosecutors to target, investigate, and prosecute domestic and foreign individuals, financial institutions, and other entities.[8]

nc/en/main-navigation/library/maastricht-principles/?tx_drblob_pi1%5BdownloadUid %5D=23 (last accessed 13 January 2017) (Maastricht Principles).

[5] There is a rapidly growing body of case law that concerns extraterritorial obligations in regional human rights courts. Some of the key cases are: *Georgia v. Russian Federation* [2008] ICJ 140; *Loizidou v. Turkey* [1995] ECHR 10; *Bankovic and others v. Belgium and others* [2001] ECHR 890; Case 9903 *Rafael Ferrer-Mazorra et al. v. United States* [2001] IACHR 51/01; *Al-Skeini and Others v. United Kingdom*, Application no. 55721/07 [2011] ECHR 1093 (7 July 2011); *Armando Alejandre Jr. and Others v. Cuba ('Brothers to the Rescue')*, Inter-American Commission of Human Rights, report No. 86/99, case no. 11.589 (29 September 1999).

[6] The Global Initiative for Economic, Social and Cultural Rights, 'Working Paper Human Rights Law Sources: UN Pronouncements on Extra-Territorial Obligations Concluding Observations General Comments and Recommendations Special Procedures UPR Recommendations' (November 2015), http://globalinitiative-escr.org/wp-content/ uploads/2015/11/151027-Human-Rights-Law-Sources-ETOs.pdf (last accessed 13 January 2017). See also CESCR, 'General Comment No. 24 on State Obligations under the International Covenant on Economic, Social and Cultural Rights in the Context of Business Activities' (23 June 2017).

[7] Sexual Offences Act 2003 (UK).

[8] A. Lakatos and J. Blöchliger, 'The Extraterritorial Reach of U.S. Anti-Terrorist Finance Laws' (2009), www.mayerbrown.com/files/Publication/bc828278-4516-41ea-bc07- 5cbcf909be56/Presentation/PublicationAttachment/6746390a-c4f7-46fe-afb3- 0a9b3cc7cccb/05_Lakatos_Bloechliger.pdf (last accessed 13 January 2017).

Similarly, in environmental law, it is now generally accepted that the obligation to cause 'no harm' in territories of another state has gained the status of customary international law and that states need to ensure that activities within their territories do not have damaging effect outside their borders.[9] Consequently, the application of ETOs within the sphere of BHR is nothing new in international law, but rather an extension of practices currently being undertaken in other areas.

Following the Human Rights Council's resolution to start the work on the drafting of a potential BHR treaty, the debates on the content and subjects of obligations have moved one step forward, and international human rights lawyers now find themselves in a situation where they have to respond to the challenges to the traditional approach to human rights obligations, and accept that the world has changed rapidly since the drafting of the international covenants on human rights in the 1950s and 1960s. But this is not merely a challenge; it is also an opportunity to move international human rights law forward. Many human rights lawyers have been frustrated by the narrow approach in traditional human rights law, and there has been a concern that developments in the international community and international relations are changing the reality within which human rights are being enjoyed or violated, and without changes to our understanding of obligations, human rights law may become less relevant for the victims of human rights. In her important contribution to the human rights obligations discourse, Margot Salomon argues that 'the proper regulation of non-state actors, notably transnational corporations (TNCs), [...] requires revisiting international standards and mechanisms to ensure that their activities are consistent with human rights',[10] and that doing so is necessary 'if human rights law is to remain relevant'.[11]

Regarding BHR, and in particular about the role of the TNC's 'home' state,[12] there has been much debate as to the current state of obligations. Those supporting a broader approach to human rights obligations reflecting the globalized world in the twenty-first century argue that current international human rights law already contain existing ETOs in this

---

[9] M. Jervan, 'The Prohibition of Transboundary Environmental Harm. An Analysis of the Contribution of the International Court of Justice to the Development of the No-harm Rule' (25 August 2014), 14–17, https://papers.ssrn.com/sol3/papers.cfm?abstract_id=2486421 (last accessed 13 January 2017).

[10] Salomon, n. 2, 11.   [11] *Ibid.*, 12.

[12] The term 'home state' will be used to indicate the state where the TNC 'or its parent or controlling company, has its centre of activity, is registered or domiciled, or has its main place of business or substantial business activities'. Maastricht Principles, n. 4, Principle 25.

field.[13] However, others have firmly argued that 'at present States are not generally required under international human rights law to regulate the extraterritorial activities of businesses domiciled in their territory and/or jurisdiction'.[14] The opportunity now being presented to the international community is not only to deal with the direct responsibility of businesses with regard to international human rights standards, but equally to clarify the role of the state as an obligation holder when regulating business activities within and beyond their borders.

In this chapter, I will address the new initiative of negotiating a BHR treaty from the perspective of states' ETOs. I will start with a consideration as to why states' ETOs are relevant for the treaty initiative, and how they manifest themselves in relationship to business enterprises. I will then examine where the debate on ETOs stands today and some of the major oppositions to such state obligations in the sphere of human rights. This chapter will explore the content of the obligation to regulate extraterritorially and then deal with some of the difficulties that may be encountered when attempting to get acceptance for the obligation to regulate.

12.2   Why State Regulation of Transnational Corporations?

In June 2014, the Human Rights Council adopted two resolutions concerning BHR: Resolution 26/9 established an open-ended intergovernmental working group to negotiate a legally binding international instrument on BHR, while Resolution 26/22 extended the mandate of the Working Group on Business and Human Rights. However, neither of these resolutions refers to ETOs of states to regulate the conduct of business outside their borders. It is worth noting though that the preamble to Resolution 26/9 emphasized that '. . .. *the obligations and primary responsibility* to promote and protect human rights and fundamental freedoms *lie with the State*, and that States must protect against human rights abuse *within their territory and/or jurisdiction*

---

[13] Principles 24 of the 'Maastricht Principles (n. 4), for instance, provides: 'All States must take necessary measures to ensure that non-State actors which they are in a position to regulate, as set out in Principle 25, such as private individuals and organisations, and transnational corporations and other business enterprises, do not nullify or impair the enjoyment of economic, social and cultural rights.'

[14] Human Rights Council, 'Guiding Principles on Business and Human Rights: Implementing the United Nations "Protect, Respect and Remedy" Framework', A/HRC/17/31 (21 March 2011), Commentary to Principle 2.

by third parties, including transnational corporations'.[15] Furthermore, the Preamble to Resolution 26/22 confirmed that:

> *policies and proper regulation,* including through national legislation, of transnational corporations and other business enterprises and their responsible operation can contribute to the promotion, protection and fulfilment of and respect for human rights and assist in channelling the benefits of business towards contributing to the enjoyment of human rights and fundamental freedoms.[16]

What these two quotes show is the recognition that states have obligations to promote human rights and protect against violations by third parties, within their territory and/or jurisdiction, and that one way in which this can be done is through proper regulation. It is clear that Resolution 26/9 confirms that the concepts of 'territory' and 'jurisdiction' are not considered synonymous or necessarily to be fully overlapping. This is essential in a discussion on ETOs. Resolution 26/22 confirms the role of regulation to address the human rights impacts of TNCs activities.

However, why do we need regulation beyond borders and compliance with ETOs in this context? The International Chamber of Commerce has rightly pointed out that 'a "fundamental problem" in establishing accountability for corporate abuses is the state's failure to meet obligations under current international human rights law, and lack of enforcement of domestic laws.'[17] The sentiment in this quote is true: if all states managed to meet their obligations under current international human rights law, we would not be discussing this issue at all. In other words, international human rights law requires states to regulate the conduct of public and private entities within their territory to the extent that all human rights for all individuals are protected. This is the essence of the obligation to protect, which is generally accepted in the human rights community.[18] However, the reality is that many states are unwilling or unable to implement the

---

[15] Emphasis added.   [16] Emphasis added.

[17] The International Organisation of Employers (IOE), the International Chamber of Commerce (ICC) and the Business and Industry Advisory Committee (BIAC), 'Joint IOE-ICC-BIAC Comments on the Draft Guiding Principles' (January 26, 2011), https://business-humanrights.org/sites/default/files/media/documents/ruggie/ioe-icc-biac-comments-on-guiding-principles-26-jan-2011.pdf (last accessed 13 January 2017), quoted in N. R. Tuttle, 'Human Rights Council Resolutions 26/9 and 26/22: Towards Corporate Accountability?' (2015) 19 (20) *American Society of International Law: Insight* (3 September 2015), www.asil.org/insights/volume/19/issue/20/human-rights-council-reso lutions-269-and-2622-towards-corporate (last accessed 13 January 2017).

[18] Both the UN Human Rights Committee and the UN Committee on Economic, Social and Cultural Rights confirm this obligation. The Human Rights Committee's General

standards to which they have agreed by ratifying international human rights treaties. Those unable tend to be the states that struggle with lack of resources to carry out the implementation; those unwilling are the states that have the opportunity to protect human rights, but fail to do so, either because of domestic structural opposition or because priorities other than human rights take precedence in the domestic political struggle. Yet, while the tripartite classification of obligations (the obligation to protect being the 'middle' one) is now generally accepted in the domestic setting, there is still opposition to this typology of obligations being applied to activities over which states have influence, but which take place outside their territory. Thus, the concept of 'unwillingness' may also extend to states that are home states to TNCs engaging in business practices abroad, but who fail to regulate the conduct of these TNCs for practices which would not be acceptable at home. For instance, the home state of a TNC producing garments regulates against employing children under the age of 16 when they operate within the home state, but the same state tacitly (due to lack of regulation) accepts that the same company employ 11-year-olds abroad. Thus, it is the failure of states to implement the agreed human rights standards that necessitates further attention to regulation of business operations outside their respective territories.

12.3   Extraterritorial Obligations and Regulation of Business

The question of states' extraterritorial human rights obligations has received considerable attention in recent years, and this reflects a growing practical concern over the effects of activities of states and of actors over which states exercise jurisdiction and/or control outside their own borders. It also reflects a philosophical return to the concept of *universal*

Comment No. 31 provides that 'the positive obligations on States Parties to ensure Covenant rights will only be fully discharged if individuals are protected by the State, not just against violations of Covenant rights by its agents, but also against acts committed by private persons or entities that would impair the enjoyment of Covenant rights in so far as they are amenable to application between private persons or entities.' UN Human Rights Committee, 'The Nature of the General Legal Obligation Imposed on States Parties to the Covenant', CCPR/C/21/Rev.1/Add.13 (26 May 2004), para. 8. The Committee on Economic, Social and Cultural Rights' General Comment No. 12 provides: 'The right to adequate food, like any other human right, imposes three types or levels of obligations on States parties: the obligations to *respect*, to *protect* and to *fulfil* [. . .] The obligation to protect requires measures by the State to ensure that enterprises or individuals do not deprive individuals of their access to adequate food.' UN Committee on Economic, Social and Cultural Rights, 'General Comment No. 12 Right to Adequate Food as a Human Right', E/C.12/1999/5 (12 May 1999), para. 15.

human rights, and recognition that such universal human rights are an illusion if obligations are considered to be only territorial.[19] In the words of Mark Gibney, 'Universality means, quite simply, [. . ..] that while states are responsible for the human rights violations they carry out within their own domestic borders, they can also be responsible for violating human rights outside their own borders.'[20] However, while the attention has been growing regarding states' ETOs for their own conduct,[21] and indeed to regulate the conduct of TNCs, no explicit international human rights law exists which imposes direct liability on TNCs for human rights violations.[22] The developments that have come about in the last few years include significant attention to and a growing recognition of extraterritorial human rights obligations on the part of states by academics, NGOs, the regional and UN human rights systems, and also states themselves.[23]

Regional courts, most notably the European Court of Human Rights (ECtHR) and the Inter-American Court of Human Rights, are increasingly hearing cases that relate to states' activities internationally, including control of their agents when acting abroad. These decisions tend to focus on civil and political human rights due to the conventional mandates of these courts. Furthermore, the Maastricht Principles – which according to the preamble are 'drawn from international law and aim to clarify the content of extraterritorial States obligations to realize economic, social and cultural rights' – are increasingly being used by international human rights bodies, such as the UN human rights committees

---

[19] S. Skogly, 'Extraterritoriality: Universal Human Rights without Universal Obligations' in S. Joseph and A. McBeth (eds.), *Research Handbook on International Human Rights Law* (Edward Elgar, 2010); M. Gibney, *International Human Rights Law: Returning to Universal Principles*, 2nd edn. (Rowman and Littlefield, 2015), 2.

[20] Gibney, *Returning to Universal Principles, ibid.*

[21] While the case law on extraterritorial obligations of states is growing, most of the cases relate to states' behaviour in other states' territory either through military occupation, military or police activity, or through their own agents. For a review of case law and this predominance of attention to these kinds of operations, see G. O. Cuinn and S. Skogly, 'Understanding Human Rights Obligations of States Engaged in Public Activity Overseas: The Case of Transnational Education' (2016) 20 *International Human Rights Journal* 761.

[22] McCorquodale and Simons, n. 2, 599.

[23] In Germany and the Netherlands, an Independent Complaint Mechanism has been set up to address environmental, social and related issues arising from business activities by German and Dutch companies requiring them to establish and administer appropriate mechanisms to address project-related complaints from affected communities. For further information, see Deutsche Investitions- und Entwicklungsgesellschaft mbH (DEG), 'Independent Complaints Mechanism DEG' (February 2014), www.deginvest.de/DEG-Documents-in-English/About-DEG/Responsibility/DEG_Complaints-Mechanism_2014_05.pdf (last accessed 13 January 2017).

and special rapporteurs.[24] While focused on economic, social and cultural rights, the Maastricht Principles emphasize that 'All States have obligations to respect, protect and fulfil human rights, including civil, cultural, economic, political and social rights, both within their territories and extraterritorially'.[25]

Before moving into the specific discussion as to what states ETOs are or should be in terms of regulation of TNCs, the debate on the existence of extraterritorial human rights obligations should be visited to address some of the concerns of those that are opposed to this idea. These concerns relate to the concepts of sovereignty, jurisdiction and universalism/neo-colonialism.

12.3.1   Sovereignty

The concept of sovereignty is fundamental in international relations and in international law. In its basic content, sovereignty implies political independence and territorial integrity as recognized in Article 2 of the United Nations Charter (UN Charter).[26] In terms of the functioning of international law, the principle confirms that states are able to accept freely international law obligations through ratification of treaties or tacit acceptance of customary law, and that agreements or membership in international organizations that may reduce a state's sovereignty shall be entered into on a voluntary basis. However, as the purpose of international law is to regulate the conduct between and among states, the content and functioning of international law will inevitably have an effect on a state's ability to exercise its sovereignty with respect to the substantive content of the treaties entered into and customary law accepted and the obligations contained therein.

International human rights law in its early days, following the adoption of the UN Charter, challenged traditional notions of sovereignty. States had by that time become accustomed to cooperating with each other through treaties to carry out their international affairs. However,

---

[24] For a compilation of references to the Maastricht Principles and extraterritorial obligations by UN institutions, see Global Initiative for Economic, Social and Cultural Rights, *Human Rights Law Sources*, n. 6.

[25] Maastricht Principles, n. 4, Principle 3.

[26] Article 2(7) of the UN Charter provides: 'Nothing contained in the present Charter shall authorize the United Nations to intervene in matters which are essentially within the domestic jurisdiction of any state or shall require the Members to submit such matters to settlement under the present Charter; but this principle shall not prejudice the application of enforcement measures under Chapter VII.'

the way in which each state treated its citizens and residents domestically was, before the Second World War, considered to be the sole domain for the domestic authorities. The adoption of the UN Charter, the Universal Declaration on Human Rights and subsequent human rights treaties eroded the full sovereignty in this regard, and it has become accepted that human rights law sets limits for a state's legitimate treatment of its own population. In essence, the way in which states treat their own population is now an issue of legitimate international concern.[27]

The challenge to sovereignty on the basis of ETOs is different though. What is being considered here is the effects on human rights enjoyment of individuals of one state's action or omission within the territory of another state, and arguments are put forward that this may infringe upon the other state's ('host state') sovereignty. If state A regulates the conduct of a corporation (corporation Z) under its jurisdiction when that corporation operates in state B, the concern is that this will infringe upon the sovereignty of state B. The argument is that state B should be able to accept whatever behaviour of corporation Z no matter how it treats its employees, for instance, and that this is a consequence of state B's sovereignty. Thus, while it is now generally accepted that the international community (and indeed foreign states) has a legitimate interest in the way in which a state treats its own citizens, requiring certain behaviour by TNCs to ensure that they do not breach international human rights standards when operating in other states is still seen to be a threat to the sovereignty of that foreign state. Writing about ETOs generally, Gibney posits that 'now it is more likely that countries will be able to hide behind the sovereignty of another state in order to remove themselves from any and all responsibility in assisting an outlaw state'.[28] Translated into the topic of concern for this chapter, it would imply that states 'hide behind the sovereignty of another state' in order to remove themselves from any and all responsibility regarding the human rights effect of the actions or omissions of TNCs over which they have regulatory power. States are concerned that by regulating the conduct of private parties (whether individuals or corporations) when they act within the territory of another state, they somehow breach the sovereignty of that state. While a legitimate consideration, the conclusion that states

---

[27] W. M. Reisman, 'Sovereignty and Human Rights in Contemporary International Law' (1990) 84 *The American Journal of International Law*, 866 at 869.

[28] Gibney, *Returning to Universal Principles*, n. 19, 2.

should not regulate the conduct of such actors fails to take into account several aspects of these relationships.

First, the home state of the TNC is not being asked to direct the host state as to how to legislate or carry out policies. The home state only deals with the conduct of the entity over which it has regulatory control. Thus, it is the effect of the conduct of the TNC that is in question,[29] rather than the conduct of the host state. Indirectly, it could be seen as a criticism of the host state as such regulation by the home state could be considered to be an implicit criticism of the way the host state fails to control the conduct within their territory.

However, this leads to the second point: if the way in which a state treats its own citizens is now a legitimate human rights concern for other states and the international community generally, then it would surely be a legitimate concern for any state to regulate the behaviour of the TNCs under its control, whether it operates within or outside its borders. At the end of the day, the concern is for the welfare and indeed the rights of individuals in that other state – a legitimate concern – and not breaching sovereignty.

Third, in a number of other areas of international law, states accept that treaties and agreements contain significant clauses concerning domestic regulation and conduct. This is clearly the case for international trade agreements, international agreements in the area of the environment, and treaties concerning terrorism. As detailed in introduction to this chapter, a number of areas of international concern now regularly accept that regulation of conduct by private parties and agents of the state across borders is necessary to comply with international law obligations. Somehow, there seems to be more resistance to introducing international standards regarding human rights regulation into bilateral and multilateral agreements than is the case for other areas of international cooperation.[30]

---

[29] O. De Schutter et al., 'Commentary to the Maastricht Principles on Extraterritorial Obligations of States in the Area of Economic, Social and Cultural Rights' (Maastricht Commentary) (2012) 34 *Human Rights Quarterly* 1084. The Maastricht Commentary provides that an 'approach to regulating the conduct of transitional corporations consists of a state imposing on a parent corporation domiciled in that state an obligation to comply with certain norms wherever they operate (i.e., even if they operate in other countries) or an obligation to impose compliance with such norms on the different entities they control (their subsidiaries, or even in certain cases their business partners)'. *Ibid.* at 1141.

[30] Ming Du discusses how the WTO accepts limitations to trade based on 'public morals', when the same is not the case for concerns for human rights. M. Du, 'Permitting Moral

12.3.2   The Question of Jurisdiction

In many of the debates on ETOs, attention is given to the concept of jurisdiction. The question of jurisdiction has often produced a 'doctrinal bar' against the acceptance of extraterritorial human rights obligations, while at the same time jurisdiction has on occasion been the catalyst for 'permissive or even prescriptive exercise of extraterritorial conduct'.[31] This discussion has its origins in the questions of sovereignty as indicated above, but also in the wording in some international human rights treaties that refer to jurisdiction as one of the qualifications for the reach of obligations. For example, Article 2(1) of the International Covenant on Civil and Political Rights (ICCPR) stipulates that 'Each State Party to the present Covenant undertakes to respect and to ensure to all individuals *within its territory and subject to its jurisdiction* the rights recognized in the present Covenant'; Article 1 of the European Convention on Human Rights prescribes that 'The High Contracting Parties shall secure to *everyone within their jurisdiction* the rights and freedoms defined in Section I of this Convention'; and Article 1 of the American Convention on Human Rights provides that 'The States Parties to this Convention undertake to respect the rights and freedoms recognized herein and to ensure to *all persons subject to their jurisdiction* the free and full exercise of those rights and freedoms'.[32]

We see that the reference to jurisdiction has been used in all these three human rights treaties, while the reference to territory can only be found in the ICCPR. The African Charter on Human and Peoples' Rights does not contain any reference to territory or jurisdiction, and this is also the case for the International Covenant on Economic, Social and Cultural Rights (ICESCR).[33]

It is outside the scope of this chapter to give a detailed account of the debates that have taken place regarding the understanding of jurisdiction related to extraterritorial human rights obligations – this has been thoroughly done elsewhere.[34] However, it should be noted that the

---

Imperialism? The Public Morals Exception to Free Trade at the Bar of the World Trade Organization' (2016) 50 *Journal of World Trade*, 675.

[31] De Schutter et al., 'Maastricht Commentary', n. 29, 1105.

[32] Emphasis added in all quotes.

[33] It is worth noting that the ICESCR specifically refers to states parties' obligations to 'take steps, individually and through international assistance and co-operation . . .. to achieving progressively the full realization of the rights recognized in the present Covenant . . ..' International Covenant on Economic, Social and Cultural Rights, art. 2(1).

[34] See in particular section II 'Jurisdiction' in Langford et al., n. 2.

ECtHR has dealt with these issues in a number of prominent cases,[35] and this is also the case for the Inter-American Commission and Court on Human Rights,[36] and the UN Human Rights Committee.[37] Based on this jurisprudence, it is submitted that concepts of 'territory' and 'jurisdiction' are now recognized to be different and not necessarily overlapping. The ECtHR has determined that in exceptional circumstances the reach of the European Convention can go beyond the geographic area covered by the territories of the Contracting States.[38] This is also the case for the other judicial bodies mentioned.[39] The perceived change in the approach to what is covered by jurisdiction is a reflection of the more complex world within which we live, and where states' actions and omissions may have further ramifications outside their territorial borders than what has traditionally been the case in international law. An understanding of jurisdiction that includes

---

[35] See *Georgia v. Russian Federation* [2008] ICJ 140; *Loizidou v. Turkey* [1995] ECHR 10; *Bankovic and others v. Belgium and others* [2001] ECHR 890; *Issa v. Turkey* App No 31821/96 [2004] ECHR 629 Case 9903 *Rafael Ferrer-Mazorra et al. v. United States* [2001] IACHR 51/01.

[36] See, for instance, Case 9903 *Rafael Ferrer-Mazorra et al. v. United States* [2001] IACHR 51/01; *Armando Alejandre Jr. and Others v. Cuba ('Brothers to the Rescue')* Inter-American Commission of Human Rights, report No. 86/99, case no. 11.589 (29 September 1999).

[37] One of the first cases before the UN Human Rights Committee where the territoriality of jurisdiction was rejected was *Lopez Burgos v. Uruguay* (52/79) A/36/40, 184.

[38] *Bankovic*, n. 5, para. 71.

[39] In the *Coard case* the Inter-American Commission on human rights held:

> under certain circumstances, the exercise of its jurisdiction over acts with an extraterritorial locus will not only be consistent with but required by the norms which pertain. The fundamental rights of the individual are proclaimed in the Americas on the basis of the principles of equality and non-discrimination – "without distinction as to race, nationality, creed or sex". Given that individual rights inhere simply by virtue of a person's humanity, each American State is obliged to uphold the protected rights of any person subject to its jurisdiction. While this most commonly refers to persons within a state's territory, it may, under given circumstances, refer to conduct with an extraterritorial locus where the person concerned is present in the territory of one state, but subject to the control of another state – usually through the acts of the latter's agents abroad. In principle, the inquiry turns not on the presumed victim's nationality or presence within a particular geographic area, but on whether, under the specific circumstances, the State observed the rights of a person subject to its authority and control.

> *Coard et al. v. United States*, Case 10.951, Report No 109/99 (29 September 1999), Inter-Am.C.H.R; para. 37.

control not only over territory but also of persons (natural as well as legal) is now gaining recognition.[40]

Part of the complexity related to jurisdiction that has hampered the acceptance of ETOs is the division between domestic jurisdiction which is compulsory for governments and permissible extraterritorial jurisdiction (e.g., where states may choose to adopt extraterritorial legislation, such as extending criminal responsibility).[41] In terms of the case-law on ETOs, courts have generally accepted that, apart from exceptional circumstances, states' jurisdiction is mainly territorial: when acting outside their borders directly or indirectly, they are not within the jurisdiction as defined by the various treaties (this has in particular been the stance taken by the ECtHR), and the courts lose their jurisdiction to hear such cases. The critics of this approach argue that once states' actions have effect outside their territory, these actions (or indeed omissions) represent an exercise of the state's jurisdiction. This reflects what Gondek refers to as the 'most common meaning of jurisdiction by states [which] concerns the scope of competence of a state, delimited by international law, to regulate the conduct of physical and legal persons, and to enforce such regulation'.[42]

The Maastricht Principles contain the following definition of the 'scope of jurisdiction' in the context of extraterritorial human rights obligations:

A State has obligations to respect, protect and fulfil economic, social and cultural rights in any of the following:

a) situations over which it exercises authority or effective control, whether or not such control is exercised in accordance with international law;
b) situations over which State acts or omissions bring about foreseeable effects on the enjoyment of economic, social and cultural rights, whether within or outside its territory;
c) situations in which the State, acting separately or jointly, whether through its executive, legislative or judicial branches, is in a position to exercise decisive influence or to take measures to realize

---

[40] In *Al-Skeini*, the Court distinguished between 'state agent and control' over persons on the one hand, and 'effective control over an area' on the other. *Al-Skeini and Others v. The United Kingdom*, Application no. 55721/07 [2011] ECHR 1093 (7 July 2011), paras. 133 and 138. For a thorough discussion on the changes in approach to jurisdiction through the case law of the ECtHR, see Cuinn and Skogly, n. 21.

[41] S. Lagoutte, 'New Challenges Facing States within the Field of Human Rights and Business' (2015) 33 *Nordic Journal of Human Rights* 176.

[42] Gondek, n. 2, 47 (emphasis in original).

economic, social and cultural rights extraterritorially in accordance with international law.[43]

This passage from the Maastricht Principles emphasizes that jurisdiction relates to a state's authority or effective control, where the state's acts or omissions bring about foreseeable effects, and situations where the state may exercise decisive influence. Referring to the work of the Human Rights Committee in its interpretation of the ICCPR, the commentary to the Maastricht Principles notes:

> For the purpose of defining applicability of the Covenant, the notion of jurisdiction refers to the relationship between the individual and the state in connection with a violation of human rights, wherever it occurred, so that acts of states that take place or produce effects outside of the national territory may be deemed to fall within the jurisdiction of the state concerned.[44]

Thus, practice shows that there is now a far more nuanced approach to jurisdiction than a straight overlap between a state's territory and its jurisdiction. Indeed, in his individual opinion submitted in the *Lopez Burgos v. Uruguay* case,[45] Mr Tomuchat held:

> To construe the words 'within its territory' pursuant to their strict literal meaning as excluding any responsibility for conduct occurring beyond the national boundaries would, however, lead to utterly absurd results. The formula was intended to take care of objective difficulties which might impede the implementation of the Covenant in specific situations. Thus, a State party is normally unable to ensure the effective enjoyment of the rights under the Covenant to its citizens abroad, having at its disposal only the tools of diplomatic protection with their limited potential. [. . .] Never was it envisaged, however, to grant States parties unfettered discretionary power to carry out wilful and deliberate attacks against the freedom and personal integrity against their citizens living abroad.[46]

This observation refers to a state's obligation to its citizens abroad, as this was the focus in the relevant case (a Uruguayan citizen being kidnapped by Uruguayan security forces in Argentina and subsequently brought

---

[43] Maastricht Principles, n. 4, Principle 9. Please note that the Principles focus on economic, social and cultural rights, hence the reference in the principle.

[44] De Schutter et al., 'Maastricht Commentary', n. 29, 1106.

[45] *Sergio Euben Lopez Burgos v. Uruguay*, Communication No. R.12/52, U.N. Doc. Supp. No. 40 (A/36/40) at 176 (1981).

[46] *Ibid.*, Individual opinion submitted by a member of the Human Rights Committee under rule 94 (3) of the Committee's provisional rules of procedure; Communication No. R.12/52; Appendix.

back to Uruguay and tortured). However, almost 40 years after this individual opinion was delivered, it would be reasonable to hold that the approach to jurisdiction as expressed by Tomuchat would not only relate to the treatment of a state's citizens living abroad, but indeed also the citizens of other states. It is important to emphasize the part of the quote that relates to the practical difficulties of implementing the ICCPR abroad, and that this was seen as the main reason for the limitation in the Covenant. It is submitted that when a state is in a position to exercise jurisdiction outside its own borders (without breaching the sovereignty of another state), there is no jurisdictional bar against doing so.[47]

12.3.3 Neo-Colonialism and Universalism

The final areas of concern for those that are hesitant to the concept of ETOs moves us out of the sphere of international law and into international relations, namely, the concern that a regulation of TNCs' behaviour when operating outside of industrialized countries can be conceived of as imperialism or neo-colonialism. More specifically, the argument is that Western states (or other industrialized states) will impose their standards for treatment of individuals onto other states. This represents a dictation of moral/ ethical standards reflecting a Western individualistic ideology which may be different or alien to other cultures. The objection to ETOs on this ground represents more of an ideological opposition than the question of

---

[47] The Inter-American Commission has taken a similar view in several cases. For instance, in the *Armando Alejandre v. Cuba*, where the Cuban military had shot down two civilian aircrafts in international territory, the Commission held:

> It should be specified, however, that under certain circumstances the Commission is competent to consider reports alleging that agents of an OAS member state have violated human rights protected in the inter-American system, even when the events take place outside the territory of that state. In fact, the Commission would point out that, in certain cases, the exercise of its jurisdiction over extraterritorial events is *not only consistent with but required* by the applicable rules. . . . Because individual rights are inherent to the human being, all the American states are obligated to respect the protected rights of any person subject to their jurisdiction. Although this usually refers to persons who are within the territory of a state, in certain instances it can refer to extraterritorial actions, when the person is present in the territory of a state but subject to the control of another state, generally through the actions of that state's agents abroad.

Armando Alejandre Jr. and Others v. Cuba ('Brothers to the Rescue'), Inter-American Commission of Human Rights, report No. 86/99, case no. 11.589 (29 September 1999), para. 22 (emphasis added).

sovereignty. However, both objections fail to recognize the fundamental aspect of human rights, which is not the interests of states, but rather a standard of treatment of individual human beings no matter where or who they are.[48] They fail to recognize the original understanding of universalism and of non-discrimination. Human rights standards are not aimed at dictating to any government their policy choices or direction of society, as long as human rights standards as recognized, adopted and committed to by the international community and all individual states are adhered to.[49] Put differently, human rights recognize that torture, censorship and lack of access to potable drinking water and basic health care affect all human beings equally no matter where they live. This is the fundamental understanding of universal human rights. However, the universal concept has only been recognized in half – and this is what possibly fuels the argument of neo-colonialism. If universal human rights mean that all individuals are supposed to be able to enjoy human rights no matter where they live, but only the domestic state has obligations, then human rights protection becomes limited to what the home state is able or willing to do. Furthermore, it becomes a political and ideological game to criticize and shame foreign states for their human rights violations, while ignoring the human rights violations that could have been prevented if non-state actors such as TNCs over which a foreign state has jurisdiction are not considered.

Another aspect of neo-colonialism that is often voiced in this context is the problem of conditionality. Countries that have traditionally received assistance from industrialized states or from international financial institutions (IFIs) such as the World Bank and the International Monetary Fund (IMF) are wary of what they consider to be conditions for assistance or investment. From the experience of conditionality linked to loans and 'bailouts' from the IFIs (the gatekeeper role that these institutions have traditionally played in terms of access to international financial resources),[50] these recipient countries are concerned that industrialized countries where most of the TNCs have their headquarters will use regulations of the corporations as another form of conditions regarding their domestic policies. From the historic discourse on human rights where industrialized

---

[48] Gibney, *Returning to Universal Principles*, n. 19, 3.
[49] Council of Europe Commissioner for Human Rights, 'Safeguarding Human Rights in Times of Economic Crisis' (November 2013), 8, https://wcd.coe.int/com.instranet.Instra Servlet?command=com.instranet.CmdBlobGet&InstranetImage=2664103&SecMode=1 &DocId=2215366&Usage=2 (last accessed 13 January 2017).
[50] S. Skogly, *The Human Rights Obligations of the World Bank and the International Monetary Fund* (Cavendish Publishing, 2001), 10.

states have been very vocal (although not necessarily consistent) in terms of how other states behave regarding human rights, such a reaction is understandable. This partly relates back to the policies of the United States under President Carter in the late 1970s, whereby the Unites States introduced rules to prevent financial support for countries where massive human rights violations took place.[51] Similarly, this became a policy for the IFIs as well, as a result of the influence of the United States within these institutions.

While probably introduced with good intentions, these policies have skewed the debate, and not least because such policies were:

- seen to represent interference within the internal affairs of states (which could potentially be legitimate, given the discussion about the legitimacy of international attention to human rights violations as reflected upon above);
- the policies were not implemented consistently, and therefore smaller and less strategically important states often felt as 'victims' of these policies, rather than as a consistent and systematic attempt to improve the human rights situation worldwide; and
- when the conditionality concerning the domestic human rights situation was the only focus (i.e., how the 'recipient' state performed) and attention with respect to other actors' influence on the human rights situation (for instance TNCs), the neo-colonial or neo-imperialist conclusion was fairly easy to draw. However, similar to the question of sovereignty, if the attention is on the activities of TNCs, and not what the host state is doing, the question of conditionality is not really relevant in this context.

12.4   Content of the Obligation to Regulate

Having now considered some of the controversies regarding extraterritorial human rights obligations generally, and those pertaining to the regulation of TNCs activities abroad more specifically, this chapter will now move to the key questions regarding the role of the state in regulating the conduct of TNCs when they operate beyond the home state's national borders, and how these could be framed in a future BHR treaty. As stated by Lagoutte 'it is so far unclear what this instrument will focus on',[52] and thus the extent of the emphasis on the state is

---

[51] *Ibid.*, 6.   [52] Lagoutte, n. 41, 179.

as of yet uncertain. However, it is submitted that leaving the state out of the equation when drafting the treaty would be counter productive. The problem with leaving the state out of a treaty that aims at regulating the relationship between business and human rights is the danger that this may remove the state's position as the primary obligation holder for the protection and promotion of human rights, as clearly laid down in the UN Charter and subsequent international human rights law. There is now a growing recognition that human rights obligations are complex, and that the focus on 'one violator and one violation' is not sufficient. However, while the obligations debate has become more sophisticated, it is clear that the state still has the focal position in complying with human rights obligations. The articulation of shared or joint obligations (combined with an increased attention to complicity in violations[53]) entails that more than one state may be responsible for human rights violations, and indeed that obligations can be shared between states and non-state actors.[54] Yet, the obligation to regulate the conduct of third parties to ensure individuals' enjoyment of human rights is an essential part of a state's role, and therefore the treaty should ensure that this element is given a strong position.[55]

While the Maastricht Principles were drafted by a group of experts, and is not per se a legally binding document, it is reflective of current international human rights law.[56] On that basis, the text of the Maastricht Principles could well be used as an inspiration for the drafting of relevant parts of the proposed treaty on BHR. There is certainly a strong case for using the commonly accepted tripartite classification of human rights obligations (*respect, protect* and *fulfil*). De Schutter contends that the duty of the state 'to protect human rights by regulating the behaviour of private (non-state) actors [. . .] belong to the acquis of international human rights law'.[57] This expression of the

---

[53] J. G. Stewart, 'Complicity in Business and Human Rights', *American Society of International Law Proceedings* (9 April 2015), http://ssrn.com/abstract=2676192 (last accessed 13 January 2017).

[54] Salomon, n. 2; A. Vandenbogaerde, *Towards Shared Accountability in International Human Rights Law: Law Procedures and Principles* (Intersentia, 2016); B. A. Andreassen and V. K. Vinh (eds.), *Duties across Borders: Advancing Human Rights in Transnational Business* (Intersentia, 2016).

[55] O. De Schutter, 'Towards a New Treaty on Business and Human Rights' (2016) 1 *Business and Human Rights Journal* 45.

[56] Maastricht Principles, n. 4, Preamble.

[57] De Schutter, 'Towards a New Treaty', n. 55, 44.

obligation to protect is also relevant for ETOs.[58] While states may be responsible for violations of the obligation to respect human rights beyond their own borders, for instance through belligerent occupation, other control over foreign territory and/or persons, etc., for the purpose of the present chapter, the focus is on the obligation to *protect*. According to the Maastricht Guidelines on Violations of Economic, Social and Cultural Rights,[59] the obligation to protect 'requires States to prevent violations of [economic, social and cultural rights] by third parties'.[60] This has been confirmed for ETOs in the Maastricht Principles, and the discussion below will apply the relevant provisions of these Principles to analyse how the regulation of TNCs could work in a future BHR treaty.

Section IV of the Maastricht Principles concerns the obligation to protect, and stipulates clearly in Principle 23 that 'all states must take action, separately, and jointly through international cooperation, to protect economic, social and cultural rights of persons within their territories and extraterritorially'. The subsequent principles detail how the obligation to protect should be understood and implemented. Notably, Principle 24 entitled 'Obligation to regulate' provides that:

> All States must take necessary measures to ensure that non-State actors which they are in a positon to regulate [. . .] such as private individuals and organisations, and transnational corporation and other business enterprises, do not nullify or impair the enjoyment of economic, social and cultural rights. These include administrative, legislative, adjudicatory and other measures. All other States have a duty to refrain from nullifying or impairing the discharge of the obligation to protect.

Thus, this Principle deals directly with the obligation to regulate TNCs, and Principle 25 gives the bases for protection and specifies in terms of TNCs that states must adopt and enforce measures to protect economic, social and cultural rights *inter alia* where 'a) the harm or threat of harm originates or occurs on its territory; b) where the non-state actor has the nationality of the State concerned; and c) regarding business enterprises, where the corporation, or its parent or controlling company, has its centre of activity, is registered or domiciled, or has its main place of business or substantial business activities, in the State concerned. [. . .]'[61]

---

[58] Maastricht Principles, n. 4, Principle 9.

[59] Maastricht Guidelines on Violations on Economic, Social and Cultural Rights (Maastricht Guidelines) (January 1997), www1.umn.edu/humanrts/instree/Maastrichtguidelines_.html (last accessed 13 January 2017).

[60] *Ibid.*, Guideline 6.   [61] Maastricht Principles, n. 4, Principle 25.

The obligation to regulate the conduct of non-state actors, including TNCs, comes from a state's general international law obligation to 'control the activities of private persons within its state territory and the duty is no less applicable where the harm is caused to persons or other legal interests within the territory of another state'.[62] This approach has been confirmed by a number of UN human rights committees, including the Committee on Economic, Social and Cultural Rights, which, among others, in its concluding observation on a report from Austria observed that:

> The Committee is concerned at the lack of oversight over Austrian companies operating abroad with regard to the negative impact of their activities on enjoyment of economic, social and cultural rights in host countries (art.2).
>
> The Committee urges the State party to ensure that all economic, social and cultural rights are fully respected and rights holders adequately protected in the context of corporate activities, including by establishing appropriate laws and regulations, together with monitoring, investigation and accountability procedures to set and enforce standards for the performance of corporations, as underlined in the Committee's statement on the obligations of States parties regarding the corporate sector and economic, social and cultural rights.[63]

---

[62] I. Brownlie, *System of the Law of Nations: State Responsibility (Part 1)* (Oxford University Press, 1983), 165, as quoted in De Schutter et al., 'Maastricht Commentary', n. 29, 1136.

[63] UN Committee on Economic, Social and Cultural Rights, 'Concluding Observations – Austria', E/CN.12/2011/1, para. 12. The Committee now regularly points to the lack of regulation by states of the TNCs over which they have regulatory control, and this also goes further to include international investments. In the concluding observations on the report from Norway in 2013, the Committee commented on Norway's sovereign fund:

> The Committee is concerned that the various steps taken by the State party in the context of the social responsibility of the Government Pension Fund Global have not included the institutionalization of systematic human rights impact assessments of its investments. The Committee recommends that the State party ensure that investments by the Norges Bank Investment Management in foreign companies operating in third countries are subject to a comprehensive human rights impact assessment (prior to and during the investment). The Committee also recommends that the State party adopt policies and other measures to prevent human rights contraventions abroad by corporations that have their main offices under the jurisdiction of the State party, without infringing the sovereignty or diminishing the obligations of the host States under the Covenant. The Committee draws the attention of the State party to its statement on the obligations of State parties regarding the corporate sector and economic, social and cultural rights.

  UN Committee on Economic, Social and Cultural Rights, 'Concluding Observations – Norway', E/2012/22, annex VI, section A.

It is not merely the Committee on Economic, Social and Cultural Rights that is now including recommendations to states to regulate the activities of TNCs over which they exert control. This is now also common practice for the Human Rights Committee, which, for instance, in its discussion of the German report noted that 'The State party is encouraged to set out clearly the expectation that all business enterprises domiciled in its territory and/or its jurisdiction respect human rights standards in accordance with the Covenant throughout their operations.'[64] Furthermore, the Committee on Elimination of all Forms of Discrimination against Women,[65] the Committee on the Rights of the Child,[66] and the Committee on Elimination of Racial Discrimination[67] all question, when examining state reports, the lack of regulation of TNCs' extraterritorial activities that may impact upon the enjoyment of human rights.

In terms of the basis for regulation, the Commentary to the Maastricht Principles notes that what is reflected in Principle 25 is the active personality principle whereby a state may regulate the conduct of its nationals abroad.[68] However, as it is at times hard to determine the actual nationality of some business enterprises, Principle 25 provides that such regulation by a state may be carried out if that TNC has its 'centre of activity, is registered or domiciled, or has its main place of business or substantial business activities, in the State concerned'. This rationale will allow states to regulate the conduct of companies that use the separation of legal personality to avoid or limit the scope of their legal liability.[69]

An issue related to this was raised in the Commentary to Principle 2 of the Guiding Principles on Business and Human Rights, where it was suggested that 'there are strong policy reasons for home States to set out clearly the expectation that businesses respect human rights abroad, especially where the State itself is involved in or support those businesses'.[70] From an obligation to protect human rights as part of the tri-

---

[64] UN Human Rights Committee, 'Concluding Observations on the Sixth Periodic Report of Germany', CCPR/C/DEU/CO/6 (12 November 2012), para. 16.

[65] Committee on the Elimination of Discrimination against Women, 'Concluding Observations on the Combined Fourth and Fifth Periodic Reports of India', CEDAW/C/IND/CO/4-5 (24 July 2014), para. 15.

[66] Committee on the Rights of the Child, 'Concluding Observations: Australia', CRC/C/AUS/CO/4 (28 August 2012), para. 27.

[67] Committee on the Elimination of all forms of Racial Discrimination, 'Concluding Observations: United Kingdom', CERD/C/GBR/CO/18-20 (14 September 2011), para. 29.

[68] De Schutter et al., 'Maastricht Commentary', n. 29, 1139.   [69] Ibid., 1140.

[70] Guiding Principles, n. 14, Commentary to Principle 2.

partite classification of human rights obligations, and the clear acceptance that this level of obligation relates to a state's duty to ensure that third parties (such as private TNCs) do not infringe the enjoyment of human rights of individuals, the distinction between enterprises that are fully private or partially 'state involved or supported' does not make much difference. The focus is on the state's obligation to regulate the conduct of private entities as well as their own behaviour. Therefore, in terms of regulation, both fully private and partially state-owned companies should be included.

In addition to situations where states are in a position to regulate the conduct of TNCs when operating abroad, the Maastricht Principles also contain reference to situations where this is not directly the case, but where they are in a 'position to influence'. By this, the Principles refers to situations where a state can influence the conduct of a non-state actor (including TNCs), for instance, through their public procurement system or through international diplomacy.[71]

12.5   Overcoming Problems of Extraterritorial Regulation

It is essential to also deal with some of the predictable problems that will occur in the drafting process of the proposed BHR treaty, and also in terms of the arguments that will be used to oppose the obligations of states to regulate the activities of 'their' businesses abroad. Going from permissible regulation based on principles of prescriptive jurisdiction that clearly have no territorial limitations,[72] what an obligation on state regulation of TNCs activities abroad would in essence do is to make such regulation not only 'permissible' but rather 'mandatory'. It would remove the discretion of states whether or not to regulate. At the same time, it would enhance the global human rights protection and ensure that those standards that states have accepted through the international bill of human rights become truly universal.

However, difficulties will arise, and a few of those will be addressed briefly here. First, states will be hesitant to accept responsibility to

[71] This has been suggested by the GPs. *Ibid.*, Commentary to Principle 6. See also Committee on Economic, Social and Cultural Rights, 'Concluding Observations – Norway', n. 63.

[72] According to Dixon and McCorquodale, 'As a general rule, a State's prescriptive jurisdiction is unlimited and a State may legislate for any matter irrespective of where it occurs (even if in the territory of another State) or the nationality of persons involved. [. . . .] Enforcement jurisdiction is, on the other hand, generally considered to be territorial.' M. Dixon and R. McCorquodale, *Cases and Materials on International Law*, 3rd edn. (Blackstone Press, 2000), 281.

regulate for 'predicted effect'. Principle 13 of the Maastricht Principles articulates states obligation to avoid causing harm as follows:

> States must desist from acts and omissions that create a real risk of nullifying or impairing the enjoyment of economic, social and cultural rights extraterritorially. The responsibility of States is engaged where such nullification or impairment is a foreseeable result of their conduct. Uncertainty about potential impacts does not constitute justification for such conduct.[73]

Invoking this principle in relation to state regulation of TNCs, it will be a breach of obligation if the state failed to regulate conduct by these actors that might predictably create risk of nullifying or impairing the enjoyment of human rights. This implies that the state needs to be proactive and consider what the content of regulation may bring about in terms of human rights respect or violations, as the lack of regulation (omission) which leads to human rights violations would indeed be a breach of their obligations.[74] Case law confirms that while acts cannot be attributed to a state just by the fact that they took place on their territory, they nevertheless may be expected to 'give an explanation' if the state knew or should have known that 'activities unlawful under international law' were perpetrated on its territory and caused damage to another state.[75] Thus, in such situations, a state's obligation to exercise due diligence will be triggered. For example, in a report by the Council of Europe on the allegations of European states' involvement in extraordinary rendition of terrorist suspects by the United States, the following was critically noted:

> It has to be said that most governments did not seem particularly eager to establish the alleged facts. The body of information gathered makes it unlikely that European states were completely unaware of what was happening, in the context of the fight against international terrorism, in some of their airports, in their airspace or at American bases located on their territory. Insofar as they did not know, they did not want to know. It is inconceivable that certain operations conducted by American services could have taken place without the active participation, or at least the collusion, of national intelligence services. If this were the case,

---

[73] Maastricht Principles, n. 4, Principle 13.

[74] The Maastricht Principles reflects this through an 'obligation to avoid causing harm': 'States must desist from acts and omissions that create a real risk of nullifying or impairing the enjoyment of economic, social and cultural rights extraterritorially. The responsibility of States is engaged where such nullification or impairment is a foreseeable result of their conduct. Uncertainty about potential impacts does not constitute justification for such conduct.' 'Maastricht Principles', *ibid.*, Principle 13.

[75] *The Corfu Channel Case*, 1949 I.C.J. 4, 22, at 18.

one would be justified in seriously questioning the effectiveness, and therefore the legitimacy, of such services.[76]

Consequently, there is now acceptance that there is a duty upon states reasonably to ensure that activities originating or taking place within their jurisdiction do not breach international law provisions, including human rights enjoyment in the territory of another state.[77] The acceptance of the precautionary principle (particularly in international environmental law) also demonstrates that uncertainty about the full effect of planned measures is not an acceptable defence against taking mitigating action if future harm may ensue.[78]

Another problem that may come to the fore in discussion on the proposed BHR treaty is the problem of joint or shared obligations. Will states be willing to accept the entire responsibility for violations of international human rights standards on the part of TNCs just because they did not regulate the relevant conduct? Since traditional human rights law has focused uniquely on violations by the domestic state in situations where the legal relationship between the victim of the violation and the state has been fairly straightforward, it will be a rather new step to introduce concepts of shared or joint obligations in the treaty. Depending on how the treaty will be framed, and in particular how the obligations of subjects will be conceptualized, such an introduction of shared or joint obligations may be necessary. It may be that two states (the home and the host) may be jointly responsible, and indeed part of the responsibility may also lie with a particular company. This is a

---

[76] Council of Europe, Committee on Legal Affairs and Human Rights, 'Alleged Secret Detentions and Unlawful Inter-state Transfers Involving Council of Europe Member States' AS/Jur (2006) 16 Part II (7 June 2006), http://assembly.coe.int/committeedocs/2006/20060606_ejdoc162006partii-final.pdf (last accessed 13 January 2017), para. 230.

[77] The UN Committee on Economic, Social and Cultural Rights affirms that states parties should 'prevent third parties from violating the right[s protected under the International Covenant on Economic, Social and Cultural Rights] in other countries, if they are able to influence these third parties by way of legal or political means, in accordance with the Charter of the United Nations and applicable international law.' General Comment No. 14 'The Right to the Highest Attainable Standard of Health (Art. 12)', E/C.12/2000/4 (11 August 2000), para. 39.

[78] Marr makes a distinction between the 'preventive principle' and the 'precautionary principle' in the following manner: 'the preventive principle provides for an obligation of state to prevent known or foreseeable harm outside their territory', while 'the precautionary principle [....] requires environmental action at an earlier step: It provides a tool for dealing with situations where there is a potential hazard, but scientific uncertainty as to the impact of the environmentally sensitive activity does not allow a clear prediction of the degree of the hazards to the environment.' S. Marr, *The Precautionary Principle in the Law of the Sea* (Martinus Nijhoff Publishers, 2003), 9.

complex situation, but one that may well need to be tackled, including by evolution or clarification subsequently by a treaty body looking at concrete circumstances.

12.6   Concluding Remarks

The analysis made in this chapter has attempted to bring the role of the state back into the discussion on TNCs and human rights. It has been demonstrated that a rejection of states' ETOs is contrary to the fundamental principle of universality of human rights. The objections to ETOs have been addressed, and proposals for how future regulation by states for the behaviour of TNCs over which they exert control have been made.

The environment within which international human rights law is now operating is far more complex in terms of international interaction and the actors involved on a global scale than was the case immediately after the Second World War. As stated at the outset, unless international human rights law manages to make necessary changes in its structures and modes of operation, it is in danger of becoming irrelevant for thousands of victims in real life conditions that would be considered serious human rights violations by non-lawyers. It is, therefore, particularly important that a BHR treaty drafted at the current point in time takes this challenge on board and ensures that the provisions of the treaty contribute to this renewed relevance of international human rights law.

Building on the Maastricht Principles, I propose below how the international human rights community could use the BHR treaty as a real opportunity to get a positive codification of states' obligations to protect human rights extraterritorially. What ETOs do in this context is to emphasize that the state has obligations both domestically and abroad when they affect human rights enjoyment, or when they can influence human rights enjoyment through regulation, for instance. The recognition of ETOs thus removes the argument that certain actors' behaviour is 'beyond the control' of a state when that state clearly has a regulatory opportunity to improve human rights enjoyment.

States' regulation of corporation activities to be in compliance with international human rights standards both when they operate at 'home' and in another country, will have a positive impact on universal human rights enjoyment. Moreover, it will create a level playing field for companies and thus the 'race to the bottom' in terms of human rights and environmental protection for those affected by the activities of TNCs and other business practices will lose much of its energy.

The problem with opposition to ETOs is that states hesitate to accept the responsibility that comes with acting within their jurisdiction, while wishing to retain the liberty to act internationally. This is where we return to the early days of international human rights law development as mentioned in the introduction: states had initially rejected the idea of human rights being a matter of legitimate international concern on the ground that these issues were for domestic sovereignty and jurisdiction. Yet, that objection was not accepted, and states now (reluctantly) recognize that the international community has a legitimate interest in the way in which individuals are treated by their own government. The task at the present juncture in international human rights law development is to achieve a similar acceptance for extraterritorial activities: that the international human rights standards set limits for what states can legitimately do in their international relations as well as domestically.

12.7   Draft Treaty Provisions

States' Obligation to Protect Human Rights[79]

1. In compliance with the obligation to protect human rights, all states must take necessary administrative, legislative, investigative and adjudicatory measures to ensure that transnational corporations and other business enterprises, which they are in a position to regulate, do not nullify or impair the enjoyment of human rights while operating within their territories or extraterritorially. State parties to this Convention also have a duty to refrain from nullifying or impairing the discharge of this obligation to protect human rights on the part of a state.
2. States must adopt and enforce measures to protect human rights through legal and other means, including diplomatic means, in the following circumstances:
   a) when the harm or threat of harm originates or occurs on its territory;
   b) where the transnational corporation or another business enterprise, or its parent or controlling company, has its centre of activity, is registered or domiciled, or has its main place of business or substantial business activities in the state concerned.

---

[79] The proposed text is adapted from the Maastricht Principles, n. 4, Principles 23–26.

3. States that are in a position to influence the conduct of transnational corporations and other business enterprises even if they are not in a position to regulate such conduct, such as through their public procurement system or international diplomacy, should exercise such influence, in accordance with the Charter of the United Nations and general international law, in order to protect human rights.

The Impact of a Business and Human Rights Treaty on Investment Law and Arbitration

PETER MUCHLINSKI

13.1 Introduction

The accountability of corporate actors for violations of human rights is becoming a growth industry. As public concern over the operations of corporations in the global economy increases, so too does the desire to see them answer for the more egregious abuses that are laid at their feet. A major initial step has been taken by the adoption, in 2011, of the UN Guiding Principles on Business and Human Rights (GPs).[1] This instrument operationalizes a framework (UN Framework) based on three pillars: a binding state duty to protect against human rights abuses by business enterprises, a corporate responsibility to respect human rights and access to an effective remedy. The GPs do not create binding international duties for corporate actors to observe human rights. Rather, they rely on corporate human rights risk assessment through the due diligence procedure outlined in Principle 17 of the GPs.[2] In addition, the access to remedy

---

[1] Human Rights Council (HRC), 'Guiding Principles on Business and Human Rights Implementing the United Nations "Protect, Respect and Remedy" Framework', A/HRC/17/31 (21 March 2011).

[2] Principle 17 reads:

> In order to identify, prevent, mitigate and account for how they address their adverse human rights impacts, business enterprises should carry out human rights due diligence. The process should include assessing actual and potential human rights impacts, integrating and acting upon the findings, tracking responses, and communicating how impacts are addressed. Human rights due diligence:
>
> (a) Should cover adverse human rights impacts that the business enterprise may cause or contribute to through its own activities, or which may be directly linked to its operations, products or services by its business relationships;
>
> (b) Will vary in complexity with the size of the business enterprise, the risk of severe human rights impacts, and the nature and context of its operations;

pillar, which flows from the previous two pillars, covers both judicial and non-judicial remedies, including corporate-based grievance mechanisms. It does not direct states or corporations towards the development of any particular type of remedy but notes the major obstacles that states, in particular, should respond to. These obstacles include the problem of extraterritorial enforcement of obligations, corporate group liability issues and financial obstacles to access to remedies.

To legal minds, this has appeared as an incomplete approach, one that may rely too much upon the hope that changes in corporate culture, without binding legal duties, will provide the necessary impetus to avoid and mitigate adverse human rights impacts of corporate activities.[3] By contrast, John Ruggie, the former UN Special Representative of the Secretary General on Business and Human Rights (SRSG), has noted that the GPs represent the limits of what may be politically possible in a world where non-state actors have traditionally not been subject to binding international obligations.[4] In addition, in a world of polycentric governance, the development of corporate procedures that avoid or at least mitigate operational human rights risks may be a practical way forward that avoids many of the pitfalls that attempts at the creation of binding international treaty norms will undoubtedly bring up.[5]

Notwithstanding such concerns, in 2013, the Government of Ecuador proposed to the UN Human Rights Council (Council) that a new international instrument be negotiated outlining the obligations of multinational enterprises (MNEs) and other business enterprises in relation to human rights. In June 2014, the Council established an Open-ended Intergovernmental Working Group, 'to elaborate an international legally binding instrument to regulate, in international human

---

(c)   Should be ongoing, recognizing that the human rights risks may change over time as the business enterprise's operations and operating context evolve.

[3] See S. Deva and D. Bilchitz (eds.), *Human Rights and Obligations of Business: Beyond the Corporate Responsibility to Respect?* (Cambridge University Press, 2013).

[4] J. Ruggie, 'A UN Business and Human Rights Treaty?' Harvard University, Kennedy School of Government (28 January 2014), www.hks.harvard.edu/m-rcbg/CSRI/UNBusinessandHumanRightsTreaty.pdf (last accessed 8 January 2017).

[5] See J. Ruggie, 'Life in the Global Public Domain: Response to Commentaries on the UN Guiding Principles and the Proposed Treaty on Business and Human Rights' (23 January 2015), http://ssrn.com/abstract=2554726 or http://dx.doi.org/10.2139/ssrn.2554726 (last accessed 8 January 2017).

On polycentric governance and the GPs, see further J. D. Prenkert and S. J. Shackelford, 'Business, Human Rights, and the Promise of Polycentricity' (2014) 47 *Vanderbilt Journal of Transnational Law* 451.

rights law, the activities of transnational corporations and other business enterprises'.[6] Should such an instrument ever be concluded, which remains a significant 'If' in the historical development of the law relating to business and human rights (BHR), its impact may be considerable in numerous fields of international law. Not least of these would be in international investment law and arbitration.

What would those impacts be? The present chapter seeks to shed some light on this issue. The illumination involved will necessarily be somewhat faint, as the probable nature, structure and content of the proposed instrument is open to a large range of variations, all of which have important consequences for its interaction with other areas of international law.[7] Therefore, the chapter must necessarily concentrate on some broad themes based on a small number of key variants.

The first task will be to offer a brief account of where human rights fits into the current system of investment law and arbitration, if only to show human rights' limited impact to date. Then, the chapter will focus on the probable 'impact routes' that the proposed instrument might take in relation to investment law and arbitration. Three such routes can be distilled, from the strongest to the weakest formulation of corporate obligations.

First, a binding statement of corporate human rights obligations may be laid out in the proposed instrument. Direct duties to take into account human rights obligations of corporate claimants might be imposed on negotiators, when drafting investment agreements, and tribunals, in making arbitral decisions. This may be achieved by mandating the incorporation of corporate human rights obligations into investment agreements. Second, the proposed instrument might follow the approach of the GPs and seek to clarify certain issues that remain open. In particular, this may involve the development of state obligations to further the aims of the GPs in domestic law as part of the first pillar of the UN Framework. However, it

---

[6] Human Rights Council, 'Elaboration of an International Legally Binding Instrument on Transnational Corporations and Other Business Enterprises with respect to Human Rights', A/HRC/Res/26/9 (26 June 2014), para. 1.

[7] For a valuable overview see further A. Ramasastry and D. Cassel, 'White Paper: Options for a Treaty on Business and Human Rights' (2015) 6 *Notre Dame Journal of International & Comparative Law* 1; See also O. De Schutter, 'Towards a New Treaty on Business and Human Rights' (2016) 1 *Business and Human Rights Journal* 41; International Commission of Jurists (ICJ), 'Needs and Options for a New International Instrument on Business and Human Rights' (June 2014), http://icj.wpengine.netdna-cdn.com/wp-con tent/uploads/2014/08/International-Instrument-BHR-Exec-Sum-elec-version-light.pdf (last accessed 8 January 2017).

would not raise the corporate responsibility to respect human rights under the GPs into a set of binding international law duties. As will be discussed below, this may have indirect impacts on international investment law and arbitration. Third, it is possible that any future treaty might remain silent as to its impact on corporate obligations, focusing solely on weak procedural modalities such as state reporting mechanisms. It is uncertain what impact this approach could have on investment law and arbitration.

13.2   Human Rights in Investment Law and Arbitration: The Story to Date

To date, human rights issues have made relatively little impact on the content of international investment law. The principal source of such law rests in the myriad provisions of international investment agreements (IIAs) and in arbitral interpretations of these provisions in the course of investor–state disputes.

13.2.1   Human Rights in IIAs

As regards the content of IIAs, human rights issues are virtually non-existent in IIA provisions. Few, if any, IIAs do more than refer to human rights in the Preamble.[8] Some of the most recent model agreements,

---

[8] See, for example, the Preamble of Norway's Draft Model BIT 2007: '*Reaffirming* their commitment to democracy, the rule of law, human rights and fundamental freedoms in accordance with their obligations under international law, including the principles set out in the United Nations Charter and the Universal Declaration of Human Rights'. Available at: http://investmentpolicyhub.unctad.org/Download/TreatyFile/2873 (last accessed 20 January 2017). See also Article 7.2.d. of the Investment Agreement for the COMESA Common Investment Area (CCIA Agreement), cited in H. Mann, *International Investment Agreements, Business and Human Rights: Key Issues and Opportunities* (International Institute of Sustainable Development, 2008), 10. This enables the COMESA Committee for the Common Investment Area to consider and make:

> recommendations to the [COMESA] Council on any policy issues that need to be made to enhance the objectives of this Agreement. For example the development of common minimum standards relating to investment in areas such as:
>
> (i) environmental impact and social impact assessments
> (ii) labour standards
> (iii) respect for human rights
> (iv) conduct in conflict zones
> (v) corruption
> (vi) subsidies.

which have been drafted since the adoption of the GPs, contain some references to human rights, though these are rather limited. For example, the Indian draft Model Bilateral Investment Treaty (BIT) of 2015 only refers to sustainable development in its Preamble and mentions human rights specifically in relation to corporate compliance with host state laws.[9] Article 12 of the Indian Model BIT provides:

12.1 Investors and their Investments shall be subject to and comply with the Law of the Host State. This includes, but is not limited to, the following:

(i) Law concerning payment of wages and minimum wages, employment of contract labour, prohibition on child labour, special conditions of work, social security and benefit and insurance schemes applicable to employees;

(ii) information sharing requirements of the Host State concerning the Investment in question and the corporate history and practices of the Investment or Investor, for purposes of decision making in relation to that Investment or for other purposes;

. . .

(v) Law relating to human rights;

. . .

(vii) relevant national and internationally accepted standards of corporate governance and accounting practices.

12.2 Investors and their Investments shall strive, through their management policies and practices, to contribute to the development objectives of the Host State. In particular, Investors and their Investments should recognise the rights, traditions and customs of local communities and indigenous peoples of the Host State and carry out their operations with respect and regard for such rights, traditions and customs.

This provision falls short of a strong commitment to human rights as an integral part of the agreement, though it goes beyond traditional, first-generation IIAs, which omit any mention of human rights. The extent of the human rights obligations of investors falls to be determined by reference to domestic law of the 'host' state, though the reference to

This is the first time that any investment agreement has expressly included human rights issues related to investment as a possible future working item under the Agreement.

[9] See 'India Model BIT 2015', https://mygov.in/sites/default/files/master_image/Model%20Text%20for%20the%20Indian%20Bilateral%20Investment%20Treaty.pdf (last accessed 20 January 2017). The final version of the Indian Model BIT of 2016 replaced this provision with a general Article 12 on corporate social responsibility that contains a commitment on the part of investors to voluntarily include human rights standards into their practices and internal policies: http://indiainbusiness.nic.in/newdesign/upload/Model_BIT.pdf (last accessed 15 July 2017).

relevant internationally accepted standards of corporate governance might be interpreted – on a broad reading of this provision – to include the developing international corporate responsibility to respect human rights.

A further indirect reference to such international standards could be read into the disclosure requirements laid out in Article 10.6 of the Indian Model BIT. This requires the investor to offer timely disclosures of, among other matters:

(x) policies and other codes of conduct to which the Investment sub-scribes, their date of adoption and the countries and entities to which such statements apply;

(xi) its performance in relation to these statements and codes; and

(xii) information on internal audit, risk management and legal compliance systems.

Again, on a broad reading, it could involve an obligation on the investor to disclose their human rights policy. Given that, by Article 8.3 of the Model BIT, 'Investors and their Investments must comply with the obligations in Articles 9, 10, 11, and 12 to benefit from the provisions of this Treaty', failure to do so could have implications for the protection offered to the investor and their investment under a BIT signed by India. From an investor protection perspective, such significant consequences would require considerable effort to produce the relevant information, a cost that some investors might find unattractive. Indeed, the Indian Law Commission had criticized the draft Model BIT on such grounds, demanding that the final version be more explicit as to the types of disclosures required, their purposes and the clarification of consequences of non-compliance.[10]

The most recent investment agreements entered into by Brazil also refer to corporate social responsibility (CSR) and human rights. For example, the Brazil-Chile Investment Promotion and Co-operation Agreement of 2015 contains a best efforts commitment to CSR in Article 15.[11] This provision notes the importance that the Contracting

---

[10] Law Commission of India, 'Report No.260 Analysis of the 2015 Draft Model Indian Bilateral Investment Treaty' (August 2015), 32–33 http://lawcommissionofindia.nic.in/reports/Report260.pdf (last accessed 8 January 2017). Article 8.3. was deleted from the final 2016 Model BIT: see note 9.

[11] La República Federativa del Brasil, 'Acuerdo de Cooperación y Facilitación de Inversiones entre la República Federativa del Brasil y la República de Chile' (23 November 2015), http://investmentpolicyhub.unctad.org/Download/TreatyFile/3557 (last accessed 8 January 2017).

Parties place on the promotion of CSR and sustainable development in the
host country. In addition, direct reference is made to the OECD Guidelines
on Multinational Enterprises as a source of best efforts policies on the part
of investors. Such best efforts include *inter alia* respect for the human
rights of those involved in the activities of the companies concerned and
abstaining from seeking or accepting exemptions other than those established in the law of the host party with respect to human rights, the
environment, health, safety, labour, financial incentives or other matters.[12]
Finally, companies are exhorted to encourage, whenever possible, their
business partners, including suppliers and outsourced services, to apply
principles of business conduct consistent with the principles provided for
in Article 15.[13] Similar provisions are found in other recent Brazilian
Investment and Co-operation Agreements, though the construction of
these provisions is somewhat different. For instance, the Brazil-
Mozambique and Brazil-Angola Agreements opt for a general hortatory
provision on CSR which is supplemented by a more detailed Annex with
the same substantive content as found in the Brazil-Chile Agreement, but
omitting any reference to the OECD Guidelines on Multinational
Enterprises.[14] Although these agreements, again, represent a considerable
development over first-generation IIAs, the hortatory and best efforts
nature of these obligations leaves little room for such agreements providing a source of new binding international obligations on corporate actors.
Rather, the approach remains one of leaving substantive legal obligations
to the realm of the domestic law of the Contracting Parties.

13.2.2   Human Rights in Investment Arbitration

So far, human rights issues have not made much headway in investor–
state arbitrations.[15] Nonetheless, a number of human rights-based

---

[12] *Ibid.*, art. 15(2)(b)/(e).   [13] *Ibid.*, art. 15(2)(j).

[14] Article 10 reads: 'The investors and their investments shall strive to carry out the highest
level possible of contributions to the sustainable development of the host State and the
local community, by means of the adoption of a high degree of socially responsible
practices, taking as a reference the voluntary principles and standards defined in Annex
II – "Corporate Social Responsibility".' See International Institute for Sustainable
Development (IISD), 'Side-by-side Comparison of the Brazil-Mozambique and Brazil-
Angola Cooperation and Investment Facilitation Agreements' (Unofficial Translation by
M. D. Brauch June 2015), www.iisd.org/library/side-side-comparison-brazil-mozambi
que-and-brazil-angola-cooperation-and-investment (last accessed 8 January 2017).

[15] The following paragraphs are taken from P. Muchlinski, 'Towards a Coherent
International Investment System: Key Issues in the Reform of International Investment

arguments have been put to tribunals over recent years in relation to the legality of an expropriation, and human rights case law has been considered by tribunals as a guide to their analysis of the proportionality of the respondent states actions towards the investor.[16] Equally, in several awards arising out of the Argentine Peso crisis of 2001, the Argentine government sought to defend its emergency legislation, which caused significant financial losses to foreign investors, on the grounds that these measures protected the human rights of citizens by ensuring basic order and/or access to those services which are instrumental to public health and welfare. Thus, measures taken in response to the financial crisis were deemed necessary to uphold Argentina's constitutional order, as well as basic rights and liberties of the Argentine public.[17] This argument met with mixed responses from tribunals, most of which made little significant contribution to answering the question whether human rights issues were integral to BIT interpretation. Indeed, the tribunal in *Aguas Argentinas SA, Suez, Sociedad General de Aguas de Barcelona SA and Vivendi* noted that:

> Argentina and the amicus curiae submissions received by the Tribunal suggest that Argentina's human rights obligations to assure its population

Law' in R. Echandi and P. Sauve (eds.), *Prospects in International Investment Law and Policy* (Cambridge University Press, 2013), 411 at 425–426.

[16] See generally United Nations Conference on Trade and Development (UNCTAD), 'Selected Developments in IIA Arbitration and Human Rights', UNCTAD IIA MONITOR No. 2 (2009), www.unctad.org/en/docs/webdiaeia20097_en.pdf (last accessed 8 January 2017). See also L. Peterson and K. Gray, 'International Human Rights in Bilateral Investment Treaties and in Investment Treaty Arbitration' (Winnipeg, International Institute for Sustainable Development, 2005) (April 2003), www.iisd.org/pdf/2003/investment_int_human_rights_bits.pdf (last accessed 9 January 2017); C. Reiner and C. Schreuer, 'Human Rights and International Investment Arbitration' in P. Dupuy, F. Francioni and E. Petersmann (eds.), *Human Rights in International Investment Law and Arbitration* (Oxford University Press, 2009), 82; A. Kulick, *Global Public Interest in International Investment Law* (Cambridge University Press, 2012), 269.

[17] UNCTAD, 'Selected Developments', *ibid.*, 8. For a more recent award that suggests human rights counterclaims may have a place in international investment law, see *Urbaser v Argentina*, ICSID Case No. ARB/07/26 (8 December 2016), https://www.ita law.com/sites/default/files/case-documents/italaw8136_1.pdf (last accessed 28 June 2017). See also Edward Guntrip, 'Urbaser v Argentina: The Origins of a Host State Human Rights Counterclaim in ICSID Arbitration?', *EJIL: Talk!* (10 February 2017), https://www.ejiltalk.org/urbaser-v-argentina-the-origins-of-a-host-state-human-rights-counterclaim-in-icsid-arbitration/ (last accessed 28 June 2017); Kevin Crow and Lina Lorenzoni Escobar, 'International Corporate Obligations, Human Rights and the Urbaser Standard: Breaking New Ground?', SSRN, https://papers.ssrn.com/sol3/papers.cfm?abstract_id=2984987 (last accessed 28 June 2017).

the right to water somehow trumps its obligations under the BITs and that the existence of the human right to water also implicitly gives Argentina the authority to take actions in disregard of its BIT obligations. The Tribunal does not find a basis for such a conclusion either in the BITs or international law. Argentina is subject to both international obligations, i.e. human rights and treaty obligation, and must respect both of them equally. Under the circumstances of these cases, Argentina's human rights obligations and its investment treaty obligations are not inconsistent, contradictory, or mutually exclusive. Thus, as discussed above, Argentina could have respected both types of obligations.[18]

A further issue that has arisen concerns the state's duty to promote and protect various individual human rights obligations and the impact of such action on investor rights. In *Biwater v. United Republic of Tanzania* the tribunal accepted, at the procedural stage, that human rights considerations might be raised by the dispute, in that it concerned the operation of a privatized water company and that this involved significant public interests in relation to the right to water and to health.[19] However, when making the 2008 award, while the tribunal noted that the public interest issues surrounding the right to water in this case were admissible,[20] it did not explore the United Republic of Tanzania's human rights law obligations in further detail. The tribunal decided the case against the claimant on the basis that the claimant had not shown that the actions taken by the Tanzanian authorities in breach of the United Kingdom (UK)–Tanzania BIT had actually caused the losses complained of.

Equally, in the case of *Foresti and others v. the Republic of South Africa*, significant issues arose relating to the right of the host state to legislate so as to correct historic injustices involving gross violations of human rights.[21]

---

[18] *Aguas Argentinas SA, Suez, Sociedad General de Aguas de Barcelona SA and Vivendi v. Argentina*, Case No. ARB/03/19 Decision on Responsibility (28 July 2010), para. 261. By contrast, the Tribunal in *Urbaser v Argentina* (note 17) admitted Argentina's counterclaim that the claimant's failure to provide adequate investment in its concession to supply water and sewage services to Buenos Aires led to violations of the human right to water, and held that a BIT should, 'be construed in harmony with other rules of international law of which it forms part, including those relating to human rights'(para.1200). However, the counterclaim was rejected on the merits.

[19] See *Biwater Gauff* (Tanzania) *Ltd. v. United Republic of Tanzania* (Procedural Order No.5), ICSID Case No. ARB/05/22 (2 February 2007), para. 52. On water rights in investment arbitration, see further *Aguas Argentinas SA*, n. 18, paras. 255–265.

[20] *Biwater Gauff* (Tanzania) *Ltd. v. United Republic of Tanzania* (Award), ICSID Case No. ARB/05/22 (24 July 2008), para. 358.

[21] *Foresti and others v. the Republic of South Africa* (Award), ICSID Case No ARB (AF)/07/1 (4 August 2010). This summary is taken from Muchlinski in Echandi and Sauve (eds.), *Prospects in International Investment Law and Policy*, n.15, 434–435.

This claim was brought before International Centre for Settlement of Investment Disputes (ICSID) by Italian mining investors, who had invested after the fall of apartheid, and who argued that their investment had been indirectly expropriated as a result of South Africa's post-apartheid equal opportunities and land rights policy. Since the end of apartheid, comprehensive efforts have been made to promote Black Economic Empowerment (BEE) in South Africa, so as to transform the economy and overcome the socio-economic legacy of apartheid.[22] In the mining sector, the Minerals and Petroleum Resources Development Act (MPRDA) converted existing mining rights into 'new order' mining rights and required 26 per cent of mining assets to be transferred to black owners over the next decade.[23] The Italian claimants were major holders of mining rights in the South African granite industry. They argued that their rights in a number of quarries could be expropriated and also that as foreign investors they were being subjected to more onerous BBE requirements than domestic firms in breach of the fair and equitable and national treatment principles.[24] The government of South Africa passed the MPRDA as part of its constitutional obligations to put right the injustices of the apartheid era. As such the Act represents part of a wider policy to observe human rights in the development of the new post-apartheid era. Is it therefore open to an investor to use the narrow terms of a BIT to require compensation for the effects of such a policy?[25]

---

[22] See further L. E. Peterson, 'South Africa's Bilateral Investment Treaties Implications for Development and Human Rights', Dialogue on Globalization Occasional Papers of the Friedrich-Ebert-Stiftung, (November 2006), 16, http://library.fes.de/pdf-files/iez/global/04137-20080708.pdf (last accessed 9 January 2017) on which this summary draws. According to this study, 'BEE measures include traditional affirmative action measures, such as employment equity and preferential procurement policies, as well as sector-specific charters which gauge the progress of companies in meeting specific indicators and targets, and in meeting targets for divestiture of minority equity stakes to BEE partners'. See further South Africa Department of Trade Industry, 'Broad-Based Black Empowerment', www.thedti.gov.za/economic_empowerment/bee.jsp (last accessed 9 January 2017).

[23] Economist Intelligence Unit, 'Country Commerce Report: South Africa' (2005), 10.

[24] See Claimants' Request for the registration of arbitration proceedings in accordance with Article 2(1) of the Arbitration (Additional Facility) Rules of ICSID's Additional Facility, dated 1 November 2006. Not publicly available but summarized in Petition for limited participation as non-disputing parties in terms of Articles 41(3), 27, 39, and 35 of the ICSID's Additional Facility Rules, Case number: ARB(AF)/07/01, para. 4.2, http://ita.law.uvic.ca/documents/ForestivSAPetition_000.pdf (last visited 20 January 2017). See also *Foresti and others* n. 21, paras. 54–78.

[25] Claimant's request for arbitration proceedings, *Foresti and others*, n. 24, paras. 4.6–4.18.

The Claimants informed ICSID of their wish to discontinue proceedings in 2009. The reason given was that although the Claimants had not been provided with full relief for their alleged injuries, they nevertheless sought discontinuance because, pursuant to a December 2008 agreement with the Respondent, they had been granted partial relief. The Claimants also asserted that they had tried to settle the case with the Respondent, but to no avail. Therefore, the Claimants argued, given that they had received partial relief, and given the costs of the arbitration and current economic conditions, it was now appropriate to seek discontinuance of these proceedings.[26]

Given the very sensitive policy issues raised by the *Foresti* case, and the involvement of a coalition of non-governmental organizations (NGOs) and the International Commission of Jurists as third parties, perhaps there were other reasons as well for the discontinuance of arbitration proceedings. South Africa objected to the claimants' request for discontinuance and filed an application for a default award.[27] The tribunal awarded the default ordering a partial recovery of fees and costs by South Africa from the Claimants on the basis that, 'while claimants in investment arbitrations are in principle entitled to the costs necessarily incurred in the vindication of their legal rights, they cannot expect to leave respondent States to carry the costs of defending claims that are abandoned'.[28]

A further area in which the relationship between investment treaties and human rights has been examined by investment tribunals concerns the rights of indigenous peoples and communities affected by an investment. For example, in *Glamis Corp v. US*,[29] an investment by the claimant Canadian mining company in the Californian Imperial Desert was subjected to review by the US Solicitor of the Interior Department on the grounds *inter alia* that it violated the rights of the indigenous Quechuan Indian Nation to the use of their sacred ancestral sites for spiritual and ceremonial practices, thereby depriving future generations of their cultural heritage. The US Bureau of Land Management decided to reverse its earlier decision to approve the investment and, on 17 January 2001, the Secretary of the Department of the Interior, Bruce Babbitt, denied the mining permit given the Glamis Gold due to the cumulative adverse impacts of the project on Quechuan religious sites.[30] Glamis initiated an appeal against the

---

[26] *Ibid.*, paras. 79–80. [27] *Ibid.*, para. 81. [28] *Ibid.*, para. 132.

[29] *Glamis Gold Ltd v United States*, UNCITRAL Rules Arbitration Award (7 May 2009), www.italaw.com/cases/487 (last accessed 20 January 2017).

[30] *Ibid.*, paras. 153–156.

reversal. The new Presidential Administration rescinded the prior decision and in November 2001 the project was reinstated.[31] However, the California State Legislature passed a law requiring that all pending mining projects that might affect historic indigenous lands should require the backfilling of open-cast mining sites to their approximate original contours.[32]

As a result, Glamis claimed under the investment provisions of North American Free Trade Agreement (NAFTA), arguing that it incurred losses arising out of project development in reliance on earlier approvals and in the expectation that its investment would not be harmed by subsequent regulation. The tribunal held that Glamis had not made out its claims. The economic loss suffered as a result of the US government and State Legislative measures was insufficient to warrant a finding of expropriation under Article 1110.[33] Moreover, there was no breach of the fair and equitable treatment standard in Article 1105 of NAFTA, in that the measures complained of did not amount to a breach of the international minimum standard of treatment as prescribed by that provision, since they did not amount to the kinds of egregious acts of maladministration that would constitute a violation of that standard.[34]

The tribunal did not address the human rights aspects of the case directly, though it had admitted *amicus* briefs on behalf of the Quechuan Nation.[35] This is consistent with the procedural caveats with which the submissions of the Quechuan Nation and other third parties were received, namely, that 'acceptance of a non-disputing submission does not require the Tribunal to consider that submission at any point in the arbitration, nor does it entitle the non-disputing party to make any further submissions'.[36] The tribunal, in addition, 'expressed its intent to ensure that the incorporation of any submission, or parts thereof, would not unduly burden the Parties or delay the proceedings'.[37] Though it is possible to say that the rejection of the claims in this case may have been motivated implicitly by considerations of the rights of the Quechuan Nation,[38] the better explanation is to take the tribunal's views at face value and to assume that it remains bound by its procedural limitations,

---

[31] *Ibid.*, paras. 157–159.

[32] For the legislative history of these measures, see *ibid*, paras.166–185.

[33] *Ibid.*, paras. 535–536.   [34] *Ibid.*, paras. 824–829.

[35] *Ibid.*, paras. 267–286. On the impact of *amicus* submissions in investor–state arbitration, see J. Harrison, 'Human Rights Arguments in *Amicus Curiae* Submissions: Promoting Social Justice?' in Dupuy et al (eds.), n. 16, 396–421.

[36] *Glamis Gold*, n. 29, para. 286.   [37] *Ibid.*   [38] See, for example, Kulick, n. 16, 284–285.

and that it need not address human rights issues when making decisions in accordance with the requirements of NAFTA.

On the other hand, the acceptance of *amicus* briefs offers a positive procedural step which may allow for the presentation of wider human rights issues to the tribunal. Arbitrators will read these submissions and that may well influence their view of the facts. But it falls short of any requirement in law to address human rights-based arguments in the award, given that third parties are only heard to the extent that the parties to the arbitration consent, and that the arbitrators are bound by the arbitration agreement as to the limits of their subject-matter jurisdiction. Thus, unless the contesting parties themselves offer human rights-based arguments, tribunals cannot be expected to raise and use them independently.

However, tribunals can still resist the introduction of *amicus* briefs based on human rights arguments. Such was the situation in the cases of *Border Timbers and others v. Zimbabwe* and *Bernhard von Pezold and others v. Zimbabwe*.[39] The claims were brought before an ICSID Tribunal by German and Swiss investors under their respective BITs with Zimbabwe. The claims arose out of the compulsory acquisition of timber plantations, owned by the claimants, by the government of Zimbabwe as part of its land reform programme. In June 2012, the European Center for Constitutional and Human Rights (ECCHR) and the chiefs of four indigenous communities inhabiting the contested lands, in the area of Chimanimani in south-eastern Zimbabwe, sought leave to present *amicus* briefs before the tribunal. These briefs would present evidence and argument based on the rights, in international law, of the indigenous peoples to the disputed lands and to prior consultation, and on how the outcome of the arbitration would impact on those rights. The petitioners contended that 'in light of the "interdependence of international investment law and international human rights law", any decision in these conjoined arbitrations which neglects the content of the international human rights norms will be "legally incomplete".'[40]

---

[39] *Border Timbers and others v. Zimbabwe* and *Bernhard von Pezold and others v. Zimbabwe*, ICSID CASE NO. ARB/10/15 (28 July 2015), www.italaw.com/cases/1472 (last accessed 20 January 2017). See also European Center for Constitutional and Human Rights (ECCHR), 'Human Rights Inapplicable in International Investment Arbitration?' (July 2012), www.ecchr.eu/en/our_work/business-and-human-rights/worldbank.html?file=tl_files/Dokumente/Wirtschaft%2520und%2520Menschenrechte/ICSID%2520tribunal%2520-%2520Human%2520Rights%2520Inapplicable_A%2520Commentary.pdf (last accessed 9 January 2017).

[40] *Border Timbers and Pezold v. Zimbabwe*, n. 39, Annex 2 Procedural order No.2. (26 June 2012) para. 26.

Accordingly, they urged the arbitral tribunal to give due consideration to the duties of states and the responsibilities of companies with respect to the rights of indigenous communities. But the tribunal rejected the petition and denied the Petitioners the opportunity to submit written legal arguments, attend oral hearings or access the submissions of the disputing parties. The tribunal steered itself by the terms of Rule 37(2) of the ICSID Rules of Procedure for Arbitration Proceedings, which requires that the tribunal shall consider, among other things, the extent to which:

(a) the non-disputing party submission would assist the Tribunal in the determination of a factual or legal issue related to the proceeding by bringing a perspective, particular knowledge or insight that is different from that of the disputing parties;
(b) the non-disputing party submission would address a matter within the scope of the dispute;
(c) the non-disputing party has a significant interest in the proceeding.[41]

Following these requirements, the Tribunal held that there was sufficient doubt as to the independence of one of the Petitioners, the Nyahode Union Learning Centre, whose founder and director, Rob Sacco, was a leading activist in the indigenous land reform movement (though it was not shown by the Claimant that this body acted directly with the Respondent State), and that the ECCHR's mission and experience, as an NGO dedicated to issues of international corporate social responsibility, 'do not, in the context of these proceedings, as presently constituted, satisfy the requirement of a "significant interest in the proceedings"'.[42]

Furthermore, the tribunal doubted whether the Petitioner's submissions would assist in its determination of the factual or legal issues before it. The tribunal agreed with the Claimants that the reference to 'such rules of general international law as may be applicable' in the BITs 'does not incorporate the universe of international law into the BITs or into disputes arising under the BITs.'[43] Moreover, neither party had put the identity and/or treatment of indigenous peoples, or the indigenous communities in particular, under international law, including international human rights

---

[41] *Ibid.*, para. 48.   [42] *Ibid.*, paras. 55–56 and 61.
[43] *Ibid.*, para. 57. But see *Urbaser v Argentina* (n. 17) where the Tribunal held that disputes under the applicable BIT could not be limited to claims made by the investor only and could admit counterclaims made by the host state including human rights-based claims (paras. 1182–1192).

law on indigenous peoples, in issue in these proceedings.[44] This made irrelevant references to state obligations under Article 26 of the UN Declaration on the Rights of Indigenous Peoples, which requires states to give legal recognition and protection to lands, territories and resources possessed by indigenous peoples by reason of traditional ownership or other traditional occupation or use.[45]

Moreover, the tribunal rejected the view that international investment law and international human rights law were interdependent, 'such that any decision of these Arbitral Tribunals which did not consider the content of international human rights norms would be legally incomplete'.[46] Equally, the argument that its mandate derived from 'powers delegated to it by Contracting Parties with concrete human rights obligations under international law' was rejected.[47] The tribunal was not persuaded that consideration of the foregoing was in fact part of their mandate under either the ICSID Convention or the applicable BITs.[48]

From the above, it is clear that human rights issues have not had a uniformly positive reception in investment arbitrations. This has been explained as being attributable to the predominantly private law nature of this method of dispute settlement, the commercial law background of its principal practitioners and arbitrators, and the resulting differences in social networks and values that they espouse.[49] In contrast, human rights law is predominantly a creature of public law, whose practitioners are similarly placed in a public law-oriented field and work in networks geared to public policy accountability and change.[50] However, given that the BHR discourse has become louder in recent years and that investment arbitrators are more regularly exposed to human rights-related questions surrounding the cases before them, these initial explanations appear increasingly incomplete. A more likely explanation lies in

---

[44] *Ibid.*   [45] *Ibid.*, para. 58.   [46] *Ibid.*   [47] *Ibid.*

[48] *Ibid.*, para. 59. In *Urbaser v Argentina* (n. 17), the Tribunal held that on the basis of manifest factual links between the claims and the human rights based counterclaim, the jurisdiction of ICSID extended to the latter (paras. 1143–1155).

[49] See further M. Hirsch, 'Interactions between Investment and Non-investment Obligations' in P. Muchlinski, F. Ortino and C. Schreuer (eds.), *The Oxford Handbook of International Investment Law* (Oxford University Press, 2008), 154; M. Hirsch, 'Investment Tribunals and Human Rights: Divergent Paths' in Dupuy et al (eds.), n. 16, 97; M. Hirsch, 'The Interaction between International Investment Law and Human Rights Treaties: A Sociological Perspective' in Y. Shany et al (eds.), *Multi-Sourced Equivalent Norms* (Hart Publishing, 2011), 211.

[50] Hirsch, 'The Interaction' in Y. Shany et al (eds.), *ibid.*

the unwillingness of arbitrators to stray beyond the narrow jurisdictional brief conferred upon them by the investment agreements under which they must work.

Thus, in the *Channel Tunnel Award*, the Tribunal was asked to consider the implications of the European Convention on Human Rights on the obligations of the state parties. The case arose out of repeated complaints from the Claimant, the Channel Tunnel Group, that the tunnel was not being protected from incursions by illegal migrants. The Claimant argued *inter alia* that its right to peaceful enjoyment of its possessions under the Convention was being infringed, as well as its rights under the Tunnel Concession Agreement. The Tribunal rejected this argument on jurisdictional grounds:

> The Tribunal would observe in this context that the Concession Agreement does not contain any contractual commitment by the States Parties that they will comply with their own or with European law. Whether or not they did so would be a matter for their own courts or for the European courts. This contrasts with the commitment by the Concessionaires in Clause 41.2 to comply inter alia with "the laws in force from time to time in each of the two States" and with binding requirements imposed under those laws, it being stipulated that only "extremely serious" breaches of this commitment could give rise to measures under Clause 37 ("Termination by reason of the Fault of the Concessionaires"). In short, national and European law claims against the States are to be the subject of proceedings before the appropriate national or European forums. By contrast it is for the Tribunal to deal with disputes involving the application of the Concession Agreement.[51]

It is this jurisdictional bottleneck that lies at the heart of the general non-reception of substantive human rights-based arguments in investment arbitrations. The source of this bottleneck lies in the absence of clear provisions in IIAs that mandate the tribunal to look at human rights issues in the course of claims made under the agreement. Thus, the solution would appear to lay in the introduction of human rights clauses into IIAs and the consequential extension of subject-matter jurisdiction for tribunals. It may be argued, however, that tribunals as international dispute settlement bodies are already under a duty to apply international

---

[51] *Channel Tunnel Group v. Governments of the United Kingdom and France*, Permanent Court of Arbitration Partial Award (30 January 2007), para. 148, http://archive.pca-cpa .org/ET_PAena0a9.pdf?fil_id=218 (last visited 20 January 2017). But see *Urbaser v Argentina* (n. 17) for a broader view that includes human rights based counterclaims within the legitimate jurisdiction of an investment tribunal.

law, as did the claimants in the above-mentioned cases against
Zimbabwe. But this route is fraught with problems, as it can always be
argued that such claims are so remote from the claims before the tribunal
as to be irrelevant. Therefore, the need for clarification of the relationship
between human rights and international investment law becomes a
pressing issue that a new international BHR treaty could impact upon.
How this can and might be done is the focus of the next part of this
chapter.

13.3   Bringing Human Rights into International Investment Law: The Possible Impact of a New Treaty

The divide between human rights and investment issues is narrower than
might be suggested from the preceding analysis. The subject matter of
investment claims has a mixed public-private character and important
issues of public policy, including human rights claims of affected third
parties (and of the corporate actors themselves), can be involved and can
lie at the heart of any resolution of the dispute.[52] Equally, as argued above,
the sociological explanation for divergence can only go so far. Arbitrators
do not live in a hermetically sealed world and, at a time when the very
legitimacy of their enterprise is under scrutiny, they may well be receptive
to new ways of re-establishing that legitimacy, including through the
hearing of human rights-based arguments. The key issue remains whether
such receptiveness will lead to decisions that take human rights actively
into account or whether, as suggested from the previous section, arbitrators might continue to find ways to sidestep such issues.

In addition, resistance from some more commercial law-oriented
arbitrators cannot be fully discounted.[53]

The current efforts to develop a more normative system for BHR will
no doubt seek to have real consequences, and one of these might be the
reform of the issues that investment treaties and investment tribunals can

---

[52] On the essentially public character law of investment claims, see G. van Harten and M.
Loughlin, 'Investment Treaty Arbitration as a Species of Global Administrative Law'
(2006) 17 *European Journal of International Law* 121; M. Sornarajah, *Resistance and
Change in the International Law on Foreign Investment* (Cambridge University Press,
2015), 318–324; B. Simma, 'Foreign Investment Arbitration: A Place for Human Rights?'
(2011) 60 *International and Comparative Law Quarterly* 573. On the conceptual similarities between the two fields, see J. D. Fry, 'International Human Rights Law in Investment
Arbitration: Evidence of International Law's Unity' (2007–2008) 18 *Duke Journal of
Comparative & International Law* 1.
[53] See Sornarajah, *ibid.*

review. Before the options for such an impact are considered, it should be pointed out that were a future investment law regime to integrate human rights into its subject matter, it is probably inescapable that not only will the human rights responsibilities of corporate actors towards third parties affected by their operations become relevant, but that the human rights responsibilities of home and host states towards those third parties and the corporate actors themselves will become matters of significance. It is hard to imagine that human rights questions will not cover all these eventualities. Thus, one consequence of the move towards greater corporate accountability in this field may well be the rise of corporate human rights-based claims, such as that made in the *Channel Tunnel Case*.[54] Whether or not the assertion of human rights claims by corporate actors is desirable, or a price worth paying for corporate human rights responsibilities is a discussion requiring a further chapter, but it is a matter that negotiators of a BHR treaty ought to be aware of.

Against this background, the remainder of this section will consider three main options available for introducing human rights issues into investment law and arbitration through a treaty instrument. These range from high impact to low impact options with the strongest option being for a treaty with binding corporate human rights obligations, through an intermediate option involving a treaty commitment to state duties to protect and voluntary corporate responsibilities (essentially following the GPs model) and a third, low impact option, of a best efforts agreement, which would leave the status quo essentially intact.

13.3.1   High Impact Binding Obligations

To achieve this end, the proposed BHR treaty would need to contain a series of provisions that state expressly the nature and scope of corporate human rights obligations. The level of specificity would depend on negotiating outcomes.[55]

---

[54] See J. Alvarez, 'Are Corporations "Subjects" of International Law' (2010) 9 *Santa Clara Journal of International Law* 1, at 27–31 (who warns that the inclusion of human rights-based arguments in investor–state arbitration is likely to result in the extension of human rights to corporate actors, especially if they are seen as having a measure of international personality). On the human rights of corporate actors in international investment law, see N. Klein, 'Human Rights and International Investment Law: Investment Protection as Human Right?' (2012) 4 *Goettingen Journal of International Law* 1. On corporate claims to human rights, see P. Muchlinski, *Multinational Enterprises and the Law*, 2nd edn. (Oxford University Press, 2007), 509–514 and the references cited therein.

[55] See Ramasastry and Cassel, n. 7, 41–42; De Schutter, n. 7, 58–62.

The precedent of the UN Norms on the Responsibilities of Transnational Corporations and Other Business Enterprises with Regard to Human Rights suggests that a list of obligations could be drawn up.[56] However, the content of the UN Norms proved highly controversial in that it transposed obligations from existing human rights instruments that were directed at states and asserted that these applied to corporations as well.[57] In addition, certain obligations, not commonly understood as human rights obligations, such as consumer rights, were tagged on.[58] The result was easy to criticize on the grounds that it conflated state responsibility with corporate responsibility, and invented new obligations that had never been accepted as such under international law.[59] This was a major reason behind the adoption of a non-binding 'responsibility to respect' human rights under the GPs.[60] That said, the advantage of having a list of normative obligations in a treaty directed at corporations is to create binding norms, as it is possible, under international law, to create direct obligations upon non-state actors through the treaty route.[61]

Assuming that such a list of obligations exists, this does not resolve, by itself, the question of their applicability to investment treaties or to investment arbitration. Here the type of obligation becomes important. A distinction needs to be made between fundamental human rights

---

[56] Commission of Human Rights, 'Norms on the Responsibilities of Transnational Corporations and Other Business Enterprises with Regard to Human Rights', UN Doc. E/CN.4/Sub.2/2003/12/Rev.2(2003) (13 August 2003). See also D. Weissbrodt and M. Kruger, 'Norms on the Responsibilities of Transnational Corporations and Other Business Enterprises with Regard to Human Rights' (2003) 97 *American Journal of International Law* 901.

[57] See also Muchlinski, *Multinational Enterprises*, n. 54, 521–524 and 532.   [58] *Ibid.*, 524.

[59] *Ibid.*, 534 and 535–536. See also Commission on Human Rights, 'Interim Report of the Special Representative of the Secretary-General on the Issue of Human Rights and Transnational Corporations and Other Business Enterprises', E/CN.4/2006/97 (2006)' (22 February 2006).

[60] 'Nothing in these Guiding Principles should be read as creating new international law obligations, or as limiting or undermining any legal obligations a State may have undertaken or be subject to under international law with regard to human rights.' Guiding Principles, n. 1.

[61] See, for example, D. J. Harris, *Cases and Materials on International Law*, 7th edn. (Sweet & Maxwell, 2010), 127 (citing the direct liability of ships owners for oil pollution under Article 1 of the International Convention on Civil Liability for Oil Pollution Damage 1969). For an analysis of corporate obligations under international law, see R. G. Steinhardt, 'Multinational Corporations and Their Responsibilities under International Law' in L. Blecher, N. K. Staffor and G. C. Bellamy (eds.), *Corporate Responsibility for Human Rights Impacts: New Expectations and Paradigms* (American Bar Association, 2014), 27–50.

obligations that represent *jus cogens* and are, therefore, directly binding on all as peremptory norms of international law, and other human rights obligations which may need further implementing rules to be directly effective against non-state actors under international law.[62]

In relation to *jus cogens* norms, as these can be directly binding on all, it is arguable that any corporate action which violates such norms cannot be allowed to stand and must incur a penalty. In relation to protections under an IIA, this could be interpreted to mean that the benefits of the agreement would become unavailable where it can be shown that the corporate investor has acted in contravention of these norms. This outcome could already be accommodated under IIAs which specify that investments must be made 'in accordance with the law'. This phrase has been interpreted to mean that where corporate actions fall short of this requirement, the investor cannot bring a claim under the applicable IIA.[63] In some arbitral awards, the phrase 'in accordance with the law' has also been interpreted to include situations where the investor's action can be said to violate 'international public policy' as where evidence of gross corruption exists.[64] It would not be a major step to add that where an investor is seen to be in violation of peremptory norms of human rights law, the protection of the IIA is lost as it would be against public policy to allow for such protection in the circumstances of the case.

---

[62] *Jus cogens* norms in the field of human rights include 'the prohibition of aggression, slavery and the slave trade, genocide, racial discrimination apartheid and torture, as well as basic rules of international humanitarian law applicable in armed conflict and the right to self-determination'. International Law Commission, *Fragmentation of International Law: Difficulties Arising from the Diversification and Expansion of International Law*, A/CN.5/L.702 (18 July 2006), para. 33.

[63] 'The requirement in Article 1(1) of the Ukraine-Lithuania BIT that investments be made in compliance with the laws and regulations of the host state is a common requirement in modern BITs'. *Salini Construction v. Morocco* (Decision on Jurisdiction), ICSID Case No ARB/00/4 (23 July 2001), 42 ILM 609 (2003), para. 46. See also *Tokios Tokeles v. Ukraine* (Decision on Jurisdiction), ICSID Case No. ARB/02/18 (29 April 2004), para. 84 (the purpose of such provisions, as explained by the Tribunal in *Salini Costruttori S.p.A and Italstrade S.p.A v. Morocco*, is 'to prevent the Bilateral Treaty from protecting investments that should not be protected, particularly because they would be illegal').

[64] 'In light of domestic laws and international conventions relating to corruption, and in light of the decisions taken in this matter by courts and arbitral tribunals, this Tribunal is convinced that bribery is contrary to the international public policy of most, if not all, States or, to use another formula, to transnational public policy. Thus, claims based on contracts of corruption or on contracts obtained by corruption cannot be upheld by this Arbitral Tribunal.' *World Duty Free v. The Republic of Kenya* (Award), ICSID Case No ARB/00/07 (4 October 2006), para. 157.

As regards non-peremptory human rights norms, something more is still needed. The major issue concerns how new corporate obligations could be operationalized in IIAs. The obvious method is through a specific human rights clause in the investment agreement, which requires corporate investors to observe their human rights obligations, as expressed in the new BHR treaty, as a concomitant to their enjoyment of investor and investment protection under the treaty. A model for such a clause has been offered by UNCTAD as an option for negotiators.[65] According to UNCTAD, to correct the asymmetry created by existing IIAs, which only set out obligations for states, 'an IIA could also set out investor obligations or responsibilities, noting the evolving views on the capacity of international law to impose obligations on private parties'.[66] As Section 7.1.1. of the UNCTAD's Investment Policy Framework for Sustainable Development proposes, an IIA could:

> Require that investors comply with host State laws at both the entry and the post-entry stage of an investment.
>   Establish sanctions for non-compliance:
>
> - deny treaty protection to investments made in violation of the host State law
> - deny treaty protection to investments operating in violation of those host State laws that reflect international legally binding obligations (e.g. core labour standards, anti-corruption, environment conventions) and other laws as identified
> - consider investor conduct when interpreting IIA protection standards
> - provide for States' right to bring counterclaims in ISDS arising from investors' violations of host State law.[67]

UNCTAD's Framework states that these options will condition treaty protection upon certain investor behaviour and raise the obligation to comply with domestic laws to the international level, thereby increasing its relevance in arbitration.[68] This formulation is made taking account of existing circumstances, hence the emphasis on host state laws. However, were such a clause to refer directly to the new BHR treaty as well as

---

[65] UNCTAD, 'Investment Policy Framework for Sustainable Development', (2015), http://unctad.org/en/PublicationsLibrary/diaepcb2015d5_en.pdf (last accessed 9 January 2017).

[66] *Ibid.*, 109.

[67] *Ibid.* See further *Urbaser v Argentina* (n. 17) where the Tribunal accepted the principle that a corporate investor could have human rights obligations and that the state can bring a human rights based counterclaim alleging a violation of such obligations. On the limitations of this decision, see further Crow and Lorenzoni, n. 17.

[68] See n. 65, 108.

domestic laws, the impact would be that much greater. Neither the negotiators or any future investment tribunal tasked with the interpretation of the IIA in question could doubt that the intent was to subject investors to the human rights obligations contained in the new treaty. The jurisdictional problems identified in the previous section of this chapter (i.e., that arbitrators are not bound to consider human rights issues as they are not mentioned in most first-generation IIAs) would then simply disappear.

The foregoing discussion relates to the content of new IIAs. Most existing IIAs do not have any such investor obligations clause. Thus, the question remains whether the existence of a new BHR treaty, which contains a base of binding norms, would need to be taken into account when interpreting such a first-generation IIA. Here the general rules of treaty interpretation come into play. Article 31(3) of the Vienna Convention on the Law of Treaties provides that treaty interpretation shall take into account not only the treaty's context but also '(a) any subsequent agreement between the parties regarding the interpretation of the treaty or the application of its provisions... (b) any subsequent practice in the application of the treaty which establishes agreement of the parties regarding interpretation.'

Should both the Contracting Parties to an IIA be signatories of a new treaty on BHR, Article 31(3) could form the basis of an obligation on the tribunal to consider the impact of that treaty upon any claims before it.[69] It may be objected that to expect investment tribunals to limit investor rights by reference to a BHR treaty would be inconsistent with the object and purpose of an IIA. However, there is no reason why the Contracting Parties, who have agreed upon the scope of investor rights in the IIA, could not reconsider that scope in the light of new developments, such as a greater emphasis on the investor's human rights responsibilities. Indeed, the interpretation of an international treaty is in the hands of the parties as much as in the hands of any tribunal that is tasked with its application. Given that investment tribunals have considered the subsequent practice of a Contracting Party when, for example, analysing the scope of the most-favoured nation (MFN) clause, it seems hard to say that this cannot be done when considering the impact of the investor's conduct on the merits of their claim.[70] The main objection to such an

---

[69] On the use of Article 31(3) in investment arbitration, see A. Roberts, 'Power and Persuasion in Investment Treaty Interpretation: The Dual Role of States' (2010) 104 *American Journal of International Law* 179.

[70] Thus, in *Mafezzini v. Spain*, ICSID Case No. Arb (AF)/00/2 (29 May 2003), the Tribunal considered Argentina's subsequent practice of excluding the exhaustion of local remedies

approach to the new BHR treaty would be that it does not purport to interpret the scope of any IIAs to which the Contracting States are parties. Thus, much would depend on whether the new treaty contained language that would offer a clear indication that its content was to be used as an aid to the interpretation of IIAs, and of investor rights and duties in particular.[71]

More problematic is the case where only one of the parties to the IIA has signed the BHR treaty. In the absence of a clear provision in the IIA which extends the operation of that treaty to the IIA in question, it would appear that a tribunal would have to ignore arguments based on the new treaty. To do otherwise would be to impose obligations on a sovereign state against its will. Then the only possible impact route would be that the new treaty reflects customary international law and so can be used as an aid to interpretation of the IIA under Article 31(3)(c) of the Vienna Convention on the Law of Treaties. This argument appears rather strained.

A new BHR treaty would most probably cover the applicability of peremptory norms of human rights law, and other human rights norms, to corporate actors. The applicability of peremptory human rights norms to non-state actors would reflect existing customary international law. However, in asserting the applicability of non-peremptory human rights norms, the new treaty would undoubtedly be setting new standards in relation to the human rights responsi-bilities of corporations. The question then arises whether references to these standards could be seen as generating new rules of custom-ary international law.

Although it is possible to see customary law emerging out of the progressive development of international law though treaties, whether the new treaty would meet the criteria of a customary law making treaty is

---

rule form its more recent BITs as evidence in favour of ignoring that rule in the Argentina-Spain BIT under which the claim in that case was brought. See further Muchlinski, *Multinational Enterprises*, n. 54, 631–635.

[71] In this connection in may be noted that the GPs state the following in the Commentary on Principle 9: 'the terms of international investment agreements may constrain States from fully implementing new human rights legislation, or put them at risk of binding interna-tional arbitration if they do so. Therefore, States should ensure that they retain adequate policy and regulatory ability to protect human rights under the terms of such agreements, while providing the necessary investor protection.' Therefore, new IIAs should not ignore any new obligations states choose to assume in relation to business and human rights and ensure that this is reflected in the language of the treaty.

open to debate.[72] These criteria were examined by the International Court of Justice (ICJ) in the *North Sea Continental Shelf* case.[73] These include that the provisions in question be of 'a fundamentally norm-creating character such as could be regarded as forming the basis of a general rule of law' and that 'a widespread and representative participation in the Convention might suffice of itself, provided it included that of States whose interests were specially affected'.[74] Moreover, the ICJ noted that:

> although the passage of only a short period of time is not necessarily, or of itself, a bar to the formation of a new rule of customary international law on the basis of what was originally a purely conventional rule, an indispensable requirement would be that within the period in question, short though it might be, State practice, including that of States whose interests are specially affected, should have been both extensive and virtually uniform in the sense of the provision invoked – and should have occurred in such a way as to show a general recognition of a rule or law or legal obligation is involved.[75]

The strongest argument in favour of viewing a new BHR treaty as constitutive of customary law would be the normative nature of human rights obligations. However, this very argument was used to justify the UN Norms and was rejected by the SRSG when he examined the normative basis for the GPs.[76] Whether, now, this objection could be overcome depends on how far states are willing to concede that the human rights responsibilities of business enterprises have acquired normative status. A more basic problem will lie in the number of states that might sign up to the new treaty and whether they would represent an 'extensive and virtually uniform practice' as required by the ICJ. Given the avowed opposition of the main home states of MNEs to the proposed treaty, states who have an undoubted interest in such a treaty, this test seems likely to fall at this hurdle.[77]

---

[72] The ICJ observed that it is possible for a treaty provision to be norm-creating, and to be seen as binding even for countries that have never, and do not, become parties to that treaty, and that this 'constitutes indeed one of the methods by which new rules of customary international law may be formed. At the same time this result is not lightly to be regarded as having been attained.' *North Sea Continental Shelf Case* [1969] *ICJ Reports* 3, para. 71.

[73] *Ibid.*, paras. 72–74.   [74] *Ibid.*, para. 74.   [75] *Ibid.*

[76] See text at n. 56–59. But see Steinhardt, 'Multinational Corporations', n. 61; and D. Bilchitz, 'A Chasm Between "Is" and "Ought"? A Critique of the Normative Foundations of the SRSG's Framework and the Guiding Principles' in Deva and Bilchitz (eds.), n. 3, 107.

[77] Resolution 26/9 was adopted at the HRC by a recorded vote of 20 to 14, with 13 abstentions. HRC, 'Elaboration of an International Legally Binding Instrument', n. 6.

From the above analysis it is clear that, in the absence of a specialized BHR provision in an IIA, even a high impact binding obligation treaty may have limited effect upon investor obligations and how they might be interpreted by an arbitral tribunal, especially where not all the Contracting Parties to the IIA in question are also parties to the new treaty. However, the proposed treaty may not be a high impact normative instrument but may pursue more modest aims, which in themselves, might impact on how tribunals see investor behaviour. Two alternatives are possible, a treaty that clarifies certain aspects of the GPs by way of improving international cooperation on standards and access to remedies, and an even lower impact treaty that offers a hortatory commitment to furthering business responsibilities for human rights, possibly including a state reporting function.

13.3.2 Limited Impact Treaty: Improving International Cooperation on Standards and Access to Remedies

A high impact treaty, as described, appears at this stage to be an unlikely outcome of the continuing treaty discussions in the UN. A more probable option is for a treaty that seeks to clarify certain aspect of the GPs with a view to enhancing their effectiveness. This would be in line with the avowed aims of the UN Working Group on BHR, set up to continue the work of embedding the GPs.[78] Such a treaty would most likely not have a section devoted to corporate human rights obligations, retaining the non-binding corporate responsibility to respect human rights from the GPs, but would concentrate on strengthening the state duty to protect and access to remedies pillars.[79]

In particular, certain issues that were left open by the GPs could be further developed. In relation to the state duty to protect, this would require a clearer obligation on both home and host states to pass laws that would increase the domestic legal obligations of corporations to observe human rights, whether through specialist legislation and/or amendments to corporate and securities laws, to make grants of state assistance or investment risk insurance by the home-state subject to effective human

---

[78] See Human Rights Council, 'Twenty-ninth Session Report of the Working Group on the Issue of Human Rights and Transnational Corporations and Other Business Enterprises', A/HRC/29/28 (28 April 2015).

[79] See De Schutter, n. 7, 44–55; Ramasastry and Cassel, n. 7, 20–24; ICJ, n. 7, 43–44.

rights risk assessments,[80] and to require, as a matter of host state law, that all investment proposals be accompanied by such a risk assessment. Furthermore, the issue of extraterritorial application of home-state domestic human rights obligations to the overseas activities of MNEs domiciled in that state could be addressed.[81] In particular, the risk of a clash of obligations for the MNE, caused by differences in home and host state laws concerning corporate liabilities for human rights violations, could be addressed. Ideally, this would entail a harmonization of corporate human rights liabilities for all signatory states so as to remove that risk. At the very least the treaty could provide for a consultation procedure for the resolution of any extraterritoriality disputes arising between the home and host states.

In relation to access to remedies, the major obstacles cited in the GPs to the availability of formal legal remedies could be dealt with. These obstacles include the question of extraterritorial jurisdiction over claims made by affected groups or individuals in the host state, the removal of the obstacle of separate corporate personality and limited liability in claims made against the parent company for the acts of its overseas subsidiaries, and the availability of legal aid for the bringing of such claims.[82] Removing these obstacles may not have a direct impact on IIA content. However, dealing with them might avoid possible future IIA-based investor claims, arising out of the application of domestic law to an investor for alleged human rights infringements, on the grounds that the bringing of such a claim violated treaty protections, given the uncertain and unusual nature of the law and procedure surrounding the domestic action. Resolving these uncertainties would ensure that domestic legal actions concerning corporate human rights responsibilities were based on internationally agreed procedural and substantive norms, thereby obviating the possibility of a challenge under an IIA.

---

[80] See Simma, n. 52, 594–596; International Finance Corporation (IFC), 'Guide to Human Rights Impact Assessment and Management (HRIAM)' (September 2011), www.unglobal compact.org/docs/issues_doc/human_rights/GuidetoHRIAM.pdf (last accessed 9 January 2017); J. Harrison, 'Establishing a Meaningful Human Rights Due Diligence Process for Corporations : Learning from Experience of Human Rights Impact Assessment' (2013) 31 (2) *Impact Assessment and Project Appraisal* 107.

[81] For further elaboration, see Chapter 12 in this volume.

[82] See De Schutter, n. 7, 44–55. On legal aid issues, see R. Meeran, 'Access to Remedy: The United Kingdom Experience of MNC Tort Litigation for Human Rights Violations' in Deva and Bilchitz (eds.), n. 3, 378 at 395-401 (citing J. Ruggie's criticism of the UK Legal Aid Sentencing and Punishment of Offenders Act 2012 for limiting access to legal aid and its impact on human rights cases against MNEs).

Were such a treaty to be adopted, its impact on investment treaties would again depend on how far its provisions would be reproduced within an IIA. The UNCTAD model, cited earlier, offers one example. In that model, the failure of an investor to observe the legal obligations imposed upon it by reason of home and/or host state laws would disentitle it from protection under the IIA in question. In this regard, the impact on the investor would be similar to that which would arise if direct international legal obligations were imposed, but with the difference that the source of legal obligation would be the domestic law of one or both of the Contracting Parties to the IIA. A tribunal faced with evidence of the non-observance of such laws by the investor could conclude that this disentitles the latter from protection under the treaty, especially where the IIA contains an 'in accordance with the law' condition on its protection. Regarding the access to remedy issue, it is uncertain how that would affect the outcome of any claim made before an investor–state tribunal, though, as discussed above, some harmonization of substantive and procedural rules applicable to domestic human rights claims against corporations would reduce the risk of an IIA-based challenge against such a claim. On the other hand, the alleged victim of the human rights violation would, surely, have a claim against the home/host state for failure to provide a remedy in breach of their commitments under the new BHR treaty (should such a claim be available under the applicable domestic law), a claim that would not concern an investor–state tribunal.

13.3.3   Low Impact Treaty: Best Efforts and Reporting

At the lowest impact level, a future BHR treaty could include little more than a restatement of commitments to the GPs, and a hortatory commitment for states to use their best efforts to further the observance of human rights by corporate actors. This might be accompanied by an obligation on the signatory states to make regular reports on progress made to further this aim, in line with the practice of other human rights instruments, most notably the International Covenant on Economic, Social and Cultural Rights. According to De Schutter, such a system could be made more demanding than under existing human rights treaties citing the World Health Organization Framework Convention on Tobacco Control as a model of a convention that sets general aims and requires states to submit reports detailing *inter alia* legislative efforts to meet those aims. However, he views such a development as being of questionable political feasibility.[83] Furthermore, so far as impact on investment law and arbitration is concerned, such a convention would appear to have none. Were this option to be followed, the most likely impact would be to continue the status quo described in the first part of this chapter.

13.4 Concluding Remarks

There is little doubt that the human rights responsibilities of business will play an increasingly important role in international law. The extent to which this trend impacts upon international investment law and arbitration remains open to discussion. Much depends on whether any future treaty on BHR expressly addresses the interaction of this area with investment law obligations and, especially, its impact on the drafting of new IIAs. To date few IIAs mention human rights, and, those that do take a mostly hortatory approach. The best method to ensure that human rights obligations and responsibilities of business are taken into account is to have an express human rights clause in the IIA that makes the observance of human rights by the investor a precondition for the enjoyment of protection. As discussed in this chapter, UNCTAD's Framework has pointed the way with its draft clause.

A new treaty could take this further. A number of matters could be addressed. For example, the treaty could clarify that a reference to host state laws in an IIA includes the core international human rights instruments, thereby ensuring that failure to comply with their content by an investor would nullify their protection under the agreement. In addition, at the post-entry stage, any changes in host state law relating to the furtherance of human rights protection could be protected from a challenge by an investor on the grounds that they amounted to a breach of the applicable IIA. The human rights undertaking in the Baku-Tbilisi-Ceyhan Pipeline Agreement could provide a negotiating template.[84] Though appearing in an investor–state contract, its provisions could be adapted to ensure that subsequent host state action aimed at protecting human rights is not subjected to legal challenge under the applicable investment treaty.[85]

---

[83] See De Schutter, n. 7, 55–58.

[84] 'Protocol between BP Exploration (Caspian Sea) Ltd and the Government of the Republic of Azerbaijan on the Implementation of Security and Human Rights Principles', www.bp.com/content/dam/bp-country/en_az/pdf/legalagreements/Bilateral_Security_Protocol_ signed_en.pdf (last accessed 9 January 2017).

[85] See S. Leader, 'Human Rights, Risks, and New Strategies for Global Investment' (2006) 9 *Journal of International Economic Law* 657.

Furthermore, the proposed BHR treaty might consider whether to use principles taken from administrative law, such as the proportionality principle, in determining the balance to be struck between the human rights responsibility of corporations and their rights as investors. Finally, the relationship between human rights norms and investment law norms could be further addressed. In order to avoid uncertainty over the question of which norm has precedence, the new treaty could declare that where there is a conflict between the requirements of investment treaty rights and human rights, the latter shall prevail. Such an approach has already been taken in some investment treaties in relation to international environmental standards found in multilateral environmental agreements and it could be adapted to the BHR treaty.[86]

In the absence of a commitment to express BHR clauses in IIAs, arbitrators can already take account of human rights-based arguments. They can allow *amicus* briefs to be admitted with the consent of the parties to the dispute. They can also consider how far an investor's conduct that does not uphold fundamental human rights is illegal and so outside the protection of an IIA. More recently, the Tribunal in *Urbaser v. Argentina* admitted a counterclaim based on human rights arguments by the Respondent State, though it did not uphold it on the merits.[87] However, the extent to which arbitrators are bound to consider human rights-based arguments remains very tentative and leaves much to their discretion. Thus, a BHR treaty that falls short of demanding express BHR clauses in IIAs is unlikely to have great impact unless it includes a commitment to develop binding domestic law obligations on business, which in turn can reinforce the need for an investor to observe human rights as a condition of its legality. However, this approach still leaves the ultimate discretion to the arbitrator when interpreting the IIA before them. Not all IIAs condition the enjoyment of investor rights on their being 'in accordance with the law'. In such cases, arbitrators may not feel bound to apply human rights standards to their assessment of investor action.

Therefore, if a BHR treaty is to have real impact on investment law and arbitration, the conclusion of an obligation on signatory states to include a BHR clause in all future IIAs, and to amend existing agreements to include one, would appear essential. Whether sufficient consensus to have such a clause exists is open to doubt, but, if the will were there, the means to do so is clearly visible.

---

[86] See Muchlinski, *Multinational Enterprises*, n. 54, 571–572.
[87] *Urbaser v. Argentina*, n. 17.

PART V

Improving Access to Remedies for Victims

14

Access to Remedy

Treaty Talks and the Terms of a New Accountability Accord

ERIKA R GEORGE AND LISA J LAPLANTE

14.1 Introduction

Assuring fair and equitable redress for serious human rights violations forms the bedrock of any human rights system. Whether this harm can be attributed to a state or private actor should not matter if the action violated the human rights of an individual. Regardless who the perpetrator may be, an affected individual or community should be able to count on a prompt and adequate response, as the access to fair and equitable redress is a stand-alone human right. Responses could include compensation, an apology or other measures that provide satisfaction and a sense of justice. The ability of individuals to enforce this right goes towards assuring the whole protective system operates effectively.

Yet, the resurrection of failed attempts to advance a binding instrument in the area of business and human rights (BHR) points to a particular weakness with current efforts to assure access to adequate and effective remedies for rights violations. Although a significant segment of the international community has agreed that business enterprises have a responsibility to respect human rights and that states must protect human rights,[1] more often than not victims of violations remain without access to an adequate and effective remedy. States hosting companies alleged to be responsible for serious human rights abuses are often ineffective venues for redress, Moreover, some forums for redress have been further limited by court decisions in the United States foreclosing a previously open avenue for victims of rights violations to bring their claims against business enterprises under the Alien Tort Claims Act

---

[1] Human Rights Council, 'Guiding Principles on Business and Human Rights: Implementing the United Nations "Protect, Respect and Remedy" Framework', A/HRC/17/31 (21 March 2011).

(ATCA).[2] The result is that thousands of victims are left without recourse and businesses operate with impunity.

For this reason, the authors of this chapter contend that the BHR treaty negotiation must prioritize the question of remedies. This chapter traces the narrative of remedies in the recent efforts to negotiate a legally binding international instrument to regulate the conduct of transnational corporations (TNCs) in international human rights law. The authors offer a descriptive account of the different positions taken by various stakeholders on the question of remedies during the first session of the Open-ended Intergovernmental Working Group (OEIGWG) held in July 2015 in order to offer an objective evaluation of the overall inclusion, understanding and positioning of the concept of remedies in the treaty negotiation process. By analysing the public positions of civil society organizations (CSOs), victim groups and governments, the authors provide a historical record of the initial issues related to assuring an adequate remedy.

We argue that the proposed treaty must provide guidance to states on how to assist victims in overcoming obstacles to accessing remedies regardless of the size, nationality or location of the business enterprise implicated in human rights violations. The authors explore different options for including the right to remedy by looking comparatively at other treaty regimes and monitoring bodies. We believe that whatever is the outcome of the treaty negotiations with regard to an actual binding instrument, it is an important moment in solidifying the international right to an adequate and effective remedy. Finally, this unique opportunity could help to create a culture of accountability which also recognizes that a restorative justice approach will better respect diversity and pluralism through complementary dispute resolution processes while directly addressing power asymmetry between alleged victims and alleged violators.

First, we offer a brief overview of some of the present barriers to access to remedy. Next, we review the stand of different stakeholders involved in negotiating a BHR treaty and the range of perspectives presented at the initial round of treaty talks regarding access to remedy. We show that despite consistent reference to the issue of remedies during the talks, stakeholders did not appear to share a common concept of remedy.

---

[2] *Esther Kiobel v. Royal Dutch Petroleum* 133 S Ct 1659 (2013); *Balintulo v. Ford Motor Co.* 796 F.3d 160 (2015); *Doe v. Drummond Co.* 782 F.3d 576 (2015); *Du Daobin v. Cisco Sys. Inc.* 2 F. Supp. 3d 717 (2014); *Jovic v. L-3 Servs., Inc.* 69 F. Supp. 3d 750 (2014); *Adhikari v. Daoud & Partners* 95 F. Supp. 3d 1013 (2015); *Cardona v. Chiquita Brands Intern'l*, Inc. 760 F.3d 1185 (2014).

Having identified this challenge, we present a typology of the features of existing human rights instruments on the issue of remedies to provide a framework to inform future debates on how remedies could be incorporated into a legally binding international instrument. We explain the substantive right to remedy and the procedural requirements of various enforcement mechanisms of human rights instruments. Finally, we propose specific remedy provisions for a BHR treaty.

14.2   A Right to Remedy: Righting a Wrong

The primary impetus for the creation of a BHR treaty arises out of the failure by the international community to get remedy right, that is, to ensure survivors of rights abuses receive fair and just compensation when their human rights are violated. Indeed, practitioners and researchers remind us of the dismal plight of individuals who have had their rights trampled upon by business actors and yet encounter daunting obstacles when trying to get relief through local courts or administrative bodies.[3] The result is not only injustice for the wronged but also a complete lack of accountability of the business actors. Yet, there is universal consensus that access to adequate remedies is not only important, but also an essential right of all individuals as reflected in both treaty and customary law.[4] Indeed, the theory of remedies recognizes that a right can only be vindicated if there exist adequate and effective remedies to not only make the victim whole but also ensure enforcement of the rights framework, assuring prevention of future wrongs.[5]

For that reason, the Guiding Principles on Business and Human Rights (GPs), endorsed unanimously by the United Nations Human Rights Council (HRC) in 2011, acknowledge the importance of remedy as central to support efforts to improve business conduct and increase respect for

---

[3] *Esther Kiobel v. Royal Dutch Petroleum* 133 S Ct 1659 (2013); *Balintulo v. Ford Motor Co.* 796 F.3d 160 (2015); *Doe v. Drummond Co.* 782 F.3d 576 (2015); *Du Daobin v. Cisco Sys. Inc.* 2 F. Supp. 3d 717 (2014); *Jovic v. L-3 Servs., Inc.* 69 F. Supp. 3d 750 (2014); *Adhikari v. Daoud & Partners* 95 F. Supp. 3d 1013 (2015); *Cardona v. Chiquita Brands Intern'l*, Inc. 760 F.3d 1185 (2014).

[4] D. Shelton, *Remedies in International Human Rights Law*, 3rd edn. (Oxford University Press, 2015).

[5] L. J. Laplante, 'Bringing Effective Remedies Home: The Inter-American Human Rights System, Reparations, and the Duty of Prevention' (2004) 22 *Netherlands Quarterly of Human Rights* 347.

human rights.[6] For example, with respect to the obligation of states, the GPs provide in Pillar three that: 'As a part of their duty to protect against business-related human rights abuse, States must take appropriate steps to ensure, through judicial, administrative, legislative or other appropriate means, that when such abuses occur within their territory and/or jurisdiction those affected have access to effective remedy.'[7] Pillar three also engages business as it provides guidance on principles fundamental to creating fair non-state-based grievance mechanisms. Additionally, the GPs emphasize that business enterprises have a constructive role to play in redressing wrongs by providing that businesses should 'make it possible for grievances to be addressed early and remediated directly, business enterprises should establish or participate in effective operational-level grievance mechanisms for individuals and communities who may be adversely impacted.'[8] Finally, given the importance of remedy in realizing rights and in promoting the enjoyment of rights, Pillar three of the GPs is devoted to the concern of accessing remedies and offers comprehensive guidance on this topic. While Pillar one represents the duty of the state, and Pillar two embodies responsibility of the business world, it is Pillar three that most closely represents the role and interests of affected individuals and communities in the 'Protect, Respect and Remedy' Framework – even if not explicitly named as such.[9] It is, of course, the victims and their advocates who vigilantly seek remedies, and they are thus the lynchpin of assuring that the machinery of human rights accountability functions well.

Yet, commentators have observed that the GPs do not go far enough to adequately protect the interests of victims and their right to adequate and effective remedies. For example, speaking at the concluding session of the 2014 UN Annual Forum on Business and Human Rights, a representative from Amnesty International observed that not enough was being done for victims and that business enterprises continued to evade accountability for rights violations.[10] Similarly, the International Federation for Human Rights (FIDH), a coalition representing over 160 different human rights

---

[6] J. Drimmer and L. J. Laplante, 'The Third Pillar: Remedies, Reparations and the Ruggie Principles' in J. Martin and K. E. Bravo (eds.), *The Business And Human Rights Landscape: Moving Forward, Looking Back* (Cambridge University Press, 2015), 316.

[7] Guiding Principle, n. 1, Principle 25.   [8] *Ibid.*, Principle 29.

[9] Author Laplante's conversation with Tyler Giannini, Director, Harvard Human Rights Clinic.

[10] United Nations Forum on Business and Human Rights, 'Closing Conversation: Strategic Paths Forward and Next Steps for the Global Business and Human Rights Regime' (3 December 2014).

organizations on five continents, criticized Professor John Ruggie, the former United Nations Secretary General's Special Representative on the issue of human rights and business (SRSG), for putting forward a 'weak and ambiguous interpretation of the right to an effective remedy, and for focusing too much on non-judicial remedies, falling short of providing strong recommendations to bring justice and reparations to victims'.[11]

Arguably, the alleged weaknesses in Pillar three may reflect the lack of victims' voices in the development of the framework. For example, Surya Deva has questioned that the 'manufactured consensus' around the SRSG's process came through the exclusion of dissenting points of view and in particular the views of victims of human rights violations.[12] He has observed that 'one issue of concern here relates to the SRSGs conscious decision not to engage directly with victims of corporate human rights violations, thus denying them an opportunity to raise their concerns directly'.[13]

If we listen to the voices of victims, we learn that far too often they remain without access to an adequate and effective remedy despite the hardship and suffering caused by corporate abuses. For decades, human rights advocates working with victimized populations have recognized the challenges and obstacles standing in the way of victims accessing adequate remedies.[14] Indeed, it is arguably the raison d'être of these organizations to call for investigating, prosecuting and providing reparations for human rights violations. Likewise, advocates, researchers and practitioners aligned with the growing BHR movement have started to produce a growing number of reports and studies which document how survivors of human rights abuse face a wide range of legal and practical barriers to gaining access to both judicial and non-judicial bodies to remedy their violation of rights.[15]

---

[11] V. V. Der Plancke et al., *Corporate Accountability for Human Rights Abuses – A Guide for Victims and NGOs on Recourse Mechanisms*, 3rd edn. (Worldwide Movement for Human Rights, 2016), 29.

[12] S. Deva, 'Treating Human Rights Lightly: A Critique of the Consensus Rhetoric and Language Employed by the Guiding Principles' in S. Deva and D. Bilchitz (eds.), *Human Rights Obligations of Business: Beyond the Corporate Responsibility to Respect?* (Cambridge University Press, 2013), 83.

[13] *Ibid.*, 84.

[14] Business and Human Rights Resource Centre, 'In the Courtroom & Beyond: New Strategies to Overcome Inequality and Improve Access to Justice – Corporate Legal Accountability Annual Briefing' (29 February 2016), http://business-humanrights.org/sites/default/files/documents/Corporate%20Legal%20Accountability%20Briefing%202016%20FINAL_0.pdf (last accessed 24 January 2017).

[15] G. Skinner et al., *The Third Pillar: Access to Judicial Remedies for Human Rights Violations by Transnational Business* (International Corporate Accountability Roundtable, 2013).

One of the obvious obstacles to accessing remedy arises due to the corruption and ineffectiveness of courts and administrative bodies in less developed countries, where often multinationals decide to operate often due to relaxed regulations that benefit their bottom line.[16] Alternatively, courts in these countries often do not have the capacity, knowledge or resources to devote to lengthy and costly dispute resolution processes. These courts also may not be the fairest forums for vulnerable victims where interests of local communities are perceived to be in conflict with providing investment opportunities to international investors and the promotion of economic growth. Reports documenting the plight of individuals and communities confronting big companies with less knowledge, resources and time to pursue their grievances paint a grim picture.[17]

Where victims fail to find a local remedy in the host state of TNCs, they may seek a foreign venue. However, the home countries of TNCs show increasing reluctance to assume extraterritorial jurisdiction over claims arising out of conduct occurring overseas. For example, the United States was for a time an available forum for victims of human rights violations to seek redress under the ATCA, a jurisdictional statue that allows foreign nationals to file suits for damages in the US federal courts for violations of the laws of nations. Recent rulings by the US Supreme Court, most notably in *Kiobel v. Royal Dutch Petroleum*, have held that extending federal court jurisdiction beyond the territorial borders of country is to be disfavoured.[18] In the case of the ATCA, any dispute must 'touch and concern' the United States to be heard by a federal court. This judicial pronouncement has dramatically reduced the possibility of invoking the ATCA to hold companies accountable for human rights violations outside the United States.

---

[16] See, e.g., K. Macdonald, 'The Reality of Rights: Barriers to Accessing Remedies When Business Operates Beyond Borders', Corporate Responsibility Coalition & London School of Economics and Political Science (2009), http://corporate-responsibility.org/wp-content/uploads/2014/07/LSE_reality-of-rights.pdf (last accessed 24 January 2017).

[17] 'Human rights defenders often face threats aimed at silencing their work, such as counter-lawsuits by companies aimed at derailing human rights defenders' work; threats of death, arrest or physical harm; and technological threats to privacy and confidentiality.' Business and Human Rights Resource Centre, 'Annual Briefing – Corporate Legal Accountability' (2013). See also C. Bader, 'Suing corporations should be a last resort', *Reuters* (23 February 2012), http://blogs.reuters.com/great-debate/2012/02/23/suing-corporations-should-be-a-last-resort/ (last accessed 24 January 2017).

[18] *Esther Kiobel v. Royal Dutch Petroleum*, 133 S Ct 1659 (2013).

Even if a court determines that it has the power to properly exert jurisdiction over a claim, it can nevertheless refuse to exercise its power in favour of ceding the claim to a more convenient forum for the parties or where the disputed facts at issue are more readily found. The doctrine of *forum non conveniens* as a practical matter can present a challenge for victims when cases are dismissed and the more convenient forum is not a fair one or the victim is not free to bring a claim.[19] Indeed, empirical examination of the disposition of cases dismissed on the ground of the *forum non conveniens* doctrine has revealed that 95 per cent of such cases are never filed again in any forum.[20]

Many of the challenges related to accessing remedy are now on the agenda of the Office of the High Commissioner for Human Rights (OHCHR), and the UN Working Group on Business and Human Rights (UNWG) responsible for putting the GPs into practice. In 2014, when the HRC adopted a resolution to extend the UNWG mandate for another three-year period, it expressed concern over 'the legal and practical barriers to remedies for business-related human rights abuses which may leave those aggrieved without opportunity for effective remedy including through judicial and non-judicial avenues, and recognizing that it may be further considered whether relevant legal frameworks would provide more effective avenues of remedy for affected individuals and communities'.[21]

With a view to strengthen domestic judicial remedies, in 2014, the OHCHR launched the Accountability and Remedy Project. In June 2016, the OHCHR presented its report to the HRC noting that the question of remedies has 'arguably received the least attention' and made a series of recommendations for strengthening horizontal and vertical policy coherence to assure better protection of the right to remedy.[22] The HRC also requested the UNWG to include as an item on the agenda of the Forum on BHR 'the issue of access to remedy, judicial and non-judicial, for victims of business-related human rights abuses, in order to achieve more

---

[19] Skinner et al., n. 15.   [20] *Ibid.*, 34.
[21] Human Rights Council, 'Human Rights and Transnational Corporations and Other Business Enterprises', A/HRC/26/L.1 (15 July 2014).
[22] Human Rights Council, 'Improving Accountability and Access to Remedy for Victims of Business-Related Human Rights Abuse – Report of the United Nations High Commissioner for Human Rights', A/HRC/32/19 (16 June 2016), para. 8; Human rights Council, 'Business and Human Rights: Improving Accountability and Access to Remedy', A/HRC/32/L.19 (29 June 2016).

effective access to judicial remedies'.[23] In fact, the 2017 Forum on BHR will have a special focus on access to remedy. Given the increasing attention being given to remedies, it is timely and appropriate that this topic is also included in the treaty negotiations.

14.3   The Stakes for Stakeholders: Debates on Remedy and a Binding Treaty

On the same day that the HRC extended the mandate of the UN Working Group, it also adopted Resolution 26/9 to elaborate 'an internationally legally binding instrument on transnational corporations and other business enterprises with respect to human rights'.[24] Drafted by Ecuador and South Africa, the resolution was adopted on 26 June 2014 by a majority vote with 20 votes in support,[25] 14 opposed[26] and 13 abstentions.[27] Resolution 26/9 acknowledged the progressive developments around efforts to address the issues associated with adverse impacts on human rights due to transnational corporations. To operationalize the mandate, the HRC created the OEIGWG to begin the process of negotiating 'a legally binding international instrument to regulate, in international human rights law, the activities of transnational corporations and other business enterprises'.[28]

Resolution 26/9 adopts the allocation of responsibilities offered in the protect and respect pillars of the UN Framework.[29] However, it omits direct reference to the remedy pillar, stating instead 'that civil society actors have an important and legitimate role in promoting corporate

---

[23] Human Rights Council, 'Human Rights and Transnational Corporations and Other Business Enterprises', A/HRC/26/L.1 (23 June 2014), para. 10.

[24] Human Rights Council, 'Elaboration of an Internationally Legally Binding Instrument on Transnational Corporations and Other Business Enterprises with Respect to Human Rights', A/HRC/26/L.22/Rev.1 (25 June 2014). The resolution was put forward by Bolivia, Cuba, Ecuador, South Africa and Venezuela.

[25] Algeria, Benin, Burkina Faso, China, Congo, Côte d'Ivoire, Cuba, Ethiopia, India, Indonesia, Kazakhstan, Kenya, Morocco, Namibia, Pakistan, Philippines, Russia, South Africa, Venezuela and Vietnam.

[26] Austria, Czech Republic, Estonia, France, Germany, Ireland, Italy, Japan, Montenegro, South Korea, Romania, the Former Yugoslavia, UK and USA.

[27] Argentina, Botswana, Brazil, Chile, Costa Rica, Gabon, Kuwait, Maldives, Mexico, Peru, Saudi Arabia, Sierra Leone and the United Arab Emirates.

[28] 'Elaboration of an Internationally Legally Binding Instrument', n. 24, para. 1.

[29] For instance, by stressing 'that the obligations and primary responsibility to promote and protect human rights and fundamental freedoms lie with the State' and by emphasizing 'that transnational corporations and other business enterprises have a responsibility to respect human rights'. *Ibid.*

social responsibility, and in preventing, mitigating and seeking remedy for the adverse human rights impacts of transnational corporations and other business enterprises'.[30] This resolution emphasizes the need to include the question of remedy and yet leaves ambiguous whether it views remedy as a right, a critical aspect that needs to be assured by the involvement of stakeholder advocacy. Certainly, that opportunity is already becoming available as the OEIGWG follows its mandate to convene 'relevant stakeholders' in order to contribute ideas and share information towards the aim of drafting the proposed treaty. Including different constituencies perhaps responds to the criticism levelled against the GP processes that were perceived to diminish concerns of victims, as mentioned above. In the next section, we explore whether this dialogue effectively took place during the first session of the OEIGWG.

14.3.1   The First Treaty Negotiating Session

Resolution 26/9 provides that the OEIGWG will first 'conduct constructive deliberations on the *content, scope nature and form* of the future international instrument'.[31] It goes further to instruct that the Chairperson-Rapporteur of the Working Group must 'prepare elements for draft[ing] [the] legally binding instrument, for substantive negotiations'.[32] To fulfil its mandate, the OEIGWG convened its first meeting in July 2015. Interested constituencies gathered in Geneva for a five-day 'Programme of Work'. Each day was designated to a particular aspect, with an afternoon panel specifically dedicated to the theme of remedy entitled, 'Building National and international mechanisms for access to remedy, including international judicial cooperation, with respect to human rights violations by TNCs and other business enterprises – The OHCHR accountability and remedy project'.[33]

A preliminary study of the first OEIGWG session reveals that the theme of remedies threaded throughout the week of discussions. In the following section, we map the nascent narratives that arose by examining the contributions of key stakeholders during the first session. We have taken an ethnographic approach in our research, by relying on both participant observations based on author Laplante's attendance during

---

[30] *Ibid.*   [31] *Ibid.* (emphasis added).   [32] *Ibid.*
[33] Human Rights Council, 'First session of the open-ended intergovernmental working group on transnational corporations and other business enterprises with respect to human rights' www.ohchr.org/EN/HRBodies/HRC/WGTransCorp/Pages/Session1.aspx (last accessed 20 January 2017).

portions of this session in July 2015 as well as a detailed analysis of the transcript of this session. We also analysed the various materials and statements distributed by interested stakeholder constituencies at the meeting. In analysing the debates at the first session, we sought to assess both the frequency of the mention of remedies along with the depth and content of these references. What follows is an initial summary of remedy narratives as they relate to the treaty negotiation process during the OEIGWG's first session.

14.3.2   Competing Concerns: The Positions of Participating Country, Corporate and Civil Society Representatives

Access to remedy emerged early in treaty discussions as a central concern. Indeed, in the first session of the OEIGWG, the United Nations Special Rapporteur on the Rights of Indigenous Peoples underscored the 'paramount importance' of creating a treaty in order to address the lack of access to remedy procedures particularly where business enterprises are alleged to be involved with rights abuses.[34] A diverse range of participants with varied interests and stake in this theme attended the first session, each stating his or her support for attention to the topic of access to remedy. We have broken down the constituencies into four groups: civil society (which includes victims and their advocates); representatives of states; representatives of the business community; and finally, representatives of international and intra-governmental bodies.

14.3.3   Civil Society: Victims and Their Advocates

A diverse range of human rights CSOs raised issues of access to remedy and called for attention to be given to clarifying the legal liability of corporations under international law. CSOs stressed that remedy must be understood as 'requisite to rights protection'.[35] They recognized the importance of remedies for vindicating rights and halting impunity. As might be expected, many of these rights advocates pointed to the many challenges victims of violations confront while seeking redress for their injuries. Human rights defenders were particularly adept at detailing the difficulties victims confront when trying to vindicate their rights.

---

[34] UN Special Rapporteur on the Rights of Indigenous Peoples, 'Oral Intervention of Victoria Tauli-Corpuz' (6 July 2015).

[35] 'Oral Intervention of Papua Indonesian Development Organization' (8 July 2015).

As discussed earlier, in many respects, their remarks mirrored the fact that the dialogue on this issue is still in the diagnostic stage. That said, a few interventions offered some concrete general solutions to the problem, although not per se outlining how these proposals would look like in a treaty. For example, some participants proposed tests to determine the level of corporate responsibility for human rights abuses.[36] Many speakers emphasized the importance of having access to forums to resolve disputes and adjudicate claims in the home countries of TNCs alleged to be involved in abuses.[37] One participant suggested the creation of a legal aid fund to enable victims to hire counsel and defray the costs of dispute resolution.[38] Another participant proposed exploring provisions that would extend responsibility beyond business enterprises to the individual corporate officers.[39] Other participants supported the creation of a new independent institution to complement national and regional instruments with the authority to receive claims and issue judgements on compensation.[40]

Overall, civil society expressed strong support for ensuring access to an effective adjudicatory authority. The intervention of Franciscans International is illustrative of this stand:

> We are especially concerned that the treaty must require states to provide civil damage remedies for victims of human rights abuses in which business enterprises are involved ... we recommend that the Treaty requires states to ensure that through judicial, administrative, legislative or other appropriate means, victims have access to effective judicial remedy.[41]

While participating states also acknowledged remedy as a relevant issue, CSOs often offered stronger and more substantive statements concerning the importance of effective remedy, whether through judicial, administrative or other means. Thus, as compared to government representatives, CSOs appeared to place higher priority on issues related to an effective remedy.

---

[36] 'Oral Intervention of Bonita Meyersfield, Director of the Center for Applied Legal Studies, University of Witswatersrand' (7 July 2015).

[37] See, e.g., General Statements of SOMO, CIDSE, Brot für die Welt, IBFAN, IBFAN-GIFA & Global Policy Forum (7 July 2015).

[38] 'Oral Intervention by Chip Pitts, Professor Stanford University Law School' (9 July 2015).

[39] 'Oral Intervention by Carlos Lopez, Head of the Programme on Business and Human Rights, International Commission of Jurists' (9 July 2015).

[40] 'Oral Intervention of FIAN International' (7 July 2015).

[41] 'Oral Intervention on behalf of Franciscans International, First Session on the Working Group of Transnational Corporations and Human Rights, Panel VII' (8 July 2015).

14.3.4   Interests Protected by Governments

The United States and several European Union governments (home to most of the most profitable TNCs) elected not to participate in the first session of the OEIGWG. While the United States representatives were not present, and only 9 of the 28 European Union states appeared during the first day of the meeting, Ecuador and South Africa played prominent roles in setting forth an understanding of remedy which could inform the elements to be included in an internationally legally binding document.[42] The governments which were actively participating in the meeting predominantly represented emerging market economies and developing nations in the Global South.

Importantly, Ecuador (host to some of the most profitable transnational businesses) set the tone by framing access to remedy as a right stating that it is 'another fundamental right which we hope will serve as the guiding principle for a legally binding instrument on transnational business and human rights'.[43] However, the Ecuadorian representative perceived remedies more narrowly as the 'mechanisms of legal protection and remediation ... against acts of violation of ... fundamental human rights'.[44] South Africa emphasized the need for this remedy to be adequate, noting that 'the victims of corporate violations and abuse [should] have maximum protection, access and provision of adequate remedies. This will also ensure universal application of uniform standards, on a global scale'.[45] South Africa expressed support for developing a direct set of obligations to be placed on business enterprises including, among other things, providing redress for human rights abuses occasioned by business operations.[46] Similarly, the representative of the Bolivian delegation argued that the treaty should set forth the grounds for corporate liability and accountability under both international human rights law

---

[42]   C. Lopez and B. Shea, 'Negotiating a Treaty on Business and Human Rights: A Review of the First Intergovernmental Session' (2016) 1 *Business and Human Rights Journal* 111; Human Rights Council, 'Report on the First Session of the Open-ended Intergovernmental Working Group on Transnational Corporations and Other Business Enterprises with Respect to Human Rights, with the Mandate of Elaborating an International Legally Binding Instrument', A/HRC/31/50 (5 February 2016).

[43]   'Oral Intervention on behalf of Ecuador, First Session on the Working Group of Transnational Corporations and Human Rights, Panel II' (6 July 2015) (translated from Spanish).

[44]   *Ibid.*

[45]   'Oral Intervention on behalf of South Africa, First Session on the Working Group of Transnational Corporations and Human Rights, Panel VIII' (10 July 2015).

[46]   'Oral Intervention of South African Delegation Representative' (8 July 2015).

and international humanitarian law.[47] Ecuador also underscored the importance that any proposal advanced must be accompanied by a 'robust monitoring and enforcement mechanism' and that victims must have legal representation to assist in asserting any claims.

The Algerian Representative, speaking on behalf of the Africa Group of nations, expressed appreciation for the economic benefits brought by the activities of TNCs but emphasized that the ill-effects associated with economic activity could not always be compensated by monetary damage awards.[48] Algeria's intervention could be understood to signal the importance of a conception of remedy that goes beyond rewarding financial damages to also include more creative restorative remedies to resolve disputes.

Overall, these statements made by state representatives helped to reinforce the idea that remedy is not an afterthought but rather an essential aspect of a human rights regime to both protect victims' rights as well as hold businesses accountable. However, the majority of states did not weigh in on the topic of access to remedy: it could be that such states were not supportive of a legally binding international instrument to regulate the human rights conduct of business in the first instance.

14.3.5   Industry Representatives

Relative to other constituencies, only a few representatives of the business community actively participated in the first OEIGWG session or provided oral interventions. The International Organization for Employers (IOE), a trade association representing the interests of large commercial entities, did observe that a problem-solving and pragmatic approach centred on victims would be the most constructive approach.[49] For the IOE, to the extent that victim redress is addressed in a legally binding instrument, it is critically important for definitions to be clear and precise concerning 'violations' and 'liability standards'.[50] On behalf of the IOE, a representative explained:

> the question of which conduct and what standard of liability should be applied in a binding instrument should be driven by a victim-centered [approach] to be consistent with UN Guiding Principles' Pillar three ...

[47] 'Oral Intervention of Bolivian Delegation Representative' (8 July 2015).
[48] 'Oral Intervention of UN Representative for Algeria on Behalf of the African Group of Nations' (6 July 2015).
[49] 'Oral Intervention by Roberto Suarez, Deputy Secretary General of the International Organization of Employers' (9 July 2015).
[50] Ibid.

arguably we have reached agreement on which norms we want to cover in
the binding instrument, we will need to postpone the discussion on what
kinds of liability to impose.[51]

Significantly, this IOE representative pointed towards one very important but unclear issue with regard to this treaty: how businesses will be
held accountable and for what kinds of violations. At the time of writing
this chapter, the IOE had not issued any statement supportive of a BHR
treaty to regulate the conduct of business enterprises.

14.3.6   Statements by Other United Nations Procedures

While not technically parties to a treaty negotiation debate, representatives from various international and intra-state institutions including
United Nations agencies and the International Labour Organizations
(ILO) enjoyed a visible presence at the first OEIGWG session, lending
their support for the overall initiative and in particular the discussion on
remedies.

The Deputy High Commissioner for Human Rights provided the
following statement: 'Our organization fully supports all constructive
efforts to enhance the protection of human rights in the context of
business activities and to ensure accountability and access to effective
remedies when rights have been abused.'[52] Michael Addo, the then Chair
of UNWG, observed that any 'efforts to strengthen international standards should build upon and be complementary to the framework set out
in the Guiding Principles'.[53]

In particular, many of these actors participated in the panel dedicated
exclusively to the theme of reparations. For example, Lene Wendland of
the OHCHR provided details about the Accountability and Remedy
Project about exploring shortcomings in access to redress and strengthening Pillar three of the GPs. She announced plans for the publication of
'good practice guidance' to inform states how to develop procedures to
better meet Pillar three obligations.[54]

---

[51] 'Presentation by Roberto Suarez acting as the Deputy Secretary-General on behalf of the
International Organisation of Employers, Panel VII' (8 July 2015).
[52] 'Statement of Deputy High Commissioner for Human Rights' (6 July 2015).
[53] 'Oral Intervention of Michael Addo, Chair of the Working Group on the Issue of Human
Rights and Transnational Corporations and Other Business Enterprises, Panel I' (6 June
2015).
[54] Lene Wendland, 'The OHCHR Accountability and Remedy Project', Panel VIII (9 July
2015). See also Human Rights Council, 'Improving Accountability', n. 22.

In general, this special session on reparations focused primarily on highlighting the problem of inadequate and ineffective remedies. Participants contributed to outlining the challenges victims confront in receiving redress for violations. Several participants emphasized the importance of access to remedy in general. However, few participants offered detailed proposals for substantive remedy provisions and procedures at this very early stage of treaty discussions.

14.3.7   Analysis

While different constituencies emphasized different considerations and attached varying relative importance to the various issues and interests articulated over the course of the first session of the OEIGWG, there was a cross-constituency consensus on the importance of clarity and precision with reference to defining key terms in relation to access to remedy for the victims. However, most participants spoke of remedies in terms of access to some form of remedial process contemplating judicial, administrative or other means of enforcing rights and ensuring accountability.[55]

Overall, the theme of remedies was raised on a frequent and consistent basis, and came to play a visible role in the first session of the OEIGWG. This observation gives hope that this issue will not be side-lined by other pressing topics but is clearly on the treaty agenda. However, it remains open how the many issues surrounding obstacles to accessing adequate and effective remedies will be addressed moving forward, as there were very few concrete proposals as to how these obstacles would be overcome by the treaty provisions. Moreover, not all of the contentious points of this treaty debate are yet clear, so it is uncertain where it may become necessary to battle for or make concessions regarding particular aspects of the remedy schemata.

The common concern for the availability of a remedy may mask potential points of dissent later in the process because usage of the term 'remedy' varied, despite frequent reference to the term. For instance, a potential point of contest may arise over the treatment of international trade and TNCs and accusations of state protectionism. Similarly, questions of accountability around international or bilateral investment treaties raise many issues regarding business accountability. It is, therefore, unclear at this stage that there is a clear trajectory for a treaty provision on remedy. As

---

[55] The authors reviewed public interventions made at the first OEIGWG session.

the terms of this debate have yet to be set, the authors seek to begin to address this gap in the following section.

14.4   Getting Remedy Right: An Accord for Accountability

Our analysis of the discussions regarding remedy makes it clear that not all speakers shared the same view or concept of the term 'remedy'. Thus, the first step in organizing debates around remedy should be to identify a common language and concept of remedy. In this section, we offer an overview and typology of these features of existing human rights instruments to provide a framework for the evolving debates on how remedies should be incorporated into a BHR treaty. We discuss both the substantive and procedural aspects of access to remedy as points of reference for future debates on ensuring that an accountability accord may emerge from the OEIGWG process. In providing these benchmarks, we offer concrete suggestions on what considerations must be taken with regard to how the right to remedy and reparations should fit into this new human rights treaty regime. We also offer model language for a provision on remedies as well as an appropriate mechanism for enforcing these norms.

14.4.1   Assuring an Adequate and Effective Remedy

The creation of the international human rights regime in many ways presented a revolution in international law by introducing individuals as actors in an area of law that previously only regulated the behaviour of states vis-à-vis other states. Most historic accounts of human rights law recognize that the turning point in its development followed the Second World War and the evident atrocities that a government can inflict upon its own people, as epitomized during the Nazi Regime. Importantly, this new system also set up the basic two-tier system where governments first had the opportunity to provide remedies to redress these serious harms, but where they fail to do so, states may be subject to international scrutiny through a monitoring body. This system solidified through the development of comprehensive human rights treaty law.

The first significant step in the development of human rights law came with the drafting of the Universal Declaration on Human Rights (UDHR), which contains a wide range of rights: from the civil and political to the economic, social and cultural. Yet, this instrument was not a binding treaty, but rather aspirational in nature. In the following decades, binding human rights treaties were negotiated.

As a starting point, it is important that the treaty debate begins with the basic premise that accessing remedies constitutes a stand-alone human right. If a violation of a right does not correspond with a mechanism to remedy it, then it remains dead letter. Not surprisingly, almost all human rights treaties contain reference to remedy in not only their text but also in the jurisprudence developed by the bodies that monitor their implementation.

There are common features to all of these treaties, which offer important benchmark for any new human rights treaty. One of the most notable of these features is the clear directive that *all* victims are entitled to a remedy for injuries incurred when their human rights are violated.[56] This admonition means that there cannot be a discrimination based on race, gender, sexual orientation or other identity categories when it comes to accessing remedies. However, the underlying objective of this universal principle is to encourage, and at times mandate, that states begin to assure adequate remedies at the domestic level so that victims do not need to resort to an international forum. For example, a victim should be able to file a criminal complaint and be guaranteed a minimal level of due process including investigations if he or she alleges a prima facie crime arising out of human rights violations. The same victim may also wish to seek civil damages for these violations. The importance of the local remedy can be seen in the procedural requirement of first exhausting domestic remedies before accessing an international forum. This requirement goes to the spirit of both encouraging states to provide adequate and effective remedies and also highlighting when states will be held accountable for not providing such remedies.

Victims may have a cause of action against the company that caused them harm as well as against the state for failing to protect them from this third party. Indeed, human rights law places a duty upon states to ensure and guarantee human rights which includes preventing harm by third parties including non-state actors. Thus, a central aspect of any new treaty should be that remedies may be asserted against both state and private, non-state actors. There may be situations where a state will impose sanctions (e.g., an administrative fine following a government investigation) on a company that does not per se relate directly to a victim

---

[56] See S. Djajic, 'Victims and Promise of Remedies: International Law Fairytale Gone Bad' (2008) 9 *San Diego International Law Journal* 329.

exercising their right to a remedy.[57] However, these state actions may still serve a reparative effect and go towards satisfying the victim's sense of justice.

As discussed in the next sections, most human rights treaties contain specific features related to remedy, both in substantive and procedural terms. Understanding this nuance also is important for making sure that the proposed BHR treaty adequately contemplates adequate and effective remedies.

14.4.2   The Procedural Right to a Remedy

Remedy can be understood as a procedural right creating mechanisms that allow victims to vindicate and enforce their rights through judicial and non-judicial venues. Most of the formulations of a remedy right contained in the core international human rights treaties are concerned with access to a form of dispute resolution organized by the state, such as judicial and non-judicial mechanisms.

For example, Article 2(3) of the ICCPR provides that states must:

(a)   ensure that any person whose rights or freedoms as herein recognized are violated shall have an effective remedy, notwithstanding that the violation has been committed by persons acting in an official capacity;

(b)   ensure that any person claiming such a remedy shall have his right *thereto determined by competent judicial, administrative or legislative authorities, or by any other competent authority provided for by the legal system of the State, and to develop the possibilities of judicial remedy;* and

(c)   ensure that the competent authorities shall enforce such remedies when granted.[58]

Most other human rights treaties mirror this language by emphasizing a victim's right to some mechanism to resolve a claim. However, some of these provisions focus more squarely on judicial mechanisms. For example, Article 6 of the Convention on the Elimination of Racial

---

[57]   R. McCorquodale, 'Survey of the Provision in the United Kingdom of Access to Remedies for Victims of Human Rights Harms Involving Business Enterprises', British Institute of International and Comparative Law (2015).

[58]   International Covenant on Civil and Political Rights (entered into force 23 March 1976) 999 UNTS 171 (ICCPR) (emphasis added).

Discrimination frames remedy as access to adjudicatory authorities as follows:

> States Parties shall assure to everyone within their jurisdiction effective protection and remedies, through the competent national tribunals and other State institutions, against any acts of racial discrimination which violate his human rights and fundamental freedoms contrary to this Convention, as well as the right to seek from such tribunals just and adequate reparation or satisfaction for any damage suffered as a result of such discrimination.[59]

The Convention Against Torture also speaks of remedy in Article 13 in terms of claims adjudication:

> Each State Party shall ensure that any individual who alleges he has been subjected to torture in any territory under its jurisdiction has the right to complain to, and to have his case promptly and impartially examined by, its competent authorities. Steps shall be taken to ensure that the complainant and witnesses are protected against all ill-treatment or intimidation as a consequence of his complaint or any evidence given.[60]

Other provisions offer a much more general provision that folds remedy into the idea of protection. For example, Article 2(c) of the Convention on the Elimination of Discrimination Against Women provides that state parties must 'establish legal protection of the rights of women on an equal basis with men and to ensure through competent national tribunals and other public institutions the effective protection of women against any act of discrimination'.[61]

All of these treaty provisions relate to the procedural right to a remedy which assures the enforcement mechanisms and fair rules of procedure to vindicate adequately and promptly the substantive right to a remedy.

14.4.3 The Substantive Right to Remedy

The second aspect of the right to remedy refers to explicit provisions that refer to reparations, which most often refers to compensation for specific

---

[59] Convention on the Elimination of Racial Discrimination (entered into force 4 January 1969) 660 UNTS 195, art. 6 (CERD).

[60] Convention Against Torture and Other Cruel, Inhuman or Degrading Treatment or Punishment (entered into force 26 June 1987) 1465 UNTS 85, art. 13 (CAT).

[61] Convention on the Elimination of All Forms of Discrimination Against Women (entered into force 3 September 1981) 1249 UNTS 13, art. 2(c) (CEDAW).

harms.[62] These references also refer to stand-alone human rights: the right to reparation. Usually reparation is conceived narrowly as monetary compensation. For example, article 9 (5) of the ICCPR proclaims: 'Anyone who has been the victim of unlawful arrest or detention shall have an enforceable right to compensation.' Some treaties refer to compensation but only in reference to specific types of violations. For example, Article 10 of the American Convention on Human Rights reads: 'Every person has the right to be compensated in accordance with the law in the event he has been sentenced by a final judgment through a miscarriage of justice.' Significantly, this explicit reference to the substantive remedy is limited to the specific instance of unlawful arrest and detention and there is no other mention of reparations in the American Convention. Thus, the Inter-American Court of Human Rights has interpreted Article 8 (pertaining to due process rights) and Article 25 (access to procedural remedies) of the American Convention together to create a general right to adequate remedies.[63]

More recent treaties provide further elaboration of what measures constitute reparations in the fullest extent. For example, the Convention Against Torture (CAT) contains more details relevant to the substantive content of the remedy right by outlining that 'fair and adequate compensation' and 'rehabilitation' are relevant considerations. Article 14 of the CAT provides that:

> Each State Party shall ensure in its legal system that the victim of an act of torture obtains redress and has an enforceable right to fair and adequate compensation, including the means for as full rehabilitation as possible. In the event of the death of the victim as a result of an act of torture, his dependents shall be entitled to compensation.

Some treaties combine both procedural and substantive aspects in one provision. For example, the Convention on Enforced Disappearances (CED) is distinctive among the international human rights instruments in that it makes express reference not only to 'reparation' in the procedural sense, but also includes more details about what that reparation may entail. The language of the Preamble alludes to 'the right of victims to justice and reparation'.[64] Article 24 of the CED provides that state parties must ensure that 'the victims of enforced disappearance have the

---

[62] See also the chapter by Stephens in this volume.
[63] *Albán-Cornejo et al. v. Ecuador* [2008] IACHR Series C No. 183.
[64] International Convention for the Protection of All Persons from Enforced Disappearance (entered into force 23 December 2010) 2716 UNTS 3, Preamble (CED).

right to obtain reparation and prompt, fair and adequate compensation'.[65] The right to obtain reparation in the CED is expansive, extending to 'material and moral damages'. The right to reparation may, where appropriate, include a range of alternatives: '(a) Restitution; (b) Rehabilitation; (c) Satisfaction, including restoration of dignity and reputation; [and] (d) Guarantees of non-repetition.'[66]

Finally, some treaties empower the treaty's monitoring body to order reparations for victims who bring claims to the international oversight system. However, the international body is ordering the state party to grant these reparations because it was liable for failing to prevent the human rights violation (or causing it through its agents) as well as for failing to provide an adequate remedy. For example, Article 63 of the American Convention reads:

> If the Court finds that there has been a violation of a right or freedom protected by this Convention, the Court shall rule that the injured party be ensured the enjoyment of his right or freedom that was violated. It shall also rule, if appropriate, that the consequences of the measure or situation that constituted the breach of such right or freedom *be remedied and that fair compensation be paid to the injured party.*[67]

Indeed, it is through these provisions that monitoring bodies have been able to develop a rich jurisprudence related to reparations.[68] Ultimately, if a victim does not receive reparations at the local level, the international monitoring body may order a state to make good on this right.

14.4.4 Enforcement Mechanisms

One other important aspect of the principle of an adequate remedy in international human rights law relates to the opportunity to complain to an external body when the state fails to provide an adequate remedy through domestic law and procedures. In essence, these international mechanisms serve as an additional remedy for victims. Significantly, the European Convention on Human Rights (ECHR) has a provision directing the European Court of Human Rights (ECtHR) to allow any individual who is

---

[65] *Ibid.*, art. 24(4).   [66] *Ibid.*, art. 24(5).   [67] Emphasis added.

[68] The Inter-American Court of Human Rights has developed the concept of 'transformative reparations' to ensure a holistic approach to redress. I. Alvarez et al., 'Reparations in the Inter-American System: A Comparative Approach Conference' (2007) 56(6) *American University Law Review* 1376.

subject to the ECHR to submit a claim to the European Court.[69] The ability to lodge individual complaints is considered a significant development in international law because it empowered individuals to become limited subjects of international law.

Most international human rights instruments were crafted without an enforcement mechanism. It was presumed that state parties were to meet the commitments assumed by virtue of adopting and implementing a given instrument. In the case of these treaties, an additional treaty (an optional protocol) supplements the original treaty to include a monitoring body. In this situation, the state party must sign and ratify these additional protocols and consent to the competence (jurisdiction) of a given body to hear claims. The challenge presented by an optional protocol procedure is that not all state parties opt to participate in complaint mechanisms.

Presently, within the United Nations system, seven international human rights treaties have committees with the capacity to receive complaints from individuals or communities about alleged violations of the rights that are contained in the particular instrument overseen by the Committee.[70] The CAT, the CMW and the CERD are unique in that the potential for asserting individual complaints are contained in the text of the initial treaty and were not added as an option at a subsequent point in time, as was the case for the ICCPR, ICESCR, CEDAW and CRPD. For example, Article 14 of CERD provides that a:

> State Party may at any time declare that it recognizes the competence of the Committee to receive and consider communications from individuals or groups of individuals within its jurisdiction claiming to be victims of a violation by that State Party of any of the rights set forth in this Convention. No communication shall be received by the Committee if it concerns a State Party which has not made such a declaration.[71]

Article 22 of the CAT and Article 77 of the CMW contain a similar provision.

---

[69] European Convention for the Protection of Human Rights and Fundamental Freedoms, as amended by Protocols Nos. 11 and 14 (entered into force 3 September 1953) Europe Treaty Series 005, art. 34. (ECHR).

[70] The International Covenant on Civil and Political Rights (ICCPR), the International Covenant on Economic Social and Cultural Rights, the Convention on the Elimination of All forms of Racial Discrimination (CERD), the Convention on the Elimination of All Forms of Discrimination Against Women (CEDAW), the Convention Against Torture (CAT), the International Convention on the Protection of the Rights of Migrant Workers and Members of their Families (CMW) and the Convention on the Rights of Persons with Disabilities (CRPD) all have committees entertaining individual complaints.

[71] CERD, n. 59, art. 14.

Even when a treaty includes a monitoring body, there may still be a delay in its being able to receive complaints. To illustrate, the CERD procedure for accepting communications from individuals did not come into operation until 1982, decades after the treaty was adopted and entered into force, when ten states parties agreed to accept the Committee's complaints authority under Article 14.[72] The CERD has more state parties than the CMW or the CAT, but it is not as widely ratified as the ICCPR or the ICESR, which are often considered the core human rights treaties and make up the 'international bill of rights' along with the UDHR.

While the CAT is widely ratified by a range of states, only 65 states parties have agreed to be bound by the Article 22 complaints provision. The result is that there may be an uneven terrain of enforcement that can undermine the weight of the treaty in influencing local state enforcement of these important norms. There is a risk that any future BHR treaty could also face a patchwork of uneven ratifications and uneven enforcement leaving certain victims with less access to remedy.

The regional human rights systems also include monitoring bodies. In fact, these systems include courts which have more binding power but also require consent to their contentious jurisdiction. For example, the European system includes the ECtHR, established through the ECHR, recognizes the important role of remedy and provides procedures. In the case of the Inter-American System, there is both a commission (the Inter-American Commission on Human Rights) and a court (the Inter-American Court of Human Rights) under the American Convention on Human Rights. Similarly, the African System includes a commission (the African Commission on Human and People's Rights) as well as a court (the African Court on Human and Peoples' Rights). With these bifurcated processes, victims must first submit a claim to the commission and run through various steps in the adjudication before possibility having the case forwarded to the court, although this is not necessarily guaranteed.

14.4.5 Procedural Requirements

Disputes brought before the complaints mechanisms of international human rights instruments are subject to procedural requirements.

---

[72] Office of the High Commissioner for Human Rights, 'Fact Sheet No.12, The Committee on the Elimination of Racial Discrimination', www.ohchr.org/Documents/Publications/FactSheet12en.pdf (last accessed 24 January 2017).

Some treaties include these rules directly in the text of their treaty, while others delegated to their enforcement bodies the power to draft such procedure.

Individual complaints brought by human rights victims must conform to certain conditions in order to be considered by each committee, commission or tribunal to which it is submitted. As a general matter, any individual may lodge a complaint provided the state alleged to be responsible for the violation at issue has ratified, accepted or otherwise approved the treaty instrument.[73] The individual must also fall within the territory or jurisdiction of that state and where the alleged harm occurred. The state alleged to be responsible for the violation must also have accepted the competence of the committee, commission or tribunal to entertain individual complaints.[74]

With some variations, committees accepting complaints operate under some basic common principles. Complaining individuals cannot make anonymous submissions before most mechanisms. An identifiable individual or entity must sign communications to the committees but can request that any identifying information be kept confidential by the committee. The facts and arguments in complaints must be substantiated with supporting facts. Treaty bodies do not allow complaints in defence of general abstract public or collective interests. Rather, the direct victim(s) of the alleged human rights violations must make a specific complaint of injury. The complainant must demonstrate that he or she is personally and directly affected in an adverse manner by the decisions, acts or omissions of the state at issue.

In cases of unlawful detention, disappearance and extrajudicial killings – where direct victims are unable to bring claims – the committees have granted standing to close relatives of the victims. In other special circumstances, certain treaty bodies will consider complaints lodged on behalf of victims that are not able to act on their own provided the complaining party obtains the consent to proceed from the victims. The Human Rights Committee has been reluctant to grant standing to representatives acting or speaking on behalf of victims.[75] The CEDAW Committee is distinct in that it has authority to allow a complaining party to proceed without the victim's consent where the

---

[73] See Der Plancke et al., n. 11, 37.   [74] See, e.g., CAT, n. 60, art. 21 (1).
[75] A. R. Harrington, 'Don't Mind the Gap: The Rise of Individual Complaints Mechanisms within International Human Rights Treaties' (2012) 22 *Duke Journal of Comparative & International Law* 153 at 160.

party can provide a sufficient explanation to the Committee to proceed with the complaint.

Most bodies do not allow claims that are submitted in other international or intra-national forums, or have already been heard in these venues. Moreover, complaints in most instances must exhaust domestic remedies before invoking review by a committee. Committees will make occasional exceptions to this rule. For instance, the CED sets aside the domestic exhaustion rule where there are unreasonable delays.[76] The Inter-American System includes various exceptions such as when the remedy is unavailable, unreasonably delayed as well as if the victim is indigent or in great fear. The importance of this complementary principle lies in the fact that the international human rights regime ultimately aims to give states not only an opportunity to resolve their own disputes but also emphasize their obligation to provide recourse to effective remedies. When a state fails to provide such a remedy, the victim then may have recourse to an international body. If reparations are ordered by the international body, they may in part be because of the state failed to provide an adequate remedy (and in turn failed to protect this very right).

14.5 An Accord for Accountability: Providing Remedy to Protect Rights

The push for a specialized BHR treaty responds to the fact that the existing treaty-based complaints mechanisms have not yet been fully or effectively utilized to raise issues where businesses have allegedly committed rights violations.[77] Moreover, the types of remedies that some of these treaty-based complaints mechanisms can provide may be quite limited and not as responsive to situations of harm, especially involving multiple people. For instance, treaty bodies do not have the authority to issue enforceable sanctions against violators especially if they are non-state actors. Nevertheless, treaty bodies still can give voice to victims and contribute to elevating an issue in the public consciousness in cooperation with other advocacy constituencies. For that reasons, the authors offer a series of recommendations concerning the inclusion of remedy provisions in the proposed BHR treaty. It will be critical that such a treaty does not replicate the shortcomings of earlier instruments.

---

[76] CED, n. 64, art. 31(d).   [77] Der Plancke et al., n. 11, 25.

14.5.1   Proposal for Substantive Provisions

Most of the existing human rights treaties set forth a formulation of remedy that is rather narrow, emphasizing primarily access to tribunal type adjudication. Furthermore, the explicit text of the few treaty articles relevant to remedy tend to focus exclusively on the idea of compensation.

An exception to this trend arises out of the jurisprudence developed by international monitoring bodies which have expanded the notion of 'reparation'. The Inter-American Court of Human Rights follows the principle of *restitutio in integrum*, which means that a full repair may require a full scope of measures to put the victim back in the position he/she would have been if there was no violation.[78] Moreover, the right to remedy has greatly evolved since most human rights treaties were originally drafted, which warrants the issuance of more guidelines from international bodies. Most notably, the United Nations Basic Principles and Guidelines on the Right to a Remedy and Reparation for Victims of Gross Violations of International Human Rights Law and Serious Violations of International Humanitarian Law (Basic Principles), approved by the UN General Assembly in 2005, establish standards that must be taken into consideration.[79] Although the Basic Principles might be considered soft law, they explicitly clarify that the right to a remedy and reparations is not discretionary, but rather is obligatory under treaty and customary law.[80] In other words, states must respect, protect and fulfil the right to remedy. While we are at the early stages of determining legal tests for how these standards are met, they arguably require a more pluralistic approach that takes into account the justice needs of victims.[81] Namely, remedies for serious human rights violations

---

[78] 'Redressing the damage caused by the breach of an international duty requires, as far as possible, *restitutio in integrum*, which means restoring the situation to that prior to the violation. Should this be impossible, it is for the international court to establish a series of measures aimed not only at ensuring respect for the violated rights, but also at redressing the consequences of the breach and ordering the payment of compensation for the damage suffered.' *Almonacid Arellano et al. v. Chile* [2006] IACHR Series C No. 154, para. 136.

[79] UN General Assembly, 'Basic Principles and Guidelines on the Right to a Remedy and Reparation for Victims of Gross Violations of International Human Rights Law and Serious Violations of International Humanitarian Law', A/RES/60/147 (16 December 2005).

[80] The Inter-American Court established this fact in its first contentious case of reparations. See *Velásquez-Rodríguez v. Honduras* [1989] IACHR Series C No. 7.

[81] L. J. Laplante, 'Just Repair' (2015) 48 (3) *Cornell International Law Journal* 513.

must be 'adequate, effective, prompt and appropriate'.[82] Significantly, the Basic Principles do not claim to be merely aspirational, but rather articulate and codify pre-existing law.[83]

In light of these developments, we propose that the BHR treaty includes not only a provision specifically dedicated to assuring the right to reparations in the substantive sense of remedy, but also the standards outlined in the Basic Principles. Thus, a model article may read as follows: '*Every individual has a right to adequate, effective, prompt and appropriate reparations, which includes the principle of restitutio in integrum.*'

Ultimately, this right would be read in conjunction with a general provision that it is the obligation of states to guarantee this right within its judicial, administrative and legislative processes.

14.5.2 *Procedural Considerations*

Any provision regarding remedies should be included in the text of the primary BHR instrument and not left to be integrated through a separate instrument at a later point in time. Time is of the essence for individuals and communities who continue to suffer the effects of rights violations. One challenge to assuring an effective remedy goes beyond the physical infrastructure and explicit law in any country, and relates to the psycho-social-economic realities of most survivors of human rights violations. Those who suffer human rights violations tend to be the already marginalized in terms of education, ethnicity, gender, language and class. They often do not have the knowledge or expertise to exercise their right to a remedy, nor can they afford to hire professionals to help them. There may also be a lack of access to information, not only about their rights but also about the details of the harm that caused their grievance.[84] Moreover, they may need to make very practical decisions between working to support their families or dedicating precious time to fighting a legal cause. Some live in remote areas, far from government offices and cannot

---

[82] UN General Assembly, 'Basic Principles and Guidelines on the Right to a Remedy and Reparation for Survivors of Violations of International Human Rights and Humanitarian Law', G.A. Res. A/RES/60/147 (21 March 2006) (Basic Principles).

[83] *Ibid.*

[84] A. Gaughran, 'Obstacles to Effective Remedy in Cases of Corporate Abuse of Human Rights, Delivered at the OHCHR Consultation on Business and Human Rights' (6 October 2009), www2.ohchr.org/english/issues/globalization/business/docs/AudreyGaughran_AI. doc. (last accessed 24 January 2017).

spare the time or resources to spend prolonged time in administrative quagmire to arrive at a fair settlement.[85] Ultimately, these types of conditions lead to a power imbalance between the victims of abuses, and the corporations they seek to challenge.

Therefore, it will not be enough if the proposed BHR treaty merely requires functioning courts and the legal right to access them: states must also be tasked with addressing some of the underlying socio-economic factors that stand in the way of survivors accessing remedies. In addition to including provisions commonly found in most human rights treaties that assure access to a judicial and non-judicial remedy, we also recommend that the BHR treaty include language which recognizes the state's obligation to address the socio-economic barriers to accessing these remedies. In the clause relating to the right to remedy, the additional obligation on the part of states may be framed as follows: '*To advance access to justice for aggrieved parties and fair resolution of disputes for all parties, states shall endeavor to remove existing procedural and practical barriers to bring greivances before legitimate arbiters with an authority to grant remedy.*'

Another concern is that traditional treaty mechanisms, which focus squarely on traditional state apparatus to resolve disputes, may overlook some of the alternative approaches to reaching a favourable outcome for victims, such as non-judicial grievance mechanisms provided by the state, by the company or a sort of hybrid between the two.

Considering the diversity of forms of business enterprises, the complexity of supply chains production and the range of rights put at risk by irresponsible business conduct, it is important to craft a provision that does not reduce dispute resolution solely to litigation or adjudication alone. A point of departure for a remedy provision might mirror model arbitral and conciliation rules for private disputes.[86] There may be more room for this type of expansive view of remedies because the proposed treaty, unlike most of the other existing international human rights

[85] Author Laplante shares these observations from her field work study in Peru regarding the reality of victims seeking reparations for violations of their mental health during that country's internal armed conflict. While the context did not relate specifically to victims of corporate abuse, the general observations remain the same given that the same demographics of this group also apply to the typical victim of corporate abuse. See L. J. Laplante and M. Rivera, 'The Peruvian Truth Commission's Mental Health Reparations: Empowering Survivors of Political Violence to Impact the Public Health Policy' (2006) 9 *Harvard International Journal of Health and Human Rights* 137.

[86] See, e.g., UNCITRAL Model Law on International Commercial Conciliation (2002); UNCITRAL Model Law on International Commercial Arbitration (2006)

instruments, will engage the conduct of private actors. That said, the primacy of protecting remedies lies with the state that ratifies the treaty. Therefore, the state should retain final review and responsibility for enforcement of judgements or settlement agreements fairly negotiated or otherwise arbitrated. The state should also have power to compel parties alleged to have committed violations to participate in proceedings to provide redress to victims, but also to review these agreements to assure fairness.[87] The state should not condition access to non-judicial grievance mechanisms on waiver of judicial forums.

To achieve the above objectives, model provision in the BHR treaty may read as follows:

(1) If a human rights violation results from an action or omission of a business enterprise, parties involved shall in good-faith work to redress the injury and resolve related disputes. Parties shall consult and negotiate a just and equitable solution satisfactory to all affected parties.

(2) If a resolution and remedy is not reached within a reasonable period of time, a victim may seek an order from the State with jurisdiction over the case to direct the alleged violator and victims to participate in arbitration, mediation or conciliation of the dispute. States shall order arbitration, mediation or conciliation in accordance with principles of equal treatment and fair process.

(3) Where parties conclude an agreement resolving a dispute, the agreement shall be binding and enforceable as well as reviewable by state authorities to assure fairness.

This model language attempts to address issues of unreasonable delay and uncooperative parties and is obligatory in that it provides for state enforcement. We recognize that should a BHR treaty include an accountability provision like the one we propose, it will raise other issues that will need to be further explored as the debate develops. For example, it may become imperative to explore who is a party to a dispute: will it only be victims and the corporate actor involved, or should it also include others having an interest like CSOs? Future clarity would also be needed as to the institutional setting within which consultation and negotiation between parties should occur and what a reasonable period of time should be for resolving disputes. Last but not least, issues of jurisdiction

---

[87] L. Laplante, 'Privatizing Human Rights Enforcement through Company Level Grievance Mechanisms' (forthcoming). (manuscript on file with the authors)

and authority for reviewing the fairness of processes and outcomes would need to be considered by the treaty drafters.

14.5.3   International Oversight

Any proposal for a substantive remedy provision should avoid the problems associated with the existing individual complaints mechanisms of the treaty bodies. While the majority of human rights treaties did not include specific provisions for individual complaint mechanisms, we recommend that the BHR treaty contemplate such a mechanism within its text. The question of state consent always raises important issues with regard to accountability and we recognize the importance of state buy-in to this oversight mechanism. However, we recommend that the mechanism be automatically binding upon signing and ratifying the treaty, while acknowledging that states may be left with a discretion to make reservations to these provisions as long as doing does not undermine the spirit of the treaty.[88]

The most important issue will be whether a new monitoring body will be established to receive these complaints, or whether such complaints will go to an existing treaty monitoring bodies or alternatively to another international body such as the UNWG, which we doubt currently has the capacity to handle this new role. We recommend that a new body could be created that mirrors the rank of other committees overseeing specialized treaties, and tasked with other important assignments such as receiving country reports and naming special rapporteurs to study particular issues related to business and human rights.[89]

We suggest that the procedure for this body also follow similar rules already established by most human rights monitoring bodies, for example, that claimants may need to prove that they have exhausted domestic remedies. Moreover, if claims have already gone before other bodies like National Contact Points operating under the OECD Guidelines for Multinational Enterprises or the Ombudsman of the World Bank, these procedures may bar a claim in this new body unless there is a demonstrated procedural defect or fundamentally unfair outcome that fails to provide

---

[88] The Genocide Convention took this approach. See *Case Concerning Application of the Convention on the Prevention and Punishment of The Crime Of Genocide, Bosnia and Herzegovina v. Serbia and Montenegro* [2007] ICJ 921.

[89] An international mechanism may go beyond just contemplating cases against states and even provide a forum for complaints against businesses. See, for example, M. Steinitz, 'The Case for an International Court of Civil Justice' (2015) 67 *Stanford Law Review Online* 75.

redress. The same rule may apply to instances where victims have sought to resolve their claims through an operational-level grievance mechanism.

14.6 Conclusion: Beyond Infrastructure Addressing the Context of Remedy

This chapter has traced the narrative of remedies in recent efforts to determine the elements that should be given emphasis in a BHR treaty. A significant segment of concerned stakeholders agree that business enterprises have a responsibility to respect human rights. Significantly, participants in the first session of the OEIGWG identified access to remedy as a central concern. Nevertheless, there did not appear to be a common understanding of the substantive content of remedy or its procedural dimensions. Despite the constructive interventions during the first session about the current barriers to victims accessing remedy, no party made any clear statements of solution to the issue, which is a necessary step in the drafting of a treaty.[90]

Based on our research we conclude that interested stakeholders must seize the opportunity to avoid the shortcomings of existing human rights instruments. Our proposal builds upon the strengths of existing instruments in order to advance justice for aggrieved parties and fair resolution of disputes to call for the express acknowledgement of the right to adequate and effective forms of reparation in the proposed BHR treaty. Doing so would contribute to further cementing the place of remedy in international human rights law. We have argued that a substantive right to remedy should be integral to any future legally binding international instrument on BHR. This chapter has outlined some model treaty provisions and a range of potential mechanisms for ensuring that effective access to remedy takes into account diversity and power differentials with a view towards a more expansive understanding of remedy rooted in dispute resolution. As the terrain of the BHR landscape changes, it would be desirable to give greater attention to restorative forms of dispute resolution when speaking of remedy in future treaty talks.

---

[90] The written contributions submitted to the OEIGWG before the second session though provide specific elements that should inform the treaty text. Human Rights Council, 'Second session – Written contributions' www.ohchr.org/EN/HRBodies/HRC/WGTransCorp/Session2/Pages/WrittenContributions.aspx (last accessed 20 January 2017).

Making Remedies Work

Envisioning a Treaty-Based System of Effective Remedies

BETH STEPHENS[*]

15.1 Introduction

The right to an effective remedy is at the heart of international human rights law. Without remedies to make whole those who are injured, punish those responsible and deter further violations, human rights norms offer empty promises. In practice, however, rights are frequently violated and effective remedies rarely available. Where the perpetrator is a corporation, the situation is, if anything, even more bleak. In many parts of the world, corporations violate human rights with impunity. Corporations use their financial power to promote favourable legal regimes and to influence government officials, including judges. They create elaborate corporate structures to escape legal responsibility for their actions. When remedies do exist on paper, injured individuals and communities rarely have the resources necessary to access them – and often risk additional physical or economic harm if they attempt to do so.

The latest effort to articulate norms governing business and human rights (BHR), the 2011 United Nations Guiding Principles on Business and Human Rights (Guiding Principles),[1] has perpetuated the gap between the promise of remedies and the reality of corporate impunity. In the Guiding Principles, states once again recognize a duty to ensure that corporations do not violate human rights and to ensure access to remedies,[2] and businesses are told that they have the 'responsibility' to respect human rights.[3] That rhetoric, however, is not backed by a commitment by states or corporations to take any concrete steps to

---

[*] I would like to thank my research assistant, Brian Gilligan, for his excellent research support for this chapter.
[1] Human Rights Council (HRC), 'Guiding Principles on Business and Human Rights: Implementing the United Nations "Protect, Respect, and Remedy" Framework', A/HRC/17/31 (21 March 2011) (Guiding Principles).
[2] *Ibid.*, Principles 1–10.   [3] *Ibid.*, Principles 11–24.

implement effective remedies: the Guiding Principles are phrased as soft law, not binding obligations, contain no enforcement mechanisms and rely heavily on voluntary procedures designed and implemented by corporations with no state supervision.

The UN Human Rights Council decision in 2014 to begin discussion of a legally binding instrument governing BHR[4] offers an opportunity to envision a system that could actually offer effective remedies for corporate human rights violations.[5] The challenge is daunting. A legal system capable of deterring, punishing and providing remedies for corporate abuses would require major reforms to domestic and international law and a wholesale change in political and economic power structures. Neither corporations nor states have demonstrated any interest in such radical change. Widespread ratification and enforcement of a treaty containing the strong measures necessary to guarantee remedies would require a political will that seems nowhere in evidence at the moment.

Nevertheless, articulating what would be necessary to guarantee effective remedies is an essential first step. This chapter focuses on what is needed, not what is politically feasible. If we do not articulate clearly, at the start of the process, the scope of the necessary changes, we risk adoption of a treaty that does little more than reiterate an unenforceable right to remedies. A treaty that is less than ideal could include useful reforms. The difficult task still ahead for advocates is to determine the essential provisions without which a treaty would not be worth the effort.

The views expressed in this chapter reflect my participation in an international legal group convened by the Treaty Initiative, a joint project of the International Network for Economic, Social and Cultural Rights (ESCR-Net) and the International Federation for Human Rights (FIDH).[6] In a series of meetings in 2015 and 2016, the legal group consulted about treaty

---

[4] Human Rights Council, 'Elaboration of an International Legally Binding Instrument on Transnational Corporations and Other Business Enterprises with respect to Human Rights', A/HRC/26/L.22/Rev.1 (25 June 2014).

[5] In this chapter, I do not explore the many additional issues the treaty must address, some of which are discussed in other chapters of this book. One such issue is whether the treaty will recognize that human rights norms bind corporations directly or will impose on states the obligation to require that corporations abide by those norms (see Chapter 7 by Bilchitz in this volume). My use of the term 'corporate human rights violations' is intended to encompass whichever concept the treaty adopts: direct corporate human rights obligations and/or obligations imposed by states.

[6] For more information about the Treaty Initiative and the legal group, see International Network for Economic, Social and Cultural Rights (ESCR-Net), 'Corporate Accountability Treaty Initiative', www.escr-net.org/corporateaccountability/treatyinitiative (last accessed 13 January 2017).

options with representatives of over 100 organizations from the Global South, including both members of impacted communities and civil society organizations (CSOs) that work alongside them. I do not speak for the Treaty Initiative's legal group or the people we met, but my views articulated in this chapter are heavily influenced by what I learned from them.

To set the stage for my discussion of possible treaty provisions, this chapter begins with an overview of the right to a remedy and the obstacles to effective remedies for corporate abuses. It then highlights a prerequisite for effective remedies: access to information about both corporate operations and available remedies. The next two sections of the chapter address in detail the treaty provisions that would, if fully implemented, provide effective remedies for corporate human rights abuses. After addressing the substantive content of effective remedies, I explain why the remedial mechanisms must be safe, independent, affordable and timely, with the power to enforce orders. The chapter then discusses different categories of mechanisms: non-state and state, judicial and non-judicial, domestic and international. The final section (Appendix) offers suggestions as to how these different remedies might interact in a BHR treaty that would bring the international community into compliance with its longstanding, long-unfulfilled commitment to provide effective remedies to those injured by corporate human rights abuses.

15.2 The Right to an Effective Remedy

The right to an effective remedy is a cornerstone of the international human rights system. The Universal Declaration of Human Rights states that '[e]veryone has the right to an effective remedy'.[7] In the International Covenant on Civil and Political Rights, states agree to ensure an effective remedy, access to a competent authority to obtain the remedy, and enforcement of remedies.[8] Similar commitments are found in virtually all of the major international human rights instruments.[9]

---

[7] Universal Declaration of Human Rights (adopted 10 December 1948) (UDHR), art. 8.

[8] International Covenant on Civil and Political Rights (entered into force 23 March 1976) 999 UNTS 171 (ICCPR), art. 2(3).

[9] See, for example, International Convention on the Elimination of All Forms of Racial Discrimination (entered into force 4 January 1969) 660 UNTS 195 (ICERD), art. 6; Convention on the Rights of the Child (entered into force 2 September 1990) 1577 UNTS 3 (CRC), art. 39; Convention Against Torture and Other Cruel, Inhuman or Degrading Treatment or Punishment (entered into force 26 June 1987) 1465 UNTS 85, art. 14(1). See also Committee on Economic, Social and Cultural Rights, 'Statement on the Obligations of States Parties Regarding the Corporate Sector and Economic, Social and

In 2005, the UN General Assembly adopted a detailed resolution affirming the right to a remedy[10] and stating explicitly that business entities should provide reparations to victims of human rights abuses.[11] 'Access to remedy' is one of three pillars of the 'protect, respect and remedy' framework endorsed by the UN Human Rights Council in 2008.[12] The Guiding Principles, which were developed to implement that framework, recognize that the right to an effective remedy is fundamental to corporate accountability, asserting that states must ensure that 'when [corporate] abuses occur within their territory and/or jurisdiction those affected have access to effective remedy'.[13]

The Guiding Principles also recognize that corporations have the responsibility to provide redress for human rights violations caused by their business operations.[14] Corporations 'should address adverse human rights impacts with which they are involved',[15] which requires 'taking adequate measures for their... remediation'[16] and having in place '[p]rocesses to enable the remediation of any adverse human rights impacts they cause or to which they contribute'.[17]

15.3 Obstacles to Effective Remedies

The strong language about the right to an effective remedy in international law instruments has had little impact on the ground. A report of the UN High Commissioner for Human Rights recently concluded that remedies are 'elusive'.[18] Multiple studies have

---

Cultural Rights', E/C.12/2011/1 (20 May 2011), para. 5. ('It is of the utmost importance that States parties ensure access to effective remedies to victims of corporate abuse of economic, social and cultural rights', including 'tak[ing] steps to prevent human rights contraventions abroad by corporations which have their main offices under their jurisdiction'.)

[10] UN General Assembly, 'Basic Principles and Guidelines on the Right to a Remedy and Reparation for Victims of Gross Violations of International Human Rights Law and Serious Violations of International Humanitarian Law', A/RES/60/147 (16 December 2005) (UN Basic Principles).

[11] Ibid., para. 15.

[12] Human Rights Council, 'Protect, Respect and Remedy: A Framework for Business and Human Rights', A/HRC/8/5 (7 April 2008), para. 84; Guiding Principles, n. 1, Pillar III.

[13] Guiding Principles, n. 1, Principle 25.   [14] Ibid., Principles 11, 13, 15 and 22.

[15] Ibid., Principle 11.   [16] Ibid., Commentary on Principle 11.

[17] Ibid., Principle 15(c). See also Principle 22.

[18] Human Rights Council, 'Improving Accountability and Access to Remedy for Victims of Business-Related Human Rights Abuse: Report of the United Nations High

demonstrated the inadequacies of the status quo.[19] Although states
clearly have a legal obligation to ensure effective remedies for human
rights violations committed by business entities, corporations violate
human rights with impunity. Communities lose their land, their
homes and their livelihoods, and have no recourse to remedies at
all in practice.

A major problem with the existing system is its reliance on voluntary
measures that largely depend on corporate good will and on requests that
they be good corporate citizens. Corporations are designed to produce
profit for their owners. Expecting them to voluntarily choose to be
responsible social actors, despite the cost, is naive. As John Ruggie
wrote in 2015, 'Forty years of pure voluntarism should be a long enough
period of time to conclude that it cannot be counted on to do the job by
itself.'[20] Ruggie was writing about one particular remedial procedure, but
his indictment of voluntary mechanisms applies broadly. They do not
work.

Corporations do not merely decline to volunteer to comply with
human rights norms, including the right to an effective remedy. They
also actively work to undermine enforcement measures. Through their
outsized influence on domestic and international decision-makers,
corporations have been able to dictate the terms of their relationship
with the societies in which they operate. Using both lawful political
pressure and unlawful/corrupt persuasion, corporations have side-
tracked efforts to impose binding, enforceable human rights obligations
and have obtained favourable procedural and substantive protections

Commissioner for Human Rights' (HRC, 'Improving Accountability'), A/HRC/32/19 (10
    May 2016), para. 2.
[19] See, for example, G. Skinner, R. McCorquodale and O. De Schutter, *The Third Pillar:
    Access to Judicial Remedies for Human Rights Violations by Transnational Business (The
    Third Pillar)* (2013), http://icar.ngo/wp-content/uploads/2013/12/The-Third-Pillar-
    FINAL1.pdf (last accessed 13 January 2017); J. Zerk, 'Corporate Liability for Gross
    Human Rights Abuses Towards a Fairer and More Effective System of Domestic Law
    Remedies: A Report Prepared for the Office of the UN High Commissioner for Human
    Rights' (Corporate Liability) (2014), www.ohchr.org/Documents/Issues/Business/
    DomesticLawRemedies/StudyDomesticLawRemedies.pdf (last accessed 13 January
    2017); Amnesty International, *Injustice Incorporated: Corporate Abuses and the Human
    Right to Remedy* (2014), www.amnesty.org/en/documents/POL30/001/2014/en/ (last
    accessed 13 January 2017).
[20] J. Ruggie and T. Nelson, 'Human Rights and the OECD Guidelines for
    Multinational Enterprises: Normative Innovations and Implementation Challenges'
    (2015), 21, www.hks.harvard.edu/index.php/content/download/76202/1711396/ver
    sion/1/file/workingpaper66.pdf (last accessed 20 January 2017).

for their operations. Communities complain about 'corporate capture': their governments, including the judiciary, are under the sway of corporate interests, and their home-state institutions are not capable of affording justice to those injured by corporate human rights violations.

Where mechanisms exist to challenge corporate misdeeds, those impacted are often unable to access them effectively. They may be unaware of the existence of the available procedures or lack the necessary legal assistance, funding or other resources. Moreover, corporations generally control information about their operations and the potential impact on human rights. Communities may be blindsided by corporate activities and face irreparable harm before they are even aware of the impending crisis, and they may have difficulty gathering evidence to prove a link between corporate operations and the injuries they suffer.

The most chilling obstacle to effective remedies is the danger that human rights defenders face. In 2015, at least 156 human rights defenders were killed or died in detention.[21] In mid-2016, more than 300 were actively at risk.[22] In Honduras alone, over 100 environmental activists were killed between 2010 and 2014.[23] States' abysmal failure to protect the lives of those who seek remedies for human rights abuses makes a mockery of the international norm alleging a right to an effective remedy.

Even when affected communities are able to lodge a complaint against a corporation, the petitioners rarely receive satisfaction. Company-based grievance mechanisms generally lack transparency, independence and the capacity to resolve disputes with enforceable, effective remedies.[24] Administrative and judicial systems in the state where the abuses take place are often understaffed and subject to corporate pressure. Host-state courts may not have jurisdiction over the parent companies that have the financial ability to remedy widespread abuses, and, if they do assert jurisdiction, are often unable to enforce their orders. For all but a handful of impacted communities, judicial remedies in the home state of the

---

[21] Frontline Defenders, 'Annual Report 2016' (14 January 2016), 7, www.frontlinedefenders .org/en/resource-publication/2016-annual-report (last accessed 13 January 2017).

[22] Frontline Defenders, 'Open Cases', www.frontlinedefenders.org/open-cases (last accessed 13 January 2017).

[23] J. Blitzer, 'The Death of Berta Cáceres', *The New Yorker* (11 March 2016), www.new yorker.com/news/news-desk/the-death-of-berta-caceres (last accessed 13 January 2017).

[24] See discussion later in the chapter.

corporation[25] are blocked by lack of information, inadequate legal and financial resources, and lack of access to the evidence necessary to prove their case. Moreover, the courts of the corporation's home state may refuse to assert jurisdiction over the corporation's extraterritorial conduct or claim that the challenged activities are those of a subsidiary, not the parent corporation. In addition, courts apply the doctrine of *forum non conveniens* to dismiss litigation on the ground that the claims can be more conveniently litigated in another state.

A few international mechanisms exist to resolve human rights claims against corporations. Several human rights treaties include committees authorized to hear complaints against states, and some expressly permit claims based on a state's failure to prevent or remedy corporate misconduct.[26] Several international mechanisms establish systems to review complaints about corporate abuses, including international finance institutions such as the World Bank, the Organization for Economic and Community Development (OECD) and some multistakeholder initiatives. But these remedies, where they exist, have the same problems as those discussed above: communities rarely even know they exist; if they do know, they rarely have the resources to present a complaint; and if they can access the system, the process is slow and cumbersome and generally designed to mediate disputes or

---

[25] Although, for convenience, I refer to 'home state' in the singular throughout this chapter, the Maastricht Principles call on states to regulate business enterprises 'where the corporation, or its parent or controlling company, has its centre of activity, is registered or domiciled, or has its main place of business or substantial business activities', not merely in the state where registered or domiciled. 'Maastricht Principles on Extraterritorial Obligations of States in the Area of Economic, Social and Cultural Rights' (Maastricht Principles) (February 2012), para. 25, www.etoconsortium.org/en/main-navigation/library/maastricht-principles/ (last accessed 13 January 2017).

[26] For example, the complaint mechanism created by the Third Optional Protocol to the Convention on the Rights of the Child addresses violations of the rights protected by the Convention. Optional Protocol to the Convention on the Rights of the Child on a Communications Procedure (entered into force 14 April 2014), A/RES/66/138, art. 5(1)(a). This includes state obligations to '[e]nsure that the activities and operations of business enterprises do not adversely impact on children's rights' and '[e]nsure access to effective remedy for children whose rights have been infringed by a business enterprise acting as a private party or as a State agent'. Committee on the Rights of the Child, 'General Comment No. 16 on State Obligations Regarding the Impact of the Business Sector on Children's Rights', CRC/C/GC/16 (17 April 2013), paras. 5(a) and 5(c). The Inter-American human rights system also hears complaints alleging violations by business enterprise. For an overview, see K. Salazar, 'Business and Human Rights: A New Challenge for the OAS?' (14 October 2015), www.dplfblog.com/2015/10/14/business-and-human-rights-a-new-challenge-for-the-oas/ (last accessed 13 January 2017).

issue recommendations, not to produce enforceable judgements. Finally, in those few cases in which a decision is enforced, the remedies it provides are rarely sufficient to fully restore the community to the conditions existing before the violations.

15.4   Access to Information: A Prerequisite

One of the most basic prerequisites for effective remedies is access to information.[27] This begins, fundamentally, with information about corporate activities, so that impacted communities know what the corporation is planning before the harm occurs, and know what the corporation has done so they can file informed complaints about how it has impacted their lives. In addition, in order to assess the corporation's liability for the injuries they have suffered, communities need information about corporate structures and supply chains, the corporation's own impact assessments, and prior human rights complaints and legal actions. Access to information also encompasses the right to information about remedies: there is no 'access to remedy' if those in need of a remedy do not know their rights or how to enforce them.

The Guiding Principles make only passing reference to the right to information, leaving it to the discretion of the business enterprise to decide what impacts require disclosure.[28] Principle 3 says that, 'where appropriate', states should require corporations to communicate how they address human rights impacts,[29] but the Guiding Principles neither require advance disclosure of threats to human rights nor specify when a threat is significant enough to mandate disclosure.[30] And the Guiding Principles make no reference to the additional, essential information that is within the control of corporations.

---

[27] For a thorough discussion of the issues addressed in this section, see N. Jägers, 'Will Transnational Private Regulation Close the Governance Gap' in S. Deva and D. Bilchitz, *Human Rights Obligations of Business: Beyond the Corporate Responsibility to Respect?* (Cambridge University Press, 2013), 295.

[28] Principle 17 calls on corporations to 'account for' how they address 'adverse human rights impacts' and 'communicat[e]' that information. When their operations 'pose risks of severe human rights impacts', they should 'report formally on how they address them'. Guiding Principles, n. 1, Principle 21.

[29] *Ibid.*, Principle 3(d).

[30] The Commentary states that a disclosure requirement would be 'particularly appropriate where the business operations . . . pose a significant threat to human rights', but does not require disclosure even in such situations. *Ibid.*, Commentary on Principle 3.

To address the need for information, the treaty should require corporate disclosure of all information relevant to current or future human rights abuses and to holding corporations accountable for their actions, and should provide a means by which impacted communities can learn about their rights and remedial mechanisms.

15.5   The Substance of an Adequate, Effective Remedy

When communities and individuals are able to obtain some remedy, it is often inadequate or ineffective. Adequate, effective remedies include enforceable interim measures to halt and prevent violations, reparation and punishment of those responsible.[31] To implement this right, the treaty should specify that those injured by corporate human rights violations must have access to the full range of remedies, as appropriate to the particular harms they have suffered.

15.5.1   Interim or Provisional Measures of Protection

The possibility of future compensation is an inadequate remedy for people faced with harm to their health and safety, their community, their property or the land and water that they depend upon for their livelihood. The treaty should require that communities have access to quick, affordable, enforceable interim measures to halt abusive activities, prevent further violations and protect the safety of those raising the complaints. Currently, such provisional measures are often ineffective;[32] strengthening protective measures must be a priority in treaty discussions.

15.5.2   Reparation

Reparation encompasses a broad range of measures to restore the situation that would have existed prior to the wrongful act, including restitution, compensation, rehabilitation, satisfaction and guarantees of non-

---

[31] This section draws heavily on the UN Basic Principles, n. 10, The Commentary on Principle 25 of the Guiding Principles contains similar language.
[32] Honduran human rights defender Berta Cáceres was killed in March 2016 despite two requests for precautionary measures issued by the Inter-American Commission on Human Rights. Blitzer, 'Death of Berta Cáceres', n. 23.

repetition.[33] Monetary compensation is often insufficient. If a community has been forced from its land or lost access to fields, water, or other essential resources, money will rarely enable them to re-establish the situation that existed before the violation of their rights. A full remedy includes rebuilding houses, replacing lost property and means of employment, and restoring access to the resources on which the community depends.

Where it is not possible to restore the situation existing before the violations, monetary compensation must be sufficient to enable community members to rebuild lives comparable to what they had before the unlawful violations. Compensation equal to the market value of resources lost does not constitute full compensation if the community is left without a means of livelihood. Nor would resettlement in new homes be sufficient if community members are deprived of crucial community ties on which they had depended. Compensation should also address non-property injuries, including physical, mental or cultural harm and the costs of legal, medical and psychological services.

Satisfaction, a key component of reparation, includes full public disclosure of the truth about abusive acts, apology and acceptance of responsibility. Confidential settlements and monetary payments without an admission of responsibility allow the corporation and its employees, in effect, to purchase the right to commit abuses, and to continue to do so as long as they have sufficient funds. Equally important, guarantees of non-repetition require institutional reforms to prevent future violations.

Reparations, along with the process by which they are negotiated and assessed, must be culturally appropriate, taking into account the values of the community impacted by the corporate abuses. In general, remedies must be sensitive to gender, age and the needs of minorities, as well as indigenous people. For example, indigenous people's access to sacred locations may be irreplaceable, and a full remedy must offer the possibility of re-establishing traditional customs and activities.[34] Remedies must also take into account the particular vulnerability of some community members. Women, persons with disabilities and children, for example,

---

[33] UN Basic Principles, n. 10, para. 18. The aim of remedies is 'to counteract or make good any human rights harms that have occurred'. Guiding Principles, n. 1, Commentary on Principle 25.

[34] See generally C. M. Doyle (ed.), *Business and Human Rights: Indigenous Peoples' Experiences with Access to Remedy* (AIPP, Almáciga: IWGIA, 2015).

cannot be relocated to situations in which they would face physical obstacles, danger, or other heightened risks.

15.5.3 Punishment of both the Business Entity and Corporate Officials

An effective remedy includes sanctions against those responsible for the violations, both to punish them and to deter future violations. The corporation itself and the individuals involved in the violations must be punished through civil sanctions, criminal prosecutions and administrative penalties. Corporations can face criminal prosecution, fines or other sanctions that limit their operations or require them to alter their business plans to ensure respect for human rights. Of course, states can impose the 'corporate death penalty': dissolving a corporation by cancelling its registration or incorporation. Corporate employees can be punished with imprisonment, fines, recovery of unjust enrichment and the full range of criminal sanctions.

15.6 Remedial Mechanisms

Communities around the world are in desperate need of safe and effective mechanisms through which to obtain remedies for corporate human rights violations. Effective remedies require safe, independent, affordable, timely procedures, guided by the rule of law, and a mechanism empowered to enforce remedial orders. Currently, the systems supposedly designed to provide remedies rarely come close to that standard.

After discussing requirements common to all remedial mechanisms, this section discusses and critiques a broad range of possible procedures – non-state and state, non-judicial and judicial, domestic and international – that could be part of the treaty, from local operational grievance mechanisms to new international criminal or civil courts. The options are not interchangeable and are not all equal. State-based remedies are essential, regardless of whether non-state based mechanisms are available.[35] Judicial remedies – impartial, independent state-based tribunals – are also crucial.[36] Non-judicial mechanisms are, in general, only effective if a state judicial remedy

---

[35] 'State-based judicial and non-judicial grievance mechanisms should form the foundation of a wider system of remedy'. Guiding Principles, n. 1, Commentary on Principle 25.
[36] 'Effective judicial mechanisms are at the core of ensuring access to remedy'. *Ibid.*, Commentary on Principle 26.

is available as a backdrop, providing a threat and incentive to spur good-faith engagement.[37]

The discussion ends with a discussion of how the various mechanisms might work together in an effective BHR treaty.

15.6.1   Core Requirements

A few core requirements are common to all remedial mechanisms.[38]

Safety: Complainants, witnesses, advocates and the community at large must be protected from physical harm, economic reprisals or other retribution. Human rights defenders must be protected.

Accessibility: Remedial mechanisms must be affordable, including the costs of legal assistance, preparing and filing complaints, gathering evidence, travel and translation.

Collective actions: An effective remedy must include the possibility of class, representative or other collective actions (rather than require that individuals bring separate complaints) both to reduce costs and to protect community members who may be subject to reprisals if they file complaints as individuals.

Independence: The process must be protected from corporate or political interference, and must follow fair procedures laid down beforehand.

Prompt procedures: The mechanism must also operate promptly, to prevent further harm and to provide a timely remedy

Enforceable judgements: The remedial mechanism must have some means to enforce its orders and final judgements.

In practice, some of these core principles may conflict. The least expensive, most accessible remedies are often those available in the community: company-based operational-level grievance mechanisms. But they are not independent, and they present the highest risk of danger to complainants. At the other end of the spectrum, international mechanisms may be more independent of corporate pressure, but access may be time-consuming and costly. A treaty will have to include varied options and responses to the multiple obstacles, in order to maximize the likelihood that, one way or

---

[37] C. Rees, 'Corporations and Human Rights Accountability Mechanisms for Resolving Complaints and Disputes' (April 2007), 6, 18, www.hks.harvard.edu/content/download/67692/1243578/version/1/file/report_15_accountabilitymechanisms.pdf (last accessed 13 January 2017).

[38] The UN Basic Principles, n. 10, contain detailed discussions of these basic requirements. See also the Commentary on Principle 25 of the Guiding Principles, and Principle 31 (applying similar criteria for non-judicial grievance mechanisms).

another, a community injured by a corporate human rights violation will obtain the remedy guaranteed to it by international law.[39]

15.6.2   Non-State-Based Mechanisms

Communities impacted by corporate human rights abuses view existing non-state mechanisms with great scepticism. To the extent that they could be useful in some circumstances, two preconditions are essential. First, participation in a non-state mechanism can never be either a prerequisite for or a bar to access to a state-based remedy. In particular, access to a non-state procedure must not be conditioned on waiver of the right to seek judicial remedies.[40] Second, where corporate conduct is criminal – and corporate human rights abuses often constitute crimes – non-state remedies are not a substitute for state criminal prosecution of the corporation and its employees.[41]

15.6.2.1   Operational-Level Grievance Mechanisms

The simplest, least expensive response to an imminent or current human rights abuse is to complain directly to the entity responsible for the violation: the local business. The Guiding Principles place great emphasis on operational-level grievance mechanisms.[42] Unfortunately, these mechanisms are, in most cases, inherently flawed and viewed with distrust and even fear by communities impacted by corporate abuses. Most troubling, community members may put their lives at risk when they approach corporate representatives with their complaints. More broadly, they generally do not trust a process operated by the business enterprise. As one report stated succinctly, '[r]emedy cannot rely on the willingness of the party who

---

[39] Deva, for example, has articulated an integrated theory of regulation which requires employment of multiple regulatory mechanisms in tandem. S. Deva, *Regulating Corporate Human Rights Violations: Humanizing Business* (Routledge, 2012),

[40] See Guiding Principles, n. 1, Commentary on Principle 29 (operational-level grievance mechanisms should not 'preclude access to judicial or other non-judicial grievance mechanisms'.)

[41] See Human Rights Council, 'Report from an Expert Workshop entitled "Business Impacts and Non-judicial Access to Remedy: Emerging Global Experience" held in Toronto in 2013' (HRC, Workshop Report), A/HRC/26/25/Add.3 (28 April 2014), para. 15 (remedies obtained through a non-judicial mechanism are without prejudice to criminal liability or judicial action against the perpetrators).

[42] Principle 31 of the Guiding Principles and the accompanying Commentary provide detailed guidelines for designing an operational-level grievance procedure.

committed the abuse'.[43] Companies have incentives to design grievance mechanisms to advantage the company, not those injured by its misdeeds:

> Dealing with grievances in-house has many advantages for companies: they design and control the grievance mechanism; they or their appointed agents investigate the claim; they adjudicate on whether a claim is valid; they determine the type of remedy and – for example, when financial compensation is offered – the level at which it is set. Most importantly, companies access and control all information relating to a claim, from personal details about the victim, through to provisions of any final settlement, invariably bound-up by confidentiality clauses that allow the company to decide what will be made public. The process is less about achieving justice for victims, but about containment to minimize damage to a company's reputation.[44]

In a 2014 assessment of access to remedies, the UN Working Group reported a similar long list of concerns about company-based mechanisms,[45] including lack of transparency, dependence on cooperation from the business enterprise, failure to monitor compliance or enforce judgements, structural power imbalances, lack of access to independent counsel, failure to consult with victims in designing the mechanisms, requirements that participants waive their right to take further legal action, and remedies that were not appropriate to the severity of the harm suffered.

Any provision for operational-level grievance mechanisms in the treaty, therefore, would need to significantly strengthen the model, starting by requiring supervision by an independent state oversight body; that body would need the authority to ensure that the corporation acts in good faith and the power to protect the safety of those who present complaints. Procedures must be transparent, participants must have the right to independent legal counsel, agreements or judgements must be enforceable, and complainants must not be required to waive their right to seek other remedies.

If the affected communities can engage safely and participate on an equal footing with corporate representatives, participation is voluntary,

---

[43] The Centre for Research on Multinational Corporations (SOMO), 'The Patchwork of Non-Judicial Grievance Mechanisms: Addressing the Limitations of the Current Landscape' (SOMO, Patchwork) (1 December 2014), 6, www.somo.nl/news-en/the-patch work-of-non-judicial-grievance-mechanisms (last accessed 13 January 2017).

[44] Rights and Accountability in Development (RAID), 'Principles Without Justice: The Corporate Takeover of Human Rights' (March 2016), 57, www.raid-uk.org/sites/default/files/principles_without_justice.pdf (last accessed 13 January 2017).

[45] See UN General Assembly, 'Report of the Working Group on the issue of human rights and transnational corporations and other business enterprises', A/HRC/26/25 (5 May 2014), paras. 36–42. See also HRC, Workshop Report, n. 41.

and communities do not waive other remedial rights, they might find the possibility – even if remote – of a quick, local remedy to be worth the attempt. But to have any support from the community, operational-level grievance mechanisms must respond to the needs of the victims of corporate abuses. Principle 31(h) of the Guiding Principles recommends that corporations 'engag[e] with affected stakeholder groups about [the] design' of the mechanism. Many CSOs see this as essential to the success of the process, so that the community accepts it as legitimate and any resulting remedies actually address the needs of those injured.

EarthRights International (ERI) is working on developing a model of 'community-driven' operational grievance mechanisms in which the corporation engages community members in 'a participatory process', rather than in 'top-down' remedies.[46] Under this model, to avoid the conflict of interest inherent in remedial mechanisms designed and implemented by the companies themselves, the process is 'designed and approved by the affected persons – the rights-holders – rather than those who are believed to have caused the problems in the first place'.[47] Community-directed remedial mechanisms affirm that remedies are not gifts from the company, but rather implement the community's right to remedies under international law.[48]

Strengthening corporate grievance procedures would result in a mechanism that is more complex than one designed and implemented under the complete control of the corporation. But if corporations are not willing to offer a remedy that communities can possibly trust, the dispute should be resolved through state-based mechanisms.

15.6.2.2   Multi-Stakeholder Initiatives

In multi-stakeholder initiatives (MSIs), representatives of business and civil society set standards for corporate behaviour. Corporations voluntarily agree to join the initiatives, and monitoring of compliance, if any, is generally confidential and controlled by the corporation or by a governing body in which corporations usually play a dominant role. The Guiding Principles recommend that MSIs include grievance mechanisms through which complainants can seek remedies for violations of MSI standards.[49]

---

[46] J. Kaufman and K. McDonnell, 'Community-Driven Operational Grievance Mechanisms' (2015) 1 *Business and Human Rights Journal* 127 at 128–129.

[47] *Ibid.*, 128. See also EarthRights International and SOMO, 'Community Driven Operational Grievance Mechanisms: Discussion Paper for a New Model' (2014), www.earthrights.org/sites/default/files/documents/ogm_discussion_paper.pdf (last accessed 13 January 2017).

[48] Kaufman and McDonnell, n. 46, 131.   [49] Guiding Principles, n. 1, Principle 30.

MSIs present the same sets of problems as company-led grievance mechanisms. Voluntary procedures, under the control of corporations, are likely to bolster the corporate image, not to provide effective redress to those injured by corporate abuses. The mechanisms are unlikely to be transparent or protective of the rights and safety of complainants, or to produce enforceable judgements. To the extent that MSI grievance mechanisms were included in some form in the treaty, they would have to be placed under robust state supervision, with meaningful community involvement in their design, a complaint procedure, protection for participants, and enforceable rules and judgements.

15.6.3 State-Based Remedies

State-based remedies play an essential role in protecting human rights. The efficacy of these remedies, however, depends on whether the state institution is truly independent of the corporation and willing and able to protect individuals and communities from corporate activities. Concerns about corporate capture and scepticism about the government's commitment to human rights frequently undermine the community's trust of state-based remedies.

15.6.3.1 Non-Judicial Remedies

The treaty could require host or homes states to offer a range of non-judicial remedial mechanisms, although, as emphasized in the introduction to this section, non-judicial remedies cannot be either a prerequisite for or a bar to judicial remedies. In theory, non-judicial remedies could offer a fast, accessible remedy. In practice, however, non-judicial remedies are often a waste of time and resources; produce no response or unenforceable recommendations; put the lives of complainants at risk; and enable corporations to continue to violate human rights, increasing the harm to the communities and rendering any future relief more expensive and harder to implement.

Many CSOs are unlikely to support the inclusion of non-judicial remedies in a BHR treaty unless those remedies are substantially strengthened to provide a transparent process that is independent, accessible and timely; protects the lives and property of complainants; and has the power to either issue enforceable decisions or provide quick access to a judicial process that can enforce a non-judicial decision. State agencies could, at least, play a useful role in explaining rights and available remedies – but only if impacted communities trust that they are independent, not representing corporate interests.

National Human Rights Institutions (NHRIs): Whether called a national human rights commission or institution, an ombudsperson, or a human rights defender, a national state-based agency can be empowered to offer remedies for injuries caused by corporate human rights violations.[50] Although many NHRIs are limited to conducting research, issuing policy recommendations and perhaps mediating disputes, some receive complaints and issue decisions on the merits.[51] The treaty should not rely on NHRIs unless it protects their independence and strengthens their authority to resolve complaints and issue enforceable decisions through timely, safe procedures that communities can access easily.

Government Ministries or Other Administrative Bodies: Specialized government bodies – such as the ministries of health, labour or the environment, the agencies charged with granting applications for corporate registration or incorporation, or agencies that regulate imports, exports and trade – could receive complaints and order remedies for human rights violations. These administrative remedies for corporate human rights abuses can be useful only if the community views the process as independent and the agencies are granted sufficient authority and funding to investigate, operate efficiently, protect complainants and enforce their orders.

OECD National Contact Points: States that belong to the OECD[52] are obligated to create National Contact Points (NCPs) to receive complaints of violations of the OECD Guidelines for Multinational Enterprises (OECD Guidelines), which include human rights standards.[53] NCP

---

[50] United Nations Office of the High Commissioner for Human Rights, 'OHCHR and NHRIs' (26 January 2016), www.ohchr.org/EN/Countries/NHRI/Pages/NHRIMain.aspx (last accessed 15 January 2017).

[51] See generally OHCHR, 'Business and Human Rights: A Survey of NHRI Practices–Results from a Survey Distributed by the Office of the United Nations High Commissioner for Human Rights' (23 May 2008), www.reports-and-materials.org/OHCHR-National-Human-Rights-Institutions-practices-Apr-2008.doc (last accessed 15 January 2017).

[52] The OECD was formed in 1960 by the United States, Canada and 18 European states, and has since added 14 members from around the world. *See* OECD, 'Members and Partners', www.oecd.org/about/membersandpartners/ (last accessed 15 January 2017).

[53] OECD, 'OECD Guidelines for Multinational Corporations' (OECD Guidelines) (2011), 68, http://dx.doi.org/10.1787/9789264115415-en (last accessed 15 January 2017). The OECD Guidelines were revised in 2011 to incorporate the standards contained in the Guiding Principles. *Ibid.*, 31–34.

complaints trigger a dialogue intended to facilitate a voluntary resolution: rather than issue a binding decision, the NCP makes recommendations to the corporation.[54] This is one of the fundamental problems with the NCP process: it has no teeth.[55] Canada is apparently the only state that has announced *any* negative consequences for companies when a NCP complaint process finds violations.[56] As John Ruggie himself wrote recently about the NCPs, experience has shown that purely voluntary mechanisms are not effective.[57] Moreover, with rare exceptions, the NCPs cannot stop ongoing human rights violations or provide remedies for violations already committed by corporations.[58] The NCP process also fails a number of the core preconditions for a functioning grievance mechanism: the process has too many barriers to access, lacks impartiality and transparency, fails to produce timely decisions and cannot enforce its decisions.[59]

To the extent that the treaty tries to builds upon the OECD model, it would need to substantially strengthen the NCP system and grant significant additional powers to resolve complaints and award remedies through binding decisions.

15.6.3.2 Judicial Civil Remedies

Judicial remedies are 'at the core of ensuring access to remedy',[60] but currently beyond reach of most of those impacted by corporate abuses. In addition to the barriers common to all remedial mechanisms, obstacles to judicial remedies include a long list of practical problems that impact both host-state and home-state litigation, such as the high cost of litigation, endemic delays, limited access to evidence and lack of legal assistance.[61] In order to facilitate access to judicial remedies, a treaty will need to address these problems, requiring states to take steps such as permitting contingency

---

[54] *Ibid.*, 71–74.

[55] For a detailed study of NCP complaints and the weaknesses of the system, see OECD Watch, 'Remedy Remains Rare' (2015), 5, http://www.oecdwatch.org/publications-en/Publication_4201 (last accessed 13 January 2017).

[56] Ruggie and Nelson, *Human Rights*, n. 20, 21. [57] *Ibid.*

[58] OECD Watch, 'Remedy Remains Rare', n. 55, 17. Only 1 per cent of NCP complaints filed on behalf of impacted communities produced a resolution 'that directly improved conditions for the victims of corporate misconduct'. *Ibid.* 19.

[59] *Ibid.*, 5. OECD Watch concludes that the NCP process has potential, but only if these significant problems are addressed. *Ibid.*, 50.

[60] Guiding Principles, n. 1, Commentary on Principle, 26.

[61] Many of the obstacles to effective judicial remedies are referenced in the Guiding Principles, Commentary on Principle 26. In addition, see HRC, 'Improving Accountability', n. 18, paras. 4–5; Zerk, 'Corporate Liability', n. 19, 7.

fees or other fee-shifting rules and funding legal aid programs; mandating disclosure of relevant evidence in the control of corporate defendants; and authorizing class, representative or other collective actions.

In addition to these common problems, corporate-defendant litigation faces particular obstacles in both host and home states.

Host-State Judicial Remedies: When available, judicial remedies in the host state, the country where the abuses occurred and the injuries were inflicted, are generally preferable to remedies that require those harmed to travel to a foreign state to litigate their claims. However, communities impacted by corporate human rights violations often find the courts of their own state unable to provide effective remedies. Domestic judicial systems are often short-staffed and underfunded and thus incapable of offering timely and effective remedies, particularly in cases involving complex corporate litigation. Even more problematic, however, is the fact that many courts succumb to pressure from politicians or corporations, either through outright corruption or the powerful influence of the economic benefits that foreign investment can bring to those positioned to profit from it.

Legal restrictions also impede access to justice in host states. Multinational corporations (MNCs) increasingly rely on elaborate corporate structures that insulate different branches of their operations from the legal obligations incurred by others. As a result, host-state courts may not have jurisdiction over the parent corporation that benefits from the unlawful activities and has sufficient resources to provide a remedy to those harmed by the violations.

In light of these hurdles, many of those injured by corporate human rights violations view remedies in their own state as impossible. A BHR treaty cannot address the myriad judicial, economic and political obstacles that undermine access to effective remedies. But a treaty that does not recognize the scope of the problem would be meaningless.[62] As an initial

---

[62] As the UN High Commissioner for Human Rights wrote in a report to the HRCL:

> Rectifying these deficiencies – which, in many cases, are rooted in wider social, economic and legal challenges – will not be straightforward. It will require concerted and multifaceted efforts from all States, encompassing actions relating to law reform and legal development, improvements to the functioning of judicial mechanisms, law enforcement, policy development and closer international co-operation. However, this is essential work towards realizing the imperatives of accountability and remedy for business-related human rights abuses.

HRC, 'Improving Accountability', n. 18, para. 7.

step, the treaty could emphasize the importance of an independent, transparent, functioning judicial system capable of issuing enforceable decisions in cases addressing corporate human rights abuses.[63] The treaty could reiterate states' pre-existing obligations to provide such a system and link it to the obligation to provide remedies for corporate human rights violations. It could mandate legal assistance between judicial systems, so that evidence can be obtained across borders, and require that judgements rendered by a foreign legal system be enforced. Furthermore, as discussed in the following sections, the treaty could address the jurisdictional issues and corporate structures that make it difficult to hold accountable the corporate entity responsible for the violations.

Finally, the treaty could make clear that the lack of a domestic judicial system capable of providing effective redress for corporate human rights violations will trigger the right to seek remedies in other states and through international mechanisms. For now and for the immediate future, a remedy in the judicial system of a MNC's home state may be the most accessible remedy of all.

Home-State Judicial Remedies: Seeking remedies in an MNC's home state will usually present daunting financial and logistical challenges. How will the complainants connect with lawyers, finance the litigation, travel to the foreign state to participate in the proceedings, translate documents, and transport evidence and witnesses to the foreign court? Moreover, home-state mechanisms are not immune from the political and economic pressures that undermine host-state legal systems.

Despite these difficulties, the inadequacies of a host-state legal system may make it preferable to bring claims against large MNCs in their home state, rather than in the states in which they operate. The home-state judiciary may be more independent, more efficiently operated and better able to enforce the law against a large business enterprise. The parent corporation may not be subject to suit in the place where its subsidiaries or other business partners operate. Given that the corporation generally has assets in its home state, any resulting judgement is likely to be enforceable, whereas host-state remedies are often stymied by corporate structures that leave the local entities insufficient resources to provide redress for the harms they have inflicted.

---

[63] For guidance on improving domestic judicial remedies, see HRC, 'Improving Accountability', *ibid.*; Human Rights Council, 'Improving Accountability and Access to Remedy for Victims of Business-Related Human Rights Abuse: Explanatory Notes for Guidance' (HRC, Improving Accountability: Explanatory Notes), A/HRC/32/19/Add.1 (12 May 2016).

Considering the complexity of the global economy and the cross-border movement of goods, financial assets and personnel, remedial systems cannot be successful if cabined within national borders.[64]

As a result, and despite the well-known difficulties of litigation in a foreign country, access to remedies in a corporation's home state is a central demand from communities impacted by corporate human rights abuses. Several comprehensive reports have detailed the legal and practical barriers to home-state litigation against MNCs and have recommended means of addressing these obstacles.[65] A new treaty on BHR would be well-positioned to address these necessary reforms, which include both substantive and procedural law.

An important requirement for meaningful home-state remedies is to recognize substantive legal norms that hold parent corporations liable for the unlawful actions of their subsidiaries and for abuses in their supply chains. Several legal doctrines could implement these concepts. Most obviously, the parent corporation should be held liable when it has been directly involved in the human rights violations. Similarly, parent corporations should be held liable for conspiring with, assisting or otherwise furthering conduct that violates the rights of others.

Legal reforms could also make it easier to pierce the corporate veil: to find that the parent is liable for the obligations of its subsidiary, because the subsidiary is not, in reality, an entirely separate legal entity. The laws governing agency could be strengthened to make it easier to show that a subsidiary or supplier is acting as an agent for the parent corporation. Parent companies could be held liable for failing to effectively control

---

[64] As summarized in a report on dismal efforts to seek redress for people in the Ivory Coast injured by the dumping of toxic waste, '[t]he abuses were transnational but the remedies were not'. Amnesty International and Greenpeace Netherlands, *The Toxic Truth* (2012), 172, www.greenpeace.org/international/en/publications/Campaign-reports/Toxics-reports/The-Toxic-Truth/ (last accessed 13 January 2017).

[65] For thorough discussions and critiques of the options mentioned in this section, see G. Skinner, 'Rethinking Limited Liability of Parent Corporations for Foreign Subsidiaries' Violations of International Human Rights Law' (2015) 72 *Washington and Lee Law Review* 1769 at 1819-1847; Skinner et al., *The Third Pillar*, n. 19, 5–12, 68–69; D. Cassell and A. Ramasastry, 'White Paper: Options for a Treaty on Business and Human Rights' (White Paper) (May 2015), 41–44, business-humanrights.org/sites/default/files/documents/whitepaperfinal%20ABA%20LS%206%2022%2015.pdf (last accessed 13 January 2017); O. De Schutter, 'Extraterritorial Jurisdiction as a Tool for Improving the Human Rights Accountability of Transnational Corporations' (1 December 2006), http://business-humanrights.org/en/pdf-extraterritorial-jurisdiction-as-a-tool-for-improving-the-human-rights-accountability-of-transnational-corporations (last accessed 15 January 2017).

their subsidiaries or business partners. More broadly, the legal system could impose enterprise liability, finding that a set of interconnected corporations constitute a single business enterprise and that the whole is legally liable for human rights violations committed by any of the parts.

Another broad approach would impose a presumption of parent company liability that could be overcome only if the parent corporation has conducted effective due diligence to identify, prevent and mitigate adverse human rights impacts throughout their affiliated operations. This presumption of liability would create a parent company duty of care and shift the burden of proof from those injured by human rights violations to the corporation, requiring the parent to prove that it has taken reasonable steps to avoid and remedy such violations. The requirement of due diligence could be imposed on affiliates and throughout the supply chain by requiring that it be included in contracts for goods or services. People impacted by corporate human rights violations would view this approach with scepticism, however, unless it includes measures to ensure that the supposed 'due diligence' is not just a perfunctory means to ward off liability.

In addition to standards of liability that hold parent corporations accountable, access to home-state remedies requires that the home-state judiciary assert jurisdiction over claims based on conduct that occurred outside the territory of the home state. Legal standards holding parent corporations liable for abuses committed by subsidiaries or other affiliates should make clear that the home state will assert jurisdiction over such claims. In addition, the treaty could require states to recognize that corporations are subject to suit in multiple states. That is, as reflected in the Maastricht Principles, states could recognize that corporations can be sued 'where the corporation, or its parent or controlling company, has its centre of activity, is registered or domiciled, or has its main place of business or substantial business activities', not merely in the state where a particular corporate subdivision is registered or domiciled.[66] To facilitate home-state litigation, the treaty could also discourage dismissals of suits based on the doctrine of *forum non conveniens*, according to which a court may dismiss a case if the defendant shows that it can be more conveniently litigated in another forum. Plaintiffs should also be able to rely on the doctrine of jurisdiction by necessity, which holds that a court should assert jurisdiction over claims if no other forum is available to resolve the complaint.

Treaty language about the appropriate forum for human rights litigation should take into account the dearth of effective remedies for

[66] Maastricht Principles, n. 25, para. 25.

corporate human rights violations. States are not writing on a blank slate on this issue, but rather addressing the longstanding and pernicious inadequacies of the current remedial options. The goal must be to open more and less expensive litigation options. As discussed in the final section of this chapter, although plaintiffs can be encouraged to consider the possibility of obtaining remedies in the place where the abuses occurred, when they choose to file lawsuits in the home state of the corporation involved in human rights abuses, their decision to do so should be granted deference.

The Importance of Clear Standards and Jurisdictional Rules: A BHR treaty should strive for consistent rules to govern jurisdiction, substantive liability and damages. Litigation against MNCs is often delayed at the outset by time-consuming, expensive battles over jurisdiction and choice of law, to the disadvantage of the complainants, who have limited resources. Uniform rules would simplify the search for remedies by specifying which legal systems will hear a claim and what legal standards will govern. Although diverse legal systems need not apply identical procedures, a treaty would make a significant contribution to improving access to effective remedies if it provided clear rules to decide these issues.

15.6.3.3   Corporate Criminal Liability in Domestic Law

Many of the human rights violations committed by corporations constitute crimes. Criminal prosecutions are an essential remedial mechanism, in part because they satisfy the truth-telling and punishment aspects of remedies. In addition, in many jurisdictions, convicted criminals can be ordered to take remedial actions or pay compensation to those harmed by their crimes; civil claims can be joined to criminal prosecutions; or civil lawsuits can rely on a criminal conviction to satisfy the civil burden of proof.

   Although criminal prosecution of corporations is a possibility in most, but not all, states,[67] corporations are rarely prosecuted.[68] One reason is a lack of resources: criminal prosecutions of corporations, particularly well-resourced multinational corporations, are likely to be expensive and complex. Unnecessarily high standards for attributing conduct to the corporation pose an additional hurdle. As a report of the UN High Commissioner for Human Rights has noted, domestic law standards of

---

[67] A. Ramasastry and R. C. Thompson, *Commerce, Crime and Conflict: Legal Remedies for Private Sector Liability for Grave Breaches of International Law* (September 2006), 13, www.biicl.org/files/4364_536.pdf (last accessed 13 January 2017).

[68] HRC, 'Improving Accountability', n. 18, para. 2.

intent and secondary liability focus excessively on pinpointing the criminal activity of particular employees, rather than on systematic actions within the corporation that lead to criminal behaviour.[69]

A BHR treaty could take several steps to spur corporate criminal prosecutions.[70] It could mandate legal reforms to enable criminal prosecutions of business entities and require states to commit sufficient resources to fund prosecutions. The treaty could define a set of international crimes that will be subject to domestic criminal prosecutions and standardize rules for the assertion of jurisdiction over such crimes when committed by entities affiliated with a local corporation. Finally, the proposed treaty could adopt a uniform definition of corporate complicity to make clear when a corporation has committed a crime.

15.6.4   International Mechanisms

Some sort of international remedial mechanism is a persistent demand from CSOs working on BHR issues. With good reason, communities impacted by corporate abuses do not trust corporations to voluntarily regulate themselves, and they do not trust their own governments to regulate the corporations. Even though an international mechanism might be able to address only a small number of complaints, many local groups see it as an essential fall back in a system that is so sharply tilted against them.

Establishing any international mechanism, even the most modest of these proposals, will be a daunting task. To begin, proposals for international supervision will face the same political and economic forces that have made domestic remedies in both host and home states so unreliable. Those forces will surely work overtime to block creation of an international mechanism and to weaken its authority. Even if a treaty establishes a new mechanism that is insulated from undue outside interference and is authorized to take strong action, the sheer volume of potential complaints could overwhelm it. In 2008, John Ruggie estimated that there were 77,000 TNCs in the world, plus 800,000 subsidiaries, millions of

---

[69] HRC, Improving Accountability: Explanatory Notes, n. 63, paras. 10-20. See also Zerk, 'Corporate Liability', n. 21, 33–37.

[70] See discussion of criminal liability in Cassel and Ramasastry, 'White Paper', n. 65, 22–24, and the list of suggested legal reforms in Ramasastry and Thompson, Commerce, Crime, n. 67, 28–29 as well as in Amnesty International and International Corporate Accountability Roundtable, *Corporate Crimes Principles: Advancing Investigations and Prosecutions in Human Rights Cases* (October 2016).

suppliers and millions of national companies.[71] An international mechanism would find it difficult to sort through the thousands of complaints it would receive, much less respond to any significant number of them.

Nevertheless, resolution of even a small number of representative complaints could have outsized resonance for impacted communities around the world. During the heyday of human rights litigation in the United States, the courts resolved only a handful of cases each year.[72] Those cases resonated with people suffering from similar human rights abuses and helped trigger an ever-growing number of cases filed in domestic court systems around the world. Potential defendants were acutely aware of the cases and the possibility that they might be sued. Given this multiplier effect, an international body charged with acting on complaints of corporate human rights abuses could play an important role, even if only able to address a tiny subset of such abuses.

This section discusses several proposals for international mechanisms, some of which have strong support among groups working with communities impacted by corporate human rights violations. The relationship between these international mechanisms and domestic remedies is discussed in the final section of this Part.

15.6.4.1   International Criminal Court

In addition to requiring that states provide for corporate criminal prosecutions in their domestic law, many participants in the discussions of a new treaty have argued that the treaty should authorize international criminal prosecutions. One proposal is to create a new Corporate International Criminal Court; a second is to propose an amendment to the current International Criminal Court (ICC) to expand its jurisdiction to include corporate defendants.[73] Both options would be expensive and politically difficult to accomplish. Moreover, experience to date with the ICC makes clear that international criminal prosecutions are slow and cumbersome. But even a small number of successful prosecutions could

---

[71] J. Ruggie, 'Treaty Road Not Travelled' (2008) *Ethical Corporation* 42 at 43.
[72] For discussion of the issues raised in this paragraph, see B. Stephens, 'Translating Filártiga: A Comparative and International Law Analysis of Domestic Remedies for International Human Rights Violations' (2002) 27 *Yale Journal of International Law* 1; B. Stephens, 'The Curious History of the Alien Tort Statute' (2014) 89 *Notre Dame Law Review* 1467.
[73] Cassel and Ramasastry, White Paper, n. 65, 33; Ramasastry and Thompson, n. 67, 28.

have a significant impact on the corporate world and could increase interest in improving domestic remedies as a way to avoid the risk of international criminal proceedings.

15.6.4.2 International Civil Court

The treaty could establish a new International Civil Court empowered to decide cases involving corporate human rights violations. One detailed proposal for an International Court of Civil Justice suggests that corporations would welcome it as an alternative to ineffective legal systems in states in which they operate.[74] Creating a new court from scratch would be politically difficult, time consuming and expensive. Although a civil court could hear more cases than a criminal court, it would still be able to resolve only a small percentage of the cases that arise around the world. However, even a handful of cases could send a message to other corporate violators and help encourage development of domestic judicial remedies.

15.6.4.3 International Arbitration Procedure

Arbitration is potentially a faster and less expensive means to resolve disputes than litigation.[75] The fairness of the outcome depends heavily on the independence of the arbitrators and of the rules under which they operate. Human rights organizations are understandably wary of arbitration as a means to resolve human rights complaints against corporations, given the widespread view that the current investor-state arbitration process favours business and has been used to override human rights.[76]

A BHR treaty could include an agreement to create an arbitration tribunal and require that corporations agree to submit to its jurisdiction.[77] Although a complex task, creating an arbitration process

---

[74] M. Steinitz and P. Gowder, 'Transnational Litigation as a Prisoner's Dilemma' (2016) 94 *North Carolina Law Review* 751 (proposing international court to resolve cross-border disputes, including business-to-business disputes). For a proposal for an international civil court focused on state human rights violations, see M. Gibney, 'On the Need for an International Civil Court' (2002) 26 *Fletcher Forum of World Affairs* 47.

[75] A common arbitration structure involves a panel of three arbitrators, with each side picking one arbitrator and those two agreeing on a third. Generally, there is no means to appeal an arbitration decision, and subsequent panels are not bound by earlier decisions.

[76] For an overview, see L. E. Peterson, 'Human Rights and Bilateral Investment Treaties: Mapping the Role of Human Rights Law within Investor-State Arbitration' (1 February 2009), http://publications.gc.ca/site/archivee-archived.html?url=http://publications.gc.ca/collections/collection_2012/dd-rd/E84-36-2009-eng.pdf (last accessed 13 January 2017).

[77] For a proposal for an International Arbitration Tribunal on Business and Human Rights, with trained human rights arbitrators, procedures tailored to respect human rights, and

would be far less expensive than establishing a new international criminal or civil court, and arbitration would be able to resolve many more claims than a court. The likelihood that it could impact many MNCs, however, might make them wary of supporting the proposal. It is also unclear whether impacted communities would trust such a system.

15.6.4.4   Treaty-Based Committee with the Power to Hear Complaints

A treaty on BHR could create a committee empowered to monitor compliance with the treaty, similar to the existing committees created by several human rights treaties. A proposal merely to grant such a committee authority to review and comment on regular reports from state parties would presumably be less controversial than a more ambitious proposal for a new complaint mechanism, but it would also be deeply unsatisfying to communities harmed by corporate human rights violations. For those groups, some sort of complaint procedure is a core requirement. Moreover, even a complaint procedure would be disappointing if, based on the current common model, it resulted only in recommendations from the treaty committee to the offending state. Impacted communities seek enforceable remedies, not more voluntary recommendations.

If the treaty does establish a complaint procedure, a key question is whether complaints could be filed directly against corporations, as well as against states. As discussed earlier, many CSOs have no confidence in their state's will or capacity to ensure effective remedies for corporate human rights violations. Others view enforcement of human rights norms as a state function, however, and might prefer that the international remedial mechanisms be addressed to states, not corporations. A corporate complaint mechanism would face the same problem of overwhelming volume discussed above, with hundreds of thousands of MNCs and millions of national corporations as potential targets.

---

financial support for complainants, see C. Cronstedt and R. C. Thompson, 'An International Arbitration Tribunal on Business and Human Rights' (13 April 2015), www.l4bb.org/news/TribunalV5B.pdf (last accessed 13 January 2017); C. Cronstedt and R. C. Thompson, 'A Proposal for an International Arbitration Tribunal on Business and Human Rights' (21 July 2015), www.ihrb.org/commentary/proposal-for-international-arbitration-tribunal.html (last accessed 13 January 2017).

15.6.4.5   Global Ombudsperson/Mediator

While a global ombudsperson authorized to receive complaints, intervene on behalf of impacted communities and mediate disputes would be a minimal advance over the status quo,[78] it would be disappointing to impacted communities if it did not have the power to enforce decisions. With sufficient resources and independence, such an office could at least play a role in disseminating information and advising about how to access the remedial mechanisms that do exist.

15.6.5   *Putting the Pieces Together: Modified Complementarity*

Encouraging provision of remedies at a local level is a laudable goal that is fully consistent with human rights principles. Remedies close in space and time to the abuses that cause injuries, when possible, are generally more efficient than remedies far from home. Most international enforcement mechanisms require exhaustion of adequate and available domestic remedies. Similarly, complementarity is a foundational principle of the ICC, which will defer to domestic proceedings 'unless the State is unwilling or unable genuinely to carry out the investigation or prosecution'.[79]

Grim experience, however, has shown that local remedies are often not possible. In recognition of this reality, exhaustion of domestic remedies is excused when remedies are not adequate and available, and the ICC need not defer when the State is 'unwilling or unable' to prosecute. Efforts to hold corporations accountable for human rights violations repeatedly confront inadequate, unavailable local remedies and both corporations and governments that are unwilling or unable to provide remedies. Communities impacted by corporate human rights abuses express a deep mistrust of corporate-sponsored remedial mechanisms and of the remedies offered by their own states. Many of these advocates demand a treaty that provides immediate access to remedies in a MNC's home state and to international mechanisms, without requiring that they first exhaust domestic remedies or attempt to access corporate grievance procedures.

---

[78] For a discussion of the potential advantages and difficulties surrounding this proposal, see C. Rees, 'Grievance Mechanisms for Business and Human Rights: Strengths, Weaknesses and Gaps' (January 2008), 34–37, www.hks.harvard.edu/m-rcbg/CSRI/publications/workingpaper_40_Strengths_Weaknesses_Gaps.pdf (last accessed 13 January 2017).

[79] Rome Statute of the International Criminal Court (entered into force 1 July 2002), A/CONF.183/9, art. 17(1)(a).

As noted earlier, recourse to private grievance mechanisms should never be a prerequisite to accessing state or international remedies. Furthermore, to the extent that states insist on some form of exhaustion of remedies requirement or complementarity, the barrier for access to home-state or international mechanisms must be low. If states require onerous, time-consuming preliminary steps before those injured can access a mechanism that they trust, remedies will be unduly delayed, abuses will continue and the corporation, with its greater resources, will thwart access to redress.

In recognition of the difficulties faced by those harmed by corporate human rights abuses and the disproportionate economic and political might of business enterprises, the treaty should establish a low threshold to show that host-state remedies are unavailable, inadequate, dangerous, excessively expensive or ineffective. The threat of quick access to international remedies could provide an incentive for states to improve domestic remedies and for corporations to prevent and remedy such harms.

15.7   Conclusion

Effective remedies for corporate human rights violations are rare. The litany of what is wrong with the current system is long and shameful, including delays, obfuscation, deceit and, tragically, the deaths of human rights defenders. To give effect to the seemingly simple promise of adequate, effective and prompt remedies for corporate violations would require systematic economic and political changes that a BHR treaty is unlikely to accomplish. But a treaty must at least begin to address the power imbalance that allows corporations to decide whether they should, or more often should not, choose to provide remedies for the human rights violations they commit. Communities engaged in fighting corporate abuses will not be fooled by a treaty that merely calls on corporations, yet again, to voluntarily provide remedies or relies on government officials who are under the sway of those corporations. Envisioning what a truly rights-respecting remedial system would look like is one step on the long path towards achieving it.

15.8   Appendix: Proposed Provisions Regarding Access to Remedies

As discussed at length in this chapter, a treaty is unlikely to resolve all the daunting challenges facing those who seek remedies for corporate human rights abuses. Nevertheless, the proposed provisions below are an effort to suggest some of the basic commitments that a treaty should include.

'Each State Party shall take legislative, administrative, judicial or other measures to ensure that those injured by corporate activities have access to adequate, effective, prompt and appropriate remedies, including interim measures to halt violations, reparation, and punishment of individuals and business entities responsible for violations.

(a) Interim measures must be prompt, affordable and accessible, able to halt ongoing violations and prevent future violations, and enforceable by the state.
(b) Reparation shall include restitution, compensation, rehabilitation, satisfaction and guarantees of non-repetition.
(c) Punishment of corporate employees and business entities shall include civil and criminal sanctions and serve both to punish and to deter future violations.
(d) Remedies shall be culturally appropriate and sensitive to gender, age, and disability and to the special needs of minorities and indigenous peoples.

Each State Party shall ensure that remedial mechanisms are safe, independent, affordable and accessible, and that such mechanisms operate in a timely manner and are capable of issuing adequate, effective and appropriate remedies.

Each State Party shall ensure that its judicial system is capable of issuing independent, timely, effective, enforceable remedies to those injured by corporate activities. States shall provide legal and financial assistance to those seeking remedies, and ensure that complainants have access to information about corporate structures and activities.

State Parties shall ensure that those injured by corporate activities can seek judicial remedies in both the State where the injuries occurred and the State in which the corporation or its parent or controlling company has its centre of activity, is registered or domiciled, or has its main place of business or substantial business activities.

State parties shall provide for the criminal liability of both business entities and corporate employees where the harms inflicted constitute crimes.

Each State Party shall ensure that individuals and organizations that raise complaints about corporate activities are protected against harm to their person or property and that those who retaliate against such activities are prosecuted and punished.

Each State Party shall ensure that State non-judicial mechanisms do not require that participants waive the right to seek a judicial remedy, provide complainants assistance to seek independent legal advice, are transparent about both procedures and outcomes, and have the authority to enforce agreements or judgments.

Each State Party shall ensure that corporate operational-level grievance mechanisms are subject to state regulation and supervision, with State oversight of the design and operation of the mechanisms and State guarantees that any resulting agreements or judgments will be enforced.

The State shall ensure that corporate grievance mechanisms (a) are not a prerequisite to seeking other remedies, including judicial remedies, (b) do not require that participants waive the right to seek a judicial remedy, (c) provide complainants assistance to obtain independent legal advice (d) and are transparent and rights-compatible about procedures as well as outcomes.

The Business and Human Rights Committee created pursuant to this Treaty shall have the authority to (a) review State compliance with the provisions of the Treaty, (b) hear and resolve complaints of State violations of the Treaty, and (c) hear and resolve complaints of corporate violations of the Treaty. State Parties shall ensure that Committee decisions are enforceable in their judicial systems.

State Parties agree to begin, in good faith, negotiations for the creation of a Business and Human Rights Court empowered to resolve civil claims against business entities for damages arising out of corporate activities.'

16

The Potential Role of Criminal Law in a Business and Human Rights Treaty

SHANE DARCY

International human rights law has long recognized the role of criminal law in ensuring accountability for human rights abuses. An obligation to employ criminal law at the national level to hold companies to account for violations of human rights is foreseeable in the context of a proposed business and human rights treaty. This point applies regardless of whether the scope of the treaty is broad, encompassing the full range of human rights, or whether it focuses only on 'gross human rights abuses', as has been suggested by the former United Nations Special Representative to the Secretary-General on business and human rights, John Ruggie.[1] Criminal law is ultimately only relevant for those human rights violations which are viewed as being so serious as to attract criminal liability. Not all violations of human rights are recognized in positive law as criminal acts, and corresponding offences for violations of socio-economic rights, for example, tend not be found in national criminal codes or in the statutes of the various international criminal courts.[2] International criminal law is concerned only with the prosecution of a particular class of serious crimes, what the Rome Statute of the International Criminal Court refers to as 'the most serious crimes of concern to the international community as a whole', specifically genocide, crimes against humanity, war crimes and the crime of aggression.[3] Despite such thresholds, how a treaty on business and human rights might engage criminal law merits consideration given the increased role of both international and national criminal law in punishing human rights violations.

---

[1] J. Ruggie, 'A UN Business and Human Rights Treaty?' Harvard Kennedy School Issues Brief, 28 January 2014, 5.

[2] See however E. Schmid, *Taking Economic, Social and Cultural Rights Seriously in International Criminal Law* (Cambridge University Press, 2015).

[3] Rome Statute of the International Criminal Court (entered into force 1 July 2002), 2187 UNTS 90, preamble, Articles 5–8.

The institutional commitment to developing a business and human rights treaty is found in United Nations Human Rights Council Resolution 26/9 of June 2014, which established an Intergovernmental Working Group with a mandate to 'elaborate an international legally binding instrument to regulate, in international human rights law, the activities of transnational corporations and other business enterprises'.[4] In light of the resolution's language and the context of its adoption, it would seem likely that the proposed business and human rights treaty will be modelled along similar lines to the core human rights treaties, thus creating general obligations for states, including, potentially, a requirement to bring criminal law to bear on serious human rights violations involving companies.[5] The drafters of a business and human rights treaty will have to grapple with a number of challenging questions even within the relatively narrow debate on the precise role of criminal law in the context of a proposed treaty. How prescriptive and detailed should the relevant provisions be when it comes to matters of offences, prosecution and punishment? In the area of criminal law, should the treaty demonstrate caution or ambition? A treaty could merely include a general obligation requiring states parties to ensure that human rights violations already considered as criminal offences at the international level are investigated and prosecuted where a business enterprise is implicated. At the other end of the spectrum, the proposed treaty could devise a list of human rights violations to be designated as offences under national law, impose an obligation to extradite, investigate or prosecute individual corporate officers or employees, clarify the precise contours of modes of liability (including the requisite mental element), require the establishment of corporate criminal liability in domestic law and elaborate on issues of attribution, identify appropriate forms of punishment and even address issues related to extraterritorial jurisdiction, extradition and mutual legal assistance. While international criminal law has engaged at some level with all of the above, international human rights law itself has been more conservative and has displayed deference to the national legal traditions of states when it comes to matters of criminal law.

---

[4] United Nations Human Rights Council, Resolution 26/9, 25 June 2014, A/HRC/26/L.22/ Rev. 1.

[5] Regarding various possible approaches see O. De Schutter, 'Towards a New Treaty on Business and Human Rights' (2016) 1(1) *Business and Human Rights Journal* 41; D. Cassell and A. Ramasastray, 'White Paper: Options for a Treaty on Business and Human Rights', Prepared for the American Bar Association, Centre for Human Rights and the Law Society of England and Wales, May 2015.

International criminal law is frequently invoked in the context of business and human rights, and although having developed in recent years into a detailed body of law, there has been limited practical application to corporate activities.[6] This relatively new body of international law has borrowed from national criminal law to create a somewhat self-contained international legal regime, which is primarily applied by the existing international criminal courts. As a matter of treaty law, contemporary international criminal law does not squarely address corporate criminal liability, although its norms and institutions can be brought to bear on the actions of individuals, whether as company directors, officers or employees. Substantive rules of international criminal law have also been relied upon in civil cases against companies.[7] There is some limited case law from the post-Second World War period and a handful of more recent national cases where individual business people have been prosecuted for their companies' complicity in international crimes.[8] Nevertheless, international criminal law must be taken into consideration when considering the criminal aspects of a business and human rights treaty, especially in regard to its subject matter and how it addresses modes of criminal liability.

This chapter takes as its point of departure the criminal law components of existing human rights treaties, rather than international or national criminal law, that may be of relevance to a business and human rights treaty. The chapter explores how international human rights law has incorporated criminal law into existing instruments. It then turns to consider the acts that give rise to criminal liability and what might be understood by 'gross human rights violations' in international law. The chapter's third section examines the issue of criminal liability, and considers how a treaty

---

[6] See generally W. A. Schabas, 'Enforcing international humanitarian law: Catching the Accomplices' (2001) vol. 83 no. 842 *International Review of the Red Cross* 439; A. Ramasastry, 'Corporate Complicity: From Nuremberg to Rangoon: An Examination of Forced Labor Cases and Their impact on the Liability of Multinational Corporations' (2002) 20 *Berkeley Journal of International Law* 91; J. G. Stewart, *Corporate War Crimes: Prosecuting the Pillage of Natural Resources* (Open Society Justice Initiative, 2011).

[7] A. Clapham, 'Extending International Criminal Law beyond Individuals to Corporations and Armed Opposition Groups' (2010) 6 *Journal of International Criminal Justice* 899.

[8] See W. Kaleck and M. Saage-Maaβ, 'Corporate Accountability for Human Rights Violations Amounting to International Crimes' (2010) 8 *Journal of International Criminal Justice* 699; W. Huisman and E. van Sliedregt, 'Rogue Traders: Dutch Businessman, International Crimes and Corporate Complicity' (2010) 8 *Journal of International Criminal Justice* (2010) 803; H. Vest, 'Business Leaders and the Modes of Individual Criminal Responsibility under International Law', (2010) 8 *Journal of International Criminal Justice* 851.

might address both the modes of liability for individual employees, officers or directors of a company, and that of the company itself as a legal person, through the doctrine of corporate criminal liability. The chapter will also draw on other areas of international law of relevance to this issue, including treaties relating to corruption, terrorism and organized crime. While national legal systems provide numerous examples of the application of criminal law to companies or associated individuals, this chapter consciously focuses on existing international law, particularly human rights law, in order to determine the extent of international agreement regarding the modalities of the application of criminal law to corporate activities that violate human rights. In light of this approach, the concluding section includes a suggested article on criminal liability for legal persons for inclusion in the potential business and human rights treaty.

16.1   The Criminal Law Aspects of International Human Rights Law

International human rights law has focused predominantly on laying down the obligations of states themselves regarding human rights, and elaborating a number of treaties to address various types of violations. The core instruments of international human rights law give rise to State responsibility for breaches of human rights, although the instruments do acknowledge that other entities, as well as individuals, can be implicated in such violations. The International Convention on the Elimination of Racial Discrimination, for example, requires states parties to 'prohibit and bring to an end, by all appropriate means, including legislation as required by circumstances, racial discrimination by any persons, group or organization'.[9] The Convention for the Elimination of All Forms of Discrimination Against Women requires states parties to take appropriate measures to address such discrimination by 'any person, organization or enterprise'.[10] While obligations of non-State actors can be read into these provisions,[11] existing treaties have on the whole tended to focus

---

[9] Convention on the Elimination of Racial Discrimination (entered into force 4 January 1969) 660 UNTS 195, Article 2(d).

[10] Convention on the Elimination of All Forms of Discrimination Against Women (entered into force 3 September 1981) 1249 UNTS 13, Article 2(e).

[11] See, for example, D. Bilchitz, 'A chasm between 'is' and 'ought'? A critique of the normative foundations of the SRSG's Framework and the Guiding Principles' in S. Deva and D. Bilchitz, *Human Rights Obligations of Business; Beyond the Corporate Responsibility to Respect* (Cambridge University Press, 2013), 107 at 111–112.

more on specific human rights and types of violations than with those who perpetrate or contribute to them.

The existing human rights treaties have occasionally treated certain violations as being so serious that states parties are obliged to adopt legislation to provide for substantive offences in their domestic criminal law. Initial efforts refrained from addressing in any great detail the types of entities that might be implicated in the particular crimes and from defining modes of criminal liability that might be applied. This approach is exemplified in Article 4(1) of the Convention Against Torture and Other Cruel, Inhuman or Degrading Treatment or Punishment:

> Each State Party shall ensure that all acts of torture are offences under its criminal law. The same shall apply to an attempt to commit torture and to an act by any person which constitutes complicity or participation in torture.[12]

The Convention's primary concerns here are to ensure the criminalization of torture and that criminal liability not be limited only to the physical perpetrators of this crime. The Convention arguably only has natural persons in mind as offenders, referring as it does to issues of nationality, extradition and custody, notwithstanding that the treaty 'does not exclude any criminal jurisdiction exercised in accordance with internal law'.[13] While obliging states parties to introduce the necessary legislation on torture as a crime, the Convention is not overly prescriptive and implicitly acknowledges differing national approaches to certain legal questions, such as jurisdiction.

More recent human rights instruments have gone further than the Convention Against Torture in terms of addressing various forms of criminal liability, as well as broaching the issue of the criminal liability of corporate entities for breaches of human rights. This wider approach would seem to be a reflection of parallel developments in international criminal law and in other areas of international law. In addition to requiring that states parties take 'the necessary measures to ensure that enforced disappearance constitutes an offence under its criminal law', the International Convention for the Protection of All Persons from Enforced Disappearances obliges each State party to 'take the necessary measures to hold criminally responsible [. . .] [a]ny person who commits, orders, solicits or induces the commission of, attempts to commit, is an

---

[12] Convention Against Torture and Other Cruel, Inhuman or Degrading Treatment or Punishment (entered into force 26 June 1987)1465 UNTS 85, Article 5(1).
[13] *Ibid.*, Article 5(3).

accomplice to or participates in an enforced disappearance'.[14] The Convention also provides for the doctrine of superior responsibility in a provision that borrows its language from Article 28 of the Rome Statute of the International Criminal Court.[15] This level of detail in relation to criminal law is unique amongst the core human rights treaties and confirms the expanded role given to criminal law for the protection of human rights. The Convention on Enforced Disappearances entered into force in 2010 and has 51 states parties at the time of writing.[16]

In the context of the potential criminal law provisions of a business and human rights treaty, the Optional Protocol to the Convention on the Rights of the Child on the Sale of Children, Child Prostitution and Child Pornography is especially relevant. The Protocol, which has 171 states parties, requires that the prohibited acts are 'fully covered under its criminal or penal law, whether such offences are committed domestically or transnationally or on an individual or organized basis'.[17] States parties must ensure that criminal liability can arise for attempts, complicity and participation in such offences, in language borrowed from the Convention Against Torture.[18] The Optional Protocol addresses the liability of legal persons in Article 3(4):

> Subject to the provisions of its national law, each State Party shall take measures, where appropriate, to establish the liability of legal persons for offences established in paragraph 1 of the present article. Subject to the legal principles of the State Party, such liability of legal persons may be criminal, civil or administrative.[19]

The proviso 'Subject to the provisions of the national law of a State party' also appears in relation to other modes of liability in the Optional Protocol. As will be seen further below, this is a common approach in international instruments which address the liability of legal persons, whereby the obligation is stated in general terms, and deference is

---

[14] International Convention for the Protection of All Persons from Enforced Disappearances (entered into force 23 December 2010) 2716 UNTS 3, Articles 4 and 6(1)(a).

[15] *Ibid.*, Article 6(1)(b).

[16] See United Nations Treaty Collection, https://treaties.un.org/pages/ViewDetails.aspx?src=IND&mtdsg_no=IV-16&chapter=4&lang=en, (last accessed 31 January 2016).

[17] Optional Protocol to the Convention on the Rights of the Child on the Sale of Children, Child Prostitution and Child Pornography (entered into force 18 December 2002) 2171 UNTS 227, Article 3(1).

[18] *Ibid.*, Article 3(2).

[19] *Ibid.* Article 3(1) refers to the offering, delivering or accepting a child for the purpose of sexual exploitation, transfer of organs for profit or for forced labour.

accorded to national preferences and legal traditions when it comes to giving effect to the obligation. This latitude may explain why no states parties expressly objected to this potentially far-reaching provision by way of a reservation upon ratification of the instrument.

This brief survey of relevant core human rights treaties demonstrates that the obligation to criminalize and prosecute certain human rights violations is an occasional component of those instruments. This obligation has been set down in somewhat broad terms, leaving a degree of discretion to states parties regarding, for example, appropriate modes of criminal liability or how the liability of legal persons might be provided for. It is also clear that these human rights instruments have adopted criminal liability for especially serious human rights violations: torture, enforced disappearances and the exploitation of children. If the drafters of a business and human rights treaty are to include provisions implicating criminal law, they will first have to consider which violations of human rights should give rise to criminal liability for business enterprises or their directors, officers or employees, a question to which I turn in the next section.

16.2 'Gross Human Rights Abuses'

In the debate on a treaty on business and human rights, former United Nations Special Representative for the Secretary-General John Ruggie has argued that at the present stage in the development of international law, a binding instrument should focus only on 'gross human rights abuses'.[20] Ruggie has advocated for 'carefully constructed precision tools' and has expressed his preference for an instrument that would deal with 'the worst of the worst' in terms of human rights violations.[21] This would include violations that amount to international crimes, such as genocide, extrajudicial killings and slavery-type practices.[22] He has explained that 'the underlying prohibitions already enjoy widespread consensus among states yet there remains considerable confusion about how they should be implemented in practice when it comes to legal

---

[20] Ruggie, 'A UN Business and Human Rights Treaty?' n. 1, 5.

[21] *Ibid.*, J. Ruggie, 'Life in the Global Domain: Response to the Commentaries on the UN Guiding Principles and the Proposed Treaty on Business and Human Rights' (2015), http://papers.ssrn.com/sol3/papers.cfm?abstract_id=2554726 (last accessed 31 January 2016) 5.

[22] Ruggie, 'A UN Business and Human Rights Treaty?' n. 1, 5.

persons'.[23] The narrowness of this approach can be criticized given the range of human rights violations in which business can be implicated.[24] This view was frequently expressed by non-governmental organizations at the first session of the Inter-Governmental Working Group tasked with developing a binding business and human rights treaty. An instrument focusing only on gross human rights violations, it was argued, 'could be limited to crimes under international law, which does not cover most corporate human rights abuses'.[25] From a criminal law perspective, however, it is not especially relevant whether the scope of the proposed treaty goes beyond 'gross human rights violations', given that criminal liability tends to arise only for violations that are already considered of such seriousness as to merit criminal sanction. Even so, the concept of gross abuses of human rights is not perfectly synonymous with violations that attract criminal liability, and, accordingly, it is worth considering what meaning is given to gross, serious or grave human rights abuses or violations under international law.

During the discussions at the first session of the Inter-Governmental Working Group, it was pointed out that there is 'no definition of grave violations of human rights in international law'.[26] The phrase 'gross violations of international human rights law' is prominent in the United Nations Basic Principles and Guidelines on the Right to a Remedy and Reparation for Victims of Gross Violations of International Human Rights Law and Serious Violations of International Humanitarian Law.[27] Despite the centrality of the concept, the Basic Principles and Guidelines do not offer a definition of what is meant by gross violations. Its preamble merely notes that such violations 'by their very grave nature, constitute an affront to human dignity'. Other instruments do give some indication of what is understood by gross violations and offer examples. For instance, the 1993 Vienna Declaration and Programme of Action points out that:

---

[23] Ruggie, 'Life in the Global Domain', n. 21, 5.

[24] See, for example, International Commission of Jurists, *Needs and Options for a New International Instrument in the Field of Human Rights*, Geneva, June 2014, 35, 41–43; D. Bilchitz, 'The Necessity for a Business and Human Rights Treaty' (2016) 1(2) *Business and Human Rights Journal* 203, 225–227.

[25] Report of the Open-ended Intergovernmental Working Group on Transnational Corporations and Other Business Enterprises (Draft), 10 July 2015, paragraph 27. See also paragraphs 41, 56, 74.

[26] *Ibid.*, paragraph 56.

[27] *Basic Principles and Guidelines on the Right to a Remedy and Reparation for Victims of Gross Violations of International Human Rights Law and International Humanitarian Law (2005)*, UN Doc. A/RES/60/147, 21 March 2006.

gross and systematic violations and situations that constitute serious obstacles to the full enjoyment of all human rights continue to occur in different parts of the world [...] Such violations and obstacles include, as well as torture and cruel, inhuman and degrading treatment or punishment, summary and arbitrary executions, disappearances, arbitrary detentions, all forms of racism, racial discrimination and apartheid, foreign occupation and alien domination, xenophobia, poverty, hunger and other denials of economic, social and cultural rights, religious intolerance, terrorism, discrimination against women and lack of the rule of law.[28]

There is little doubt regarding the validity of the claim that the examples provided constitute either serious violations of international law or serious obstacles to the realization of human rights, but for present purposes, it is clear that not all of the gross violations of human rights in this expansive list give rise to criminal liability under either international or domestic criminal law. For example, while certain acts of racism and discrimination may attract a criminal sanction in a number of national legal systems, "all forms" of racism and racial discrimination are not necessarily criminalized, even if rightly classified as a gross violation of human rights.

Drafters of a business and human rights treaty would be on firmer ground if they were to interpret 'gross human rights abuses' as including, at least as a starting point, those norms that are considered as *jus cogens* in nature, as well as the principal offences falling within the jurisdiction of contemporary international criminal courts, namely genocide, war crimes and crimes against humanity. There is some overlap between the two. With regard to peremptory norms of international law, the International Law Commission has acknowledged that relatively few such norms have been established, and that those that are 'clearly accepted and recognized' as such include 'the prohibitions of aggression, genocide, slavery, racial discrimination, crimes against humanity and torture, and the right to self-determination'.[29] With regard to international crimes as set out in the Rome Statute of the International Criminal Court, both genocide and grave breaches of the 1949 Geneva Conventions are long-established as a matter of treaty law. Crimes against humanity and war crimes in non-international armed conflicts had a more limited basis in conventional international law prior to the adoption of the Rome Statute in 1998 and

---

[28] UN General Assembly, *Vienna Declaration and Programme of Action*, 12 July 1993, A/CONF.157/23, paragraph 30.
[29] International Law Commission, 'Responsibility of States for Internationally Wrongful Acts', II *Yearbook of the International Law Commission* (2001) 31, 85.

generated some debate in the jurisprudence.[30] That being said, there is little doubt regarding the seriousness of such crimes and their entrenchment within international law, even if some of their finer points may continue to be debated. In terms of international agreement concerning such international crimes, it bears noting that the Rome Statute has over 120 states parties and a strong argument can be made that its subject-matter jurisdiction reflects customary international law.[31]

If the drafters of the business and human rights treaty were to draw on the crimes within the jurisdiction of the International Criminal Court, they would not necessarily have to be bound by the jurisdictional definitions and gravity thresholds which arise for that particular judicial institution. Torture, for example, only falls within the jurisdiction of the International Criminal Court if committed as a war crime, a crime against humanity or as an act of genocide. War crimes can only arise in the context of an armed conflict, and Article 8 of the Rome Statute gives the court jurisdiction over war crimes 'in particular when committed as part of a plan or policy or as part of a large scale commission of such crimes'. For torture to constitute a crime against humanity, such an act must be committed as part of a widespread or systematic attack directed against any civilian population. Individual acts of torture not meeting the 'chapeau' requirements would not fall within the court's jurisdiction, although the obligations for individual states under the Convention Against Torture would remain relevant, in that cases should be 'submitted to the competent authorities for the purpose of prosecution'.[32] Although the crimes under the Rome Statute may not reflect the full range of human rights violations in which business may be implicated, certain crimes are of particular relevance in the context of a business and human rights instrument, including the crimes against humanity of enslavement, forcible transfer and '[o]ther inhumane acts of a similar character intentionally causing great suffering, or serious injury to body or to mental or physical health'.[33]

---

[30] See, for example, L. van den Herik, 'Using Custom to Reconceptualize Crimes against Humanity', *in* S. Darcy and J. Powderly (eds.), *Judicial Creativity at the International Criminal Tribunals* (Oxford University Press, 2010) 80; S. Darcy, *Judges, Law and War; the Judicial Development of International Humanitarian Law* (Cambridge University Press, 2014) 265–292.

[31] See, for example, *Prosecutor v. Furundzija*, Case No. IT-95-17/1-T, Trial Chamber Judgment, 10 December 1998, paragraph 227; W. A. Schabas, *The International Criminal Court; A Commentary on the Rome Statute* (Oxford University Press, 2011) 271.

[32] Convention Against Torture, Article 7(1).

[33] Rome Statute of the International Criminal Court, Articles 7(1)(c)(d) & (k).

That international crimes and gross human rights abuses are not coterminous is aptly illustrated by the Arms Trade Treaty which has recently entered into force.[34] Under Articles 6(3), states parties are required to refrain from authorizing transfers of conventional arms and related items if they would be used for committing certain international crimes. A State party must not allow such transfers if:

> it has knowledge at the time of authorization that the arms or items would be used in the commission of genocide, crimes against humanity, grave breaches of the Geneva Conventions of 1949, attacks directed against civilian objects or civilians protected as such, or other war crimes as defined by international agreements to which it is a Party.

A number of states declared at the time of ratification that, in their understanding, this paragraph would include serious violations of Common Article 3 of the 1949 Geneva Conventions, as well as other war crimes set out in instruments such as Additional Protocol I and the Rome Statute.[35] Article 7 of the Arms Trade Treaty covers instances not addressed by Article 6, and requires states parties to consider whether a transfer of arms could be used to commit a 'serious violation' of international humanitarian law or international human rights law.[36] If there remains an 'overriding risk' that such a violation will occur, following an assessment and consideration of potential mitigating measures, the State party 'shall not authorize the export'.[37] The treaty does not define what such a 'serious violation' involves, although the drafters clearly envisaged a category of harms that fell below what might constitute international crimes.[38] The Arms Trade Treaty may have deliberately been constructively ambiguous when it came to such key terminology, an approach that is not uncommon in international instruments or agreements.[39]

---

[34] Arms Trade Treaty, UN Doc. A/CONF.217/2013/L.3 (entered into force 24 December 2014). See further L. Lustgarten, 'The Arms Trade Treaty: Achievements, Failings, Future' (2015) 64(4) *International and Comparative Law Quarterly* 569; A. Clapham et. al., *The Arms Trade Treaty: A Commentary* (Oxford University Press, 2016).

[35] See the declarations of Lichtenstein, New Zealand and Switzerland, *available at*: https://treaties.un.org/pages/ViewDetails.aspx?src=TREATY&mtdsg_no=XXVI-8&chapter=26&lang=en.

[36] Arms Trade Treaty, Article 7(1).   [37] Ibid., Article 7(3).

[38] See further T. Karimova, 'What amounts to "a serious violation of international human rights law"? An analysis of practice and expert opinion for the purpose of the 2013 Arms Trade Treaty', Geneva Academy Briefing No. 6, August 2014.

[39] See, for example, C. Kress, 'The Procedural Law of the International Criminal Court; Anatomy of a Unique Compromise' (2003) 1(3) *Journal of International Criminal Justice* 603; C. Bell and K. Cavanaugh, '"Constructive Ambiguity" or Internal

Drafters of a business and human rights treaty will thus find little precision in international law on the concept of 'gross human rights abuses' if they seek to go beyond what has been designated as international crimes under treaty and customary international law, as well as those violations of human rights which give rise to a treaty obligation for states to ensure they are designated as offences under national law. In deciding on the scope of a potential treaty, the pragmatic route would be to base the subject matter of the proposed instrument as it relates to criminal offences and sanctions on prevailing international law. Defining gross human rights abuses or proposing the creation of new human rights crimes would of course be open to the drafters, but such undertakings are likely to be time-consuming, not to mention fraught with potential disagreement and division. In any event, there is perhaps greater concern that the proposed treaty provides the means for holding corporate actors to account when violations do arise; the instrument needs to focus as much on the actor as the acts. In this regard, the next section considers how criminal liability for the involvement of corporate actors in serious violations of human rights might be addressed in a potential treaty.

16.3   Criminal Liability

The third pillar of the United Nations Guiding Principles on business and human rights – access to a remedy – recognizes the role of criminal sanctions.[40] The commentary which accompanies the Guiding Principles points out the legal risks that might arise for companies or individual directors, officers or employees implicated in certain human rights violations. Business enterprises are warned of the growing potential for criminal or civil liability if they are complicit in gross human rights abuses. The commentary refers to:

> the expanding web of potential corporate legal liability arising from extraterritorial civil claims, and from the incorporation of the provisions of the Rome Statute of the International Criminal Court in jurisdictions that provide for corporate criminal responsibility. In addition, corporate directors, officers and employees may be subject to individual liability for acts that amount to gross human rights abuses.[41]

Self-Determination? Self-Determination, Group Accommodation, and the Belfast Agreement' (1998) 22 *Fordham Journal of International Law* 1345.

[40] Guiding Principles, 22–23.   [41] *Ibid.*, 21.

The varying approaches of different jurisdictions on these matters are also acknowledged; for example, 'most national jurisdictions prohibit complicity in the commission of a crime, and a number allow for criminal liability of business enterprises in such cases'.[42] The stern sanctions of the criminal law are increasingly applicable to companies and individuals for acts that violate human rights. Criminal law provides not only tangible punishment, but also the social condemnation of particularly serious wrongs.

The relevance of criminal law in the context of business and human rights is clearly recognized by the Guiding Principles, as are the barriers to the effective implementation of this form of judicial remedy. The Commentary to the Guiding Principles notes the following barriers of relevance to criminal proceedings:

- The attribution of legal responsibility among members of a corporate group according to domestic criminal and civil laws may facilitate the avoidance of accountability
- Claimants may be denied justice in a host State, but cannot access the courts of the business enterprise's home State despite the claim's merits
- Prosecutors may lack sufficient resources, expertise and support to investigate individual and business involvement in human rights-related offences.[43]

It is not possible within the confines of this chapter to address how a potential treaty might address each of the barriers that prevents the effective application of criminal law to corporate wrongdoing.[44] Consequently, this section will focus on what a binding instrument could add in relation to the issue of criminal liability for individual directors, officers or employees and the corporation itself.

A binding business and human rights treaty could provide a means for ensuring that states establish the legal liability of companies in their national laws and, it has been suggested, for clarifying the modes of criminal liability therein. According to the draft report of the first session of the Intergovernmental Working Group, a number of NGOs urged that States be 'required to establish legislation that defines appropriate criminal and civil liability to sanction companies that have caused or

---

[42] *Ibid.*, 17.   [43] *Ibid.*, 23.

[44] See further G. Skinner, R. McCorquodale and O. De Schutter, *The Third Pillar; Access to Judicial Remedies for Human Rights Violations by Transnational Business*, International Corporate Accountability Roundtable, CORE and European Coalition for Corporate Justice, 2013.

contributed to human rights abuses'.[45] There was said to be a need to 'clarify criminal liability of legal entities' in the proposed treaty.[46] One participant suggested that a binding business and human rights instrument should incorporate the following:

> the obligation of States to incorporate in criminal legislation illegal acts, which should be those already defined under international law; the need to include in national legislation sanctions for human rights abuses that aren't defined as criminal acts; standards of complicity or conspiracy; and explicit recognition of legal responsibility of a company as a legal person, which doesn't exclude individual legal responsibility of directors and managers for decision making in a corporation.[47]

Those who would undertake the preparation of a business and human rights treaty will have to decide on the extent to which the instrument addresses these matters. Will it be necessary, for example, to specify in fine detail the relevant forms of criminal liability and the applicable modes of attribution to be relied upon if the instrument provides for the criminal liability of corporate entities? As Section 16.1 has demonstrated, international human rights law has generally deferred to national jurisdiction regarding appropriate modes of liability and the liability of legal persons.

Were a business and human rights treaty to require states parties to provide for corporate criminal liability in their national legal systems, it would not be an especially novel requirement. The concept is already present in many national criminal laws,[48] and States have, at times, been required to provide for criminal or other forms of legal liability in their national legislation by international treaties to which they are a party.[49] That companies can commit crimes is no longer as contested a concept as it once was.[50] According to the United Nations Office of Drugs and Crime:

> The principle that corporations cannot commit crimes (*societas delinquere non potest*) used to be universally accepted. [. . .] Today, the age-old debate on whether legal entities can bear criminal responsibility has

---

[45] Draft Report of the Open-ended Intergovernmental Working Group, July 2015, paragraph 73.
[46] *Ibid.*, paragraph 81.   [47] *Ibid.*, paragraph 77.
[48] See generally M. Pieth and R. Ivory, *Corporate Criminal Liability; Emergence, Convergence and Risk* (Springer, 2011).
[49] See Section 16.3.2 below.
[50] See generally C. Wells, *Corporations and Criminal Responsibility*, Oxford University Press, 2001.

shifted more widely to the question of how to define and regulate such responsibility.[51]

That being said, there is a demonstrable lack of consistency across national legal systems as to the presence and form of such liability.[52] The International Commission of Jurists has noted that while a number of states provide for the liability of legal persons, 'many others do not or only partially provide for it'.[53] Although company directors, officers or employees might be prosecuted nationally or internationally as natural persons, overall there is a 'patchy system of legal accountability that leads to protection gaps that are more acute in certain jurisdictions than in others'.[54] International criminal law and human rights law can provide some guidance as to how a business and human rights treaty could contribute to remedying such deficiencies in relation to the application of criminal law to corporate human rights abuses.

16.3.1   Modes of Criminal Liability

Modes of criminal liability is the term used to refer to the various ways in which an individual might participate in criminal activity and be subject to criminal responsibility therefor. This is arguably the most discussed and debated topic in international criminal law.[55] The established modes of liability in international criminal law are primarily addressed to individuals as natural persons. That being said, they may also be relevant in the context of corporate criminal responsibility, discussed in the next section, for purposes of holding companies to account, including parent companies for the acts of subsidiary companies. Parent companies are generally not legally liable in civil or criminal law for the acts of subsidiaries or subcontractors, because of the doctrine of limited liability: some national jurisdictions have, however, provided for parental liability

---

[51] *Legislative Guidance for the Implementation of the United Nations Convention Against Corruption*, United Nations Office of Drugs and Crime, Division for Treaty Affairs, 2006, 108.

[52] See generally J. Zerk, *Corporate Liability for Gross Human Rights Abuses; Towards a fairer and more effective system of domestic law remedies*, Report prepared for the Office of the High Commissioner for Human Rights, 2013.

[53] ICJ, *Needs and Options*, n. 24, 20.   [54] *Ibid.*

[55] See, for example, R. Cryer et al., *An Introduction to International Criminal Law and Procedure*, 3rd edn. (Cambridge University Press, 2014) 353–396; J. Stewart, 'The End of "Modes of Liability"' (2012) 25 (1) *Leiden Journal of International Law* 165.

in certain situations, including in the context of criminal sanctions.[56] In a study prepared for the Office of the High Commissioner for Human Rights, Jennifer Zerk pointed to the role that complicity might play in this context:

> ... even if the parent may not be held responsible on the basis that it owned the subsidiary it might potentially be liable under other legal principles of accessory liability (depending on the applicable domestic law rules) if it ordered, incited, organized, assisted or facilitated the offences. In other words, offences of aiding and abetting and criminal conspiracy provide a way of allocating criminal liability to the parent in a way that respects, rather than undermines, the doctrine of separate corporate personality.[57]

While modes of criminal liability that are present in international law were developed with individual persons in mind, their application need not be so limited.

International criminal law's modes of liability are largely drawn from domestic criminal law, although the doctrine of superior responsibility can be considered as somewhat unique to international law, at least in its inception.[58] Articles 25 and 28 of the Rome Statute of the International Criminal Court provide a widely accepted enunciation of modes of liability applicable to international crimes, albeit without any claim to comprehensiveness. At first glance, the Rome Statute seems to define modes of liability such as commission, ordering, aiding and abetting, common purpose liability and superior responsibility in great detail, at least as compared to the statutes of the *ad hoc* international criminal tribunals. However, aside from a few specific instances,[59] the relevant provisions of the Statute serve mainly to identify the modes of liability that the Court may apply, without clarifying the precise meaning of each of these. The Statutes of the ICTY and ICTR were notoriously skeletal when it came to modes of liability, allowing for expansive interpretations

---

[56] See, for example, G. Skinner, *Parent Company Accountability; Ensuring Justice for Human Rights Violations*, International Corporate Accountability Roundtable, November 2015, p. 12. For a general discussion of this question, see Chapters 8 and 9 in this collection.

[57] Zerk, *Corporate Liability for Gross Human Rights Abuses*, n. 52, 37.

[58] The doctrine was first relied upon in *Trial of General Tomoyuki Yamashita*, United States Military Commission, Manila, 8 October – 7 December 1945, Case No. 21, IV *Law Reports of Trials of War Criminals* 1, and codified in Article 86, Protocol Additional to the Geneva Conventions of 12 August 1949, and Relating to the Protection of Victims of International Armed Conflicts (Protocol I), (entered into force 7 December 1978) 1125 UNTS 3.

[59] See, for example, Rome Statute, Article 25(3)(d) and Article 28.

by the Tribunals, not to mention fractious judicial disagreement at times.[60] The Rome Statute provides a more demarcated framework for the International Criminal Court, while inevitably leaving some latitude for judicial interpretation. In contrast to treaties of international humanitarian law or human rights law which also address modes of criminal liability, the Rome Statute was prepared for the specific purpose of being applied by an international criminal tribunal with a broad jurisdictional reach, covering crimes potentially committed by nationals or on the territory of many of the states which were involved in its drafting. This explains the greater elaboration of substantive law in the Rome Statute. It bears noting that there is no clear statutory obligation that the modes of liability in the Rome Statute be replicated in national criminal law, although the principle of complementarity could be interpreted as creating an impetus to do so.[61]

Other international treaties which have addressed modes of criminal liability have demonstrated a greater concern for establishing particular crimes in positive international law, rather than elaborating on the substance of modes of liability. Nonetheless, these are important precedents to be considered in the context of a potential treaty on business and human rights. The Convention on the Prevention and Punishment of the Crime of Genocide reflects an approach of its time that did not fully distinguish between substantive crimes and modes of liability. Article III makes punishable the crime of genocide itself, as well as conspiracy to commit genocide, direct and public incitement to commit genocide, attempt to commit genocide and complicity in genocide.[62] In the context of war crimes, the 1949 Geneva Conventions identify a series of 'grave breaches' and treat as criminally liable those 'committing or ordering to be committed' such breaches of the Conventions.[63] At the Diplomatic Conference leading to the adoption of the Geneva Conventions, it was decided that the drafters should not concern themselves with codifying

---

[60] See, for example, *Prosecutor v. Perišić*, Case No. IT-04-81-A, Appeals Chamber Judgment, 28 February 2013; *Prosecutor v. Šainović et al.*, Case No. IT-05-87-A, Appeals Chamber Judgment, 23 January 2014.

[61] See S. M. H. Nouwen, *Complementarity in the Line of Fire; The Catalysing Effect of the International Criminal Court in Uganda and Sudan* (Cambridge University Press, 2013) 41, 51–59.

[62] Convention on the Prevention and Punishment of the Crime of Genocide (entered into force 12 January 1951) 78 UNTS 277, Article III.

[63] See, for example, First Geneva Convention, Article 50; Second Geneva Convention, Article 50; Third Geneva Convention, Articles 129; Fourth Geneva Convention, Article 146.

applicable modes of liability, and that this 'should be left to the judges who would apply the national laws'.[64] Additional Protocol I adds to the list of grave breaches, but stands apart from other treaties of international humanitarian law, in that it elaborates in some detail superior responsibility as a means for disciplining or holding criminally liable military commanders who fail to prevent crimes by their subordinates.[65]

Amongst the core human rights treaties, the International Convention for the Protection of All Persons from Enforced Disappearances provides the most detailed articulation of the ways in which liability can arise for criminal conduct. Article 6 provides as follows:

1. Each State Party shall take the necessary measures to hold criminally responsible at least:

   (a) Any person who commits, orders, solicits or induces the commission of, attempts to commit, is an accomplice to or participates in an enforced disappearance;
   (b) A superior who:
   (i) Knew, or consciously disregarded information which clearly indicated, that subordinates under his or her effective authority and control were committing or about to commit a crime of enforced disappearance;
   (ii) Exercised effective responsibility for and control over activities which were concerned with the crime of enforced disappearance; and
   (iii) Failed to take all necessary and reasonable measures within his or her power to prevent or repress the commission of an enforced disappearance or to submit the matter to the competent authorities for investigation and prosecution.[66]

To be precise, the Convention creates an obligation for states parties to hold to account persons who are involved in an enforced disappearance in any of the ways described. Although not clearly stated, this obligation may require legislative action at the national level to ensure that these modes of liability are present in domestic law in order to allow for criminal prosecution in all these circumstances. Even then, the modes

---

[64] Fourth Report drawn up by the Special Committee of the Joint Committee, 12 July 1949, *Final Record of the Diplomatic Conference of Geneva of 1949*, Federal Political Department, Berne, Vol. II, Section B, 114, p. 115.
[65] Additional Protocol I, Article 86.
[66] Convention for the Protection of All Persons from Enforced Disappearances, Article 6.

of liability in the Convention are largely reflective of those already found in national criminal laws and in the treaties of international criminal law.

The United Nations Trafficking Protocol goes further than the Convention on Enforced Disappearances and requires states parties, of which there are 169 at the time of writing, to 'adopt such legislative and other measures as may be necessary to establish as criminal offences' attempting, participating as an accomplice, organizing or directing another person to commit the offence of trafficking in persons.[67] This obligation must be read in line with the proviso 'Subject to the basic concepts of its legal system', which is included in the relevant article of the Protocol. Similar language is found in the preamble of the EU Directive on trafficking, which requires Member States to 'take the necessary measures to ensure that inciting, aiding and abetting or attempting to commit an offence . . . is punishable'.[68] These instruments provide key illustrative examples of the reluctance of international law to impose an absolute obligation on State parties to modify national criminal laws as they relate to modes of liability.

In the context of business and human rights, the concept of complicity has featured significantly. For example, Principle 2 of the UN Global Compact asks companies to 'make sure they are not complicit in human rights abuses', while the Draft Norms on the Responsibilities of Transnational Corporations and Other Business Enterprises with Regard to Human Rights suggested that companies should neither 'engage in nor benefit from' international crimes.[69] As complicity has 'both legal and non-legal meanings',[70] discussion of the concept has been marked by a lack of precision at times. With regard to the legal meaning of complicity, John Ruggie wrote in a 2008 report to the United Nations Human Rights Council that this was an area of considerable uncertainty:

> Owing to the relatively limited case history in relation to companies rather than individuals, and given the variations in definitions of complicity

---

[67] Protocol to Prevent, Suppress and Punish Trafficking in Persons, Especially of Women and Children, Supplementing the United Nations Convention Against Transnational Organized Crime (entered into force 25 December 2003) 2237 UNTS 319, Article 5(2).

[68] Directive 2011/36/EU of the European Parliament and the Council of 5 April 2011 on preventing and combatting trafficking in human beings and protecting its victims, and replacing Council Framework Decision 2002/629/JHA, Article 3. See also preamble, paragraph 14.

[69] Draft Norms on the Responsibilities of Transnational Corporations and Other Business Enterprises with Regard to Human Rights, E/CN.4/Sub.2/2003/12 (2003), Article 3.

[70] Guiding Principles, 17.

within different legal contexts, it is not possible to specify exacting tests for
what constitutes complicity even within the legal sphere.[71]

Ruggie considered that international criminal law could offer some
guidance in this regard, via the notion of 'aiding and abetting' as a widely
recognized mode of criminal liability. It was singled out in the commentary of the UN Guiding Principles, wherein it states that '[t]he weight of
international criminal law jurisprudence indicates that the relevant standard for aiding and abetting is knowingly providing practical assistance
or encouragement that has a substantial effect on the commission of a
crime'.[72] It bears emphasizing that Ruggie drew on international case
law, a subsidiary source of international law, to elaborate the meaning of
aiding and abetting, given the absence of a precise standard for this mode
of liability in existing treaty law.

Since the Guiding Principles were endorsed by the Human Rights
Council in 2011, aiding and abetting as a mode of liability has generated
serious disagreement within and between the *ad hoc* international criminal tribunals.[73] In particular, there was judicial disagreement within the
Appeals Chamber of the ICTY as to whether practical assistance must be
'specifically directed' towards international crimes in order for liability to
arise.[74] The jurisprudence seems to have become settled subsequently on
the point that specific direction is not an element of aiding and abetting,[75]
although it bears noting that the International Criminal Court has not
provided any in-depth consideration of this mode of liability to date. The
Rome Statute provides that criminal liability might arise for an individual
who '[f]or the purpose of facilitating the commission of such a crime,
aids, abets or otherwise assists in its commission or its attempted

---

[71] See 'Clarifying the Concepts of "Sphere of Influence" and "Complicity"', *Report of the
Special Representative of the Secretary-General on the issues of human rights and transnational corporations and other business enterprises, John Ruggie*, 15 May 2008, A/HRC/8/
16, p. 10.

[72] Guiding Principles, 17.

[73] See, for example, S. Darcy, 'Assistance, Direction and Control: Untangling International
Judicial Opinion on Individual and State Responsibility for War Crimes by Non-State
Actors', (2014) vol. 96 no. 893, *International Review of the Red Cross* 243.

[74] *Prosecutor v. Perišić*, Case No. IT-04-81-A, Appeals Chamber Judgment, 28 February
2013; *Prosecutor v. Šainović et al.*, Case No. IT-05-87-A, Appeals Chamber Judgment, 23
January 2014; *Prosecutor v. Stanišić and Simatović*, Case No. IT-03-69-A, Appeals
Chamber Judgment, 9 December 2015.

[75] See Special Court for Sierra Leone, *Prosecutor v. Taylor*, Case No. SCSL-03-1-A,
Judgment (Appeals Chamber), 26 September 2013, paragraphs 471-479; Extraordinary
Chambers in the Courts of Cambodia, Case File/Dossier No. 002/19-09-2007/ECCC/TC,
Case 002/01 Judgment, 7 August 2014, paragraphs 707-710.

commission, including providing the means for its commission'.[76] Courts in the United States assessing claims under the Alien Torts Statute have relied upon an aiding and abetting standard, but there has been division as to whether knowledge of the crime and a substantial contribution to it will suffice, or whether purpose is also required, which is a higher *mens rea* standard requiring that the contribution was intentionally made with a view to the crime's commission.[77]

A treaty on business and human rights that addresses the question of criminal liability will inevitably have to address the concept of complicity, given its ubiquity in the debate on corporate accountability. The drafters could take the lead from existing human rights treaties which have adopted something of a minimalist approach, by setting down the obligation to hold to account persons that are complicit in certain human rights abuses. For example, the Convention Against Torture requires that 'complicity' be an offence under criminal law, while the Convention on Enforced Disappearances speaks of the obligation to hold responsible anyone who is an 'accomplice' to an enforced disappearance. The Genocide Convention criminalizes 'complicity in genocide', while the Apartheid Convention goes further and speaks of liability for persons who '[c]ommit, participate in, directly incite or conspire in the commission of the acts [...] [d]irectly abet, encourage or co-operate in the commission of the crime of apartheid'.[78] The failure of these instruments to define complicity has contributed to the uncertainty as to its precise contours.

The more developed definitions of aiding and abetting in international criminal law, such as in the Rome Statute of the International Criminal Court, do not fully dispel any uncertainty and must be read in conjunction with the relevant jurisprudence of those courts. A maximalist approach may not be open to drafters of a business and human rights treaty seeking to bring clarity to the legal meaning of complicity. It would not seem likely that agreement on a detailed definition could be achieved in a treaty given the lack of uniformity and precision in existing international treaties, as well as the differing approaches of national

---

[76] Rome Statute, Article 25(3)(c).

[77] Compare *John Doe v. Exxon Mobil Corporation*, United States Court of Appeal for the District of Columbia Circuit, 8 July 2011 with *The Presbyterian Church of Sudan v. Talisman Energy, Inc.*, United States Court of Appeals for the Second Circuit, 2 October 2009.

[78] International Convention on the Suppression and Punishment of the Crime of Apartheid (entered into force 18 July 1976) 1015 UNTS 243, Article III.

jurisdictions.[79] A less arduous route might be to seek the iteration of a general obligation on states to investigate, prosecute and punish complicity in serious human rights violations, whether committed by individual directors, officers or employees and/or the company itself. The treaty could provide an illustrative list of modes of criminal liability drawn from existing international law, with accompanying legislative guidance, as is the case with the United Nations Convention on Corruption.[80] This approach would ultimately allow for states to defer to their national legal tradition in determining how the treaty obligation is met. Such discretion, however, could be tempered by granting an interpretive role to a monitoring or judicial body to be set up pursuant to the treaty.[81]

16.3.2   Corporate Criminal Liability

In considering the potential role of criminal law in a business and human rights treaty, the issue of corporate criminal liability is of particular relevance. There are strong rationales behind holding a corporate entity criminally liable. When crimes are committed by or through a business, the wrongdoing of the company may be more than the sum of its parts and individual contributions might not be sufficient to give rise to criminal liability by themselves.[82] As Hin-Yan Liu has put it, corporate criminal liability 'can articulate and capture the additional dimension of organisation that characterize international crimes, as well as the simultaneously individual and collective nature of the corporate juridical person'.[83] Such liability can be seen as complementary to individual criminal responsibility, which itself might be out of reach where it is not possible to apprehend or try individual perpetrators. Corporate criminal liability can also serve a preventive function. According to the United Nations Office of Drugs and Crime, '[c]riminal liability of a legal entity may also have a deterrent effect, partly because reputational damage and monetary sanctions can be very costly and partly because it may act as a catalyst for more effective management and supervisory

---

[79] Zerk, *Corporate Liability for Gross Human Rights Abuses*, n. 52, 37–39.

[80] See *Legislative Guidance for the Implementation of the United Nations Convention Against Corruption*, n. 51, 108.

[81] For a similar suggestion in relation to corporate obligations see Bilchitz, 'The Necessity of a Business and Human Rights Treaty', n. 24, 212.

[82] See further R. C. Slye, 'Corporations, Veils and International Criminal Liability' (2008) 33 *Brooks Journal of International Law* 955.

[83] Hin-Yan Liu, *Law's Impunity; Responsibility and the Modern Private Military Company* (Hart, 2015) 255.

structures to ensure compliance with the law'.[84] Without doubt, the prospect of criminal liability tends to attract the attention of individuals or entities whose activities may place them at risk of such legal action. Corporate criminal liability is not unknown in international law, as certain treaties already call on states parties to provide for the criminal liability of legal persons in their national legal systems. As will be elaborated in this section, this requirement has been limited to a number of defined criminal acts and, moreover, has been formulated such that it allows for civil or administrative liability as an alternate means of meeting a treaty obligation to provide for the liability of legal persons.

Corporate criminal responsibility is not presently found in the principal instruments of international criminal law, such as the Rome Statute, and companies cannot be prosecuted before the International Criminal Court as its jurisdiction stands. That being said, the Special Tribunal for Lebanon is pursuing corporate entities for offences against the administration of justice,[85] and corporate criminal liability for international crimes can be found in a number of national jurisdictions.[86] An unsuccessful attempt to include the criminal liability of legal persons in the Rome Statute was made during the drafting of that instrument.[87] Leaving aside the substance of this proposal for a moment, it bears considering briefly whether the Rome Statute should be the focus of a renewed attempt to introduce corporate criminal liability in international law. For the International Criminal Court to exercise jurisdiction over companies, the Statute would have to be amended by way of a fairly cumbersome amendment process,[88] something that could not be done by way of another international instrument, such as a business and human rights treaty.

While there would be obvious merit to amending the Rome Statute so as to include corporate criminal liability, there are also reasons to avoid focusing solely on this institution: the International Criminal Court's jurisdiction is constrained in terms of the crimes it can prosecute, as well as the nationals and territories over which the Court has jurisdiction.

---

[84] *Legislative Guidance for the Implementation of the United Nations Convention Against Corruption*, n. 51, 108.

[85] See N. Bernaz, 'Corporate Criminal Liability under International Law; the *NEW TV S.A.L.* and *Akbhar Beirut S.A.L.* Cases at the Special Tribunal for Lebanon' (2015) 13 (2) *Journal of International Criminal Justice* 313.

[86] See, for example, J. Kyriakakis, 'Corporations and the International Criminal Court: The Complementarity Objection Stripped Bare' (2008) 19 (1) *Criminal Law Forum* 115, 147.

[87] Schabas, *The International Criminal Court*, n. 31, 424–427.

[88] See Article 121, Rome Statute.

From a practical perspective, the Court can only ever prosecute a few individuals because of resource constraints, and it is heavily reliant on state cooperation for the fulfilment of its mandate. Although the Rome Statute recalls 'the duty of every State to exercise its criminal jurisdiction over those responsible for international crimes', the Court is not designed to ensure that national prosecutions occur, or to monitor those that do so, except perhaps where the Prosecutor is conducting a preliminary examination. The Court is focused squarely on the prosecution of international crimes, not their prevention, a principal reason why the International Law Commission is undertaking work on a crimes against humanity convention.[89] The focus of the International Criminal Court has tended to be on 'those who bear the greatest responsibility' for international crimes.[90] Within the already narrow jurisdictional constraints of the International Criminal Court, the prosecution of accomplices to international crimes, even if they are corporations, might not garner much prosecutorial attention. Finally, the 'insurmountable obstacle' which prevented agreement on corporate criminal liability in 1998, namely, the absence of such liability from a number of national legal systems, could stifle any attempted amendment,[91] even if this objection has been challenged as a matter of law.[92]

A business and human rights treaty is arguably a more promising route towards ensuring the introduction of corporate criminal liability in national legal systems for serious violations of human rights. It has been said that by addressing corporate criminal liability, a business and human rights treaty could 'solve a persistent ambiguity in the field'.[93] It will be open to the drafters to decide how to approach the subject of corporate criminal liability and how prescriptive the proposed instrument would be. A treaty could approach the issue by requiring states parties to provide for corporate criminal liability, or an alternative form of legal liability in national law, while leaving it to states to work out the

---

[89] International Law Commission, *First report on crimes against humanity*, by Sean D. Murphy, Special Rapporteur, 17 February 2015, A/CN.4/680, paragraph 10.
[90] International Criminal Court, Office of the Prosecutor, *Report on Prosecutorial Strategy*, The Hague, 14 September 2006, 5.
[91] Schabas, *The International Criminal Court*, n. 31, 424.
[92] See generally Kyriakakis, 'Corporations and the International Criminal Court', n. 86.
[93] N. Bernaz, 'Including Corporate Criminal Liability for International Crimes in the Business and Human Rights Treaty: Necessary but Insufficient', Debate the Treaty blog series, October 2015, http://business-humanrights.org/en/including-corporate-criminal-liability-for-international-crimes-in-the-business-and-human-rights-treaty-necessary-but-insufficient (last accessed 31 January 2016).

precise modalities of such liability in accordance with their national legal systems. Alternatively, the treaty could specify in detail how corporate criminal liability might arise, by setting out how criminal acts might be attributed to a company itself and what the necessary mental elements might be. These are areas where there is much divergence in national legal systems, with differing approaches to the modalities of corporate criminal liability, including attribution and the relationship between individual and corporate liability.[94] Certain doctrinal differences are also discernible:

> There are still concerns over the attribution of intent and guilt, the determination of the degree of collective culpability, the type of proof required for the imposition of penalties on corporate entities and the appropriate sanctions, in order to avoid the penalization of innocent parties. In some jurisdictions, it is considered artificial to treat a corporation as having a blameworthy state of mind.[95]

Given such varied approaches nationally, it is instructive to consider how existing international treaties have successfully included the obligation of states to provide for the legal liability of legal persons in their national systems.

The Optional Protocol to the Convention on the Rights of the Child on the Sale of Children, Child Prostitution and Child Pornography, as outlined in Section 16.1, requires states parties to provide for the liability of legal persons in their national laws. The obligation is couched in language which defers to national legal traditions:

> Subject to the provisions of its national law, each State Party shall take measures, where appropriate, to establish the liability of legal persons for offences established in paragraph 1 of the present article. Subject to the legal principles of the State Party, such liability of legal persons may be criminal, civil or administrative.[96]

The Optional Protocol is not the only international instrument to adopt this approach, but it does stand out amongst the core international human rights treaties and protocols as being the sole instrument to address corporate criminal liability. The Committee on the Rights of the Child has sought to extend the obligation beyond the Protocol itself, by recommending that states 'consider the adoption of criminal legal

---

[94] Zerk, *Corporate Liability for Gross Human Rights Abuses*, n. 52, 32–43.
[95] *Legislative Guidance for the Implementation of the Convention Against Corruption*, n. 51, 108.
[96] Optional Protocol, Article 3(4).

liability – or another form of legal liability of equal deterrent effect – for legal entities, including business enterprises, in cases concerning serious violations of the rights of the child, such as forced labour'.[97] The Committee urged that states ensure that national courts have jurisdiction over such serious violations 'in accordance with accepted rules of jurisdiction'.[98] The Optional Protocol does not elaborate in any detail the substance or requirements for corporate criminal liability or how it might relate to individual criminal responsibility. Such issues are, however, addressed elsewhere in international law.

The United Nations Convention against Corruption requires State parties to establish criminal offences for corrupt acts, such as giving or receiving bribes by national or foreign public officials.[99] The Convention is noticeably deferential to national legal systems where it broaches matters of criminal law. In setting out the obligation of each State party to provide for certain offences in national law, the Convention uses caveats such as '[s]ubject to its constitution and the fundamental principles of its legal system',[100] 'in accordance with fundamental principles of its domestic law' and '[s]ubject to the basic concepts of its legal system'.[101] A similar approach is taken in Article 26, which contains the obligation concerning the liability of legal persons:

1. Each State Party shall adopt such measures as may be necessary, consistent with its legal principles, to establish the liability of legal persons for participation in the offences established in accordance with this Convention.
2. Subject to the legal principles of the State Party, the liability of legal persons may be criminal, civil or administrative.
3. Such liability shall be without prejudice to the criminal liability of the natural persons who have committed the offences.
4. Each State Party shall, in particular, ensure that legal persons held liable in accordance with this article are subject to effective, proportionate and dissuasive criminal or non-criminal sanctions, including monetary sanctions.

---

[97] Committee on the Rights of the Child, General Comment No. 16 (2013) on states' obligations regarding the impact of the business sector on children's rights, CRC/C/GC/16, 17 April 2013, paragraph 70.

[98] *Ibid.*

[99] United Nations Convention against Corruption (entered into force 14 December 2005) 2349 UNTS 41, Articles 15, 16, 17, 18, 19, 21, 22 and 25.

[100] *Ibid.*, Article 20.   [101] *Ibid.*, Article 23.

This article reiterates that the liability of legal persons and natural persons are not mutually exclusive. It also goes further than the Optional Protocol by setting out principles to be applied in the sanctioning of legal persons found liable of relevant offences. Sanctions can include fines, exclusion from Government procurement, forfeiture, confiscation, restitution, debarment or the 'closing down of legal entities'.[102] However, its formulation raises the question as to whether a State party's 'legal principles' can absolve it of the obligation to provide for the legal liability of persons, criminal or otherwise. According to the *Legislative Guidance* prepared by the United Nations Office of Drugs and Crime, the obligation to provide for the liability of legal entities is mandatory 'to the extent that this is consistent with each State's legal principles'.[103] It notes that 'there is no obligation to establish criminal liability, if that is inconsistent with a State's legal principles. In those cases, a form of civil or administrative liability will be sufficient to meet the requirement'.[104]

The Convention against Corruption has been widely ratified, with 178 states parties at the time of writing, including most of the home states of the world's largest companies, such as those in Europe and North America. The obligation in the Convention to introduce liability for legal persons in accordance with national legal principles is similarly also found in other treaties, including the OECD Convention on Combating Bribery of Foreign Public Officials in International Business Transactions and the United Nations Convention against Transnational Organized Crime.[105] Other instruments have gone a little further, specifying in greater detail the modalities of how corporate criminal liability might arise and how it interacts with individual criminal responsibility. For example, the International Convention for the Suppression of the Financing of Terrorism ties the liability of a legal person to the commission of an offence by a senior individual:

---

[102] *Legislative Guidance for the Implementation of the Convention Against Corruption*, n. 51, 113.

[103] *Ibid.*, p. 112.   [104] *Ibid.* (footnote omitted).

[105] Article 2, OECD Convention on Combating Bribery of Foreign Public Officials in International Business Transactions (entered into force 15 February 1999); Article 10, United Nations Convention against Transnational Organized Crime (entered into force 29 September 2003) 2225 UNTS 209, See also Article 9, Council of Europe Convention on the Protection of the Environment through Criminal Law (1998), *not entered into force*; Article 17, Protocol Against the Illegal Exploitation of Natural Resources, International Conference on the Great Lakes Region, 30 November 2006.

1. Each State Party, in accordance with its domestic legal principles, shall take the necessary measures to enable a legal entity located in its territory or organized under its laws to be held liable when a person responsible for the management or control of that legal entity has, in that capacity, committed an offence set forth in article

2. Such liability may be criminal, civil or administrative.[106]

The Convention requires that states parties ensure that legal persons are subject to 'effective, proportionate and dissuasive criminal, civil or administrative sanctions', and notes that the liability of legal persons is without prejudice to the criminal liability of individuals.

It can be confidently asserted that the consensus that has been achieved in international law on the question of corporate criminal liability is embodied in the relevant provisions of the widely ratified Convention for the Suppression of the Financing of Terrorism, the United Nations Convention against Corruption and the Optional Protocol to the Convention on the Rights of the Child. Pursuant to these instruments, as well as other international treaties, states are required to provide for the criminal liability of a legal person in national law, although this obligation is not absolute, in that it incorporates deference to national legal traditions, such that civil or administrative liability may suffice. In other words, states parties must only provide for corporate criminal liability if it accords with their domestic legal system. The obligation is also presented in general terms, with the treaties not specifying in any significant detail how a legal person can be held liable for criminal offences. Were the drafters of a business and human rights treaty to seek to go beyond the consensus as encapsulated in these instruments, and spell out in greater detail the substance of corporate criminal liability, resort could be made to regional treaties or national legislation for guidance. For example, the Council of Europe Criminal Law Convention on Corruption (1999) provides that liability for legal persons will arise where the offences in question were:

> committed for their benefit by any natural person, acting either individually or as part of an organ of the legal person, who has a leading position within the legal person, based on:
>
> – a power of representation of the legal person; or
> – an authority to take decisions on behalf of the legal person; or

---

[106] International Convention for the Suppression of the Financing of Terrorism (entered into force 10 April 2002) 2178 UNTS 197, Article 5.

– an authority to exercise control within the legal person;

as well as for involvement of such a natural person as accessory or instigator in the above-mentioned offences.[107]

In addition, states parties to this Convention, of which there are fourteen, shall ensure that legal persons can be liable where lack of supervision or control by an individual occupying a leading position made the offence possible.[108] The European Union 2011 Directive on trafficking in persons replicates these modes of attributing wrongdoing to a legal person, and does so without any reference to national legal traditions.[109]

International criminal law, it will be recalled, does not provide for corporate criminal liability, but if greater detail is sought for a business and human rights treaty, it may be useful to have recourse to the original proposal to include the criminal liability of 'juridical persons' in the Rome Statute. The final draft of the provision on the criminal liability of 'juridical persons' put to the delegates at the 1998 Rome Conference proposed that such liability would only arise if a natural person had already been convicted of the crime charged, and:

(b) The natural person charged was in a position of control within the juridical person under the national law of the State where the juridical person was registered at the time the crime was committed; and

(c) The crime was committed by the natural person acting on behalf of and with the explicit consent of that juridical person and in the course of its activities.[110]

The proposal did not succeed, but it is notable that the draft article had envisaged corporate criminal liability only where the criminal act was committed by a person in a controlling position within the legal entity. A provision on criminal liability for corporations has successfully been included in the Draft Protocol on Amendments to the Protocol on the Statute of the African Court of Justice and Human Rights, although the

---

[107] Council of Europe Criminal Law Convention on Corruption (entered into force 1 July 1972) ETS No. 173, Article 18(1).

[108] *Ibid.*, Article 18(2).

[109] Directive 2011/36/EU of the European Parliament and the Council of 5 April 2011 on preventing and combatting trafficking in human beings and protecting its victims, and replacing Council Framework Decision 2002/629/JHA, Article 5.

[110] Working Paper on article 25, paragraphs 5 and 6, Document A/CONF.183/C.1/WGGP/L.5/Rev.2, 3 July 1998.

instrument has not entered into force.[111] As a precedent, however, the relevant provisions, especially regarding the mental element or *mens rea*, are far from a model of clarity:

> 2. Corporate intention to commit an offence may be established by proof that it was the policy of the corporation to do the act which constituted the offence.
> 3. A policy may be attributed to a corporation where it provides the most reasonable explanation of the conduct of that corporation.
> 4. Corporate knowledge of the commission of an offence may be established by proof that the actual or constructive knowledge of the relevant information was possessed within the corporation.
> 5. Knowledge may be possessed within a corporation even though the relevant information is divided between corporate personnel.[112]

These provisions would have benefitted from greater elaboration in order to clarify some of the key questions which arise for corporate criminal liability. For example, in establishing knowledge of an offence, is it envisaged that it might be possessed by any corporate employee or only those in a position of authority and control? It has been suggested that a business and human rights treaty could resolve uncertainty regarding the attribution to a company of the necessary elements of a crime, including the mental element.[113] The Draft Protocol's formulation demonstrates the challenge of doing so, rather than providing a feasible solution.

Corporate criminal liability raises complex legal issues which have the potential to bog down negotiations on a binding business and human rights treaty. While there may be political objections to creating a binding instrument on business and human rights, in the area of criminal law there may be *bona fide* law-based objections to insisting on corporate criminal liability or requiring a particular model of attribution. While there are certainly innovative approaches to be found in national legislation concerning corporate criminal liability, including legislation which focuses on corporate culture as well as individuals in positions of authority or control,[114] the practice of international treaty-making to date demonstrates an aversion by states to overly prescriptive approaches to

---

[111] Draft Protocol on Amendments to the Protocol on the Statute of the African Court of Justice and Human Rights, (2014), STC/Legal/Min/7(1) Rev. 1.

[112] *Ibid.*, Article 46C.   [113] Bernaz, 'Including Corporate Criminal Liability', n. 93.

[114] See, for example, Australia's Criminal Code Act, 1995, Section 3, Part 2.5, Division 12.3(2). See further Clapham, 'Extending International Criminal Law beyond Individuals', n. 7, 917–918; Zerk, *Corporate Liability for Gross Human Rights Abuses*, n. 52, 33–35.

the question of liability for legal person. States would likely be more receptive, or at least less hostile, to a general obligation to provide for corporate legal liability in their national legal systems, including criminal liability, for serious human rights violations, but with deference to national authorities on the form and precise modalities of such liability. John Ruggie has expressed the view that 'criminalization is not necessary', and that adopting the approach of the UN and OECD treaties would leave states 'free to consider appropriate forms of liability in line with the fundamental principles of their national legal systems, which could include civil or administrative liability, with corporate dissolution as the ultimate penalty'.[115] This approach would not provide for universal standards regarding corporate criminal liability, although these may not be attainable if the practice to date is anything to go by. Creating a general obligation for states to provide domestically for the liability of legal persons, but without specifying the finer details of such liability, would not foreclose the possibility of further elaboration and clarification by way of legislative guidance and judicial or expert interpretation of the obligation.

16.4   Conclusion

A business and human rights treaty which seeks to advance corporate accountability and remedies for victims of human rights abuses will be incomplete if it fails to draw on criminal law for this purpose. The Guiding Principles correctly note that the State duty to protect human rights can become 'weak or meaningless' if states fail to investigate, punish and redress human rights abuses related to business activities.[116] A society's opprobrium towards particular conduct is often represented by its criminalization, with criminal sanctions serving to punish, deter and stigmatize such wrongdoing. International law has already designated particular acts as amounting to international crimes or as requiring their criminalization in domestic legal systems, and has identified the actors that can be liable for their commission, including states, individuals and legal persons. Within international human rights law specifically, a number of treaties have established obligations for states to ensure that offences corresponding to certain serious human rights abuses are

---

[115] Ruggie, 'Life in the Global Domain', n. 21, p. 6. See also Draft Report of the Open-ended Intergovernmental Working Group, July 2015, paragraph 75.
[116] Guiding Principles, 22.

present in domestic criminal law. Illustrative examples of modes of liability can also be found within this body of law, although it is less common for states to be mandated by international law to provide for certain modes of criminal liability in their national laws. The Optional Protocol to the Convention on the Rights of the Child on the exploitation of children requires states parties to ensure the liability of legal persons in national legal systems, although it does not insist that such liability is criminal in nature. This approach mirrors that which is found in a raft of international treaties which can be almost uniformly characterized by their deference to national legal traditions on matters relating to criminal liability. The variance in domestic approaches is presented as a barrier to international law insisting in absolute terms on the provision of corporate criminal liability in national law.

The drafting of a treaty on business and human rights presents an opportunity for assessing the present state of domestic laws concerning appropriate modes of liability for corporate involvement in human rights abuses. In light of the growing number of treaties requiring the implementation of liability for legal persons, there may be a greater receptiveness among states to obligations of this nature too. In view of the approach adopted by international human rights law to date regarding serious violations of human rights and the liability of legal persons, the following article is proposed for a potential business and human rights treaty:

> Subject to the provisions of its national law, each State Party shall take measures, where appropriate, to establish the liability of legal persons for serious violations of human rights including slavery, trafficking in persons, forced labour, torture, enforced disappearances, sexual exploitation of children and for international crimes, namely genocide, crimes against humanity, grave breaches of the Geneva Conventions of 1949 or other war crimes as defined by international agreements to which it is a Party.
>
> Subject to the legal principles of the State Party, such liability of legal persons may be criminal, civil or administrative.
>
> Such liability shall be without prejudice to the criminal liability of the natural persons who have committed the offences.
>
> Each State Party shall, in particular, ensure that legal persons held liable in accordance with this article are subject to effective, proportionate and dissuasive criminal or non-criminal sanctions, including monetary sanctions.

Such an article would serve to advance corporate accountability for serious human rights abuses by requiring for the first time that states ensure that legal liability arises for all of such acts in their domestic legal systems. It would expand the class of acts for which such an obligation already exists in international law, by including those human rights violations which require criminalization but where a requirement of liability for legal persons has not been laid down in treaty law. The article consciously defers to national legal traditions concerning the precise modalities of liability for legal persons, with a view to its greater acceptance. It is cautiously ambitious. While it does not address key criminal law issues such as defences, extraterritorial application and parent company liability,[117] it provides a general obligation which could conceivably be supplemented elsewhere in the treaty itself, in a subsequent instrument or by the authoritative findings of relevant judicial, monitoring or advisory bodies.

---

[117] For a discussion of aspects of these issues, see Chapters 8, 9, 10 and 12 in this book.

CONCLUSION

Connecting the Dots

How to Capitalize on the Current High Tide for a Business and Human Rights Treaty

SURYA DEVA

C.1 Introduction

The relevance and the exact role of international law in regulating human rights abuses by business – especially by transnational corporations (TNCs) – has been discussed at the United Nations (UN) and other intergovernmental bodies since the early 1970s.[1] One prominent strand of this discussion has been attempts to adopt a legally binding international instrument that obligates TNCs (and other business enterprises) to comply with agreed human rights norms. Such recurrent attempts – the most recent being triggered by a June 2014 resolution of the Human Rights Council (HRC)[2] – could be compared to tides,[3] with the momentum of negotiating a binding international instrument coming in and going out.

---

[1] In addition to chapter by Hamdani and Ruffing in this volume, see T. Sagafi-nejad and J. Dunning, *The UN and Transnational Corporations: From Code of Conduct to Global Compact* (Indiana University Press, 2008); D. Bilchitz and S. Deva, 'The Human Rights Obligations of Business: A Critical Framework for the Future' in S. Deva and D. Bilchitz (eds.), *Human Rights Obligations of Business: Beyond the Corporate Responsibility to Respect?* (Cambridge University Press, 2013) 1; K. Hamdani and L. Ruffing, *United Nations Centre on Transnational Corporations: Corporate Conduct and the Public Interest* (Routledge, 2015).

[2] Human Rights Council, 'Elaboration of an international legally binding instrument on transnational corporations and other business enterprises with respect to human rights', A/HRC/RES/26/9 (26 June 2014), para. 1, http://daccess-dds-ny.un.org/doc/UNDOC/GEN/G14/082/52/PDF/G1408252.pdf?OpenElement (last accessed 20 January 2017).

[3] See S. Deva, 'The Human Rights Obligations of Business: Reimagining the Treaty Business', http://business-humanrights.org/sites/default/files/media/documents/reimagine_int_law_for_bhr.pdf (last accessed 10 October 2016).

The contributing authors to this volume have grappled with various aspects of the current business and human rights (BHR) treaty project: from why such a treaty is required to certain considerations that should be kept in mind while negotiating the treaty (including lessons from the past failed attempts), and the potential contours of several elements of the treaty. This concluding chapter seeks to connect the dots, build synergy between divergent perspectives canvassed in this volume and propose certain principles that should guide negotiations about the form as well as content of the proposed treaty.

Before proceeding further, I should clarify at the outset the role of the proposed BHR treaty in regulating human rights violations by corporations, because some of the scepticism towards the treaty might be due to misinformed assumptions or apprehensions about the treaty. A BHR treaty is not an end in itself; rather, it is an important means to achieve certain ends about which there should not be much dispute. Multiple arguments have been provided in this book for why a treaty is necessary.[4] In particular, it seems to me that one of the key goals of any treaty must be to strengthen access to effective remedies for the victims of corporate human rights violations and to create more opportunities to hold business actors accountable for such violations. The treaty should not be seen as a panacea to fix all existing regulatory gaps. Nor should the idea of a legally binding international instrument be seen as being in competition with other current regulatory initiatives, including the Guiding Principles on Business and Human Rights (GPs).[5] Rather, the idea – if it materializes – will be a powerful additional tool in our armour to regulate more effectively the activities of difficult regulatory targets. The proposed BHR treaty should be seen as part of an evolutionary process consistent with the idea of an integrated theory of regulation: this idea implies that since all regulatory tools have certain limitations, the key is to employ multiple tools simultaneously in a coordinated manner.[6]

In the next section of this chapter, I compare the nature of the current high tide for a BHR treaty with two such previous high tides and suggest that the chances of securing a treaty are brighter this time as compared to

---

[4] In addition to Bilchitz's Introduction, see, for example, Chapters 2 and 3 by Simons and Leader, respectively.

[5] Human Rights Council, 'Guiding Principles on Business and Human Rights: Implementing the United Nations "Protect, Respect and Remedy" Framework', A/HRC/17/31 (21 March 2011) (GPs).

[6] See S. Deva, *Regulating Corporate Human Rights Violations: Humanizing Business* (Routledge, 2012).

previous attempts. I then outline a number of principles which might help in riding the waves in this current treaty tide to reach a fruitful conclusion. The subsequent section explores the potential format as well as the content of the proposed treaty. This chapter concludes with some observations to situate the recurrent high tide for a binding instrument in the context of the wider BHR landscape.

C.2   The Current High Tide versus the Previous Ones[7]

As noted above, the UN has been grappling with the demands for a legally binding international instrument concerning corporate human rights violations for over four decades. At least three high tides for such a binding instrument are discernible during this period. The HRC Resolution 26/9 triggered the third high tide, the earlier two high tides being the 1990 UN Code of Conduct on Transnational Corporations (Code)[8] and the 2003 Norms on the Responsibilities of Transnational Corporations and Other Business Enterprises with Regard to Human Rights (Norms). These tides at the UN level could be compared to a 'cycle of high and low tides'. The three high tides differ from each other in terms of the driving force, the focal point and the key participating actors. Reviewing briefly the nature of these tides may be helpful in assessing the prospects of success of the third tide as well as to articulate principles that should guide negotiations so as to bring this high tide to a fruitful conclusion.

C.2.1   First High Tide

The first high tide was represented by the 1990 Code. However, the preparation for this tide began in the early 1970s when the UN's Economic and Social Council requested the Secretary General to constitute a Group of Eminent Persons to study the impact of TNCs on the development process (especially in developing countries) and international relations.[9] The Group recommended that the UN establish a

---

[7] This section draws upon S. Deva, 'Alternatives Ways to Getting a Business and Human Rights Treaty' in N. Carrillo-Santarelli and J. L. Černič (eds.), *Perspectives on the Proposed UN Treaty on Business and Human Rights* (Intersentia, forthcoming).

[8] 'Draft Code on Transnational Corporations' in United Nations Centre on Transnational Corporations (UNCTC), *Transnational Corporations, Services and the Uruguay Round*, Annex IV, p. 231 (1990).

[9] P. Muchlinski, *Multinational Enterprises and the Law* (Blackwell Publishing, 1999), 593.

Commission on TNCs, which, amongst other things, should formulate a code of conduct for them.[10] This recommendation led to the establishment of the Commission on Transnational Corporations and the United Nations Centre on Transnational Corporations (UNCTC) in 1974. The quest to establish an agreeable code under the aegis of these UN bodies continued for more than one decade, but the 1990 Code could not be adopted due to significant differences between developed and developing countries.[11] Later on, the negotiations on the Code were suspended and the Commission as well as the UNCTC were dismantled.[12] Thus, the first high tide started receding around 1992–1993.

During the first high tide, the proposed code sought to deal with *both* responsibilities (linked to TNCs' activities) and rights (linked to TNCs' treatment by host states). In fact, there was an apparent clash between the push for recognizing the 'rights' and 'responsibilities' of TNCs. While developing countries were more interested in solidifying their right to regulate TNCs and outlining the responsibilities of TNCs, developed countries were keener to secure a level playing field for their TNCs operating in emerging markets.[13]

Consistent with the then prevailing view of international law, states were the principal actors which pushed for such a binding code and negotiated its content (with non-state actors mostly staying in the background). Furthermore, human rights were not the primary concern of the 1990 Code.[14] However, the main regulatory focus of binding instruments was set to change during the next two high tides. As we will see, there has been almost no discussion about the rights of TNCs in such binding instruments: this was perhaps not needed because TNCs are now

---

[10] *Ibid.*   [11] *Ibid.*, 593–597.

[12] Economic and Social Council, 'Integration of the Commission on Transnational Corporations into the Institutional Machinery of the United Nations Conference on Trade and Development', Resolution 1994/1 (14 July 1994).

[13] For detailed insights, see Chapter 1 by Hamdani and Ruffing in this volume.

[14] This perhaps contributed to the former Special Representative of the Secretary General on human rights and transnational corporations and other business enterprises (SRSG) asserting that '[h]uman rights did not feature' in the code formulation. J. Ruggie, 'Business and Human Rights: The Evolving International Agenda' (2007) 101 *American Journal of International Law* 819. This assertion does not seem to be entirely correct though, because paragraph 14 of the Code had stated that TNCs '*shall respect human rights* and fundamental rights and fundamental freedoms in the countries in which they operate.' 'Draft Code on Transnational Corporations' in UNCTC, *Transnational Corporations, Services and the Uruguay Round* (1990), Annex IV, p. 231 at 234, para. 14 (emphasis added). See also paras. 25, 37 and 41–43.

able to secure their rights through bilateral investment treaties (BITs) that have mushroomed since the mid-1990s.[15]

C.2.2   Second High Tide

The second high tide was reflected in the approval of the Norms[16] by the erstwhile Sub-Commission on the Promotion and Protection of Human Rights in 2003.[17] The roots of the second tide could be traced to August 1998 when the Human Rights Commission's Sub-Commission on the Promotion and Protection of Human Rights decided to establish a five-member Working Group on the Working Methods and Activities of Transnational Corporations.[18] Against the backdrop of criticisms of voluntary initiatives like the Global Compact,[19] the Working Group drafted detailed substantive provisions as to the human rights responsibilities of TNCs and other business enterprises and also incorporated provisions for the implementation of these responsibilities.[20] Although the Sub-Commission approved the Norms, the Commission on Human Rights in its 2004 session resolved that the Norms have 'no legal standing'.[21] The Commission then, in its 2005 session, requested the UN Secretary General to appoint a SRSG,[22] who felt the need to discard the Norms for their conceptual flaws and divisive nature and built a new

---

[15] See D. Bishop, J. Crawford and M. Reisman, *Foreign Investment Disputes: Cases, Materials and Commentary* (Kluwer Law International, 2005), 1–10.

[16] Sub-Commission on the Promotion and Protection of Human Rights, 'Norms on the Responsibilities of Transnational Corporations and Other Business Enterprises with Regard to Human Rights', UN Doc E/CN.4/Sub.2/2003/12/Rev.2 (13 August 2003) (UN Norms).

[17] Sub-Commission on the Promotion and Protection of Human Rights, 'Resolution 2003/16' (13 August 2003), E/CN.4/Sub.2/2003/L.11, 52–55.

[18] D. Weissbrodt and M. Kruger, 'Norms of the Responsibilities of Transnational Corporations and Other Business Enterprises with Regard to Human Rights' (2003) 97 *American Journal of International Law* 901, at 903–904.

[19] J. Nolan, 'The United Nations' Compact with Business: Hindering or Helping the Protection of Human rights?' (2005) 24 *University of Queensland Law Journal* 445; S. Deva, 'Global Compact: A Critique of UN's "Public-Private" Partnership for Promoting Corporate Citizenship' (2006) 34 *Syracuse Journal of International Law and Commerce* 107.

[20] See Weissbrodt and Kruger, n. 18, 903-907.

[21] Commission on Human Rights, 'Agenda Item 16', E/CN.4/2004/L.73/Rev.1 (16 April 2004), para. (c).

[22] Commission on Human Rights, 'Promotion and Protection of Human Rights', E/CN.4/2005/L.87 (15 April 2005).

framework underpinned by 'principled pragmatism'.[23] Therefore, the second high tide also receded quickly without fulfilling the promise of delivering a human rights instrument that imposed binding obligations on TNCs.

In comparison with the first high tide, the primary focus of the second high tide – which lasted for a much shorter period than the first one – was on cataloguing the human rights responsibilities of TNCs and other business enterprises. As noted above, the omission of TNCs' rights from the drafting debate during this period could be explained by the proliferation of BITs and the establishment of the Word Trade Organization (WTO) in 1995. These two developments allowed TNCs to demand – directly or through their home states – fair and equal treatment from host states as well protection for their investments under the WTO or investor–state dispute settlement mechanism. It did not, therefore, remain equally critical to catalogue the rights of TNCs. As compared to the first high tide, the second high tide also provided good evidence of the emerging importance of non-state actors in moulding the contours of international law: TNCs, business organizations and NGOs played an active role in mobilizing opinion for or against the Norms (though they did not get enough opportunities to engage during the drafting process of the Norms). In a way, this is consistent with the idea that non-state actors can help craft international law from the 'bottom-up'.[24]

C.2.3   Third High Tide

The momentum for the current third high tide began in September 2013 when the Republic of Ecuador made a statement at the HRC's 24th session stressing the importance of a legally binding international

---

[23] Commission on Human Rights, 'Interim report of the Special Representative of the Secretary-General on the issue of human rights and transnational corporations and other business enterprises', E/CN.4/2006/97 (22 February 2006), paras. 55–69 and 81. 'Principled pragmatism' means 'an unflinching commitment to the principle of strengthening the promotion and protection of human rights as it relates to business, coupled with a pragmatic attachment to what works best in creating change where it matters most – in the daily lives of people.' *Ibid.*, para. 81.

[24] See S. Deva, 'Multinationals, Human Rights and International Law: Time to Move beyond the "State-Centric" Conception?' in Jernej Letnar Černič and Tara Van Ho (eds.), *Human Rights and Business: Direct Corporate Accountability for Human Rights* (Wolf Legal Publishers, 2015) 27.

framework.[25] Apart from the support of at least 85 states, this Ecuadorian initiative was supported by hundreds of CSOs[26] which have since then formed a Treaty Alliance.[27] This resurgence in the demand for an international binding instrument came quite close after the unanimous endorsement of the GPs by the HRC in June 2011 and the subsequent wide uptake of the GPs by states, international institutions, businesses and CSOs alike.[28] In fact, the fear that an attempt to negotiate a treaty will fracture the highly prized 'consensus' built around the GPs is one of the arguments raised against the utility of the current treaty process.[29]

It is difficult to predict at this stage how long this tide will last and whether it might deliver the text of a treaty. However, looking at the developments so far – including the stand taken by states during the first two sessions of the OEIGWG[30] – it appears that the divisions that were visible between developed countries and developing during the first and second high tides are resurfacing again. All the developed countries (invariably from the Global North) had voted against Resolution 26/9, while all the

---

[25] Republic of Ecuador, 'Statement on behalf of a Group of Countries at the 24th Session of the Human Rights Council' (September 20013), http://business-humanrights.org/media/documents/statement-unhrc-legally-binding.pdf (last accessed 2 February 2014).

[26] 'Call for an International Legally Binding Instrument on Human Rights, Transnational Corporations and Other Business Enterprises', www.business-humanrights.org/media/call-for-binding-instrument.pdf (accessed 2 February 2014). See also '100+ groups publicly call on United Nations to develop new binding instrument to address corporate human rights abuses', www.escr-net.org/news/2013/100-groups-publicly-call-united-nations-develop-new-binding-instrument-address-corporate (last accessed 2 February 2014) and 'Statement to the Human Rights Council in Support of the Initiative of a Group of States for a Legally Binding Instrument on Transnational Corporations', www.stopcorporateimpunity.org/?p=3830 (last accessed 2 February 2014).

[27] The information about the Treaty Alliance and its statements on the issue are available at www.treatymovement.com/ (last accessed 20 January 2017).

[28] John Ruggie, 'Life in the Global Public Domain: Response to Commentaries' (5 February 2015), http://jamesgstewart.com/author/john-g-ruggie/ (last accessed 20 January 2017).

[29] See D. Cassel and A. Ramasastry, 'White Paper: Options for a Treaty on Business and Human Rights' (May 2015), 8, https://business-humanrights.org/sites/default/files/documents/whitepaperfinal%20ABA%20LS%206%2022%2015.pdf (last accessed 20 January 2017). For a critique of this 'consensus' narrative, see Surya Deva, 'Treating Human Rights Lightly: A Critique of the Consensus Rhetoric and the Language Employed by the Guiding Principles' in Surya Deva and David Bilchitz (eds.), *Human Rights Obligations of Business: Beyond the Corporate Responsibility to Respect?* (Cambridge: Cambridge University Press, 2013), 78, 81–91.

[30] See Chapter 14 in this volume by George and Laplante, and Human Rights Council, 'Second session of the open-ended intergovernmental working group on transnational corporations and other business enterprises with respect to human rights', www.ohchr.org/EN/HRBodies/HRC/WGTransCorp/Session2/Pages/Session2.aspx (last accessed 20 January 2017).

resolution supporters were developing countries from the Global South. Even after the resolution was passed, hardly any country from the Global North participated in the OEIGWG's first session.[31] While the exclusion of local business enterprises from the scope of the treaty was the supposed reason for such disengagement,[32] in reality the opposition to any binding international instrument ran deeper. The opposition seemingly goes to the very idea of international law imposing *binding* human rights obligations on corporations. For example, the very same states are against a legally binding instrument to regulate the conduct of private military and security companies, even though the proposed instrument is not limited to TNCs.[33]

Unlike the second tide, the current high tide for a legally binding instrument is led and controlled by states, though independent experts have been invited to share their perspectives during OEIGWG sessions. There is, however, one key difference. Both pro-treaty and anti-treaty states have operated in alliance with like-minded non-state actors: whereas pro-treaty states have found support in CSOs, anti-treaty states have been courting business associations. A defining feature of the third high tide has been the momentum built by the collective global mobilization of CSOs in the form of a Treaty Alliance which has played an unprecedented role in this high tide.[34] In the absence of support from the Global North states, the main sponsors of the HRC Resolution 26/9 (Ecuador and South Africa) have relied on civil society power to push forward the treaty project and also mount pressure on the European Union (EU) to engage with the treaty process. This tactic has worked to some extent as the EU showed a somewhat softer stance during the second session of the OEIGWG. At the same time, CSOs' resistance to corporations and business associations participating in the treaty process – due to the fear of the corporate capture of states – has raised concerns about lack of inclusive consultation with business.

C.2.4   Third High Tide versus Previous Two High Tides

In view of the differences in the nature of the three high tides highlighted above, I will argue that the current high tide offers better chances of

---

[31] See C. Lopez and B. Shea, 'Negotiating a Treaty on Business and Human Rights: A Review of the First Intergovernmental Session' (2015) 1 *Business and Human Rights Journal* 111.

[32] For details, see Deva's Chapter 6 in this volume.

[33] 'United Nations Human Rights Council', www.ohchr.org/EN/HRBodies/HRC/WGMilitary/Pages/OEIWGMilitaryIndex.aspx (last accessed 20 January 2017).

[34] Aragão and Roland in Chapter 5 of this volume trace the counter-hegemonic role played by civil society.

getting us closer to a BHR treaty if creative diplomacy is shown by the treaty proponents.[35] At least three such differences are noteworthy.

First, unlike the previous two tides, the third high tide has the 'springboard' of the GPs. Considering that there is a broad consensus about the GPs, the proposed treaty drafted by the OEIGWG should build on useful elements of the GPs to gain political support. In fact, it is highly unlikely that any treaty will not include provisions about the state duty to protect human rights violations by business enterprises (Pillar I) and enhancing access to effective remedies for the affected rights-holders (Pillar III). The concept of human rights due diligence under Pillar II of the GPs will also be relevant for the proposed treaty, irrespective of whether it imposes 'direct' obligations on TNCs or not. Therefore, if the GPs are used as a springboard to build the treaty provisions, states supportive of the GPs would find it quite difficult to oppose the treaty, especially if the treaty-sponsoring states too show sincerity in implementing the GPs within their respective domestic jurisdictions.

Second, the current high tide for a binding international instrument has been supported by the Treaty Alliance's unprecedented global campaign for corporate accountability. This campaign – which also seeks to 'dismantle corporate power' and fight 'corporate capture'[36] – is exposing the limitations of the existing regulatory initiatives by focusing on the victims' struggle for holding corporations accountable for human rights violations, thus countering the state-centric narrative against the need for a binding instrument. More importantly, the Treaty Alliance campaign has put several developed states in the Global North opposing the treaty process in a very uncomfortable situation: how to reconcile their position as the torchbearers of human rights and the key funders of CSOs with their opposition to developing binding human rights norms for TNCs. In other words, this strong civil society advocacy for a binding instrument might help in softening the opposition of certain states.

Third, many states (including developed countries) have started experiencing the side effects of arbitration triggered by TNCs under

---

[35] Of course, there are also differences which would work against the possibility of securing a BHR treaty. For example, business associations are now much more organized in their opposition to binding rules. Moreover, as compared to the first two tides, the mandate to negotiate an instrument during the third high tide is fractured from the very outset. See also the challenges highlighted by Backer and Mares in Chapters 4 and 10, respectively, in this volume.

[36] See 'Dismantle Corporate Power', www.stopcorporateimpunity.org/ (last accessed 20 January 2017).

BITs:[37] for example, 60 per cent of the investor–state disputes in 2015 were decided on the merits in favour of investors.[38] Thus, asymmetries between the 'rights' and 'obligations' of TNCs are no longer a matter of academic argument or mere speculation, as TNCs have even challenged legislative reforms in some investment disputes. Moreover, it is quite possible that, in future, TNCs from the Global South may turn the table on developed countries by taking them before arbitration tribunals under BITs. These possibilities may encourage even treaty-sceptic states to claw back the pendulum a little bit towards human rights. The proposed BHR treaty may offer such an opportunity by striking a better balance between states' legitimate role in safeguarding human rights and the need to protect investors' rights.

C.3   Principles to Turn the Treaty Tide

What principles should guide negotiations of the proposed BHR treaty as well as its content? Backer in Chapter 4, for example, argues that 'principled pragmatism' – skilfully employed by the former SRSG to craft the GPs – should be the guiding torch for the treaty negotiators. Simons, in Chapter 2, also reminds us of the need to move on the treaty road 'in a careful and strategic manner'. Similarly, Mares, in Chapter 10, cautions that the legalization project under the treaty should not dismiss lightly the legal separation of entities principle or ignore national sovereignty concerns. Drawing on insights underlying these cautionary principles, I will propose below not just one principle but a 'basket of principles' which should underpin the substance of the treaty as well as the process employed to achieve that substance.

C.3.1   *Capturing as Many Human Rights and Businesses as Possible*

Although it might be easier to negotiate a treaty that is limited to 'gross' or 'serious' business-related human rights violations, such a treaty will not be able to cover most of the current corporate abuses of human rights.[39] Therefore, the proposed treaty should cover all international

---

[37] 'Prior to 2013, fewer cases were brought against developed countries.' But now about 40 per cent cases have been brought against them. UNCTAD, *World Investment Report 2016 – Investor Nationality: Policy Challenges* (UNCTAD, 2016), 104–105.

[38] *Ibid.*, 107.

[39] Unless such a narrow treaty is agreed upon as part of a clear framework to adopt sequential treaties covering different sets of rights.

human rights abuses potentially committed by corporations. Achieving this outcome should not be difficult, at least in theory, because the GPs – which were unanimously endorsed by states and are widely supported by corporations – adopt this premise. The treaty may of course differentiate amongst human rights in terms of remedies available for their breach: for certain human rights violations, only civil and/or administrative remedies should suffice, whereas additional criminal remedies might be desirable for more serious abuses.

As far as the treaty's applicability to business is concerned, again it will be ideal to apply this to all types of business enterprises, because the form of an entity matters little for the victims of corporate human rights abuses. However, considering significant divisions amongst states on this particular point, a 'hybrid option' mooted in Chapter 6 may be the way to break the stalemate: while the main treaty could apply only to TNCs and other business enterprises with a transnational character, an Optional Protocol could extend its relevant provisions to all other types of business enterprises.

C.3.2   Focusing on Rights-Holders

The proposed BHR treaty should adopt an approach that keeps the rights-holders central both to the treaty content as well as the process adopted to draft this content. For instance, the treaty should respond to the suffering of victims of business-related human rights abuses and their need to seek justice against corporate actors. Only then could it make some difference to the lives of victims.

In terms of the process, states should consult the rights-holders. Such consultations with rights-holders (including victims) should be genuine and effective (i.e., allowing them an opportunity to inform the content of the treaty) rather than aimed at merely providing legitimacy to a pre-defined content. The treaty process so far has provided channels to engage with victims' voices both during the OEIGWG sessions and outside.[40] More challenging, however, would be to align the treaty's content with the needs of victims (e.g., imposing binding human rights obligations on corporations; establishing effective remedial mechanisms at the regional and international levels), as this might entail including some

---

[40] For a non-session engagement with victims, see, for example, the ESCR-Net and FIDH project: 'Treaty Initiative', www.escr-net.org/corporateaccountability/treatyinitiative (last accessed 20 January 2017).

provisions which are not politically feasible or acceptable to business. To achieve this objective, the position of states as well as business associations should be informed, at least partially, by the interests of rightsholders. In other words, pragmatism should yield to normative principles on this front.

C.3.3 Bridging the Cleavage between the GPs and the Treaty

The proposed BHR treaty should build on the GPs rather than trying to reinvent the wheel all over again.[41] By using the GPs as a 'springboard', the treaty project would enhance not only the political legitimacy but also consensus around the text of the proposed treaty. For example, if the treaty requires states to develop appropriate laws and policies to institutionalize mandatory human rights due diligence on the part of all business enterprises domiciled within their territory and/or jurisdiction, this should not be highly controversial or problematic.[42]

Although the GPs should be the 'starting point' for the treaty, they need not be the 'end point', because the treaty could plug in some of the gaps of the GPs or strengthen their implementation by both states and business enterprises. Let us take a concrete example. Principle 9 of the GPs reminds states to 'maintain adequate domestic policy space to meet their human rights obligations when pursuing business-related policy objectives with other states or business enterprises'. If the BHR treaty requires states to (i) include explicitly human rights provisions in BITs, (ii) conduct a human rights impact assessment before signing BITs, and (iii) make protection of investors rights subject to compliance with national and international human rights norms, this will help in implementing the GPs in this respect.

The potential of a mutually complementary relation[43] between the GPs and the proposed BHR treaty is, however, undermined by the current

---

[41] Among others, see IOE, ICC, BIAC and WBCSD, 'UN Treaty Process on Business and Human Rights: Further Considerations by the International Business Community on a Way Forward' (September 2016), www.ioe-emp.org/fileadmin/ioe_documents/publications/Policy%20Areas/business_and_human_rights/EN/_2016-09-29__IOE-ICC-BIAC-WBCSD_Paper_on_further_considerations_re_the_UN_TREATY_PROCESS_ON_BUSINESS_AND_HUMAN_RIGHTS_final.pdf (last accessed 20 January 2017).

[42] While the UK and France have already enacted laws with some form of required human rights due diligence, others states like Australia, the Netherlands and Switzerland are considering to enact such a law.

[43] See J. Martens and K. Seitz, *The Struggle for a UN Treaty: Towards Global Regulation on Human Rights and Business* (Global Policy Forum, 2016), 18–19.

cleavage seen in practice between the two processes.[44] Instead of having an 'either or' mind-set, the proposed treaty should be treated as a 'logical evolution' of the GPs. In fact, any state or corporation which supports the GPs should not oppose the idea of a treaty: doing so would only imply that it is not sincere about the GPs.[45] Conversely, pro-treaty states should implement effectively the GPs, otherwise doubts would be cast about their motives behind the treaty.

C.3.4   Clarifying and Strengthening States' Obligations

States remain a weak link in holding corporations accountable for human rights violations, especially when they compete to attract foreign investment or while dealing with TNCs. The treaty should enhance the regulatory position of states vis-à-vis TNCs in several ways. It could, for instance, prescribe appropriate tests for states to invoke extraterritorial jurisdiction. In addition, an obligation could be imposed on states to offer mutual assistance and cooperation involving cross-border human rights abuses. The treaty should enable states to preserve their regulatory space to protect human rights while negotiating trade or investment agreement, but also strengthen their legal position in disputes with corporate investors. As Muchlinski highlights in his chapter, a number of options are available to achieve this objective.[46]

C.3.5   Reducing Regulatory Dependency on States

Despite the best efforts to beef up the position of states, it is inevitable that some states will be unwilling or unable to exercise effectively their duty to protect the human rights of individuals from violations by corporations. The proposed BHR treaty should reduce this regulatory dependency of

---

[44] See Deva's Chapter 6 in this volume.

[45] To illustrate, the G-7 Leaders in their Elmau Declaration of June 2015 acknowledged their strong support for a responsible supply chain, including by implementing the GPs. 'G-7 Leaders' Declaration' (8 June 2015), www.whitehouse.gov/the-press-office/2015/06/08/g-7-leaders-declaration (last accessed 20 January 2017). If these developed states as well as TNCs based therein really wish to walk the talk on the GPs, the proposed treaty should not worry them; rather they should support the treaty as a complementary tool in the armory to accomplish the common goal of promoting business compliance with human rights.

[46] See also ESCR-Net and FIDH, ESCR-Net and FIDH, 'Ten Key Proposals for the Treaty' (October 2016), 17–25, www.escr-net.org/sites/default/files/attachments/tenkeyproposals_final.pdf (last accessed 20 January 2017).

international law on states by taking a number of measures. Obligating states to regulate the extraterritorial activities of corporations incorporated or domiciled in one's jurisdiction would, for example, ensure that at least some state is able to control the corporate behaviour. Moreover, the treaty should consider imposing direct obligations on corporations and conceive of regional as well as international monitoring mechanisms. The role of CSOs in exercising oversight over corporate behaviour could also be institutionalized.[47]

C.3.6 Removing Barriers in Access to Effective Remedies

The treaty should strengthen access to effective remedies for victims of corporate human rights abuses by removing well-known barriers in accessing judicial remedies.[48] The GPs acknowledge these barriers and remind states to consider 'ways to reduce legal, practical and other relevant barriers that could lead to a denial of access to remedy',[49] but hardly provide any guidance on removing these barriers. The treaty should, therefore, provide states with concrete guidance on how some of these barriers – for example, the liability of a parent company for violations by its subsidiary; the doctrine of *forum non conveniens*; the lack of class actions and legal aid; the burden of proof resting on victims; delays in the judicial process; the overseas enforcement of judgements – could be minimized if not removed completely.[50] It should also pay special attention to unique challenges faced by marginalized or vulnerable groups of society (e.g., women, children, indigenous peoples, people with disabilities and migrant workers) in seeking remedies.

C.3.7 Adopting an Inclusive Process Free from Corporate Capture

While the corporate capture of state agencies and regulatory processes is very real at both domestic and international levels, any arguments about barring TNCs and business associations from the treaty consultation

---

[47] Article 33(3) of the Convention on the Rights of Person with Disabilities, for example, provide that civil society shall be involved in the monitoring process.

[48] See discussion in Stephens's Chapter 15 in this volume.

[49] Guiding Principles, n. 5, Principle 26.

[50] This OHCHR's Accountability and Remedy Project provides useful recommendations in this regard. Human Rights Council, 'Improving accountability and access to remedy for victims of business-related human rights abuse, Report of the United Nations High Commissioner for Human Rights', A/HRC/32/19 (10 May 2016).

process may not be worth the price: if the states have already been captured, there is not much that would be gained by merely keeping TNCs outside the negotiation tent. Rather, the key lies in engaging with businesses and convincing them why human rights norms are not optional any more. At the same time, safeguards against corporate capture of the treaty process should be built into the consultation process (e.g., posting draft text on a website; joint engagement with CSOs and business associations) and – if necessary – the gap in the promises and practices of corporations concerning human rights should be exposed.

C.3.8   Avoiding an 'All or Nothing' Attitude

Perhaps the most important principle guiding the proposed BHR treaty negotiations should be to avoid an 'all or nothing' attitude, as this treaty may be only the first of many further legally binding instruments that might be needed to regulate effectively the activities of business enterprises. Current negotiations in pursuance of Resolution 26/9 should be seen as part of this evolutionary process. States (as well as CSOs) should also adopt a flexible attitude because all negotiations at the international level involve give and take, as long as certain 'red lines' are not breached. Managing expectations of CSOs and communicating to them as well as the rights-holders about the limitations of any treaty will also be crucial. Experiences from previous failed attempts should be instructive too. For example, the 2003 Norms failed to garner support, among other reasons, because they tried to impose excessive human rights obligations on corporations.

C.4   Form and Content of the Proposed BHR Treaty

Regarding the form of the proposed BHR treaty, a range of options have been canvased by scholars.[51] Out of these options, Simons in Chapter 2 in this volume and De Schutter[52] in a journal article have suggested that a frame-work convention may be the most promising way forward, considering that no thick consensus for a strong conventional treaty currently exists amongst states. It is doubtful, however, whether a framework treaty would be an

---

[51] See, for example, Cassel and Ramasastry, n. 29, 14–36. See also ICJ, 'Needs and Options for a New International Instrument in the Field of Business and Human Rights' (June 2014), www.icj.org/wp-content/uploads/2014/06/NeedsandOptionsinternationalinst _ICJReportFinalelecvers.compressed.pdf (last accessed 20 January 2017).

[52] O. De Schutter, 'Towards a New Treaty on Business and Human Rights' (2016) 1 *Business and Human Rights Journal* 41.

adequate response to deal with current regulatory gaps. As far as the content of the treaty is concerned, again several concrete proposals have been put on the discussion table.[53] The contributions in this volume should also be seen as part of this 'pool of proposals' to assist the Chairperson-Rapporteur of the OEIGWG in preparing the elements of the proposed BHR treaty.

The views of the contributing authors to this volume about the form or content of the treaty can be placed on a spectrum with two extreme ends being what is 'politically feasible' and what is 'normatively desirable'. As I have tried to show in Chapter 6 about the scope of the proposed BHR treaty, it is not impossible to strike a balance between these two competing underlying considerations. It is critical, however, not to start with what is politically feasible: rather, the negotiations about the form as well as the content of the BHR treaty should begin by looking at what is normatively desirable from the perspective of individuals whose human rights are impinged upon by business activities. Then attempts should be made to pull, as much as possible, political considerations surrounding feasibility towards normativity. Such a process would ensure that the interests of rights-holders remain central to the treaty process.

Adopting this approach, I will suggest that the proposed BHR treaty should respond to deficits in the current regulatory environment in terms of what I call the '5As':

1) *Alignment*: the treaty should require an alignment of states' laws and policies as well as corporate policies and practices with the human rights norms stipulated therein.
2) *Assessment*: the treaty should create reporting and peer-learning processes which allow an assessment of the conduct of both states and corporations by independent parties.
3) *Access to remedies*: the treaty should require states to strengthen both judicial and non-judicial remedial mechanisms at various levels, create a range of sanctions (civil, administrative and criminal) against wrongdoers, and propose measures to remove barriers in access to effective remedies.
4) *Assistance and cooperation*: the treaty should introduce tools to facilitate mutual assistance and cooperation amongst states, build capacity of both states and corporations to internalize human rights,

---

[53] See, for example, Martens and Seitz, n. 43; ICJ, 'Proposals for Elements of a Legally Binding Instrument on Transnational Corporations and Other Business Enterprises' (October 2016); ESCR-Net and FIDH, 'Ten Key Proposals for the Treaty', n. 46; and South Centre's policy briefs on the treaty. See also the submissions made before the second session of the OEIGWG: 'Second Session – Written Contributions' www.ohchr.org/EN/HRBodies/HRC/WGTransCorp/Session2/Pages/WrittenContributions.aspx (last accessed 20 January 2017).

and assist affected individuals and communities in holding corporations accountable for human rights violations.

5) *Alliances*: the treaty should encourage building alliances amongst states as well as between other stakeholders to deal with complex and powerful regulatory targets.

Taking into account, among others, the proposals made in this book, I provide below a broad birds-eye view of how these '5As' could be included within different sections of the treaty.

C.4.1   Preamble

In its Preamble, the proposed BHR treaty should, among others, (i) acknowledge that all types of business enterprises can violate all universal, inalienable, interrelated, interdependent and indivisible human rights; (ii) assert the primacy of human rights norms over norms related to the conduct of business, trade and investment; (iii) refer to the evolution of standards in the BHR area, including the GPs, the 2011 OECD Guidelines for Multinational Enterprises and the 2017 ILO Tripartite Declaration of Principles Concerning Multinational Enterprises and Social Policy; (iv) highlight that TNCs and other business enterprises with a 'transnational character' pose special regulatory challenges and hence the treaty only applies to them; (v) affirm that the human rights norms laid down in this treaty should be treated as good practices for all types of business enterprises; and (vi) encourage states to ratify the Optional Protocol to this treaty so as to extend its provisions to all other business enterprises with no transnational character.

The Preamble should also outline the key objectives behind the treaty, and stress the need to show special sensitivity while dealing with the human rights of marginalized or vulnerable groups of society.

C.4.2   Scope

As explained in Chapter 6, the proposed treaty should apply to (i) states and intergovernmental organizations; and (ii) TNCs and other business enterprises with a 'transnational character'. The treaty provisions may also apply, as far as relevant, to all other non-transnational business enterprises if a state party ratifies the Optional Protocol to this treaty.

In terms of the subject matter, the treaty's scope should extend to all human rights instruments specified in its annexure.

C.4.3 Definitions

The treaty would need to provide definitions of certain key terms used therein, e.g., human rights, victims, TNC, business enterprise with a transnational character, home/host state, and human rights due diligence. Most of these definitions could draw on other existing instruments. For example, a definition of 'multinational enterprise' under the OECD Guidelines on Multinational Enterprises could be used as a reference point to define a 'TNC'.

C.4.4 General Principles

The treaty should reaffirm (i) the non-delegable duty of states to protect human rights from violations by non-state actors within their territory and/or jurisdiction, and (ii) an independent duty of business enterprises to comply with their human rights obligations, including a duty to exercise effective human rights due diligence over their subsidiaries and suppliers.[54]

In addition, the proposed BHR treaty should reiterate the obligation (i) of states to provide prompt, accessible and effective remedies to the victims of business-related human rights abuses,[55] and (ii) of corporations to cooperate in good faith with the provision of remedies by states.

The treaty should also declare that in cases of any irreconcilable conflict between the provisions of this treaty and any prior or subsequent trade or investment agreement, the former shall prevail. Moreover, it should affirm the non-derogation principle: that nothing in this instrument shall be taken to limit or dilute the human rights obligations of both states and business enterprises under other relevant domestic laws and regional or international instruments.

C.4.5 Obligations of States

The proposed treaty should impose an obligation on state parties to:[56]

(a) align their national laws and policies with their obligations under international human rights law and the GPs;

---

[54] For details about the second element, see Chapters 8 and 9 by McCorquodale/Smit and Nolan, respectively, in this volume.

[55] See Chapters 14 and 15 by George/Laplante and Stephens, respectively, in this volume.

[56] For further discussion and specific proposals, see Chapters 3, 8, 9, 11, 12, 13, 14, 15 and 16 in this volume by Leader, McCorquodale/Smit, Nolan, Lopez, Skogly, Muchlinski, George/Laplante, Stephens and Darcy, respectively.

(b) ensure that trade and investment agreements do not undermine human rights under domestic or international law;

(c) develop appropriate standards to attribute civil, administrative and criminal liability to corporations and their officials for human rights violations;

(d) require all business enterprises incorporated or domiciled within their territory and/or jurisdiction to conduct human rights due diligence;

(e) reform corporate laws to ensure that they do not encourage corporations to give priority to profit over human rights;

(f) enact laws to require corporations to disclose information, in an accessible manner, about their human rights policies and practices;

(g) enact laws to protect whistle-blowers and human rights defenders;

(h) regulate extraterritorial activities of corporations incorporated or domiciled within their territory by taking appropriate legislative, administrative and other measures to ensure their compliance with human rights standards;

(i) ensure state-owned enterprises, on their own or in collaboration with others, do not violate human rights throughout their operations;

(j) integrate human rights into their procurement policies;

(k) provide access to effective judicial and non-judicial remedies to the victims of corporate human rights violations, including by removing barriers in access to remedy;

(l) make provisions for adequate, effective and prompt reparation to individuals and communities affected by business-related human rights abuses;

(m) provide sanctions – civil, criminal or administrative as the case may be – against corporations for violating human rights;[57] and

(n) offer, on request, appropriate assistance to other state parties in matters related to collection of evidence, investigation, prosecution, extradition of individuals and enforcement of overseas judgements.

---

[57] For corporate criminal liability, see Amnesty International and ICAR, 'The Corporate Crimes Principles: Advancing Investigations and Prosecutions in Human Rights Cases' (October 2016), www.commercecrimehumanrights.org/wp-content/uploads/2016/10/CCHR-0929-Final.pdf (last accessed 20 January 2017).

C.4.6   Obligations of Corporations

The treaty should affirm that corporations have an obligation to respect all human rights, and specify circumstances in which they also incur an obligation to protect and fulfil human rights.[58] The treaty should lay down some general principles which could help in ascertaining the exact human rights obligations of corporations with reference to the texts of international human rights instruments directed primarily at the conduct of states.

It should also require corporations to:

(a) develop, in consultation with stakeholders, and implement effective human rights due diligence policies throughout their global operations;[59]

(b) exercise extra diligence while operating in weak governance zones or in conflict-affected areas;

(c) conduct regular human rights impact assessments of their business activities on the affected communities and take appropriate remedial measures;

(d) disclose, in an accessible manner, the findings of their human rights impact assessments as well as the measures taken to address any concerns;

(e) respect the principle of 'free, prior and informed consent'; and

(f) provide remedies at the company-level in appropriate cases, and co-operate with other judicial or non-judicial mechanisms established by states.

C.4.7   Barriers in Access to Remedy

The proposed BHR treaty should reiterate access to an effective remedy as a human right available to all individuals and affected communities without any discrimination based on sex, sexual orientation, race, colour, language, religion, political or other opinion, national or social origin, disability, birth or other status.[60] Special attention should be paid to unique obstacles experienced by marginalized or vulnerable groups of

---

[58] On the latter point, see discussion in Bilchitz's Chapter 7 in this volume.

[59] For detailed discussion, see Chapters 8 and 9 by McCorquodale/Smit and Nolan, respectively, in this volume.

[60] See discussion in Chapters 14 and 15 by George/Laplante and Stephens, respectively, in this volume.

society such as women, children, indigenous peoples, people with disabilities and migrant workers in accessing remedies.

The treaty should also impose a duty on states to review and revise their laws as well as policies to remove barriers in access to judicial remedies, including those related to:

(a) access to information;
(b) availability of legal aid;
(c) cost of litigation;
(d) delays in judicial process;
(e) options to file a class or collective action against corporations;
(f) causation and burden of proof;
(g) limitation period;
(h) liability of a company for the conduct of its subsidiaries and suppliers; and
(i) availability of a suitable, independent and well-resourced forum.[61]

The treaty should consider establishing a mechanism to develop Model Laws to provide states with concrete guidance in how to remove barriers in the areas identified above.

C.4.8 Monitoring, Implementation and Enforcement

The proposed BHR treaty should obligate states to strengthen or put in place effective mechanisms – judicial, quasi-judicial and administrative – at the national level to monitor the implementation of human rights norms by business and enforce these norms. Furthermore, it should encourage states to harness the potential of CSOs to operate as a watchdog of corporate behaviour with agreed human rights norms.

In addition, the treaty should establish a committee of experts with the power to issue authoritative interpretation of the treaty provisions, develop further standards, provide advice and assist in building capacity of state parties, and accept individual complaints against both states and corporations.

States should also be required to submit periodic reports to the treaty committee and include, as part of universal period review, information about steps taken to implement the treaty obligations.

---

[61] The treaty text could draw on recommendations made in the OHCHR's Accountability and Remedy Project. Human Rights Council, 'Improving accountability and access to remedy for victims', n. 50.

Moreover, the treaty should require states to continue exploring, in good faith, the possibility of establishing a new international court, or extend the jurisdiction of the International Criminal Court, to provide for criminal liability for gross human rights violations by corporations.[62]

C.4.9 International Cooperation and Mutual Assistance

The treaty should require states to cooperate with other state parties and to provide them, in good faith and in consonance with the relevant international law as well as domestic laws, with mutual assistance concerning collection of evidence, investigation, prosecution, extradition of individuals and enforcement of overseas judgements in cases related to human rights violations by corporations (including state-owned enterprises).[63]

It should also encourage state parties to share information about good practices, provide technical assistance, collaborate in conducting research and offering training, and support capacity building.

Moreover, the proposed BHR treaty should establish a global network of pro bono lawyers who are willing to assist the victims of human rights abuses in seeking effective remedies against powerful corporations.

C.4.10 Miscellaneous Provisions

The final section of the treaty should contain standard provisions related to signature by state parties, entry into force, amendment, reservations and language.

C.4.11 Annexure

The annexure to the treaty should list all international human rights instruments with reference to which the human rights obligations of states as well as corporations under this treaty shall be ascertained.[64]

C.5 Conclusion

The repeated demands as well as attempts to negotiate a legally binding international instrument show that all other existing regulatory

---

[62] Darcy's Chapter 16 in this volume explores the need for corporate criminal liability at the domestic level as well, which is a more realistic goal in the interim.

[63] For past precedents in this area, see K. Mohamadieh, 'Approaching States' Obligations under a Prospective Legally Binding Instrument on TNCs and Other Business Enterprises in regard to Human Rights', *South Centre Policy Brief*, No. 30 (October 2016), 4–5.

[64] For details, see Deva's Chapter 6 in this volume.

initiatives – including the GPs – do not offer effective 'preventive' and/or 'redressive' remedies to the victims of corporate human rights abuses and that there is some merit in swimming the current treaty high tide. As the GPs were endorsed unanimously by states and have been supported widely by business as well as by civil society, one would think that both states and corporations will be under pressure from several 'push and pull' factors to deliver on what they have promised in terms of implementing the GPs. In practice, however, this is not happening enough in terms of both scale and speed.

In the regulatory domain of the BHR field, the real challenge for states would be to act in situations where there is no clear business case for human rights and corporations on their own are not internalizing human rights norms into their business operations. Similarly, corporations' commitment to upholding human rights would be tested in situations where states are unwilling or unable to take decisive steps to protect human rights. The proposed BHR treaty would be a critical addition to the existing 'push and pull' factors in pushing both states and corporations to match their human rights pledges with concrete actions.

This book has shown why a treaty is needed and what its potential content could be. In this chapter I have tried to connect dots and outline a number of principles that should guide the treaty negotiations. The proposed BHR treaty should build on what is already there and try to plug in existing regulatory gaps seen from the eyes of the bearers of human rights. Although we may perhaps need more than one legally binding instrument, the international community should come together to take the first decisive step. One should also bear in mind that high tides by their nature do not last for ever. Therefore, a draft of the proposed treaty should be negotiated within a reasonable period, otherwise the current momentum might be lost.

The era of playing a game of 'hide and seek' in the BHR field should come to an end for both states and companies, for the rights-holders have been suffering for too long from the conduct of profit-driven business actors. The current corporate impunity for human rights violations must end if human rights mean anything in the era of free market economy in which corporations have come to assume an all-pervasive role and unmatched power. Not taking decisive steps is not an option for the viability of international human rights law.

INDEX